ISBN 978-1-5280-0057-4
PIBN 10927708

FB &c Ltd, Dalton House, 60 Windsor Avenue, London, SW19 2RR.
Company number 08720141. Registered in England and Wales.

For support please visit www.forgottenbooks.com

A CATALOGUE

OF

THE CHINESE TRANSLATION

OF

THE BUDDHIST TRIPIṬAKA

THE SACRED CANON

OF THE

BUDDHISTS IN CHINA AND JAPAN

COMPILED

BY ORDER OF THE SECRETARY OF STATE FOR INDIA

BY

BUNYIU NANJIO

PRIEST OF THE TEMPLE, EASTERN HONGWANZI, JAPAN,
MEMBER OF THE ROYAL ASIATIC SOCIETY, LONDON

THIS BOOK IS A REPRINT, MADE PHOTOGRAPHICALLY IN JAPAN BY PERMISSION OF THE CLARENDON PRESS, OF THE BOOK PUBLISHED BY THE CLARENDON PRESS AT OXFORD IN 1883.

Oxford

AT THE CLARENDON PRESS

M DCCC LXXXIII

TO

PROFESSOR MAX MÜLLER,

IN GRATEFUL AND RESPECTFUL REMEMBRANCE

OF

HIS KIND INSTRUCTION, HELP, AND SYMPATHY,

THIS CATALOGUE IS

DEDICATED

BY

HIS PUPIL

BUNYIU NANJIO.

CONTENTS.

CATALOGUE.

FIRST DIVISION.

經藏 *Kiṅ-tsâṅ*, or Sûtra-piṭaka.

SECOND DIVISION.

律藏 Lüh-tsâṅ, Vinaya-piṭaka.

CONTENTS.

THIRD DIVISION.

論藏 Lun-tsâṅ, Abhidharma-pitaka.

FOURTH DIVISION.

雜藏 Tsâ-tsâṅ ('Samyukta-pitaka?')[1], Miscellaneous Works.

APPENDIX I.

APPENDIX II.

APPENDIX III.

---

[1] 雜藏 Tsâ-tsâṅ, 'Samyukta-pitaka (?).' This Chinese term for miscellaneous Indian and Chinese works is used by a Chinese priest named K'-sü, in his valuable work entitled Yuen-tsâṅ-k'-tsiṅ, or Guide for the Examination of the Canon. It consists of 48 fasciculi. The compilation of this work was finished by him in A. D. 1654, after he had spent about twenty years in a careful examination of the whole Canon, beginning from his thirtieth year. I have a copy of the Japanese edition in my possession, sent to me from the temple Eastern Hongwanzi last year.

[2] For the Southern and Northern Collections of the Tripitaka under the Miṅ dynasty, see my introduction to this Catalogue, p. xxii.

INTRODUCTION.

THE OBJECT OF THIS CATALOGUE.

This is a complete Catalogue of the Chinese Translation of the Buddhist Tripiṭaka, the Sacred Canon of the Buddhists in China and Japan. It contains not only the titles of 1662 different works (of which 342, however, are miscellaneous works), but also the names of the authors and translators, together with their dates. The arrangement and classification of these works are the same as in the original Chinese Catalogue, i. e. No. 1662. Notes taken from various sources are added under each title with their full references. A list of the principal authorities consulted by me will be found on p. xxxii. Though I gladly and gratefully acknowledge the assistance received from my predecessors, there still remain such difficulties as were pointed out by the Rev. J. Summers in his Descriptive Catalogue of the Chinese, Japanese, and Manchu books in the Library of the India Office, 1872 (p. iv), when he says: 'The title of a [Chinese] book is often untranslatable; the author's name is frequently out of sight, and has to be sought for in some obscure corner or work; the date of the publication is alike often doubtful, and in the case of Buddhist Literature the identification of the Chinese title with the Sanskrit original is sufficiently troublesome.' This quotation will to a certain extent explain the imperfection of my own work, for which I have to crave the indulgence of those who may use it.

My principal object in making this compilation has been to show the original, though it may be not quite scientific, arrangement of this great Collection of our Sacred Canon, made in China under the Miṅ dynasty, A. D. 1368–1644. A copy of the Japanese edition of this Chinese Collection, published in Japan in A. D. 1678–1681, is now in the Library of the India Office in London. 'It is this copy of the Sacred Books,' says the Rev. S. Beal, 'that (in 1874) I requested His Excellency Iwakura Tomomi to procure for the India Office Library. In 1875 the entire Tripiṭaka was received at the India Office, in fulfilment of the promise made by the Japanese ambassador[1].' Immediately after this, Mr. Beal prepared a Catalogue of the books 'for practical purposes[2],' which was completed in June 1876, within the time of six months[3].

In the same month (viz. June), I left Japan for England, where I arrived in August of the same year. At that time I did not know English at all. So I spent about two years and a half in London to learn it, before I could begin my study of Sanskrit. Before I left London for Oxford in February 1879, I had an opportunity of seeing Mr. Beal's Catalogue, but I did not visit the India Office Library till April 1880. In September of the same year, I received special permission to examine the whole Collection (except a few works which I have not been able to see to the present day) in the Library. I at once perceived some grave mistakes that had been made concerning the arrangement of the works in this Collection, on the part of some Japanese who had been charged to send this copy from Japan to England. I felt it my duty to correct this wrong arrangement. The original arrangement is by no means so irrational as Mr. Beal thinks, when he says in his Catalogue (p. 1, note 2): 'The travels of the Buddhist Pilgrims, for example, are arranged under the heading of King or Sûtras, but it is evident that this arrangement is purely Chinese, and comparatively modern.' Such an arrangement, however, is neither modern nor Chinese, but simply erroneous! If Mr. Beal had adopted what he calls the third method (in his Catalogue, p. 2),

---

[1] Abstract of Four Lectures on Buddhist Literature in China, delivered at University College, London, by Rev. S. Beal, 1882, p. vii.

[2] Ibid., p. viii.

[3] The Buddhist Tripiṭaka, as it is known in China and Japan. A Catalogue and Compendious Report, by Rev. S. Beal, 1876.

b 2

taking the works in the order of the Index, or of the original Catalogue, i.e. No. 1662, the proper arrangement would have been at once restored, though it would of course have required nearly an entire re-adjustment of the contents of the 'one hundred and three cases.' Moreover, this original arrangement exactly corresponds with the order of 'determining characters,' taken from the 'Thousand Character Composition.'

The present compilation is the result of my own examination of the Collection in September 1880. I regret, however, that I have been unable to give a more complete account of each work, or to show the contents of the whole Collection more fully. Nevertheless, with the help of several learned works, I think I have succeeded in identifying a number of the Chinese titles[1]. In a few cases I was also able to compare the Chinese translations with the original Sanskrit texts. The Sanskrit titles thus identified are given in the first Index. In the second Index, the names of the Indian and Chinese authors and translators are arranged alphabetically. These two Indices, together with three Appendices which precede them, will, I hope, be of some use in determining the dates of certain authors and their works.

I have made a distinction between the authors and translators. There are some Chinese authors who not only translated Sanskrit works into Chinese, but also composed original treatises in Chinese. In this case their names are mentioned in the second Appendix as well as in the third.

THE CHINESE BUDDHIST LITERATURE.

The Chinese Buddhist literature is somewhat different in its style from the classical and historical works of China. It dates from the first century of the Christian era, while the Chinese classics and some of their historical works were written long before. Now the Chinese Buddhist literature chiefly consists of translations of Sanskrit works; so that it is not only full of transliterations, but also of quite literal renderings of technical terms and proper names. These require special study. As the sound of the Chinese characters has been changing in successive periods and in different parts of China, the transliteration varies in various translations, made from the first century A.D. down to the thirteenth. The older transliteration is generally less full, so that it is more difficult to restore it to its Sanskrit original, unless it is first compared with a later and fuller transliteration. For this kind of study there are six useful works in the present Collection, namely:—

(1) No. 1604, Shâo-hhiṅ-*k*uṅ-tiâo-tâ-tsâṅ-yin, or a dictionary of the Buddhist Canon, republished in the Shâo-hhiṅ period, A.D. 1131–1162. 3 fasciculi.

(2) No. 1605, Yi-tshië-*k*iṅ-yin-i, or a dictionary of the whole Canon. Dates from A.D. 649. 26 fasciculi.

(3) No. 1606, Hwâ-yen-*k*iṅ-yin-i, or a dictionary of the Buddhâvatamsaka-sûtra, No. 88. Dates from A.D. 700. 4 fasciculi.

(4) No. 1621, Tâ-miṅ-sân-tsâṅ-fâ-shu, or a concordance of numerical terms and phrases of the Law of the Tripiṭaka, collected under the great Miṅ dynasty, A.D. 1368–1644. 40 fasciculi.

(5) No. 1636, *K*iâo-shaṅ-fâ-shu. This is a later collection similar to No. 1621. Dates from A.D. 1431. 12 fasciculi.

(6) No. 1640, Fân-i-miṅ-i-tsi, lit. 'a collection of the meanings of the (Sanskrit) names translated (into Chinese).' Dates from A.D. 1151. 20 fasciculi. This is a very useful dictionary of the technical terms and proper names, both in Sanskrit and Chinese Buddhist literature, though it requires much correction.

Beside these, I must not omit two valuable works of European scholars, namely:—

(1) Méthode pour déchiffer et transcrire les noms Sanskrits, par M. Stanislas Julien, 1861.

(2) Handbook for the Student of Chinese Buddhism, by Rev. E. J. Eitel, 1870.

DIFFERENT COLLECTIONS AND EDITIONS OF THE CHINESE TRANSLATION OF THE BUDDHIST TRIPIṬAKA AND THE THIRTEEN CATALOGUES NOW IN EXISTENCE.

There still remain two questions, namely: Who collected the Chinese Translation of the Buddhist Tripiṭaka, and when was such a Collection published in China, Corea, and Japan? In answering these questions, I must give an historical sketch of our Collection.

[1] Whenever the meaning of the Chinese title is not quite the same as that of the Sanskrit title, it has been translated quite literally into English, or sometimes into Sanskrit. All these renderings are printed in small type with inverted commas, under the Chinese titles.

We have in the present Collection thirteen Catalogues or Indices of the Chinese Translation of the Buddhist Tripitaka. A chronological table of these Catalogues with their titles, and those of different Collections and Editions, will be found towards the end of this Introduction.

Beside these, there are said to have been thirty-one Lists or Indices compiled before A. D. 730, all of which were lost at that time. The titles, however, and compilers, and even contents of some of them are mentioned in the Khâi-yuen-lu, No. 1485, fasc. 10, fol. 1 a seq. The two oldest Lists are said to have dated from the Tshin and the Former or Western Hân dynasties, B. C. 221–206 and 202–A. D. 9, respectively. These and some of the rest are of course very doubtful. I shall therefore not dwell on the missing Lists or Indices, but proceed at once to examine the more substantial materials.

TRANSLATIONS NOW IN EXISTENCE, AND MENTIONED IN THE OLDEST CATALOGUE OF ABOUT 520 A. D.

The following works in existence in the present Collection seem to be the same as those mentioned in the *Kh*u-sân-tsâñ-*k*i-tsi, No. 1476, the oldest Catalogue of the Chinese Translation of the Buddhist Tripitaka, compiled in about 520, under the Liâñ dynasty, A. D. 502–557.

Sûtras of the Mahâyâna.

*Kh*u-sân-tsâñ-*k*i-tsi.

No.		Fasc.	Page
3	Pañ*kk*avimsati-sâhasrikâ pra*gñ*âpâramitâ	2	21 b
4	,, ,,	,,	8 b
5	Dasasâhasrikâ pra*gñ*âpâramitâ	,,	4 b
6	,, ,,	,,	22 a
7	,, ,,	,,	19 b
8	,, ,,	,,	7 a
10	Va*g*ra*kkh*edikâ ,,	,,	22 b
23 (3)	Tathâgatâ*k*intya-*g*uhya-nirdesa	,,	9 a
23 (17)	Pûr*n*a-paripri*kkh*â	,,	22 b
23 (44)	Ratnarâsi, or Ratnaparâsi	,,	25 b
23 (47)	Ratna*k*û*d*a-paripri*kkh*â	,,	10 a
26	Amitâyusha, or -âbha, or Sukhâvatî-vyûha	,,	6 b
28	Akshobhyasya Tathâgatasya vyûha	,,	5 a
30	Samantamukha-parivarta	,,	12 b
31	Mañ*g*usrî-buddhakshetragu*n*avyûha	,,	9 b
32	Garbha-sûtra (?)	,,	12 b
33	Ugra-paripri*kkh*â	,,	5 b
34	,, ,,	,,	10 a
35	Bhadra-mâyâkâra-paripri*kkh*â, or -vyâkara*n*a	,,	,,
36	Vinayavinis*k*aya-upâli-paripri*kkh*â	,,	27 b
39	Sumati-dârikâ-paripri*kkh*â	,,	11 a
41	Vimaladattâ-paripri*kkh*â	,,	10 a
42	Asokadattâ-vyâkara*n*a	,,	13 b
43	Surata-paripri*kkh*â	,,	8 a
47	Sush*th*itamati-paripri*kkh*â, or Mâyopama-samâdhi	,,	12 b
50	Subâhu-paripri*kkh*â	3	12 a
52	*G*ñânottara-bodhisattva-paripri*kkh*â	2	11 a
53	Bhadrapâla-sresh*th*i-paripri*kkh*â	,,	10 a
55	Maitreya-paripri*kkh*â	,,	12 b

*Kh*u-sân-tsâñ-*k*i-tsi.

No.		Fasc.	Page
57	Kâsyapa-parivarta	2	5 a
59	*S*rîmâlâ-devî-si*m*hanâda	,,	30 a
61	Mahâvaipulya-mahâsannipâta-sûtra	,,	24 a
66	Sumerugarbha	3	2 a (?)
68	Âkâsagarbha-bodhisattva-sûtra	2	24 a
70	'Âkâsagarbha-bodhisattva-dhyâna-sûtra'	,,	29 a
71	Bodhisattva-buddhânusmriti-samâdhi	,,	31 b
73	Pratyutpanna-buddhasammukhâvasthita-samâdhi	,,	4 b
74	Akshayamati-nirdesa-sûtra	,,	13 b
79	Tathâgata-mahâkâru*n*ika-nirdesa	,,	9 a
80	'Ratnastrî-paripri*kkh*â'	,,	10 b
81	'Mûka-kumâra-sûtra'	,,	11 a
82	'Îsvararâ*g*a-bodhisattva-sûtra'	,,	22 b
87	Buddhâvata*m*saka - mahâvaipulya-sûtra	,,	25 b
92	'Sûtra on the appearance of the Tathâgata'	,,	10 b
100	'Sûtra on the original action of the Bodhisattva'	,,	6 b
102	'Sûtra on the Tathâgata-visesha*n*a (?)'	,,	5 a
104	'Sûtra of the chapter on going across the world'	,,	9 a
105	Dasabhûmika-sûtra	,,	22 a
108	'Sûtra of the chapter on the way of practice in the ten dwellings (i. e. the earlier steps) of a Bodhisattva (which lead on to the ten Bhûmis)'	,,	13 a
110	Dasabhûmika-sûtra	,,	9 a
112	'Sûtra on the office of the Bodhisattva, asked by Mañ*g*usrî'	,,	5 a

No.		Fasc.	Page
113	Mahâparinirvâ*n*a-sûtra	2	24 a
116	*K*aturdâraka-samâdhi-sûtra	„	11 a
120	Mahâparinirvâ*n*a-sûtra	„	26 a
122	'Sûtra of Buddha's last instruction'	„	23 a
127	Suvar*n*aprabhâsa-sûtra	„	24 b
128	Sarvapu*n*yasamu*kk*aya-samâdhi-sûtra	„	10 a
133	'Amitârtha-sûtra'	„	32 b
134	Saddharmapu*nd*arîka-sûtra	„	22 a
136	„ „	3	12 a
138	„ „	2	9 a
142	Karu*n*âpu*nd*arîka-sûtra	„	24 b
143	'Sha*t*pâramitâ-sannipâta-sûtra'	„	8 a
145	Vimalakîrtti-nirdesa	„	11 b
146	„ „	„	22 a
150	Avaivartya (?), or Aparivartya-sûtra	„	9 b
154	Sandhinirmo*k*ana-sûtra	„	30 b
157	Avaivartya (?), or Aparivartya-sûtra	3	15 b
158	„ „	2	29 b
160	Lalitavistara	„	9 a
164	Sarvadharma-prav*ri*tti-nirdesa-sûtra	„	22 b
165	'Vasudhara-bodhisattva-paripr*i*kkhâ-sûtra'	„	11 b
166	'Vasudhara-sûtra'	„	22 a
168	Ratnakâra*nd*akavyûha-sûtra	„	9 b
174	A*g*âtasatru-kaukr*i*tya-vinodana	„	5 a
175	Laṅkâvatâra-sûtra	„	30 b
182	A*g*âtasatru-kaukr*i*tya-vinodana	„	9 b
183	„ „	3	13 b
184	Mañ*g*usrî-vikrî*d*ita-sûtra	2	10 a
190	Viesha*k*inta-brahma-paripr*i*kkhâ	„	22 a
194	Hastikakshyâ	„	13 a
197	Viesha*k*inta-brahma-paripr*i*kkhâ	„	9 a
200	Sukhâvatyamr*i*tavyûha-sûtra, or Sukhâvatîvyûha	„	22 b
202	'A later translation of the Sûtra consisting of verses on Amitâyus'	4	41 a
204	'Sûtra about the meditation on the Bodhisattva Maitreya's going up to be born in the Tushita heaven'	2	31 a
205	Maitreya-vyâkara*n*a	„	22 b
206	„ „	3	13 a
208	'Sûtra about the meditation on the Bodhisattva Maitreya's coming down to be born (in this world)'	2	12 a
209	'Sûtra on Maitreya's becoming Buddha'	„	22 b
214	Strîvivarta-vyâkara*n*a-sûtra	„	12 a
216	'Sûtra on the Bodhisattva who was the son who took a look at (his blind father)'	3	10 a
219	'Kumâra-mûka-sûtra'	2	12 b
224	'Sûtra spoken by Buddha at (the request of) an old woman'	„	7 a
230	*K*andraprabha-kumâra-sûtra	„	11 a
233	Vatsa-sûtra		7 b
234	„ „	„	13 a
238	Gayâsîrsha	„	22 b
242	'Sûtra on the determined Dhâra*n*î'	„	10 b
244	Mahâmegha-sûtra	„	24 b
252	'Sarvavaipulyavidyâsiddha-sûtra'	„	10 b
255	Tathâgata*g*ñânamudrâ-samâdhi	4	46 b
256	„ „		6 b
257	'Anantaratna-samâdhi-sûtra'	„	13 b
281	*S*âlisambhava-sûtra	„	7 b
283	'Sûtra on the Samâdhi called vow, realised by the Tathâgata alone'	„	13 b
297	'Sûtra on the girl Nâgadattâ'	„	7 b
309	Mahâmayûrî-vidyârâ*g*ñî	„	19 a
310	'Mahâmayûrî-râ*g*ñî-sa*m*yuktarddhi-dhâra*n*î-sûtra'	„	„
342	*S*rîmatî-brâhma*n*î-paripr*i*kkhâ	„	10 b
354	Anantamukha-sâdhaka-dhâra*n*î (?)	„	31 b
355	„ „	„	6 b
356	„ „	„	26 a
376	'Sûtra on cutting the tie (of passions) in the ten dwellings (i.e. the earlier steps of a Bodhisattva which lead on to the ten Bhûmis)'	„	21 a
377	'Bodhisattva-bodhivr*i*ksha-sûtra'	„	6 b
379	'Sûtra on (the history of) Poh (or Pushya ?)'	„	7 a
381	'Pûr*n*aprabhâsa-samâdhimati-sûtra'	„	5 a
384	Tathâgatagarbha-sûtra	„	25 b
385	Ratna*g*âli-paripr*i*kkhâ	„	12 a
388	'Sûtra on (the characteristic marks on Buddha's) person as (the results of) fifty causes of the practice of a Bodhisattva'	„	11 a
392	'*K*aturdurlabha-sûtra'		12 b
393	'Su*k*inti (?)-devaputra-sûtra'	„	10 a
395	'Avalokitesvara-bodhisattva-mahâsthâmaprâpta-bodhisattva-vyâkara*n*a-sûtra'	„	27 b
397	'Sûrya*g*ihmîkara*n*aprabhâ-samâdhi-sûtra'	„	17 b
399	*S*ûraṅgama-samâdhi		22 a
401	Buddhasaṅgîti-sûtra		10 a
403	Bhadrakalpika-sûtra	„	8 b
405	'Atîta-vyûhakalpa-sahasrabuddhanâma-sûtra'	4	4 a
406	'Pratyutpanna-bhadrakalpa-sahasrabuddhanâma-sûtra'	„	

No.		Fasc.	Page
407	‘Anâgata-nakshatratârâkalpa-sahasrabuddhanâma-sûtra’	4	4 a
412	‘A*k*intyaguna - sarvabuddha - parigraha-sûtra’	„	45 b
416	‘*S*resh*th*i-dharma*k*âri-bhâryâ-sûtra’	3	15 b
421	Pratyutpanna - buddha - sammukhâvasthita-samâdhi-sûtra	2	27 a
425	Kusalamûla-samparigraha, or -paridhara-sûtra	„	22 a
430	‘Buddhadhyâna - samâdhisâgara-sûtra’	„	25 b
432	‘Bodhisattva-pûrva*k*aryâ-sûtra’	3	17 b
433	Garbha-sûtra (?)	2	21 a
434	Aṅgulimâlîya-sûtra	„	30 b
437	Anavatapta-nâgarâ*g*a-pariprikkhâ	„	9 b
438	‘Sûtra on fifty countings of clear measure (?)’	„	3 b
440	Mahâbherî-hâraka-parivarta	„	30 a
445	‘Sûtra of the garland of the Bodhisattva’	„	21 a
456	Sâgara-nâgarâ*g*a-paripri*kkh*â	„	9 b
468	‘Sûtra on the changes of the future’	„	13 a
469	‘Sûtra on the Pi*n*dapâtika of a Buddha of the past’	„	13 b
470	‘Sûtra on the destruction of the law’	4	31 a
472	‘Sûtra on Phi-lo (Vela ?), the crown-prince of a heavenly king’	3	18 b
478	‘Sûtra on the spiritual Mantra for keeping the house safe’	4	44 a
480	‘Sûtra on the Vidyâ or spell for avoiding and removing the injury (caused) by a thief’	„	„
481	‘Sûtra on relieving epidemic by a spell’	„	43 b
483	*K*akshur-visodhana-vidyâ	„	44 a
484	‘Sûtra on relieving a (sick) child by a spell’	„	43 b
513	‘*K*andraprabha-bodhisattva-sûtra’	2	6 b
514	‘Sûtra on *K*ittaprabhâ (?)’	„	13 a
515	Dasadigandhakâra - vidhva*m*sana-sûtra	„	11 b
517	‘Sûtra on the opposition of the Mâra’	„	10 b
518	Râsh*t*ravara - paripri*kkh*â - gu*n*aprabha-kumâra-sûtra’	„	„

Sûtras of the Hînayâna.

No.		Fasc.	Page
542	Madhyamâgama-sûtra	2	21 b
543	Ekottarâgama-sûtra	„	20 b
544	Sa*m*yuktâgama-sûtra	„	30 a
545	Dîrghâgama-sûtra	2	23 b
548	‘Sûtra on the law of ten rewards in the Dîrghâgama’	„	3 a
551	‘Sûtra on the Lokadhâtu (?)’	„	6 a
553	‘Sûtra on the Avidyâ, T*ri*sh*n*â, and *G*âti of man’	„	3 a
558	‘Sûtra on the salt-water comparison’	3	13 a
559	‘Sûtra on the cause of all the Âsravas or sins’	2	4 a
565	‘Sûtra on the law, true and not true’	„	
567	‘Sûtra on the explanation of Âsrava (?)’	„	3 a
577	‘Sûtra on fasting (Upavasatha, Uposatho in Pâli)’	„	7 a
578	‘Sûtra on the Du*h*kha-skandha (?)’	4	30 a
580	‘Sûtra on the cause’	2	7 a
583	‘Sûtra on G*ri*hapati, being a man possessed of eight cities and ten families (?)’	„	18 a
586	‘Sûtra on the universal meaning of the law’	„	3 a
594	‘Sûtra on the (G*ri*hapati) Râsh*t*rapâla (?) or Râsh*t*ravara’	„	8 a
600	‘Sûtra on the Bhikshu *K*ampa’	„	3 a
601	‘Sûtra on the fundamental relationship or causation’	„	4 a
609	‘Sûtra on the honourable one (?)’	„	6 b
611	‘Sûtra on or to Teu-thiâo (Devadatta ?)’	3	9 b
616	‘Sûtra on Sumati (?)’	2	7 a (?)
621	‘Sûtra on Aṅgulimâlya’	„	13 a
623	‘Sûtra on the (500) Mallas or wrestlers who were trying to move a mountain’	„	11 b
639	‘Sûtra on a *S*râma*n*era’	3	18 b
647	‘Sûtra on the secret importance of curing the (heart) disease of those who engage in contemplation’	2	31 a
648	‘Sûtra on seven Âyatanas and three subjects for contemplation’	„	3 b
652	‘Sûtra on the holy seal of the law’	„	11 b
653	‘Sûtra on the comparison of the five Skandhas’	„	3 b
656	‘Sûtra on Pûr*n*amaitrâya*n*îputra’	4	49 b
657	Dharma*k*akra-pravartana (-sûtra)	2	3 b
659	‘Ash*t*âṅga-sa*m*yañ-mârga-sûtra’	„	„
661	‘Sûtra on three characteristic marks of a (good) horse’	3	3 b (?)
662	‘Sûtra on eight characteristics of a		

No.		Fasc.	Page
	(bad) horse compared with those of a (bad) man'	3	4 a (?)
664	'Sûtra on the origin of practice (of the Bodhisattva)'	2	6 a
665	'Sûtra on the lucky fulfilment of the crown-prince'	"	"
666	'Sûtra on the cause and effect of the past and present'	"	30 b
669	*G*âtaka-nidâna	"	9 a
671	'Vaidûrya-*râg*a-sûtra'	"	12 a
674	'Sûtra on the fulness of meaning'	"	6 b
676	'Sa*m*yukta-pi*t*aka-sûtra'	"	26 b
678	'Sûtra of forty-two sections'	"	2 a
681	'Sûtra on keeping thought, in the (manner of) great Ânâpâna'	"	3 b
683	'Sûtra on perception in the law of practice of meditation'	"	4 a
689	'Sûtra on the condition (Dharma) which receives dust or impurity'	"	"
696	Sûtra (spoken to ?) Ânanda on four matters'	"	7 a
699	'Sûtra on four wishes (of mankind)'	"	7 b
702	'Sûtra on the filial child'	3	10 a
709	'Sûtra on seven women'	2	7 a
710	'Sûtra on eight teachers'	"	"
712	'Sûtra on desire being the cause of affliction'	"	13 b
722	'Sûtra on the *K*aturmahârâ*g*a'	"	29 b
729	'Sûtra on 500 disciples telling their own Nidâna or *G*âtaka'	"	12 a
746	'Sûtra on four (articles of) self-injuring'	"	11 a
758	'Sûtra on King Samantaprâpta (?)'	3	12 b
759	'Sûtra on the mother of (500) demon-children (i. e. Hâritî)'	"	11 b
760	'Sûtra on a king of the country Brâhma*n*a (?)'	"	9 b
765	'Sûtra on nine (causes of) unexpected or untimely (death)'	2	3 b
775	'Sûtra on the five kings'	4	17 a
780	'Skandha-dhâtv-âyatana-sûtra'	2	2 b

Vinaya of the Mahâyâna.

No.		Fasc.	Page
1083	'Sûtra on the manners concerning the five *S*ilas of the Bodhisattva-upâsaka'	2	28 b
1084	Paramârthasa*m*varti (-varta ?)-satyanirde*s*anâma-mahâyâna-sûtra	"	10 b
1085	Bodhisattva-*k*aryâ-nirde*s*a	"	28 b
1086	" "	"	24 b
1088	'Upâsaka-*s*îla-sûtra'	2	24 b
1091	'Ma*ñg*u*s*rî-kshamâ-sûtra'	"	11 b
1093	'Sûtra on receiving the ten good precepts or the *S*ikshâpada'	4	13 a
1095	Buddhapi*t*aka-nigrahanâma-mahâyâna-sûtra	2	22 b
1096	'Bodhisattva-pratimoksha-sûtra'	"	24 b

Vinaya of the Hînayâna.

No.		Fasc.	Page
1114	'Upâsaka-pa*ñk*a*s*îla-rûpa-sûtra'	2	28 b
1115	Sarvâstivâda-vinaya		23 b
1117	Dharmagupta-vinaya	"	"
1119	Mahâsa*n*gha (or -sa*n*ghika)-vinaya	"	26 b
1122	Mahî*s*âsaka-vinaya	"	28 a
1125	Vibhâshâ-vinaya	,	33 a
1132	Sarvâstivâda-nikâya-vinaya-mâ*t*rikâ	"	29 a
1145	'*S*râma*n*era-da*s*a*s*îla-dharmakarmavâ*k*â (?)'	4	13 a
1155	Pratimoksha of the Dharmagupta-nikâya	2	24 a
1157	Pratimoksha of the Mahî*s*âsaka-nikâya	"	28 a
1160	Pratimoksha-sûtra (?)		23 b
1161	Bhikshu*n*î-pratimoksha-sûtra (?)	"	31 a
1166	'An important use for the Bhikshu concerning the Karman of the Da*s*âdhyâya (-vinaya)'	"	31 b

Abhidharma of the Mahâyâna.

No.		Fasc.	Page
1169	'Mahâpra*gñ*âpâramitâ (-sûtra)-*s*âstra'	2	23 a
1179	Prâ*n*yamûla-*s*âstra-*t*îkâ		"
1180	'Da*s*abhûmi-vibhâshâ-*s*âstra'	"	"
1186	Dvâda*s*anikâya-*s*âstra		23 b
1188	*S*ata-*s*âstra		"

Abhidharma of the Hînayâna.

No.		Fasc.	Page
1268	*S*âriputrâbhidharma-*s*âstra	2	24 a
1273	Abhidharma-*gñ*ânaprasthâna-*s*âstra	"	21 b
1274	'Satyasiddhi-*s*âstra'	"	23 a
1279	Vibhâshâ-*s*âstra		20 a
1287	Sa*m*yuktâbhidharma-h*ri*daya-*s*âstra		28 b
1288	Abhidharma-h*ri*daya-*s*âstra	"	21 b
1289	'Ârya-vasumitra-bodhisattva-sa*ṅ*gîti-*s*âstra'	1	20 a

INDIAN MISCELLANEOUS WORKS.

No.		Fasc.	Page
1321	Avadâna (-sûtra), or Dhammapadâvadâna	2	21 a
1322	Damamûka (-nidâna-sûtra)	„	30 a
1323	'Buddhapûrvakaryâ-sûtra'	„	27 b
1325	'Karyâmârgabhûmi-sûtra'	„	9 a
1326	'Mârgabhûmi-sûtra'	„	2 b
1329	'Samyuktaratnapitaka-sûtra'	„	32 a
1336	Samantabhadrapranidhâna	„	26 a
1337	'Sûtra on six Bodhisattvas' names to be recited and kept in mind'	4	8 a(?)
1339	'Sûtra on the twelve causes as an oral explanation according to the Âgama'	2	4 a
1340	'Sûtra (or record) on the Nidâna or cause of transmitting the Dharmapitaka'	„	32 b
1341	Dharmatara (or -trâta)-dhyâna-sûtra	„	25 b
1342	'Sûtra on the important explanation of the law of meditation'	„	23 a
1346	'Abhidharma-pañkadharmakaryâ-sûtra'	„	3 a
1349	'Sûtra on the fruits of Karman briefly explained by the Bodhisattva Âryasûra'	„	29 a
1350	'Dhyânanishthita (?)-samâdhi-dharmaparyâya-sûtra'	2	23 a
1352	'Sûtra on the practice of Buddha, compiled by Sangharaksha'	„	20 a
1364	'Sûtra of a hundred comparisons'	„	33 b
1365	Dharmapada or Dhammapada	„	6 a
1366	'Samyuktâvadâna-sûtra, selected from various Sûtras'	,	23 a
1367	'Sûtra on the Nidâna or cause of the eye-destruction of Fâ-yi, the son of Asoka'	„	21 a
1381	'Explanation of an extract from the four Âgamas'	„	20 b
1382	'Pañkadvâra-dhyânasûtra-mahârthadharma'	„	29 b
1416	'Law of the Bodhisattva's blaming lustful desire'	„	23 a
1440	Ârya-nâgârguna-bodhisattva-suhrillekha	„	29 a
1451	'Pragñâpâramitâ-buddhi-sûtra-mahâsukhâmogha-samayasatya-vagra-bodhisattvâdisaptadasârya-mahâmandalavyâkhyâ'	4	13 a

A CHINESE WORK.

No.		Fasc.	Page
1496	Travels of Fâ-hhien or Fâ-hian	2	26 b

No. 1476, the oldest Catalogue in existence (see pp. xiii, xxvii), mentions 2213 distinct works, whether translations or native productions, of which 276 works may thus be identified with those in existence at the present day. This oldest Catalogue is a private compilation of a Chinese priest, named San-yiu. He lived under the reign of the Emperor Wu, A.D. 502–549, the founder of the Liân dynasty, A.D. 502–557. As we read in the Annals of the Sui dynasty, A.D. 589–618, 'This Emperor paid great honour to Buddhism. He made a large collection of the Buddhist canonical books, amounting to 5400 volumes, in the Hwâ-lin garden. The Shâman Pâo-khan compiled the Catalogue in fifty-four fascicles[1].' According to the Khâi-yuen-lu (fasc. 10, fol. 5 a), this Catalogue was compiled by Pâo-khan under the Imperial order, in 4 fasciculi, in A.D. 518; but it had been lost already in A.D. 730. The total number of the sacred books in it is said to have been about 1432, or 3395(!) distinct works in 3741 fasciculi, arranged under twenty classes. This was the first Collection of Buddhist sacred books made by an Emperor of China.

In A.D. 533–534 the second Collection of Buddhist sacred books was made by the Emperor Hhiâo-wu, of the Northern Wei dynasty, A.D. 386–534. An official, Li Kwo, compiled the Catalogue under the Imperial order. There were ten classes, including about 427(?) works in 2053 fasciculi. This Catalogue had been lost already in A.D. 730. (See Khâi-yuen-lu, fasc. 10, fol. 4 b.)

Under the Sui dynasty, A.D. 589–618, three Catalogues were compiled, in A.D. 594, 597, and 603. These Catalogues are in existence, viz. Nos. 1609, 1504, and 1608 (see p. xxvii). The number of the books in these Catalogues differs considerably. The first and the last compilations, Nos. 1609 and 1608, were made under an Imperial order. These may therefore be called the third and fourth Collections, made by Wan-ti, the first Emperor of the Sui dynasty, who reigned A.D. 589 or 581–604.

[1] Max Müller, Selected Essays, vol. ii, p. 328.

No. 1609, the second Catalogue, which is still in existence (see p. xxvii), compiled by Fâ-kiñ and others, mentions 2257 distinct works in 5310 fasciculi in nine classes, each class being subdivided into two or more heads. But the actual number is as follows:—

1. Sûtra.	Mahâyâna	. . . .	784	in	1718	fasciculi.
	Hînayâna	. . . .	845	"	1304	"
2. Vinaya.	Mahâyâna	. . . .	50	"	82	"
	Hînayâna	. . . .	63	"	381	"
3. Abhidharma.	Mahâyâna	. . . .	68	"	381	"
	Hînayâna	. . . .	116	"	482	"
4. Later works, Indian and Chinese.	Extracts	. . . .	144	"	627	"
	Records	. . . .	68	"	185	"
	Treatises	. . . .	119	"	134	"
			2257	"	5294	"

Although mention is not made of missing works in No. 1609, yet it is doubtful whether the 2257 works were all in existence in A.D. 594 (see second line from the bottom of this page).

In A.D. 597 the third Catalogue in existence, No. 1504 (see p. xxvii), was compiled by Fê Khân-fân, who was a translator of the Buddhist sacred books, appointed by the Emperor. In his compilation the following number of works is said to have been admitted into the Canon:—

1. Mahâyâna.

Sûtra, whose translators are known	. .	234	in	885	fasciculi.
" " " " unknown	. .	235	"	402	"
Vinaya, " " " known	. .	19	"	40	"
" " " " unknown	. .	12	"	14	"
Abhidharma, " " " known	. .	49	"	238	"
" " " " unknown	. .	2	"	7	"
		551	"	1586	"

2. Hînayâna.

Sûtra, whose translators are known	. .	108	in	527	fasciculi.
" " " " unknown	. .	316	"	482	"
Vinaya, " " " known	. .	39	"	285	"
" " " " unknown	. .	31	"	67	"
Abhidharma, " " " known	. .	21	"	351	"
" " " " unknown	. .	10	"	27	"
		525	"	1739	"

The fourth Catalogue in existence, No. 1608 (see p. xxvii), was compiled in A.D. 602 by priests and literati, who were then appointed by the Emperor as translators of the Buddhist sacred books. In this Catalogue the total number and classification of works are again different, namely:—

1. Works with one translation	. . . . . .	370	in	1786	fasciculi.
2. Works with two or more translations	. . . .	277	"	583	"
3. Works of the (Indian) sages	. . . . .	41	"	164	"
4. Works of separate production, or extracts	. .	810	"	1288	"
5. Works doubtful and false	. . . . . .	209	"	490	"
6. Works missing	. . . .	402	"	747	"
		2109	"	5058	"

As we read in the Sui Annals, 'In the period Tâ-yeh (A. D. 605–616) the Emperor (Yâṅ) ordered the Shâman *K*i-kwo to compose a catalogue of the Buddhist books at the Imperial Buddhist chapel within the gate of the palace. He then made some divisions and classifications, which were as follow:—

'The Sûtras which contained what Buddha had spoken were arranged under three divisions:—

'1. The Mahâyâna. 2. The Hînayâna. 3. The Mixed Sûtras.

'Other books, that seemed to be the productions of later men, who falsely ascribed their works to greater names, were classed as Doubtful Books.

'There were other works in which Bodhisattvas and others went deeply into the explanation of the meaning, and illustrated the principles of Buddha. These were called Disquisitions, or *S*âstras.

'Then there were Vinaya works, or compilations of precepts, under each division, as before, Mahâyâna, Hînayâna, Mixed.

'There were also Records, or accounts of the doings in their times of those who had been students of the system. Altogether there were eleven classes under which the books were arranged:—

'1. Sûtra.	Mahâyâna . .	617	in	2076	chapters (or fasciculi).
	Hînayâna . .	487	"	852	"
	Mixed . . .	380	"	716	"
	Mixed and doubtful	172	"	336	"
'2. Vinaya.	Mahâyâna . .	52	"	91	"
	Hînayâna . .	80	"	472	"
	Mixed . . .	27	"	46	"
'3. *S*âstra.	Mahâyâna . .	35	"	141	"
	Hînayâna . .	41	"	567	"
	Mixed . . .	51	"	437	"
	Records . .	20	"	464	"
		1962	"	6198	"[1]'

Neither the Catalogue nor the compiler is mentioned in Chinese Buddhist works. The number of books is again different from that mentioned in four earlier Catalogues still in existence. This may however be called the fifth Collection made by an Emperor of China.

In A. D. 664[2] a Chinese priest, named Tâo-süen, compiled the fifth Catalogue which has come down to us, No. 1483 (see p. xxvii). This compilation is subdivided into ten sections. In the first section he gives a list of works, whether translations or original treatises in Chinese, with a biographical note of each author, and sums up the total number of works as 2487, in 8476 fasciculi. In the second section he divides the works then in existence, in the following way:—

1. Mahâyâna.	Sûtra . .	386	in	1152	fasciculi,	8521	leaves.
	Vinaya .	22	"	34	"	461	"
	Abhidharma	72	"	500	"	9220	"
2. Hînayâna.	Sûtra . .	204	"	544	"	7674	"
	Vinaya .	35	"	274	"	5813	"
	Abhidharma	33	"	676	"	12177	"
3. Works of the (Indian) sages		47	"	184	"	1760	"
		799	"	3364	"	45626	"

In the remaining sections of No. 1483, Tâo-süen makes several divisions and classifications, which are very complicated.

The sixth Catalogue in existence, No. 1487 (see p. xxvii), was compiled about A. D. 664 by Tsiṅ-mâi. It contains all the titles of translations, whether in existence or missing, from Kâsyapa Mâtaṅga, A. D. 67, to Hhüen-*k*wâṅ or Hiouen-thsang, A. D. 645–664. The number of translators is 120, and that of their works is 1620 in 5552 fasciculi, with the exception of 298 works in 527 fasciculi, whose translators are unknown.

[1] Max Müller, Selected Essays, vol. ii, pp. 329–330.

[2] In this year the famous Hhüen-*k*wâṅ or Hiouen-thsang died.

In A.D. 695 the seventh Catalogue which we still possess, No. 1610 (see p. xxvii), was compiled by Min-*khü*en and others, under the order of the Emperor Wu Tsö-thien, A.D. 684–705. This is the sixth Collection made by a Sovereign of China. The divisions and classifications in this Catalogue are as follow:—

1 Mahâyâna.				
Sûtra of single translation . .	283	in	525	fasciculi.
Sûtra of duplicate translations .	696	„	2514	„
Vinaya	44	„	105	„
Abhidharma	108	„	611	„
2. Hînayâna.				
Sûtra of single translation . .	323	„	419	„
Sûtra of duplicate translations .	656	„	1227	„
Vinaya	104	„	428	„
Abhidharma	54	„	703	„
3. Works of the (Indian) sages .	36	„	91	„
4. Sûtras of unknown translators .	424	„	636	„
5. Sûtras missing	888	„	1262	„
	3616	„	8521	„

Besides these, the following works were then admitted into the Canon:— .

1. Mahâyâna.	Sûtra . .	452	in	1840	fasciculi,	186	cases.
	Vinaya .	23	„	47	„	6	„
	Abhidharma	83	„	516	„	51	„
2. Hînayâna.	Sûtra .	205	„	441	„	44	„
	Vinaya .	35	„	260	„	23	„
	Abhidharma	36	„	744	„	73	„
3. Works of the (Indian) sages		25	„	34	„	4	„
		859	„	3882	„	386	„

Then there follows a list of 228 spurious works, which are said to have been in 419 fasciculi.

In A.D. 730 the eighth, ninth, and tenth Catalogues in existence, Nos. 1485, 1486, 1488 (see p. xxvii), were compiled by *K'*-shan. No. 1485 is one of the best, if not the best, of Catalogues of the Chinese Translation of the Buddhist Tripiṭaka. It is generally called Khâi-yuen-lu [1]. It was originally in 20 fasciculi, now subdivided into 30 fasciculi. In the first 9 original fasciculi (subdivided into 13), 2278 works in 7046 fasciculi, with the exception of 741 in 1052 fasciculi of unknown translators, are ascribed to 176 translators or writers, who lived in China in the period of 664 years between A.D. 67 and 730. The titles of these works are given in chronological order, and 'a short account of each translator or writer (is added), being preceded by a list of his works and various miscellaneous items of information, such as the number of books (or fasciculi) into which each work is divided; variations in the title, and when and where the translation was made, etc.[2]' Then the compiler concludes with the following words (fasc. 9, fol. 36 b seq.):—'Thus under 19 dynasties, from the Eastern Hân (A.D. 25–220) to the Thân (618–907), there were produced translations of the Sûtra, Vinaya, and Abhidharma or Sâstra of the Mahâyâna and Hînayâna, as well as the works of the sages and wise men, altogether 2278 works in 7046 fasciculi. Of these 1124 works in 5048 fasciculi are now (A.D. 730) admitted into the Canon. In truth, however, the exact number is 1123 works in 5047 fasciculi, because one and the same work in one fasciculus is given both in the Pragñâpâramitâ and Ratnakûṭa classes (viz. Nos. 21 and 23 (46)). Again, 40 works in 368 fasciculi are not translations, but written originally in Chinese. At the same time the number of missing works is 1148 in 1980 fasciculi. Thus the total number is really 2271 works in 7027 fasciculi, subtracting 7 works in 19 fasciculi (which

---

[1] For the contents of this Catalogue, see also the Chrysanthemum Magazine, June 1881, p. 234 seq. Published monthly at Yokohama, in Japan.

[2] Chrysanthemum, 1881, p. 235.

are no longer independent works, being put in other works as their parts) from the number 2278 in 7946 fasciculi above mentioned.'

In fasc. 10 of the Khâi-yuen-lu, No. 1485, a list of forty-one Catalogues with a few details regarding them is given. In the next 8 original fasciculi (subdivided into 12), the following divisions and classifications are introduced:—

1. Translations (and some original Chinese works) in existence (A. D. 730).		
a. Tripiṭaka of the Bodhisattvas or the Mahâyâna	686 in 2745	fasciculi.
b. Tripiṭaka of the Srâvakas or the Hînayâna	330 " 1762	"
c. Works of the sages and wise men	108 " 541	"
	1124 " 5048	"
2. Translations missing	1148 in 1980	fasciculi.
3. Portions published separately	682 in 812	fasciculi.
4. Double copies and extracts taken away	147 " 408	"
5. Formerly not found or missing, and newly-produced works now supplied	306 " 1111	"
6, Doubtful works re-examined	14 " 19	"
7. Spurious and heterodox books	382 " 1055	"
	1531 " 3405	"

Some of these 1531 works are included in the translations then in existence (see above), while the rest are altogether excluded from the total number already alluded to.

In fasc. 19 and 20 of No. 1485, the works in existence, in A. D. 730, are arranged in the following divisions:—

1. Mahâyâna.				
Sûtra	515 (or 563)	in 2173	fasciculi, 203	cases.
Vinaya	26	" 54	" 5	"
Abhidharma	97	" 518	" 50	"
2. Hînayâna.				
Sûtra	240	" 618	" 48	"
Vinaya	54	" 446	" 45	"
Abhidharma	36	" 698	" 72	"
3. Works of the sages and wise men.				
Indian	68	in 173	" } 57	"
Chinese	40	" 368	" }	
	1076 (1124)	" 5048	" 480	"

The ninth Catalogue in existence, No. 1486 (see p. xxvii), is an abridged reproduction of the last part of No. 1485, in 5 fasciculi. 'But as it is little more than a bare enumeration of the titles of the different works mentioned in the larger catalogue, the translators' names, and the number of chapters (or fasciculi) into which each work is divided, it is not of much use to the foreign student of Buddhism. It gives the Index character (taken from the Tshien-tsz'-wan, or Thousand-character-composition) under which each work may be found in the Imperial Collection, and occasionally a few details[1].' This may be called the seventh Collection, made by order of the Emperor Hhüen-tsuṅ, A. D. 713–755, under whose reign this Index was made.

The tenth Catalogue in existence, No. 1488 (see p. xxvii), is a continuation of No. 1487 (see pp. xix, xxvii). It enumerates 163 translations in 645 fasciculi, made by twenty-one translators, who lived in China between A. D. 664 and 730.

[1] Chrysanthemum, 1881, p. 236 note.

According to the Fo-tsu-li-tâi-thuṅ-tsâi, No. 1637 (fasc. 14, fol. 2 a), Thâi-tsu, the first Emperor of the later Suṅ dynasty, who reigned A.D. 960–975, was the first who ordered the whole Buddhist Canon to be published. The blocks of wood on which the characters were cut for this edition are said to have been 130,000 in number. This event happened in A.D. 972. In the preceding year, he caused two copies of the same Canon to be made, one written in gold and the other in silver paint. This may be called the eighth Collection made by order of the Emperor of China, though no Catalogue or Index seems to have been compiled on this occasion.

The eleventh Catalogue in existence, No. 1612 (see p. xxvii), was compiled by Kiṅ-ki-siaṅ, together with some Indian, Tibetan, and Chinese priests and officials, in A.D. 1285–1287, under the Imperial order of Shi-tsu, the founder of the Yuen dynasty, who reigned A.D. 1280–1294. It is therefore the ninth Collection made by the Chinese Emperor. This Catalogue is generally called K'-yuen-lu, or the Catalogue of the K'-yuen period, A.D. 1264–1294 [1].

There are given the following divisions and classifications:—

1. Sûtra.	Mahâyâna	.	.	897	in 2980	fasciculi.
	Hînayâna	.	.	291	„ 710	„
2. Vinaya.	Mahâyâna	.	.	28	„ 56	„
	Hînayâna	.	.	69	„ 504	„
3. Abhidharma.	Mahâyâna	.	.	117	„ 628	„
	Hînayâna	.	.	38	„ 708	„
				1440	„ 5586	„

These are the translations made by 194 persons under twenty-two dynasties in the period of 1219 years, from A.D. 67 to 1285. Besides this number there are 95 Indian and 118 Chinese miscellaneous works.

The compilers of the K'-yuen-lu, No. 1612, compared the Chinese translations with the Tibetan translations (Kangur and Tangur?), and added the Sanskrit title in transliteration, and gave a note after each Chinese title, stating whether both translations were in agreement, or whether the book was wanting in the Tibetan version [2]. This comparison, however, seems to have been made only through a Catalogue of the Tibetan translations, and not actually with the translations themselves. (See the K'-yuen-lu, fasc. 1, fol. 4 a. col. 5 seq.) Nevertheless, it is curious to see that there have been (in A.D. 1300) and still are so many Chinese translations, which are similar to, though they do not agree exactly with, the Tibetan translations. I have added the result of their comparison under each title.

The twelfth Catalogue in existence, No. 1611 (see p. xxvii), was originally compiled by Wân Ku, under the Suṅ dynasty, A.D. 960–1280; and continued by Kwân-ku-pâ, in A.D. 1360, under the Yuen dynasty, A.D. 1280–1368. It depends entirely on No. 1612, and adds a short account of the contents of each work.

The thirteenth Catalogue in existence, No. 1662 (see p. xxvii), is the base of the present compilation. This was originally the Catalogue of the Southern Collection or Edition of the Chinese Buddhist Canon, published in Nanking ('Southern Capital'), under the reign of Thâi-tsu, the first Emperor of the Miṅ dynasty, who reigned A.D. 1368–1398. But it is now used also as the Catalogue of a reproduction of the Northern Collection or Edition of 1621 works (Nos. 1–1621), first published in Peking ('Northern Capital'), by the order of Khaṅ-

---

[1] For the contents of this Catalogue, see the Journal Asiatique, Novembre–Decembre, 1849, p. 37 seq.

[2] Cf. the following account, which is said to be derived from a Tibetan source, as we read in the Journal of the Asiatic Society of Bengal, 1882, p. 91:—

'Last of all, during the reign of the Tartar Emperor, Sa-chhen, the Chinese scriptures were compared with the Tibetan collections of the Kangur and Tangur. Such treatises and volumes as were wanting in the Chinese were translated from the Tibetan scriptures. All these formed one complete collection, the first part of which consisted of Buddha's teaching (Kangur). To the second part 11 volumes of translations from Tibetan, the Chinese Sâstras, and works of eminent Hwashan (Upâdhyâya or teacher?), com-

prising 153 volumes, were added. The whole collection consisted of 740 volumes. An analytic catalogue of all these books was also furnished. In this collection many Sâstras were found which did not exist in the Tibetan collections.'

This statement seems to agree to a certain extent with the account concerning the K'-yuen-lu, No. 1612, if the 'Tartar Emperor, Sa-chhen,' is meant for the Mongolian Emperor, Shi-tsu. Otherwise the 'Tartar Emperor, Sa-chhen,' could only be identified either with Shi-tsuṅ, of the Liâo dynasty, who reigned A.D. 947–950, or with Shi-tsuṅ, of the Kin dynasty, who reigned A.D. 1161–1189. The Liâo and Kin dynasties were both Tartars, while the Yuen was a Mongolian dynasty.

tsu or Thâi-tsuṅ, the third Emperor of the Miṅ dynasty, who reigned A.D. 1403–1424, together with 41 additional works (Nos. 1622–1662), published by a Chinese priest named Mi-tsâṅ[1], after some twenty or thirty years' labour, beginning from A.D. 1586. Afterwards, in A.D. 1678–1681, this edition was re-published in Japan by a Japanese priest named Dô-kô or Tetsu-gen, whose labours will be described below.

Thus there are altogether thirteen Catalogues of the Chinese Translation of the Buddhist Canon in the Collection of the India Office Library.

The Southern and Northern Collections or Editions made under the Miṅ dynasty may be called the tenth and eleventh Collections made by the Emperors of China, if the Southern Edition is the same as that which is said to have been published by Thâi-tsu, in Nanking. For in a composition by the Chinese Bhikshu Tâo-khâi, dated A.D. 1586, we read: 'The Emperor Thâi-tsu Kâo (A.D. 1368–1398) caused the whole Piṭaka to be engraved in *K*iṅ-liâṅ (Nanking); and the Emperor Thâi-tsuṅ Wan (A.D. 1403–1424) again caused a good edition to be published in Pe-piṅ (Peking)[2].'

But there is another statement about these two Collections or Editions, namely: 'In the Yuṅ-lö period, A.D. 1403–1424, of the Miṅ dynasty, an edition was published (by the Emperor) in the Capital (Peking), which is called the Northern Piṭaka or Collection of the Sanskrit Books (translated into Chinese). Again there was a private edition among the people, and the blocks for this publication were kept at *K*iâ-hhiṅ-fu in Chehkiang. This is called the Southern Piṭaka or Collection[3].'

This statement is found in an Imperial preface to the Buddhist Canon, which preface dates from the thirteenth year of the Yuṅ-*k*aṅ period, A.D. 1735. The author is the Emperor Shi-tsuṅ, the third sovereign of the present Tshiṅ dynasty, who reigned A.D. 1723–1735. If this Imperial authority may be accepted in spite of a later date, then Thâi-tsu's edition would have been quite different from the Southern Collection or Edition already alluded to.

The Imperial preface above quoted was added by the Emperor Shi-tsuṅ to a carefully-revised Edition of the Buddhist Canon, first collected and published under the Miṅ dynasty, with the addition of 54 Chinese works. The Edition was completed in the second year of the *K*ien-luṅ period, A.D. 1737, under the reign of his successor, Kâo-tsuṅ, who reigned A.D. 1736–1795. This may be called the twelfth and last Collection made by an Emperor of China[4].

It is remarkable that the whole Collection of the Buddhist Canon, which became larger and larger in the course of time, was preserved in MS. only, from the introduction of Buddhism into China in A.D. 67, till A.D. 972. At that time the first Edition was published by Thâi-tsu, the founder of the later Suṅ dynasty (see p. xxii). Thereafter it 'has been printed at various times in China from wooden blocks, which were as often destroyed by fire or civil war. It is said that during the Suṅ and Yuen dynasties (A.D. 960–1368) as many as twenty different editions had been produced, but during the troubles occurring towards the end of the Yuen period all of them perished.'

This statement is quoted from Mr. Beal's introduction (p. vii) to his 'Buddhist Literature in China (1882),'

---

[1] 密藏. For an account of his labours, see the 刻經緣叙 *Khö-kiṅ-yuen-sü*, or 'a list (or collection) of prefaces respecting the engraving of the blocks for Buddhist scriptures. They are by different authors in praise of the books and those at whose expense the great collection was published. One volume.'—Summers, Catalogue of Chinese Books in the Library of the India Office, 1872, p. 37. No. 70. In this interesting book there are added some rules observed by Mi-tsâṅ in comparing, for the sake of his own edition, four previous Chinese editions published under the Suṅ (A.D. 960–1280), Yuen (1280–1368), and the Southern and Northern Collections under the Miṅ dynasty (1368–1644).

[2] 太祖高皇帝既刻全藏于金陵太宗文皇帝復鏤善梓于北平. *Khö-kiṅ-yuen-sü*, fol. 18 a.

[3] 明永樂間刊板京師是爲梵本北藏又有民間私刊書本板在浙江嘉興府謂之南藏. See the 御製大藏序跋集 Gyô-sei-dai-zô-syô-batsu-shiu, or Collection of the Imperial Prefaces and Addenda to the Great Piṭaka or the Buddhist Canon, Tokio, 1882, fol. 26 b, cols. 4, 5.

[4] See the 大清重刻龍藏彙記 Tâ-tshiṅ-kuṅ-khö-lun-tsâṅ-wêi-ki, or Catalogue of the Buddhist Canon re-published under the great Tshiṅ dynasty. I possess a copy of this Catalogue published in Nanking, 1870. It was given to me by my learned Chinese friend, Mr. Yang Wen-hoei, who, together with a priest named Miâo-khuṅ (who died 1880), has been publishing the same collection again, about thirteen years since, collecting donations from his countrymen. According to his last letter, dated Shanghai, July 10, 1882, more than 3000 fasciculi have already been published. His edition is very carefully done, as I can judge from copies of certain works which he gave me in London and Paris, where I met him last year.

and agrees with what is found in two interesting compositions, written in Japan A.D. 1748 and 1879, and published there A.D. 1819 and 1880 respectively. The first Japanese authority is a priest called Zui-ten, who wrote an introduction to his useful Catalogue of the three Great Piṭakas or Collections [1] in the monastery Zô-ziô-zi, also called San-yen-zan, at Shiba in Tokio, the present Capital of Japan; where he was the librarian in A.D. 1748 [2]. The second authority is found in the advertisement of a Japanese Society, called Kô-kiô-sho-in, added to its new Edition of the Great Piṭaka, now in course of publication in Tokio [3]. From these sources I can draw the following sketch:—

There are three nearly complete copies of as many different foreign Collections or Editions of the Buddhist Canon, still preserved in the Library of the monastery Zô-ziô-zi. These copies were originally deposited in three different monasteries, of which we shall speak presently. In the beginning of the seventeenth century A.D., Tokugawa Iyeyasu, the first Shiogun or Commander-in-chief of Yedo, gave grants of land in exchange for these three Collections, and had them brought to Yedo, the present Tokio, where they are now.

The first of these three Collections is the best and oldest copy of all the different Editions now in existence, at least in Japan. It was published in Corea at the beginning of the eleventh century A.D., by order of the Corean King, whose personal name was *K'* (治). He greatly respected Buddhism. In A.D. 995 he sent an envoy to the Chinese Emperor and asked for a copy of the Imperial Edition (published A.D. 972?) At that time there were already three or more different Collections in Corea. One of them was that which was made under the *Kh*i-tân or Tartar dynasty (cf. p. xxii note), and two others were called Former and Latter Collections made in Corea. The *Sramana* Suṅ-*k*i and others were appointed by the King as the revisers of his new Edition, which was completed after fourteen years' labour. The copy of this Edition, now in existence in Tokio, was brought to Japan, in the Bun-mei period, A.D. 1469–1486, by a priest called Yei-gu, and then deposited in his monastery, Yen-ziô-zi, in the province of Yamato [4]. This Corean Collection consists of 1521 distinct works in 6467 or 6589 fasciculi, of which 2 fasciculi are wanting in the copy preserved there.

The second Collection in the Library of the Zô-ziô-zi, is one which was published in China, in A.D. 1239, under the Suṅ dynasty. The blocks for this edition belonged to the monastery, Fâ-pâo-sz', at Sz'-*kh*i, in Hu-*k*eu-lu [5]. The copy in Tokio was brought to Japan by a priest called Den-giô, who visited China in A.D. 1275, and then deposited in his monastery, Kwan-zan-zi, in the province of Ômi [6]. This Collection consists of 1421 distinct works in 5714 or 5916 fasciculi.

The third Collection in the Zô-ziô-zi Library is a later Chinese edition, published in A.D. 1277–1290, which was collated with two earlier editions. The blocks for this Yuen edition belonged to the monastery, Tâ-phu-nin-sz', at Nân-shân, in Hân-*k*eu-lu [7]. When and by whom the copy in Tokio was brought to Japan is not known. It was formerly deposited in the monastery, Shu-zen-zi, in the province of Idzu [8].

These second and third Collections in the Zô-ziô-zi Library might be two of the twenty different editions which were produced during the Suṅ and Yuen dynasties (A.D. 960–1368. See p. xxiii). Then followed the Miṅ dynasty (A.D. 1368–1644), under which two Imperial Editions were produced, as already mentioned. The form of books in these Editions as well as that in the previous ones is said to have followed the shape of the Sanskrit Manuscript, being folded [9], and unlike an ordinary Chinese bound book [10], so that the number of volumes became very considerable.

---

[1] They are (1) 高麗本 Kô-rai-bon (lit. hon), or Corean Collection or Edition; (2) 宋本 Sô-hon, or the Suṅ dynasty Collection or Edition; and (3) 元本 Gempon (lit. Gen-hon), or the Yuen dynasty Collection or Edition.

[2] 緣山三大藏目錄 Yen-zan-san-dai-zô-moku-roku. 3 vols. Compiled A.D. 1748. Preface dated A.D. 1763. Published A.D. 1819, when an addendum was written. For the contents of this Catalogue, see also the Chrysanthemum, June 1881, pp. 236–237.

[3] 大日本大藏經緣起 Dai-nippon-dai-zô-kiô-yen-gi. Published as a supplement to the 明教新誌 Mei-kiô-shin-shi, a Japanese newspaper, August 26, 1880.

[4] 文明中和州忍辱山圓成寺僧榮弘將來藏其寺矣.

[5] 湖州路思溪法寶寺.

[6] 建治元年近州世良田長樂寺僧傳曉入宋將來藏于其寺.

[7] 杭州路南山大普寧寺.

[8] 豆州走湯縣修禪寺藏也.

[9] 梵筴.

[10] 方筴 or 方冊.

There was then a Bhikshuṇî called Fâ-*k*an[1] in China, who first published a similar Collection in the ordinary form of Chinese books, after finding the inconvenience of the former Editions. The blocks of her publication were however gradually effaced. At length there was an active priest Mi-tsâṅ (see p. xxiii), who followed Fâ-*k*an's example and circulated his Edition most widely. Copies of his Edition were successively imported into Japan, where it is called Min-zô (Miṅ-tsâṅ), or the Piṭaka or Collection made and published under the Miṅ dynasty. It is said that the editor Mi-tsâṅ collated the Northern Collection with the Southern one for his new edition, and added five works (Nos. 1658–1662) of the latter Collection to the former. Besides these, he could only meet with a few books of the earlier Editions of the Suṅ and Yuen dynasties. It is a pity that this widely circulated Edition is in reality a reproduction only of the Northern Collection or Edition of the Miṅ dynasty with a few additions, no attempt being made to correct the blunders or fill in omissions of the earlier Edition. These errors of the Northern Collection of the Miṅ dynasty are severely remarked on by the Imperial pen in the preface to the reproduction under the present dynasty in China (see p. xxiii).

Now Buddhism was introduced into Japan from Corea, in A.D. 552, and to the latter country it had been brought from China about a century before[2]. At that time the King of Kudara (one of three kingdoms in Corea), Sei-mei by name, sent some Buddhist sacred books to the Japanese court. The titles of these books are not known. In A.D. 606 the Prince Imperial Umayado lectured, in the presence of the reigning Empress Sui-ko, his aunt, on two Sûtras, viz. the *S*rîmâlâ-devî-siṃhanâda, No. 59, translated by Guṇabhadra in A.D. 435, and the Saddharmapuṇḍarîka, No. 134, translated by Kumâra*g*îva in A.D. 406[3]. In A.D. 735, when a priest called Gen-bô returned from China, he presented to the Imperial Government the Buddhist sacred books in more than 5000 fasciculi[4]. When the Chinese priest Kan-shin arrived in Japan, A.D. 753, the ex-Emperor Shiô-mu is said to have ordered him to correct the wrongly written characters in the copies of the Buddhist Canon. All the Scriptures were then copied by some appointed copyists in China and Japan. Even the Emperors, Empresses, and Ministers of State were sometimes engaged in copying the sacred books[5]. Some fragments of such copies are still carefully preserved in old temples in Japan.

In A.D. 987, when a famous priest called Chiô-nen returned from China to Japan, he first brought with him a copy of the Edition of the Buddhist Canon in more than 5000 fasciculi, produced under the Suṅ dynasty, A.D. 960–1280[6]. Afterwards copies of Chinese and Corean Editions were gradually brought over to Japan, and deposited in the large temples or monasteries. These copies have not been allowed to be read or examined by the public since olden times; and Buddhist scholars have had to submit to this inconvenience.

In the Kwan-yei period, A.D. 1624–1643, a priest of the Ten-dai sect, Ten-kai by name (who died in his 132nd year, A.D. 1643), first caused the Great Collection of the Buddhist Canon to be printed in movable wooden types. Copies of this edition are still found in the Libraries of some old temples.

A few years later there was a priest of the Wô-baku sect, Dô-kô (or Tsû-kô), better known by another name Tetsu-gen ('Iron eye'). In A.D. 1669 he first published a letter (col. 367 (6)) expressing his wish to receive donations for his intended reproduction of Mi-tsâṅ's edition of the Great Canon (see p. xxiii). It is stated in the history of Japan, that 'from his youth Tetsu-gen wished to reproduce the Chinese Buddhist Canon in Japan; and hence he diligently collected a large number of donations, to enable him to carry out his plan. About this time, a famine prevailed in the country, and he at once gave his money to the poor, instead of keeping it for the expense of the edition. But he did not change his mind, and again collected other donations; then he was again obliged to give the money to the poor, owing to the same calamity as before. However he accomplished his desire at last. For the third time he got fresh donations, in the first year of the Tenna (lit. Ten-wa) period, A.D. 1681, and then published his long-delayed edition[7].'

Copies of this publication issued by Tetsu-gen, have been preserved in many Buddhist temples or monasteries throughout the whole country of Japan. There is a special building within the gate of a temple, for keeping this large Collection. This building is generally called in Japan Rin-zô[8], or 'revolving repository,' because it contains a large eight-angled book-case, made to revolve round a vertical axis[9].

---

[1] 法珍.

[2] See the 國史紀事本末 Koku-shi-ki-zi-hon-matsu, fasc. 13, fol. 1 a, 8 a.

[3] Ibid. fol. 7 a, b.

[4] Ibid. fasc. 16, fol. 3 a. See also the 國史略 Koku-shi-ryaku, fasc. 1, fol. 37 b.

[5] See Rev. Giô-kai's preface to the 'Collection of the Imperial Prefaces and Addenda to the Great Piṭaka,' fol. 1 a.

[6] Ibid. fol. 1 b.

[7] Koku-shi-ryaku, fasc. 5, fol. 24 b. Cf. col. 366 (1, 2).

[8] 輪藏 Lun-tsâṅ.

[9] For the plan of this building, see Tab. IV, in Siebold's great work on Japan, vol. v, Pantheon von Nippon.

This plan is said to have been invented, in A.D. 544, by a celebrated Chinese layman, named Fu Hhi (Fu Kiu, in Japan)[1], who was born in A.D. 497 and died in 569. He is commonly known as Fu Tâ-sh' (Fu Dai-zi in Japan)[2], or the Mahâsattva or noble-minded Fu. He is said to have thought, that if any pious person could touch such a book-case containing the whole of the Tripitaka and make it revolve once, he would have the same merit as if he had read the whole Collection. The statue of this Chinese inventor is generally placed in the front of the Revolving Repository; and on each side of his statue, there are added those of his two sons, Phu-kien (Fu-ken)[3] and Phu-*kh*an (Fu-ziô, in Japan)[4]. The statue of the elder is known by his pointing the finger, and that of the younger by the open palms of his hands. Their father's statue represents the impartial view which he held during his life-time, for he is represented as wearing the Taoist cap, the Confucianist shoes and Buddhist Kashâya or scarf across the shoulder[5]. There is a story, that when Fu in this dress saw Wu-ti, the founder of the Liân dynasty, who reigned A.D. 502–549, the Emperor asked him whether he was a Buddhist priest, Fu then pointed to his Taoist cap. When asked again whether he was a Taoist, he pointed to his Confucianist shoes. Being asked lastly, whether he was a Confucianist, he pointed to his Buddhist scarf[6].

It is curious that, about two centuries after the time of Tetsu-gen, a copy of his Edition (produced A.D. 1681) was sent over to England from Japan (1875), by the Japanese ambassador, now one of the three highest ministers of the Mikado, for the use of scholars in Europe. This Edition is no doubt an excellent work on the part of the editor, having been accomplished by a single Buddhist priest; but at the same time it is simply a reproduction of the Chinese publication issued by Mi-tsân, which is not quite free from blunders, as before stated.

There were formerly two Japanese priests, Nin-*k*io[7] of the *Z*iô-do sect, and *Z*un-ye[8] of the Shin-shu, who collated Tetsu-gen's Edition with that of Corea. A complete copy of the Corean Edition, being similar to that of the Zô-ziô-zi Library, was preserved in the Library of the monastery Ken-nin-zi, in Kioto. Nin-*k*io, together with more than ten assistants, spent five years in collating, A.D. 1706–1710. *Z*un-ye accomplished his collation in eleven years, in A.D. 1826–1836. In A.D. 1837 there was a calamitous conflagration in Kioto, by which the copy of the Corean Edition in the Ken-nin-zi Library was burnt, leaving only forty-nine cases out of six hundred and thirty-nine cases of the whole Collection. This copy is said to have been brought to Japan in A.D. 1458.

The new Edition of the Japanese Society, Kô-kiô-sho-in, now being published in Tokio (see p. xxiv), is a reproduction of the Corean Edition with various readings of and some additions from three different Chinese Editions, produced under the Sun, Yuen, and Min dynasties, A.D. 960–1644. The arrangement of the works in this Edition is more scientific, being the same as the one adopted by the Chinese priest *K*'-sü, in his 'Guide for the Examination of the Canon[9].' This Edition is in modern movable types, and in small-sized books, royal octavo. The preparation for the press is made by competent scholars. About sixty volumes, containing nearly four hundred distinct works, were published in June 1882. According to the Advertisement of the Society (see p. xxiv) all the remaining works are to be issued within twenty-five months from the appearance of the first wrapper or open case, containing twenty-eight works, which appeared in November 1881. A copy of this new Japanese Edition may be seen in the Bodleian Library, Oxford, where the first wrapper was received in January of this year. The present Catalogue will be, I hope, used for this new Edition also. All

---

[1] 傅翕 For his life, see the 佛祖統紀 Fo-tsu-thun-*k*i, No. 1661, and the 佛祖歷代通載 Fo-tsu-li-tâi-thun-tsâi, No. 1637, fasc. 10, fol. 21 a seq.

For the account of his plan of the Revolving Repository, see the 釋門正統 Shaku-mon-shio-tô, 釋氏稽古略 Shaku-shi-kei-ko-ryaku, 谷響集 Koku-ko-shiu, and 明教新誌 Mei-kio-shin-shi, August 4, 1880.

[2] 傅大士.

[3] 普建.

[4] 普成.

[5] For these three statues, see Tab. III, in Siebold's great work on Japan, vol. v, Pantheon von Nippon.

[6] See the Fo-tsu-thun-*k*i, fasc. 37, fol. 8 b.

[7] 忍澂.

[8] 順慧.

[9] 閱藏知津 Yueh-tsân-*k*'-tsin (Yetsu-zô-*k*i-shin, in Japan), by 智旭 *K*'-sü (Ki-kyoku). 48 fasc. Compiled A.D. 1635–1654. Published in China, A.D. 1664 and 1709; and in Japan, A.D. 1782.

that is required for this purpose is a comparative table of the arrangements of the works in both Editions, deposited in the India Office and Bodleian Libraries, and a few additional notes.

I have thus described all that I have hitherto either seen or heard about the Collections or Editions of the Chinese Translation of the Buddhist Tripi*t*aka as well as some Indian miscellaneous works, together with some Chinese ones.

I shall now add three chronological tables, which will illustrate the foregoing statement.

Chronological Table of the Thirteen Catalogues still in Existence.

	Date.	No.	Title.
(1)	A. D. 520	1476	*K*hu-sân-tsâṅ-*k*i-tsi, lit. Collection of the records of the Translation of the Tripi*t*aka. 17 fasc.
(2)	" 594	1609	Sui-*k*uṅ-*k*iṅ-mu-lu, lit. Catalogue of Buddhist sacred books (collected) under the Sui dynasty, A. D. 589–618. 7 fasc.
(3)	" 597	1504	Li-tâi-sân-pâo-*k*i, lit. Record concerning the three precious things (Triratna) under successive dynasties. 15 fasc.
(4)	" 602	1608	Sui-*k*uṅ-*k*iṅ-mu-lu, lit. Catalogue of Buddhist sacred books (collected) under the Sui dynasty, A. D. 589–618. 5 fasc.
(5)	" 664	1483	Tâ-thâṅ-nêi-tien-lu, lit. Catalogue of Buddhist books (collected) under the great Thâṅ dynasty, A. D. 618–907. 16 fasc.
(6)	" 664	1487	Ku-*k*in-i-*k*iṅ-thu-*k*i, lit. Record of the picture (of the events) of ancient and modern translations of Buddhist sacred books. 4 fasc.
(7)	" 695	1610	Wu-*k*eu-khân-tiṅ-*k*uṅ-*k*iṅ-mu-lu, lit. Revised Catalogue of Buddhist sacred books (collected) under the *K*eu dynasty of the Wu family, A. D. 690–705. 15 fasc.
(8)	" 730	1485	Khâi-yuen-shih-*k*iâo-lu, lit. Catalogue of (the books on) the teaching of *S*âkyamuni, (compiled) in the Khâi-yuen period, A. D. 713–741. 30 fasc.
(9)	" 730	1486	Khâi-yuen-shih-*k*iâo-lu-lüeh-*k*hu, or an abridged reproduction of the preceding Catalogue. 5 fasc.
(10)	" 730	1488	Suh-ku-*k*in-i-*k*iṅ-thu-*k*i, or a continuation of No. 1487. 1 fasc.
(11)	" 1285–1287	1612	*K'*-yuen-fâ-pâo-*k*ien-thuṅ-tsuṅ-lu, lit. Comparative Catalogue of the Dharmaratna or Buddhist sacred books (collected) in the *K'*-yuen period, A. D. 1264–1294. 10 fasc.
(12)	" 1306	1611	Tâ-tsâṅ-shaṅ-*k*iâo-fâ-pâo-piâo-mu, lit. Catalogue of the Dharmaratna, being the holy teaching of the Great Repository, or Buddhist sacred books. 10 fasc.
(13)	" 1600	1662	Tâ-miṅ-sân-tsâṅ-shaṅ-*k*iâo-mu-lu, lit. Catalogue of the sacred teaching of the Tripi*t*aka (collected) under the great Miṅ dynasty, A. D. 1368–1644. 4 fasc.

Chronological Table of the Different Collections of the Chinese Translation of the Buddhist Tripitaka, made by order of the Emperors of China.

(1)	A. D. 518	By Wu-ti, the founder of the Liâṅ dynasty, who reigned A. D. 502–549.
(2)	" 533–534	By the Emperor Hhiâo-wu, of the Northern Wêi dynasty, who reigned A. D. 532–534.
(3)	" 594	By Wan-ti, the founder of the Sui dynasty, who reigned A. D. 589 or 581–604.
(4)	" 602	(as above)
(5)	" 605–616	By Yâṅ-ti, the second Emperor of the Sui dynasty, who reigned A. D. 605–616.
(6)	" 695	By the Empress Wu Tsö-thien, of the Thâṅ dynasty, who reigned A. D. 684–705.
(7)	" 730	By the Emperor Hhüen-tsuṅ, of the Thâṅ dynasty, who reigned A. D. 713–755.
(8)	" 971	By Thâi-tsu, the founder of the later Suṅ dynasty, who reigned A. D. 960–975.
(9)	" 1285–1287	By Shi-tsu, the founder of the Yuen dynasty, who reigned A. D. 1280–1294.*
(10)	" 1368–1398	By Thâi-tsu, the founder of the Miṅ dynasty, who reigned A. D. 1368–1398.
(11)	" 1403–1424	By Thâi-tsuṅ, the third Emperor of the Miṅ dynasty, who reigned A. D. 1403–1424.
(12)	" 1735–1737	By the Emperors Shi-tsuṅ and Kâo-tsuṅ, of the Tshiṅ dynasty, who reigned A. D. 1723–1735 and 1736–1795 respectively.

Chronological Table of the various printed Editions of the Chinese Translation of the Buddhist Tripitaka, in China, Corea, and Japan[1].

(1)	A. D.	972	By Thâi-tsu, the founder of the later Sun dynasty, who reigned A. D. 960–975.
(2)	„	1010	By the Corean King, whose personal name is *K'* (治). (A copy still exists in Japan.)
(3)	„	1239	By unknown editor, under the Southern Sun dynasty, A. D. 1127–1280. (Ditto.)
(4)	„	1277–1290	By unknown editor, under the Yuen dynasty, A. D. 1280 (or 1260)–1368. (Ditto.)
(5)	„	1368–1398	By Thâi-tsu, the founder of the Min dynasty, who reigned A. D. 1368–1398.
(6)	„	1403–1424	By Thâi-tsun, the third Emperor of the Min dynasty, who reigned A. D. 1403–1424.
(7)	„	1500 (?)	By Fâ-*k*an, a Chinese Bhikshunî.
(8)	„	1586–1606 or 1616	By Mi-tsân, a Chinese priest. (Copied from No. 6.)
(9)	„	1624–1643	By Ten-kai, a Japanese priest.
(10)	„	1678–1681	By Dô-kô or Tetsu-gen, a Japanese priest. (Copied from No. 8.)
(11)	„	1735–1737	By the Chinese Emperors Shi-tsun and Kâo-tsun, of the present Tshin dynasty, who reigned A. D. 1723–1735 and 1736–1795 respectively. (Copied from No. 8.)
(12)	„	1869– —	By Yang Wen-hoei, a Chinese scholar, together with Miâo-khun, a Chinese priest (who died 1880). (Copied from No. 11, and now in course of publication in Nanking.)
(13)	„	1881– —	By the Kô-kiô-sho-in, or the Buddhist Bible Society, in Tokio, Japan. (Copied from No. 2, collated with Nos. 3, 4, and 8; and now in course of publication.)

In conclusion, I have to thank most sincerely my teacher, Professor Max Müller, for his kind instruction and help, through which alone I have been able to carry out this work. I did not know any Sanskrit at all before February 1879, when I became his pupil, bringing with me a letter of introduction from his friend, the late Dean Stanley.

I have also to thank Dr. Rost, the Librarian of the India Office, and the other gentlemen in that Library, for their kindness in allowing me to study the great Collection now deposited there.

Nor should I forget to express my sincere gratitude to the Delegates of the Clarendon Press in undertaking the printing and publication of this Catalogue, in conjunction with the India Office; and I have much pleasure in acknowledging the excellent manner in which the printing has been executed. The Chinese types, cast at the Clarendon Press from matrices lately acquired in China, at the recommendation of Professor Legge, have been of great service for this undertaking.

I have received valuable assistance from my two Japanese friends, Mr. Y. Ymaïzoumi and Mr. Kenjiu Kasawara, on several matters in this compilation; for which I return my best thanks.

Lastly, I most humbly ask all students of Buddhist literature to assist me in correcting any mistakes I may have made in compiling this Catalogue.

BUNYIU NANJIO.

Llantrissant House,
Kingston Road, Oxford,
16th November, 1882.

---

[1] There are said to have been as many as twenty different editions under the Sun and Yuen dynasties, A. D. 960–1368. But minute accounts concerning these editions are not found, except with reference to Nos. 1, 3, and 4 in this table.

TRANSLITERATION OF SANSKRIT AND CHINESE WORDS ADOPTED FOR THE CATALOGUE OF THE CHINESE BUDDHIST TRIPI*T*AKA.

NOTE.—For Sanskrit words, Professor Max Müller's Scheme for the Transliteration of Oriental Alphabets, as followed in the 'Sacred Books of the East,' has been adopted. For Chinese, Mr. Wells Williams' System of Orthography for the Pronunciation of Peking, as given in his Syllabic Dictionary of the Chinese Language (Shanghai, 1874), has been followed, though represented according to the same scheme of transliteration. There are several sounds which are found in Chinese only, in which case the original system of Wells Williams is for the most part retained.

VOWELS.	SANSKRIT.	CHINESE.	WELLS WILLIAMS' SYSTEM AND EXPLANATION[1].
a	अ	a	ă as in quota.
â	आ	â	a as in father.
i	इ	i	i as in pin.
î	ई		î as in machine.
u	उ	u	u as in put.
û	ऊ	û	ú as oo in fool, or o in move.
ri	ऋ	. . .	ri as in fiery[2].
rî	ॠ	. . .	rî[2].
li	ऌ	. . .	li as in friendly[2].
lî	ॡ	. . .	lî[2].
e	. . .	e	e as in men.
ê	ए[3]	ê	é as in grey.
âi	ऐ[3]	âi	ai as in aisle.
o	. . .	o	o as in long.
ô	ओ[3]	. . .	o as in note[3].
âu	औ[3]	âu	au as ow in now.
ü	. . .	ü	ü as in June.
ö	. . .	ö	ö as in könig, a German sound.
âo	. . .	âo	ao like ow in howl, prolonged.
iâ	. . .	iâ	ia as in piastre, or ya in yard.
iâi	. . .	iâi	iai and iao, each letter sounded.
iâo	. . .	iâo	
iu	. . .	iu	iu as ew in pew.
iü	. . .	iü	iü like ew in chewing, prolonged.
ie	. . .	ie	ie as in siesta.
iê	. . .	iê	ié as ea in fealty.
io	. . .	io	io as yaw in yawn.
ui	. . .	ui	ui as ewy in dewy.
ûi	. . .	ûi	úi as ooi in cooing.
üe	. . .	üe	üe as in duet; it runs into üé when a final.
üê	. . .	üê	
ei	. . .	ei	ei as in height, or i in sigh.
êi	. . .	êi	éi as eyi in greyish.
eu	. . .	eu	eu as ou in souse, shorter than au.
êu	. . .	êu	éu as au in Capernaum.
			ANOMALOUS SOUNDS.
sz'	. . .	sz'	sz', tsz', a peculiar sibilant; the first can be made by changing di in dizzy to s, and speaking it quickly.
tsz'	. . .	tsz'	
k'	. . .	*k*'	ch' and sh', like the preceding, but softer. They are often uttered by a person who stutters, as if in speaking chin or shin, he could not get out the n. They have also been compared to the sound made when chiding a child for making a noise.
sh'	. . .	sh'	
'rh	. . .	'rh	'rh, like the word err.

[1] Introduction to his Dictionary, pp. xix–xxiv. [2] Professor Max Müller's Scheme for the Transliteration of Oriental Alphabets.
[3] For these four diphthongs, however, the mark of circumflex has been omitted in this Catalogue.

CONSONANTS.	SANSKRIT.	CHINESE.	WELLS WILLIAMS' SYSTEM AND EXPLANATION.
k	क	k	k as in king, kick.
kh	ख	kh	k', nearly the same sound, but somewhat softened and aspirated.
g	ग	. . .	g as in gate[1].
gh	घ	. . .	gh as in spring-head[1].
ṅ (ng)	ङ	ṅ	ng as in sing.
k	च	*k*	ch as in church.
kh	छ	*kh*	ch', the same sound aspirated.
g	ज	. . .	j as in jolly[1].
gh	झ	. . .	jh as in bridge-house[1].
ñ	ञ	. . .	*ñ* as in new[1].
t	ट	. . .	*t* as in town[1].
th	ठ	. . .	*th* as in outhouse[1].
d	ड	. . .	*d* as in done[1].
dh	ढ	. . .	*dh* as in rodhook[1].
n	ण	. . .	*n* as in no[1].
t	त	t	t as in top, lot.
th	थ	th	t', the same sound aspirated.
d	द	. . .	d as in din[1].
dh	ध	. . .	dh as in landholder[1].
n	न	n	n as in nun.
p	प	p	p as in pot, lop.
ph	फ	ph	p', the same sound aspirated.
b	ब	. . .	b as in bed[1].
bh	भ	. . .	bh as in clubhouse[1].
m	म	m	m as in man, ham.
y	य	y	y as in yard[2].
r	र	. . .	r as in red[1].
l	ल	l	l as in lion.
v	व	. . .	v as in live[1].
s	श	. . .	*s* as in sharp[1].
sh	ष	sh	sh as in shall.
s	स	s	s as in sand.
h	ह	h	h as in hung; as a final it is nearly suppressed.
m	अं	. . .	*m* Anusvâra (slight nasal)[1].
h	अः	. . .	*h* Visarga (slight breathing)[1].
ts	. . .	ts	ts as in wits.
tsh	. . .	tsh	ts', the same sound aspirated.
w	. . .	w	w as in wind.
f		f	f as in farm.
z		z	z as in zone.
z		*z*	zh as z in azure. j as in the French jamais.
ꝁh	. . .	hh	h' before i and ü, a sibilant sound resembling an affected lisp, and easily confounded with sh[3].

[1] Professor Max Müller's Scheme for the Transliteration of Oriental Alphabets.

[2] 'In Peking, some words beginning with y change it into r before u and ŭ, as rung 容 for yung, rueh for 月 yueh; but this is exceptional.' W. Williams' Dictionary, Introduction, p. xxiv, col. 2.

[3] 'The digraph hs, adopted by Meadows and Wade, does not exactly express it, for there is no proper s in the sound, and sh is too much. If one puts the finger between the teeth, and tries to speak hing or hü, this is said to express nearly this sibilant initial. The Spanish x, as in Quixote, comes near to it, and would be much the best symbol, if it were not that it would be mispronounced by the common reader, as in xiang 香, xin 忻, &c.' W. Williams' Dictionary, Introduction, p. xxiii, col. 2.

CHRONOLOGICAL TABLE OF THE CHINESE DYNASTIES, BOTH SUCCESSIVE AND CONTEMPORANEOUS.

NOTE—In this table many less important contemporaneous dynasties are not given, except those under which some translations of the Tripiṭaka were made.

DYNASTIC TITLE.	B.C.
三皇五帝 Sân-hwân-wu-ti, or the age of the Three and Five Emperors	2852–2204
夏 Hhiâ, or the Hhiâ dynasty	2205–1766
商 or 殷 Shân or Yin	1766–1122
周 *K*eu (Chow or Châw, by others)	1122–256
秦 Tshin	221 (or 255)–206
前 or 西漢 Tshien or Si-hân, or Former or Western Hân	201 (or 206)–A.D. 9
	A.D.
後 or 東漢 Heu or Tuṅ-hân, or Latter or Eastern Hân	25–220
三國 Sân-kwo, or Three Kingdoms.	
(1) 蜀漢 Shu-hân, or Hân established in Shu (Shuh)—western	221–263
(2) 魏 Wêi—northern	220–265
(3) 吳 Wu—southern	222–280
西晉 Si-tsin, or Western Tsin	265–316
前涼 Tshien-liâṅ, or Former Liâṅ	302–376
東晉 Tuṅ-tsin, or Eastern Tsin	317–420
前秦 Tshien-tshin, or Former Tshin	350–394
後秦 Heu-tshin, or Latter Tshin	384–417
西秦 Si-tshin, or Western Tshin	385–431
北涼 Pe-liâṅ, or Northern Liâṅ	397–439
南北朝 Nân-pe-*k*âo, or Southern and Northern Dynasties.	
(1) 南朝 Nân-*k*âo, or Southern Dynasties.	
宋 Suṅ—earlier	420–479
齊 Tshi	479–502

DYNASTIC TITLE.	A.D.
梁 Liâṅ	502–557
陳 *Kh*an	557–589
(2) 北朝 Pe-*k*âo, or Northern Dynasties.	
北魏 Pe-wêi, or Northern Wêi	386–534
西魏 Si-wêi, or Western Wêi	535–557
東魏 Tuṅ-wêi, or Eastern Wêi	534–550
北齊 Pe-tshi, or Northern Tshi	550–577
北周 Pe-*k*eu, or Northern *K*eu	557–581
隋 Sui	589 (or 581)–618
唐 Thâṅ	618–907
五代 Wu-tâi, or Five Dynasties.	
(1) 後梁 Heu-liâṅ, or Latter Liâṅ	907–923
(2) 後唐 Heu-thâṅ, or Latter Thâṅ	923–936
(3) 後晉 Heu-tsin, or Latter Tsin	936–947
(4) 後漢 Heu-hân, or Latter Hân	947–951
(5) 後周 Heu-*k*eu, or Latter *K*eu	951–960
(北)宋 (Pe) Suṅ, or (Northern) Suṅ—later	960–1127
南宋 Nân-suṅ, or Southern Suṅ	1127–1280
遼 Liâo	907–1125
夏 Hhiâ	1038–1227
金 *K*in	1115–1234
西遼 Si-liâo, or Western Liâo	1125–1201
元 Yuen	1280 (or 1260)–1368
明 Miṅ	1368–1644
清 Tshiṅ	1644– —

LIST OF THE PRINCIPAL AUTHORITIES CONSULTED IN PREPARING THIS CATALOGUE AND THE THREE APPENDICES, AND TO WHICH REFERENCE IS MADE UNDER THE FOLLOWING ABBREVIATIONS.

San-*k*whan.—No. 1490 高僧傳 Kâo-san-*k*whân, or Memoirs of Eminent Priests, in 14 fasciculi. Compiled by 慧皎 Hwui-*k*iâo, in A. D. 519, under the Liân dynasty, A. D. 502–557.

Sui-shu.—隋書 or Annals of the Sui dynasty, A. D. 589–618. By 長孫無忌 *Kh*ân-sun Wu-*k*i (died A. D. 659) and others, of the Thân dynasty, A. D. 618–907. There is a section on the Buddhist Books, in fasciculus 35.

Suh-san-*k*whân.—No. 1493 續高僧傳 Suh-kâo-san-*k*whân, or a Continuation of the Memoirs of Eminent Priests, in 40 fasciculi. By 道宣 Tâo-süen (died A. D. 667), of the Thân dynasty.

Nêi-tien-lu.—No. 1483 大唐內典錄 Tâ-thân-nêi-tien-lu, or a Catalogue of the Buddhist Books collected under the great Thân dynasty, in 10 fasciculi, subdivided into 16. By the same compiler as before, in A. D. 664.

Thu-*k*i.—No. 1487 古今譯經圖紀 Ku-*k*in-i-*k*in-thu-*k*i, or a Catalogue of the Ancient and Modern Translations, in 4 fasciculi. By 靖邁 Tsin-mâi, in about A. D. 664.

Suh-thu-*k*i.—No. 1488 續古今譯經圖紀 Suh-ku-kin-i-*k*in-thu-*k*i, i. e. a Continuation of the preceding work, in 1 fasciculus. By 智昇 *K*'-shan, in A. D. 730.

Khâi-yuen-lu.—No. 1485 開元釋教錄 Khâi-yuen-shih-*k*iâo-lu, or a Catalogue of the Buddhist Books collected in the Khâi-yuen period, A. D. 713–741, in 20 fasciculi, subdivided into 30. By the same compiler in the same year as before.

Sun-san-*k*whân.—No. 1495 宋高僧傳 Sun-kâo-san-*k*whân, or Memoirs of Eminent Priests, compiled under the later or Northern Sun dynasty, A. D. 960–1127, in 30 fasciculi. By 贊寧 Tsân-nin, in A. D. 988.

Min-i-tsi.—No. 1640 翻譯名義集 Fân-i-min-i-tsi, or a Collection of the Meanings of the Sanskrit Names translated into Chinese, in 20 fasciculi. By 法雲 Fâ-yun, in A. D. 1151, under the Southern Sun dynasty, A. D. 1127–1280.

Thun-*k*i.—No. 1661 佛祖統紀 Fo-tsu-thun-*k*i, or Records of the Lineage of Buddha and the Patriarchs, in 45 fasciculi, subdivided into 55. This is a history of Buddhism. By 志磐 *K*'-phân, in about A. D. 1269–1271.

K'-yuen-lu.—No. 1612 至元法寶勘同總錄 *K*'-yuen-fâ-pâo-*k*ien-thun-tsun-lu, or a Comparative Catalogue of the Dharmaratna or the Buddhist Books collected in the *K*'-yuen period, A. D. 1264–1294, in 10 fasciculi. By 慶吉祥 *K*in-*k*i-siân and others, in A. D. 1285–1287, under the Yuen dynasty, A. D. 1280–1368.

Piâo-mu.—No. 1611 大藏聖教法寶標目 Tâ-tsân-shan-*k*iâo-piâo-mu, or a Catalogue of the Dharmaratna, being the Holy Teaching of the Great Repository or the Tripitaka, in 16 fasciculi. By 王古 Wân-ku, of the later (or Northern) or Southern Sun dynasty, A. D. 960–1280; and continued by 管主八 Kwân-*k*u-pâ, in about A. D. 1306.

Thun-tsâi.—No. 1637 佛祖歷代通載 Fo-tsu-li-tâi-thun-tsâi, or a Complete statement concerning Buddha and the Patriarchs in all ages, in 36 fasciculi. By 念常 Nien-*kh*ân, in A. D. 1333 or 1344.

Tâ-min-sân-tsân-shan-kiâo-mu-lu 大明三藏聖教目錄 No. 1662. A Catalogue of the Chinese Buddhist Tripitaka, collected under the Min dynasty, A. D. 1368–1644. 4 fasciculi. This is the original Catalogue of the Collection in the India Office Library, on which my own Catalogue is based. The classification and order of the 1662 works contained in it are therefore unaltered; while the Index-characters, taken from the 千字文 Tshien-tsz'-wan, or Thousand-character-composition, are omitted.

Min-san-*k*whân.—大明高僧傳 Tâ-min-kâo-san-*k*whân, or Memoirs of Eminent Priests, compiled under the great Min dynasty, A. D. 1368–1644, in 8 fasciculi. By 如惺 *Z*u-sin, in A. D. 1617.

K'-tsin.—閱藏知津 Yueh-tsân-*k*'-tsin, or Guide for the Examination of the Canon, in 48 fasciculi. By 智旭 *K*'-sü, in A. D. 1654, under the present Tshin dynasty, which began in A. D. 1644. For this work, see also pp. x, xxvi.

A. R.—Asiatic Researches, vol. xx, Arts. II and XI, i. e. Analysis of the Kangur, on pp. 41–93 and 393–585. By Mr. Alexander Csoma Körösi. Calcutta, 1836.

Conc.—Concordance Sinico-Sanskrite d'un nombre considérable de Titres d'ouvrages Bouddhiques, recueillie dans un Catalogue Chinois de l'an 1306 [read 1285–1287] et publiée, après le déchiffrement et la restitution des mots indiens, par M. Stanislas Julien. In the Journal Asiatique, Novembre–Decembre, 1849, pp. 353–445. The figures after 'Conc.' in the present Catalogue refer to the order of the titles in Julien's list.

Wassiljew.—Der Buddhismus, seine Dogmen, Geschichte und Literatur, von W. Wassiljew. St. Petersburg, 1860. The figures after this author's name in the Catalogue refer to the pages of the Russian Original, as printed in the margin of the German translation. In the early pages of the Catalogue, the letter 'p.' should be supplied before the figures.

Eitel.—Handbook for the Student of Chinese Buddhism, by Rev. E. J. Eitel. London, 1870.

Beal, Catena.—A Catena of Buddhist Scriptures from Chinese. By Rev. S. Beal. London, 1871.

Beal, Catalogue.—The Buddhist Tripiṭaka, as it is known in China and Japan. A Catalogue and Compendious Report. By the same author. 1876. This is the Catalogue of the Chinese Buddhist Tripiṭaka in the India Office Library, together with an interesting and useful Report on this Collection. This Catalogue is the principal guide of the present compilation.

Beal, B.L.C.—Abstract of Four Lectures on Buddhist Literature in China, delivered at University College, London. By the same author. London, 1882.

Mayers.—The Chinese Reader's Manual. A Handbook of Biographical, Historical, Mythological, and General Literary Reference. By W. F. Mayers. Shanghai, 1874.

Edkins.—Chinese Buddhism. A Volume of Sketches, Historical, Descriptive, and Critical. By Rev. J. Edkins. London, 1880.

Selected Essays.—No. xix. On Sanskrit Texts discovered in Japan, in Selected Essays on Language, Mythology, and Religion, vol. ii, pp. 313–371. By Professor Max Müller. London, 1881.

Catalogue of the Hodgson Manuscripts.—Catalogue of Sanskrit Manuscripts, collected in Nepal, and presented to various Libraries and Learned Societies, by B. H. Hodgson, Esq. Compiled by Dr. W. W. Hunter. Trübner & Co., 1881.

A. M. G.—Annales du Musée Guimet, vol. ii, pp. 131–577. Lyon, 1881. Analyse du Kandjour, traduite de l'Anglais et augmentée de diverses additions et remarques, par M. Léon Feer.

J. R. A. S.—The Journal of the Royal Asiatic Society of Great Britain and Ireland. London.

J. A. S. B.—The Journal of the Asiatic Society of Bengal.

S. B. E.—The Sacred Books of the East, translated by various Oriental Scholars, and edited by F. Max Müller. Oxford, 1879–1883.

ABBREVIATIONS IN THE APPENDICES.

S. M.—Sûtras of the Mahâyâna.
S. H.—Sûtras of the Hînayâna.
V. M.—Vinaya of the Mahâyâna.
V. H.—Vinaya of the Hînayâna.
A. M.—Abhidharma of the Mahâyâna.
A. H.—Abhidharma of the Hînayâna.
I. M.—Indian Miscellaneous Works.
C. M.—Chinese Miscellaneous Works.

Cat. Bodl. Japan.—A Catalogue of Japanese and Chinese Books and Manuscripts, lately added to the Bodleian Library. Prepared by Bunyiu Nanjio. Oxford, 1881.

ADDITIONS AND CORRECTIONS.

Col.	No.	Line	
1	1	5	for 'A. D. 659' read 'A. D. 660–663'
		7	for 'Nêi-tien-lu, fasc. 5, fol. 19' read 'Khâi-yuen-lu, fasc. 8 a, fol. 12 a'
		note 3	add 'or into Sanskrit quite literally' after 'English'
3	1	8, 13, 17, 20, 21, 24	for 'sahasrikâ' read 'sâhasrikâ'
4	2–5	4	(of Nos. 2, 3), 5 (of Nos. 4, 5) for 'sahasrikâ' read 'sâhasrikâ'
	3	6	add 'A. D. 403–404' after 'Saṅ-sui'
	4	7	add 'A. D. 286' after 'Yueh-*k*''
5	5	1	add 'A. D. 179' after 'Lokaraksha'
	6–8	4	for 'sahasrikâ' read 'sâhasrikâ'
	9	6	for '*Kh*ân' read '*Kh*an'
6	11	2	add 'A. D. 509' after 'Bodhiru*k*i'
	12	3	for '*Kh*ân' read '*Kh*an'
	13	5	add 'A. D. 648' after 'Hiouen-thsang'
	14	2	add 'A. D. 703' after 'I-tsiṅ'
7	18	5	add 'A. D. 693' after 'others'
8	20	4	add 'A. D. 649' after 'Hiouen-thsang'
9	23	6	add '706–' between 'A. D. and 713'
	(1)	4	for 'Trisam°' read 'Trisam°'
10	(2)	3	add 'A. D. 280' after 'Dharmaraksha'
11		note 2	for 'A. D. 257' read 'A. D. 258'
		5	for 'A. D. 266–313' read 'A. D. 308'
		11	for '*K*u Tâ-li' read '*K*u Fâ-li'
12	(9)	8	add 'A. D. 539' after 'Buddhasânta'
13	(14)	5	add 'A. D. 710' after 'I-tsiṅ'
14	(16)	7	add 'A. D. 568' after 'Narendrayasas'
	(17)	7	add 'A. D. 405' after 'Kumâra*g*îva'
	(19)	7	add 'A. D. 252' after 'Saṅghavarman'
15	(23)	9	add 'A. D. 541' after 'Upasûnya'
16	(29)	5	for 'Udayâna' read 'Udayana'
17	(32)	8	add 'A. D. 539' after 'Buddhasânta'
18	(38)	8	add 'A. D. 420' after 'Nandi'
	(39)	8	add 'A. D. 596' after '*Gñ*ânagupta'
20	(47)	8	add 'A. D. 290' after 'Dharmaraksha'
	24	4	for 'Trisam°' read 'Trisam°'
21	28	6	add 'A. D. 147' after 'Lokaraksha'
22	30	6	add 'A. D. 287' after 'Dharmaraksha'
	31	7	add 'A. D. 290' after 'Dharmaraksha'
	32	5	add 'A. D. 303' after 'Dharmaraksha'
	33	5	for 'An Hhüen' read 'Ân Hhüen'
		6	add 'A. D. 181' after 'Fo-thiâo'
23	37	5	add 'A. D. 595' after '*Gñ*ânagupta'
	38	4	for 'Udayâna' read 'Udayana'
24	41	7	add 'A. D. 289' after 'Dharmaraksha'
	42	9	add 'A. D. 317' after 'Dharmaraksha'
	44	2	add 'A. D. 373' after 'Sh'-lun'
25	45	5	add 'A. D. 541' after 'Prag*ñ*âru*k*i'
	46	7	add 'A. D. 693' after 'Bodhiru*k*i'
	47	5	for 'Mâyopama' read 'Mâyopamâ'

Col.	No.	Line	
25	48	6	add 'A. D. 541' after 'others'
26	51	7	add 'A. D. 595' after '*Gñ*ânagupta
	52	7	add 'A. D. 285' after 'Dharmaraksha
	53	6	add 'A. D. 680' after 'others'
27	55	6	add 'A. D. 303' after 'Dharmaraksha'
28	59	8	add 'A. D. 435' after 'Gunabhadra'
	60	6	add 'A. D. 542' after 'Prag*ñ*âru*k*i'
	62	7	add 'A. D. 584–585' after 'Narendrayasas'
			add '(or 581)' after 'A. D. 589'
29	63	6	add 'A. D. 566' after 'as before'
		7	for 'Tsi' read 'Tshi'
	64	7	add '(Hiouen-thsang)' after 'Hhuen-*k*wâṅ'
	66	6	add 'A. D. 558' after 'Dharmaprag*ñ*a'
		7	for 'Tsi' read 'Tshi'
	67	7	add 'A. D. 587' after '*Gñ*ânagupta'
			add '(or 581)' after 'A. D. 589'
30	71	7	add 'A. D. 462' after 'Hhüen-*kh*âṅ'
31	74	7	add 'A. D. 291(?)' after 'Dharmaraksha'
	75	5	add 'A. D. 594' after 'others'
	77	6	for 'Pâo-un' read 'Pâo-yun'
			add 'A. D. 427' after 'Pâo-yun'
	78	4	add 'A. D. 595' after '*Gñ*ânagupta'
32	79	6	add 'A. D. 291' after 'Dharmaraksha'
	80	5	add 'A. D. 287' after 'Dharmaraksha'
	82	4	add 'A. D. 407' after 'Kumâra*g*îva'
	84	4	for 'Prabhâmitra' read 'Prabhâkaramitra'
			for 'A. D. 628' read 'A. D. 629'
33	87	7	add 'A. D. 418–420' after 'others'
34	86	6	add 'A. D. 693' after 'Bodhiru*k*i'
35	90	2	for 'Bodhiru*k*i' read 'Dharmaru*k*i'
			add 'A. D. 504' after 'Dharmaru*k*i'
	92	4	add 'A. D. 291' after 'Dharmaraksha'
	94	5	add 'A. D. 691' after 'Devaprag*ñ*a'
36	95	4	add 'A. D. 654' after 'Hiouen-thsang'
	96	7	add 'A. D. 689' after 'Devaprag*ñ*a'
37	101	7	add 'A. D. 685' after 'Divâkara'
	104	4	add 'A. D. 291' after 'Dharmaraksha'
38	110	6	add 'A. D. 297' after 'Dharmaraksha'
39	113	5	add '416–' between 'A. D. and 423'
	115	5	add 'A. D. 664–665' after 'others'
40	116	6	add 'A. D. 269' after 'Dharmaraksha'
	117	7	add 'A. D. 558' after 'Dharmaprag*ñ*a'
41	120	5	add 'A. D. 417–418' after 'Buddhabhadra'
	121	6	add 'A. D. 593' after '*Gñ*ânagupta'
	126	6	add 'A. D. 703' after 'I-tsiṅ'
42	123	7	add 'A. D. 652' after 'Hiouen-thsang'
43	130	5	for 'Pâo-kwei' read 'Pâo-kwêi'
			add 'A. D. 597' after '*Gñ*ânagupta'
		8	add 'A. D. 552' after 'Paramârtha'
44	133	1	add 'A. D. 481' after 'Dharma*g*âtayasas'

Col.	No.	Line	
44	134	6	add 'A. D. 406' after 'Kumâragîva'
	135	4	add 'A. D. 427' after 'K'-yen'
45	138	5	add 'A. D. 286' after 'Dharmaraksha'
47	140	5	add 'A. D. 650' after 'Hiouen-thsang'
	141	5	add 'A. D. 616' after 'Dharmagupta'
	143	4	add 'A. D. 251' after 'Sań-hwui'
48	149	5	add 'A. D. 650' after 'Hiouen-thsang'
	150	3, 5	for 'Avaivarttya' read 'Avaivartya'
		7	add 'A. D. 284' after 'Dharmaraksha'
50	158	1	for '榑' read '博'
57	187	5	for '*G*ñânagupta (the same person as before), under' read '*G*ñânayasas, of'
60	203	4	for 'Zih-hhiu' read '*Z*ih-hhiu'
72	272	5	add the following note: 'It has been translated into English by Mr. Beal, in his "Buddhist Literature in China," pp. 172–178'
	273	6	add the following note: 'Cf. Beal, B. L. C., pp. 174–176'
83	324	3	for '*K*inta' read '*K*intâ'
84	327	7	for '°svaraika°' read '°svaraikâ°'
	328	4	
88	347	4	for 'Sui dynasty, A. D. 618–907' read 'Northern *K*eu dynasty, A. D. 557–581'
91	363	4	for 'Ŏ-ti-*kh*u-to' read 'Ŏ-ti-*kh*û-to'
	365	4	for 'Buddhasânta, of the Northern Wêi dynasty, A. D. 386–534' read 'Thân-wu-lân (Dharmaraksha?), of the Eastern Tsin dynasty, A. D. 317–420'
97	395	7	for 'Dharmakâra' read 'Dharmavikrama'
98	399	4, 12	for '*S*ûrâṅgama' read '*S*ûraṅgama'
		11	for '*S*ûra (hero)-aṅga (limb)' read '*S*ûraṅ (heroism)-gama (approaching)'
	401	4	add '(°saṅgati?)' after '°saṅgîti'
	402	2	for '*Kh*ân' read '*Kh*an'
103	425	6	for 'paridhara' read 'paridhâra'
105	436	7	for 'Fâ-shâń' read 'Fâ-shań'
107	446	6, 12	for 'sûrâṅgama' read 'sûraṅgama'
		7	for 'Mikasâkya' read 'Meghasikha'
	449	6	for 'Northern' read 'Eastern'
		7	for 'A. D. 386–534' read 'A. D. 534–550'
110	464	5	for 'Bodhidîpa' read 'Bodhi-tań'
115	496	4	for '*G*ñânolka' read '*G*ñânolkâ'
121	526	5	for 'Bhavasaṅkramita' read 'Bhavasaṅkrâmita'
133	543	6	for 'Dharmanandi' read 'Dharmanandin'
145	584	4	for 'Eastern Tsin' read 'earlier Suń'
		5	for 'A. D. 317–420' read 'A. D. 420–479'
146	594	3	for 'Râsh*t*rapâla' read 'Râsh*t*ravara'
147	595	4	for 'Fâ-hu (Dharmaraksha)' read 'Fâ-tu'
166	696	9	for '*S*râmanas' read '*S*ramanas'
169	711	4	for '*Kh*âń-yuen' read '*Kh*ań-yuen'
173	734	4	for 'parivra*g*aka' read 'parivrâ*g*aka'
187	808	4	for '*S*râmanera' read '*S*râmanera'
189	820	2	for 'pai' read 'pâi'
191	835	6	add 'dur' between 'sarva and gati'
192	840	7	for 'Sagara' read 'Sâgara'
196	859	8	for 'Pâszepa' read 'Pâ-sz'-pâ, or Bashpa'
199	872	3	for 'dhyâya' read 'dhyâna'
204	903	3	for 'adhimukta' read 'adhimukti'
204	904	3	for 'Mahâsatpâda' read 'Mahâsatpada'
206	922	3	for '°sraddha°' read '°sraddhâ°'
221	1004	6	for 'Tâi-tsuń, A. D. 763–779' read 'Töh-tsuń, A. D. 780–804'
		7–9	'This Emperor . . . . till 788' must be left out
224	1018	5	for '°dbhutânuttara°' read '°dbhutânuttara°'
233	1059	5	for 'pinnayaka (?)' read 'vinâyaka'
234	1064	5	for 'Ârya-(dâ)kinî (?)' read 'Ârya-ksmi'
235	1068	5	for 'mâtrikavimsati-pûga' read 'matrikaikavimsatipûgâ'
236	1073	6	for 'Fâ-hhien, A. D. 982–1001' read 'Fâ-thien, A. D. 973–981'
237	1075	5	for 'nâmâsh*t*asataka' read 'nâmâsh*t*asataka'
238	1081	5	for 'A. R., p. 486; A. M. G., p. 289' read 'Cf. A. R., p. 473; A. M. G., pp. 277, 414'
241	1090	4	for 'pratisarana' read 'pratisarana'
247	1116	4	for 'Kwâi-su' read 'Hwâi-su'
249	1128	5	
251	1137	1	for 'Pâszepa (Bâshpa)' read 'Pâ-sz'-pâ (Bashpa)'
252	1145	3	for '*S*râmanera' read '*S*râmanera'
253	1151	3	for '*S*ramanerikâ' read '*S*râmanerikâ'
254	1154	5	for 'Kwâi-su' read 'Hwâi-su'
	1156	5	
255	1162	3	for 'Mahâsrâmana' read 'Mahâsramana'
256	1166	5	for 'Sań-*kh*û' read 'Sań-*kh*u'
260	1179	6	for 'Nîla*k*akshus (? "blue-eye," or Piṅgalanetra)' read 'Nîlanetra (or Ârya Deva)'
261	1185	6	for 'Nirdesaprabha (? "distinct-brightness," or Piṅgalanetra)' read 'Nîlanetra (or Ârya Deva)'
268	1219	5	for 'Try-alakshanâ (?)' read 'Try-akâra (or -alakshana)'
269	1223	4	for 'tarka read 'târaka'
	1224	4	
	1223	6	for 'Nâgâr*g*una' read 'Mahâdignâga'
	1224	5	
	1225	3	for 'vipassanâ (or -vidarsana)' read 'vipasyana (or -vipassanâ)'
270	1228	3	for 'Pra*g*ñâpti' read 'Pra*g*ñapti'
272	1237	3	for 'sûtra' read 'sâstra'
		5	for 'A. D. 643' read 'A. D. 648'
274	1252	3	inverted comma must be left out
281	1276	5	add 'Translated by Hhüen-*k*wâń (Hiouen-thsang), A. D. 660–663' after '*S*âriputra'
	1278	6	add 'but the translator's name is lost' after 'A. D. 220–265'
283	1290	3	for '°desa' read '°desa'
286	1297	3	for 'Lokasthiti' read 'Lokasthity'
289	1306	3	for '°saṅ*g*îti' read '°saṅgîti'
	1309	5	
		6	for 'Nâgâr*g*una' read 'Mahâdignâga'
291	1317	4	for 'Pra*g*ñâpti' read 'Pra*g*ñapti'
296	1329	4	for '*K*î-*k*iâ-ye' read '*K*i-*k*iâ-yê'
	1330	4	for 'Nirvâna' read 'Parinirvâna'

Col.	No.	Line	
306	1367	5	for 'Dharmanandi' read 'Dharmanandin'
308	1376	3	for 'Mahâpranidhâ°' read 'Mahâpraṇidhâ°'
	1379	5	for '*Zih-kân*' read '*Zih-khan*'
312	1403	5	for 'dvâkâya' read 'dvikâya'
318	1436	5	for 'Tsz'-hhien' read 'Tshz'-hhien'
319	1440	8	for 'A. D. 534' read 'A. D. 434'
328	1485	6	for '1142' read '1124'
			add 'whether' after 'fasciculi'
			add 'or whether written originally in Chinese' after 'Chinese'
336	1519	8	for '*Zân-yo*' read '*Zan-yo*'
338	1527	5	for 'Wêi-*k*âi' read 'Wêi-kâi'
		11	for '*Kâi-suṅ*' read '*Kiô-sûṅ*'
343	1552	6	add '; and recorded by his disciple Kwân-tiṅ' after 'A. D. 589–618'
344	1557	5	
	1559	6	
345	1562	5	
350	1588	5	for 'Hhien-kwei' read 'Hhien-hwui'
352	1600	6	for 'A. D. 936–946' read 'A. D. 936–947'
353	1607	5	for 'Shan' read 'Shân'
	1608	5	for 'A. D. 603' read 'A. D. 602'
354	1610	8	add '(or 8521)' before 'fasciculi'
		9–11	for 'of which . . . . fasciculi' read 'with the addition of 859 works in 3910 (or 3882) fasciculi'
359	1634	4	for 'Tsz'-*khâṅ*' read 'Tsz'-*khaṅ*'
363	1649	4	for '*K*'no' read '*K*'-no'
365	1658	7	for '*S*râmaṇa' read '*S*ramaṇa'

370 Between No. 3 Nâgârguna, and No. 4 Deva, the following author and his works (taking from lines 12, 13, 21, 22) must be added: 'No. 3 a Dignâga or Mahâdignâga, whose name is translated 大域龍 Tâ-yü-luṅ, lit. 'great-region-dragon,' or 大域龍樹 Tâ-yü-luṅ-shu, lit. 'great-region-dragon-tree' (Mahâdignâgârguna?). There are 3 works ascribed to him, namely :—

No. 1223	Nyâyadvâratâraka-sâstra.	A. D. 711.
" 1224	" "	" 648.
" 1309	'Buddhamâtrika-pragñâpâramitâ-mahârthasaṅgîti-sâstra.'	A. D. 980–1000.

Col.	No.	Line	
379	1	9	for '*S*râmaṇa' read '*S*ramaṇa'
380	2	5	
381	3	5	
	4	13	
383	5, 7, 8	1	
384	9, 10	1	
	11	4	
	12	7	

A CATALOGUE OF THE CHINESE BUDDHIST TRIPIṬAKA.

大明三藏聖教目錄

Tâ-miṅ-sân-tsâṅ-shaṅ-*k*iâo-mu-lu.

'A Record of the Titles of the Sacred Teaching of the Three Repositories (Tripiṭaka, or Three Baskets, collected) under the Great Miṅ Dynasty, A.D. 1368–1644.'

FIRST DIVISION.

經藏 *K*iṅ-tsâṅ, or Sûtra-piṭaka.

PART I.

大乘經 Tâ-shaṅ-*k*iṅ, or the Sûtras of the Mahâyâna.

CLASS I.

般若部 Pân-zo-pu, or Pragñâpâramitâ class.

1 **大般若波羅蜜多經**

Tâ-pân-zo-po-lo-mi-to-*k*iṅ.

Mahâpragñâpâramitâ-sûtra[1].

See the *K*'-yuen-lu, fasc. 1, fol. 11 a; Conc. 638. Translated by Hhüen-*k*wâṅ (Hiouen-thsang), A.D. 659, of the Thâṅ dynasty, A.D. 618–907. (For the former date, see the Nêi-tien-lu, fasc. 5 b, fol. 19.) It consists of 600 fasciculi; 200,000 slokas in verse, or an equivalent number of syllables in prose. This is a collection of sixteen Sûtras, short and long. To each of them a preface is added by a Chinese priest, named Hhüen-tsö, a contemporary of the translator. The following is a summary of the contents:—

	FASC.	FASC.	CHAP.	PLACE OF THE SCENE.
(a)	400	(1–400),	79,	Gridhrakûta.
(b)	78	(401–478),	85,	
(c)	59	(479–537),	31,	
(d)	18	(538–555),	29,	
(e)	10	(556–565),	24,	
(f)	8	(566–573),	17,	
(g)	2	(574–575),		Srâvastî.
(h)	1	(576),		
(i)	1	(577),		
(j)	1	(578),		Abode of the Paranirmita-vasavartins.
(k)	5	(579–583),		Srâvastî.
(l)	5	(584–588),		
(m)	1	(589),		
(n)	1	(590),		
(o)	2	(591–592),		Gridhrakûta.
(p)	8	(593–600),		Venuvana.

[1] Whenever the meaning of the Chinese title is not quite the same as that of the Sanskrit title, it has been translated into English.

In the *K'*-yuen-lu (No. 1612), a catalogue of the Chinese Tripiṭaka (compiled A.D. 1285–1287, fasc. 1, fol. 11 b–14 a), these sixteen Sûtras (as all the rest) are compared with the Tibetan translations[1] (Kangur and Tangur?), and the following result is stated:

(a) Agrees with the Tibetan Pragñâpâramitâ in 100,000 ślokas in verse, or an equivalent number of syllables in prose (Śatasahasrikâ pragñâpâramitâ, 75 chapters, 303 bam-po, or artificial divisions). For the Sanskrit text, see Catalogue of the Hodgson Manuscripts, I. 63; VII. 52.

(b) Agrees with the Tibetan Pragñâpâramitâ in 25,000 ślokas (Pañkaviṁśati-sahasrikâ pragñâpâramitâ, 76 chapters, 78 bam-po). For the Sanskrit text, see Catalogue of the Hodgson Manuscripts, III. 2; V. 5.

(c) Agrees with the Tibetan Pragñâpâramitâ in 18,000 ślokas (Ashṭâdaśa-sahasrikâ pragñâpâramitâ, 87 chapters, 50 bam-po).

(d) Agrees with the Tibetan Pragñâpâramitâ in 8000 ślokas (Ashṭasâhasrikâ pragñâpâramitâ. But it is really the Daśasahasrikâ pragñâpâramitâ, 33 chapters, 24 bam-po. Cf. No. 7 below).

(e) Agrees with the Tibetan Pragñâpâramitâ in 8000 ślokas (Ashṭasâhasrikâ pragñâpâramitâ, 32 chapters, 24 bam-po). For the Sanskrit text, see Catalogue of the Hodgson Manuscripts, I. 1; III. 11; IV. 4, 5; VII. 54. Complete in 32 chapters.

(f) Deest in Tibetan. According to the contents, this is the Suvikrântavikrami-paripṛikkhâ.

(g) Agrees with the Tibetan Pragñâpâramitâ, in 700 ślokas (Saptaśatikâ).

(h) Deest in Tibetan. The Chinese title is a transliteration of 'Nâgaśrî.' Pañkaśatikâ?

(i) Agrees with the Tibetan Pragñâpâramitâ, in 300 ślokas. This is the Vagrakkhedikâ pragñâpâramitâ. The Sanskrit text has been published by Professor Max Müller in the Anecdota Oxoniensia, Aryan Series, vol. i, part 1, Oxford, 1881.

(j) Agrees with the Tibetan Pragñâpâramitâ, in 150 ślokas (Pragñâpâramitâ ardhaśatikâ).

(k–o) Agrees with the Tibetan Pragñâpâramitâ, in 1800 ślokas.

(p) Agrees with the Tibetan Pragñâpâramitâ, in 1200 ślokas.

The Sanskrit titles and the Tibetan accounts are given in the Index to the Kangur, published by Csoma Körösi in the Asiatic Researches, vol. xx (1836), pp. 393–397; and by L. Feer in the Annals du Musée Guimet, vol. ii (1881), pp. 199–203. For the contents of the whole Pragñâpâramitâ class, see these authorities: the former, pp. 397–400; the latter, pp. 203–208. See also Wassiljew's Buddhismus, 145; Beal's Catena of the Buddhist Scriptures from the Chinese, pp. 275–280.

Two Imperial prefaces to the Tripiṭaka are added at the beginning of this collection (No. 1), in both of which the labours of Hhüen-*k*wâṅ (Hiouen-thsang) are described by eye-witnesses, namely: 1. That by the Emperor Thâi-tsuṅ, A.D. 627–649, of the Thâṅ dynasty. 2. That by the Emperor Kâo-tsuṅ, A.D. 650–683, while he was the heir-apparent.

2 放光般若波羅蜜經

Fâṅ-kwâṅ-pân-zo-po-lo-mi-*k*iṅ.

'Pragñâpâramitâ-sûtra (with the first chapter on) emitting light.'

Pañkaviṁśati-sahasrikâ pragñâpâramitâ.

Translated by Wu-lo-*kh*â (or Mokshala, of Khoten), together with *K*u Shu-lân, A.D. 291, of the Western Tsin dynasty, A.D. 265–316. (Nâi-tien-lu, fasc. 2, fol. 31 b.) 30 fasciculi; 90 chapters.

3 摩訶般若波羅蜜經

Mo-hŏ-pân-zo-po-lo-mi-*k*iṅ.

'Mahâpragñâpâramitâ-sûtra.'

Pañkaviṁśati-sahasrikâ pragñâpâramitâ.

Translated by Kumâragîva, together with a Chinese priest, Saṅ-zui, of the Latter Tshin dynasty, A.D. 384–417. 30 fasciculi; 90 chapters.

4 光讚般若波羅蜜經

Kwâṅ-tsân pân-zo-po-lo-mi-*k*iṅ.

'Pragñâpâramitâ-sûtra (with the first chapter on) the praise of light.'

Pañkaviṁśati-sahasrikâ pragñâpâramitâ.

Translated by *K*u Fâ-hu (Dharmaraksha, of the Yueh-*k*'), of the Western Tsin dynasty, A.D. 265–316. 10 fasciculi; 21 chapters.

The above three works are earlier translations of the second Sûtra (b) of No. 1; but No. 4 is incomplete. (Preface to No. 1, fasc. 401; *K'*-yuen-lu, fasc. 1, fol. 14 b.)

5 道行般若波羅蜜經

Tâo-hhiṅ-pân-zo-po-lo-mi-*k*iṅ.

'Pragñâpâramitâ-sûtra (with the first chapter on) the practice of the way.'

Daśasahasrikâ pragñâpâramitâ.

[1] In the *K'*-yuen-lu, these Tibetan translations are called 蕃本 Fân-pan, or the Books of 西蕃 Si-fân, 'Western Fân,' i.e. 土蕃 Thu-fân, more properly 禿髮 Thu-fâh, which name was assumed for his newly-established kingdom by 倫贊索 Lun-tsân-su, in the Khâi-hwâṅ period, A.D. 581–600, of the Sui dynasty, which dynasty however did not become the sole ruler of China till A.D. 589. See the 西藏國考 Si-tsâṅ-kwo-khâo, in the 清類 Tshiṅ-lâi, fasc. 1, fol. 26 a seq. See also the Early History of Tibet, by Dr. Bushell, in the Journal of the Royal Asiatic Society, 1880, p. 435 seq.

Translated by *K*' Leu-*kiâ-kh*ân (Lokaraksha?), of the Eastern Hân dynasty, A. D. 25–220. 10 fasciculi; 30 chapters.

6 小品般若波羅蜜經
Siâo-phin-pân-*z*o-po-lo-mi-*k*in.
'Pra*gñ*âpâramitâ-sûtra of a small class.'
Da*s*asahasrikâ pra*gñ*âpâramitâ.

Translated by Kumâra*g*îva, A. D. 408, of the Latter Tshin dynasty, A. D. 384–417. (Preface to this version, by San-zui.) 10 fasciculi; 29 chapters.

7 摩訶般若波羅蜜鈔經
Mo-hö-pân-*z*o-po-lo-mi-*kh*âo-*k*in.
'An extract from the Mahâpra*gñ*âpâramitâ-sûtra.'
Da*s*asahasrikâ pra*gñ*âpâramitâ.

Conc. 365. Translated by Dharmapriya, together with *K*u Fo-nien and others, A. D. 382, of the Former Tshin dynasty, A. D. 350–394. (Nêi-tien-lu, fasc. 3 b, fol. 3 a.) 5 fasciculi; 13 chapters.

8 大明度無極經
Tâ-min-tu-wu-*k*i-*k*in.
'Sûtra of unlimited great-bright-crossing (or Mahâpra*gñ*âpâramitâ).'
Da*s*asahasrikâ pra*gñ*âpâramitâ.

Translated by *K*' *Kh*ien, of the Wu dynasty, A. D. 222–280. 6 fasciculi; 30 chapters.

The above four works are earlier translations of the fourth Sûtra (d) of No. 1; but No. 7 is incomplete. (Preface to No. 1, fasc. 538; *K*'-yuen-lu, fasc. 1, fol. 14 b.)

9 勝天王般若波羅蜜經
Shan-thien-wân-pân-*z*o-po-lo-mi-*k*in.
'Pra*gñ*âpâramitâ-sûtra, (spoken to) a heavenly king called Conquering.'
Suvikrântavikrami-paripri*kkh*â.

Translated by Upa*s*ûnya, A. D. 565, of the *Kh*ân dynasty, A. D. 557–589. (Nêi-tien-lu, fasc. 5 a, fol. 12.) 7 fasciculi; 16 chapters. This is an earlier translation of the sixth Sûtra (f) of No. 1. (Preface to No. 1, fasc. 566; *K*'-yuen-lu, fasc. 1, fol. 15 a.)

10 金剛般若波羅蜜經
*K*in-kân-pân-*z*o-po-lo-mi-*k*in.
'Diamond-pra*gñ*âpâramitâ-sûtra.'
Va*g*ra*kkh*edikâ pra*gñ*âpâramitâ.

Conc. 287. The Sanskrit text edited by Professor Max Müller in Anecdota Oxoniensia, Aryan Series, vol. i, part 1. Translated by Kumâra*g*îva, of the Latter Tshin dynasty, A. D. 384–417. 14 leaves. There is an Imperial preface to this version, by the Emperor *Kh*ân-tsu, of the Min dynasty, dated the ninth year of the Yun-lö period, A. D. 1411. An English translation by Beal in the Journal of the Royal Asiatic Society, 1864–5, Art. I.

11 The same as No. 10.

Conc. 287. Translated by Bodhiru*k*i, of the Northern Wêi dynasty, A. D. 386–534. 12 chapters; 17 leaves.

12 The same as No. 10.

Conc. 287. Translated by Paramârtha, A. D. 562, of the *Kh*ân dynasty, A. D. 557–589. (Note at the end of this version.) 17 leaves.

13 能斷金剛般若波羅蜜經
Nan-twân-*k*in-kân-pân-*z*o-po-lo-mi-*k*in.
'Well-cutting-diamond-pra*gñ*âpâramitâ-sûtra.'
Va*g*ra*kkh*edikâ pra*gñ*âpâramitâ.

Translated by Hhüen-*k*wân (Hiouen-thsang), of the Thân dynasty, A. D. 618–907. 21 leaves.

14 The same as No. 13.

Translated by I-tsin, of the Thân dynasty, A. D. 618–907. 14 leaves.

15 金剛能斷般若波羅蜜經
*K*in-kân-nan-twân-pân-*z*o-po-lo-mi-*k*in.
'Diamond-well-cutting-pra*gñ*âpâramitâ-sûtra.'
Va*g*ra*kkh*edikâ pra*gñ*âpâramitâ.

Translated by Dharmagupta, of the Sui dynasty, A. D. 589–618. 19 leaves. This translation is so literal and mot-à-mot as to be unintelligible to a Chinese without the Sanskrit text. There is a remarkable example, which puzzles the Chinese very much (as I have witnessed myself), namely, Sârdham ardha-trayodasabhir Bhikshu-satais is translated by Dharmagupta literally into 共半三十比丘百 Kun-pân-sân-shi-pi-*kh*iu-poh, 'together with-half-three-ten-Bhikshu-hundred,' instead of rendering it as usual by 千二百五十人俱 Tshien-'rh-poh-wu-shi-zan-*k*ü, 'thousand-two-hundred-five-ten-person-together with,' i.e. 'together with twelve hundred and fifty persons (or Bhikshus).' No Chinese reader could understand why 'half-three-ten-hundred' should be translated into 'twelve hundred and fifty,' unless he knew the Sanskrit text, which means 'thirteen hundred minus a half (hundred),' i.e. 1250[1]. A comparison of Dharmagupta's

[1] As to the origin of the number 1250 of Bhikshus, the following explanation by a Chinese priest named Lun-hhin is quoted in a commentary on the 'Amitâyur-dhyâna-sûtra' (fasc. 2, fol. 24 a): 'According to the Dharmagupta-vinaya (No. 1117), this number consists of 500 disciples of Uruvilva-kâsyapa, 300 of Gayâ-kâsyapa, 200 of Nadî-kâsyapa, 150 of *S*âriputra, and 100 of Maudgalyâyana. But these five teachers themselves, as well as the five Bhadravargîyas, ought also to be added to this number of Bhikshus.'

literal translation with the Sanskrit original helps in many places to make the Chinese translation intelligible, and enables us to correct the mistakes of the Chinese translator.

The above six works are earlier and later translations of the ninth Sûtra (i) of No. 1. No. 13 is merely a separate copy of the version given in No. 1. (Preface to No. 1, fasc. 577; *K'*-yuen-lu, fasc. 1, fol. 16 b.) No. 10 is comparatively short, it being a well-known character of this translator (Kumâragîva), that he seldom made a full translation, but preferred to give an abstract of the original. Nos. 11–14 are more or less full, when they are compared with the text, though No. 14 is also short. All these six translations of the *Vagrakkhedikâ* seem to have been made from a very similar text, if not from the same.

16 佛說儒首菩薩無上清淨分衛經

Fo-shwo-ṣu-sheu-phu-sâ-wu-shâṅ-tshiṅ-tsiṅ-fan-wêi-*k*iṅ.

'Sûtra on the Bodhisattva Mañgusrî's highest pure act of seeking alms, spoken by Buddha.'

Pañkasatikâ pragñâpâramitâ (?).

Translated by Siâṅ-kuṅ, of the earlier Suṅ dynasty, A.D. 420–479, at the Nân-hâi ('South-sea') district, in China. 2 fasc. This is an earlier and longer translation of the eighth Sûtra (h) of No. 1. (*K'*-yuen-lu, fasc. 1, fol. 17 a.)

17 仁王護國般若波羅蜜經

Ẕan-wâṅ-hu-kwo-pân-ṣo-po-lo-mi-*k*iṅ.

'Pragñâpâramitâ-sûtra on a benevolent king who protects his country.'

Translated by Kumâragîva, of the Latter Tshin dynasty, A.D. 384–417. 2 fasciculi; 8 chap. Doubtful (or not found) in Tibetan. (*K'*-yuen-lu, fasc. 1, fol. 16 b.)

18 實相般若波羅蜜經

Shih-siâṅ-pân-ṣo-po-lo-mi-*k*iṅ.

'Pragñâpâramitâ-sûtra of the true form.'

Pragñâpâramitâ ardhasatikâ.

Translated by Bodhiruki and others, of the Thâṅ dynasty, A.D. 618–907. 10 leaves. This is a later translation of the tenth Sûtra (j) of No. 1. (*K'*-yuen-lu, fasc. 1, fol. 16 b.)

19 摩訶般若波羅蜜大明咒經

Mo-hö-pân-ṣo-po-lo-mi-tâ-miṅ-*k*heu-*k*iṅ.

'Mahâpragñâpâramitâ-mahâvidyâ-mantra-sûtra.'

Pragñâpâramitâ-hṛidaya-sûtra.

Translated by Kumâragîva, of the Latter Tshin dynasty, A.D. 384–417. 1 leaf. For the Sanskrit text, see Max Müller's Selected Essays, vol. ii, pp. 368, 370; Anecd. Oxon., vol. i, part 1, pp. 3–11; Cat. Bodl. Japan., Nos. 45 b, 46 a, 61, 62, 63. Agrees with Tibetan. (*K'*-yuen-lu, fasc. 1, fol. 17 a. Cf. A. R., p. 397; A. M. G., p. 202.)

20 般若波羅蜜多心經

Pân-ṣo-po-lo-mi-to-sin-*k*iṅ.

Pragñâpâramitâ-hṛidaya-sûtra.

Translated by Hhüen-*k*wâṅ (Hiouen-thsang), of the Thâṅ dynasty, A.D. 618–907. 1 leaf. This is a later translation of the preceding sûtra. (*K'*-yuen-lu, fasc. 1, fol. 17 a.) An English translation by Beal in the Journal of the Royal Asiatic Society, 1864–5, Art. II; and also in his Catena of Buddhist Scriptures from the Chinese, pp. 282–284.

There are two prefaces to No. 20, namely: 1. That by the Emperor Thâi-tsu, A.D. 1368–1398, of the Miṅ dynasty. 2. That by a priest named Hwui-*k*uṅ, of the Thâṅ dynasty.

These two translations agree well with the Sanskrit text above mentioned.

21 文殊師利所說摩訶般若波羅蜜經

Wan-shu-sh'-li-ṣu-shwo-mo-hö-pân-ṣo-po-lo-mi-*k*iṅ.

'Mahâpragñâpâramitâ-sûtra, spoken by Mañgusrî.'

Saptasatikâ pragñâpâramitâ.

Conc. 797. Translated by Mandra, of the Liâṅ dynasty, A.D. 502–557. 24 leaves.

22 文殊師利所說般若波羅蜜經

Wan-shu-sh'-li-ṣu-shwo-pân-ṣo-po-lo-mi-*k*iṅ.

'Pragñâpâramitâ-sûtra, spoken by Mañgusrî.'

Saptasatikâ pragñâpâramitâ.

Translated by Saṅghapâla, of the Liâṅ dynasty, A.D. 502–557. 23 leaves.

The above two works are earlier translations of the seventh Sûtra (g) of No. 1. (Preface to No. 1, fasc. 574; *K'*-yuen-lu, fasc. 1, fol. 15 b.)

CLASS II.

寶積部 Pâo-tsi-pu, i. e. Ratnakûta Class.

23 **大寶積經**

Tâ-pâo-tsi-*k*in.

Mahâratnakû*t*a-sûtra.

K'-yuen-lu, fasc. 1, fol. 20 a; Conc. 642. Cf. A. R., p. 406; A. M. G., p. 212; Wassiljew, 154. Translated by Bodhiru*k*i, A. D. 713, of the Thân dynasty, A. D. 618–907; and by his predecessors and contemporaries, A. D. 265–713. 120 fasc. This is a collection of forty-nine Sûtras, arranged by Bodhiru*k*i, who had himself translated twenty-five of them.

There are two prefaces to this collection, namely: 1. That by the Emperor *Z*ui-tsun, A. D. 684, 710–712, who then retired from the throne, and who gives a short account concerning the life of Bodhiru*k*i. 2. That by an official, Sü Ño, a contemporary of Bodhiru*k*i.

The following is a list of the forty-nine Sûtras:—

(1) **三律儀會**

Sân-lüh-i-hwui.

'That (spoken at) an assembly on the three moral precepts.'

Trisambara-nirdesa.

K'-yuen-lu, fasc. 1, fol. 20 b; Conc. 507; A. R., p. 407; A. M. G., p. 213[1]. Translated by Bodhiru*k*i, of the Thân dynasty, A. D. 618–907. 3 fasciculi (fasc. 1–3 of No. 23).

(2) **無邊莊嚴會**

Wu-pien-*k*wân-yen-hwui.

'That (spoken at) an assembly on (the request of the Bodhisattva) Anantavyûha (?).'

Anantamukha-vinisodhana-nirdesa.

K'-yuen-lu, fasc. 1, fol. 20 b; Conc. 842; A. R., p. 407; A. M. G., p. 214. Translated by Bodhiru*k*i, of the Thân dynasty, A. D. 618–907. 4 fasciculi (fasc. 4–7).

(3) **密跡金剛力士會**

Mi-tsi-*k*in-kân-li-*k*'-hwui.

'That (spoken at) an assembly on (the request of) the wrestler Guhyapada (? or Guhyapati) Vagra.'

Tathâgatâ*k*intya-guhya-nirdesa.

K'-yuen-lu, fasc. 1, fol. 21 a; Conc. 351; A. R., p. 408; A. M. G., p. 314. Translated by *K*u Fâ-hu (Dharmaraksha), of the Western Tsin dynasty, A. D. 265–316. 7 fasciculi (fasc. 8–14).

(4) **淨居天子會**

Tsin-*k*ü-thien-tsz'-hwui.

'That (spoken at) an assembly on (the request of) a Devaputra of the pure abode (*S*uddhavâsa ?).'

(Vini)*s*odhana-nirdesa.

K'-yuen-lu, fasc. 1, fol. 21 a; Conc. 763.

Svapna-nirdesa.

A. R., p. 408; A. M. G., p. 214; Conc. 763.

Translated by *K*u Fâ-hu (Dharmaraksha), of the Tsin dynasty, A. D. 265–316. 2 fasciculi (fasc. 15, 16).

(5) **無量壽如來會**

Wu-liân-sheu-*z*u-lâi-hwui.

'That (spoken at) an assembly on the Tathâgata Amitâyus.'

Amitâyusha-vyûha.

K'-yuen-lu, fasc. 1, fol. 21 b.

Amitâbha-vyûha.

A. R., p. 408; A. M. G., p. 214; Conc. 827.

Sukhâvatî-vyûha.

Cf. A. M. G., p. 214, note 2.

Translated by Bodhiru*k*i, of the Thân dynasty, A. D. 618–907. 2 fasciculi (fasc. 17, 18).

This is the eleventh of twelve translations of the large Sukhâvatîvyûha[1]. The first and the fifth to tenth were

---

[1] These last two authorities give a full Sanskrit title, viz. Ârya-mahâratnakû*t*a-dharmaparyâya-satasahasrika-granthe Trisambara-nirdesa-parivartanâma mahâyâna-sûtram. Csoma adds the following note, which I shall follow hereafter in this Catalogue: 'To make short the titles, in the beginning the word "Ârya," meaning "the venerable," as also at the end, "Nâma mahâyâna-sûtram," will be omitted, and only that will be mentioned which necessarily belongs to the titles.'

[1] According to the Thu-*k*i (No. 1487), a catalogue of the Chinese Tripi*t*aka, compiled in about A. D. 664, Khâi-yuen-lu and *K*'-yuen-lu, the following is a list of twelve translations of this Sûtra:—

(I) Wu-liân-sheu-*k*in, 'Amitâyus-sûtra.' 2 fasc. Translated by Ân Shi-kâo, A. D. 148–170, of the Eastern Hân dynasty, A. D. 25–220. (Thu-*k*i, fasc. 1, fol. 5 b.) Lost.

(II) Wu-liân-tshin-tsin-phin-tan-kiâo-*k*in, 'Amita-suddha-samyaksambuddha-sûtra.' 3 fasc. By *K*' Leu-*k*iâ-*k*hân (Lokaraksha ?), A. D. 147–186, of the same dynasty as before. (Thu-*k*i, fasc. 1, fol. 4 a; *K*'-yuen-lu, fasc. 1, fol. 31 a.) In existence, first of the five translations. No. 25 of the Chinese Tripi*t*aka.

(III) Ö-mi-tho-*k*in, 'Amita-sûtra.' 2 fasc. By *K*' *Kh*ien, A. D. 223–253, of the Wu dynasty, A. D. 222–280. (Thu-*k*i, fasc. 1, fol. 19 a; *K*'-yuen-lu, fasc. 1, fol. 31 b.) In existence, second of the five. No. 26.

(IV) Wu-liân-sheu-*k*in, 'Amitâyus-sûtra.' 2 fasc. By Khân San-khâi (Sanghavarman), A. D. 252, of the Wêi dynasty, A. D. 220–265. (Thu-*k*i, fasc. 1, fol. 17 b; *K*'-yuen-lu, fasc. 1, fol. 31 b.) In existence, third of the five. No. 27.

already lost in China in A.D. 730, when the Khâi-yuen-lu (No. 1485), a well-known catalogue of the Chinese Tripiṭaka, was compiled; so that there are now only five in existence, of which this (No. 23. 5) is the fourth translation. For the Sanskrit text, see J. R. A. S., 1880, pp. 164, 165; Max Müller, Selected Essays, vol. ii, pp. 343–345; Catalogue of Hodgson MSS., I. 20; III. 13; IV. 3; VI. 29; VII. 71. Five MSS., as described by Professor Max Müller, have already been compared, and they are nearly the same, except a few various readings, additions, and omissions. But none of the five Chinese translations agrees entirely with the Sanskrit text, and they themselves differ from each other considerably. The following facts, however, remain unchanged throughout the text and translations, viz. the scene of the dialogue is placed at Râgagriha, on the mountain Gridhrakûṭa, and Bhagavat or Buddha, Ânanda and Maitreya are introduced as the principal speakers, the subject being the description of Sukhâvatî, together with the history of Amitâyus or Amitâbha, from his early stage of a Bhikshu with the name Dharmâkara, at the time of the Tathâgata Lokesvararâga.

(V) Wu-liân-tshiṅ-tsiṅ-phiṅ-taṅ-kiâo-kiṅ, 'Amita-suddha-samyaksambuddha-sûtra.' 2 fasc. By Po Yen, A.D. 257, of the same dynasty as before. (Thu-ki, fasc. 1, fol. 18 a.) Lost.

(VI) Wu-liâṅ-sheu-kiṅ, 'Amitâyus-sûtra.' 2 fasc. By Ku Fâ-hu (Dharmaraksha), A.D. 266–313, of the Western Tsin dynasty, A.D. 265–316. (Thu-ki, fasc. 2, fol. 2 a.) Lost.

(VII) Sin-wu-liâṅ-sheu-kiṅ, 'new Amitâyus-sûtra.' 2 fasc. By Buddhabhadra, A.D. 398–421, of the Eastern Tsin dynasty, A.D. 317–420. (Thu-ki, fasc. 2, fol. 23 b.) Lost.

(VIII) Wu-liâṅ-sheu-k'-kan-taṅ-kaṅ-kiâo-kiṅ, 'Amitâyur-arhat-samyaksambuddha-sûtra.' 1 fasc. By Ku Tâ-li, A.D. 419, of the same dynasty as before. (Thu-ki, fasc. 2, fol. 26 a.) Lost.

(IX) Sin-wu-liâṅ-sheu-kiṅ, 'new Amitâyus-sûtra.' 2 fasc. By Pâo-yun, A.D. 424–453, of the earlier Suṅ dynasty, A.D. 420–479. (Thu-ki, fasc. 3, fol. 19 a.) Lost.

(X) Sin-wu-liâṅ-sheu-kiṅ, 'new Amitâyus-sûtra.' 2 fasc. By Dharmamitra, A.D. 424–441, of the same dynasty as before. (Khâi-yuen-lu, fasc. 14, fol. 4 a.) Lost.

(XI) Wu-liâṅ-sheu-su-lâi-hwui, 'Amitâyus-tathâgata-parshad,' i.e. the Sûtra spoken by Buddha (Fo-shwo .... kiṅ understood) on the Tathâgata Amitâyus, at an assembly. 2 fasc. By Bodhiruki, A.D. 693–713, of the Thâṅ dynasty, A.D. 618–907. (K'-yuen-lu, fasc. 1, fol. 21 b.) In existence, fourth of the five. No. 23 (5).

(XII) Tâ-shaṅ-wu-liâṅ-sheu-kwâṅ-yen-kiṅ, 'Mahâyânâmitâyur-vyûha-sûtra.' 3 fasc. By Fâ-hhien, A.D. 982–1001, of the later Suṅ dynasty, A.D. 960–1280. (K'-yuen-lu, fasc. 4, fol. 11 a.) In existence, fifth of the five. No. 863.

Thus none of these twelve Chinese titles has yet shown us the meaning of the title of Sukhâvatîvyûha, or Amitâbhavyûha; but on the contrary, almost all of them agree with the title Amitâyur-vyûha, or Amitâyus-sûtra. For the above seven missing translations, see the Khâi-yuen-lu, fasc. 14, fol. 3 b seq.

(6) 不動如來會

Pu-tuṅ-su-lâi-hwui.

'That (spoken at) an assembly on the Tathâgata Akshobhya.'

Akshobhyasya Tathâgatasya vyûha.

K'-yuen-lu, fasc. 1, fol. 21 b; Conc. 500; A. R., p. 408; A. M. G., p. 214. Translated by Bodhiruki, of the Thâṅ dynasty, A.D. 618–907. 2 fasciculi (fasc. 19, 20); 6 chapters.

(7) 被甲莊嚴會

Pêi-kiâ-kwâṅ-yen-hwui.

'That (spoken at) an assembly on the adornment of wearing the armour.'

Varmavyûha-nirdesa.

K'-yuen-lu, fasc. 1, fol. 21 b; Conc. 436. Translated by Bodhiruki, of the Thâṅ dynasty, A.D. 618–907. 5 fasciculi (fasc. 21–25).

(8) 法界體性無分別會

Fâ-kiê-thi-siṅ-wu-fan-pieh-hwui.

'That (spoken at) an assembly on the indivisibility of the substance and nature of the Dharmadhâtu.'

Dharmadhâtu-hridaya-samvrita-nirdesa.

K'-yuen-lu, fasc. 1, fol. 22 a; Conc. 134.

Dharmadhâtu-prakrity-asambheda-nirdesa[1].

A. R., p. 408; A. M. G., p. 214; Conc. 134.

Translated by Mandra, of the Liâṅ dynasty, A.D. 502–557. 2 fasciculi (fasc. 26, 27).

The above eight Sûtras agree with Tibetan. K'-yuen-lu, fasc. 1, fol. 22 a.

(9) 大乘十法會

Tâ-shaṅ-shi-fâ-hwui.

'That (spoken at) an assembly on the ten Dharmas of the Mahâyâna.'

Dasadharmaka.

K'-yuen-lu, fasc. 1, fol. 22 b; Conc. 567; A. R., p. 408; A. M. G., p. 215. Translated by Buddhasânta, of the Northern Wêi dynasty, A.D. 386–534. 1 fasciculus (fasc. 28).

(10) 文殊師利普門會

Wan-shu-sh'-li-phu-man-hwui.

'That (spoken at) an assembly on (the request of) Mañgusrî on the Samantamukha.'

Samantamukha-parivarta.

K'-yuen-lu, fasc. 1, fol. 22 b; Conc. 804; A. R., p. 408; A. M. G., p. 215. Translated by Bodhiruki, of the Thâṅ dynasty, A.D. 618–907. 1 fasciculus (fasc. 29).

[1] Csoma translates this title as follows: 'The showing of the indivisibility of the root of the first moral Being.'

(11) 出現光明會

*Kh*u-hhien-kwâṅ-miṅ-hwui.

'That (spoken at) an assembly on making the light manifest.'

Rasminirhâra-saṅgirathî (or -saṅgîti ?).

K'-yuen-lu, fasc. 1, fol. 22 b; Conc. 721.

Prabhâ-sâdhanâ.

A. R., p. 408; A. M. G., p. 215.

Translated by Bodhiru*k*i, of the Thâṅ dynasty, A. D. 618–907. 5 fasciculi (fasc. 30–34).

(12) 菩薩藏會

Phu-sâ-tsâṅ-hwui.

'That (spoken at) an assembly on the Bodhisattva-piṭaka.'

Bodhisattva-piṭaka.

K'-yuen-lu, fasc. 1, fol. 23 a; Conc. 491; A. R., p. 408; A. M. G., p. 215. Translated by Hhüen-*k*wâṅ (Hiouen-thsang), A. D. 645, of the Thâṅ dynasty, A. D. 618–907. 20 fasciculi (fasc. 35–54); 12 chapters. This is the first translation made by Hhüen-*k*wâṅ (Hiouen-thsang), after his return to China from India in A. D. 645. (Nêi-tien-lu, fasc. 5 b, fol. 19 b.)

The above four Sûtras agree with Tibetan. *K*'-yuen-lu, fasc. 1, fol. 23 a.

(13) 佛為阿難說人處胎會

Fo-wei-ö-nân-shwo-*z*an-*kh*u-thâi-hwui.

'That spoken by Buddha to Ânanda at an assembly on (the state of) man's dwelling in the womb.'

Garbha-sûtra (?).

Wassiljew, 327. Translated by Bodhiru*k*i, of the Thâṅ dynasty, A. D. 618–907. 1 fasciculus (fasc. 55).

(14) 佛說入胎藏會

Fo-shwo-*z*u-thâi-tsâṅ-hwui.

'That spoken by Buddha at an assembly on entering the womb.'

Garbha-sûtra (?).

Translated by I-tsiṅ, of the Thâṅ dynasty, A. D. 618–907. 2 fasciculi (fasc. 56, 57). 'This Sûtra originally formed a part (fasc. 11 and 12) of the Sarvâstivâda-nikâya-vinaya-sa*m*yukta-vastu (No. 1121, in 40 fasciculi), translated by I-tsiṅ, who then published this Sûtra as a separate work. It was afterwards placed here as No. 23 (14) by Bodhiru*k*i, according to the order of the Sanskrit text of Mahâratnakûṭa-sûtra (No. 23).' *K*'-yuen-lu, fasc. 1, fol. 23 b.

(15) 文殊師利授記會

Wan-shu-sh'-li-sheu-*k*i-hwui.

'That (spoken at) an assembly on giving the prophecy to Mañgusrî.'

Mañgusrî-buddhakshetraguṇavyûha.

A. R., p. 409; A. M. G., p. 215; Conc. 800. Translated by *S*ikshânanda, of the Thâṅ dynasty, A. D. 618–907. 3 fasciculi (fasc. 58–60).

'The above three Sûtras are wanting in Tibetan.' *K*'-yuen-lu, fasc. 1, fol. 23 b. But the last of the three seems to be in existence in Tibetan also. See the authorities mentioned under the title.

(16) 菩薩見實會

Phu-sâ-*k*ien-shih-hwui.

'That (spoken at) an assembly on the Bodhisattva's seeing the truth.'

Pitâ-putra-samâgama.

K'-yuen-lu, fasc. 1, fol. 23 b; Conc. 480; A. R., p. 409; A. M. G., p. 215. Translated by Narendrayasas, of the Northern Tshi dynasty, A. D. 550–577. 16 fasciculi (fasc. 61–76); 29 chapters.

(17) 富樓那會

Fu-leu-nâ-hwui.

'That (spoken at) an assembly on (the request of) Pûrṇa.'

Pûrṇa-paripri*kkh*â.

K'-yuen-lu, fasc. 1, fol. 24 a; Conc. 179; A. R., p. 409; A. M. G., p. 215. Translated by Kumâra*g*îva, of the Latter Tshin dynasty, A. D. 384–417. 3 fasciculi (fasc. 77–79); 8 chapters.

(18) 護國菩薩會

Hu-kwo-phu-sâ-hwui.

'That (spoken at) an assembly on (the request of) the Bodhisattva Râshṭrapâla.'

Râshṭrapâla-paripri*kkh*â.

K'-yuen-lu, fasc. 1, fol. 24 a; Conc. 214; A. R., p. 409; A. M. G., p. 216. Translated by *G*ñânagupta, of the Sui dynasty, A. D. 589–618. 2 fasciculi (fasc. 80, 81). This Bodhisattva Râshṭrapâla (as the Chinese title tells us) is 'a demon,' in Tibetan. See the last two authorities above mentioned.

(19) 郁伽長者會

Yü-*k*ie-*kh*âṅ-*k*ö-hwui.

'That (spoken at) an assembly on (the request of) the *S*resh*th*in Ugra.'

Ugra-paripri*kkh*â.

K'-yuen-lu, fasc. 1, fol. 24 b; Conc. 859; A. R., p. 409; A. M. G., p. 216. Translated by Khâṅ Saṅ-khâi (Saṅghavarman), of the Wêi dynasty, A. D. 220–265. 1 fasciculus (fasc. 82). Agrees with Tibetan. *K*'-yuen-lu.

(20) 無盡伏藏會

Wu-tsin-fu-tsâṅ-hwui.

'That (spoken at) an assembly on the unexhausted hidden repository,' or 'Aksharakosha-sûtra (?).'

Translated by Bodhiruki, of the Thâṅ dynasty, A. D. 618–907. 2 fasciculi (fasc. 83, 84). Deest in Tibetan. K'-yuen-lu, fasc. 1, fol. 24 b.

(21) 授幻師跋陀羅記會

Sheu-hwân-sh'-poh-tho-lo-ki-hwui.

'That (spoken at) an assembly on giving the prophecy to the magician Bhadra.'

Bhadra-mâyâkâra-paripṛikkhâ.

K'-yuen-lu, fasc. 1, fol. 24 b.

Bhadra-mâyâkâra-vyâkaraṇa.

A. R., p. 409; A. M. G., p. 216; Conc. 63. Translated by Bodhiruki, of the Thâṅ dynasty, A. D. 618–907. 1 fasciculus (fasc. 85).

(22) 大神變會

Tâ-shan-pien-hwui.

'That (spoken at) an assembly on giving the great supernatural change.'

Mahâpratihâryopadeśa.

K'-yuen-lu, fasc. 1, fol. 25 a; Conc. 563; A. R., p. 409; A. M. G., p. 216. Translated by Bodhiruki, of the Thâṅ dynasty, A. D. 618–907. 2 fasciculi (fasc. 86, 87).

(23) 摩訶迦葉會

Mo-hö-kie-yeh-hwui.

'That (spoken at) an assembly on (the request of) Mahâkâśyapa.'

Mahâkâśyapi (or -kâśyapa?).

K'-yuen-lu, fasc. 1, fol. 25 a.

Mahâkâśya(pa)-saṅgîti. Conc. 363.

Maitreya-mahâsiṃhanâdana.

A. R., p. 409; A. M. G., p. 216. Translated by Upaśûnya, of the Eastern Wêi dynasty, A. D. 534–550. 2 fasciculi (fasc. 88, 89).

(24) 優波離會

Yiu-po-li-hwui.

'That (spoken at) an assembly on (the request of) Upâli.'

Vinayaviniśkaya-upâli-paripṛikkhâ.

K'-yuen-lu, fasc. 1, fol. 25 b; Conc. 862; A. R., p. 409; A. M. G., p. 216. Translated by Bodhiruki, of the Thâṅ dynasty, A. D. 618–907. 1 fasciculus (fasc. 90).

(25) 發勝志樂會

Fâ-shaṅ-k'-yâo-hwui.

'That (spoken at) an assembly on raising the excellent inclination and wish.'

Âdyâśaya-saṅkodana.

K'-yuen-lu, fasc. 1, fol. 25 b; Conc. 128; A. R., p. 410; A. M. G., p. 216. Translated by Bodhiruki, of the Thâṅ dynasty, A. D. 618–907. 2 fasciculi (fasc. 91, 92).

(26) 善臂菩薩會

Shân-phi-phu-sâ-hwui.

'That (spoken at) an assembly on (the request of) the Bodhisattva Subâhu.'

Subâhu-paripṛikkhâ.

K'-yuen-lu, fasc. 1, fol. 26 a; Conc. 58; A. R., p. 410; A. M. G., p. 216. Translated by Kumâragîva, of the Latter Tshin dynasty, A. D. 384–417. 2 fasciculi (fasc. 93, 94).

(27) 善順菩薩會

Shân-shun-phu-sâ-hwui.

'That (spoken at) an assembly on (the request of) the Bodhisattva Surata.'

Surata-paripṛikkhâ.

K'-yuen-lu, fasc. 1, fol. 26 a; Conc. 54; A. R., p. 410; A. M. G., p. 216. Translated by Bodhiruki, of the Thâṅ dynasty, A. D. 618–907. 1 fasciculus (fasc. 95). This Bodhisattva Surata (as the Chinese title tells us) is 'a chief or brave man,' in Tibetan. See the last two authorities above mentioned.

(28) 勤授長者會

Khin-sheu-kkâṅ-kö-hwui.

'That (spoken at) an assembly on (the request of) the Śreshṭhin Vîradatta.'

Vîradatta-paripṛikkhâ.

K'-yuen-lu, fasc. 1, fol. 26 a; Conc. 282; A. R., p. 410; A. M. G., p. 216. Translated by Bodhiruki, of the Thâṅ dynasty, A. D. 618–907. 1 fasciculus (fasc. 96).

(29) 優陀延王會

Yiu-tho-yen-wâṅ-hwui.

'That (spoken at) an assembly on (the request of) the King Udayâna.'

Udayâna-vatsarâga-paripṛikkhâ.

K'-yuen-lu, fasc. 1, fol. 26 b; Conc. 865; A. R., p. 410; A. M. G., p. 217. Translated by Bodhiruki, of the Thâṅ dynasty, A. D. 618–907. 1 fasciculus (fasc. 97).

(30) 妙慧童女會

Miâo-hwui-thuṅ-nü-hwui.

'That (spoken at) an assembly on (the request of) a girl named Sumati (a daughter of a Śreshṭhin in Râgagṛiha).'

Sumati-dârikâ-paripṛikkhâ.

K'-yuen-lu, fasc. 1, fol. 26 b; Conc. 356; A. R., p. 410; A. M. G., p. 217. Translated by Bodhiruki, of the Thân dynasty, A. D. 618–907. 1 fasciculus (fasc. 98 a).

(31) 恒河上優婆夷會
Hań-hö-shâń-yiu-pho-i-hwui.
'That (spoken at) an assembly on (the request of) an Upâsikâ who lived on (the bank of) the river Gaṅgâ.'
Gaṅgottaropâsikâ-paripṛikkhâ.

K'-yuen-lu, fasc. 1, fol. 27 a; Conc. 184; A. R., p. 410; A. M. G., p. 217. Translated by Bodhiruki, of the Thân dynasty, A. D. 618–907. 1 fasciculus (fasc. 98 b).

(32) 無畏德菩薩會
Wu-wêi-töh-phu-sâ-hwui.
'That (spoken at) an assembly on (giving the prophecy to) the Bodhisattva Asokadattâ (a Princess of the King Agâtasatru).'
Asokadattâ-vyâkarana.

K'-yuen-lu, fasc. 1, fol. 27 a; Conc. 835; A. R., p. 410; A. M. G., p. 217. Translated by Buddhasânta, of the Northern Wêi dynasty, A. D. 386–534. 1 fasciculus (fasc. 99).

(33) 無垢施菩薩應辯會
Wu-keu-sh'-phu-sâ-yiṅ-pien-hwui.
'That (spoken at) an assembly on the fitting eloquence of the Bodhisattva Vimaladattâ (a Princess of the King Prasenagit).'
Vimaladattâ-paripṛikkhâ.

K'-yuen-lu, fasc. 1, fol. 27 a; Conc. 819; A. R., p. 410; A. M. G., p. 217. Translated by Nieh Tâo-kan, of the Western Tsin dynasty, A. D. 265–316. 1 fasciculi (fasc. 100); 5 chapters.

(34) 功德寶華敷菩薩會
Kuṅ-töh-pâo-hwâ-fu-phu-sâ-hwui.
'That (spoken at) an assembly on (the request of) the Bodhisattva Gunaratnasaṅkusumita.'
Gunaratnasaṅkusumita-paripṛikkhâ.

K'-yuen-lu, fasc. 1, fol. 27 b; Conc. 300; A. R., p. 410; A. M. G., p. 217. Translated by Bodhiruki, of the Thân dynasty, A. D. 618–907. 6 leaves (fasc. 101 a).

(35) 善德天子會
Shân-töh-thien-tsz'-hwui.
'That (spoken at) an assembly on (the request of) the Devaputra Sadharma (? "good-virtue").'
Akintyabuddhavishaya-nirdesa.

K'-yuen-lu, fasc. 1, fol. 27 b; Conc. 62; A. R., p. 411; A. M. G., p. 217. Translated by Bodhiruki, of the Thân dynasty, A. D. 618–907. 19 leaves (fasc. 101 b.)

The above fifteen Sûtras agree with Tibetan. K'-yuen-lu, s. v.

(36) 善住意天子會
Shân-ku-i-thien-tsz'-hwui.
'That (spoken at) an assembly on (the request of) the Devaputra Sushtkitamati.'
Sushthitamati-paripṛikkhâ.

A. R., p. 411; A. M. G., p. 217; Conc. 61. Translated by Dharmagupta, of the Sui dynasty, A. D. 589–618. 4 fasciculi (fasc. 102–105); 10 chapters. 'Deest in Tibetan.' K'-yuen-lu, fasc. 1, fol. 28 a. See, however, the authorities mentioned under the title.

(37) 阿闍世王太子會
Ö-shö-shi-wâń-thâi-tsz'-hwui.
'That (spoken at) an assembly on (the request of) the Crown-Prince of the King Agâtasatru (Simha by name).'
Simha-paripṛikkhâ.

K'-yuen-lu, fasc. 1, fol. 28 a; Conc. 4; A. R., p. 411; A. M. G., p. 217.

Subâhu-paripṛikkhâ.

Conc. 4. Translated by Bodhiruki, of the Thâń dynasty, A. D. 618–907. 7 leaves (fasc. 106 a).

(38) 大乘方便會
Tâ-shań-fâń-pien-hwui.
'That (spoken at) an assembly on the good means (Upâyakausalya) of the Mahâyâna.'
Gńânottara-bodhisattva-paripṛikkhâ.

K'-yuen-lu, fasc. 1, fol. 28 a, where a longer title is given; Conc. 568; A. R., p. 411; A. M. G., p. 218. Translated by Nandi, of the Eastern Tsin dynasty, A. D. 317–420. 3 fasciculi (fasc. 106 b–108).

(39) 賢護長者會
Hhien-hu-kkâń-kö-hwui.
'That (spoken at) an assembly on (the request of) the Sreshthin Bhadrapâla.'
Bhadrapâla-sreshthi-paripṛikkhâ.

K'-yuen-lu, fasc. 1, fol. 28 b; Conc. 188; A. R., p. 411; A. M. G., p. 218. Translated by Gńânagupta, of the Sui dynasty, A. D. 589–618. 2 fasciculi (fasc. 109, 110).

The above three Sûtras agree with Tibetan. K'-yuen-lu, s. v.

(40) 淨信童女會
Tsiń-sin-thuń-nü-hwui.
'That (spoken at) an assembly on (the request of) a girl named Pure-faith,' or 'Suddhasraddhâ-dârikâ-paripṛikkhâ (?).'

Translated by Bodhiruki, of the Thâń dynasty, A. D. 618–907. 14 leaves (fasc. 111 a). Deest in Tibetan. K'-yuen-lu, fasc. 1, fol. 29 a.

(41) 彌勒菩薩問八法會

Mi-lö-phu-sâ-wan-pâ-fâ-hwui.

'That (spoken at) an assembly on the eight Dharmas asked by the Bodhisattva Maitreya.'

Maitreya-paripṛkkhâ-dharmâshṭa.

K'-yuen-lu, fasc. 1, fol. 29 a; Conc. 347; A. R., p. 411; A. M. G., p. 218. Translated by Bodhiruki, of the Northern Wêi dynasty, A. D. 386–534. 4 leaves (fasc. 111 b).

(42) 彌勒菩薩所問會

Mi-lö-phu-sâ-su-wan-hwui.

'That (spoken at) an assembly on (the request of) the Bodhisattva Maitreya.'

Maitreya-paripṛkkhâ.

K'-yuen-lu, fasc. 1, fol. 29 a; Conc. 348; A. R., p. 411; A. M. G., p. 218. Translated by Bodhiruki, of the Thân dynasty, A. D. 618–907. 13 leaves (fasc. 111 c).

The above two Sûtras agree with Tibetan. *K'*-yuen-lu, s. v.

(43) 普明菩薩會

Phu-min-phu-sâ-hwui.

'That (spoken at) an assembly on (the request of) the Bodhisattva Samantaprabha.'

Kâsyapa-parivarta.

A. R., p. 411; A. M. G., p. 218; Conc. 472. Translator's name is lost. 1 fasciculus (fasc. 112). 'Deest in Tibetan.' *K'*-yuen-lu, fasc. 1, fol. 29 b. See, however, the authorities mentioned under the title.

(44) 寶梁聚會

Pâo-liân-tsu-hwui.

'That (spoken at) an assembly on a heap of precious beams.'

Ratnarâsi.

K'-yuen-lu, fasc. 1, fol. 29 b.

Ratnaparâsi.

A. R., p. 411; A. M. G., p. 218; Conc. 411. Translated by Shih Tâo-kun, of the Northern Liân dynasty, A. D. 397–439. 2 fasciculi (fasc. 113, 114).

(45) 無盡慧菩薩會

Wu-tsin-hwui-phu-sâ-hwui.

'That (spoken at) an assembly on (the request of) the Bodhisattva Akshayamati.'

Akshayamati-paripṛkkhâ.

K'-yuen-lu, fasc. 1, fol. 29 b; Conc. 850; A. R., p. 411; A. M. G., p. 218. Translated by Bodhiruki, of the Thân dynasty, A. D. 618–907. 9 leaves (fasc. 115 a).

(46) 文殊說般若會

Wan-shu-shwo-pân-zo-hwui.

'Pragñâpâramitâ spoken by Mañgusrî at an assembly.'

Mañgusrî-buddhakshetraguṇavyûha.

K'-yuen-lu, fasc. 1, fol. 30 a; Conc. 798.

Saptasatikâ pragñâpâramitâ.

A. R., p. 412; A. M. G., p. 218; Conc. 797. Translated by Mandra, of the Liân dynasty, A. D. 502–557. 2 fasciculi (fasc. 115 b, 116). This version is exactly the same as No. 21. *K'*-yuen-lu, fasc. 1, fol. 15 b.

(47) 寶髻菩薩會

Pâo-ki-phu-sâ-hwui.

'That (spoken at) an assembly on (the request of) the Bodhisattva Ratnakûḍa.'

Ratnakûḍa-paripṛkkhâ.

K'-yuen-lu, fasc. 1, fol. 30 a; Conc. 410; A. R., p. 412; A. M. G., p. 218. Translated by Ku Fâ-hu (Dharmaraksha), of the Western Tsin dynasty, A. D. 265–316. 2 fasciculi (fasc. 117, 118).

(48) 勝鬘夫人會

Shan-mân-fu-zan-hwui.

'That (spoken at) an assembly by the Princess Srîmâlâ.'

Vyûha-paripṛkkhâ.

K'-yuen-lu, fasc. 1, fol. 30 b. This seems to be a wrong reading of the title of Vyâsa-paripṛkkhâ, i. e. that of the following work.

Srîmâlâ-devî-simhanâda.

A. R., p. 412; A. M. G., p. 218; Conc. 104. Translated by Bodhiruki, of the Thân dynasty, A. D. 618–907. 1 fasciculus (fasc. 119).

The above five Sûtras agree with Tibetan. *K'*-yuen-lu, s. v.

(49) 廣博仙人會

Kwân-poh-sien-zan-hwui.

'That (spoken at) an assembly on (the request of) the *Rishi* Vyâsa.'

Vyâsa-paripṛkkhâ.

A. R., p. 412; A. M. G., p. 218; Conc. 315. Translated by Bodhiruki, of the Thân dynasty, A. D. 618–907. 1 fasciculus (fasc. 120). 'Deest in Tibetan.' *K'*-yuen-lu, fasc. 1, fol. 31 a. See, however, the authorities mentioned under the title.

24 大方廣三戒經

Tâ-fân-kwân-sân-kie-kin.

'Mahâvaipulya-sûtra on the three moral precepts.'

Trisambara-nirdesa (or, Trisambala-n°).

Conc. 603. Translated by Dharmaraksha, of the

Northern Liân dynasty, A. D. 397–439. 3 fasciculi. This is an earlier translation of the first Sûtra of No. 23. *K'*-yuen-lu, fasc. 1, fol. 31 a.

25 佛說無量清淨平等覺經

Fo-shwo-wu-liân-tshin-tsin-phin-tan-*k*iâo-*k*in.

'Sûtra spoken by Buddha on Amita-suddha-samyaksambuddha.'

Amitâyusha-vyûha, or Sukhâvatî-vyûha.

Cf. No. 23 (5).

Amitâbha-vyûha.

Conc. 836, 837. Translated by *K'* Leu-*k*iâ-*kh*ân (Lokaraksha?), of the Eastern Hân dynasty, A. D. 25–220. 3 fasciculi.

26 佛說阿彌陀經

Fo-shwo-ŏ-mi-tho-*k*in.

'Sûtra spoken by Buddha on Amita or Amitâyus.'

Amitâyusha-vyûha, or Sukhâvatî-vyûha.

Cf. No. 23 (5).

Amitâbha-vyûha.

Conc. 9, where a longer Chinese title is given. Cf. *K'*-yuen-lu, fasc. 1, fol. 31 b. Translated by *K'Kh*ien, of the Wu dynasty, A. D. 222–280. 2 fasciculi.

27 佛說無量壽經

Fo-shwo-wu-liân-sheu-*k*in.

'Sûtra spoken by Buddha on Amitâyus.'

Aparimitâyus-sûtra.

K'-yuen-lu, fasc. 1, fol. 31 b; Conc. 828, 829.

Amitâyusha-vyûha, or Sukhâvatî-vyûha.

Cf. No. 23 (5); Conc. 828. Translated by Khân Sañ-khâi (Sañghavarman), A. D. 252, of the Wêi dynasty, A. D. 220–265. Thu-*k*i, fasc. 1, fol. 17 b. 2 fasciculi.

The above three works are earlier translations of the fifth Sûtra of No. 23. *K'*-yuen-lu, fasc. 1, fol. 31 b.

28 佛說阿閦佛國經

Fo-shwo-ŏ-*kh*u-fo-kwo-*k*in.

'Sûtra spoken by Buddha on the Buddha-country of Akshobhya.'

Akshobhyasya tathâgatasya vyûha.

Conc. 38. Translated by *K'* Leu-*k*iâ-*kh*ân (Lokaraksha?), of the Eastern Hân dynasty, A. D. 25–220. 3 fasciculi. This is an earlier translation of the sixth Sûtra of No. 23. *K'*-yuen-lu, fasc. 1, fol. 32 a.

29 佛說大乘十法經

Fo-shwo-tâ-shan-shi-fâ-*k*in.

'Sûtra spoken by Buddha on the ten Dharmas of the Mahâyâna.'

Dasadharmaka.

Conc. 567. Translated by Sañghapâla, of the Liân dynasty, A. D. 502–557. 1 fasciculus. This is an earlier translation of the ninth Sûtra of No. 23. *K'*-yuen-lu, fasc. 1, fol. 32 a.

30 佛說普門品經

Fo-shwo-phu-man-phin-*k*in.

'Sûtra spoken by Buddha being a chapter on the universal gate.'

Samantamukha-parivarta.

Conc. 470. Translated by *K*u Fâ-hu (Dharmaraksha), of the Western Tsin dynasty, A. D. 265–316. 1 fasciculus. This is an earlier translation of the tenth Sûtra of No. 23. *K'*-yuen-lu, fasc. 1, fol. 32 a.

31 文殊師利佛土嚴淨經

Wan-shu-sh'-li-fo-thu-yen-tsin-*k*in.

'Sûtra on the pureness and adornment of the Buddha-country of Mañgusrî.'

Mañ*g*us*r*î-buddhakshetragu*n*avyûha.

Conc. 861. Translated by *K*u Fâ-hu (Dharmaraksha), of the Western Tsin dynasty, A. D. 265–316. 2 fasciculi. This is an earlier translation of the fifteenth Sûtra of No. 23. *K'*-yuen-lu, fasc. 1, fol. 32 b.

32 佛說胞胎經

Fo-shwo-pâo-thâi-*k*in.

'Sûtra spoken by Buddha on the womb.'

Garbha-sûtra (?).

Translated by *K*u Fâ-hu (Dharmaraksha), of the Western Tsin dynasty, A. D. 265–316. 1 fasciculus. This is an earlier translation of the thirteenth Sûtra of No. 23. *K'*-yuen-lu, fasc. 1, fol. 32 b.

33 佛說法鏡經

Fo-shwo-fâ-*k*in-*k*in.

'Sûtra spoken by Buddha on the mirror of the Dharma.'

Ugra-pari*p*ri*kkh*â.

Conc. 136. Translated by An Hhüen together with Yen Fo-thiâo, of the Eastern Hân dynasty, A. D. 25–220. 2 fasciculi.

34 郁迦羅越問菩薩行經

Yü-*k*iâ-lo-yueh-wan-phu-sâ-hhin-*k*in.

'Sûtra on the practice of the Bodhisattva asked by Ugra(de)va (?).'

Ugra-pari*p*ri*kkh*â.

Conc. 861. Translated by *K*u Fâ-hu (Dharmaraksha), of the Western Tsin dynasty, A. D. 265–316. 1 fasciculus; 8 chapters.

The above two works are earlier and later translations of the nineteenth Sûtra of No. 23. *K'*-yuen-lu, fasc. 1, fol. 33 a.

35 幻士仁賢經

Hwân-*k*'-*s*an-hhien-*k*in.

'Sûtra (spoken on the request) of the magician Bhadra.'

Bhadra-mâyâkâra-paripri*kkh*â.

K'-yuen-lu, fasc. 1, fol. 33 a.

Bhadra-mâyâkâra-vyâkara*n*a.

Conc. 216. Translated by *K*u Fâ-hu (Dharmaraksha), of the Western Tsin dynasty, A.D. 265–316. 1 fasciculus. This is an earlier translation of the twenty-first Sûtra of No. 23. *K*'-yuen-lu, s. v.

36 佛說決定毗尼經

Fo-shwo-*k*üê-tiṅ-phi-ni-*k*iṅ.

'Sûtra spoken by Buddha on the determination of the Vinaya.'

Vinayavinis*k*aya-upâli-paripri*kkh*â.

Conc. 295. Translated by a teacher of the Tripi*t*aka, of (or at) the Thun-kwâṅ[1] district (?). 'According to *K*'-shaṅ, the compiler of the Khâi-yuen-lu, this translation was made under the Eastern Tsin dynasty, A.D. 317–420. But the other catalogues mention neither the translator's name nor the period of the translation.' This is another translation of the twenty-fourth Sûtra of No. 23. *K*'-yuen-lu, fasc. 1, fol. 33 b. 1 fasciculus.

37 發覺淨心經

Fâ-*k*iâo-tsiṅ-sin-*k*iṅ.

'Sûtra on raising and awakening the pure thought.'

Âdyâsaya-sa*ñk*oda.

Conc. 135. Translated by *G*ñânagupta, of the Sui dynasty, A.D. 589–618. 2 fasciculi. This is an earlier translation of the twenty-fifth Sûtra of No. 23. *K*'-yuen-lu, fasc. 1, fol. 33 b.

38 佛說優塡王經

Fo-shwo-yiu-thien-wâṅ-*k*iṅ.

'Sûtra spoken by Buddha on (the request of) the King Udayâna.'

Udayâna-vatsarâ*g*a-paripri*kkh*â.

K'-yuen-lu, fasc. 1, fol. 33 b; Conc. 864. Translated by Fâ-*k*ü, of the Western Tsin dynasty, A.D. 265–316. 6 leaves. This is an earlier translation of the twenty-ninth Sûtra of No. 23. *K*'-yuen-lu, fasc. 1, fol. 34 a.

39 佛說須摩提經

Fo-shwo-sü-mo-thi-*k*iṅ.

'Sûtra spoken by Buddha on (the request of) Sumati.'

Sumati-dârikâ-paripri*kkh*â.

K'-yuen-lu, fasc. 1, fol. 34 a; Conc. 532. Translated by *K*u Fâ-hu (Dharmaraksha), of the Western Tsin dynasty, A.D. 265–316. 9 leaves.

40 佛說須摩提菩薩經

Fo-shwo-sü-mo-thi-phu-sâ-*k*iṅ.

'Sûtra spoken by Buddha on (the request of) the Bodhisattva Sumati.'

Sumati-dârikâ-paripri*kkh*â.

Conc. 533. Translated by Kumâra*g*îva, of the Latter Tshin dynasty, A.D. 384–417. 11 leaves.

The above two works are earlier translations of the thirtieth Sûtra of No. 23. *K*'-yuen-lu, fasc. 1, fol. 34 a.

41 佛說離垢施女經

Fo-shwo-li-keu-sh'-nü-*k*iṅ.

'Sûtra spoken by Buddha on (the request of) the Princess Vimaladattâ.'

Vimaladattâ-paripri*kkh*â.

Conc. 321. Translated by *K*u Fâ-hu (Dharmaraksha), of the Western Tsin dynasty, A.D. 265–316. 1 fasciculus. This is an earlier translation of the thirty-third Sûtra of No. 23. *K*'-yuen-lu, fasc. 1, fol. 34 b.

42 佛說阿闍世王女阿術達菩薩經

Fo-shwo-ö-shö-shi-wâṅ-nü-ö-shu-tâ-phu-sâ-*k*iṅ.

'Sûtra spoken by Buddha on the Bodhisattva Asokadattâ, a Princess of the King A*g*âtasatru.'

Asokadattâ-vyâkara*n*a.

Conc. 3. Translated by *K*u Fâ-hu (Dharmaraksha), of the Western Tsin dynasty, A.D. 265–316. 1 fasciculus. This is an earlier translation of the thirty-second Sûtra of No. 23. *K*'-yuen-lu, fasc. 1, fol. 34 b.

43 佛說須賴經

Fo-shwo-sü-lâi-*k*iṅ.

'Sûtra spoken by Buddha on the request of Surata.'

Surata-paripri*kkh*â.

Conc. 531. Translated by Po Yen, of the Wei dynasty, A.D. 220–265. 1 fasciculus.

44 The same as No. 43.

Translated by *K*' Sh'-lun, of the Former Liâṅ dynasty, A.D. 302–376. 1 fasciculus.

The above two works are earlier translations of the twenty-seventh Sûtra of No. 23. *K*'-tsiṅ, fasc. 3, fol. 15 a.

[1] 燉煌 'a town or region at the western extreme of the Great Wall in Kansuh in Ngan-si-cheu.' Wells Williams, Chin. Dict., p. 930.

45 得無垢女經

Tŏh-wu-keu-nü-*k*iṅ.

'Sûtra (spoken on the request) of the Princess Vimaladattâ.'

Vimaladattâ-pariprikkhâ.

Conc. 736. Translated by Gautama Pragñâruki, of the Eastern Wêi dynasty, A. D. 534-550. 1 fasciculus. This is a later translation of the thirty-third Sûtra of No. 23, and also that of No. 41. *K*'-yuen-lu, fasc. 1, fol. 34 b.

46 文殊師利所說不思議佛境界經

Wan-shu-sh'-li-su-shwo-pu-sz'-i-fo-*k*iṅ-*k*ie-*k*iṅ.

'Sûtra spoken by Mañgusrî on the inconceivable place of Buddha.'

A*k*intyabuddhavishaya-nirdesa.

Conc. 808. Translated by Bodhiruki, of the Thâṅ dynasty, A. D. 618-907. 2 fasciculi. This is another translation of the thirty-fifth Sûtra of No. 23. *K*'-yuen-lu, fasc. 1, fol. 34 b.

47 佛說如幻三昧經

Fo-shwo-*z*u-hwân-sân-mêi-*k*iṅ.

'Sûtra spoken by Buddha on the Samâdhi called Like illusion.'

Sushthitamati-pariprikkhâ. Conc. 246.

Mâyopama-samâdhi.

A. R., p. 444; A. M. G., p. 249. Translated by *K*u Fâ-hu (Dharmaraksha), of the Western Tsin dynasty, A. D. 265-316. 3 fasciculi.

48 善住意天子所問經

Shan-*k*u-i-thien-tsz'-su-wân-*k*iṅ.

'Sûtra (spoken) on the request of the Devaputra Sushthitamati.'

Sushthitamati-pariprikkhâ.

Translated by Phi-mu-*k*' (Vimokshapragña ?) together with Pragñâruki and others, of the Eastern Wêi dynasty, A. D. 534-550. 3 fasciculi.

The above two works are earlier translations of the thirty-sixth Sûtra of No. 23. *K*'-yuen-lu, fasc. 1, fol. 35 a.

49 太子刷護經

Thâi-tsz'-shwa-hu-*k*iṅ.

'Sûtra (spoken on the request) of the Crown-Prince Subâhu.'

Subâhu-pariprikkhâ.

Conc. 671. Translated by *K*u Fâ-hu (Dharmaraksha), of the Western Tsin dynasty, A. D. 265-316. 5 leaves.

50 太子和休經

Thâi-tsz'-hŏ-hhiu-*k*iṅ.

'Sûtra (spoken on the request) of the Crown-Prince Subâhu.'

Subâhu-pariprikkhâ.

Conc. 672. It is stated in Saṅ-yiu's Catalogue, compiled under the Liâṅ dynasty, A. D. 502-557, that this work has been put in the list of unknown translators' works in Ân-kuṅ or Tâo-ân's Catalogue, compiled under the Eastern Tsin dynasty, A. D. 317-420. Now this is added to the list of translations made under the Western Tsin dynasty, A. D. 265-316. 4 leaves.

The above two works are earlier translations of the thirty-seventh Sûtra of No. 23. *K*'-yuen-lu, fasc. 1, fol. 35 b.

51 入法界體性經

Zu-fâ-*k*ie-thi-siṅ-*k*iṅ.

'Sûtra on entering the substance and nature of the Dharmadhâtu,' or 'Dharmadhâtu-prakrity-avatâra-sûtra (?).'

Ratnakûta-sûtra.

K'-yuen-lu, fasc. 3, fol. 9 a. Translated by Gñânagupta, of the Sui dynasty, A. D. 589-618. 11 leaves. It agrees with Tibetan. *K*'-yuen-lu, s. v.

52 慧上菩薩問大善權經

Hwui-shâṅ-phu-sâ-wan-tâ-shân-*k*hüen-*k*iṅ.

'Sûtra on the great good means asked by the Bodhisattva Gñânottara.'

Gñânottara-bodhisattva-pariprikkhâ.

Conc. 207. Translated by *K*u Fâ-hu (Dharmaraksha), of the Western Tsin dynasty, A. D. 265-316. 2 fasciculi. This is an earlier translation of the thirty-eighth Sûtra of No. 23. *K*'-yuen-lu, fasc. 1, fol. 35 b.

53 大乘顯識經

Tâ-shaṅ-hhien-shi-*k*iṅ.

'Sûtra of the Mahâyâna on the explanation of the intellectual knowledge.'

Bhadrapâla-sreshthi-pariprikkhâ.

Conc. 570. Translated by Divâkara and others, of the Thâṅ dynasty, A. D. 618-907. 2 fasciculi. This is a later translation of the thirty-ninth Sûtra of No. 23. *K*'-yuen-lu, fasc. 1, fol. 35 b. There is a preface by the Empress Wu Tsö-thien, A. D. 668-705, of the Thâṅ dynasty.

54 佛說大乘方等要慧經

Fo-shwo-tâ-shaṅ-fâṅ-taṅ-yâo-hwui-*k*iṅ.

'Sûtra of the Mahâyâna-vaipulya spoken by Buddha on the important understanding.'

Maitreya-pariprikkhâ-dharmâshta.

Conc. 569. Translated by Ân Shi-kâo, of the Eastern Hân dynasty, A. D. 25-220. 1 leaf. This is an earlier translation of the forty-first Sûtra of No. 23. *K*'-yuen-lu, fasc. 1, fol. 36 a.

55 彌勒菩薩所問本願經

Mi-lö-phu-sâ-su-wan-pan-yuen-*kiṅ*.

'Sûtra on the former prayers asked by the Bodhisattva Maitreya.'

Maitreya-pari*prikkh*â.

Conc. 349. Translated by *K*u Fâ-hu (Dharmaraksha), of the Western Tsin dynasty, A.D. 265–316. 9 leaves. This is an earlier translation of the forty-second Sûtra of No. 23. *K*'-yuen-lu, fasc. 1, fol. 36 a.

56 度一切諸佛境界智嚴經

Tu-yi-tshiê-*k*u-fo-*kiṅ*-*kie*-*k*'-yen-*kiṅ*.

'Sûtra on arranging the wisdom and adornment of the place of all Buddhas.'

Sarvabuddhavishayâvatâra.

Wassiljew, 161. Translated by Saṅghapâla, of the Liâṅ dynasty, A.D. 502–557. 1 fasciculus. Deest in Tibetan. *K*'-yuen-lu, fasc. 3, fol. 2 a.

57 佛遺日摩尼寶經

Fo-i-*z*ih-mo-ni-pâo-*kiṅ*.

'Sûtra of the sun and mani-jewel left by Buddha (?).'

Kâsyapa-parivarta.

Conc. 162. Translated by *K*' Leu-*kiâ*-*kh*ân (Lokaraksha ?), of the Eastern Hân dynasty, A.D. 25–220. 1 fasciculus.

58 佛說摩訶衍寶嚴經

Fo-shwo-mo-ho-yen-pâo-yen-*kiṅ*.

'Sûtra of the Mahâyâna spoken by Buddha on the adornment of jewels.'

Kâsyapa-parivarta.

Translated under the Western or Eastern Tsin dynasty, A.D. 265–420, but the translator's name is lost. 1 fasciculus.

The above two works are different translations of the forty-third Sûtra of No. 23. They are wanting in Tibetan. *K*'-yuen-lu, fasc. 1, fol. 36 b. But see No. 23 (43).

59 勝鬘師子吼一乘大方便方廣經

Shaṅ-mân-sh'-tsz'-heu-yi-shaṅ-tâ-fâṅ-pien-fâṅ-kwâṅ-*kiṅ*.

'Vaipulya-sûtra on the great good means, being the *S*rîmâlâ-simhanâda.'

*S*rîmâlâ-devî-si*m*hanâda.

Conc. 105, 106. Translated by Gu*n*abhadra, of the earlier Suṅ dynasty, A.D. 420–479. 1 fasciculus. This is an earlier translation of the forty-eighth Sûtra of No. 23. *K*'-yuen-lu, fasc. 1, fol. 36 b.

60 毗耶娑問經

Phi-yê-so-wan-*kiṅ*.

'Sûtra (spoken) on the request of Vyâsa.'

Vyâsa-pari*prikkh*â.

Conc. 448, 449. Translated by Gautama Pra*gñ*â-ru*k*i, of the Eastern Wêi dynasty, A.D. 534–550. 2 fasciculi. This is an earlier translation of the forty-ninth Sûtra of No. 23. Deest in Tibetan. *K*'-yuen-lu, fasc. 1, fol. 36 b. But see No. 23 (49). It is stated in a note at the beginning, that this translation was made in A.D. 542, and that it consists of 14,457 Chinese characters.

CLASS III.

大集部 Tâ-tsi-pu, or Mahâsannipâta Class.

61 大方等大集經

Tâ-fâṅ-taṅ-tâ-tsi-*kiṅ*.

Mahâvaipulya-mahâsannipâta-sûtra.

Cf. No. 72. See also Wassiljew, 162. Translated by Dharmaraksha, of the Northern Liâṅ dynasty, A.D. 397–439. 4 parts; 30 fasciculi. It agrees with Tibetan, but part 1, chapters 6, 7 are wanting in the latter. *K*'-yuen-lu, fasc. 2, fol. 2 a.

62 大乘大方等日藏經

Tâ-shaṅ-tâ-fâṅ-taṅ-*z*ih-tsâṅ-*kiṅ*.

'Mahâyâna-mahâvaipulya-sûryagarbha-sûtra.'

Sûryagarbha-sûtra.

K'-yuen-lu, fasc. 2, fol. 2 b; Conc. 609; Wassiljew, 168; A.R., p. 465; A.M.G., p. 269. Translated by Narendrayasas, of the Sui dynasty, A.D. 589–618. 10 fasciculi. This is a later and fuller translation of the fourth part of No. 61. *K*'-yuen-lu, s.v.

63 大方等大集月藏經
Tâ-fâṅ-taṅ-tâ-tsi-yueh-tsâṅ-*k*iṅ.
'Mahâvaipulya-mahâsannipâta-*k*andragarbha-sûtra.'
*K*andragarbha-vaipulya.

Conc. 659; Wassiljew, 169. Translated by Narendrayasas (the same person as before), under the Northern Tsi dynasty, A.D. 550–577. 10 fasciculi. It agrees with Tibetan. *K*'-yuen-lu, fasc. 2, fol. 2 b.

64 大乘大集地藏十輪經
Tâ-shaṅ-tâ-tsi-ti-tsâṅ-shi-lun-*k*iṅ.
'Mahâyâna-mahâsannipâta-kshitigarbha-dasa*k*akra-sûtra.'
Dasa*k*akra-kshitigarbha.

K'-yuen-lu, fasc. 2, fol. 3 a; Conc. 593; Wassiljew, 170; A. R., p. 462; A. M. G., p. 266. Translated by Hhüen-*k*wâṅ, A.D. 651, of the Thâṅ dynasty, A.D. 618–907. 10 fasciculi; 8 chapters.

65 佛說大方廣十輪經
Fo-shwo-tâ-fâṅ-kwâṅ-shi-lun-*k*iṅ.
'Mahâvaipulya-sûtra spoken by Buddha on the ten wheels (of the Bodhisattva Kshitigarbha).'
Dasa*k*akra-kshitigarbha.

Conc. 598. Translated under the Northern Liâṅ dynasty, A.D. 397–439, but the translator's name is lost. 8 fasciculi; 15 chapters. This is an earlier and shorter translation of No. 64, which latter agrees with Tibetan. *K*'-yuen-lu, fasc. 2, fol. 3 a.

66 大集須彌藏經
Tâ-tsi-sü-mi-tsâṅ-*k*iṅ.
'Mahâsannipâta-sumerugarbha-sûtra.'
Sumerugarbha.

Conc. 587. See also Wassiljew, 171. Translated by Narendrayasas together with Fâ-*k*' (Dharmapragña), of the Northern Tsi dynasty, A.D. 550–577. 2 fasciculi; 4 chapters.

67 虛空孕菩薩經
Hhü-khuṅ-yün-phu-sâ-*k*iṅ.
'Âkâsagarbha-bodhisattva-sûtra.'
Âkâsagarbha-sûtra.

K'-yuen-lu, fasc. 2, fol. 3 b; Conc. 196; Wassiljew, 171; A. R., p. 466; A. M. G., p. 270. Translated by Gñânagupta, of the Sui dynasty, A.D. 589–618. 2 fasciculi.

68 虛空藏菩薩經
Hhü-khuṅ-tsâṅ-phu-sâ-*k*iṅ.
Âkâsagarbha-bodhisattva-sûtra.

K'-yuen-lu, fasc. 2, fol. 3 b; Conc. 194. Translated by Buddhayasas, of the Latter Tshin dynasty, A.D. 384–417. 1 fasciculus.

69 虛空藏菩薩神咒經
Hhü-khuṅ-tsâṅ-phu-sâ-shan-*kh*eu-*k*iṅ.
Âkâsagarbha-bodhisattva-dhâranî-sûtra.

Conc. 195. Translated by Dharmamitra, of the earlier Suṅ dynasty, A.D. 420–479. 1 fasciculus.

The above three works are translations of the same or similar text, and agree with Tibetan. *K*'-yuen-lu, fasc. 2, fol. 4 a.

70 觀虛空藏菩薩經
Kwâṅ-hhü-khuṅ-tsâṅ-phu-sâ-*k*iṅ.
'Âkâsagarbha-bodhisattva-dhyâna-sûtra (?).'

Translated by Dharmamitra, of the earlier Suṅ dynasty, A.D. 420–479. 3 leaves.

71 佛說菩薩念佛三昧經
Fo-shwo-phu-sâ-nien-fo-sân-mêi-*k*iṅ.
'Sûtra spoken by Buddha on the Samâdhi called Bodhisattva-buddhânusmriti.'
Bodhisattva-buddhânusm*ri*ti-samâdhi.

Wassiljew, 172; Conc. 481. Translated by Kuṅ-töh-*k*ih together with Hhüen-*kh*âṅ, of the earlier Suṅ dynasty, A.D. 420–479. 6 fasciculi; 16 chapters.

72 佛說大方等大集菩薩念佛三昧經
Fo-shwo-tâ-fâṅ-taṅ-tâ-tsi-phu-sâ-nien-fo-sân-mêi-*k*iṅ.
'Mahâvaipulya-mahâsannipâta-sûtra spoken by Buddha on the Samâdhi called Bodhisattva-buddhânusm*ri*ti.'
Mahâvaipulya-mahâsannipâta-bodhisattva-buddhânusm*ri*ti-samâdhi.

K'-yuen-lu, fasc. 2, fol. 4 b; Conc. 610. Translated by Dharmagupta, of the Sui dynasty, A.D. 589–618. 10 fasciculi; 15 chapters. This is a later and incomplete translation of No. 71, which latter agrees with Tibetan. *K*'-yuen-lu, s. v.

73 般舟三昧經
Pân-*k*eu-sân-mêi-*k*iṅ.
'Sûtra on the Samâdhi called Pratyutpanna (etc.).'
Pratyutpanna-buddhasammukhâvasthita-samâdhi.

A. R., p. 444; A. M. G., p. 250. See also Conc. 404; Wassiljew, 172. Translated by *K'* Leu-*kiâ*-*khân* (Lokaraksha?), of the Eastern Hân dynasty, A. D. 25–220. 3 fasciculi; 16 chapters.

74 阿差末菩薩經
Ö-*khâ*-mo-phu-sâ-*kiṅ*.
'Sûtra (spoken) by the Bodhisattva Aksharamati.'
Aksharamati-nirdesa-sûtra.

K'-yuen-lu, fasc. 2, fol. 5 a; Conc. 35. See also A. R., p. 451; A. M. G., p. 256. Translated by *Ku* Fâ-hu (Dharmaraksha), of the Western Tsin dynasty, A. D. 265–316. 7 fasciculi.

75 大方等大集賢護經
Tâ-fâṅ-taṅ-tâ-tsi-hhien-hu-*kiṅ*.
Mahâvaipulya-mahâsannipâta-bhadrapâla-sûtra.

Conc. 608. Translated by *Gñâ*nagupta, Dharmagupta, and others, of the Sui dynasty, A. D. 589–618. 5 fasciculi; 17 chapters.

76 拔陂菩薩經
Pâ-pho-phu-sâ-*kiṅ*.
'Sûtra (spoken on the request) of the Bodhisattva Bhadrapâla.'
Bhadrapâla-sûtra.

Conc. 394. Translated by *K'* Leu-*kiâ*-*khân* (Lokaraksha), of the Eastern Hân dynasty, A. D. 25–220. 1 fasciculus.
The above two works are similar translations of No. 73, and they agree with Tibetan; but No. 76 contains the first four chapters only. *K'*-yuen-lu, fasc. 2, fol. 5 a.

77 無盡意菩薩經
Wu-tsin-i-phu-sâ-*kiṅ*.
'Sûtra (spoken) by the Bodhisattva Aksharamati.'
Aksharamati-nirdesa-sûtra.

Conc. 851. See also Wassiljew, 171. Translated by *K'*-yen and Pâo-un, of the earlier Suṅ dynasty, A. D. 420–479. 4 fasciculi. This is a later translation of No. 74. *K'*-yuen-lu, fasc. 2, fol. 5 b.

78 大集譬喩王經
Tâ-tsi-phi-yü-wâṅ-*kiṅ*.
'Mahâsannipâtâvadânarâga-sûtra (?).'

Translated by *Gñâ*nagupta, of the Sui dynasty, A. D. 589–618. 2 fasciculi. It agrees with Tibetan. *K'*-yuen-lu, fasc. 2, fol. 5 b.

79 大哀經
Tâ-âi-*kiṅ*.
'Sûtra on the great compassion.'
Tathâgata-mahâkâruṇika-nirdesa.

A. R., p. 447; A. M. G., p. 252. Translated by *Ku* Fâ-hu (Dharmaraksha), of the Western Tsin dynasty, A. D. 265–316. 8 fasciculi; 28 chapters. This is an earlier translation of part 1, chapters 1, 2 of No. 61. *K'*-yuen-lu, fasc. 2, fol. 5 b.

80 寶女所問經
Pâo-nü-su-wan-*kiṅ*.
'Sûtra (spoken) on the request of a precious woman,' or 'Ratnastri-pariprikkhâ (?).'

Translated by *Ku* Fâ-hu (Dharmaraksha), of the Western Tsin dynasty, A. D. 265–316. 4 fasciculi; 13 chapters. This is an earlier translation of part 1, chapter 3 of No. 61. *K'*-yuen-lu, fasc. 2, fol. 6 a.

81 無言童子經
Wu-yen-thuṅ-tsz'-*kiṅ*.
'Sûtra on the dumb boy,' or 'Mûka-kumâra-sûtra (?).'

Translated by *Ku* Fâ-hu (Dharmaraksha), of the Western Tsin dynasty, A. D. 265–316. 2 fasciculi. This is an earlier translation of part 1, chapter 7 of No. 61. *K'*-yuen-lu, fasc. 2, fol. 6 a.

82 自在王菩薩經
Tsz'-tsâi-wâṅ-phu-sâ-*kiṅ*.
'Îsvararâga-bodhisattva-sûtra (?).'

Translated by Kumâragîva, of the Latter Tshin dynasty, A. D. 384–417. 2 fasciculi.

83 奮迅王問經
Fân-hhün-wâṅ-wan-*kiṅ*.
'Sûtra (spoken) on the request of the powerful king.' or 'Îsvararâga-pariprikkhâ (?).'

Translated by Gautama Pragñâru*ki*, A. D. 542, of the Eastern Wêi dynasty, A. D. 534–550. 2 fasciculi. It consists of 18,341 Chinese characters. This is a later translation of No. 82, and both are similar to part 1, chapter 2 of No. 61. *K'*-yuen-lu, fasc. 2, fol. 6 b.

84 寶星陀羅尼經
Pâo-siṅ-tho-lo-ni-*kiṅ*.
'Ratnatârâ-dhârani-sûtra (?).'

Translated by Prabhâmitra, A. D. 628–630, of the Thâṅ dynasty, A. D. 618–907. 8 fasciculi. It consists of 63,882 Chinese characters. This is a later translation of part 2 of No. 61. *K'*-tsiṅ, fasc. 4, fol. 19 a. Cf. *K'*-yuen-lu, fasc. 2, fol. 6 b.

85 度諸佛境界智光嚴經

Tu-*k*u-fo-*k*iṅ-*k*iê-*k'*-kwâṅ-yen-*k*iṅ.

'Sûtra on crossing the wisdom, light, and adornment of the place of all Buddhas.'

Sarvatathâgatavishayâvatâra.

Wassiljew, 161. Translated under the three Tshin dynasties, A.D. 350–431, but the translator's name is lost. 1 fasciculus. Deest in Tibetan. *K'*-yuen-lu, fasc. 2, fol. 9 b.

86 大乘金剛髻珠菩薩修行分經

Tâ-shaṅ-*k*in-kâṅ-*k*i-*k*u-phu-sâ-siu-hhiṅ-fan-*k*iṅ.

'Mahâyâna-vagra*k*û*d*âmani-bodhisattva-*k*aryâ-varga-sûtra (?).'

Translated by Bodhiru*k*i, of the Thâṅ dynasty, A.D. 618–907. 1 fasciculus. Deest in Tibetan. *K'*-yuen-lu, fasc. 2, fol. 10 a.

CLASS IV

華嚴部 Hwâ-yen-pu, or Avata*m*saka Class[1].

87 大方廣佛華嚴經

Tâ-fâṅ-kwâṅ-fo-hwâ-yen-*k*iṅ.

'Mahâvaipulya-buddhâvatamsaka-sûtra.'

Buddhâvata*m*saka-mahâvaipulya-sûtra.

K'-yuen-lu, fasc. 2, fol. 8 a; Conc. 599; Wassiljew, 157; A. R., p. 401; A. M. G., p. 208. Translated by Buddhabhadra and others, of the Eastern Tsin dynasty, A.D. 317–420. 60 fasciculi; 34 chapters. Spoken by Buddha at eight assemblies, held in seven different places. Hence the term 七處八會 Tshi-*kh*u-pâ-hwui, or 'the seven places and eight assemblies.'

88 The same as No. 87.

Translated by *S*ikshânanda, A.D. 695–699, of the Thâṅ dynasty, A.D. 618–907. 80 fasciculi; 39 chapters. This is a later and fuller translation of No. 87, and agrees with Tibetan (45 chapters), which latter was translated from Chinese. The sixth assembly of No. 87 is divided into two in No. 88. *K'*-yuen-lu, s.v. There are two Imperial prefaces, namely: 1. That by *Kh*aṅ-tsu, the third sovereign of the Miṅ dynasty, dated A.D. 1412. 2. That by the Empress Wu Tsö-thien, A.D. 684–705, of the Thâṅ dynasty, who sent a special envoy to Khoten for the Sanskrit text of this Sûtra, and took part in the translation.

89 大方廣佛華嚴經普賢菩薩行願品

Tâ-fâṅ-kwâṅ-fo-hwâ-yen-*k*iṅ-phu-hhien-phu-sâ-hhiṅ-yuen-*k*iṅ.

'Chapter on the practice and prayer of the Bodhisattva Samantabhadra, in the Mahâvaipulya-buddhâvatamsaka-sûtra.'

Translated by Pra*g*ña, A.D. 796–798, of the Thâṅ dynasty, A.D. 618–907. 40 fasciculi. This is a later and fuller translation of a text similar to that of the last chapter of Nos. 87, 88. *K'*-tiṅ, fasc. 1, fol. 8 b. At the end there is a letter addressed to the Chinese Emperor from the King of Wu-*kh*a, i.e. Odra or Uda, in South India, who presented to the former his own copy of the Sanskrit text of this chapter, in A.D. 795. It contains 62 verses of the Samantabhadra-pra*n*idhâna, called Bhadra*k*ari, and agrees with the Sanskrit text mentioned in Catalogue of the Hodgson Manuscripts, I. 33, and Catal. Bodl. Japan., No. 56.

The above three works are generally distinguished by the number of fasciculi, as 'sixty, eighty, and forty Hwâ-yen-*k*iṅ.'

90 信力入印法門經

Sin-li-*z*u-yin-fâ-man-*k*iṅ.

'Sûtra on the gate of the law of the seal for entering the power of faith.'

*S*raddhâbaladhânâvatâramudrâ-sûtra.

[1] In the new Japanese edition of the Chinese Tripitaka, now in the course of publication in Tokio, this class forms its first part, having the following works in a different order, as they appear in the Yueh-tsâṅ-*k'*-tsiṅ, or Guide for the Examination of the Canon. See the Advertisement of the Kô-kiô-sho-in, published as a supplement to the Mei-kiô-shin-shi, a Japanese newspaper, Aug. 26, 1880.

K'-yuen-lu, fasc. 2, fol. 9 a; Conc. 527, A. R., p. 455; A. M. G., p. 260. Translated by Bodhiruki, of the Northern Wêi dynasty, A. D. 386–534. 5 fasciculi.

91 佛華嚴入如來德智不思議境界經

Fo-hwâ-yen-zu-zu-lâi-töh-k'-pu-sz'-i-kiṅ-kiê-kiṅ.

'Buddhâvataṃsaka-tathâgata .... âvatâra-sûtra.'

Tathâgataguṇagñânâkintyavishayâvatâra-nirdeśa.

Wassiljew, 161. Translated by Gñânagupta, of the Sui dynasty, A. D. 589–618. 1 fasciculus. This is a later translation of No. 85; which latter ought also to be arranged in this class, as it is so in K'-yuen-lu, fasc. 2, fol. 9 b.

92 佛說如來興顯經

Fo-shwo-zu-lâi-hhiṅ-hhien-kiṅ.

'Sûtra spoken by Buddha on the appearance of the Tathâgata.'

Translated by Ku Fâ-hu (Dharmaraksha), of the Western Tsin dynasty, A. D. 265–316. 4 fasciculi. This is an earlier translation of chapters 32 and 24 of No. 87, and chapters 37 and 29 of No. 88. K'-yuen-lu, fasc. 2, fol. 12 b.

93 大方廣入如來智德不思議經

Tâ-fâṅ-kwâṅ-zu-zu-lâi-k'-töh-pu-sz'-i-kiṅ.

'Mahâvaipulya-tathâgataguṇagñânâkintya(visaya)-avatâra-sûtra.'

Tathâgataguṇagñânâkintyavishayâvatâra-nirdeśa.

Translated by Sikshânanda, of the Thâṅ dynasty, A. D. 618–907. 1 fasciculus. This is a later translation of No. 91. K'-yuen-lu, fasc. 2, fol. 10 a.

94 大方廣佛華嚴經修慈分

Tâ-fâṅ-kwâṅ-fo-hwâ-yen-kiṅ-siu-tshz'-fan.

'Part on the practice of compassion, in the Mahâvaipulya-buddhâvataṃsaka-sûtra.'

Translated by Devapragña, of the Thâṅ dynasty, A. D. 618–907. 8 leaves. Deest in Tibetan. K'-yuen-lu, fasc. 2, fol. 10 b.

95 顯無邊佛土功德經

Hhien-wu-pien-fo-thu-kuṅ-töh-kiṅ.

'Anantabuddhakshetraguṇa-nirdeśa-sûtra (?).'

Translated by Hhüen-kwâṅ (Hiouen-thsang), of the Thâṅ dynasty, A. D. 618–907. 2 leaves. This is a similar translation of chapter 26 of No. 87, and chapter 31 of No. 88. K'-yuen-lu, fasc. 2, fol. 12 b.

96 大方廣佛華嚴經不思議境界分

Tâ-fâṅ-kwâṅ-fo-hwâ-yen-kiṅ-pu-sz'-i-kiṅ-kiê-fan.

'Part on the Akintyavishaya, in the Mahâvaipulya-buddhâvataṃsaka-sûtra.'

Translated by Devapragña, of the Thâṅ dynasty, A. D. 618–907. 1 fasciculus.

97 大方廣如來不思議境界經

Tâ-fâṅ-kwâṅ-zu-lâi-pu-sz'-i-kiṅ-kiê-kiṅ.

'Mahâvaipulya-tathâgatâkintyavishaya-sûtra.'

Translated by Sikshânanda, of the Thâṅ dynasty, A. D. 618–907. 1 fasciculus. This is a later translation of No. 96. Deest in Tibetan. K'-yuen-lu, fasc. 2, fol. 10 a.

98 大方廣普賢所說經

Tâ-fâṅ-kwâṅ-phu-hhien-su-shwo-kiṅ.

'Mahâvaipulya-sûtra spoken by Samantabhadra.'

Translated by Sikshânanda, of the Thâṅ dynasty, A. D. 618–907. 5 leaves. Deest in Tibetan. K'-yuen-lu, fasc. 2, fol. 10 b.

99 莊嚴菩提心經

Kwâṅ-yen-phu-thi-siṅ-kiṅ.

'Bodhihridaya-vyûha-sûtra.'

Translated by Kumâragîva, of the Latter Tshin dynasty, A. D. 384–417. 8 leaves. Deest in Tibetan. K'-yuen-lu, fasc. 2, fol. 10 b.

100 佛說菩薩本業經

Fo-shwo-phu-sâ-pan-yeh-kiṅ.

'Sûtra spoken by Buddha on the original action of the Bodhisattva.'

Translated by K' Khien, of the Wu dynasty, A. D. 222–280. 1 fasciculus. This is an earlier translation of chap. 7 on the 'pure practice' of No. 87, and chap. 11 of No. 88. K'-yuen-lu, fasc. 2, fol. 11 b.

101 大方廣佛華嚴經續入法界品

Tâ-fâṅ-kwâṅ-fo-hwâ-yen-kiṅ-suh-zu-fâ-kiê-phiṅ.

'A continuation of the chapter on entering the Dharmadhâtu, in the Mahâvaipulya-buddhâvataṃsaka-sûtra.'

Translated by Divâkara, of the Thâṅ dynasty, A.D. 618-907. 10 leaves.

102 佛說兜沙經

Fo-shwo-teu-sha-kiṅ.

'Sûtra spoken by Buddha on the Tathâgata-viseshana (? the names or epithets of the Tathâgata).'

Translated by K' Leu-kiâ-khân (Lokaraksha ?), of the Eastern Hân dynasty, A.D. 25-220. 6 leaves. This is an earlier and shorter translation of chap. 3 on the 'epithets of the Tathâgata' of No. 87, and of chap. 7 of No. 88. K'-yuen-lu, fasc. 2, fol. 11 a.

103 大方廣菩薩十地經

Tâ-fâṅ-kwâṅ-phu-sâ-shi-ti-kiṅ.

'Mahâvaipulya-bodhisattva-dasabhûmi-sûtra.'

Translated by Ki-kiâ-yê and Thân-yâo, of the Northern Wêi dynasty, A.D. 386-534. 8 leaves. This is a later translation of No. 99. K'-yuen-lu, fasc. 2, fol. 11 a.

104 度世品經

Tu-shi-phin-kiṅ.

'Sûtra of the chapter on going across the world.'

Translated by Ku Fâ-hu (Dharmaraksha), of the Western Tsin dynasty, A.D. 265-316. 6 fasciculi. This is an earlier translation of chap. 33 on the 'separation from the world' of No. 87, and chap. 38 of No. 88. K'-yuen-lu, fasc. 2, fol. 13 a.

105 十住經

Shi-ku-kiṅ.

'Dasabhûmi-sûtra.'

Dasabhûmika-sûtra.

Cf. K'-yuen-lu, fasc. 2, fol. 14 a; Conc. 90. Cf. also Dasabhûmîsvara, in Catalogue of the Hodgson Manuscripts, I. 3; III. 1; V. 55; VI. 5; VII. 14. Translated by Kumâragîva together with Buddhayasas, of the Latter Tshin dynasty, A.D. 384-417. 6 fasciculi. This is a similar translation of chap. 22 on the 'Dasabhûmi' of No. 87, and chap. 26 of No. 88. K'-yuen-lu, fasc. 2, fol. 12 a.

106 佛說羅摩伽經

Fo-shwo-lo-mo-kiê-kiṅ.

'Sûtra spoken by Buddha on Râmaka (? the name of a man).'

Translated by Shaṅ-kien, of the Western Tshin dynasty, A.D. 385-431. 4 fasciculi. This is an incomplete translation of chap. 34 of No. 87, and chap. 39 of No. 88. K'-yuen-lu, fasc. 2, fol. 13 a.

107 諸菩薩求佛本業經

Ku-phu-sâ-khiu-fo-pan-yeh-kiṅ.

'Sûtra on the original actions of the Bodhisattvas who are seeking the state of Buddha.'

Translated by Nieh Tâo-kan, of the Western Tsin dynasty, A.D. 265-316. 12 leaves. This is a later translation of No. 100.

108 菩薩十住行道品經

Phu-sa-shi-ku-hhiṅ-tâo-phin-kiṅ.

'Sûtra of the chapter on the way of practice in the ten dwellings or stations (not the Dasabhûmi, but still inferior) of the Bodhisattva.'

Translated by Ku Fâ-hu (Dharmaraksha), of the Western Tsin dynasty, A.D. 265-316. 9 leaves.

109 佛說菩薩十住經

Fo-shwo-phu-sâ-shi-ku-kiṅ.

'Sûtra spoken by Buddha on the ten stations of the Bodhisattva.'

Translated by Gîtamitra, of the Eastern Tsin dynasty, A.D. 317-420. 5 leaves.

The above two works are similar translations of chap. 11 on the 'ten stations' (lower than the Dasabhûmi) of No. 87, and chap. 15 of No. 88. K'-yuen-lu, fasc. 2, fol. 11 b.

110 漸備一切智德經

Tsien-pi-yi-tshiê-k'-töh-kiṅ.

'Sûtra on making gradually complete all the wisdom and virtue.'

Dasabhûmika-sûtra.

Cf. No. 105. Translated by Ku Fâ-hu (Dharmaraksha), of the Western Tsin dynasty, A.D. 265-316. 5 fasciculi. This is an earlier translation of No. 105. K'-yuen-lu, fasc. 2, fol. 11 b.

111 等目菩薩所問三昧經

Tań-mu-phu-sâ-su-wan-sân-mêi-*k*iń.

'Sûtra on a Samâdhi asked by the Bodhisattva Samakakshas (? "equal-eye").'

Translated by *K*u Fâ-hu (Dharmaraksha), of the Western Tsin dynasty, A.D. 265-316. 3 fasciculi. This is an earlier translation of chapter 24 on the 'Dasa-samâdhi' of No. 87, and chapter 27 of No. 88. *K*'-yuen-lu, fasc. 2, fol. 12 a.

112 文殊師利問菩薩署經

Wan-shu-sh'-li-wan-phu-sâ-shu-*k*iń.

'Sûtra on the office of the Bodhisattva asked by Mañjusrî.'

Translated by *K*' Leu-*k*iâ-*kh*ân (Lokaraksha ?), of the Eastern Hân dynasty, A.D. 25-220. 1 fasciculus.

CLASS V.

涅槃部 Niê-phân-pu, or Nirvâ*n*a Class.

113 大般涅槃經

Tâ-pân-niê-phân-*k*iń.

Mahâparinirvâ*n*a-sûtra.

Conc. 640. Cf. A.R., pp. 441, 487; A.M.G., pp. 247, 290. Translated by Dharmaraksha, A.D. 423, of the Northern Liań dynasty, A.D. 397-439. 40 fasciculi; 13 chapters. It agrees with Tibetan. *K*'-yuen-lu, fasc. 2, fol. 14 b. A partial English translation of fasc. 12 and 39, by Beal, in his Catena of Buddhist Scriptures from the Chinese, pp. 160-188.

114 南本大般涅槃經

Nân-pan-tâ-pân-niê-phân-*k*iń.

'Southern book of the Mahâparinirvâ*n*a-sûtra.'

This is a revision of No. 113, made in *K*ien-yeh, the modern Nankiń, or the 'Southern Capital,' by two Chinese *S*râma*n*as, Hwui-yen and Hwui-kwân, and a literary man, Sie Liń-yun, A.D. 424-453, of the earlier Suń dynasty, A.D. 420-479. 36 fasciculi; 25 chapters. This revision depends on No. 120. *K*'-yuen-lu, fasc. 2, fol. 14 b. No. 113 is sometimes called the 北本 Pe-pan, or the Northern Book, when it is compared with its revision, the Southern Book, No. 114.

115 大般涅槃經後分

Tâ-pân-niê-phân-*k*iń-heu-fan.

'Latter part of the Mahâparinirvâ*n*a-sûtra.'

Translated by *G*ñânabhadra together with Hwui-niń and others, of the Thân dynasty, A.D. 618-907. 2 fasciculi; 4 chapters and a half, i.e. a continuation of the last chapter of Nos. 113, 114. It agrees with Tibetan (?). *K*'-yuen-lu, fasc. 2, fol. 15 a, where however the most important character is written wrongly, so it means literally 'Deest (for Agrees ?) with Tibetan,' 與蕃本闕 (for 同 ?).

116 佛說方等般泥洹經

Fo-shwo-fâń-tań-pân-ni-yuen-*k*iń.

'Vaipulya-parinirvâ*n*a-sûtra spoken by Buddha.'

*K*aturdâraka-samâdhi-sûtra.

Conc. 150. Translated by *K*u Fâ-hu (Dharmaraksha), of the Western Tsin dynasty, A.D. 265-316. 2 fasciculi; 9 chapters. It agrees with Tibetan. *K*'-yuen-lu, fasc. 2, fol. 15 b.

117 大悲經

Tâ-pêi-*k*iń.

'Mahâkâru*n*ika-sûtra.'

Mahâkaru*n*âpu*n*darîka-sûtra.

K'-yuen-lu, fasc. 2, fol. 16 a; Conc. 644; A.R., p. 433; A.M.G., p. 239. Translated by Narendrayasas together with Fâ-*k*' (Dharmapra*g*ña), of the Northern Tshi dynasty, A.D. 550-577. 5 fasciculi; 13 chapters. It agrees with Tibetan. *K*'-yuen-lu, s.v.

118 大般涅槃經

Tâ-pân-niê-phân-*k*iń.

Mahâparinirvâ*n*a-sûtra.

K'-yuen-lu, fasc. 6, fol. 20 a; Conc. 639. Translated by Fâ-hhien (Fa-hian), of the Eastern Tsiń dynasty, A.D. 317-420. 3 fasciculi.

119 佛說方等泥洹經

Fo-shwo-fâń-tań-ni-yuen-*k*iń.

'Vaipulya-nirvâ*n*a-sûtra spoken by Buddha.'

Mahâparinirvâ*n*a-sûtra.

Translated under the Eastern Tsiń dynasty, A.D. 317-420; but the translator's name is lost. 2 fasciculi.

The above two works are different translations of the second Sûtra on the 'walking for pleasure,' or the

Vihâra (?), in the Dîrghâgama, No. 545, and also No. 552; and they agree with Tibetan. *K'*-yuen-lu, fasc. 6, fol. 20 a, where Nos. 118, 119 are accordingly arranged properly under the heading of the Sûtras of the Hînayâna, as the one before, and the other after No. 552. No. 118 omits the first part of No. 119, though the former is much longer than the latter. Nos. 118, 119, 545 (2), and 552 are also to be compared with the Pâli text of the Mahâparinibbâna-suttanta; for which latter, see the Sacred Books of the East, vol. xi.

120 大般泥洹經
Tâ-pân-ni-yuen-*k*in.
Mahâparinirvâ*n*a-sûtra.

K'-yuen-lu, fasc. 2, fol. 15 a. Translated by Fâ-hhien (Fa-hian) together with Buddhabhadra, of the Eastern Tsin dynasty, A.D. 317–420. 6 fasciculi; 18 chapters. This is a similar and incomplete translation of Nos. 113, 114. *K'*-yuen-lu, s. v.

121 四童子三昧經
Sz'-thuṅ-tsz'-sân-mêi-*k*iṅ.
*K*aturdâraka-samâdhi-sûtra.

K'-yuen-lu, fasc. 2, fol. 15 b; Conc. 555. Cf. A. R., p. 444; A. M. G., p. 250. Translated by *G*ñânagupta, of the Sui dynasty, A.D. 589–618. 3 fasciculi; 6 chapters. This is a later and incomplete translation of No. 116. *K'*-yuen-lu, s. v.

122 佛垂般涅槃略說教誡經
Fo-*k*hui-pân-niê-phân-liâo-shwo-*k*iâo-*k*iê-*k*iṅ.
'Sûtra of teaching spoken briefly by Buddha just before his entering Parinirvâ*n*a.'

Translated by Kumâra*g*îva, of the Latter Tshin dynasty, A.D. 384–417. 7 leaves.

123 佛臨涅槃記法住經
Fo-lin-niê-phân-*k*i-fâ-*k*u-*k*iṅ.
'Sûtra on the duration of the law foretold by Buddha just before his entering Nirvâ*n*a.'
Mahâparinirvâ*n*a.

A. R., p. 442; A. M. G., p. 247. Translated by Hhüen-*k*wâṅ (Hiouen-thsang), of the Thâṅ dynasty, A.D. 618–907. 5 leaves. It agrees with Tibetan. *K'*-yuen-lu, fasc. 4, fol. 3 a.

124 佛滅度後棺斂葬送經
Fo-mieh-tu-heu-kwân-lien-tsâṅ-suṅ-*k*iṅ.
'Sûtra on (the rules for) putting the body into the coffin and sending it in the funeral after Buddha's entering Nirvâ*n*a.'

Translated under the Western Tsin dynasty, A.D. 265–316; but the translator's name is lost. 3 leaves. Deest in Tibetan. *K'*-yuen-lu, fasc. 7, fol. 23 b, where this work is mentioned under the heading of the Sûtras of the Hînayâna.

125 般泥洹後灌臘經
Pân-ni-yuen-heu-kwân-lâ-*k*iṅ.
'Sûtra on the rules for two annual festivals to be held after Buddha's entering Parinirvâ*n*a.'

Translated by *K*u Fâ-hu (Dharmaraksha), of the Western Tsin dynasty, A.D. 265–316. 2 leaves. The two annual festivals are: 1. In 4th month, 8th day, i.e. anniversary of Buddha's birth; 2. In 7th month, 15th day, i.e. one day before the end of summer.

CLASS VI.

五大部外重譯經 Wu-tâ-pu-wâi-*k*uṅ-yi-*k*iṅ, or Sûtras of duplicate translations, excluded from the preceding five Classes.

126 金光明最勝王經
*K*in-kwâṅ-miṅ-tsui-shaṅ-wâṅ-*k*iṅ.
Suvar*n*aprabhâsottamarâ*g*a-sûtra.

K'-yuen-lu, fasc. 2, fol. 19 a; Conc. 291; A. R., p. 514; A. M. G., p. 315; Wassiljew, 315. Translated by I-tsiṅ, of the Thâṅ dynasty, A.D. 618–907. 10 fasciculi; 31 chapters. It agrees with Tibetan. *K'*-yuen-lu, s. v. For the Sanskrit text, see Catalogue of the Hodgson Manuscripts, I. 8; III. 10, 59; VI. 8; VII. 73.

127 金光明經
*K*in-kwâṅ-miṅ-*k*iṅ.
Suvar*n*aprabhâsa-sûtra.

Translated by Dharmaraksha, of the Northern Liâṅ dynasty, A.D. 397–439. 4 fasciculi; 18 chapters. This is an earlier and incomplete translation of No. 126. Cf. *K'*-yuen-lu, fasc. 2, fol. 19 b. In China this is the most popular translation, having two famous commentaries, viz. Nos. 1548, 1552. *K'*-tsin, fasc. 6, fol. 16 b.

140 分別緣起初勝法門經

Fan-pieh-yuen-khi-khu-shaṅ-fâ-man-kiṅ.

'Sûtra of explaining the first and excellent gate of the law of Nidâna.'

Translated by Hhüen-kwâṅ (Hiouen-thsang), of the Thâṅ dynasty, A.D. 618–907. 2 fasciculi.

141 佛說緣生初勝分法本經

Fo-shwo-yuen-shaṅ-khu-shaṅ-fan-fâ-pan-kiṅ.

'Sûtra spoken by Buddha on the origin of the law being the first and excellent part of Nidâna.'

Translated by Dharmagupta, of the Sui dynasty, A.D. 589–618. 2 fasciculi. This is an earlier translation of No. 140. K'-yuen-lu, fasc. 2, fol. 24 b.

142 悲華經

Pei-hwa-kiṅ.

Karunâpundarîka-sûtra.

K'-yuen-lu, fasc. 2, fol. 18 b; Conc. 431; A.R., p. 436; A.M.G., p. 242; Wassiljew, 154. Translated by Dharmaraksha, of the Northern Liâṅ dynasty, A.D. 397–439. 10 fasciculi; 6 chapters. It agrees with Tibetan. K'-yuen-lu, s.v. For the Sanskrit text, see Catalogue of the Hodgson Manuscripts, I. 21; V. 42; VI. 18; VII. 34.

143 六度集經

Liu-tu-tsi-kiṅ.

'Shatpâramitâ-sannipâta-sûtra.'

Translated by Khâṅ Saṅ-hwui, of the Wu dynasty, A.D. 222–280. 8 fasciculi. There are three prefaces, by three Chinese, named Khâṅ Wan-ku, Yü Shun-hhi, and Hhiâ Ẑih-hwhei, dated A.D. 1590, 1589, and 1588 respectively. The third man edited this Sûtra, wishing the long life of his parents by the merit of this good action. Deest in Tibetan. K'-yuen-lu, fasc. 3, fol. 5 b. It contains many Gâtakas.

144 大乘頂王經

Tâ-shaṅ-tiṅ-wâṅ-kiṅ.

'Mahâyâna-mûrddharâga-sûtra.'

Vimalakîrtti-nirdesa.

Conc. 594. Translated by Upasûnya, of the Liâṅ dynasty, A.D. 502–557. 1 fasciculus.

145 大方等頂王經

Tâ-fâṅ-taṅ-tiṅ-wâṅ-kiṅ.

'Mahâvaipulya-mûrddharâga-sûtra.'

Vimalakîrtti-nirdesa.

Conc. 616. Translated by Ku Fâ-hu (Dharmaraksha), of the Western Tsin dynasty, A.D. 265–316. 1 fasciculus.

This is an earlier translation of No. 144. K'-yuen-lu, fasc. 2, fol. 18 b.

146 維摩詰所說經

Wêi-mo-khie-su-shwo-kiṅ.

'Vimalakîrtti-nirdesa-sûtra.'

Vimalakîrtti-nirdesa.

A.R., p. 451; A.M.G., p. 256; Conc. 788; Wassiljew, 152. Translated by Kumâragîva, of the Latter Tsin dynasty, A.D. 384–417. 3 fasciculi; 14 chapters. It agrees with Tibetan. K'-yuen-lu, fasc. 2, fol. 18 a.

147 維摩詰經

Wêi-mo-khie-kiṅ.

'Vimalakîrtti-sûtra.'

Vimalakîrtti-nirdesa.

Conc. 789. Translated by K' Khien, of the Wu dynasty, A.D. 222–280. 3 fasciculi; 14 chapters. This is an earlier translation of No. 146. K'-yuen-lu, fasc. 2, fol. 18 a.

148 道神足無極變化經

Tâo-shan-tsu-wu-ki-pien-hwâ-kiṅ.

'Sûtra on the unlimited changes of the supernatural footsteps.'

Translated by Ân Fâ-khin, of the Western Tsin dynasty, A.D. 265–316. 4 fasciculi. Deest in Tibetan. K'-yuen-lu, fasc. 2, fol. 20 a.

149 說無垢稱經

Shwo-wu-keu-khan-kiṅ.

Vimalakîrtti-nirdesa.

Conc. 121. Translated by Hhüen-kwâṅ (Hiouen-thsang), of the Thâṅ dynasty, A.D. 618–907. 6 fasciculi; 14 chapters. This is a later translation of Nos. 146 and 147. K'-yuen-lu, fasc. 2, fol. 18 a.

150 阿惟越致遮經

Ö-wêi-yueh-k'-kö-kiṅ.

Avaivarttya(?)-sûtra.

K'-yuen-lu, fasc. 2, fol. 20 b.

Aparivarttya-sûtra.

Conc. 40. Translated by Ku Fâ-hu (Dharmaraksha), of the Western Tsin dynasty, A.D. 265–316. 4 fasciculi; 18 chapters. It agrees with Tibetan. K'-yuen-lu, s.v.

151 佛說寶雨經

Fo-shwo-pâo-yü-kiṅ.

'Ratnavarsha-sûtra spoken by Buddha.'

Ratnamegha-sûtra.

K'-yuen-lu, fasc. 2, fol. 20 a; Conc. 421; A.R., p. 460; A.M.G., p. 264. Translated by Dharmaruki

(i. e. the first name of Bodhiru*k*i), A. D. 693, of the Thân dynasty, A. D. 618–907. 10 fasciculi. It agrees with Tibetan. *K'*-yuen-lu, s. v.

152 佛說寶雲經

Fo-shwo-pâo-yun-*k*iṅ.

Ratnamegha-sûtra.

Conc. 423. Translated by Mandra and Saṅghapâla, A. D. 503, of the Liâṅ dynasty, A. D. 502–557. 7 fasciculi. This is an earlier translation of the preceding Sûtra. *K'*-yuen-lu, fasc. 2, fol. 20 b.

153 佛昇忉利天爲母說法經

Fo-shaṅ-tâo-li-thien-wêi-mu-shwo-fâ-*k*iṅ.

'Sûtra of Buddha's ascension to the Trayastriṁsa heaven to preach the law for his mother's sake.'

Translated by *K*u Fâ-hu (Dharmaraksha), circa A. D. 270, of the Western Tsin dynasty, A. D. 265–316. 3 fasciculi. This is a similar translation of No. 148. *K'*-yuen-lu, fasc. 2, fol. 20 a.

154 相續解脫地波羅蜜了義經

Siâṅ-suh-*k*iê-tho-ti-po-lo-mi-liâo-i-*k*iṅ.

'Sandhinirmo*k*anabhûmi-pâramitâ-satyârtha-sûtra.'

Sandhinirmo*k*ana-sûtra.

Conc. 519, 520. Translated by Guṇabhadra, of the earlier Suṅ dynasty, A. D. 420–479. 13 leaves. This is an earlier translation of the last two chapters of No. 247. *K'*-yuen-lu, fasc. 2, fol. 24 a.

155 相續解脫如來所作隨順處了義經

Siâṅ-suh-*k*iê-tho-*z*u-lâi-su-tso-sui-shun-*kh*u-liâo-i-*k*iṅ.

'Sandhinirmo*k*ana-tathâgatakrityânuvishaya-satyârtha-sûtra.'

Sandhinirmo*k*ana-sûtra.

Translated by Guṇabhadra, of the earlier Suṅ dynasty, A. D. 420–479. 9 leaves. This is an earlier translation of the fourth and fifth fasciculi of No. 247. See note under the title of this translation.

156 佛說解節經

Fo-shwo-*k*iê-tsiê-*k*iṅ.

Sandhinirmo*k*ana-sûtra.

Conc. 279. Translated by Paramârtha, of the *Kh*an dynasty, A. D. 557–589. 1 fasciculus; 4 chapters. This is an earlier translation of the first five chapters of No. 247. *K'*-yuen-lu, fasc. 2, fol. 24 a.

157 不退轉法輪經

Pu-thui-*k*wâṅ-fâ-lun-*k*iṅ.

'Avivartita-dharma*k*akra-sûtra.'

Avaivartya (?)-sûtra.

K'-yuen-lu, fasc. 2, fol. 20 b.

Aparivartya-sûtra.

Conc. 501. Translated under the Northern Liâṅ dynasty, A. D. 397–439; but the translator's name is not known. 4 fasciculi; 9 chapters.

158 廣博嚴淨不退轉法輪經

Kwâṅ-poh-yen-tsiṅ-pu-thui-*k*wâṅ-fâ-lun-*k*iṅ.

'Vaipulya-vyûhâvivartita-dharma*k*akra-sûtra.'

Avaivartya (?)-sûtra.

K'-yuen-lu, fasc. 2, fol. 20 b.

Aparivartya-sûtra.

Conc. 316. Translated by *K'*-yen and Pâo-yun, A. D. 427, of the earlier Suṅ dynasty, A. D. 420–479. 4 fasciculi.

The above two works are later translations of No. 150. *K'*-yuen-lu, fasc. 2, fol. 21 a.

159 方廣大莊嚴經

Fâṅ-kwâṅ-tâ-*k*wâṅ-yen-*k*iṅ.

'Vaipulya-mahâvyûha-sûtra.'

Lalitavistara.

A. R., p. 416; A. M. G., p. 223; Conc. 147; Wassiljew, 176. Translated by Divâkara, A. D. 683, of the Thân dynasty, A. D. 618–907. 12 fasciculi; 27 chapters. There is another title of this translation given as a note under the above title in the first fasciculus, viz. 神通遊戲(經) Shan-thuṅ-yiu-hhi(-*k*iṅ), i. e. '*R*iddhivikrî*d*ita(-sûtra).' Cf. *K'*-yuen-lu, fasc. 2, fol. 16 b; Conc. 97. But Julien gives in his Méthode (p. 33) a different reading for the second character, viz. 童 thuṅ, though it is the same in pronunciation. This reading is given in Eitel's Handbook of Chinese Buddhism, p. 61 a. The title may literally be rendered into '*R*iddhikumâra-vikrî*d*ita(-sûtra).' The contents of this translation are given in Beal's Catalogue, pp. 17–19. There is a preface by the Empress Wu Tsö-thien, A. D. 684–705, of the Thân dynasty, the same as that to No. 53. In this preface Divâkara is said to have translated ten works, together with ten Chinese assistants, whose united labours were accomplished in A. D. 685.

According to the *K'*-yuen-lu (fasc. 2, fol. 16 b), this translation agrees with the Tibetan. This Sûtra was translated into Chinese four times, but the first and third had already been lost in A. D. 730, when the Khâi-yuen-lu was compiled. The second and fourth translations are in existence, viz. Nos. 160 and 159 respectively. The two missing translations were both entitled 普曜經 Phu-yâo-*k*iṅ, i. e. 'Samanta-prabhâsa-sûtra (?),' in eight fasciculi each. The first was translated under the Latter Hân dynasty, one of the Three Kingdoms, A. D. 221–263; but the translator's name is lost. The third was translated by *K*'-yen together with Pâo-yun, of the earlier Suṅ dynasty, A.D. 420–479. Khâi-yuen-lu, fasc. 14 a, fol. 13 a. The Sanskrit text has been edited by Râjendralâla Mitra in the Bibliotheca Indica, Old Series, Nos. 51, 73, 143, 144, 145, and 237, Calcutta, 1853–1877. This edition requires a careful collation with MSS.; for which latter, see Catalogue of the Hodgson Manuscripts, I. 7; III. 14, 15; IV. 7; VII. 37. There is another MS., numbered 341, in the India Office Library, London, which was procured in Nepal by Captain Knox, and presented to the Library by T. Colebrooke, Esq. An English translation of the first few chapters by Râjendralâla Mitra in the Bibliotheca Indica. A French translation of the Tibetan version of the Lalitavistara by Foucaux.

160 普曜經
Phu-yâo-*k*iṅ.
'Samanta-prabhâsa-sûtra.'
Lalitavistara.

Translated by *K*u Fâ-hu (Dharmaraksha), A. D. 308, of the Western Tsin dynasty, A. D. 265–316. 8 fasciculi; 30 chapters. According to the *K*'-yuen-lu (fasc. 2, fol. 16 b), this is an earlier translation of No. 159. This authority gives another title as a note, viz. 方等本起經 Fâṅ-taṅ-pan-*kh*i-*k*iṅ, i. e. 'Vaipulya-nidâna-sûtra.' Cf. Conc. 151.

161 伅眞陀羅所問寶如來三昧經
Tun-*k*an-tho-lo-su-wan-pâo-*z*u-lâi-sân-mêi-*k*iṅ.
'Druma-kinnara-pariprikkhâ-ratnatathâgata-samâdhi-sûtra.'
Mahâdruma-kinnararâ*g*a-pari*pri*kkhâ.

Cf. No. 162. Translated by *K*' Leu-*k*iâ-*kh*ân (Lokaraksha ?), of the Eastern Hân dynasty, A. D. 25–220. 3 fasciculi. It agrees with Tibetan. *K*'-yuen-lu, fasc. 2, fol. 19 b.

162 大樹緊那羅王所問經
Tâ-shu-*k*in-na-lo-wâṅ-su-wan-*k*iṅ.
Mahâdruma-kinnararâ*g*a-pari*pri*kkhâ.

K'-yuen-lu, fasc. 2, fol. 19 b; Conc. 597. Translated by Kumâra*g*îva, of the Latter Tshin dynasty, A. D. 384–417. This is a later translation of No. 161. *K*'-yuen-lu, s. v.

163 諸法本無經
*K*u-fâ-pan-wu-*k*iṅ.
Sarvadharma-pravritti-nirdesa-sûtra.

K'-yuen-lu, fasc. 2, fol. 26 a; Conc. 714; A. R., p. 452; A. M. G., p. 256. Translated by *G*ñânagupta, A. D. 595, of the Sui dynasty, A. D. 589–618. 3 fasciculi.

164 諸法無行經
*K*u-fâ-wu-hhiṅ-*k*iṅ.
Sarvadharma-pravritti-nirdesa-sûtra.

Conc. 715. Translated by Kumâra*g*îva, of the Latter Tshin dynasty, A. D. 384–417. 2 fasciculi. This is an earlier translation of No. 163. *K*'-yuen-lu, fasc. 2, fol. 26 a.

165 持人菩薩所問經
Kh'-*z*an-phu-sâ-su-wan-*k*iṅ.
'Vasudhara-bodhisattva-pari*pri*kkhâ-sûtra.'

Translated by *K*u Fâ-hu (Dharmaraksha), of the Western Tsin dynasty, A. D. 265–316. 4 fasciculi.

166 持世經
Kh'-shi-*k*iṅ.
'Vasudhara-sûtra.'

Translated by Kumâra*g*îva, of the Latter Tshin dynasty, A. D. 384–417. 4 fasciculi. This is also called 法印經 Fâ-yin-*k*iṅ, i. e. 'Dharmamudrâ-sûtra,' and it is a later translation of No. 165. Deest in Tibetan. *K*'-yuen-lu, fasc. 2, fol. 22 b.

167 佛說大灌頂神咒經
Fo-shwo-tâ-kwân-tiṅ-shan-*kh*eu-*k*iṅ.
'Buddhabhâshita-mahâbhishekarddhidhârani-sûtra.'

Translated by Poh *S*rîmitra, of the Eastern Tsin dynasty, A. D. 317–420. 12 fasciculi. Each fasciculus contains a Sûtra with its own title, so that this is a collection of twelve Sûtras. All these Sûtras except the last are wanting in Tibetan. *K*'-yuen-lu, fasc. 2, fol. 27 a seq.

168 佛說文殊師利現寶藏經
Fo-shwo-wan-shu-sh'-li-hhien-pâo-tsâṅ-*k*iṅ.
'Buddhabhâshita-mañ*g*usrî-vibhâvita-ratnapi*t*aka-sûtra.'
Ratnakâra*nd*akavyûha-sûtra.

K'-yuen-lu, fasc. 2, fol. 23 a; Conc. 802; A. R., p. 437; A. M. G., p. 243; Wassiljew, 154. Translated by *K*u Fâ-hu (Dharmaraksha), A. D. 270, of the Western Tsin dynasty, A. D. 265–316. 2 fasciculi. It agrees with Tibetan. *K*'-yuen-lu, s. v. For the Sanskrit text, see Catalogue of the Hodgson Manuscripts, I. 24; III. 20, 21; IV. 1 a; VII. 31. The Sanskrit text has been edited by Satyavrata Samasrami, at Calcutta, 1873.

169 大方廣寶匧經

Tâ-fâṅ-kwâṅ-pâo-*kh*iê-*k*iṅ.

'Mahâvaipulya-ratnakâraṇḍa-sûtra.'

Ratnakâraṇḍakavyûha-sûtra.

Conc. 601. Translated by Guṇabhadra, of the earlier Suṅ dynasty, A. D. 420–479. 2 fasciculi. This is a later translation of No. 168. *K*'-yuen-lu, fasc. 2, fol. 23 a.

170 藥師如來本願經

Yâo-sh'-*z*u-lâi-pan-yuen-*k*iṅ.

'Bhesha*g*yaguru-tathâgata-pûrvapraṇidhâna-sûtra.'

Bhesha*g*yaguru-pûrvapraṇidhâna.

Cf. No. 171. Translated by Dharmagupta, A. D. 615, of the Sui dynasty, A. D. 589–618. 1 fasciculus.

171 藥師瑠璃光如來本願功德經

Yâo-sh'-liu-li-kwâṅ-*z*u-lâi-pan-yuen-kuṅ-töh-*k*iṅ.

'Bhesha*g*yaguru-vaiḍûryaprabhâsa-tathâgata-pûrvapraṇidhâna-guṇa-sûtra.'

Bhesha*g*yaguru-vaiḍûryaprabhâsa-pûrvapraṇidhâna.

K'-yuen-lu, fasc. 2, fol. 28 a; Conc. 866. Translated by Hhüen-*k*wâṅ (Hiouen-thsang), A. D. 650, of the Thâṅ dynasty, A. D. 618–907. 1 fasciculus.

172 藥師瑠璃光七佛本願功德經

Yâo-sh'-liu-li-kwâṅ-tshi-fo-pan-yuen-kuṅ-töh-*k*iṅ.

'Bhesha*g*yaguru-vaiḍûryaprabhâsa(-âdi)-saptabuddha-pûrvapraṇidhâna-guṇa-sûtra.'

Saptatathâgata-pûrvapraṇidhâna-visesha-vistara.

K'-yuen-lu, fasc. 2, fol. 28 b; Conc. 868; A. R., p. 508; A. M. G., p. 309. Translated by I-tsiṅ, A. D. 707, of the Thâṅ dynasty, A. D. 618–907. 2 fasciculi.

The above three works are later translations of the twelfth Sûtra of No. 167, and they agree with Tibetan. *K*'-yuen-lu, s. v.

173 番字藥師瑠璃光七佛本願功德經

Fân-tsz'-yâo-sh'-liu-li-kwâṅ-tshi-fo-pan-yuen-kuṅ-töh-*k*iṅ.

'Bhesha*g*yaguru-vaiḍûryaprabhâsa(-âdi)-saptabuddha-pûrvapraṇidhâna-guṇa-sûtra in the letters of Fân (i. e. Tibet).'

1 fasciculus. This seems to have been a copy of the Tibetan version of the Sûtra, but it is considered to have already been lost or left out, at the time when this whole collection was published in China, towards the end of the Miṅ dynasty, about A. D. 1600. There is a note above this title in the original Catalogue, Tâ-miṅ-sân-tsâṅ-shan-*k*iâo-mu-lu (fasc. 1, fol. 12 b), added most probably by the Japanese editor, namely: 'In the Chinese and Corean editions of the Tripiṭaka, this book is wanting.' But it must be understood, that this book was originally included in the so-called Southern and Northern Collections of the Chinese Tripiṭaka, published under the reign of the first and third Emperors of the Miṅ dynasty, A. D. 1368–1398 and 1403–1424 respectively; because there is mention of the mark-characters of this book in the original Catalogue, as they have been employed in both Collections.

174 佛說阿闍世王經

Fo-shwo-ö-shö-shi-wâṅ-*k*iṅ.

'Buddhabhâshita*g*âtasatru-râ*g*a-sûtra.'

A*g*âtasatru-kaukṛitya-vinodana.

K'-yuen-lu, fasc. 2, fol. 28 b; Conc. 1; A. R., p. 457; A. M. G., p. 262. Translated by *K*' Leu-*k*iâ-*kh*ân (Lokaraksha?), of the Eastern Hân dynasty, A. D. 25–220. 2 fasciculi. It agrees with Tibetan. *K*'-yuen-lu, fasc. 2, fol. 29 a.

175 楞伽阿跋多羅寶經

Laṅ-*k*iê-ö-poh-to-lo-pâo-*k*iṅ.

'Laṅkâvatâra-ratna-sûtra.'

Laṅkâvatâra-sûtra.

Conc. 326; A. R., p. 432; A. M. G., p. 237; Wassiljew, 151. Translated by Guṇabhadra, A. D. 443, of the earlier Suṅ dynasty, A. D. 420–479. 4 fasciculi; 1 chapter. There are two prefaces, by Tsiang *K*'-*kh*i and Su Shi, of the later Suṅ dynasty, A. D. 960–1127. The date of the latter preface corresponds to A. D. 1085.

176 入楞伽經

*Z*u-laṅ-*k*iê-*k*iṅ.

Laṅkâvatâra-sûtra.

Conc. 327. Translated by Bodhiru*k*i, A. D. 513, of the Northern Wêi dynasty, A. D. 386–534. 10 fasciculi; 18 chapters.

177 大乘入楞伽經
Tâ-shan-su-lan-kiâ-kiṅ.
Laṅkâvatâra-sûtra.

K'-yuen-lu, fasc. 2, fol. 25 a; Conc. 571. Translated by Sikshânanda, A. D. 700–704, of the Thân dynasty, A. D. 618–907. 7 fasciculi; 10 chapters. There is a preface added by the Empress Wu Tsö-thien, A. D. 684–705, of the Thân dynasty.

The above three works are similar translations, and they agree with Tibetan. K'-yuen-lu, s.v. But No. 175 is incomplete. Nos. 176 and 177 agree more or less with the Sanskrit text. For the text, see Catalogue of the Hodgson Manuscripts, I. 5; III. 9; V. 20; VI. 6; VII. 36. There are also two MSS. in the University Library, Cambridge.

178 菩薩行方便境界神通變化經
Phu-sâ-hhiṅ-fâṅ-pien-kiṅ-kiê-shan-thuṅ-pien-hwâ-kiṅ.
'Bodhisattvakaritopâyavishayarddhivikriyâ-sûtra.'

Translated by Guṇabhadra, of the earlier Suṅ dynasty, A. D. 420–479. 3 fasciculi.

179 大薩遮尼乾子受記經
Tâ-sâ-kö-ni-khien-tsz'-sheu-ki-kiṅ.
'Mahâsatya (?)-nirgrantha-putra-vyâkaraṇa-sûtra.'

Translated by Bodhiruki, A. D. 519, of the Northern Wei dynasty, A. D. 386–534. 10 fasciculi; 12 chapters.

The above two works are similar translations, and wanting in Tibetan. K'-yuen-lu, fasc. 2, fol. 25 b.

180 大乘大悲分陀利經
Tâ-shan-tâ-pêi-fan-tho-li-kiṅ.
Mahâkaruṇâpuṇḍarîka-sûtra.

K'-yuen-lu, fasc. 2, fol. 18 b; Conc. 644, 645. Translated under the (three) Tshin (dynasties, A. D. 350–431); but the translator's name is lost. 8 fasciculi; 30 chapters. This is a similar translation of No. 142. K'-yuen-lu, s. v.

181 善思童子經
Shân-sz'-thuṅ-tsz'-kiṅ.
'Sukintita (?)-kumâra-sûtra.'
Vimalakîrtti-nirdesa.

Conc. 60. Translated by Gñânagupta, A. D. 591, of the Sui dynasty, A. D. 589–618. 2 fasciculi. This is a later translation of Nos. 144 and 145. K'-yuen-lu, fasc. 2, fol. 18 b.

182 普超三昧經
Phu-khâo-sân-mêi-kiṅ.
'Samantâtikramaṇa (?)-samâdhi-sûtra.'
Agâtasatru-kaukritya-vinodana.

Conc. 496. Translated by Ku Fâ-hu (Dharmaraksha), A. D. 286, of the Western Tsin dynasty, A. D. 265–316. 4 fasciculi. This is a later translation of No. 174. K'-yuen-lu, fasc. 2, fol. 29 a.

183 放鉢經
Fâṅ-poh-kiṅ.
'Sûtra on letting the bowl go,' or 'Pâtra-gamayat-sûtra (?).'
Agâtasatru-kaukritya-vinodana.

Cf. Conc. 149, where a different reading is given for the last word of the Sanskrit title. Translated under the Western Tsin dynasty, A. D. 265–316; but the translator's name is lost. 1 fasciculus. This is a similar translation of the second chapter of No. 182.

184 佛說大淨法門品經
Fo-shwo-tâ-tsiṅ-fâ-man-phin-kiṅ.
'Buddhabhâshita-mahâsuddhadharmaparyâyâdhyâyá-sûtra.'
Mañgusrî-vikrîdita-sûtra.

Conc. 658; A. R., p. 425; A. M. G., p. 230; Wassiljew, 184. Translated by Ku Fâ-hu (Dharmaraksha), A. D. 313, of the Western Tsin dynasty, A. D. 265–316. 1 fasciculus.

185 大莊嚴法門經
Tâ-kwâṅ-yen-fâ-man-kiṅ.
'Mahâvyûhadharmaparyâya-sûtra.'
Mañgusrî-vikrîdita-sûtra.

K'-yuen-lu, fasc. 3, fol. 1 b; Conc. 654. Translated by Narendrayasas, A. D. 583, of the Sui dynasty, A. D. 589 (or 581)–618. 2 fasciculi.

The above two works are similar translations, and they agree with Tibetan. K'-yuen-lu, s. v.

186 佛說大方等大雲請雨經
Fo-shwo-tâ-fâṅ-taṅ-tâ-yun-tshiṅ-yü-kiṅ.
'Buddhabhâshita-mahâvaipulya-sûtra on asking rain of the great cloud.'
Mahâmegha-sûtra.

A. R., p. 461; A. M. G., p. 265; Conc. 612. Translated by Gñânagupta, of the Sui dynasty, A. D. 589–618. 1 fasciculus. It agrees with Tibetan. K'-yuen-lu, fasc. 2, fol. 26 a. For the Sanskrit text, see Catalogue of the Hodgson Manuscripts, I. 64; III. 12. An extract from the text with an English translation, published by Mr. C. Bendall, in the Journal of the Royal Asiatic Society, vol. xii, part ii, pp. 288–311.

187 大雲請雨經
Tâ-yun-tshiṅ-yü-*k*iṅ.
'Sûtra on asking rain of the great cloud.'
Mahâmegha-sûtra.

Conc. 668. Translated by *G*ñânagupta (the same person as before), under the Northern *K*eu dynasty, A. D. 557–581. 1 fasciculus.

188 大雲輪請雨經
Tâ-yun-lun-tshiṅ-yü-*k*iṅ.
'Sûtra on asking rain of the great-cloud-wheel.'
Mahâmegha-sûtra.

Conc. 667. Translated by Narendrayasas, A. D. 585, of the Sui dynasty, A. D. 589 (or 581)–618. 2 fasciculi.

The above two works are similar translations of No. 186. *K*'-yuen-lu, fasc. 2, fol. 26 a. An abstract English translation of No. 188, by Beal in his Catena of Buddhist Scriptures from the Chinese, pp. 419–423.

189 勝思惟梵天所問經
Shaṅ-sz'-wêi-fân-thien-su-wan-*k*iṅ.
Viseshakinta-brahma-pariprikkhâ (-sûtra).

K'-yuen-lu, fasc. 2, fol. 22 a; Conc. 110. Translated by Bodhiru*k*i, A. D. 517, of the Northern Wêi dynasty, A. D. 386–534. 6 fasciculi. It agrees with Tibetan. *K*'-yuen-lu, s. v.

190 思益梵天所問經
Sz'-yi-fân-thien-su-wan-*k*iṅ.
Viseshakinta-brahma-pariprikkhâ (-sûtra).

Conc. 551. Translated by Kumâra*g*îva, A. D. 402, of the Latter Tshin dynasty, A. D. 384–417. 4 fasciculi; 24 chapters. This is an earlier translation of the preceding Sûtra. *K*'-yuen-lu, fasc. 2, fol. 22 a.

191 月燈三昧經
Yueh-taṅ-sân-mêi-*k*iṅ.
'*K*andra-dîpa-samâdhi-sûtra.'

Translated by Narendrayasas, A. D. 557, of the Northern Tshi dynasty, A. D. 550–577. 11 fasciculi. Deest in Tibetan. *K*'-yuen-lu, fasc. 3, fol. 1 a.

192 The same as No. 191.

Translated by Shih Sien-kuṅ, of the earlier Suṅ dynasty, A. D. 420–479. 1 fasciculus. This is an earlier translation of the seventh and eighth fasciculi of the preceding Sûtra.

193 佛說象腋經
Fo-shwo-siâṅ-ye-*k*iṅ.
'Buddhabhâshita-hastikakshyâ-sûtra.'
Hastikakshyâ.

K'-yuen-lu, fasc. 3, fol. 1 b; Conc. 523; A. R., p. 456; A. M. G., p. 261. Translated by Dharmamitra, of the earlier Suṅ dynasty, A. D. 420–479. 1 fasciculus. It agrees with Tibetan. *K*'-yuen-lu, fasc. 3, fol. 1 b.

194 佛說無所希望經
Fo-shwo-wu-su-hhi-wâṅ-*k*iṅ.
'Sûtra spoken by Buddha on the absence of hope.'
Hastikakshyâ.

Translated by *K*u Fâ-hu (Dharmaraksha), of the Western Tsin dynasty, A. D. 265–316. 1 fasciculus. This is an earlier translation of the preceding Sûtra. *K*'-yuen-lu, fasc. 3, fol. 1 b.

195 佛說大乘同性經
Fo-shwo-tâ-shaṅ-thuṅ-siṅ-*k*iṅ.
Mahâyânâbhisamaya-sûtra.

K'-yuen-lu, fasc. 2, fol. 23 a; Conc. 595. Translated by *G*ñânayasas, together with Saṅ-ân, A. D. 570, of the Northern *K*eu dynasty, A. D. 557–581. 2 fasciculi. It agrees with Tibetan. *K*'-yuen-lu, s. v.

196 佛說證契大乘經
Fo-shwo-*k*aṅ-*k*'i-tâ-shaṅ-*k*iṅ.
Mahâyânâbhisamaya-sûtra.

Conc. 695. Translated by Divâkara, A. D. 680, of the Thâṅ dynasty, A. D. 618–907. 2 fasciculi. This is a later translation of the preceding Sûtra. *K*'-yuen-lu, fasc. 2, fol. 23 b. There is a preface, by the Empress Wu Tsö-thien, A. D. 684–705, of the Thâṅ dynasty. This preface is the same as that to Nos. 53 and 159.

197 持心梵天所問經
*K*h'-sin-fân-thien-su-wan-*k*iṅ.
Viseshakinta-brahma-pariprikkhâ (-sûtra).

Conc. 691. Translated by *K*u Fâ-hu (Dharmaraksha), A. D. 286, of the Western Tsin dynasty, A. D. 265–316. 4 fasciculi; 18 chapters. This is an earlier translation of Nos. 189 and 190. *K*'-yuen-lu, fasc. 2, fol. 22 a.

198 佛說觀無量壽佛經
Fo-shwo-kwâṅ-wu-liâṅ-sheu-fo-*k*iṅ.
'Buddhabhâshitâmitâyurbuddha-dhyâna (?)-sûtra.'

Translated by Kâlayasas, A. D. 424, of the earlier Suṅ dynasty, A. D. 420–479. 1 fasciculus. There was another translation of this Sûtra, made by Dharmamitra, of the same dynasty; but it was lost already in A. D. 730. Khâi-yuen-lu, fasc. 14 a, fol. 17 b. This Sûtra may be called the Sukhâvatîvyûha, according to its contents. But Conc. 311 and 830 are both very doubtful, if not wrong.

There are verses prefixed to No. 198, which verses consist of sixty lines, each line consisting of seven Chinese characters. The title of these verses is 御製無量壽佛讚 Yü-k'-wu-liâṅ-sheu-fo-tsân, i. e. 'Hymn of Buddha Amitâyus, being the Imperial composition.' This composition entirely depends on No. 198; but the Emperor's name is not mentioned.

199 稱讚淨土佛攝受經

*Kh*an-tsân-tsiṅ-tu-fo-shö-sheu-*k*iṅ.

'Sûtra of the Favour of (all) Buddhas and the Praise of the Pure Land.'

Sukhâvatîvyûha.

A. R., p. 437; A. M. G., p. 243; Conc. 699, 700, 702, which three are different titles of this translation. See *K'*-yuen-lu, fasc. 3, fol. 2 b. Translated by Hhüen-*k*wâṅ (Hiouen-thsang), A. D. 650, of the Thâṅ dynasty, A. D. 618–907. 11 leaves. It agrees with Tibetan. *K'*-yuen-lu, s. v.

200 佛說阿彌陀經

Fo-shwo-ö-mi-tho-*k*iṅ.

'Buddhabhâshitâmitâyus-sûtra.'

Sukhâvatyamṛitavyûha-sûtra.

K'-yuen-lu, fasc. 2, fol. 2 b.

Sukhâvatîvyûha.

Translated by Kumâragîva, A. D. 402, of the Latter Tshin dynasty, A. D. 384–417. 5 leaves. This is an earlier (and shorter) translation of the preceding Sûtra. *K'*-yuen-lu, s. v. But this shorter translation corresponds, with a few omissions, to the Sanskrit text, which, together with an English translation and notes, has been published by Professor Max Müller, in J. R. A. S., vol. xii, part ii, 1880, pp. 168–186, and afterwards in his Selected Essays, vol. ii, pp. 348–363, without the text. An incomplete English translation of No. 200, by Rev. S. Beal, is given in his Catena of Buddhist Scriptures from the Chinese, pp. 378–383. A French translation, by MM. Ymaïzoumi and Yamata, with the Sanskrit text, was published in the Annales du Musée Guimet, vol. ii (1881), pp. 39–64.

There was another Chinese translation of this short Sukhâvatîvyûha, made by Guṇabhadra, of the earlier Suṅ dynasty, A. D. 420–479. But it was lost already in A. D. 730. Khâi-yuen-lu, fasc. 14 a, fol. 17 b.

201 拔一切業障根本得生淨土神咒

Pa-yi-tshiê-yeh-*k*âṅ-kan-pan-töh-shaṅ-tsiṅ-tu-shan-*kh*eu.

'A spiritual Dhâraṇî for uprooting all the obstacles of Karma and for causing one to be born in the Pure Land (Sukhâvatî).'

Translated by Guṇabhadra, A. D. 453, of the earlier Suṅ dynasty, A. D. 420–479. This Dhâraṇî consists of fifty-nine Chinese characters in transliteration, and it is followed by about two columns of explanation.

202 後出阿彌陀偈經

Heu-*kh*u-ö-mi-tho-*k*iê-*k*iṅ.

'A later translation of the Sûtra consisting of verses on Amitâyus.'

Translated under the Eastern Hân dynasty, A. D. 25–220; but the translator's name is lost. 56 lines, each line consists of five characters. There was an earlier translation, but it was lost already in A. D. 730. Khâi-yuen-lu, fasc. 14 a, fol. 17 b.

203 大阿彌陀經

Tâ-ö-mi-tho-*k*iṅ.

'A large Amitâyus-sûtra.'

Compiled by Wâṅ Zih-hhiu, in A. D. 1160–1162, of the Southern Suṅ dynasty, A. D. 1127–1280. 2 fasciculi; 56 chapters. This work ought to be arranged under the heading of Chinese Works, in the Fourth Division of the Chinese Tripiṭaka; because it is not a translation made from the original text, but consists of extracts from four translations of the same or a similar text, viz. Nos. 25, 26, 27, and 863. Moreover the compiler made this, without comparing those versions with the Sanskrit text, simply from his own judgment, through the spiritual help of Avalokitesvara, for which he had always prayed in the course of his compilation. See his preface. It is curious that he does not mention Bodhiruki's translation of the same Sûtra (No. 23. 5), which was made more than four centuries before, and is much better at least than No. 863, both in contents and composition. At any rate, No. 203 has no such value as Nos. 130 and 139, which were made by men who had the Sanskrit texts before them, and who also made some additions and corrections.

204 佛說觀彌勒菩薩上生兜率陀天經

Fo-shwo-kwâṅ-mi-lö-phu-sâ-shâṅ-shaṅ-teu-shwâi-tho-thien-*k*iṅ.

'Sûtra spoken by Buddha about the meditation on the Bodhisattva Maitreya's going up to be born in the Tushita heaven.'

Translated by Tsü-*kh*ü *K*iṅ-shaṅ, A. D. 455, of the earlier Suṅ dynasty, A. D. 420–479. 9 leaves. This is arranged here, though it is a single translation, because the subject has some connection with that of the following five works. *K'*-yuen-lu, fasc. 3, fol. 3 a.

205 佛說彌勒下生經
Fo-shwo-mi-lö-hhiâ-shañ-*k*iñ.
'Sûtra spoken by Buddha on Maitreya's coming down to be born (in this world).'
Maitreya-vyâkara*n*a.

A. R., p. 480; A. M. G., p. 283. Translated by Kumâra*g*îva, of the Latter Tshin dynasty, A. D. 384–417. 8 leaves.

206 佛說彌勒來時經
Fo-shwo-mi-lö-lâi-sh'-*k*iñ.
'Sûtra spoken by Buddha on the time of Maitreya's coming (down to be born in this world).'
Maitreya-vyâkara*n*a.

See No. 205. Translated under the Eastern Tsin dynasty, A. D. 317–420; but the translator's name is lost. 3 leaves.

207 佛說彌勒下生成佛經
Fo-shwo-mi-lö-hhiâ-shañ-*kh*añ-fo-*k*iñ.
'Sûtra spoken by Buddha on Maitreya's coming down to be born (in this world) and to become Buddha.'
Ma treya-vyâkara*n*a.

See No. 205. Translated by I-tsiñ, A. D. 701, of the Thâñ dynasty, A. D. 618–907. 4 leaves.

The above three works are the fourth, third, and sixth respectively of six translations of the same or a similar text; while the first, second, and fifth were lost already in A. D. 730. Khâi-yuen-lu, fasc. 14 a, fol. 18 a; *K*'-yuen-lu, fasc. 3, fol. 3 a, where it is stated that this Sûtra is wanting in Tibetan. See, however, the authorities mentioned under No. 205.

208 佛說觀彌勒菩薩下生經
Fo-shwo-kwâñ-mi-lö-phu-sâ-hhiâ-shañ-*k*iñ.
'Sûtra spoken by Buddha about the meditation on the Bodhisattva Maitreya's coming down to be born (in this world).'

Translated by *K*u Fâ-hu (Dharmaraksha), of the Western Tsin dynasty, A. D. 265–316. 9 leaves. This is a single translation, but it is arranged here on account of the subject being similar to the preceding three works.

209 佛說彌勒成佛經
Fo-shwo-mi-lö-*kh*añ-fo-*k*iñ.
'Sûtra spoken by Buddha on Maitreya's becoming Buddha.'

Translated by Kumâra*g*îva, A. D. 402, of the Latter Tshin dynasty, A. D. 384–417. 1 fasciculus. There was an earlier translation, but it was lost already in A. D. 730. Khâi-yuen-lu, fasc. 14 a, fol. 18 a.

210 佛說第一義法勝經
Fo-shwo-ti-yi-i-fâ-shañ-*k*iñ.
'Sûtra spoken by Buddha on the excelling of the law of the first (or highest) meaning.'
Paramârthadharmavi*g*aya-sûtra.

K'-yuen-lu, fasc. 3, fol. 3 b; Conc. 741; A. R., p. 464; A. M. G., p. 268. Translated by Gautama Pra*gñ*âruki, A. D. 542, of the Eastern Wêi dynasty, A. D. 534–550. 1 fasciculus.

211 佛說大威燈光僊人問疑經
Fo-shwo-tâ-wêi-tañ-kwâñ-sien-*z*an-wan-i-*k*iñ.
'Sûtra spoken by Buddha on the question of doubt asked by the *Ri*shi Great-powerful-lamp-light.'
Paramârthadharmavi*g*aya-sûtra.

Conc. 661. Translated by *Gñ*ânagupta, A. D. 586, of the Sui dynasty, A. D. 589 (or 581)–618. 1 fasciculus.

The above two works are similar translations, and they agree with Tibetan. *K*'-yuen-lu, fasc. 3, fol. 4 a.

212 一切法高王經
Yi-tshiê-fâ-kâo-wâñ-*k*iñ.
'Sarvadharmo*kk*arâ*g*a-sûtra.'

Translated by Gautama Pra*gñ*âru*k*i, A. D. 542, of the Eastern Wêi dynasty, A. D. 534–550. 1 fasciculus.

213 佛說諸法勇王經
Fo-shwo-*k*u-fâ-yuñ-wâñ-*k*iñ.
'Buddhabhâshita-sarvadharma-nirbhayarâ*g*a-sûtra.'

Translated by Dharmamitra, of the earlier Suñ dynasty, A. D. 420–479. 1 fasciculus.

The above two works are similar translations, and are wanting in Tibetan. *K*'-yuen-lu, fasc. 3, fol. 3 b.

214 順權方便經
Shun-*kh*üen-fâñ-pien-*k*iñ.
'Upâyakausalya-sûtra.'
Strîvivarta-vyâkara*n*a-sûtra.

K'-yuen-lu, fasc. 3, fol. 4 a; Conc. 124; A. R., p. 454; A. M. G., p. 258. Translated by *K*u Fâ-hu (Dharmaraksha), of the Western Tsin dynasty, A. D. 265–316. 2 fasciculi; 4 chapters.

215 佛說樂瓔珞莊嚴方便經
Fo-shwo-lö-yiñ-lo-*k*wâñ-yen-fâñ-pien-*k*iñ.
'Sûtra spoken by Buddha on the means of adornment of a necklace of happiness (?).'
Strîvivarta-vyâkara*n*a-sûtra.

Conc. 329. Translated by Dharmayasas, of the Latter Tshin dynasty, A. D. 384–417. 1 fasciculus.

The above two works are similar translations, and they agree with Tibetan. *K*'-yuen-lu, fasc. 3, fol. 4 a.

216 菩薩睒子經

Phu-sâ-shân-tsz'-*k*iṅ.

'Sûtra on the Bodhisattva who was the son who took a look at (his blind father).'

Translated under the Western Tsin dynasty, A.D. 265–316; but the translator's name is lost. 7 leaves.

217 佛說睒子經

Fo-shwo-shân-tsz'-*k*iṅ.

'Sûtra spoken by Buddha on the son who took a look at (his blind father).'

Translated by Shaṅ-*k*ien, of the Western Tshin dynasty, A.D. 385–431. 7 leaves.

The above two works are later translations of a part of fasc. 2 of No. 143, being a *G*âtaka, concerning the Dâna-pâramitâ. *K*'-yuen-lu, fasc. 3, fol. 5 a.

218 佛說九色鹿經

Fo-shwo-*k*iu-seh-lu-*k*iṅ.

'Sûtra spoken by Buddha on the nine-coloured deer.'

Translated by *K*' *Kh*ien, of the Wu dynasty, A.D. 222–280. 3 leaves. This is a similar translation of a part of fasc. 6 of No. 143, being a *G*âtaka, concerning the Vîrya-pâramitâ. *K*'-yuen-lu, fasc. 3, fol. 5 a.

219 佛說太子沐魄經

Fo-shwo-thâi-tsz'-mu-phoh-*k*iṅ.

'Buddhabhâshita-kumâra-mûka-sûtra.'

Translated by *K*u Fâ-hu (Dharmaraksha), of the Western Tsin dynasty, A.D. 265–316. 4 leaves.

220 太子慕魄經

Thâi-tsz'-mu-phoh-*k*iṅ.

'Kumâra-mûka-sûtra.'

Translated by Ân Shi-kâo, of the Eastern Hân dynasty, A.D. 25–220. 6 leaves.

The above two works are similar translations of a part of fasc. 4 of No. 143, being the *G*âtaka of the dumb boy, concerning the *S*îla-pâramitâ. *K*'-yuen-lu, fasc. 3, fol. 5 a.

221 無字寶篋經

Wu-tsz'-pâo-*kh*iê-*k*iṅ.

'Anakshara-ratnakâra*nd*aka-sûtra.'

Anakshara-granthaka-ro*k*anagarbha-sûtra.

Conc. 849. Translated by Bodhiru*k*i, of the Northern Wêi dynasty, A.D. 386–534. 7 leaves.

222 大乘離文字普光明藏經

Tâ-shaṅ-li-wan-tsz'-phu-kwâṅ-miṅ-tsâṅ-*k*iṅ.

'Mahâyânânakshara-samantaro*k*anagarbha-sûtra.'

Anakshara-granthaka-ro*k*anagarbha-sûtra.

K'-yuen-lu, fasc. 3, fol. 5 b; Conc. 584. Translated by Divâkara, A.D. 683, of the Thâṅ dynasty, A.D. 618–907. 5 leaves.

223 大乘徧照光明藏無字法門經

Tâ-shaṅ-pien-*k*âo-kwâṅ-miṅ-tsâṅ-wu-tsz'-fâ-man-*k*iṅ.

'Mahâyâna-vairo*k*anagarbhânakshara-dharmaparyâya-sûtra.'

Anakshara-granthaka-ro*k*anagarbha-sûtra.

Conc. 584. Translated by Divâkara, of the Thâṅ dynasty, A.D. 618–907. 7 leaves.

The above three works are similar translations, and they agree with Tibetan. *K*'-yuen-lu, fasc. 3, fol. 5 b.

224 佛說老女人經

Fo-shwo-lâo-nü-*z*an-*k*iṅ.

'Sûtra spoken by Buddha at (the request of) an old woman.'

Translated by *K*' *Kh*ien, of the Wu dynasty, A.D. 222–280. 2 leaves.

225 佛說老母經

Fo-shwo-lâo-mu-*k*iṅ.

'Sûtra spoken by Buddha at (the request of) an old mother.'

Translated under the earlier Suṅ dynasty, A.D. 420–479; but the translator's name is lost. 3 leaves.

226 佛說老母女六英經

Fo-shwo-lâo-mu-nü-liu-yiṅ-*k*iṅ.

'Sûtra spoken by Buddha at (the request of) an old mother called Six-flowers (Shatpushpâ ?).'

Translated by Gu*n*abhadra, of the earlier Suṅ dynasty, A.D. 420–479. 1 leaf.

The above three works are similar translations, and are wanting in Tibetan. *K*'-yuen-lu, fasc. 3, fol. 6 a.

227 佛說長者子制經

Fo-shwo-*kh*âṅ-*k*ö-tsz'-*k*'-*k*iṅ.

'Sûtra spoken by Buddha on the son of an elder (*S*resh*th*in) *K*' (or *G*eta ?).'

Translated by Ân Shi-kâo, of the Eastern Hân dynasty, A.D. 25–220. 5 leaves.

228 佛說菩薩逝經

Fo-shwo-phu-sâ-shi-*k*iṅ.

'Sûtra spoken by Buddha on the Bodhisattva Shi (or *G*eta ?).'

Translated by Po Fâ-tsu, of the Western Tsin dynasty, A.D. 265–316. 4 leaves.

229 佛說逝童子經

Fo-shwo-shi-thuṅ-tsz'-kiṅ.

'Sûtra spoken by Buddha on the boy Shi (or *Geta* ?).'

Translated by *K'* Fâ-tu, A.D. 301, of the Western Tsin dynasty, A.D. 265–316. 4 leaves.

The above three works are similar translations, and they are wanting in Tibetan. *K'*-yuen-lu, fasc. 3, fol. a.

230 佛說月光童子經

Fo-shwo-yueh-kwâṅ-thuṅ-tsz'-kiṅ.

'Buddhabhâshita-*k*andraprabha-kumâra-sûtra.'

*K*andraprabha-kumâra-sûtra.

Conc. 870. Translated by *K*u Fâ-hu (Dharmaraksha), of the Western Tsin dynasty, A.D. 265–316. 10 leaves.

231 佛說申日兒本經

Fo-shwo-shan-zih-'rh-pan-kiṅ.

'Sûtra spoken by Buddha on the original (or *Gâtaka* ?) of the child of *S*rîgupta (?).'

*K*andraprabha-kumâra-sûtra.

Conc. 92. Translated by Gu*n*abhadra, of the earlier Sun dynasty, A.D. 420–479. 3 leaves.

232 佛說德護長者經

Fo-shwo-töh-hu-*kh*âṅ-kö-kiṅ.

'Buddhabhâshita-srîgupta-sreshthi-sûtra.'

*S*rîgupta-sûtra.

K'-yuen-lu, fasc. 3, fol. 6 b; Conc. 733; A. R., p. 458; A. M. G., p. 262. Translated by Narendrayasas, A.D. 583, of the Sui dynasty, A.D. 589 (or 581)–618. 2 fasciculi.

The above three works are similar translations; but Nos. 230 and 231 are incomplete, while No. 232 agrees with Tibetan. *K'*-yuen-lu, s. v.

233 佛說犢子經

Fo-shwo-tu-tsz'-kiṅ.

'Sûtra spoken by Buddha on the calf.'

Vatsa-sûtra.

Cf. No. 234. Translated by *K' Kh*ien, of the Wu dynasty, A.D. 220–280. 2 leaves.

234 佛說乳光佛經

Fo-shwo-zu-kwâṅ-fo-kiṅ.

'Sûtra spoken by Buddha on Buddha of milky light.'

Vatsa-sûtra.

K'-yuen-lu, fasc. 3, fol. 7 b; Conc. 232. Translated by *K*u Fâ-hu (Dharmaraksha), of the Western Tsin dynasty, A.D. 265–316. 7 leaves.

The above two are similar translations, and they agree with Tibetan. *K'*-yuen-lu, fasc. 3, fol. 7 b.

235 佛說無垢賢女經

Fo-shwo-wu-keu-hhien-nü-kiṅ.

'Sûtra spoken by Buddha on the wise girl Vimalâ.'

Strîvivarta-vyâkarana-sûtra.

K'-yuen-lu, fasc. 3, fol. 7 b; Conc. 821; A. R., p. 454; A. M. G., p. 258. Translated by *K*u Fâ-hu (Dharmaraksha), of the Western Tsin dynasty, A.D. 265–316. 4 leaves.

236 佛說腹中女聽經

Fo-shwo-fu-*k*uṅ-nü-thiṅ-kiṅ.

'Sûtra spoken by Buddha on the daughter (of Sudatta) listening (to the law), while in the womb.'

Strîvivarta-vyâkara*n*a-sûtra.

Conc. 168. Translated by Dharmaraksha, of the Northern Liâṅ dynasty, A.D. 397–439. 3 leaves.

237 佛說轉女身經

Fo-shwo-*k*wâṅ-nü-shan-kiṅ.

'Sûtra spoken by Buddha on turning the body of a woman (into man).'

Strîvivarta-vyâkara*n*a-sûtra.

Conc. 732. Translated by Dharmamitra, of the earlier Suṅ dynasty, A.D. 420–479. 1 fasciculus.

The above three works are similar translations, and they agree with Tibetan. Nos. 235 and 236 are incomplete. *K'*-yuen-lu, fasc. 3, fol. 8 a. Cf. Nos. 214 and 215.

238 文殊師利問菩提經

Wan-shu-sh'-li-wan-phu-ti-kiṅ.

'Sûtra of *Mañg*usrî's question on the Bodhi.'

Gayâsîrsha.

A. R. p. 433; A. M. G., p. 238; Conc. 498 and 499 mention two shorter Chinese titles, as given in *K'*-yuen-lu, fasc. 3, fol. 6 b. Translated by Kumâra*g*îva, of the Latter Tshin dynasty, A.D. 384–417. 8 leaves.

239 伽耶山頂經

Kiâ-ye-shân-tiṅ-kiṅ.

'Sûtra (spoken) on the top of the Gayâ mountain.'

Gayâsîrsha.

A. R., p. 433; A. M. G., p. 238; Conc. 270. Translated by Bodhiru*k*i, of the Northern Wêi dynasty, A.D. 386–534. 12 leaves.

240 佛說象頭精舍經

Fo-shwo-siâṅ-theu-tsiṅ-shö-kiṅ.

'Sûtra spoken by Buddha in the pure house (or vihâra) of the head of an elephant (or *Gag*asîrsha).'

Gayâsîrsha.

A. R., p. 433; A. M. G., p. 238; Conc. 521. Translated by Vinîtaru*k*i, A. D. 582, of the Sui dynasty, A. D. 589(or 581)–618. 11 leaves.

241　大乘伽耶山頂經

Tâ-shan-*k*iê-ye-shân-tiń-*k*iń.
'Sûtra of the Mahâyâna (spoken) on the top of the Gayâ mountain.'

Gayâśîrsha.

A. R., p. 433; A. M. G., p. 238; Conc. 573. Translated by Bodhiru*k*i, A. D. 693, of the Thâń dynasty, A. D. 618–907. 8 leaves.

The above four works are similar translations, and they are wanting in Tibetan. *K*'-yuen-lu, fasc. 3, fol. 7 a. See, however, the authorities mentioned under the title.

242　佛說決定總持經

Fo-shwo-*k*üê-tiń-tsuń-*k*i'-*k*iń.
'Sûtra spoken by Buddha on the determined Dhâranî.'

Translated by *K*u Fâ-hu (Dharmaraksha), of the Western Tsin dynasty, A. D. 265–316. 11 leaves. In this work the Dhâranî is translated into Chinese, instead of being transliterated as usual.

243　佛說謗佛經

Fo-shwo-pâń-fo-*k*iń.
'Sûtra spoken by Buddha on speaking evil of Buddha.'

Translated by Bodhiru*k*i, of the Northern Wêi dynasty, A. D. 386–534. 8 leaves.

The above two works are similar translations, and they agree with Tibetan. *K*'-yuen-lu, fasc. 3, fol. 8 b.

244　大方等大雲經

Tâ-fâń-tań-tâ-yun-*k*iń.
'Mahâvaipulya-mahâmegha-sûtra.'

Mahâmegha-sûtra.

Conc. 611. Translated by Dharmaraksha, of the Northern Liâń dynasty, A. D. 397–439. 4 fasciculi. There was an earlier translation, but it is now lost. *K*'-yuen-lu, fasc. 2, fol. 25 b.

245　如來莊嚴智慧光明入一切佛境界經

Zu-lâi-*k*wâń-yen-*k*'-hwui-kwâń-miń-*zu*-yi-tshiê-fo-*k*iń-*k*iê-*k*iń.
'Tathâgatavyûha-*g*ñânaprabhâsa-sarvabuddhavishayâvatâra-sûtra.'

Sarva*b*uddhavishayâvatâra.

Wassiljew, 161. Translated by Dharmaru*k*i, of the Northern Wêi dynasty, A. D. 386–534. 2 fasciculi.

This is an earlier translation of No. 56. *K*'-yuen-lu, fasc. 3, fol. 2 a.

246　深密解脫經

Shan-mi-*k*iê-tho-*k*iń.
'Sûtra on the deliverance of deep secret.'

Sandhinirmo*k*ana-sûtra.

K'-yuen-lu, fasc. 2, fol. 23 b; Conc. 90; A. R., p. 431; A. M. G., p. 236; Wassiljew, 152. Translated by Bodhiru*k*i, of the Northern Wêi dynasty, A. D. 386–534. 5 fasciculi; 11 chapters.

247　解深密經

*K*iê-shan-mi-*k*iń.
'Sûtra on delivering deep secret.'

Sandhinirmo*k*ana-sûtra.

Conc. 275. Translated by Hhüen-*k*wâń (Hiouen-thsang), A. D. 645, of the Thâń dynasty, A. D. 618–907. 5 fasciculi; 8 chapters.

The above two works are similar translations, and they agree with Tibetan. *K*'-yuen-lu, s. v. Chapter 2 in No. 247 is divided into four chapters in No. 246. *K*'-tsiń, fasc. 6, fol. 12 b.

248　佛說諫王經

Fo-shwo-*k*ien-wâń-*k*iń.
'Sûtra spoken by Buddha on remonstrating with the King.'

Râ*g*âvavâdaka.

A. R., p. 459; A. M. G., p. 263. Translated by Tsü-*k*hü *K*iń-shań, of the earlier Suń dynasty, A. D. 420–479. 4 leaves.

249　如來示教勝軍王經

Zu-lâi-sh'-*k*iâo-shań-*k*iün-wâń-*k*iń.
'Sûtra of the Tathâgata's instruction to the King Prasenagit.'

Râ*g*âvavâdaka.

A. R., p. 459; A. M. G., p. 263. Translated by Hhüen-*k*wâń (Hiouep-thsang), A. D. 649, of the Thâń dynasty, A. D. 618–907. 8 leaves.

250　佛爲勝光天子說王法經

Fo-wêi-shań-kwâń-thien-tsz'-shwo-wâń-fâ-*k*iń.
'Sûtra of the law of the King spoken by Buddha for the sake of the Devaputra *G*inaprabha (?).'

Râ*g*âvavâdaka.

A. R., p. 459; A. M. G., p. 263. Translated by I-tsiń, A. D. 705, of the Thâń dynasty, A. D. 618–907. 7 leaves.

The above three works are similar translations, and they are wanting in Tibetan. *K*'-yuen-lu, fasc. 3, fol. 12 a.

251 寶積三昧文殊師利菩薩問法身經

Pâo-tsi-sân-mêi-wan-shu-sh'-li-phu-sâ-wan-fâ-shan-*k*iṅ.

'Sûtra on the Ratnakûṭa-samâdhi and Dharmakâya, asked by the Bodhisattva Mañgusrî.'

Ratnakûṭa-sûtra.

K'-yuen-lu, fasc. 3, fol. 9 a; Conc. 417. Translated by Ân Shi-kâo, of the Eastern Hân dynasty, A. D. 25–220. 7 leaves. This is an earlier translation of No. 51. *K'*-yuen-lu, s. v.

252 佛説濟諸方等學經

Fo-shwo-tsi-*k*u-fâṅ-taṅ-hhio-*k*iṅ.

'Buddhabhâshita-sarvavaipulyavidyâsiddha-sûtra.'

Translated by *K*u Fâ-hu (Dharmaraksha), of the Western Tsin dynasty, A. D. 265–316. 1 fasciculus.

253 大乘方廣總持經

Tâ-shaṅ-fâṅ-kwâṅ-tsuṅ-*k*h'-*k*iṅ.

'Mahâyânavaipulyadhâranî-sûtra.'

Translated by Vinîtaru*k*i, A. D. 582, of the Sui dynasty, A. D. 589 (or 581)–618. 1 fasciculus.

The above two works are similar translations, and they are wanting in Tibetan. *K'*-yuen-lu, fasc. 2, fol. 23 a.

254 太子須大拏經

Thâi-taz'-su-tâ-nâ-*k*iṅ.

'Sûtra of the Crown-Prince Sadâna.'

Translated by Shaṅ-*k*ien, of the Western Tshin dynasty, A. D. 385–431. 1 fasciculus. This is a later translation of a part of fasc. 2 of No. 143, being a *G*âtaka concerning the Dâna-pâramitâ. *K'*-yuen-lu, fasc. 3, fol. 4 b. It is the Vessantara *G*âtaka fully told. Fâ-pâo-piâo-mu, fasc. 3, fol. 24 a; Beal, Catalogue, p. 26.

255 佛説如來智印經

Fo-shwo-*z*u-lâi-*k*'-yin-*k*iṅ.

'Buddhabhâshita-tathâgata*g*ñânamudrâ-sûtra.'

Tathâgata*g*ñânamudrâ.

K'-yuen-lu, fasc. 2, fol. 26 b.

Tathâgata*g*ñânamudrâ-samâdhi-sûtra.

A. R., p. 444; A. M. G., p. 249; Conc. 252. Translated under the earlier Suṅ dynasty, A. D. 420–479; but the translator's name is lost. 1 fasciculus.

256 佛説慧印三昧經

Fo-shwo-hwui-yin-san-mêi-*k*iṅ.

'Buddhabhâshita-*g*ñânamudrâ-samâdhi-sûtra.'

Tathâgata*g*ñânamudrâ.

K'-yuen-lu, fasc. 2, fol. 26 b.

Tathâgata*g*ñânamudrâ-samâdhi-sûtra.

A. R., p. 444; A. M. G., p. 249; Conc. 209. Translated by *K'* *Kh*ien, of the Wu dynasty, A. D. 222–280. 1 fasciculus.

The above two works are similar translations, and they agree with Tibetan. *K'*-yuen-lu, s. v.

257 佛説無極寶三昧經

Fo-shwo-wu-*k*i-pâo-sân-mêi-*k*iṅ.

'Buddhabhâshita-anantaratna-samâdhi-sûtra.'

Translated by *K*u Fâ-hu (Dharmaraksha), A. D. 307, of the Western Tsin dynasty, A. D. 265–316. 2 fasciculi.

258 寶如來三昧經

Pâo-*z*u-lâi-sân-mêi-*k*iṅ.

'Ratnatathâgata-samâdhi-sûtra.'

Translated by Gîtamitra, of the Eastern Tsin dynasty, A. D. 317–420. 2 fasciculi.

The above two works are similar translations, and they are wanting in Tibetan. *K'*-yuen-lu, fasc. 2, fol. 26 b.

259 無上依經

Wu-shâṅ-i-*k*iṅ.

'Sûtra of the highest reliance.'

Translated by Paramârtha, A. D. 557, of the Liâṅ dynasty, A. D. 502–557. 2 fasciculi; 7 chapters.

260 佛説未曾有經

Fo-shwo-wêi-tshaṅ-yiu-*k*iṅ.

'Sûtra spoken by Buddha on wonderfulness.'

Adbhuta-dharmaparyâya.

A. R., p. 476; A. M. G., p. 279. Translated under the Eastern Hân dynasty, A. D. 25–220; but the translator's name is lost. 4 leaves.

261 佛説甚希有經

Fo-shwo-shan-hhi-yiu-*k*iṅ.

'Sûtra spoken by Buddha on the extreme rareness.'

Adbhuta-dharmaparyâya.

Translated by Hhüen-*k*wâṅ (Hiouen-thsang), A. D. 649, of the Thâṅ dynasty, A. D. 618–907. 6 leaves.

The above two works are similar translations of the first and seventh chapters of No. 259, and they agree with Tibetan. *K'*-yuen-lu, fasc. 3, fol. 8 b; *K'*-tsiṅ, fasc. 10, fol. 7 b.

262 佛説如來師子吼經

Fo-shwo-*z*u-lâi-sh'-taz'-heu-*k*iṅ.

'Buddhabhâshita-tathâgatasiṁhanâda-sûtra.'

Simhanâdika-sûtra.

K'-yuen-lu, fasc. 3, fol. 9 a; Conc. 251; A. R., p. 456; A. M. G., p. 261. Translated by Buddhasânta, A. D. 524, of the Northern Wêi dynasty, A. D. 386–534. 6 leaves.

263 佛說大方廣師子吼經

Fo-shwo-tâ-fâṅ-kwâṅ-sh'-tsz'-heu-*k*iṅ.

'Buddhabhâshita-mahâvaipulya-simhanâda-sûtra.'

Si*m*hanâdika-sûtra.

Conc. 604. Translated by Divâkara, A. D. 680, of the Thâṅ dynasty, A. D. 618–907. 6 leaves.

The above two works are similar translations, and they agree with Tibetan. *K'*-yuen-lu, fasc. 3, fol. 9 b.

264 佛說大乘百福相經

Fo-shwo-tâ-shaṅ-pâi-fu-siâṅ-*k*iṅ.

'Sûtra of the Mahâyâna spoken by Buddha on the hundred prosperous marks.'

Mañ*g*usrî-pariprikkhâ.

K'-yuen-lu, fasc. 3, fol. 9 b; Conc. 581. Translated by Divâkara, A. D. 683, of the Thâṅ dynasty, A. D. 618–907. 8 leaves.

265 佛說大乘百福莊嚴相經

Fo-shwo-tâ-shaṅ-pâi-fu-*k*wâṅ-yen-siâṅ-*k*iṅ.

'Sûtra of the Mahâyâna spoken by Buddha on the hundred prosperous marks of adornment.'

Mañ*g*usrî-pariprikkhâ.

Conc. 582. Translated by Divâkara, of the Thâṅ dynasty, A. D. 618–907. 9 leaves.

The above two works are similar translations, and they agree with Tibetan. *K'*-yuen-lu, fasc. 3, fol. 9 b.

266 佛說大乘四法經

Fo-shwo-tâ-shaṅ-sz'-fâ-*k*iṅ.

'Buddhabhâshita-mahâyâna-*k*aturdharma-sûtra.'

*K*atushka-nirhâra-sûtra.

K'-yuen-lu, fasc. 3, fol. 10 a; Conc. 588; A. R., p. 465; A. M. G., p. 268. Translated by Divâkara, A. D. 680, of the Thâṅ dynasty, A. D. 618–907. 2 leaves.

267 佛說菩薩修行四法經

Fo-shwo-phu-sâ-siu-hhiṅ-sz'-fâ-*k*iṅ.

'Buddhabhâshita-bodhisattva-*k*aryâ-*k*aturdharma-sûtra.'

*K*atushka-nirhâra-sûtra.

Translated by Divâkara, A. D. 681, of the Thâṅ dynasty, A. D. 618–907. 1 leaf.

The above two works are similar translations, and they agree with Tibetan. *K'*-yuen-lu, fasc. 3, fol. 10 a.

268 佛說希有校量功德經

Fo-shwo-hhi-yiu-*k*iâo-liâṅ-kuṅ-töh-*k*iṅ.

'Sûtra spoken by Buddha on the good qualities of rare comparison or measure.'

Translated by *G*ñânagupta, A. D. 586, of the Sui dynasty, A. D. 589 (or 581)–618. 7 leaves.

269 佛說最無比經

Fo-shwo-tsui-wu-pi-*k*iṅ.

'Sûtra spoken by Buddha on the greatest incomparableness.'

Translated by Hhüen-*k*wâṅ (Hiouen-thsang), A. D. 649, of the Thâṅ dynasty, A. D. 618–907. 10 leaves.

The above two works are similar translations, and they are wanting in Tibetan. *K'*-yuen-lu, fasc. 3, fol. 10 b.

270 佛說前世三轉經

Fo-shwo-tshien-shi-sân-*k*wâṅ-*k*iṅ.

'Sûtra spoken by Buddha on three changes of his former births.'

Translated by Fâ-*k*ü, of the Western Tsin dynasty, A. D. 265–316. 8 leaves. This Sûtra contains three *G*âtakas, namely:—1. The Bodhisattva was once a woman of excellent (or silver) colour; and having cut off her breasts she saved one who was just going to eat his own child. 2. The Bodhisattva was once a king, and governed his country according to the right law, giving his body as charity to birds and beasts. 3. He was once the son of a Brâhma*n*a; and by fasting he asked to be allowed to become an ascetic. Throwing away his body he saved a hungry tigress.

271 佛說銀色女經

Fo-shwo-yin-seh-nü-*k*iṅ.

'Sûtra spoken by Buddha on the silver-coloured woman.'

Translated by Buddhasânta, A. D. 539, of the Eastern Wêi dynasty, A. D. 534–550. 8 leaves.

The above two works are similar translations, and they are wanting in Tibetan. *K'*-yuen-lu, fasc. 3, fol. 10 b.

272 佛說阿闍世王受決經

Fo-shwo-ö-shö-shi-wâṅ-sheu-*k*iê-*k*iṅ.

'Buddhabhâshita-a*g*âtasatru-râ*g*a-vyâkara*n*a-sûtra.'

Translated by Fâ-*k*ü, of the Western Tsin dynasty, A. D. 265–316. 5 leaves.

273 採華違王上佛受決經

Tshâi-hwâ-wêi-wâṅ-shâṅ-fo-sheu-*k*iê-*k*iṅ.

'Sûtra of prophecy received (from Buddha) by one who offered a flower to Buddha, and did not follow the King (A*g*âtasatru).'

Translated by Thân-wu-lân (Dharmaraksha?), of the Eastern Tsin dynasty, A. D. 317–420. 3 leaves.

The above two works are similar translations, and they agree with Tibetan. K'-yuen-lu, fasc. 3, fol. 11 a. But No. 272 is incomplete.

274 佛說正恭敬經
Fo-shwo-kan-kun-kin-kin.
'Sûtra spoken by Buddha on the right respectfulness.'

Translated by Buddhasânta, A.D. 539, of the Eastern Wêi dynasty, A.D. 534–550. 6 leaves.

275 佛說善恭敬經
Fo-shwo-shân-kun-kin-kin.
'Sûtra spoken by Buddha on the good respectfulness.'

Translated by Gñânagupta, A.D. 586, of the Sui dynasty, A.D. 589 (or 581)–618. 8 leaves.

The above two works are similar translations, and they are wanting in Tibetan. K'-yuen-lu, fasc. 3, fol. 11 a.

276 稱讚大乘功德經
Khân-tsân-tâ-shan-kun-töh-kin.
'Sûtra of the praise of the good qualities of the Mahâyâna.'

Translated by Hhüen-kwân (Hiouen-thsang), A.D. 654, of the Thân dynasty, A.D. 618–907. 5 leaves.

277 妙法決定業障經
Miâo-fâ-kiê-tin-yeh-kân-kin.
'Sûtra of the good law which determines the obstacle of Karma.'

Translated by K'-yen, A.D. 721, of the Thân dynasty, A.D. 618–907. 4 leaves.

The above two works are similar translations, but the comparison with Tibetan is not given in K'-yuen-lu, fasc. 3, fol. 11 b.

278 佛說貝多樹下思惟十二因緣經
Fo-shwo-pei-to-shu-hhiâ-sz'-wêi-shi-'rh-yin-yuen-kin.
'Sûtra spoken by Buddha on the twelve causes (Nidânas) discovered under the Tâla tree.'
Pratîtyasamutpâda-sûtra (?).

Cf. A.R., p. 457; A.M.G., pp. 261, 534. Translated by K' Khien, of the Wu dynasty, A.D. 222–280. 5 leaves.

279 佛說緣起聖道經
Fo-shwo-yuen-khi-shan-tâo-kin.
'Buddhabhâshita-nidânâryamârga-sûtra.'
Pratîtyasamutpâda-sûtra (?).

Translated by Hhüen-kwân (Hiouen-thsang), A.D. 649, of the Thân dynasty, A.D. 618–907. 5 leaves.

The above two works are similar translations, and they are wanting in Tibetan. There were four more similar translations, two of which dating from the Eastern Hân dynasty, A.D. 25–220; but they were lost already in A.D. 730. Khâi-yuen-lu, fasc. 14 a, fol. 20 a, b. K'-yuen-lu, fasc. 3, fol. 12 b.

280 佛說稻稈經
Fo-shwo-tâo-kân-kin.
'Sûtra spoken by Buddha on the paddy straw.'
Sâlisambhava-sûtra.

K'-yuen-lu, fasc. 3, fol. 12 b; Conc. 666; A.R., p. 457; A.M.G., p. 261. Translated under the Eastern Tsin dynasty, A.D. 317–420; but the translator's name is lost. 8 leaves.

281 佛說了本生死經
Fo-shwo-liâo-pan-shan-sz'-kin.
'Sûtra spoken by Buddha on understanding the origin of birth and death.'
Sâlisambhava-sûtra.

Conc. 323. Translated by K' Khien, of the Wu dynasty, A.D. 222–280. 6 leaves.

The above two works are similar translations, and they agree with Tibetan. There was another translation, but it was lost already in A.D. 730. Khâi-yuen-lu, fasc. 14 a, fol. 20 b; K'-yuen-lu, fasc. 3, fol. 13 a.

282 佛說自誓三昧經
Fo-shwo-tsz'-shi-sân-mêi-kin.
'Sûtra spoken by Buddha on the Samâdhi called Tsz'-shi or vow.' Cf. Fân-i-min-i-tsi, fasc. 11, fol. 2 a.

Translated by Ân Shi-kâo, of the Eastern Hân dynasty, A.D. 25–220. 9 leaves.

283 如來獨證自誓三昧經
Zu-lâi-tu-kan-tsz'-shi-sân-mêi-kin.
'Sûtra on the Samâdhi called Tsz'-shi or vow, realised by the Tathâgata alone.'

Translated by Ku Fâ-hu (Dharmaraksha), of the Western Tsin dynasty, A.D. 265–316. 8 leaves.

The above two works are similar translations, and they are wanting in Tibetan. There was another translation, but it was lost already in A.D. 730. Khâi-yuen-lu, fasc. 14 a, fol. 20 b; K'-yuen-lu, fasc. 3, fol. 13 a.

284 佛說轉有經
Fo-shwo-kwân-yiu-kiṅ.
'Sûtra spoken by Buddha on transmigration.'
Bhavasaṅkrâmita (?).
A. R., p. 460; A. M. G., p. 264. Translated by
Buddhasânta, A. D. 539, of the Eastern Wêi dynasty,
A. D. 534-550. 2 leaves.

285 大方等修多羅王經
Tâ-fâṅ-taṅ-siu-to-lo-wâṅ-kiṅ.
'Mahâvaipulya-sûtrarâga-sûtra.'
Bhavasaṅkrâmita (?).
Translated by Bodhiruki, of the Northern Wêi
dynasty, A. D. 386-534. 3 leaves.
The above two works are similar translations, and
they are wanting in Tibetan. K'-yuen-lu, fasc. 3, fol. 12 a.

286 佛說文殊師利巡行經
Fo-shwo-wan-shu-sh'-li-sün-hhiṅ-kiṅ.
'Sûtra spoken by Buddha on Mañgusrî's going round (to
examine the Bhikshus' rooms).'
Translated by Bochiruki, of the Northern Wêi
dynasty, A. D. 386-534. 7 leaves.

287 佛說文殊尸利行經
Fo-shwo-wan-shu-sh'-li-hhiṅ-kiṅ.
'Sûtra spoken by Buddha on Mañgusrî's going (round to
examine the Bhikshus' rooms).'
Translated by Gñâragupta, A. D. 586, of the Sui
dynasty, A. D. 589 (or 531)-618. 9 leaves.
The above two works are similar translations, and
they agree with Tibetan K'-yuen-lu, fasc. 3, fol. 12 b.

288 大乘造像功德經
Tâ-shaṅ-tsâo-siâṅ-kuṅ-töh-kiṅ.
'Sûtra of the Mahâyâna on the good qualities or virtue of
making the images (of Buddha).'
Tathâgata-pratibimba-pratishthânusamsâ.
A. R., p. 476; A. M. G., p. 279. Translated by
Devapragña, A. D. 691, of the Thâṅ dynasty, A. D. 618-
907. 2 fasciculi.

289 佛說作佛形像經
Fo-shwo-tso-fo-hhiṅ-siâṅ-kiṅ.
'Sûtra spoken by Buddha on making Buddha's images.'
Tathâgata-pratibimba-pratishthânusamsâ.
A. R., p. 476; A. M. G., p. 279. Translated under
the Eastern Hâu dynasty A. D. 25-220. 3 leaves.

290 佛說造立形像福報經
Fo-shwo-tsâo-li-hhiṅ-siâṅ-fu-pâo-kiṅ.
'Sûtra spoken by Buddha on the happy reward of making or
setting up (Buddha's) images.'
Tathâgata-pratibimba-pratishthânusamsâ.
Translated under the Eastern Tsin dynasty, A. D.
317-420. 5 leaves.
The above two works are similar translations, and
they agree with Tibetan. K'-yuen-lu, fasc. 3, fol. 13 b.
They are perhaps earlier translations of a part of
No. 288.

291 佛說灌佛經
Fo-shwo-kwân-fo-kiṅ.
'Sûtra spoken by Buddha on sprinkling (water on the images
of) Buddha.'
Translated by Fâ-kü, of the Western Tsin dynasty,
A. D. 265-316. 2 leaves.

292 佛說灌洗佛經
Fo-shwo-kwân-si-fo-kiṅ.
'Sûtra spoken by Buddha on sprinkling (water on) and washing
(the images of) Buddha.'
Translated by Shaṅ-kien, of the Western Tshin
dynasty, A. D. 385-431. 4 leaves.
The above two works are similar translations, and
they are wanting in Tibetan. K'-yuen-lu, fasc. 3, fol. 13 b.

293 佛說浴像功德經
Fo-shwo-yü-siâṅ-kuṅ-töh-kiṅ.
'Sûtra spoken by Buddha on the good qualities of washing the
images (of Buddha).'
Translated by Ratnakinta, A. D. 705, of the Thâṅ
dynasty, A. D. 618-907. 4 leaves.

294 浴像功德經
Yü-siâṅ-kuṅ-töh-kiṅ.
'Sûtra on the good qualities of washing the images (of Buddha).'
Translated by I-tsiṅ, A. D. 710, of the Thâṅ dynasty,
A. D. 618-907. 5 leaves.
The above two works are similar translations, and
they are wanting in Tibetan. K'-yuen-lu, fasc. 3, fol. 15 a.

295 佛說校量數珠功德經
Fo-shwo-kiâo-liâṅ-shu-ku-kuṅ-töh-kiṅ.
'Sûtra spoken by Buddha on counting the good qualities of a
rosary.'
Translated by Ratnakinta, A. D. 705, of the Thâṅ
dynasty, A. D. 618-907. 2 leaves.

296 曼殊室利咒藏中校量數珠功德經

Mân-shu-shih-li-*kh*eu-tsâṅ-*k*un-*k*iâo-liâṅ-shu-*k*u-kuṅ-töh-*k*iṅ.

'Sûtra on counting the good qualities of a rosary in the Mañgusrî-dhâranî-piṭaka.'

Translated by I-tsiṅ, A.D. 703, of the Thâṅ dynasty, A.D. 618–907. 2 leaves.

The above two works are similar translations, and they agree with Tibetan. *K*'-yuen-lu, fasc. 3, fol. 15 a.

297 佛說龍施女經

Fo-shwo-luṅ-sh'-nü-*k*iṅ.

'Sûtra spoken by Buddha on the girl Nâgadattâ.'

Translated by *K*' *Kh*ien, of the Wu dynasty, A.D. 222–280. 3 leaves.

298 佛說龍施菩薩本起經

Fo-shwo-luṅ-sh'-phu-sâ-pan-*kh*i-*k*iṅ.

'Sûtra spoken by Buddha on the Gâtaka of the Bodhisattva Nâgadattâ.'

Translated by *K*u Fâ-hu (Dharmaraksha), of the Western Tsin dynasty, A.D. 265–316. 5 leaves.

The above two works are similar translations, and they are wanting in Tibetan. *K*'-yuen-lu, fasc. 3, fol. 14 a.

299 佛說八吉祥神咒經

Fo-shwo-pâ-*k*i-siâṅ-shan-*kh*eu-*k*iṅ.

'Sûtra spoken by Buddha on the eight lucky and spiritual Mantras or Dhâranîs.'

Ash*t*abuddhaka.

A. R., p. 469; A. M. G., p. 272. Translated by *K*' *Kh*ien, of the Wu dynasty, A.D. 222–280. 4 leaves.

300 佛說八陽神咒經

Fo-shwo-pâ-yâṅ-shan-*kh*eu-*k*iṅ.

'Sûtra spoken by Buddha on the eight pure and spiritual Mantras or Dhâranîs.'

Ash*t*abuddhaka.

Translated by *K*u Fâ-hu (Dharmaraksha), of the Western Tsin dynasty, A.D. 265–316. 3 leaves.

301 佛說八吉祥經

Fo-shwo-pâ-*k*i-siâṅ-*k*iṅ.

'Sûtra spoken by Buddha on the eight lucky (Mantras).'

Ash*t*abuddhaka.

Translated by Saṅghapâla, of the Liâṅ dynasty, A.D. 502–557. 3 leaves.

302 佛說八佛名號經

Fo-shwo-pâ-fo-miṅ-hâo-*k*iṅ.

'Sûtra spoken by Buddha on the names of eight Buddhas (of the eastern quarter).'

Ash*t*abuddhaka.

Translated by *G*ñânagupta, A.D. 586, of the Sui dynasty, A.D. 589 (or 581)–618. 5 leaves.

The above four works are similar translations, and they agree with Tibetan. There was still another translation, but it was lost already in A.D. 730. Khâi-yuen-lu, fasc. 14 a, fol. 21 a; *K*'-yuen-lu, fasc. 3, fol. 14 b. No. 301 omits the question asked by *S*âriputra.

303 佛說盂蘭盆經

Fo-shwo-yü-lân-phan-*k*iṅ

'Sûtra spoken by Buddha on (offering) the vessel (of eatables to Buddha and Saṅgha for the benefit of Pretas) being in suspense.'

Translated by *K*u Fâ-hu (Dharmaraksha), of the Western Tsin dynasty, A.D. 265–316. 2 leaves. This Sûtra was addressed to Maudgalyâyana, when he asked Buddha for the way of saving his unfortunate mother, whose state of being a Preta had been perceived by her son. The phrase 盂蘭 yü-lân in the Chinese title is generally understood as a transliteration of Ullambana, and translated by 倒懸 tâo-hhüen, 'to hang upside down,' or 'to be in suspense.' At the same time the character 盆 phan, 'vessel,' is explained as not being a part of the transliteration. But this character may have been used here by the translator in both ways. On the one hand, it may stand for the last two syllables of Ullambana; on the other, it may mean the 'vessel' of eatables to be offered to Buddha and Saṅgha for the benefit of those being in the Ullambana. See, however, Fâṅ-i-miṅ-i-tsi, fasc. 9, fol. 17 b, where a fuller and more correct transliteration is quoted, viz. 烏藍婆拏 wu-lan-pho-na, i. e. Ullambana. Cf. Eitel, Handbook, p. 154 b seq.; Wells Williams, Chin. Dict., p. 232, col. 2; Edkins, Chinese Buddhism, pp. 126, 210, 268.

304 佛說報恩奉盆經

Fo-shwo-pâo-an-faṅ-phan-*k*iṅ.

'Sûtra spoken by Buddha on offering the vessel (of eatables to Buddha and Saṅgha) for recompensing the favour (of the parents).'

Translated under the Eastern Tsin dynasty, A.D. 317–420. 1 leaf.

The above two works are similar translations, and they are wanting in Tibetan. *K*'-yuen-lu, fasc. 3, fol. 14 b.

305 佛說觀藥王藥上二菩薩經

Fo-shwo-kwân-yâo-wâṅ-yâo-shâṅ-'rh-phu-sâ-*k*iṅ.

'Sûtra spoken by Buddha about the meditation on the two Bodhisattvas, Bhaishagyarâ*g*a and Bhaishagyasamudgata.'

Bhaisha*g*yarâ*g*a-bhaisha*g*yasamudgati (or -gata)-sûtra.

K'-yuen-lu, fasc. 3, fol. 19 a; Conc. 312. Translated by Kâlayasas, A. D. 424, of the earlier Suṅ dynasty, A. D. 420–479. 1 fasciculus. It agrees with Tibetan. There was an earlier translation, but it was lost already in A. D. 730. Khâi-yuen-lu, fasc. 14 b, fol. 3 a; *K*'-yuen-lu, fasc. 3, fol. 19 a, b.

306 佛說大孔雀咒王經

Fo-shwo-tâ-khuṅ-tshioh-*kh*eu-wâṅ-*k*iṅ.

'Buddhabhâshita-mahâmayûrî-mantrarâ*g*a-sûtra.'

Mahâmayûrî-vidyârâ*g*ñî.

K'-yuen-lu, fasc. 4, fol. 21 b; Conc. 631, where 'dhâranî' is added to the title; A. R., p. 516; A. M. G., p. 316. Translated by I-tsiṅ, A. D. 705, of the Thâṅ dynasty, A. D. 618–907. 3 fasciculi. For the Sanskrit text, see Catalogue of the Hodgson Manuscripts, VII. 45, where it is called Mahâmâyûrî.

307 佛母大孔雀明王經

Fo-mu-tâ-khuṅ-tshioh-miṅ-wâṅ-*k*iṅ.

'Buddhamâtrikâ-mahâmayûrî-vidyârâ*g*ñî-sûtra.'

Mahâmayûrî-vidyârâ*g*ñî.

Translated by Amoghava*g*ra, of the Thâṅ dynasty, A. D. 618–907. 3 fasciculi.

308 佛說孔雀王咒經

Fo-shwo-khuṅ-tshioh-wâṅ-*kh*eu-*k*iṅ.

'Buddhabhâshita-mahâmayûrî-râ*g*ñî-mantra-sûtra.'

Mahâmayûrî-vidyârâ*g*ñî.

Translated by Saṅghapâla, of the Liâṅ dynasty, A. D. 502–557. 2 fasciculi

309 佛說大孔雀王神咒經

Fo-shwo-tâ-khuṅ-tshioh-wâṅ-shan-*kh*eu-*k*iṅ.

'Buddhabhâshita-mahâmayûrî-ra*g*ñy-ridhimantra-sûtra.'

Mahâmayûrî-vidyârâ*g*ñî.

Translated by Poh *S*rîmitra, of the Eastern Tsin dynasty, A. D. 317–420. 7 leaves.

310 佛說大孔雀王雜神咒經

Fo-shwo-tâ-khuṅ-tshioh-wâṅ-tsâ-shan-*kh*eu-*k*iṅ.

'Buddhabhâshita-mahâmayûrî-râ*g*ñî-samyuktarddhidhâranî-sûtra.'

Translated by Poh *S*rîmitra, of the Eastern Tsin dynasty, A. D. 317–420. 13 leaves.

311 大金色孔雀王咒經

Tâ-*k*in-seh-khuṅ-tshioh-wâṅ-*kh*eu-*k*iṅ.

'Mahâsuvarnavarna-mayûrî-râ*g*ñî-dhâranî-sûtra.'

Mahâmayûrî-vidyârâ*g*ñî.

Conc. 628. Translated by Kumâra*g*îva, of the Latter Tshin dynasty, A. D. 384–417. 13 leaves.

The above six works are similar translations (complete and incomplete), and they agree with Tibetan. There were three earlier translations made under the Eastern Tsin dynasty, A. D. 317–420, but they were lost already in A. D. 730. Khâi-yuen-lu, fasc. 14 a, fol. 21 b; *K*'-yuen-lu, fasc. 4, fol. 22 b. According to the *K*'-yuen-lu, the Chinese Tripi*t*aka, collected under the Yuen dynasty, A. D. 1280–1368, seems to have had an interesting work[1], namely, 唐梵相對孔雀經 Thâṅ-fân-siâṅ-tui-khuṅ-tshioh-*k*iṅ, i. e. 'the peacock (or rather peahen) sûtra in Sanskrit and Chinese facing each other, or in parallel columns.' Translated by Amoghava*g*ra, of the Thâṅ dynasty, A. D. 618–907. 3 fasciculi. This translation may have been the same as No. 307.

312 佛說不空羂索咒經

Fo-shwo-pu-khuṅ-*k*üen-soh-*kh*eu-*k*iṅ.

'Buddhabhâshita-amoghapâsa-mantra-sûtra.'

Amoghapâsahridaya.

A. R., p. 535; A. M. G., p. 333.

Amoghapâsa-dhâranî.

Conc. 467. Translated by *G*ñânagupta and others, A. D. 587, of the Sui dynasty, A. D. 589 (or 581)–618. 1 fasciculus.

313 不空羂索心咒王經

Pu-khuṅ-*k*üen-soh-sin-*kh*eu-wâṅ-*k*iṅ.

'Amoghapâsa-hridaya-mantrarâ*g*a-sûtra.'

Translated by Ratna*k*inta, A. D. 693, of the Thâṅ dynasty, A. D. 618–907. 3 fasciculi.

314 不空羂索陀羅尼經

Pu-khuṅ-*k*üen-soh-tho-lo-ni-*k*iṅ.

'Amoghapâsa-dhâranî-sûtra.'

---

[1] There exists in Japan one copy of nearly the whole collection of the Yuen dynasty; so that this work may still be found there, and added to the new Japanese edition of the Buddhist Canon, now in course of publication in Tokio.

Cf. Conc. 469. Translated by Li Wu-thâo, A. D. 700, of the Thân dynasty, A. D. 618–907. 2 fasciculi; 17 chapters. According to the note at the end, the last chapter was translated by a Chinese priest named Hwui-zih, together with an Indian, *S*rîmat by name.

The above two works are similar translations. *K'*-yuen-lu, fasc. 4, fol. 19 b. These may be compared with the Tibetan version of the Amoghapâsa-pâramitâ-shat-paripurâya(?)-dhâranî. A. R., p. 532; A. M. G., p. 330.

315 不空羂索咒心經

Pu-khun-*k*üen-soh-*kh*eu-sin-*k*in.

Amoghapâsa-h*ri*daya-sûtra.

See No. 312. Translated by Bodhiru*k*i, of the Thân dynasty, A. D. 618–907. 1 fasciculus.

316 不空羂索神咒心經

Pu-khun-*k*üen-soh-shan-*kh*eu-sin-*k*in.

'Amoghapâsarddhimantra-h*ri*daya-sûtra.'

Amoghapâsa-h*ri*daya. See Nos. 312, 315.

Amoghapâsa-dhâranî.

Conc. 468. Translated by Hhüen-*k*wân (Hiouen-thsang), A. D. 659, of the Thân dynasty, A. D. 618–907. 1 fasciculus.

The above two works, together with No. 312, are similar translations of the first chapter of No. 317. *K'*-yuen-lu, fasc. 4, fol. 19 a.

317 不空羂索神變眞言經

Pu-khun-*k*üen-soh-shan-pien-*k*an-yen-*k*in.

'Amoghapâsarddhivik*ri*ti-mantra-sûtra.'

Amoghapâsa-kalparâ*g*a.

K'-yuen-lu, fasc. 4, fol. 18 b; A. R., p. 537; A. M. G., p. 335.

Amoghapâsa-dhâranî.

Conc. 466. Translated by Bodhiru*k*i, A. D. 707–709, of the Thân dynasty, A. D. 618–907. 30 fasciculi; 78 chapters. It agrees with Tibetan. *K'*-yuen-lu, s. v.

318 千眼千臂觀世音菩薩陀羅尼神咒經

Tshien-yen-tshien-phi-kwân-shi-yin-phu-sâ-tho-lo-ni-shan-*kh*eu-*k*in.

'Sahasrâksha-sahasrabâhv-avalokitesvara-bodhisattva-dhâranyriddhi-mantra-sûtra.'

Nîlaka*nth*a.

K'-yuen-lu, fasc. 4, fol. 19 b; Conc. 773. Translated by *K'*-thun, A. D. 627–649, of the Thân dynasty, A. D. 618–907. 2 fasciculi.

319 千手千眼觀世音菩薩姥陀羅尼身經

Tshien-sheu-tshien-yen-kwân-shi-yin-phu-sâ-mu-tho-lo-ni-shan-*k*in.

'Sahasrabâhu-sahasrâksha-avalokitesvara-bodhisattva-v*ri*ddhâ-(or 'old woman') dhâranî-kâya-sûtra.'

Nîlaka*nth*a.

Conc. 770. Translated by Bodhiru*k*i, A. D. 709, of the Thân dynasty, A. D. 618–907. 1 fasciculus.

The above two works are similar translations, and they agree with Tibetan. *K'*-yuen-lu, fasc. 4, fol. 19 b. These or No. 320 may be compared with a Tibetan work, having no Sanskrit title, explained as follows: 'The minute rituals and ceremonies of Avalokitesvara, who has a thousand hands, and as many eyes.' A. R., p. 532; A. M. G., p. 330.

320 千手千眼觀世音菩薩廣大圓滿無礙大悲心陀羅尼經

Tshien-sheu-tshien-yen-kwân-shi-yin-phu-sâ-kwân-tâ-yuen-mân-wu-nâi-tâ-pêi-sin-tho-lo-ni-*k*in.

'Sahasrabâhu-sahasrâksha-avalokitesvara-bodhisattva-mahâpûrnâpratihata-mahâkâru*n*ikah*ri*daya-dhâranî-sûtra.'

Translated by *K*iâ-fân-tâ-mo (Bhagavaddharma?), of the Thân dynasty, A. D. 618–907. 1 fasciculus. At the end, there is added a transliteration of the 大悲咒 Tâ-pêi-*kh*eu, or the 'Mahâkâru*n*ika-mantra (or -dhâranî).' 4 leaves. A preface is added by the Emperor *Kh*ân-tsu, of the Min dynasty, dated A. D. 1411. According to the *K'*-yuen-lu (fasc. 4, fol. 20 a), there was a later translation of this Sûtra, and they both agree with Tibetan. But the later translation, made by Amoghavagra, is not found in this collection. No. 320 has been a very popular work in China, since the later Sun dynasty, A. D. 960–1127. *K'*-tsin, fasc. 14, fol. 11 a seq. Cf. Edkins, Chinese Buddhism, p. 132; where, however, the work is mentioned, as if it were the later translation above mentioned.

321 觀世音菩薩秘密藏神咒經

Kwân-shi-yin-phu-sâ-pi-mi-tsân-shan-*kh*eu-*k*in.

'Avalokitesvara-bodhisattva-guhyagarbharddhimantra (or dhâranî)-sûtra.'

Padma*k*intâma*n*i-dhâra*n*î-sûtra.

Conc. 306. Translated by *S*ikshânanda, of the Thân dynasty, A. D. 618–907. 10 leaves; 6 chapters.

322 觀世音菩薩如意摩尼陀羅尼經

Kwân-shi-yin-phu-sâ-zu-i-mo-ni-tho-lo-ni-*k*in.

'Avalokitesvara-bodhisattva-*k*intâmani-dhâranî-sûtra.'

Padma*k*intâma*n*i-dhâra*n*î-sûtra.

Conc. 307. Translated by Ratna*k*inta, of the Thân dynasty, A.D. 618–907. 9 leaves.

323 觀自在菩薩如意心陀羅尼經

Kwân-tsz'-tsâi-phu-sâ-zu-i-sin-tho-lo-ni-*k*in.

'Avalokitesvara-bodhisattva-*k*intâhridaya (or -manas for mani?)-dhâranî-sûtra.'

Padma*k*intâma*n*i-dhâra*n*î-sûtra.

Conc. 310. Translated by I-tsin, A.D. 710, of the Thân dynasty, A.D. 618–907. 4 leaves.

324 如意輪陀羅尼經

*Z*u-i-lun-tho-lo-ni-*k*in.

'*K*inta*k*akra-dhâranî-sûtra.'

Padma*k*intâma*n*i-dhâra*n*î-sûtra.

K'-yuen-lu, fasc. 4, fol. 20 b. Cf. Conc. 247, where however another Sanskrit title is mentioned. Translated by Bodhiru*k*i, A.D. 709, of the Thân dynasty, A.D. 618–907. 1 fasciculus; 10 chapters.

The above four works are similar translations, and they agree with Tibetan. *K*'-yuen-lu, s. v.

325 觀自在菩薩怛嚩多唎隨心陀羅尼經

Kwân-tsz'-tsâi-phu-sâ-ta-fo-to-li-sui-sin-tho-lo-ni-*k*in.

'Avalokitesvara-bodhisattva-(saman) tabhadrânuhridaya (?)-dhâranî-sûtra.'

Translated by *K*'-thun, A.D. 653, of the Thân dynasty, A.D. 618–907. 1 fasciculus.

326 請觀世音菩薩消伏毒害陀羅尼咒經

Tshin-kwân-shi-yin-phu-sâ-siâo-fu-tu-hâi-tho-lo-ni-*k*heu-*k*in.

'Sûtra of the Dhâranî-mantra for asking the Bodhisattva Avalokitesvara to counteract the injury of a poison.'

Translated by *K*u Nandi, A.D. 420, of the Eastern Tsin dynasty, A.D. 317–420. 15 leaves. There was an earlier translation; but it was lost already in A.D. 730. Khâi-yuen-lu, fasc. 14 a, fol. 22 b; *K*'-yuen-lu, fasc. 5, fol. 3 b.

327 佛說十一面觀世音神咒經

Fo-shwo-shi-yi-mien-kwân-shi-yin-shan-*k*heu-*k*in.

'Buddhabhâshita-ekadasamukhâvalokitesvara-bodhisattvarddhi-mantra-sûtra.'

Avalokitesvaraikadasamukha-dhâranî.

A. R., p. 533; A. M. G., p. 330. Translated by Yasogupta, of the Northern *K*eu dynasty, A.D. 557–581. 13 leaves.

328 十一面神咒心經

Shi-yi-mien-shan-*k*heu-sin-*k*in.

'Ekadasamukharddhimantra-hridaya-sûtra.'

Avalokitesvaraikadasamukha-dhâranî.

Translated by Hhüen-*k*wân (Hiouen-thsang), A.D. 656, of the Thân dynasty, A.D. 618–907. 13 leaves.

The above two works are similar translations of a Sûtra in fasciculus 4 of No. 363; and they are wanting in Tibetan. *K*'-yuen-lu, fasc. 4, fol. 23 a seq.

329 千轉陀羅尼觀世音菩薩咒經

Tshien-*k*wân-tho-lo-ni-kwân-shi-yin-phu-sâ-kheu-*k*in.

'Sahasrapravartana-dhâranî-avalokitesvara-bodhisattva-mantra-sûtra.'

Translated by *K*'-thun, A.D. 653, of the Thân dynasty, A.D. 618–907. 5 leaves. This is a similar translation of a Mantra or Dhâranî, in No. 347, and in fasciculus 5 of No. 363; and it is wanting in Tibetan. *K*'-yuen-lu, fasc. 4, fol. 23 b seq.

330 咒五首經

*K*heu-wu-sheu-*k*in.

'Sûtra of five Mantras.'

Translated by Hhüen-*k*wân (Hiouen-thsang), A.D. 664, of the Thân dynasty, A.D. 618–907. 3 leaves. The first three of the five Mantras are similar to those of Nos. 329, 331, and 344, and the fifth is to that of No. 325; while the fourth seems to be a single translation or transliteration. Cf. *K*'-tsin, fasc. 14, fol. 30 b.

331 六字神咒經

Liu-tsz'-shan-*k*heu-*k*in.

'Shadaksharardhimantra-sûtra.'

Sha*d*aksharavidyâmantra.

A. R., p. 526; A. M. G., p. 325. Translated by Bodhiru*k*i, A.D. 693, of the Thân dynasty, A.D. 618–907. 4 leaves. This is a similar translation of a Mantra or

Dhâranî, in No. 347, and in fasciculus 6 of No. 363. It agrees with Tibetan. *K'*-yuen-lu, fasc. 4, fol. 23 b seq.

332 咒三首經

*Kh*eu-sân-sheu-*k*in.

'Sûtra of three Mantras.'

Translated by Divâkara, of the Thân dynasty, A. D. 618–907. 1 leaf. The first and third Mantras are similar to those in No. 363; while the second seems to be an independent translation or transliteration. Cf. *K'*-tsin, fasc. 14, fol. 30 a.

333 大方廣菩薩藏經中文殊師利根本一字陀羅尼法

Tâ-fân-kwân-phu-sâ-tsân-*k*in-*k*un-wan-shu-sh'-li-kan-pan-yi-tsz'-tho-lo-ni-fâ.

'Mañgusrî-mûlaikâkshara-dhâranî-dharma, in the Mahâvaipulya-bodhisattva-pitaka-sûtra.'

Translated by Ratna*k*inta, A. D. 702, of the Thân dynasty, A. D. 618–907. 5 leaves.

334 曼殊室利菩薩咒藏中一字咒王經

Mân-shu-shih-li-phu-sâ-*kh*eu-tsân-*k*un-yi-tsz'-*kh*eu-wân-*k*in.

'Ekâkshara-mantrarâga-sûtra, in the Mañgusrî-bodhisattva-mantra-pitaka.'

Translated by I-tsin, A. D. 703, of the Thân dynasty, A. D. 618–907. 5 leaves.

The above two works are similar translations, and they are wanting in Tibetan. *K'*-yuen-lu, fasc. 4, fol. 21 a.

335 十二佛名神咒校量功德除障滅罪經

Shi-'rh-fo-min-shan-*kh*eu-*k*iâo-liân-kun-töh-*kh*u-*k*an-mieh-tsui-*k*in.

'Sûtra of the spiritual Mantra of the names of twelve Buddhas, which recounts their good qualities, removes obstacles, and destroys sin.'

Dvâdasabuddhaka-sûtra.

K'-yuen-lu, fasc. 4, fol. 21 b; Conc. 67; A.R., p. 469; A. M. G., p. 273. Translated by *G*ñânagupta, A. D. 587, of the Sui dynasty, A. D. 589 (or 581)-618. 7 leaves.

336 佛說稱讚如來功德神咒經

Fo-shwo-*kh*ân-tsân-*z*u-lâi-kun-töh-shan-*kh*eu-*k*in.

'Buddhabhâshita-prasamsita-tathâgata-gunarddhi-mantra-sûtra.'

Dvâdasabuddhaka-sûtra. See No. 335.

Dvâdasabuddhaka-dhâranî.

Conc. 701. Translated by I-tsin, A. D. 711, of the Thân dynasty, A. D. 618–907. 5 leaves.

The above two works are similar translations, and they are wanting in Tibetan. *K'*-yuen-lu, fasc. 4, fol. 21 b. See, however, the last two authorities mentioned under the title of No. 335.

337 華積陀羅尼神咒經

Hwâ-tsi-tho-lo-ni-shan-*kh*eu-*k*in.

'Pushpakûta-dhârany-riddhimantra-sûtra.'

Pushpakû*t*a.

A. R., p. 526; A.M. G., p. 325. Translated by *K'* *Kh*ien, of the Wu dynasty, A. D. 222–280. 3 leaves.

338 師子奮迅菩薩所問經

Sh'-tsz'-fan-hhün-phu-sâ-su-wan-*k*in.

'Simharshabha (?)-bodhisattva-pariprikkhâ-sûtra.'

Pushpakûta.

See No. 337. Translated under the Eastern Tsin dynasty, A. D. 317–420; but the translator's name is lost. 4 leaves.

339 佛說華聚陀羅尼經

Fo-shwo-hwâ-tsü-tho-lo-ni-*k*in.

'Buddhabhâshita-pushpakûta-dhâranî-sûtra.'

Pushpakû*t*a.

See No. 337. Translated under the Eastern Tsin dynasty, A. D. 317–420; but the translator's name is lost. 3 leaves.

The above three works are similar translations, and they are wanting in Tibetan. *K'*-yuen-lu, fasc. 5, fol. 2 a. See, however, the authorities mentioned under the title of No. 337.

340 六字咒王經

Liu-tsz'-*kh*eu-wân-*k*in.

'Shadakshara-mantrarâga-sûtra.'

Sha*d*akshara-vidyâmantra.

A. R., p. 526; A. M. G., p. 325. Translated under the Eastern Tsin dynasty, A. D. 317–420; but the translator's name is lost. 7 leaves.

341 六字神咒王經
Liu-tsz'-shan-kheu-wâṅ-kiṅ.
'Shadaksharavidyâmantrarâga-sûtra.'
Shadakshara-vidyâmantra.

See No. 340. Translated under the Liâṅ dynasty, A.D. 502-557; but the translator's name is lost. 9 leaves.

The above two works are similar translations of No. 331, and they agree with Tibetan. K'-yuen-lu, fasc. 4, fol. 24 a.

342 梵女首意經
Fân-nü-sheu-i-kiṅ.
'Brâhmanî-srîmatî-sûtra.'
Srîmatî-brâhmanî-pariprikkhâ.

A. R., p. 450; A. M. G., p. 255. Translated by Ku Fâ-hu (Dharmaraksha), of the Western Tsin dynasty, A.D. 265-316. 7 leaves.

343 有德女所問大乘經
Yiu-töh-nü-su-wan-tâ-shaṅ-kiṅ.
'Srîmatî-strî-pariprikkhâ-mahâyâna-sûtra.'
Srîmatî-brâhmanî-pariprikkhâ.

See No. 342. Translated by Bodhiruki, A.D. 693, of the Thâṅ dynasty, A.D. 618-907. 5 leaves. This work is mentioned in Wassiljew's Buddhismus, 175.

The above two works are similar translations, and they agree with Tibetan. Cf. K'-yuen-lu, fasc. 4, fol. 4 b; K'-tsiṅ, fasc. 8, fol. 17 a seq.

344 佛說七俱胝佛母心大準提陀羅尼經
Fo-shwo-tshi-kü-k'-fo-mu-sin-tâ-kun-thi-tho-lo-ni-kiṅ.
'Buddhabhâshita-saptakoṭibuddhamâtrika-hridaya-mahâkundî-dhâranî-sûtra.'
Kundî-devî-dhâranî.

A. R., p. 518; A. M. G., p. 318. Translated by Divâkara, A.D. 685, of the Thâṅ dynasty, A.D. 618-907. 4 leaves.

345 佛說七俱胝佛母準提大明陀羅尼經
Fo-shwo-tshi-kü-k'-fo-mu-kun-thi-tâ-miṅ-tho-lo-ni-kiṅ.
'Buddhabhâshita-saptakoṭibuddhamâtrika-kundî-mahâvidyâ-dhâranî-sûtra.'
Kundî-devî-dhâranî.

See No. 344. Translated by Vagrabodhi, A.D. 723, of the Thâṅ dynasty, A.D. 618-907. 1 fasciculus.

346 七俱胝佛母所說準提陀羅尼經
Tshi-kü-k'-fo-mu-su-shwo-kun-thi-tho-lo-ni-kiṅ.
'Saptakoṭibuddhamâtrika-bhâshita-kundî-dhâranî-sûtra.'
Kundî-devî-dhâranî.

See No. 344. Translated by Amoghavagra, of the Thâṅ dynasty, A.D. 618-907. 1 fasciculus.

The above three works are similar translations, and they agree with Tibetan. K'-yuen-lu, fasc. 4, fol. 24 b. Nos. 345 and 346 have an additional part called the 'law of the practice of meditation.'

347 種種雜咒經
Kuṅ-kuṅ-tsâ-kheu-kiṅ.
'Nânâ-samyuktamantra-sûtra.'

Translated by Gñânagupta, of the Sui dynasty, A.D. 618-907. 11 leaves. It contains twenty-three Mantras or Dhâranîs, of which the fifteenth is similar to that of No. 329, the twentieth to that of Nos. 344-346, and the twenty-second to that of Nos. 331, 340, 341. Cf. K'-yuen-lu, fasc. 4, fol. 25 a; K'-tsiṅ, fasc. 14, fol. 30 b seq.

348 佛頂尊勝陀羅尼經
Fo-tiṅ-tsun-shaṅ-tho-lo-ni-kiṅ.
'Sûtra of the honourable and excelling Dhâranî of Buddha's head.'
Sarvadurgatiparisodhana-ushnîsha-vigaya-dhâranî.

K'-yuen-lu, fasc. 4, fol. 25 b; Conc. 173. Translated by Buddhapâla, A.D. 676, of the Thâṅ dynasty, A.D. 618-907. 8 leaves. There are two prefaces, namely: 1. That by the Emperor Khâṅ-tsu, of the Miṅ dynasty, dated A.D. 1411. 2. That by a priest named K'-tsiṅ, of the Thâṅ dynasty.

349 The same as No. 348.

Translated by Tu Hhiṅ-i, A.D. 679, of the Thâṅ dynasty, A.D. 618-907. 9 leaves.

350 佛說佛頂尊勝陀羅尼經
Fo-shwo-fo-tiṅ-tsun-shaṅ-tho-lo-ni-kiṅ.
'Sûtra spoken by Buddha on the honourable and excelling Dhâranî of Buddha's head.'
Sarvadurgatiparisodhana-ushnîsha-vigaya-dhâranî.

See No. 348. Translated by I-tsiṅ, A.D. 710, of the Thâṅ dynasty, A.D. 618-907. 9 leaves.

351 最勝佛頂陀羅尼淨除
　　　業障經

Tsui-shaṅ-fo-tiṅ-tho-lo-ni-tsiṅ-khu-
yeh-kâṅ-kiṅ.

'Sûtra of the most excelling Buddha's head's Dhâraṇî, which
purifies the obstacle of Karma.'

Sarvadurgatiparisodhana-ushnîsha-vigaya-
dhâraṇî.

Conc. 782. Translated by Divâkara, of the Thâṅ
dynasty, A.D. 618–907. 16 leaves.

352 佛頂最勝陀羅尼經

Fo-tiṅ-tsui-shaṅ-tho-lo-ni-kiṅ.

'Sûtra of the most excelling Dhâraṇî of Buddha's head.'

Sarvadurgatiparisodhana-ushnîsha-
vigaya-dhâraṇî.

Conc. 173. Translated by Divâkara, A.D. 682, of the
Thâṅ dynasty, A.D. 618–907. 7 leaves. This is Divâkara's first translation, while No. 351 is his second and
fuller version.

The above five works are similar translations, and
they agree with Tibetan. K'-yuen-lu, fasc. 4, fol. 25 b.

353 舍利弗陀羅尼經

Shö-li-fu-tho-lo-ni-kiṅ.

'Sâriputra-dhâraṇî-sûtra.'

Anantamukha-sâdhaka-dhâraṇî (?).

A. R., p. 445; A. M. G., p. 250. Translated by
Sanghapâla, of the Liâṅ dynasty, A. D. 502–557.
12 leaves.

354 佛說無量門破魔陀
　　　羅尼經

Fo-shwo-wu-liâṅ-man-pho-mo-tho-
lo-ni-kiṅ.

'Buddhabhâshita-amitamukha-mâragid (?)-dhâraṇî-sûtra.'

Anantamukha-sâdhaka-dhâraṇî (?).

See No. 353. Translated by Kuṅ-töh-kih, together
with Hhüen-khâṅ, A. D. 462, of the earlier Suṅ dynasty,
A. D. 420–479. 13 leaves.

355 佛說無量門微密持經

Fo-shwo-wu-liâṅ-man-wêi-mi-kh'-kiṅ.

'Buddhabhâshita-amitamukha-guhyadhara-sûtra.'

Anantamukha-sâdhaka-dhâraṇî (?).

See No. 353. Translated by K' Khien, of the Wu
dynasty, A.D. 222–280. 7 leaves.

356 佛說出生無量門持經

Fo-shwo-khu-shaṅ-wu-iiâṅ-man-kh'-kiṅ.

'Buddhabhâshita-gâtâmitamukhadhara-sûtra.'

Anantamukha-sâdhaka-dhâraṇî (?).

See No. 353. Translated by Buddhabhadra, of the
Eastern Tsin dynasty, A. D. 317–420. 11 leaves.

357 阿難陀目佉尼訶離陀
　　　隣尼經

Ö-nân-tho-mu-khü-ni-hö-li-tho-
lin-ni-kiṅ.

'Anantamukhanirhâri (?)-dhâraṇî-sûtra.'

Anantamukha-sâdhaka-dhâraṇî (?).

See No. 353. Translated by Buddhasânta, of the
Northern Wêi dynasty, A.D. 386–534. 14 leaves.

358 阿難陀目佉尼訶離陀經

Ö-nân-tho-mu-khü-ni-hö-li-tho-kiṅ.

'Anantamukhanirhâri-dhâ (raṇî ?)-sûtra.'

Anantamukha-sâdhaka-dhâraṇî (?).

See No. 353. Translated by Gunabhadra, of the
earlier Suṅ dynasty, A.D. 420–479. 12 leaves.

359 佛說一向出生菩薩經

Fo-shwo-yi-hhiâṅ-khu-shaṅ-phu-sâ-kiṅ.

'Buddhabhâshita-ekamukhagâta-bodhisattva-sûtra.'

Anantamukha-sâdhaka-dhâraṇî (?).

See No. 353. Translated by Gñânagupta, A.D. 585, of
the Sui dynasty, A.D. 589 (or 581)–618. 1 fasciculus.

360 出生無邊門陀羅尼經

Khu-shaṅ-wu-pien-man-tho-lo-ni-kiṅ.

'Gâtânantamukha-dhâraṇî-sûtra.'

Anantamukha-sâdhaka-dhâraṇî (?).

See No. 353. Translated by K'-yen, A.D. 721, of
the Thâṅ dynasty, A. D. 618–907. 1 fasciculus.

The above eight works are similar translations, long
and short. K'-tsiṅ, fasc. 13, fol. 20 b.

361 勝幢臂印陀羅尼經

Shaṅ-kwâṅ-phi-yin-tho-lo-ni-kiṅ.

'Su-dhvaga-bâhu-mudrâ-dhâraṇî-sûtra.'

Translated by Hhüen-kwâṅ (Hiouen-thsang), A.D. 654,
of the Thâṅ dynasty, A.D. 618–907. 4 leaves.

362 妙臂印幢陀羅尼經
Miâo-phi-yin-*k*wâṅ-tho-lo-ni-*k*iṅ.
'Subâhu-mudrâ-dhvaga-dhâranî-sûtra.'

Translated by *S*ikshânanda, of the Thâṅ dynasty, A. D. 618–907. 2 leaves.

The above two works are similar translations, and they are wanting in Tibetan. *K*'-yuen-lu, fasc. 5, fol. 1 a.

363 佛說陀羅尼集經
Fo-shwo-tho-lo-ni-tsi-*k*iṅ.
'Buddhabhâshita-dhâranî-saṅgraha-sûtra.'

Translated by Ö-ti-*k*ku-to (Atigupta?), A. D. 653–654, of the Thâṅ dynasty, A. D. 618–907. 13 fasciculi. Deest in Tibetan. *K*'-yuen-lu, fasc. 4, fol. 22 b. Some of the Dhâranîs in this work are similar to those of Nos. 327–329, etc. This work may be compared with some Nepalese MSS. mentioned in Catalogue of the Hodgson Manuscripts, I. 55, 59, 79; III. 36; IV. 6 a; VI. 21.

364 佛說持句神咒經
Fo-shwo-*k*h'-*k*ü-shan-*k*heu-*k*iṅ.
'Buddhabhâshita-padadhararddhimantra-sûtra.'

Translated by *K*' *K*hien, of the Wu dynasty, A. D. 222–280. 4 leaves.

365 佛說陀鄰尼鉢經
Fo-shwo-tho-lin-ni-poh-*k*iṅ.
'Buddhabhâshita-dhâranî-pâtra-sûtra.'

Translated by Buddhasânta, of the Northern Wêi dynasty, A. D. 386–534. 4 leaves.

366 東方最勝燈王如來助護持世間神咒經
Tuṅ-fâṅ-tsui-shaṅ-taṅ-wâṅ-zu-lâi-*k*u-hu-*k*h'-shi-*k*ien-shan-*k*heu-*k*iṅ.
'Sûtra of the spiritual Mantra (or Dhâranî) of the Tathâgata Anuttaradîparâga, who helps, protects, and holds the world.'

Translated by *G*ñânagupta, of the Sui dynasty, A. D. 589–618. 15 leaves.

The above three works are similar translations, and they are wanting in Tibetan. *K*'-yuen-lu, fasc. 5, fol. 3 a.

367 如來方便善巧咒經
Zu-lâi-fâṅ-pien-shan-*k*hiâo-*k*heu-*k*iṅ.
'Tathâgatopâyakausalya-mantra-sûtra.'
Saptabuddhaka-sûtra.

K'-yuen-lu, fasc. 5, fol. 2 a; Conc. 248; A. R., p. 469; A. M. G., p. 272. Translated by *G*ñânagupta, A. D. 587, of the Sui dynasty, A. D. 589 (or 581)–618. 12 leaves.

368 虛空藏菩薩問七佛陀羅尼咒經
Hhü-khuṅ-tsâṅ-phu-sâ-wan-tshi-fo-tho-lo-ni-*k*heu-*k*iṅ.
'Âkâsagarbha-bodhisattva-paripr*kkh*â-saptabuddha-dhâranî-mantra-sûtra.'
Saptabuddhaka-sûtra.

Conc. 198. Translated under the Liâṅ dynasty, A. D. 502–557; but the translator's name is lost. 13 leaves.

The above two works are similar translations, and they agree with Tibetan. *K*'-yuen-lu, fasc. 5, fol. 2 b.

369 善法方便陀羅尼咒經
Shan-fâ-fâṅ-pien-tho-lo-ni-*k*heu-*k*iṅ.
'Saddharmopâya-dhâranî-mantra-sûtra.'

Translated by *G*ñânagupta, of the Sui dynasty, A. D. 589–618. 6 leaves.

370 金剛祕密善門陀羅尼經
*K*in-kâṅ-pi-mi-shan-man-tho-lo-ni-*k*iṅ.
'Vagraguhya-sad (dharma) paryâya-dhâranî-sûtra.'

Translated by *G*ñânagupta, of the Sui dynasty, A. D. 589–618. 7 leaves.

371 護命法門神咒經
Hu-miṅ-fâ-man-shan-*k*heu-*k*iṅ.
'Âyushpâla-dharmaparyâyarddhimantra-sûtra.'

Translated by Bodhiru*k*i, A. D. 693, of the Thâṅ dynasty, A. D. 618–907. 14 leaves.

The above three works are similar translations, and they are wanting in Tibetan. *K*'-yuen-lu, fasc. 5, fol. 3 a.

372 金剛場陀羅尼經
*K*in-kâṅ-*k*hâṅ-tho-lo-ni-*k*iṅ.
'Vagramanda-dhâranî-sûtra.'
Vagra-mantra (or -ma*nd*ala)-dhâra*n*î.
K'-yuen-lu, fasc. 5, fol. 1 b.
Vagrama*nd*a-dhâra*n*î.

A. R., p. 445; A. M. G., p. 250; Conc. 289. Translated by *G*ñânagupta, A. D. 587, of the Sui dynasty, A. D. 589 (or 581)–618. 1 fasciculus.

373 金剛上味陀羅尼經
*K*in-kâṅ-shâṅ-wêi-tho-lo-ni-*k*iṅ.
'Vagrottararasa-dhâranî-sûtra.'
Vagramantra (or -ma*nd*ala)-dhâra*n*î.
Vagrama*nd*a-dhâra*n*î.

Conc. 283. Translated by Buddhasânta, A. D. 524, of the Northern Wêi dynasty, A. D. 386–534. 1 fasciculus.

The above two works are similar translations, and they agree with Tibetan. *K'*-yuen-lu, fasc. 5, fol. 1 b.

374 佛說無涯際總持法門經
Fo-shwo-wu-yâi-tsi-tsuṅ-*kh*'-fâ-man-*k*iṅ.

'Buddhabhâshita-ananta-dhâraṇî-dharmaparyâya-sûtra.'

Translated by Shaṅ-*k*ien, of the Western Tshin dynasty, A. D. 385–431. 1 fasciculus.

375 尊勝菩薩所問一切諸法入無量法門陀羅尼經
Tsuṅ-shaṅ-phu-sâ-su-wan-yi-tshiê-*k*u-fâ-*z*u-wu-liâṅ-fâ-man-tho-lo-ni-*k*iṅ.

'Ârya-*g*ina (?)-bodhisattva-paripṛikkhâ-sarvadharmâvatârâmita-dharmaparyâya-dhâraṇî-sûtra.'

Translated by Wân Thien-i, A. D. 562–563, of the Northern Tshi dynasty, A. D. 550–577. 1 fasciculus.

The above two works are similar translations, and they are wanting in Tibetan. *K'*-yuen-lu, fasc. 5, fol. 1 b.

CLASS VII.

單譯經 Tân-yi-*k*iṅ, or Sûtras of which there exists one translation only, and which are excluded from the five Classes.

376 十住斷結經
Shi-*k*u-twân-*k*iê-*k*iṅ.

'Sûtra on the cutting of the tie (of passions) in the ten dwellings (i. e. steps of a Bodhisattva lower than the ten Bhûmis).'

Translated by Fo-nien, of the Latter Tshin dynasty, A. D. 384–417. 14 fasciculi; 33 chapters. It agrees with Tibetan. *K'*-yuen-lu, fasc. 3, fol. 20 a.

377 菩薩道樹經
Phu-sâ-tâo-shu-*k*iṅ.

'Bodhisattva-bodhivṛiksha-sûtra.'

Translated by *K' Kh*ien, of the Wu dynasty, A. D. 222–280. 1 fasciculus. Deest in Tibetan. *K'*-yuen-lu, fasc. 3, fol. 15 a seq.

378 菩薩生地經
Phu-sâ-shaṅ-ti-*k*iṅ.

'Bodhisattva-*g*âtabhûmi-sûtra.'

Kshâmâkâra-bodhisattva-sûtra.

Conc. 484. Translated by *K' Kh*ien, of the Wu dynasty, A. D. 222–280. 4 leaves. Deest in Tibetan. *K'*-yuen-lu, fasc. 3, fol. 16 a.

379 佛說孛經
Fo-shwo-poh-*k*iṅ.

'Sûtra spoken by Buddha on (the history of) Poh (or Pushya ?).'

Translated by *K' Kh*ien, of the Wu dynasty, A. D. 222–280. 1 fasciculus. At the beginning of this work a well-known account concerning *G*etavana, or the Prince *G*eta's grove, and Anâthapiṇḍada's Ârâma or garden is given; then follows a life of Poh (or Pushya ?), the third son of a Brahma*k*ârin of the Gautama family, one of Buddha's former births. This *G*âtaka was spoken by Buddha to the King Prasena*g*it, on the eighth day after Buddha had met with the ill-fame concerning the woman Sundarî, as the consequence of his former deed. *K'*-tsiṅ, fasc. 31, fol. 22 a, where this work is taken as a Hînayâna-sûtra.

380 無垢淨光大陀羅尼經
Wu-keu-tsiṅ-kwâṅ-tâ-tho-lo-ni-*k*iṅ.

'Vimalasuddhaprabhâsa-mahâdhâraṇî-sûtra.'

Translated by Mi-tho-shan (Mitrasânta ?), A. D. 705, of the Thâṅ dynasty, A. D. 618–907. 1 fasciculus.

381 成具光明定意經
*Kh*âṅ-*k*ü-kwâṅ-miṅ-tiṅ-i-*k*iṅ.

'Pûrṇaprabhâsa-samâdhimati-sûtra.'

Translated by *K'* Yâo, A. D. 185, of the Eastern Hân dynasty, A. D. 25–220. 1 fasciculus.

382 摩訶摩耶經
Mo-hö-mo-ye-*k*iṅ.
Mahâmâyâ-sûtra.

Conc. 364. Translated by Thân-*k*iṅ, of the Northern Tshi dynasty, A. D. 550–577. 2 fasciculi. This work is also called the 'Sûtra of Buddha's ascent to the

Trayastrimsa heaven to preach the law to his mother.' It is stated in the note at the end (dated A. D. 1283), that 'there was a chapter on dividing Buddha's relics among eight places, which formed the latter part of this work. But it ought to have belonged to the Nirvâna-sûtra, and it was not given in the Indian text; so that the chapter is now omitted in this book.' It agrees with Tibetan. *K'*-yuen-lu, fasc. 3, fol. 18 a.

383 諸德福田經

*K*u-töh-fu-thien-*k*iṅ.

'Sarvaguna-punyakshetra-sûtra.'

Translated by Fâ-li and Fâ-*k*ü, of the Western Tsin dynasty, A. D. 265–316. 7 leaves. Deest in Tibetan. *K'*-yuen-lu, fasc. 3, fol. 16 b. Conc. 727 gives wrongly to this work the Sanskrit title of No. 385.

384 大方等如來藏經

Tâ-fâṅ-taṅ-zu-lâi-tsâṅ-*k*iṅ.

'Mahâvaipulya-tathâgatagarbha-sûtra.'

Tathâgatagarbha-sûtra.

K'-yuen-lu, fasc. 3, fol. 16 b; Conc. 606; A. R., p. 466; A. M. G., p. 269. Translated by Buddhabhadra, of the Eastern Tsin dynasty, A. D. 317–420. 13 leaves. It agrees with Tibetan. *K'*-yuen-lu, s. v.

385 佛說寶網經

Fo-shwo-pâo-wâṅ-*k*iṅ.

'Buddhabhâshita-ratnagâli-sûtra.'

Ratnagâli-pariprikkhâ.

K'-yuen-lu, fasc. 3, fol. 16 a; Conc. 419; A. R., p. 449; A. M. G., p. 254. Translated by *K*u Fâ-hu (Dharmaraksha), of the Western Tsin dynasty, A. D. 265–316. 1 fasciculus. It agrees with Tibetan. *K'*-yuen-lu, s.v.

386 佛說內藏百寶經

Fo-shwo-nêi-tsâṅ-pâi-pâo-*k*iṅ.

'Sûtra spoken by Buddha on a hundred precious things in the inner repository.'

Lokânuvartana-sûtra.

K'-yuen-lu, fasc. 3, fol. 15 a; Conc. 382.

Lokânusamânâvatâra-sûtra.

A. R., p. 455; A.M.G., p. 259; Conc. 382. Translated by *K'* Leu-*k*iâ-*kh*ân (Lokaraksha ?), of the Eastern Hân dynasty, A. D. 25–220. 8 leaves. It agrees with Tibetan. *K'*-yuen-lu, s. v.

387 佛說温室洗浴衆僧經

Fo-shwo-wan-shih-sien-yü-*k*uṅ-saṅ-*k*iṅ.

'Sûtra spoken by Buddha on (Gîva's inviting) many priests to wash themselves in a bath-house.'

Translated by Ân Shi-kâo, of the Eastern Hân dynasty, A. D. 25–220. 4 leaves. It agrees with Tibetan. *K'*-yuen-lu, fasc. 3, fol. 15 b. Conc. 795 gives wrongly to this work the Sanskrit title of No. 386.

388 佛說菩薩行五十緣身經

Fo-shwo-phu-sâ-hhiṅ-wu-shi-yuen-shan-*k*iṅ.

'Sûtra spoken by Buddha on (the characteristic marks on) his person as (the results of) fifty causes of the practice of Bodhisattva.'

Translated by *K*u Fâ-hu (Dharmaraksha), of the Western Tsin dynasty, A. D. 265–316. 8 leaves. Deest in Tibetan. *K'*-yuen-lu, fasc. 3, fol. 16 b.

389 佛說菩薩修行經

Fo-shwo-phu-sâ-siu-hhiṅ-*k*iṅ.

'Buddhabhâshita-bodhisattvakaryâ-sûtra.'

Translated by Po Fâ-tsu, of the Western Tsin dynasty, A. D. 265–316. 11 leaves. Deest in Tibetan. *K'*-yuen-lu, fasc. 3, fol. 16 b.

390 佛說金色王經

Fo-shwo-*k*in-seh-wâṅ-*k*iṅ.

'Buddhabhâshita-kanakavarnarâga-sûtra.'

Kanakavarna-pûrvayoga.

A. R., p. 483; A. M. G., p. 286. Translated by Gautama Pragñâruki, A. D. 542, of the Eastern Wêi dynasty, A. D. 534–550. 11 leaves, consisting of 3,514 Chinese characters. Deest in Tibetan. *K'*-yuen-lu, fasc. 3, fol. 17 a. See, however, the authorities mentioned under the title.

391 佛語法門經

Fo-yü-fâ-man-*k*iṅ.

'Buddhavakana-dharmaparyâya-sûtra.'

Translated by Bodhiruki, of the Northern Wêi dynasty, A. D. 386–534. 6 leaves.

392 佛說四不可得經

Fo-shwo-sz'-pu-kho-töh-*k*iṅ.

'Buddhabhâshita-katurdurlabha-sûtra.'

Translated by *K*u Fâ-hu (Dharmaraksha), of the Western Tsin dynasty, A. D. 265–316. 7 leaves. Deest in Tibetan. *K'*-yuen-lu, fasc. 3, fol. 16 a.

393　　**須 眞 天 子 經**
Sü-kan-thien-tsz'-kiṅ.
'Sukinti (?)-devaputra-sûtra.'

Translated by Ku Fâ-hu (Dharmaraksha), A. D. 266, of the Western Tsin dynasty, A. D. 265–316. 2 fasciculi; 10 chapters. It agrees with Tibetan. K'-yuen-lu, fasc. 3, fol. 17 b.

394　**佛 說 觀 普 賢 菩 薩 行 法 經**
Fo-shwo-kwân-phu-hhien-phu-sâ-hhiṅ-fâ-kiṅ.
'Sûtra spoken by Buddha on the law of practice of meditation on the Bodhisattva Samantabhadra.'

Translated by Dharmamitra, of the earlier Suṅ dynasty, A. D. 420–479. 1 fasciculus. Deest in Tibetan. K'-yuen-lu, fasc. 3, fol. 18 b seq.

395　**觀 世 音 菩 薩 得 大 勢 菩
薩 受 記 經**
Kwân-shi-yin-phu-sâ-töh-tâ-shi-phu-sâ-sheu-ki-kiṅ.
'Avalokitesvara-bodhisattva-mahâsthâmaprâpta-bodhisattva-vyâkaraṇa-sûtra.'

Translated by Thân-wu-kiĕ (Dharmâkâra ?), of the earlier Suṅ dynasty, A. D. 420–479. 1 fasciculus. Deest in Tibetan. K'-yuen-lu, fasc. 3, fol. 18 a seq.

396　**不 思 議 光 菩 薩 所 說 經**
Pu-sz'-i-kwân-phu-sâ-su-shwo-kiṅ.
Akintyaprabhâsa-(bodhisattva)-nirdesa-sûtra.

K'-yuen-lu, fasc. 3, fol. 19 a; Conc. 495; A. R., p. 430; A. M. G., p. 235. Translated by Kumâragîva, of the Latter Tshin dynasty, A. D. 384–417. 1 fasciculus. It agrees with Tibetan. K'-yuen-lu, s. v.

397　　**超 日 明 三 昧 經**
Kâo-zih-miṅ-sân-mêi-kiṅ.
'Sûtra on the Samâdhi called Surpassing the brightness of the sun (or, Sûryagihnikaraṇa-prabhâ ?).'

Translated by Neih Khaṅ-yuen, of the Western Tsin dynasty, A. D. 265–316. 1 fasciculus. Deest in Tibetan. K'-yuen-lu, fasc. 3, fol. 20 a.

398　　**除 恐 災 患 經**
Khu-khuṅ-tsâi-hwân-kiṅ.
'Sûtra on removing fear, misfortune, and anxiety.'
Srîkaṇṭha-sûtra.

K'-yuen-lu, fasc. 3, fol. 18 a; Conc. 724. Translated by Shaṅ-kien, of the Western Tshin dynasty, A. D. 385–

431. 1 fasciculus. It agrees with Tibetan. K'-yuen-lu, s. v.

399　**佛 說 首 楞 嚴 三 昧 經**
Fo-shwo-sheu-lâṅ-yen-sân-mêi-kiṅ.
'Buddhabhâshita-sûrâṅgama-samâdhi-sûtra.'
Sûrâṅgama-samâdhi.

K'-yuen-lu, fasc. 3, fol. 18 b; Conc. 65; A. R., p. 444; A. M. G., p. 249; Wassiljew, p. 175. Translated by Kumâragîva, of the Latter Tshin dynasty, A. D. 384–417. 3 fasciculi. It agrees with Tibetan. K'-yuen-lu, s. v. In his version of the Mahâpragñâpâramitâ-sâstra (No. 1169), Kumâragîva translates the term Sheu-lâṅ-yen into 健相 kien-siâṅ, lit. strong-form, i. e. Sûra (hero)-aṅga (limb). The term Sûrâṅgama has therefore no connection whatever with Sûra, the sun, as Mr. Beal thinks in his Catena of Buddhist Scriptures from Chinese, p. 284, note 2. See Fân-i-miṅ-i-tsi, fasc. 9, fol. 16 b.

400　　**未 曾 有 因 緣 經**
Wêi-tshaṅ-yiu-yin-yuen-kiṅ.
'Adbhuta-hetu-pratyaya-sûtra.'
Adbhutadharmaparyâya (?).

A. R., p. 476; A. M. G., p. 279. Translated by Thân-kiṅ, of the Tshi dynasty, A. D. 479–502. 2 fasciculi. It agrees with Tibetan. K'-yuen-lu, fasc. 3, fol. 19 b seq.

401　　**諸 佛 要 集 經**
Ku-fo-yâo-tsi-kiṅ.
'Sûtra of the important collection of Buddhas'
Buddhasaṅgîti-sûtra.

K'-yuen-lu, fasc. 3, fol. 19 b; Conc. 720; A. R., p. 460; A. M. G., p. 264. Translated by Ku Fâ-hu (Dharmaraksha), of the Western Tsin dynasty, A. D. 265–316. 2 fasciculi. It agrees with Tibetan. K'-yuen-lu, s. v.

402　**稱 揚 諸 佛 功 德 經**
Khân-yâṅ-ku-fo-kuṅ-töh-kiṅ.
'Sûtra on the praise of the good qualities of Buddhas.'
Kusumasañkaya-sûtra.

K'-yuen-lu, fasc. 3, fol. 17 b; Conc. 703; A. R., p. 468; A. M. G., p. 271. Translated by Ki-kiâ-yĕ, together with Thân-yâo, of the Northern Wêi dynasty, A. D. 386–534. 3 fasciculi. It agrees with Tibetan. K'-yuen-lu, s. v.

403 賢刧經
Hhien-*k*iê-*k*iñ.
Bhadrakalpika-sûtra.

K'-yuen-lu, fasc. 3, fol. 20 a; Conc. 190; A. R., p. 413; A. M. G., p. 220. Translated by *K*u Fâ-hu (Dharmaraksha), A.D. 300, of the Western Tsin dynasty, A.D. 265–316. 10 fasciculi. It agrees with Tibetan. *K*'-yuen-lu, s.v.

404 佛說佛名經
Fo-shwo-fo-miñ-*k*iñ.
'Buddhabhâshita-buddhanâma-sûtra.'

Translated by Bodhiru*k*i, of the Northern Wêi dynasty, A.D. 386–534. 12 fasciculi. In this work Buddha enumerates Buddhas, Bodhisattvas, and Pratyekabuddhas, 11,093 in number. *K*'-tsiñ, fasc. 5, fol. 13 b. Deest in Tibetan. *K*'-yuen-lu, fasc. 3, fol. 20 b seq. Cf. Wassiljew, p. 174; where 11,073 seems to be a misprint.

405 過去莊嚴刧千佛名經
Kwâ-*k*hü-*k*wâñ-yen-*k*iê-tshien-fo-miñ-*k*iñ.
'Atîta-vyûhakalpa-sahasrabuddhanâma-sûtra.'

Translated under the Liâñ dynasty, A.D. 502–557; but the translator's name is lost. 1 fasciculus. There is an additional and older part, entitled Sân-*k*iê-sân-tshien-fo-yuen-*k*hi, or 'Trikalpa-trisahasra-buddhanidâna;' which was translated by Kâlayasas, of the earlier Suñ dynasty, A.D. 420–479.

406 現在賢刧千佛名經
Hhien-tsâi-hhien-*k*iê-tshien-fo-miñ-*k*iñ.
'Pratyutpanna-bhadrakalpa-sahasrabuddhanâma-sûtra.'

Translated under the Liâñ dynasty, A.D. 502–557; but the translator's name is lost. 1 fasciculus.

407 未來星宿刧千佛名經
Wêi-lâi-siñ-siu-*k*iê-tshien-fo-miñ-*k*iñ.
'Anâgata-nakshatratârâkalpa-sahasrabuddhanâma-sûtra.'

Translated under the Liâñ dynasty, A.D. 502–557; but the translator's name is lost. 1 fasciculus.

The above three works are sometimes collectively called Sân-*k*iê-sân-tshien-*k*u-fo-miñ-*k*iñ, or 'Trikalpa-trisahasra-(sarva) buddhanâma-sûtra; and they are wanting in Tibetan. *K*'-yuen-lu, fasc. 3, fol. 20 b seq. Cf. Wassiljew, p. 174.

408 佛說五千五百佛名神咒除障滅罪經
Fo-shwo-wu-tshien-wu-pâi-fo-miñ-shan-*k*heu-*k*u-*k*añ-mieh-tsâi-*k*iñ.
'Sûtra spoken by Buddha on the names of 5,500 Buddhas and spiritual Mantras which remove obstacles and destroy sin.'

Translated by *G*ñânagupta, together with Dharmagupta and others, A.D. 593, of the Sui dynasty, A.D. 589–618. 8 fasciculi. Deest in Tibetan. *K*'-yuen-lu, fasc. 3, fol. 21 a. But this work may be compared with the Tibetan version of the Buddhanâma-sahasrapañ*k*asata*k*atus-tripañ*k*adasa (or -tripañ*k*âsat ?), i. e. the names of 5,453 Buddhas, as mentioned in A. R., p. 466; A. M. G., p. 270. The names of Buddhas in No. 408, however, are counted 4,704 only. *K*'-tsiñ, fasc. 5, fol. 13 b seq.; Wassiljew, p. 174.

409 力莊嚴三昧經
Li-*k*wâñ-yen-sân-mêi-*k*iñ.
'Balavyûha-samâdhi-sûtra.'

Translated by Narendrayasas, A.D. 585, of the Sui dynasty, A.D. 589 (or 581)–618. 3 fasciculi. It agrees with Tibetan. *K*'-yuen-lu, fasc. 3, fol. 21 b.

410 佛說八部佛名經
Fo-shwo-pâ-pu-fo-miñ-*k*iñ.
'Buddhabhâshita-ashtavargabuddhanâma-sûtra.'
Ash*t*abuddhaka-sûtra.

K'-yuen-lu, fasc. 4, fol. 5 a; Conc. 395; A. R., p. 469; A. M. G., p. 272. Translated by Gautama Prag*ñ*âru*k*i, A.D. 542, of the Eastern Wêi dynasty, A.D. 534–550. 3 leaves. It agrees with Tibetan. *K*'-yuen-lu, s.v. In this Sûtra Buddha tells the *S*resh*t*hin or elder (rich merchant) Shan-tso (Sukara ?) the names and good qualities of eight Buddhas of the eastern quarter.

411 百佛名經
Pâi-fo-miñ-*k*iñ.
'*S*atabuddhanâma-sûtra.'

Translated by Narendrayasas, A.D. 582, of the Sui dynasty, A.D. 589 (or 581)–618. 9 leaves. Deest in Tibetan. *K*'-yuen-lu, fasc. 3, fol. 17 b.

412 佛說不思議功德諸佛所護念經
Fo-shwo-pu-sz'-i-kuñ-töh-*k*u-fo-su-hu-nien-*k*iñ.
'Buddhabhâshita-a*k*intyaguna-sarvabuddha-parigraha-sûtra.'

Translated by *G*ñânagupta, of the Sui dynasty, A. D. 589–618. 2 fasciculi. Deest in Tibetan. *K*'-yuen-lu, fasc. 3, fol. 21 a; where this work is said to have been translated under the Wâi dynasty, A. D. 220–265; but the translator's name is lost. In this Sûtra the names of 1,120 Buddhas are mentioned. *K*'-tsiṅ, fasc. 5, fol. 18 b.

413 金剛三昧本性清淨不壞不滅經

*K*in-kâṅ-sân-mêi-pan-siṅ-tshiṅ-tsiṅ-pu-hwâi-pu-mieh-*k*iṅ.

'Sûtra on the Vagrasamâdhi, the original nature (of which being) pure and free from destruction.'

Translated under the three Tshin dynasties, A. D. 350–431; but the translator's name is lost. 8 leaves. Deest in Tibetan. *K*'-yuen-lu, fasc. 4, fol. 5 b seq.

414 佛說師子月佛本生經

Fo-shwo-sh'-tsz'-yueh-fo-pan-shaṅ-*k*iṅ.

'Buddhabhâshita-simhakandra-buddha-gâtaka-sûtra.'

Translated under the three Tshin dynasties, A. D. 350–431; but the translator's name is lost. 9 leaves. Deest in Tibetan. *K*'-yuen-lu, fasc. 4, fol. 6 a seq.

415 演道俗業經

Yen-tâo-su-yeh-*k*iṅ.

'Sûtra on explaining the actions of priests and laymen.

Translated by Shaṅ-*k*ien, of the Western Tshin dynasty, A. D. 385–431. 12 leaves. Deest in Tibetan. *K*'-yuen-lu, fasc. 3, fol. 17 a seq.

416 佛說長者法志妻經

Fo-shwo-*k*hâṅ-kö-fâ-*k*'-tshi-*k*iṅ.

'Buddhabhâshita-sreshṭhi-dharmakâri-bhâryâ-sûtra.'

Translated under the Northern Liâṅ dynasty, A. D. 302–439. 4 leaves. Deest in Tibetan. *K*'-yuen-lu, fasc. 4, fol. 6 a seq.

417 佛說薩羅國經

Fo-shwo-sâ-lo-kwo-*k*iṅ.

'Buddhabhâshita-(ko)sala (?)-desa-sûtra.'

Translated under the Eastern Tsin dynasty, A. D. 317–420; but the translator's name is lost. 4 leaves. Deest in Tibetan. *K*'-yuen-lu, fasc. 4, fol. 6 a seq. It states that Buddha went to the country of (Ko)sala (?) from *G*etavana, and taught the king and his subjects; so that they knew pain and raised their thoughts towards the Bodhi. *K*'-tsiṅ, fasc. 9, fol. 21 b.

418 佛說十吉祥經

Fo-shwo-shi-*k*i-shâṅ-*k*iṅ.

'Buddhabhâshita-dasasri-sûtra.'

Translated under one of the three Tshin dynasties, A. D. 350–431; but the translator's name is lost. 2 leaves. Deest in Tibetan. *K*'-yuen-lu, fasc. 4, fol. 6 a seq. In this Sûtra Buddha tells the noble-minded Vimalâvarana (?) the names and good qualities of ten Buddhas of the eastern quarter. *K*'-tsiṅ, fasc. 5, fol. 16 b.

419 佛說長者女菴提遮師子吼了義經

Fo-shwo-*k*hâṅ-kö-nü-ṅân-thi-*k*ö-sh'-tsz'-heu-liâo-i-*k*iṅ.

'Sûtra spoken by Buddha on the clear meaning of the lion-roaring (preaching, or discussion) of Ṅân-thi-kö (?), the daughter of a Sreshṭhin.'

Translated under the Liâṅ dynasty, A. D. 502–557; but the translator's name is lost. 8 leaves. It is stated at the beginning under the title, namely: 'This translation seems to have been made by Kumâragîva (of the Latter Tshin dynasty, A. D. 384–417).' Deest in Tibetan. *K*'-yuen-lu, fasc. 4, fol. 6 b seq.

420 佛說一切智光明仙人慈心因緣不食肉經

Fo-shwo-yi-tshiê-*k*'-kwâṅ-miṅ-sien-*z*an-tshz'-sin-yin-yuen-pu-shi-*z*eu-*k*iṅ.

'Sûtra spoken by Buddha on the abstaining from meat, being the Nidâna of the compassionate thought of the Rishi Sarvagñâprabha.'

Translated under one of the three Tshin dynasties, A. D. 350–431, 5 leaves. Deest in Tibetan. *K*'-yuen-lu, fasc. 4, fol. 6 b seq.

421 大方等陀羅尼經

Tâ-fâṅ-tâṅ-tho-lo-ni-*k*iṅ.

'Mahâvaipulya-dhâraṇî-sûtra.'

Pratyutpanna-buddha-sammukhâvasthita-samâdhi-sûtra.

K'-yuen-lu, fasc. 5, fol. 3 b; Conc. 614; A. R., p. 444; A. M. G., p. 250. Translated by Fâ-*k*un, of the Northern Liâṅ dynasty, A. D. 397–439. 4 fasciculi. It agrees with Tibetan. *K*'-yuen-lu, s. v.

422 大法炬陀羅尼經

Tâ-fâ-*k*ü-tho-lo-ni-*k*iṅ.

'Mahâdharmolkâ-dhâraṇî-sûtra.'

Translated by *Gñânagupta*, A. D. 592, of the Sui dynasty, A. D. 589–618. 20 fasciculi. Deest in Tibetan. *K'*-yuen-lu, fasc. 5, fol. 4 a.

423 大威德陀羅尼經
Tâ-wêi-töh-tho-lo-ni-*k*iṅ.
'Mahâbaladharma-dhâraṇî-sûtra.'

Translated by *Gñânagupta*, A. D. 595, of the Sui dynasty, A. D. 589–618. 20 fasciculi. Deest in Tibetan. *K'*-yuen-lu, fasc. 5, fol. 4 a. This work is mentioned by Wassiljew, in his Buddhismus, p. 177.

424 觀察諸法行經
Kwân-tsâ-*k*u-fâ-hhiṅ-*k*iṅ.
'Sarvadharma*k*aryâ-dhyâna (?)-sûtra.'

Translated by *Gñânagupta*, A. D. 595, of the Sui dynasty, A. D. 589–618. 4 fasciculi. It agrees with Tibetan. *K'*-yuen-lu, fasc. 3, fol. 22 a.

425 佛說華手經
Fo-shwo-hwâ-sheu-*k*iṅ.
'Buddhabhâshita-pushpa-hasta-sûtra.'
Kusalamûla-samparigraha-sûtra.

K'-yuen-lu, fasc. 3, fol. 21 a; Conc. 201.

Kusalamûla-paridhara-sûtra.

A. R., p. 429; A. M. G., p. 234. Translated by Kumâra*g*îva, of the Latter Tshin dynasty, A. D. 384–417. 10 fasciculi. It agrees with Tibetan. *K'*-yuen-lu, s. v.

426 法集經
Fâ-tsi-*k*iṅ.
Dharmasaṅgîti-sûtra.

K'-yuen-lu, fasc. 3, fol. 22 a; Conc. 140; A. R., p. 462; A. M. G., p. 266. Translated by Bodhiru*k*i, A. D. 515, of the Northern Wêi dynasty, A. D. 386–534. 6 fasciculi. It agrees with Tibetan. *K'*-yuen-lu, s. v.

427 大方廣圓覺修多羅了義經
Tâ-fâṅ-kwâṅ-yuen-*k*iâo-sheu-to-lo-liâo-i-*k*iṅ.
'Mahâvaipulya-pûrṇabuddha-sûtra-prasannârtha-sûtra.'

Translated by Buddhatrâta, A. D. 7th century, of the Thâṅ dynasty, A. D. 618–907. 2 fasciculi. There are two prefaces, which, however, belong to a Chinese commentary on this Sûtra, No. 1629.

428 佛說施燈功德經
Fo-shwo-*k'*-tâṅ-kuṅ-töh-*k*iṅ.
'Buddhabhâshita-pradîpadânaguṇa-sûtra.'
Pradîpadânîya-sûtra.

K'-yuen-lu, fasc. 3, fol. 23 a; Conc. 89; A. R., p. 456; A. M. G., p. 260. Translated by Narendrayasas, A. D. 558, of the Northern Tshi dynasty, A. D. 550–577. 1 fasciculus. Doubtful in Tibetan. *K'*-yuen-lu, s. v. See, however, the last two authorites mentioned under the title.

429 金剛三昧經
*K*in-kâṅ-sân-mêi-*k*iṅ.
'Va*g*rasamâdhi-sûtra.'

Translated under the Northern Liâṅ dynasty, A. D. 397–439; but the translator's name is lost. 2 fasciculi; 8 chapters. Deest in Tibetan. *K'*-yuen-lu, fasc. 4, fol. 6 b.

430 觀佛三昧海經
Kwân-fo-sân-mêi-hâi-*k*iṅ.
'Buddhadhyâna-samâdhisâgara-sûtra.'

Translated by Buddhabhadra, of the Eastern Tsin dynasty, A. D. 317–420. 10 fasciculi; 12 chapters. Deest in Tibetan. *K'*-yuen-lu, fasc. 3, fol. 21 b seq.

431 大方便佛報恩經
Tâ-fâṅ-pien-fo-pâo-an-*k*iṅ.
'Sûtra of the great good means (mahopâya) by which Buddha recompenses the favour (of his parents).'

Translated under the Eastern Hân dynasty, A. D. 25–220; but the translator's name is lost. 7 fasciculi; 9 chapters. Deest in Tibetan. *K'*-yuen-lu, fasc. 3, fol. 22 a.

432 菩薩本行經
Phu-sâ-pan-hhiṅ-*k*iṅ.
'Bodhisattva-pûrva*k*aryâ-sûtra.'

Translated under the Eastern Tsin dynasty, A. D. 317–420; but the translator's name is lost. 3 fasciculi; 11 sections. Deest in Tibetan. *K'*-yuen-lu, fasc. 3, fol. 22 a.

433 菩薩處胎經
Phu-sâ-*k*hu-thâi-*k*iṅ.
'Bodhisattva-garbhastha-sûtra.'
Garbha-sûtra (?).

Wassiljew, p. 327. Translated by Fo-nien, of the Latter Tshin dynasty, A. D. 384–417. 5 fasciculi; 38 chapters. Deest in Tibetan. *K'*-yuen-lu, fasc. 3, fol. 22 b.

434 央掘魔羅經

Yâṅ-*k*hü-mo-lo-*k*iṅ.

Aṅgulimâlîya-sûtra.

K'-yuen-lu, fasc. 3, fol. 23 a; Conc. 227; A. R., p. 457; A. M. G., p. 261; Wassiljew, p. 154. Translated by Gunabhadra, of the earlier Suṅ dynasty, A. D. 420–479. 4 fasciculi. It agrees with Tibetan. *K'*-yuen-lu, s. v.

435 菩薩內習六波羅蜜經

Phu-sâ-nêi-si-liu-po-lo-mi-*k*iṅ.

'Sûtra on the Bodhisattva's inner practice (?) of the six Pâramitâs.'

Translated by Yen Fo-thiâo, of the Eastern Hân dynasty, A. D. 25–220. 3 leaves. Deest in Tibetan. *K'*-yuen-lu, fasc. 4, fol. 5 b seq.

436 菩薩投身飼餓虎起塔因緣經

Phu-sâ-theu-shan-sz'-ṅö-hu-*k*hi-thâ-yin-yuen-*k*iṅ.

'Sûtra on the Nidâna of the *K*aitya erected in the place where the Bodhisattva threw his body to feed a hungry tiger.'

Translated by Fâ-shâṅ, of the Northern Liâṅ dynasty, A. D. 397–439. 12 leaves. This is a *G*âtaka, in which the Bodhisattva was the crown-prince *K*andanavat, who sold his person as a slave and got the sandal-wood to cure the disease of the king of another country. Then becoming an ascetic, he fed a tiger with his body; and on the remaining bones a *K*aitya was erected. *K'*-tsiṅ, fasc. 6, fol. 17 a. Deest in Tibetan. *K'*-yuen-lu, fasc. 4, fol. 5 b seq.

437 三昧弘道廣顯定意經

Sân-mêi-huṅ-tâo-kwâṅ-hhien-tiṅ-i-*k*iṅ.

'Sûtra on the Samâdhi, widely explaining the thought of meditation and promulgating the way.'

Anavatapta-nâgarâ*g*a-pariprikkhâ-sûtra.

K'-yuen-lu, fasc. 3, fol. 22 b; A. R., p. 448; A. M. G., p. 253. Translated by *K*u Fâ-hu (Dharmaraksha), A. D. 308, of the Western Tsin dynasty, A. D. 265–316. 4 fasciculi; 12 chapters.

438 佛說明度五十校計經

Fo-shwo-miṅ-tu-wu-shi-*k*iâo-*k*i-*k*iṅ.

'Sûtra spoken by Buddha on fifty countings of clear measure (?).'

Translated by Ân Shi-kâo, A. D. 151, of the Eastern Hân dynasty, A. D. 25–220. 2 fasciculi. Deest in Tibetan. *K'*-yuen-lu, fasc. 3, fol. 23 b seq.

439 無所有菩薩經

Wu-su-yiu-phu-sâ-*k*iṅ.

'Sûtra on the Bodhisattva Akiñkana (?).'

Translated by *G*ñânagupta, of the Sui dynasty, A. D. 589–618. 4 fasciculi. It agrees with Tibetan. *K'*-yuen-lu, fasc. 3, fol. 23 b.

440 大法鼓經

Tâ-fâ-ku-*k*iṅ.

'Sûtra of the great law-drum.'

Mahâbherî-hâraka-parivarta.

A. R., p. 458; A. M. G., p. 262; Wassiljew, p. 162. Translated by Gunabhadra, of the earlier Suṅ dynasty, A. D. 420–479. 2 fasciculi. Deest in Tibetan. *K'*-yuen-lu, fasc. 3, fol. 24 a. See, however, the authorities mentioned under the title.

441 月上女經

Yueh-shâṅ-nü-*k*iṅ.

'Sûtra on the girl *K*androttarâ.'

*K*androttarâ-dârikâ-vyâkarana-sûtra.

K'-yuen-lu, fasc. 3, fol. 24 a; Conc. 867; A. R., p. 454; A. M. G., p. 258. Translated by *G*ñânagupta, A. D. 591, of the Sui dynasty, A. D. 589–618. 2 fasciculi. It agrees with Tibetan. *K'*-yuen-lu, s. v.

442 文殊師利問經

Wan-shu-sh'-li-wân-*k*iṅ.

'Mañgusrî-pariprikkhâ-sûtra.'

A. R., p. 451; A. M. G., p. 255; Conc. 810. Translated by Saṅghapâla, of the Liâṅ dynasty, A. D. 502–557. 2 fasciculi. Deest in Tibetan. *K'*-yuen-lu, fasc. 3, fol. 24 a. See, however, the authorities mentioned under the title.

443 大方廣如來秘密藏經

Tâ-fâṅ-kwâṅ-*z*u-lâi-pi-mi-tsâṅ-*k*iṅ.

'Mahâvaipulya-tathâgata-guhyagarbha-sûtra.'

Tathâgata-garbha-sûtra.

A. R., p. 466; A. M. G., p. 269; Conc. 600. Translated under the three Tshin dynasties, A. D. 350–431; but the translator's name is lost. 2 fasciculi. It agrees with Tibetan. *K'*-yuen-lu, fasc. 3, fol. 24 a seq.

444 大乘密嚴經

Tâ-shaṅ-mi-yen-*k*iṅ.

'Sûtra of the Mahâyâna on the secret adornment.'

Ghanavyûha-sûtra.

K'-yuen-lu, fasc. 3, fol. 24 b; Conc. 577; A. R., p. 433; A. M. G., p. 239; Wassiljew, p. 160. Translated by Divâkara, of the Thân dynasty, A. D. 618–907. 3 fasciculi. It agrees with Tibetan. *K'-yuen-lu*, s. v.

445 菩薩瓔珞經

Phu-sâ-yiṅ-lo-*k*iṅ.

'Sûtra of the garland of the Bodhisattva.'

Translated by Fo-nien, A. D. 376, of the Latter Tshin dynasty, A. D. 384–417, under the Former Tshin dynasty, A. D. 350–394. 13 fasciculi, now subdivided into 20; 40 chapters. Deest in Tibetan. *K'-yuen-lu*, fasc. 3, fol. 20 a.

446 大佛頂如來密因修證了義諸菩薩萬行首楞嚴經

Tâ-fo-tiṅ-*ǳ*u-lâi-mi-yin-sheu-*k*aṅ-liâo-i-*k*u-phu-sâ-wân-hhiṅ-sheu-lâṅ-yen-*k*iṅ.

'Mahâbuddhoshṇîsha-tathâgata-guhyahetu-sâkshâtkṛita-prasannârtha-sarvabodhisattvakaryâ-sûrâṅgama-sûtra.'

tr. in A.D. 705

Translated by Pâramiti and Mikaśâkya, of the Thân dynasty, A. D. 618–907. 10 fasciculi. Deest in Tibetan. *K'-yuen-lu*, fasc. 5, fol. 4 b. A partial English translation of the first four or five fasciculi is given by Beal, in his Catena of Buddhist Scriptures from Chinese, pp. 286–369. For the term *S*ûrâṅgama, see No. 399.

447 七佛所說神咒經

Tshi-fo-su-shwo-shan-*kh*eu-*k*iṅ.

'Saptabuddhabhâshitarddhimantra-sûtra.'

Translated under the Eastern Tsin dynasty, A. D. 317–420; but the translator's name is lost. 4 fasciculi. Deest in Tibetan. *K'-yuen-lu*, fasc. 5, fol. 5 b.

448 文殊師利寶藏陀羅尼經

Wan-shu-sh'-li-pâo-tsâṅ-tho-lo-ni-*k*iṅ.

'Mañgusrî-ratnagarbha-dhâraṇî-sûtra.'

Translated by Bodhiru*k*i, A. D. 710, of the Thân dynasty, A. D. 618–907. 1 fasciculus. Deest in Tibetan. *K'-yuen-lu*, fasc. 5, fol. 5 b.

449 僧伽吒經

Saṅ-*k*iê-*kh*a-*k*iṅ.

'Saṅghâṭa (or -ṭî ?)-sûtra.'

Saṅghâṭî-sûtra-dharmaparyâya.

A. R., p. 429; A. M. G., p. 235; Conc. 517. Translated by Upaśûnya, A. D. 538, of the Northern Wêi dynasty, A. D. 386–534. 4 fasciculi. It agrees with Tibetan. *K'-yuen-lu*, fasc. 3, fol. 21 b.

450 出生菩提心經

*Kh*u-shaṅ-phu-thi-sin-*k*iṅ.

'Utpâdita-bodhi*k*itta-sûtra.'

Translated by *G*ñânagupta, A. D. 595, of the Sui dynasty, A. D. 589–618. 1 fasciculus.

451 佛印三昧經

Fo-yin-sân-mêi-*k*iṅ.

'Buddhamudrâ-samâdhi-sûtra.'

Translated by Ân Shi-kâo, of the Eastern Hân dynasty, A. D. 25–220. 5 leaves. Deest in Tibetan. *K'-yuen-lu*, fasc. 4, fol. 1 a.

452 佛說十二頭陀經

Fo-shwo-shi-'rh-theu-tho-*k*iṅ.

'Buddhabhâshita-dvâdasadhûta-sûtra.'

Translated by Guṇabhadra, of the earlier Suṅ dynasty, A. D. 420–479. 7 leaves. Deest in Tibetan. *K'-yuen-lu*, fasc. 4, fol. 7 b seq. The following is a comparative table of the order of the twelve Dhûtas in three different works:—

MAHÂVYUTPATTI, § 45.	DHARMASAṄGRAHA.	No. 452.
(1) Pâmsukûlika	11	7
(2) Traikîvarika	2	8
(3) Nâmatika	12	2 (?)
(4) Paiṇḍapâtika	1	3 (?)
(5) Ekâsanika	7	4
(6) Khalupaskâdbhaktika (or -paskânnabhaktika ?)	3	6
(7) Âraṇyaka	9	1
(8) Vṛikshamûlika	6	10
(9) Abhyavakâśika	8	11
(10) Smâśânika	10	9
(11) Naishadika	4	12
(12) Yathâsamstarika	5	5 (?)

The 2nd, 3rd, and 5th in No. 452 (i. e. 3rd, 4th, and 12th in Sanskrit) are literally begging alms constantly, begging alms in order (or from house to house), and eating food moderately. Cf. also Childers, Pâli Dictionary, p. 123 a, under Dhûtaṅgam, where thirteen names are mentioned.

453 佛說樹提伽經

Fo-shwo-shu-thi-*k*iê-*k*iṅ.

'Sûtra spoken by Buddha on (the *S*reshṭhin) Gyotishka (?).'

Translated by Guṇabhadra, of the earlier Suṅ dynasty, A. D. 420–479. 3 leaves. Deest in Tibetan. *K'-yuen-lu*, fasc. 4, fol. 7 b seq.

454 佛說法常住經

Fo-shwo-fâ-*kh*âṅ-ku-*k*iṅ.

'Sûtra spoken by Buddha on the constancy of the law.'

Translated under the Western Tsin dynasty, A. D. 265–316; but the translator's name is lost. 3 leaves. Deest in Tibetan. *K'-yuen-lu*, fasc. 4, fol. 8 a.

455 佛說長壽王經

Fo-shwo-*kh*ân-sheu-wân-*k*in.

'Sûtra spoken by Buddha on the king of long life.'

Translated under the Western Tsin dynasty, A.D. 265–316; but the translator's name is lost. 7 leaves. Deest in Tibetan. *K'*-yuen-lu, fasc. 4, fol. 7 b seq. This is a *G*âtaka of Buddha.

456 佛說海龍王經

Fo-shwo-hâi-lun-wân-*k*in.

'Buddhabhâshita-sâgara-nâgarâ*g*a-sûtra.'

Sâgara-nâgarâ*g*a.

K'-yuen-lu, fasc. 3, fol. 18 b.

Sâgara-nâgarâ*g*a-paripri*kkh*â.

A. R., p. 448; A. M. G., p. 253; Conc. 182. Translated by *K*u Fâ-hu (Dharmaraksha), of the Western Tsin dynasty, A. D. 265–316. 4 fasciculi; 20 chapters. It agrees with Tibetan. *K'*-yuen-lu, s. v.

457 佛爲海龍王說法印經

Fo-wêi-hâi-lun-wân-shwo-fâ-yin-*k*in.

'Sûtra on the seal of the law spoken by Buddha for the sake of Sâgara-nâgarâ*g*a.'

Sâgara-nâgarâ*g*a-paripri*kkh*â.

K'-yuen-lu, fasc. 4, fol. 4 b; Conc. 177. Translated by I-tsin, A.D. 711, of the Thân dynasty, A. D. 618–907. 1 leaf. It agrees with Tibetan. *K'*-yuen-lu, s. v.

458 佛說右繞佛塔功德經

Fo-shwo-yiu-*z*âo-fo-thâ-kun-töh-*k*in.

'Sûtra spoken by Buddha on the merits of turning round the Kaitya of Buddha to the right.'

*K*aitya-pradakshi*n*a-gâthâ.

A. R., p. 476; A. M. G., p. 279. Translated by *S*ikshânanda, of the Thân dynasty, A. D. 618–907. 4 leaves. It agrees with Tibetan. *K'*-yuen-lu, fasc. 4, fol. 4 a.

459 佛說妙色王因緣經

Fo-shwo-miâo-seh-wân-yin-yuen-*k*in.

'Buddhabhâshita-suvar*n*a-râ*g*a-nidâna-sûtra.'

Translated by I-tsin, A. D. 701, of the Thân dynasty, A. D. 618–907. 4 leaves. It agrees with Tibetan. *K'*-yuen-lu, fasc. 4, fol. 4 b seq.

460 師子素馱娑王斷肉經

Sh'-tsz'-su-tho-so-wân-twân-*z*eu-*k*in.

'Sûtra on the lion-king Sudarsana's cutting his flesh (to feed others).'

Translated by *K'*-yen, A. D. 721, of the Thân dynasty, A. D. 618–907. 5 leaves. It agrees with Tibetan. *K'*-yuen-lu, fasc. 4, fol. 5 a. This is a *G*âtaka of Buddha. Piâo-mu, fasc. 5, fol. 18 a.

461 佛說差摩婆帝受記經

Fo-shwo-*kh*a-mo-po-ti-sheu-*k*i-*k*in.

'Buddhâshita-kshamâvatî-vyâkara*n*a-sûtra.

Kshamâvatî-vyâkara*n*a-sûtra.

K'-yuen-lu, fasc. 4, fol. 3 b; Conc. 679; A. R., p. 454; A. M. G., p. 258. Translated by Bodhiru*k*i, A. D. 519–524, of the Northern Wêi dynasty, A. D. 386–534. 6 leaves. It agrees with Tibetan. *K'*-yuen-lu, s. v. It is stated that when Buddha, together with Maitreya, went to Râ*g*agriha to beg alms, and arrived at the palace of Bimbisâra, the queen Kshamâvatî spread excellent clothes and asked Buddha to sit down on them. Then Buddha spoke with her on the meaning of the adornment of trees, and finally gave her the prophecy. *K'*tsin, fasc. 9, fol. 22 a.

462 佛說師子莊嚴王菩薩請問經

Fo-shwo-sh'-tsz'-*k*wân-yen-wân-phu-sâ-tsin-wan-*k*in.

'Buddhabhâshita-simhavyûharâ*g*a-bodhisattva-paripri*kkh*â-sûtra.'

Translated by Nadi, A. D. 663, of the Thân dynasty, A.D. 618–907. 4 leaves. Deest in Tibetan. *K'*-yuen-lu, fasc. 4, fol. 3 a.

463 中陰經

*K*un-yin-*k*in.

Antarâ-bhava-sûtra.

K'-yuen-lu, fasc. 3, fol. 23 b; Conc. 710. Translated by Fo-nien, of the Latter Tshin dynasty, A. D. 384–417. 2 fasciculi; 12 chapters. It agrees with Tibetan. *K'*-yuen-lu, s. v.

464 占察善惡業報經

*K*ân-tsâ-shan-ṅoh-yeh-pâo-*k*in.

'Sûtra on the consideration by divination about the results of good and bad (actions).'

Translated by Bodhidîpa (?), of the Sui dynasty, A. D. 589–618. 2 fasciculi.

465 佛說蓮華面經

Fo-shwo-lien-hwâ-mien-*k*in.

'Sûtra spoken by Buddha on (one called) Lotus-face (Padmamukha or Pu*nd*arîkamukha ?).'

Translated by Narendrayasas, A. D. 584, of the Sui dynasty, A. D. 589 (or 581)–618. 2 fasciculi. Buddha spoke this Sûtra just before he entered Nirvâ*n*a, in which he foretold that Lotus-face would in a future time break the bowl of Buddha. *K'*-tsin, fasc. 25, fol. 21 b.

466 佛說三品弟子經

Fo-shwo-sân-phin-ti-tsz'-kiṅ.

'Sûtra spoken by Buddha on the three classes of (lay) disciples (highest, middle, and lowest).'

Translated by K' Khien, of the Wu dynasty, A.D. 220–280. 3 leaves. Deest in Tibetan. K'-yuen-lu, fasc. 4, fol. 7 a seq.

467 佛說四輩經

Fo-shwo-sz'-pêi-kiṅ.

'Sûtra spoken by Buddha on the four classes (of his disciples, viz. Bhikshu, Bhikshunî, Upâsaka, and Upâsikâ).'

Translated by Ku Fâ-hu (Dharmaraksha), of the Western Tsin dynasty, A.D. 265–316. 5 leaves. Deest in Tibetan. K'-yuen-lu, fasc. 4, fol. 7 a seq.

468 佛說當來變經

Fo-shwo-tâṅ-lâi-pien-kiṅ.

'Sûtra spoken by Buddha on the changes of the future.'

Translated by Ku Fâ-hu (Dharmaraksha), of the Western Tsin dynasty, A.D. 265–316. 4 leaves. Deest in Tibetan. K'-yuen-lu, fasc. 4, fol. 7 b seq.

469 過去佛分衞經

Kwâ-khü-fo-fan-wêi-kiṅ.

'Sûtra of the Paiṇḍapâtika of a Buddha of the past.'

Translated by Ku Fâ-hu (Dharmaraksha), of the Western Tsin dynasty, A.D. 265–316. 2 leaves. Deest in Tibetan. K'-yuen-lu, fasc. 4, fol. 7 b seq.

470 佛說法滅盡經

Fo-shwo-fâ-mieh-tsin-kiṅ.

'Sûtra spoken by Buddha on the destruction of the law.'

Translated under the earlier Suṅ dynasty, A.D. 420–479; but the translator's name is lost. 4 leaves. Deest in Tibetan. K'-yuen-lu, fasc. 4, fol. 6 b seq.

471 佛說甚深大回向經

Fo-shwo-shan-shan-tâ-hwui-hhiṅ-kiṅ.

'Sûtra spoken by Buddha on the very deep and great act of making (the stocks of merits) to ripen (Avaropita-kuśalamûla).'

Translated under the earlier Suṅ dynasty, A.D. 420–479; but the translator's name is lost. 5 leaves. Deest in Tibetan. K'-yuen-lu, fasc. 4, fol. 6 b seq.

472 天王太子辟羅經

Thien-wâṅ-thâi-tsz'-phi-lo-kiṅ.

'Sûtra of Phi-lo (Vela?) the crown-prince of a heavenly king.'

Translated under one of the three Tshin dynasties, A.D. 350–431; but the translator's name is lost. 2 leaves. Deest in Tibetan. K'-yuen-lu, fasc. 4, fol. 7 a seq.

473 大吉義神咒經

Tâ-kie-i-shan-kheu-kiṅ.

'Sûtra of the spiritual Mantra of great lucky meaning.'

Translated by Thân-yâo, of the Northern Wêi dynasty, A.D. 386–534. 2 fasciculi. Deest in Tibetan. K'-yuen-lu, fasc. 5, fol. 5 b seq.

474 阿吒婆拘鬼神大將上佛陀羅尼經

Ö-khâ-pho-kü-kwêi-shan-tâ-tsiâṅ-shâṅ-fo-tho-lo-ni-kiṅ.

'Sûtra of the Dhâraṇî presented to Buddha by the general of Asuras Ö-khâ-pho-kü (Âṭavika?).'

Translated under the Liâṅ dynasty, A.D. 502–557; but the translator's name is lost. 7 leaves.

475 佛說大普賢陀羅尼經

Fo-shwo-tâ-phu-hhien-tho-lo-ni-kiṅ.

'Buddhabhâshita-mahâ-samantabhadra-dhâraṇî-sûtra.'

Samantabhadra-dhâraṇî.

A. R., p. 533; A. M. G., p. 331. Translated under the Liâṅ dynasty, A.D. 502–557; but the translator's name is lost. 4 leaves. It agrees with Tibetan. K'-yuen-lu, fasc. 5, fol. 6 a.

476 佛說大七寶陀羅尼經

Fo-shwo-tâ-tshi-pâo-tho-lo-ni-kiṅ.

'Buddhabhâshita-mahâsaptaratna-dhâraṇî-sûtra.'

Translated under the Liâṅ dynasty, A.D. 502–557; but the translator's name is lost. 1 leaf. It agrees with Tibetan. K'-yuen-lu, fasc. 5, fol. 6 a.

477 六字大陀羅尼咒經

Liu-tsz'-tâ-tho-lo-ni-kheu-kiṅ.

'Shaḍakshara-mahâdhâraṇî-mantra-sûtra.'

Translated under the Liâṅ dynasty, A.D. 502–557; but the translator's name is lost. 3 leaves. Cf. Nos. 331, 340, 341.

478 佛說安宅神咒經

Fo-shwo-ân-tsö-shan-kheu-kiṅ.

'Sûtra spoken by Buddha on the spiritual Mantra for keeping the house safe.'

Translated under the Eastern Hân dynasty, A.D. 25–220; but the translator's name is lost. 5 leaves. Deest in Tibetan. K'-yuen-lu, fasc. 5, fol. 6 b.

479 幻師颰陀神咒經

Hwân-sh'-fu-tho-shan-kheu-kiṅ.

'Mâyâkâra-bhadra-riddhimantra-sûtra.'

Translated by Thân-wu-lân (Dharmaraksha?), of the Eastern Tsin dynasty, A. D. 317–420. 2 leaves. Deest in Tibetan. *K'*-yuen-lu, fasc. 5, fol. 6 b.

480 佛說辟除賊害咒經

Fo-shwo-phi-*kh*u-tsö-hâi-*kh*eu-*k*iṅ.

'Sûtra spoken by Buddha on the Vidyâ or spell for avoiding and removing the injury (caused) by a thief.'

Translated under the Eastern Tsin dynasty, A. D. 317–420; but the translator's name is lost. 1 leaf.

481 佛說咒時氣病經

Fo-shwo-*kh*eu-sh'-*kh*i-piṅ-*k*iṅ.

'Sûtra spoken by Buddha on relieving epidemic by a spell.'

Translated by Thân-wu-lân (Dharmaraksha?), of the Eastern Tsin dynasty, A. D. 317–420. 1 leaf.

482 佛說咒齒經

Fo-shwo-*kh*eu-*kh*'-*k*iṅ.

'Sûtra spoken by Buddha on relieving toothache by a spell.'

Translated by Thân-wu-lân (Dharmaraksha?), of the Eastern Tsin dynasty, A. D. 317–420. Half a leaf.

483 佛說咒目經

Fo-shwo-*kh*eu-mu-*k*iṅ.

'Sûtra spoken by Buddha on relieving eye (disease) by a spell.'

*K*akshur-visodhana-vidyâ.

A.R., p. 525; A.M.G., p. 324. Translated by Thân-wu-lân (Dharmaraksha?), of the Eastern Tsin dynasty, A. D. 317–420. Half a leaf.

484 佛說咒小兒經

Fo-shwo-*kh*eu-siâo-'rh-*k*iṅ.

'Sûtra spoken by Buddha on relieving a (sick) child by a spell.'

Translated by Thân-wu-lân (Dharmaraksha?), of the Eastern Tsin dynasty, A. D. 317–420. Half a leaf.

485 阿彌陀鼓音聲王陀羅尼經

Ö-mi-tho-ku-yin-shaṅ-wâṅ-tho-lo-ni-*k*iṅ.

'Amitadundubhisvararâ*g*a-dhâraṇî-sûtra.'

Translated under the Liâṅ dynasty, A. D. 502–557; but the translator's name is lost. 5 leaves. In this Sûtra, Buddha is introduced as living in the great city of *K*ampâ, and telling Bhikshus the names of the parents, son, disciples and Mâra of Amitâbha; he also teaches a spiritual Mantra or Vidyâ by the practice or recital of which for ten days a man would certainly be born in his country (Sukhâvatî). *K'*-tsiṅ, fasc. 3, fol. 20 a.

486 佛說摩尼羅亶經

Fo-shwo-mo-ni-lo-tân-*k*iṅ.

'Buddhabhâshita-manirata (?)-sûtra.'

Translated by Thân-wu-lân (Dharmaraksha?), of the Eastern Tsin dynasty, A. D. 317–420. 3 leaves. Deest in Tibetan. *K'*-yuen-lu, fasc. 5, fol. 6 b. This Sûtra explains rules for curing several diseases caused by evil spirits. Piâo-mu, fasc. 5, fol. 11 b.

487 佛說檀持羅麻油述經

Fo-shwo-thân-*kh*'-lo-mo-yiu-shu-*k*iṅ.

'Buddhabhâshita-dan*d*a-lo-mo-yiu-shu (?)-sûtra.'

Translated by Thân-wu-lân (Dharmaraksha?), of the Eastern Tsin dynasty, A. D. 317–420. 3 leaves. This Sûtra seems to be similar to No. 800, i.e. the Mahâda*nd*a-dhâraṇî; as it states that when Râhula was disturbed by evil spirits in the night, Buddha spoke a Mantra or spell and protected him against the spirits. *K'*-tsiṅ, fasc. 14, fol. 28 b.

488 佛說護諸童子陀羅尼經

Fo-shwo-hu-*k*u-thuṅ-tsz'-tho-lo-ni-*k*iṅ.

'Sûtra spoken by Buddha on the Dhâraṇî-mantra for protecting boys or children.'

Translated by Bodhiru*k*i, of the Northern Wêi dynasty, A. D. 386–534. 4 leaves. Deest in Tibetan. *K'*-yuen-lu, fasc. 4, fol. 6 b.

489 諸佛心陀羅尼經

*K*u-fo-sin-tho-lo-ni-*k*iṅ.

'Sûtra of the Dhâraṇî of the heart of Buddhas.'

Buddha-h*r*idaya-dhâraṇî.

K'-yuen-lu, fasc. 5, fol. 6 b; Conc. 717; A. R., p. 516; A. M. G., p. 311. Translated by Hhüen-*k*wâṅ (Hiouen-thsang), A. D. 650, of the Thâṅ dynasty, A. D. 618–907. 3 leaves. It agrees with Tibetan. *K'*-yuen-lu, s. v.

490 拔濟苦難陀羅尼經

Fu-tsi-ku-nân-tho-lo-ni-*k*iṅ.

'Sûtra of the Dhâraṇî of uprooting and saving pain and difficulty (of beings).'

Translated by Hhüen-*k*wâṅ (Hiouen-thsang), A. D. 654, of the Thâṅ dynasty, A. D. 618–907. 2 leaves. It agrees with Tibetan. *K'*-yuen-lu, fasc. 5, fol. 7 a.

491 八名普密陀羅尼經

Pâ-miṅ-phu-mi-tho-lo-ni-*k*iṅ.

'Ash*t*anâma-samantaguhya-dhâraṇî-sûtra.'

Translated by Hhüen-*k*wâň (Hiouen-thsang), A. D. 654, of the Thâň dynasty, A. D. 618–907. 3 leaves. It agrees with Tibetan. *K*'-yuen-lu, fasc. 5, fol. 7 a.

492 佛說持世陀羅尼經
Fo-shwo-*kh*'-shi-tho-lo-ni-*k*iň.
'Sûtra spoken by Buddha on the Dhâranî of holding the world.'
Vasudhara-dhâranî.

K'-yuen-lu, fasc. 5, fol. 6 a; Conc. 686; A. R., p. 530; A. M. G., p. 328. Translated by Hhüen-*k*wâň (Hiouen-thsang), A. D. 654, of the Thâň dynasty, A. D. 618–907. 4 leaves. It agrees with Tibetan. *K*'-yuen-lu, s. v.

493 佛說六門陀羅尼經
Fo-shwo-liu-man-tho-lo-ni-*k*iň.
'Sûtra spoken by Buddha on the Dhâranî of six gates.'
Shanmukhî-dhâranî.

A. R., p. 526; A. M. G., p. 325. Translated by Hhüen-*k*wâň (Hiouen-thsang), A. D. 645, of the Thâň dynasty, A. D. 618–907. 1 leaf. Deest in Tibetan. *K*'-yuen-lu, fasc. 5, fol 7 b. See, however, the authorities mentioned under the title.

494 清淨觀世音菩薩普賢陀羅尼經
Tshiň-tsiň-kwân-shi-yin-phu-sâ-phu-hhien-tho-lo-ni-*k*iň.
'The pure Avalokitesvara-bodhisattva-samantabhadra-dhâranî-sûtra.'
Samantabhadra-dhâranî.

K'-yuen-lu, fasc. 5, fol. 7 b; Conc. 775; A. R., p. 533; A. M. G., p. 331. Cf. also No. 475. Translated by *K*'-thuň, A. D. 653, of the Thâň dynasty, A. D. 618–907. 8 leaves. It agrees with Tibetan. *K*'-yuen-lu, s. v.

495 諸佛集會陀羅尼經
*K*u-fo-tsi-hwui-tho-lo-ni-*k*iň.
'Sûtra of the Dhâranî of the assembly of Buddhas.'
Sarvabuddhâṅgavatîdhâranî.

K'-yuen-lu, fasc. 5, fol. 8 a; Conc. 719; A. R., p. 511; A. M. G., p. 311. Translated by Devapragña and others, A. D. 691, of the Thâň dynasty, A. D. 618–907. 4 leaves. It agrees with Tibetan. *K*'-yuen-lu, s. v.

496 佛說智炬陀羅尼經
Fo-shwo-*k*'-*k*ü-tho-lo-ni-*k*iň.
'Sûtra spoken by Buddha on the Dhâranî of the torch of wisdom.'
Gñânolka-dhâranî-sarvadurgati-parisodhanî.

K'-yuen-lu, fasc. 5, fol. 7 b; Conc. 690; A. R., p. 543; A. M. G., p. 340. Translated by Devapragña and others, A. D. 691, of the Thâň dynasty, A. D. 618–907. 5 leaves. It agrees with Tibetan. *K*'-yuen-lu, s. v.

497 佛說隨求卽得大自在陀羅尼神咒經
Fo-shwo-sui-*kh*u-tsi-töh-tâ-tsz'-tsâi-tho-lo-ni-shan-*kh*eu-*k*iň.
'Sûtra spoken by Buddha on the Dhâranî-riddhimantra of great freedom to be obtained as soon as one wishes for it.'

Translated by Ratna*k*inta, A. D. 693, of the Thâň dynasty, A. D. 618–907. 1 fasciculus. It agrees with Tibetan. *K*'-yuen-lu, fasc. 5, fol. 8 a.

498 佛說一切法功德莊嚴王經
Fo-shwo-yi-tshi-fâ-kuň-töh-*k*wâň-yen-wâň-*k*iň.
'Buddhabhâshita-sarva . . . râga-sûtra.'
Sarvadharmagunavyûharâga.

A. R., p. 436; A. M. G., p. 242. Translated by I-tsiň, A. D. 705, of the Thâň dynasty, A. D. 618–907. 1 fasciculus.

499 佛說拔除罪障咒王經
Fo-shwo-fu-*kh*u-tsâi-*k*âň-*kh*eu-wâň-*k*iň.
'Sûtra spoken by Buddha on the Mantra-râga of uprooting and removing sin and obstacles.'

Translated by I-tsiň, A. D. 710, of the Thâň dynasty, A. D. 618–907. 4 leaves.

500 佛說善夜經
Fo-shwo-shan-yê-*k*iň.
'Sûtra spoken by Buddha on the good night.'
Bhadrakâ-râtrî.

A. R., p. 476; A. M. G., p. 279. Translated by I-tsiň, A. D. 701, of the Thâň dynasty, A. D. 618–907. 4 leaves. In this Sûtra the Devaputra *K*andana awakened Bhikshus and caused them to ask Buddha a question, then Buddha spoke the Sûtra together with three Mantras or spells. *K*'-tsiň, fasc. 13, fol. 16 a.

501 佛說虛空藏菩薩能滿諸願最勝心陀羅尼求聞持法
Fo-shwo-hhü-khuň-tsâň-phu-sâ-naň-mân-*k*u-yuen-tsâi-shaň-sin-tho-lo-ni-*kh*iu-wan-*kh*'-fâ.
'Law or rules spoken by Buddha for seeking to hear and hold the Dhâranî of the most excellent heart, and of fulfilling all prayers belonging to the Bodhisattva Âkâsagarbha.'

Translated by *S*ubhakarasimha, A. D. 717, of the Thâṅ dynasty, A. D. 618–907. 5 leaves. Deest in Tibetan. *K'*-yuen-lu, fasc. 5, fol. 9 a seq.

502 佛說佛地經

Fo-shwo-fo-ti-*k*iṅ.

'Buddhabhâshita-buddhabhûmi-sûtra.'

Buddhabhûmi.

A. R., p. 469; A. M. G., p. 273. Translated by Hhüen-*k*wâṅ (Hiouen-thsang), A. D. 645, of the Thâṅ dynasty, A. D. 618–907. 12 leaves.

503 百千印陀羅尼經

Pâi-tshien-yin-tho-lo-ni-*k*iṅ.

'*S*atasahasramudrâ-dhâraṇî-sûtra.'

Translated by *S*ikshânanda, of the Thâṅ dynasty, A. D. 618–907. 3 leaves. Deest in Tibetan. *K'*-yuen-lu, fasc. 5, fol. 8 a seq.

504 莊嚴王陀羅尼經

*K*wâṅ-yen-wâṅ-tho-lo-ni-*k*iṅ.

'Vyûharâ*g*a-dhâraṇî-sûtra.'

Sarvatathâgatâdhish*th*âna-sattvâvalokana-buddhakshetrasandar*s*ana-vyûharâ*g*a-sûtra.

K'-yuen-lu, fasc. 5, fol. 8 b.

°kshetravyûha-nirde*s*ana.

A. R., p. 425; A. M. G., p. 231.

°kshetra-nirde*s*ana-vyûha.

Conc. 708. Translated by I-tsiṅ, A. D. 701, of the Thâṅ dynasty, A. D. 618–907. 4 leaves. It agrees with Tibetan. *K'*-yuen-lu, s. v.

505 香王菩薩陀羅尼經

Hhiaṅ-wâṅ-phu-sâ-tho-lo-ni-*k*iṅ.

'Gandharâ*g*a-bodhisattva-dhâraṇî-sûtra.'

Translated by I-tsiṅ, A. D. 705, of the Thâṅ dynasty, A. D. 618–907. 4 leaves.

506 優婆夷淨行法門經

Yiu-pho-i-tsiṅ-hhiṅ-fâ-man-*k*iṅ.

'Upâsikâ-brahma*k*aryâ-dharmaparyâya-sûtra.'

Translated under the Northern Liâṅ dynasty, A. D. 397–439; but the translator's name is lost. 2 fasciculi; 3 chapters. Deest in Tibetan. *K'*-yuen-lu, fasc. 4, fol. 7 a seq.

507 諸法最上王經

*K*u-fâ-tsui-shâṅ-wâṅ-*k*iṅ.

'Sarvadharmânuttararâ*g*a-sûtra.'

Translated by *G*ñânagupta, A. D. 595, of the Sui dynasty, A. D. 589–618. 1 fasciculus. Deest in Tibetan. *K'*-yuen-lu, fasc. 4, fol. 2 b.

508 文殊師利般湼槃經

Wan-shu-sh'-li-pân-niê-phân-*k*iṅ.

'Ma*ñg*usrî-parinirvâṇa-sûtra.'

Translated by Nieh Tâo-*k*an, of the Western Tsin dynasty, A. D. 265–316. 5 leaves. Deest in Tibetan. *K'*-yuen-lu, fasc. 4, fol. 1 a seq.

509 異出菩薩本起經

I-*k*hu-phu-sâ-pan-*kh*i-*k*iṅ.

'A different translation of the Sûtra on the origin or former history of the Bodhisattva.'

Abhinishkrama*n*a-sûtra (?).

A. R., p. 474; A. M. G., p. 277. Translated by Nieh Tâo-*k*an, of the Western Tsin dynasty, A. D. 265–316. 10 leaves. Deest in Tibetan. *K'*-yuen-lu, fasc. 4, fol. 1 a seq. This work is a similar translation of Nos. 664–666; so that it ought to be arranged under the heading of the Sûtras of the Hînayâna, as it is in *K'*-tsiṅ, fasc. 29, fol. 18 b.

510 佛說賢首經

Fo-shwo-hhien-sheu-*k*iṅ.

'Sûtra spoken by Buddha on (the request of) Bhadrasrî (a queen of Bimbisâra).'

Translated by Shaṅ-*k*ien, of the Western Tshin dynasty, A. D. 385–431. 3 leaves. Deest in Tibetan. *K'*-yuen-lu, fasc. 4, fol. 1 b.

511 千佛因緣經

Tshien-fo-yin-yuen-*k*iṅ.

'Sahasrabuddha-nidâna-sûtra.'

Translated by Kumâra*g*îva, of the Latter Tshin dynasty, A. D. 384–417. 22 leaves. This work is mentioned by Wassiljew, in his Buddhismus, p. 175, Deest in Tibetan. *K'*-yuen-lu, fasc. 4, fol. 1 a seq.

512 八大人覺經

Pâ-tâ-*z*an-*k*iâo-*k*iṅ.

'Sûtra on the eight understandings of the great men (such as Buddhas and Bodhisattvas).'

Translated by Ân Shi-kâo, of the Eastern Hân dynasty, A. D. 25–220. 2 leaves. Deest in Tibetan. *K'*-yuen-lu, fasc. 4, fol. 7 a seq.

513 佛說月明菩薩經

Fo-shwo-yueh-miṅ-phu-sâ-*k*iṅ.

'Buddhabhâshita-*k*andraprabha-bodhisattva-sûtra.'

Translated by K' Khien, of the Wu dynasty, A.D. 222–280. 4 leaves. Deest in Tibetan. K'-yuen-lu, fasc. 4, fol. 1 b.

514 佛說心明經
Fo-shwo-sin-miṅ-kiṅ.

'Sûtra spoken by Buddha on Heart-brightness (or Kittaprabhâ?, the wife of a Brahmakârin, who received from Buddha the prophecy).'

Translated by Ku Fâ-hu (Dharmaraksha), of the Western Tsin dynasty, A.D. 265–316. 4 leaves. Deest in Tibetan. K'-yuen-lu, fasc. 4, fol. 1 b.

515 佛說滅十方冥經
Fo-shwo-mieh-shi-fâṅ-miṅ-kiṅ.

'Sûtra spoken by Buddha on destroying the darkness of the ten quarters.'

Dasadigandhakâra-vidhvamsana-sûtra.

K'-yuen-lu, fasc. 4, fol. 1 b; Conc. 360; A.R., p. 468; A.M.G., p. 272. Translated by Ku Fâ-hu (Dharmaraksha), A.D. 306, of the Western Tsin dynasty, A.D. 265–316. 8 leaves. It agrees with Tibetan. K'-yuen-lu, s.v.

516 佛說鹿母經
Fo-shwo-lu-mu-kiṅ.

'Sûtra spoken by Buddha on the mother of deer.'

Translated by Ku Fâ-hu (Dharmaraksha), of the Western Tsin dynasty, A.D. 265–316. 9 leaves. Deest in Tibetan. K'-yuen-lu, fasc. 4, fol. 2 a. This is a Gâtaka of Buddha.

517 佛說魔逆經
Fo-shwo-mo-ni-kiṅ.

'Sûtra spoken by Buddha on the opposition of the Mâra.'

Translated by Ku Fâ-hu (Dharmaraksha), A.D. 289, of the Western Tsin dynasty, A.D. 265–316. 1 fasciculus. It agrees with Tibetan. K'-yuen-lu, fasc. 4, fol. 2 a.

518 佛說賴吒和羅所問德光太子經
Fo-shwo-lâi-khâ-hö-lo-su-wan-töh-kwâṅ-thâi-tsz'-kiṅ.

'Buddhabhâshita-râshtravara (? bhikshu)-paripṛikkhâ-gunaprabha-kumâra-sûtra.'

Cf. Conc. 735. Translated by Ku Fâ-hu (Dharmaraksha), A.D. 276, of the Western Tsin dynasty, A.D. 265–316. 1 fasciculus. It agrees with Tibetan. K'-yuen-lu, fasc. 4, fol. 2 a seq.

519 商主天子經
Shâṅ-ku-thien-tsz'-kiṅ.

'Banikpati (?)-devaputra-sûtra.'

Translated by Gñânagupta and others, A.D. 595, of the Sui dynasty, A.D. 589–618. 1 fasciculus. Deest in Tibetan. K'-yuen-lu, fasc. 4, fol. 2 b.

520 大乘四法經
Tâ-shaṅ-sz'-fâ-kiṅ.

'Mahâyâna-katurdharma-sûtra.'

Katushka-nirhâra-sûtra.

K'-yuen-lu, fasc. 4, fol. 4 b, Conc. 588; A.R., p. 465; A.M.G., p. 268. Translated by Sikshânanda, of the Thâṅ dynasty, A.D. 618–907. 11 leaves. It agrees with Tibetan. K'-yuen-lu, s.v. This work is not a similar translation of Nos. 266 and 267, though the title is the same. See No. 1488, fol. 9 a.

521 離垢慧菩薩所問禮佛法經
Li-keu-hwui-phu-sâ-su-wan-li-fo-fâ-kiṅ.

'Sûtra on the law of the worship of Buddha, asked by the Bodhisattva Vimalagña.'

Translated by Nadi, A.D. 663, of the Thâṅ dynasty, A.D. 618–907. 7 leaves. Deest in Tibetan. K'-yuen-lu, fasc. 4, fol. 3 a.

522 寂照神變三摩地經
Tsi-kâo-shan-pien-sân-mo-ti-kiṅ.

Prasântaviniskaya-pratihârya-samâdhi-sûtra.

K'-yuen-lu, fasc. 4, fol. 3 b; Conc. 768; A.R., p. 443; A.M.G., p. 249. Translated by Hhüen-kwâṅ (Hiouen-thsang), A.D. 663, of the Thâṅ dynasty, A.D. 618–907. 1 fasciculus. It agrees with Tibetan. K'-yuen-lu, s.v.

523 佛說造塔功德經
Fo-shwo-tsâo-thâ-kuṅ-töh-kiṅ.

'Sûtra spoken by Buddha on the merit of erecting a Kaitya.'

Translated by Divâkara, A.D. 680, of the Thâṅ dynasty, A.D. 618–907. 3 leaves. Buddha spoke this Sûtra to the Bodhisattva Avalokitesvara, while he was in the Trayastrimsa heaven, in which he explains the following famous Gâthâ, to be written down and placed in a Kaitya, being the Dharmakâya of Buddha: Ye dharmâ hetuprabhavâ hetum teshâm Tathâgataḥ, by avadat teshâm ka yo nirodha evam vâdî Mahâsramanaḥ. (K'-tsiṅ, fasc. 10, fol. 5 b seq.) An English translation of this Gâthâ by Csoma is quoted in Burnouf's Lotus de Bonne Loi, p. 522, which is as follows: 'Whatever moral (or human) actions arise from some cause, the cause of them has been declared by Tathâgata: what is the check to these actions is thus set forth by the great Srâmana.' No. 523 agrees with Tibetan. K'-yuen-lu, fasc. 4, fol. 4 a.

524 佛說不增不減經

Fo-shwo-pu-tsaṅ-pu-kien-kiṅ.

'Sûtra spoken by Buddha on neither increasing nor decreasing.'

Translated by Bodhiruki, A. D. 519–524, of the Northern Wêi dynasty, A. D. 618–907. 7 leaves. It agrees with Tibetan. K'-yuen-lu, fasc. 4, fol. 3 b seq.

525 佛說堅固女經

Fo-shwo-kien-ku-nü-kiṅ.

'Sûtra spoken by Buddha on (the prophecy given to) the Upâsikâ Firm-minded (or Sthiradhî?).'

Translated by Narendrayasas, A. D. 582, of the Sui dynasty, A. D. 589 (or 581)–618. 8 leaves. Deest in Tibetan. K'-yuen-lu, fasc. 4, fol. 2 b.

526 佛說大乘流轉諸有經

Fo-shwo-tâ-shaṅ-liu-kwân-ku-yiu-kiṅ.

'Sûtra of the Mahâyâna spoken by Buddha on the transmigration through several states of existence.'

Bhavasaṅkramita (or -krânti)-sûtra.

K'-yuen-lu, fasc. 4, fol. 4 b. Conc. 576 gives the title of 'Bhavasaṅgirathî,' but see A. R., p. 460; A. M. G., p. 264. Translated by I-tsiṅ, A. D. 701, of the Thâṅ dynasty, A. D. 618–907. 3 leaves. It agrees with Tibetan. K'-yuen-lu, s. v.

527 佛說大意經

Fo-shwo-tâ-i-kiṅ.

'Buddhabhâshita-mahâmati-sûtra.'

Translated by Guṇabhadra, of the earlier Suṅ dynasty, A. D. 420–479. 7 leaves. Deest in Tibetan. K'-yuen-lu, fasc. 4, fol. 2 b. This is a Gâtaka of Buddha, who then emptied the sea to seek for a pearl. K'-tsiṅ, fasc. 9, fol. 15 b.

528 受持七佛名號所生功德經

Sheu-kh'-tshi-fo-miṅ-hâo-su-shaṅ-kuṅ-töh-kiṅ.

'Sûtra on the merits produced from keeping the names of seven Buddhas.'

Translated by Hhüen-kwâṅ (Hiouen-thsang), A. D. 651, of the Thâṅ dynasty, A. D. 618–907. 6 leaves. Deest in Tibetan. K'-yuen-lu, fasc. 4, fol. 3 a. In this Sûtra, Buddha told Sâriputra the names of seven Buddhas, five in the eastern, and two in the southern quarter. K'-tsiṅ, fasc. 5, fol. 17 b seq.

529 金剛光焰止風雨陀羅尼經

Kin-kâṅ-kwâṅ-yen-k'-faṅ-yü-tho-lo-ni-kiṅ.

'Sûtra of the Dhâraṇî of the diamond-light which stops the wind and rain.'

Translated by Bodhiruki, A. D. 710, of the Thâṅ dynasty, A. D. 618–907. 1 fasciculus. Deest in Tibetan. K'-yuen-lu, fasc. 5, fol. 5 b seq.

530 大毗盧遮那成佛神變加持經

Tâ-phi-lu-kö-nâ-khâṅ-fo-shan-pien-kiâ-kh'-kiṅ.

'Sûtra on Mahâvairokana's becoming Buddha and the supernatural formula called Yugandhara (? lit. adding-holding).'

Mahâvairokanâbhisambodhi.

A. R., p. 506; A. M. G., p. 307. Translated by Subhakarasimha, together with the Chinese priest Yi-hhiṅ A. D. 724, of the Thâṅ dynasty, A. D. 618–907. 7 fasciculi; 36 chapters. The 7th fasciculus has its own title, and five chapters in it are numbered separately. Deest in Tibetan. K'-yuen-lu, fasc. 5, fol. 4 b seq. See, however, the authorities mentioned under the title. This work is commonly called 大日經 Tâ-zih-kiṅ, or the Great Sun Sûtra, i. e. Mahâvairokana-sûtra.

531 蘇婆呼童子經

Su-pho-hu-thuṅ-tsz'-kiṅ.

'Subâhu-kumâra-sûtra.'

Cf. Conc. 541. Translated by Subhakarasimha, together with the Chinese priest Yi-hhiṅ, A. D. 724, of the Thâṅ dynasty, A. D. 618–907. 3 fasciculi; 12 chapters. Deest in Tibetan. K'-yuen-lu, fasc. 5, fol. 5 a.

The above two works are very important Sûtras of the Mantra school.

532 一字佛頂輪王經

Yi-tsz'-fo-tin-lun-wân-*k*in.

Ekâkshara-buddhoshnîsharâ*g*a-sûtra.'

Translated by Bodhiru*k*i, A.D. 709, of the Thân dynasty, A.D. 618–907. 6 fasciculi; 13 chapters. Deest in Tibetan. *K*'-yuen-lu, fasc. 5, fol. 4 a seq.

533 蘇悉地羯羅經

Su-shih-ti-*k*iê-lo-*k*in.

'Susiddhikâra-sûtra.'

Susiddhikâra-mahâtantra-saddhanopâsikâ-pa*t*ra.

K'-yuen-lu, fasc. 5, fol. 5 a; Conc. 542.

°tantra-sâdhanopamâyika-vitala.

A. R., p. 544; A. M. G., p. 341. Translated by *S*ubhakarasi*m*ha, A.D. 724, of the Thân dynasty, A.D. 618–907. 3 fasciculi; 38 chapters. It agrees with Tibetan. *K*'-yuen-lu, fasc. 5, fol. 5 a. This is also an important Sûtra of the Mantra school.

534 金剛頂瑜伽中略出念誦經

*K*in-kân-tin-yü-*k*iê-*k*un-liâo-*kh*u-nien-sun-*k*in.

'Sûtra for reciting, being an abridged translation of the Va*g*ra-sekhara-yoga (-tantra).'

Translated by Va*g*rabodhi, A.D. 723, of the Thân dynasty, A.D. 618–907. 4 fasciculi.

535 廣大寶樓閣善住秘密陀羅尼經

Kwân-tâ-pâo-leu-kö-shan-*k*ü-pêi-mi-tho-lo-ni-*k*in.

'Vipula-mahâma*n*i-vimâna-supratish*th*ita-guhya-dhâra*n*î-sûtra.'

Mahâma*n*i-vipulavimâna-vi*s*va-supratish*th*ita-guhya-parama-rahasya-kalparâ*g*a-dhâra*n*î.

Cf. *K*'-yuen-lu, fasc. 5, fol. 11 a; A. R., p. 509; A. M. G., p. 310. Translated by Bodhiru*k*i, A.D. 706, of the Thân dynasty, A.D. 618–907. 3 fasciculi; 12 chapters. Deest in Tibetan. *K*'-yuen-lu, fasc. 5, fol. 4 a seq. See, however, the last two authorities mentioned under the title. Cf. also *K*'-tsin, fasc. 12, fol. 2 b seq., where No. 535 is said to be a similar translation of Nos. 536 and 1028.

536 牟梨曼陀羅咒經

Meu-li-mân-tho-lo-*kh*eu-*k*in.

'Mûla (?)-mandala-mantra-sûtra.'

For the Sanskrit title, see No. 535.

Translated under the Liân dynasty, A.D. 502–557; but the translator's name is lost. 2 fasciculi. Deest in Tibetan. *K*'-yuen-lu, fasc. 5, fol. 5 a seq. See, however, A. R., p. 509; A. M. G., p. 310. No. 536 has not the introductory chapter, while the later two similar translations (Nos. 535 and 1028) have it. *K*'-yuen-lu, fasc. 12, fol. 3 a seq.

537 金剛頂經曼殊室利菩薩五字心陀羅尼品

*K*in-kân-tin-*k*in-mân-shu-shih-li-phu-sâ-wu-tsz'-sin-tho-lo-ni-phin.

'Va*g*ra-sekhara-sûtra-mañ*g*usrî-bodhisattva-pañ*k*âkshara-h*ri*daya-dhâra*n*î-varga.'

Translated by Va*g*rabodhi, A.D. 730, of the Thân dynasty, A.D. 618–907. 13 leaves. Deest in Tibetan. *K*'-yuen-lu, fasc. 5, fol. 9 b.

538 觀自在如意輪菩薩瑜伽法要

Kwân-tsz'-tsâi-*z*u-i-lun-phu-sâ-yü-*k*iê-fâ-yâo.

'The importance of the law of Yoga of the Bodhisattva Avalokitesvara*k*intâ*k*akra (or -ma*n*i ?).'

Translated by Va*g*rabodhi, A.D. 730, of the Thân dynasty, A.D. 618–907. 16 leaves. Deest in Tibetan. This is said to be an extract from the Va*g*ra-sekhara-sûtra, which consists of 100,000 slokas in verse, or an equivalent number of syllables in prose. *K*'-yuen-lu, fasc. 5, fol. 9 b.

539 佛說救面然餓鬼陀羅尼神咒經

Fo-shwo-*k*iu-mien-*z*ân-nö-kwêi-tho-lo-ni-shân-*kh*eu-*k*in.

'Buddhabhâshita-*g*vâlâmukha-preta-paritrâ*n*a-dhâra*n*y-*ri*ddhimantra-sûtra.'

Translated by *S*ikshânanda, of the Thân dynasty, A.D. 618–907. 3 leaves. It agrees with Tibetan. *K*'-yuen-lu, fasc. 5, fol. 8 b.

540 佛說甘露經陀羅尼

Fo-shwo-kân-lu-*k*in-tho-lo-ni.

'Buddhabhâshitâm*ri*ta-sûtra-dhâra*n*î.'

Translated by Sikshânanda, of the Thân dynasty, A. D. 618–907. Half a leaf.

541 佛說大陀羅尼末法中一字心咒經

Fo-shwo-tâ-tho-lo-ni-mo-fâ-kuṅ-yi-tsz'-sin-kheu-kiṅ.

'Ekâkshara-hridaya-mantra-sûtra, spoken by Buddha in the last dharma of the great Dhâranî.'

Translated by Ratnakinta, of North India, A. D. 705, of the Thân dynasty, A. D. 618–907. 1 fasciculus. Deest in Tibetan. K'-yuen-lu, fasc. 5, fol. 4 b. According to the K'-tsiṅ (fasc. 14, fol. 3 a), this Mantra is given in the Mañgusrî-mûla-garbha-tantra, No. 1056. For this Tantra, see the K'-yuen-lu, fasc. 5, fol. 14 b; A. R., p. 512; A. M. G., p. 313. For the date of the translation of No. 541, see the Khâi-yuen-lu, fasc. 9, fol. 15 b.

PART II.

小乘經 Siâo-shaṅ-kiṅ, or the Sûtras of the Hînayâna.

CLASS I.

阿含部 Ö-hân-pu, or Âgama Class.

542 中阿含經

Kuṅ-ö-hân-kiṅ.

Madhyamâgama-sûtra.

K'-yuen-lu, fasc. 6, fol. 18 a; Conc. 709; Wassiljew, pp. 115–117. Translated by Gautama Saṅghadeva, A.D. 397–398, of the Eastern Tsin dynasty, A.D. 317–420. 60 fasciculi; 5 adhyâyas; 18 vargas; 222 Sûtras collected. It agrees with Tibetan. *K'*-yuen-lu, s. v. There was an earlier translation made by Dharmanandi, A.D. 384–391, of the Former Tshin dynasty, A.D. 350–394; but it was lost already in A.D. 730. Khâi-yuen-lu, fasc. 15 a, fol. 1 a. No. 542 is to be compared with the Pâli text of the Maggħima-nikâya, collection of middle Suttas, 152 in number. See Sacred Books of the East, vol. x, p. xxviii. The following is a summary of the contents, with a literal translation of the Chinese titles of the 222 Sûtras:—

TITLE.	FASC.	FOL.
ADHYÂYA 1; 64 Sûtras.		
Varga 1, on the seven Dharmas.		
(1) On the good law	1	1 a–4 b
(2) „ day-measuring tree (comparison)		4 b–6 b
(3) „ (Râgagriha) city comparison		6 b–11 b
(4) „ water comparison		11 b–15 a
(5) „ tree-heap comparison		15 a–21 b
(6) „ good men's going and coming	2	1 a–3 b
(7) „ (seven) worldly good (actions)		4 a–6 b
(8) „ seven suns (to appear at the end of a Kalpa)		6 b–10 b
(9) „ seven carts (comparison)		11 a–17 a
(10) „ Âsrava-kshaya		17 a–21 a
Varga 2, on the consequence of Karma.		
(11) On the salt comparison	3	1 a–4 b
(12) „ (instruction to the Tîrthaka) Agreement-breaking (?)		4 b–8 b
(13) „ measurement		8 b–11 b
(14) „ (warning to) Râhula (against lying)		11 b–16 a
(15) On thought		16 a–19 a
(16) On the (instruction to the people of) *Kiâ*-lân (Karâsa?)		19 a–24 a
(17) On the (instruction to the Devaputra) Gâmin (?)	3	24 b–27 b
(18) „ (instruction to the minister) Simha	4	1 a–7 a
(19) „ (refutation of) Nirgrantha		7 a–16 a
(20) „ (instruction to) Po-lo-lâo (?)		16 a–28 a
Varga 3, on the fitness of Sâriputra (who is the chief speaker in the Sûtras of this Varga).		
(21) On the (address of the Deva) Samakitta (?)	5	1 a–4 a
(22) „ perfection of the Sîla		4 a–8 b
(23) On wisdom		8 b–14 a
(24) On the lion-roaring (or preaching)		14 a–19 a
(25) „ water comparison		19 a–22 a
(26) „ (Bhikshu) *Khâ*-ni-sh' (?)	6	1 a–5 b
(27) „ (instruction to the) Brahma*k*ârin Tho-sân (?)		5 b–13 b
(28) „ instruction to the diseased (Anâthapiṇḍada)		13 b–23 b
(29) „ (answer to Sâriputra by) Mahâkaushṭhila	7	1 a–11 a
(30) „ elephant-footprint comparison		11 a–21 a
(31) „ explanation of the (four) holy Satyas or truths		21 a–29 b
Varga 4, on the Adbhuta-dharma.		
(32) On the Adbhuta or that which has never existed before	8	1 a–8 b
(33) „ attendant (Ânanda)	8	8 b–19 b
(34) „ (answer to a Tîrthaka's question by) Vakkula		19 b–22 a
(35) „ (preaching by Buddha to an) Asura		22 a–28 a
(36) „ earthquake	9	1 a–4 a
(37) „ (country of) Kampâ'(?)		4 a–8 b
(38) „ Sreshṭhin Ugra, part 1		8 b–14 b
(39) „ Sreshṭhin Ugra, part 2		14 b–19 a
(40) „ Sreshṭhin Hand (Hasta?), part 1		19 a–25 b
(41) „ Sreshṭhin Hand (Hasta?), part 2		26 a–27 a
Varga 5, on the fitness of practice.		
(42) On the (answer by Buddha to Ânanda's question, saying) what is the meaning (of keeping the Sîla)?	10	1 a–2 b
(43) „ uselessness of anxiety		2 b–3 b
(44) „ intense thought		3 b–4 a
(45) „ shamefulness, part 1		4 a–4 b
(46) „ shamefulness, part 2		4 b–6 a

	TITLE.	FASC.	FOL.
(47)	On the *S*îla, part 1	10	6 a–6 b
(48)	„ *S*îla, part 2		6 b–7 a
(49)	On respectfulness, part 1		7 a–7 b
(50)	On respectfulness, part 2		8 a–8 b
(51)	On the fundamental limit, or causation		8 b–10 b
(52)	„ food (comparison), part 1		10 b–15 a
(53)	„ food (comparison), part 2		15 a–17 b
(54)	„ (Âsrava)-kshaya wisdom (?)		17 b–19 b
(55)	„ Nirvâna		19 b–21 b
(56)	„ (instruction to) Mi-hhi (an attendant of Buddha)		21 b–25 a
(57)	„ instruction to the Bhikshus (on the same subject as the preceding)		25 a–26 b

Varga 6, on the fitness of the King.

(58)	On the seven precious things (of the *K*akravarti-râga, compared with the seven Bodhyaṅgas)	11	1 a–1 b
(59)	„ thirty-two characteristic marks		1 b–5 b
(60)	„ four continents		5 b–11 b
(61)	„ cow-dung comparison		11 b–16 a
(62)	„ King Bimbisâra's coming to meet or inviting Buddha		16 a–21 b
(63)	„ (village) Pi-pho-li-liṅ-*kh*i (?)	12	1 a–15 a
(64)	„ (five) heavenly messengers (of the King Yama)		15 b–26 a

ADHYÂYA 2; 52 Sûtras.

(65)	On the crow and another bird (?) comparison	13	1 a–9 a
(66)	„ account of the former cause (spoken by Aniruddha, and that of the future Buddha Maitreya, told by Buddha)		9 a–19 b
(67)	„ forest of the great heavenly (*K*akravarti-râga) Nârâ(yana?)	14	1 a–13 a
(68)	„ King Mahâsudarsana. Cf. the Mahâsudassana-suttam, the Great King of Glory, S. B. E., vol. xi, pp. 247–289		13 a–24 b
(69)	„ thirty comparisons	15	1 a–7 a
(70)	„ *K*akravarti-râga (Saṅkha)		7 a–23 a
(71)	„ King Pi-ss' (?)	16	1 a–27 a

Varga 7, on the King of Long Age.

(72)	On the Ityukta of the King of Long Age	17	1 a–24 b
(73)	„ heaven, or state of Deva	18	1 a–5 b
(74)	„ eight intense thoughts (of a great man)		5 b–10 b
(75)	„ pure and unshakable way		10 b–15 a
(76)	„ (instruction to the Bhikshu) Yü-*kie*-*k*'-lo (?)		15 a–18 a
(77)	„ (instruction to the) three sons of the *S*âkya family (?)		18 a–26 b
(78)	„ Deva Brahman's asking Buddha	19	1 a–8 b
(79)	„ excellent heavens		9 a–18 a
(80)	„ Ka*th*ina or robe (presented to Anuruddha by Buddha and eight hundred Bhikshus)		18 a–27 a
(81)	„ intense thought on the body	20	1 a–11 b
(82)	„ (instruction by Kaush*th*ila to the unrespectable Bhikshu) *K*'-li-mi-li (?)		11 b–17 b

	TITLE.	FASC.	FOL.
(83)	On the sleepiness of the Sthavira (Maudgalyâyana)	20	17 b–20 b
(84)	„ freedom from thorns	21	1 a–3 a
(85)	„ true man		3 a–6 a
(86)	„ subject of instruction		6 b–19 b

Varga 8, on the uncleanness (of the human passion).

(87)	On the uncleanness (of the human passion)	22	1 a–14 a
(88)	„ seeking of the law		14 a–20 a
(89)	„ Bhikshu's asking (other worthies)	23	1 a–5 a
(90)	„ knowledge of the law		5 a–7 a
(91)	„ question and perception of *K*unda		7 a–11 a
(92)	„ blue and white lotus comparison		11 a–13 a
(93)	„ Brahma*k*ârin who thinks water pure		13 a–16 a
(94)	„ Bhikshu Black (Kâla ?)		16 b–20 a
(95)	„ existence of the law		20 a–22 a
(96)	„ nothingness (of the state of existence)		22 a–23 b

Varga 9, on the cause.

(97)	On the great cause. Cf. No. 545 (13)	24	1 a–14 b
(98)	„ Smrityupasthâna		15 a–22 b
(99)	„ Du*h*kha-skandha (?), part 1	25	1 a–6 b
(100)	„ Du*h*kha-skandha (?), part 2		6 b–12 a
(101)	„ increasing thought		12 a–15 b
(102)	On thought		16 a–20 a
(103)	On the roaring of lion (or preaching)	26	1 a–5 a
(104)	„ Udumbara (flower)		5 a–19 b
(105)	„ prayer or wish (of a Bhikshu)		20 a–22 a
(106)	On consciousness		21 a–23 b

Varga 10, on the forest.

(107)	On the forest, part 1	27	1 a–4 a
(108)	„ forest, part 2		4 a–6 a
(109)	„ meditation on one's own thought, part 1		6 a–8 a
(110)	„ meditation on one's own thought, part 2		8 a–9 b
(111)	„ understanding of the Brahma*k*aryâ		9 b–13 b
(112)	„ (village) Anupâ(ta? where Buddha foretold Devadatta's falling into hell)		14 a–20 b
(113)	„ origin of Sarva-dharma	28	1 a–2 a
(114)	„ (ignorance of) Udâra(ka?)		2 a–3 b
(115)	„ honey-pill comparison		3 b–9 a
(116)	„ (account of) Gautamî (Buddha's aunt)		9 a–17 b

ADHYÂYA 3; 35 Sûtras.

Mahâ-varga 11.

(117)	On softness	29	1 a–3 a
(118)	On the Nâga (dragon or elephant)		3 b–5 b
(119)	„ three subjects of preaching (viz. the times of past, present, and future)		5 b–7 b
(120)	„ Anitya or impermanency (of the five Skandhas)		7 b–8 b
(121)	„ repeated asking (lit. asking-asking)		8 b–11 b
(122)	„ (Bhikshu) *K*ampa		11 b–15 a
(123)	„ *S*râmanas, twenty Kotis in number		15 a–19 b
(124)	„ eight difficulties (on the learning of the way)		19 b–22 b
(125)	„ poor (comparison)		22 b–25 b
(126)	„ practice of desire	30	1 a–4 a
(127)	„ Punya-kshetra, or happy field		4 a–5 a
(128)	„ Upâsaka		5 a–9 a
(129)	„ enemy (viz. anger)		9 a–12 b
(130)	„ instruction to (the Bhikshu) Dharmamitra		12 b–18 b

	TITLE.	FASC.	FOL.
(131)	On the subjugation of the Mâra (who had entered the belly of Maudgalyâyana)	30	19 a–27 b
(132)	„ (G*ri*hapati) Râsh*t*rapâla (?, whose son became the disciple of Buddha)	31	1 a–18 a
(133)	„ (G*ri*hapati) Upâli	32	1 a–17 a
(134)	„ question asked by *S*akra	33	1 a–20 b
(135)	„ (instruction to the G*ri*hapati) Sugâta (or *S*rigâla?) Cf. No. 545 (16), and the Sigâlo-vâda-sutta, in the Sept Suttas Pâlis, text, pp. 297–310, and an English translation by Gogerly, pp. 311–320; and another translation by Childers, in the Contemporary Review (February, 1876), vol. xxvii, pp. 417–424		20 b–32 b
(136)	„ merchant's seeking treasure	34	1 a–11 b
(137)	„ world (where whatever the Tathâgata has spoken is all true)		11 b–12 a
(138)	On happiness		12 a–16 a
(139)	On the way of stopping (human passion)		16 a–17 b
(140)	„ extreme one-sidedness		17 b–18 b
(141)	On comparison		18 b–20 b

Varga 12, on the Brahma*k*ârin.

	TITLE.	FASC.	FOL.
(142)	On the (minister) Rain-power (Varshabala?, who was sent to Buddha by the King A*g*âtasatru to ask about the country of Poh-*kh*i)	35	1 a–8 b
(143)	„ (Mânava) *S*ankara		8 b–14 b
(144)	„ (instruction to) Sañkhyâ-maudgalyâyana		14 b–20 a
(145)	„ (question of) Goman-maudgalyâyana (whom Ânanda answers after Buddha's Nirvâna)	36	1 a–9 a
(146)	„ elephant's footprint comparison		9 a–16 b
(147)	„ merit of hearing		16 b–20 b
(148)	„ (question, saying), 'What is pain?'		20 b–24 a
(149)	„ (question, saying), 'What do they desire?'	37	1 a–2 a
(150)	„ (instruction to the Brahma*k*ârin) Yü-sheu-ko-lo (?, about the equality of the four castes)		2 a–11 a
(151)	„ (instruction to the Brahma*k*ârin) Asva (?)		11 a–22 a

Adhyâya 4; 35 Sûtras.

	TITLE.	FASC.	FOL.
(152)	On the (instruction to the Mânava) *S*uka	38	1 a–12 b
(153)	„ (instruction to the Tîrthaka) Sukânti (?)		12 b–23 a
(154)	„ (instruction to the ascetic) Balavat (?)	39	1 a–14 a
(155)	„ (instruction to the G*ri*hapati) Sudatta		14 a–18 a
(156)	„ (instruction to the) Brahma*k*ârin Parâya(na?)		18 a–21 a
(157)	„ (instruction given in the) yellow reed garden (Pîtave*n*uvana?, where an old Brahma*k*ârin became Buddha's disciple)	40	1 a–5 a
(158)	„ (instruction to) Tuna (?)		5 a–9 b
(159)	„ (instruction to) Akalkana (?)		9 b–11 b
(160)	On the (story of the Brahma*k*ârin) Âlâna (one of Buddha's former births)	40	11 b–19 b
(161)	„ (conversion of the Brahma*k*ârin) Brahman (?)	41	1 a–18 b

Mûla-nirdesa-varga 13.

	TITLE.	FASC.	FOL.
(162)	„ description of six Dhâtus	42	1 a–9 a
(163)	„ description of six Vishayas		9 a–15 a
(164)	„ description of the law of meditation		15 b–22 a
(165)	„ Deva of a hot-spring-forest	43	1 a–8 a
(166)	„ worthy in the Vihâra of Sâkya(muni?)		8 a–12 a
(167)	„ preaching of Ânanda		12 a–14 b
(168)	„ practice of thought		14 b–17 b
(169)	„ Arana (? 'not quarrelling or disputing,' spoken to) Krosa (?)		17 b–25 b
(170)	„ (instruction to the Mânava) *S*uka (whose father was re-born as a dog and barked at Buddha)	44	1 a–9 b
(171)	„ description of the great Karma		9 b–18 b

Varga 14, on thought.

	TITLE.	FASC.	FOL.
(172)	On thought	45	1 a–3 b
(173)	On the (instruction to) Bhûmi		4 a–9 a
(174)	„ law of receiving (results of former deeds), part 1		9 a–13 a
(175)	„ law of receiving (results of former deeds), part 2		13 a–17 a
(176)	„ practice of meditation	46	1 a–10 a
(177)	„ explanation (of the meditation)		10 a–17 a
(178)	„ hunter (comparison)	47	1 a–7 a
(179)	„ (instruction to the) owner of five things		7 a–12 b
(180)	„ (gift of) Gautamî (Mahâpra*g*âpatî)		12 b–16 b
(181)	„ many (or eighteen) Dhâtus		16 b–22 a

Twin Varga 15.

	TITLE.	FASC.	FOL.
(182)	On the (instruction given at the) horse village (?), part 1	48	1 a–4 b
(183)	„ (instruction given at the) horse village (?), part 2		4 b–8 a
(184)	„ Gosriṅga-sâla forest, part 1		8 b–18 a
(185)	„ Gosriṅga-sâla forest, part 2		18 a–23 b
(186)	„ search for understanding		23 b–26 a

Adhyâya 5; 36 Sûtras.

	TITLE.	FASC.	FOL.
(187)	On the explanation of wisdom	49	1 a–8 a
(188)	„ (Tîrthaka) A*g*ina (?)		8 a–13 a
(189)	„ holy path (40 great articles)		13 a–17 b
(190)	On emptiness in short (lit. small)		17 b–21 a
(191)	On emptiness in full (lit. large)		21 a–30 b

Latter Mahâ-varga 16.

	TITLE.	FASC.	FOL.
(192)	On the (instruction to) Kâlodayin	50	1 a–12 a
(193)	„ (instruction to Bhikshu) Meu-li-po-*kh*itn-na (?)		12 b–20 b
(194)	„ (instruction to Bhikshu) Bhadrapâla	51	1 a–11 b
(195)	„ (instruction to Bhikshu) Ô-shi-*k*ü (Asvaghosha?)		11 b–20 b
(196)	„ (instruction to Ânanda and) *K*unda	52	1 a–11 b
(197)	„ (dialogues between Buddha and) Upâli		11 b–15 b
(198)	„ (Purusha-)damya-sârathi-bhûmi		15 b–23 a
(199)	„ state of wisdom and foolishness	53	1 a–15 a

	TITLE.	FASC.	FOL.
(200)	On the (warning to the Bhikshu) Artha	54	1 a–12 b
(201)	„ (instruction to the Bhikshu) *Kh*â-ti (?)		12 b–24 a

Varga 17, on (the instruction to) Pu-li-to (V*ri*ddha ?, and others).

	TITLE.	FASC.	FOL.
(202)	On the keeping of the fast-day (Uposatho, in Pâli)	55	1 a–11 a
(203)	„ (instruction to the G*ri*hapati) V*ri*ddha (?)		11 a–20 a
(204)	„ (instruction to the Bhikshus at the house of the Brahma*k*ârin) Râma	56	1 a–11 b
(205)	„ five lower knots (to be cut off)		11 b–17 b
(206)	„ impurity of the (human) thought		17 b–21 a
(207)	„ (instruction to the Tîrthaka) Arrow-hair, part 1	57	1 a–8 a
(208)	„ (instruction to the Tîrthaka) Arrow-hair, part 2		8 a–17 b
(209)	„ (instruction to the Tîrthaka) Vimanas (?)		17 b–23 a
(210)	„ (dialogues between the) Bhikshunî Dharmaratî (? and Vaisâkhya ?)	58	1 a–8 b
(211)	„ (dialogues between *S*âriputra and) Mahâ-kaushth*i*la		8 b–16 b

Varga 18, on example.

	TITLE.	FASC.	FOL.
(212)	On the all-knowing (Sarva*gñ*â)	59	1 a–10 b
(213)	„ law-adornment (Dharma-vyûha)		10 b–18 a
(214)	„ Vihati (or friend ?)		18 a–24 b
(215)	„ first obtainment		24 b–28 b
(216)	„ production of love	60	1 a–5 a
(217)	„ (instruction of Ânanda to the G*ri*hapati possessed of) eight cities (?)		5 a–8 a
(218)	„ (preaching to the Bhikshus by) Anaruddha, part 1		8 a–9 a
(219)	„ (preaching to the Bhikshus by) Anaruddha, part 2		9 a–11 a
(220)	„ seeing or view (of the Tathâgata, which Ânanda spoke to the Tîrthakas)		11 a–12 b
(221)	„ arrow comparison		12 b–17 b
(222)	„ examples (spoken by Buddha)		17 b–30 a

543 增壹阿含經

Tsan-yi-ö-hân-*k*in.

Ekottarâgama-sûtra.

K'-yuen-lu, fasc. 6, fol. 19 a; Conc. 762. Wassiljew, p. 115, reads Ekottarikâgama. Translated by Dharmanandi, A. D. 384–385, of the Former Tshin dynasty, A.D. 350–394. 50 fasciculi; 52 chapters. There is the note at the end, viz. that the text consisted of 250,000 slokas in verse, or an equivalent number of syllables in prose; and the Sûtra has 'Evam mayâ *s*rutam ekasmin samaye' 555 times, i. e. as many short Sûtras collected. It agrees with Tibetan. *K'*-yuen-lu, s. v. According to the Khâi-yuen-lu (fasc. 15 a, fol. 1 a) and *K'*-yuen-lu, there was an earlier translation made by Dharmanandi, A. D. 384; but it was lost already in A. D. 730; while a later translation in existence is said to have been made by Gautama Pra*gñ*âru*k*i, A. D. 397, of the Eastern Tsin dynasty, A. D. 317–420. Cf. Khâi-yuen-lu, fasc. 3, fol. 9 a. But now there is a preface to No. 543 by the Chinese priest Tâo-ân, a contemporary of Dharmanandi, in which he not only describes the date of this translation, as A. D. 384–385, but gives also an account of the translator; while the later translation is not found in the present collection. No. 543 is to be compared with the Pâli text of the Aṅguttara-nikâya, miscellaneous suttas, in divisions the length of which increases by one. See Sacred Books of the East, vol. x, p. xxviii. The following is a summary of the contents, with a literal translation of the Chinese titles of the 52 chapters:—

	TITLE.	FASC.
(1)	Introduction	1
(2)	On the ten intense thoughts	
(3)	„ wide explanation	
(4)	„ disciples or Bhikshus	
(5)	„ Bhikshunîs	
(6)	„ Upâsakas	
(7)	„ Upâsikâs	
(8)	„ Asuras	
(9)	„ only son (and daughter comparison)	
(10)	„ protection of thought	
(11)	„ Anâgâmin	
(12)	On once entering the path	
(13)	On the profitable support	6
(14)	„ five *S*îlas (*S*ikshâpadas)	7
(15)	„ (faults of the belief in) existence and non-existence	
(16)	„ extinguishing of the fire	
(17)	„ Ân-pân or Ânâpâna-sm*ri*ti-karmasthâna, or meditation on breath inhaled and exhaled. (See Spence Hardy, Eastern Monachism, pp. 267–269. Cf. Miṅ-i-tsi, fasc. 17, fol. 17 a seq.; Childers, Pâli Dict., p. 31 b.)	8
(18)	On shamefulness	9
(19)	On the persuading and asking (of Brahman to Buddha to turn the wheel of the law)	10
(20)	„ good teacher	11
(21)	„ Triratna	12
(22)	„ three objects worshipped (viz. the Tathâgata, Arhat, and *K*akravarti-râga)	
(23)	„ lord of the earth	13
(24)	„ high banner	14–16
(25)	„ *K*atus-satya (four truths)	17
(26)	„ four thought-cuttings (?)	18–19
(27)	„ equally going (or treating ?) of the four truths	
(28)	„ *S*râvakas	20
(29)	On happiness and pain	21
(30)	On the (account of the *S*râmanera) Suda (?)	22
(31)	„ higher increasing	23
(32)	„ collection of good (qualities)	24
(33)	„ five kings	25
(34)	„ equal view	26
(35)	„ collection of unjust things	27
(36)	„ hearing of the law	28
(37)	„ six degrees	29–30

TITLE.	FASC.
(38) On the (six) powers (as crying of a child, anger of a woman, pâtience of a Srâmana and Brahmakârin, pride of a king, intelligence of an Arhat, and the great compassion of Buddha)	31–32
(39) „ equal law	33
(40) „ seven suns (to appear at the end of a Kalpa)	34–35
(41) On (the instruction as) not to be feared	
(42) On the eight difficulties (Ashtâkshana)	36–37
(43) „ (instruction to the) Devaputra Horse-blood	38–39
(44) „ dwellings of nine (sorts of) beings	40
(45) „ horse-king	41
(46) „ establishment of prohibition	42
(47) „ (ten) good and bad (actions)	43
(48) „ ten bad (actions)	44
(49) „ pasturing to cows	45–46
(50) „ worship of the Triratna	47
(51) „ Anitya or non-eternity	48
(52) „ Parinirvâna of Mahâpragâpatî	49–50

N. B. The above titles show the contents of the first Sûtra of each chapter.

544 雜阿含經

Tsâ-ö-hân-*k*in.

Samyuktâgama-sûtra.

K'-yuen-lu, fasc. 6, fol. 19 a; Conc. 755; Wassiljew, p. 115. Translated by Gunabhadra, of the earlier Sun dynasty, A. D. 420–479. 50 fasciculi. It agrees with Tibetan. *K*'-yuen-lu, s.v. About half of this Sûtra is the same as or similar to Nos. 542, 543; and the composition in Chinese is more perfect. But the titles of chapters are not complete. *K*'-tsin, fasc. 29, fol. 9 b. No. 544 is to be compared with the Pâli text of the Samyutta-nikâya, collection of joined Suttas. See Sacred Books of the East, vol. x, p. xxviii.

545 佛說長阿含經

Fo-shwo-*k*hân-ö-hân-*k*in.

'Buddhabhâshita-dîrghâgama-sûtra.'

Dîrghâgama-sûtra.

K'-yuen-lu, fasc. 6, fol. 17 b; Conc. 680; Wassiljew, p. 115. Translated by Buddhayasas, together with *K*u Fo-nien, A. D. 412–413, of the Latter Tshin dynasty, A. D. 384–417. 22 fasciculi; 4 vargas; 30 Sûtras collected. It agrees with Tibetan. *K*'-yuen-lu, s. v. No. 545 is to be compared with the Pâli text of the Dîgha-nikâya, collection of long Suttas, 34 in number. See Sacred Books of the East, vol. x, p. xxviii. The following table will show the difference of the order of the 30 and 34 Sûtras in No. 545 and the Pâli text; for which latter, see Sept Suttas Pâlis, by Grimblot:—

NO. 545: TITLE.	FASC.	FOL.	PÂLI.
Varga 1; 4 Sûtras.			
(1) Sûtra on the first-great-original-nidâna	1	1 a–38 b	(14) Mahâpadhâna-sutta. S.S.P., pp. 343–4
(2) On going for pleasure, or Vihâra(?), or Mahâparinirvâna-sûtra. Cf. Nos. 118, 119, 545	2 3 4	1 a–19 b 1 a–25 b 1 a–24 a	(16) Mahâparinibbâna-sutta. S.S.P., p. 344; S.B.E., vol. xi
(3) On (the minister named) Tien-tsun (lit. ruling worthy)	5	1 a–15 a	(19) Mahâgovinda-sutta. S.S.P., p. 345
(4) On (the demon) *G*anesa		15 a–22 b	(18) *G*anavasabha-suttanta. S.S.P., p. 345
Varga 2; 15 Sûtras.			
(5) On the four castes	6	1 a–10 a	
(6) On the practice of the holy *K*akravarti-râ*g*a		10 a–22 a	(26) *K*akkavatti-sihanâda-sutta. S.S.P., p. 347–8
(7) On (the Brâhmana) Pi-su (i. e. Pâyasika?)	7	1 a–16 b	(23) Pâyâsi-sutta. S.S.P., p. 346
(8) On (the Grihapati) Sandhâna	8	1 a–9 b	(25) Udumbarika-sihanâda-sutta. S.S.P., p. 347
(9) On the Sangîti		9 b–20 b	(33) Sangîti-suttanta. S.S.P., p. 349
(10) On the Dasottara (-dharma)	9	1 a–17 b	(34) Das'uttara-suttanta. S.S.P., p. 349
(11) On the Ekottara (-dharma)	10	1 a–7 b	
(12) On the Trirâsi (-dharma)		7 b–10 b	
(13) On the Mahânidâna-upâya		10 b–18 b	(15) Mahânidâna-sutta. S.S.P., pp. 245–262 (text), 263–279 (a Fr. translation)
(14) On the question of Sakra Devânâm Indra		18 b–29 b	(21) Sakkâ-pamhâ-sutta. S.S.P., pp. 345–6
(15) On (the city) Ŏ-tho-i (?)	11	1 a–15 a	
(16) On (the Grihapati-putra) Sugâta (? 'well born'). Cf. No. 542 (135)		15 a–23 b	(31) Sigâlo-vâda-sutta, S.S.P., pp. 297–310 (text), 311–320 (an English translation)
(17) On the pureness (of practice)	12	1 a–14 a	
(18) On the self-joyfulness		14 a–23 b	(28) Sampadânîya-sutta. S.S.P., p. 348
(19) On the Mahâsamaya (great assembly)		24 a–31 b	(20) Mahâsamaya-sutta, pp. 280–288 (text), 289–296 (an English translation)

Varga 3; 10 Sûtras.

NO. 545: TITLE.	FASC.	FOL.	PÂLI.
(20) On (the Mânava) Ambash*th*a (?)	13	1 a–23 a	(3) Amba*tth*a-sutta. S. S.P., pp. 339–340
(21) On the Brahma-*g*âla (lit. Brahma-moving)	14	1 a–21 a	(1) Brahma*g*âla-sutta. S.S.P., pp. 1–58 (text), 59–112 (an English trans.)
(22) On (the Brâhmana named) Planting virtue (?)	15	1 a–10 a	(4) Sona*da*n*d*a-sutta. S. S. P., p. 340
(23) On (the Brâhmana) Kuladanta		10 a–26 a	(5) Kutadanta-sutta. S. S. P., pp. 340–341
(24) On (the G*r*hapati-putra named) Firmness (Sthira ?)	16	1 a–6 a	(11) Kevaddha (?)-suttanta. S. S. P., p. 342
(25) On the Akela-brahma*k*ârin (whose patronymic was Kâsyapa)		6 a–12 b	(8) Kassapa-sîhanâda-sutta. S. S. P., p. 342
(26) On the Traividya		12 b–21 a	(13) Tevi*gg*a-suttanta. S. S. P., p. 343; S. B. E., vol. xi
(27) On the *S*râmanya-phala	17	1 a–10 b	(2) Samañña-phala-sutta. S.S.P., pp. 113–154 (text), 166–186 (an Eng. trans.), 187–244 (a French trans.)
(28) On (the Brahma-*k*ârin) Pu-*k*hâ-pho-leu (i.e. Putapâla, or Pustapâda ?)		10 b–20 b	(9) Po*tth*apâda-suttanta. S. S. P., p. 342
(29) On (the Brâhmana) Lu-*k*ŏ (?)		21 a–26 a	(12) Lohi*kk*a-suttanta. pp. 342–3

Varga 4; 1 Sûtra.

(30) On the record of the world:—

NO. 545: TITLE.	FASC.	FOL.
Chap. 1, on *G*ambudvîpa	18	1 a–13 a
" 2, on Uttarakuru		13 a–19 b
" 3, on the holy *K*akravarti-râ*g*a		19 b–26 b
" 4, on the Narakas	19	1 a–20 a
" 5, on the Nâga and birds		20 b–27 a
" 6, on the Asuras	20	1 a–4 b
" 7, on the *K*aturdivya (or Mahârâ*g*as)		4 b–7 a
" 8, on the Trayastrimsas		7 a–29 a
" 9, on the three misfortunes	21	1 a–14 b
" 10, on the fighting (of the Devas and Asuras)		14 b–24 b
" 11, on the three middle Kalpas	22	1 a–3 b
" 12, on the original cause of the world		4 a–21 a

Thus six Sûtras in No. 545 (viz. 5, 11, 12, 15, 17, 30) seem not to be given in the Pâli text, or at least with different titles. At the same time, the following ten Suttas seem to be left out in No. 545:—(6) Mahâli-suttanta, S. S. P., p. 341; (7) *G*âliya-suttanta, pp. 341–2; (10) Subha-sutta, pp. 154–165; (17) Mahâsudassana-sutta, pp. 344–5,—this is, however, found in No. 542 (68); (22) Mahâsatipa*tth*âna-sutta, p. 346; (24) Pâ*t*ika-sutta, pp. 346–7; (27) Aggañña-suttanta, p. 348; (29) Pâsâdika-sutta, p. 348; (30) Lakkhana-suttanta, p. 348; (32) Â*t*ânâtiya-sutta, pp. 321–337. It is, however, possible that if No. 545 is compared with the Pâli text minutely, some of these Suttas may still be found.

546 別譯雜阿含經

Pieh-i-tsâ-ö-hân-*k*in.

'A different translation of Samyuktâgama-sûtra.'

Saktavargâgama-sûtra (?).

K'-yuen-lu, fasc. 6, fol. 19 b; Conc. 451. Translated under the three Tshin dynasties, A. D. 350–431; but the translator's name is lost. 20 fasciculi. It agrees with Tibetan. *K*'-yuen-lu, s. v.

547 雜阿含經

Tsâ-ö-hân-*k*in.

Sa*m*yuktâgama-sûtra.

Translated under the Wêi and Wu dynasties, A. D. 220–280; but the translator's name is lost. 1 fasciculus. 25 short Sûtras collected.

The above two works are extracts from a full text as that of No. 544. *K*'-tsin, fasc. 29, fol. 9 b.

548 長阿含十報法經

*Kh*ân-ö-hân-shi-pâo-fâ-*k*in.

'Sûtra on the law of ten rewards in the Dîrghâgama.'

Translated by Ân Shi-kâo, of the Eastern Hân dynasty, A. D. 25–220. 2 fasciculi. This is an earlier translation of No. 545 (10), i.e. the Dasottara-sûtra. It contains 550 dharmas. Piâo-mu, fasc. 6, fol. 19 b; *K*'-tsin, fasc. 29, fol. 7 a.

549 起世因本經

*Kh*i-shi-yin-pan-*k*in.

'Sûtra on the original cause of raising the world (?).'

Translated by Dharmagupta, of the Sui dynasty, A. D. 589–618. 10 fasciculi; 12 chapters.

550 起世經

*Kh*i-shi-*k*in.

'Sûtra on raising the world (?).'

Translated by *G*ñânagupta, of the Sui dynasty, A. D. 589–618. 10 fasciculi; 12 chapters.

551 佛說樓炭經

Fo-shwo-leu-thân-*k*in.

'Sûtra on the Lokadhâtu (?) spoken by Buddha.'

Translated by Fâ-li, together with Fâ-*k*ü, of the

Western Tsin dynasty, A.D. 265–316. 6 fasciculi; 13 chapters.

The above three works are earlier translations of No. 545 (30), i. e. the Sûtra on the record of the world, in the Dîrghâgama. K'-yuen-lu, fasc. 6, fol. 22 a; K'-tsiṅ, fasc. 29, fol. 8 b.

552 佛般泥洹經
Fo-pân-ni-yuen-*k*iṅ.
'Buddha-parinirvâṇa-sûtra.'
Mahâparinirvâ*n*a-sûtra.

K'-yuen-lu, fasc. 6, fol. 20 a; Conc. 166. Translated by Po Fâ-tsu, A.D. 290–306, of the Western Tsin dynasty, A.D. 265–316. 2 fasciculi. This is an earlier translation of Nos. 118, 119, 545 (2); and it agrees with Tibetan. K'-yuen-lu, fasc., s. v. For the comparison with the Pâli text of the Mahâparinibbâna-sutta, see the Sacred Books of the East, vol. xi, pp. xxxvi–xxxix.

553 佛說人本欲生經
Fo-shwo-*z*an-pan-yü-shaṅ-*k*iṅ.
'Sûtra spoken by Buddha on the Avidyâ, Trishṇâ, and Gâti (i. e. three of the twelve Nidânas) of man.'

Translated by Ân Shi-kâo, A.D. 146, of the Eastern Hân dynasty, A.D. 25–220. 1 fasciculus. This is an earlier translation of No. 545 (13), i. e. the Mahânidâna-upâya-sûtra, in the Dîrghâgama. K'-yuen-lu, fasc. 6, fol. 20 b.

554 佛說梵網六十二見經
Fo-shwo-fân-wâṅ-liu-shi-'rh-*k*ien-*k*iṅ.
'Sûtra spoken by Buddha on sixty-two (different) views of the net of Brahma.'
Brahma-*g*âla-sûtra.

A. R., p. 483; A. M. G., p. 286. Translated by K' Khien, of the Wu dynasty, A.D. 222–280. 1 fasciculus. This is an earlier translation of No. 545 (21). K'-yuen-lu, fasc. 6, fol. 21 a.

555 佛說尸迦羅越六方禮經
Fo-shwo-sh'-*k*iâ-lo-yueh-liu-fâṅ-li-*k*iṅ.
'Sûtra spoken by Buddha on the worship of six quarters (i. e. four cardinal points and zenith and nadir), being the Sîgâlo (or Srigâla ?)-vâ(da).'

Translated by Ân Shi-kâo, of the Eastern Hân dynasty, A.D. 25–220. 8 leaves. This is an earlier and shorter translation of Nos. 542 (135) and 545 (16). K'-yuen-lu, fasc. 6, fol. 20 b. A partial English translation has been published by Mr. Beal, in his Catalogue, p. 112.

556 中本起經
Kuṅ-pan-*kh*i-*k*iṅ.
'Madhyama-ityukta-sûtra.'

Translated by Thân-kwo (Dharmaphala), together with Khâṅ Maṅ-siâṅ, A.D. 207, of the Eastern Hân dynasty, A.D. 25–220. 2 fasciculi; 15 chapters. This is said to be an extract from a full text of the Dîrghâgama, No. 545. K'-yuen-lu, fasc. 6, fol. 22 a. This is a life of Sâkyamuni. The subject of the first chapter is his turning the wheel of the law, and that of the fifteenth is his eating the horse-barley.

557 佛說七知經
Fo-shwo-tshi-*k*'-*k*iṅ.
'Sûtra spoken by Buddha on the seven kinds of knowledge.'

Translated by K' Khien, of the Wu dynasty, A.D. 222–280. 3 leaves. This is an earlier translation of No. 542 (1), i. e. the Sûtra on the good law, in the Madhyamâgama. K'-yuen-lu, fasc. 6, fol. 22 a.

558 佛說鹹水喻經
Fo-shwo-hhien-shui-yü-*k*iṅ.
'Sûtra spoken by Buddha on the salt-water comparison.'

Translated under the Western Tsin dynasty, A.D. 265–316; but the translator's name is lost. 2 leaves. This is an earlier translation of No. 542 (4), i. e. the Sûtra on the water comparison, in the Madhyamâgama. K'-yuen-lu, fasc. 6, fol. 22 b.

559 佛說一切流攝守因經
Fo-shwo-yi-tshiê-liu-shö-sheu-yin-*k*iṅ.
'Sûtra spoken by Buddha on the cause of all the Âsravas or sins.'

Translated by Ân Shi-kâo, of the Eastern Hân dynasty, A.D. 25–220. 5 leaves. This is an earlier translation of No. 542 (10), i. e. the Âsrava-kshaya-sûtra, in the Madhyamâgama. K'-yuen-lu, fasc. 6, fol. 22 b.

560 佛說閻羅王五天使者經
Fo-shwo-yen-lo-wâṅ-wu-thien-sh'-*k*ö-*k*iṅ.
'Sûtra spoken by Buddha on the five heavenly messengers of the King Yama.'

Translated by Hwui-*k*ien, of the earlier Suṅ dynasty, A.D. 420–479. 4 leaves.

561 佛說鐵城泥犁經
Fo-shwo-thie-*kh*âṅ-ni-li-*k*iṅ.
'Sûtra spoken by Buddha on the iron-castle Naraka.'

Translated by Thân-wu-lân (Dharmaraksha ?), of the Eastern Tsin dynasty, A.D. 317–420. 6 leaves.

The above two works are similar translations of No. 542 (64), i. e. the Sûtra on the heavenly messengers, in the Madhyamâgama. *K'*-yuen-lu, fasc. 6, fol. 23 b.

562 佛說古來世時經

Fo-shwo-ku-lâi-shi-sh'-*k*iṅ.

'Sûtra spoken by Buddha on the world and time of the past and future.'

Translated under the Western Tsin dynasty, A.D. 265–316. 6 leaves. This is an earlier translation of No. 542 (13), i. e. the Sûtra on the account of the former cause (etc.), in the Madhyamâgama. *K'*-yuen-lu, fasc. 6, fol. 24 a.

563 佛說阿那律八念經

Fo-shwo-ŏ-nâ-liu-pâ-nien-*k*iṅ.

'Sûtra spoken by Buddha on the eight intense thoughts of Anuruddha.'

Translated by *K'* Yâo, A.D. 185, of the Eastern Hân dynasty, A.D. 25–220. 5 leaves. This is an earlier translation of No. 542 (74), i.e. the Sûtra on the eight intense thoughts, in the Madhyamâgama. *K'*-yuen-lu, fasc. 6, fol. 24 a.

564 佛說離睡經

Fo-shwo-li-shui-*k*iṅ.

'Sûtra spoken by Buddha on the freedom from sleep.'

Translated by *K*u Fâ-hu (Dharmaraksha), of the Western Tsin dynasty, A.D. 265–316. 3 leaves. This is an earlier translation of No. 542 (83), i. e. the Sûtra on the sleepiness of the Sthavira (Maudgalyâyana), in the Madhyamâgama. *K'*-yuen-lu, fasc. 6, fol. 24 a.

565 佛說是法非法經

Fo-shwo-sh'-fâ-fê-fâ-*k*iṅ.

'Sûtra spoken by Buddha on the law, true and not true.'

Translated by Ân Shi-kâo, of the Eastern Hân dynasty, A.D. 25–220. 4 leaves. This is an earlier translation of No. 542 (85), i. e. the Sûtra on the true man, in the Madhyamâgama. *K'*-yuen-lu, fasc. 6, fol. 24 a.

566 佛說樂想經

Fo-shwo-lŏ-siâṅ-*k*iṅ.

Sûtra spoken by Buddha on the idea of happiness.'

Translated by *K*u Fâ-hu (Dharmaraksha), of the Western Tsin dynasty, A.D. 265–316. 2 leaves. This is an earlier translation of No. 542 (106), i. e. the Sûtra on consciousness, in the Madhyamâgama. *K'*-yuen-lu, fasc. 6, fol. 25 b.

567 佛說漏分布經

Fo-shwo-leu-fan-pu-*k*iṅ.

'Sûtra spoken by Buddha on the explanation of Âsrava (?).'

Translated by Ân Shi-kâo, of the Eastern Hân dynasty, A.D. 25–220. 7 leaves. This is an earlier translation of No. 542 (111), i. e. the Brahma*k*aryâ-sûtra, in the Madhyamâgama. *K'*-yuen-lu, fasc. 6, fol. 25 b.

568 佛說阿耨颰經

Fo-shwo-ŏ-neu-fu-*k*iṅ.

'Sûtra spoken by Buddha on (the village) Anupâ (ta ?).'

Translated by Thân-wu-lân (Dharmaraksha ?), of the Eastern Tsin dynasty, A.D. 317–420. 7 leaves. This is an earlier translation of No. 542 (112), i. e. the Sûtra on Anupâ (ta ?), in the Madhyamâgama. *K'*-yuen-lu, fasc. 6, fol. 25 b.

569 佛說求欲經

Fo-shwo-*k*hiu-yü-*k*iṅ.

'Sûtra spoken by Buddha on desire.'

Translated by Fâ-*k*ü, of the Western Tsin dynasty, A.D. 265–316. 12 leaves. This is an earlier translation of No. 542 (87), i. e. the Sûtra on the uncleanness, in the Madhyamâgama. *K'*-yuen-lu, fasc. 6, fol. 24 b.

570 佛說受歲經

Fo-shwo-sheu-sui-*k*iṅ.

'Sûtra spoken by Buddha on receiving the year (?).'

Translated by *K*u Fâ-hu (Dharmaraksha), of the Western Tsin dynasty, A.D. 265–316. 5 leaves. This is an earlier translation of No. 542 (89), i. e. the Sûtra on the Bhikshu's asking (other worthies), in the Madhyamâgama. *K'*-yuen-lu, fasc. 6, fol. 24 b.

571 佛說梵志計水淨經

Fo-shwo-fân-*k'*-*k*i-shui-tsiṅ-*k*iṅ.

'Sûtra spoken by Buddha on the Brahma*k*ârin who thinks water pure.'

Translated under the Western Tsin dynasty, A.D. 265–316; but the translator's name is lost. 3 leaves. This is an earlier translation of No. 542 (93), i. e. the Sûtra of a similar title to that of No. 571, in the Madhyamâgama. *K'*-yuen-lu, fasc. 6, fol. 25 a.

572 佛說伏婬經

Fo-shwo-fu-yin-*k*iṅ.

'Sûtra spoken by Buddha on overcoming lust.'

Translated by Fâ-kü, of the Western Tsin dynasty, A. D. 265–316. 4 leaves. This is an earlier translation of No. 542 (126), i. e. the Sûtra on the practice of desire, in the Madhyamâgama. K'-yuen-lu, fasc. 6, fol. 26 b.

573 佛說魔嬈亂經
Fo-shwo-mo-žâo-lwân-kiṅ.
'Sûtra spoken by Buddha on (Maudgalyâyana's) temptation by the Mâra.'

Translated under the Eastern Hân dynasty, A. D. 25–220; but the translator's name is lost. 10 leaves.

574 佛說弊魔試目連經
Fo-shwo-pi-mo-sh'-mu-lien-kiṅ.
'Sûtra spoken by Buddha on Maudgalyâyana's temptation by the wicked Mâra.'

Translated by K' Khien, of the Wu dynasty, A. D. 222–280. 7 leaves.

The above two works are earlier translations of No. 542 (131), i. e. the Sûtra on the subjugation of the Mâra, in the Madhyamâgama. K'-yuen-lu, fasc. 6, fol. 26 b.

575 佛說泥犁經
Fo-shwo-ni-li-kiṅ.
'Sûtra spoken by Buddha on the Naraka.'

Translated by Thân-wu-lân (Dharmaraksha ?), of the Eastern Tsin dynasty, A. D. 317–420. 14 leaves. This is a similar translation of No. 542 (199), i. e. the Sûtra on the state of wisdom and foolishness, in the Madhyamâgama. K'-yuen-lu, fasc. 7, fol. 2 a.

576 佛說優婆夷墮舍迦經
Fo-shwo-yiu-pho-i-to-shö-kiâ-kiṅ.
'Sûtra spoken by Buddha to the Upâsikâ To-shö-kiâ (?).'

Translated under the earlier Suṅ dynasty, A. D. 420–479; but the translator's name is lost. 4 leaves.

577 佛說齋經
Fo-shwo-kâi-kiṅ.
'Sûtra spoken by Buddha on fasting (Uposatho in Pâli).'

Translated by K' Khien, of the Wu dynasty, A. D. 222–280. 4 leaves.

The above two works are similar translations of No. 542 (202), i. e. the Sûtra on keeping a fast, in the Madhyamâgama. K'-yuen-lu, fasc. 7, fol. 2 a.

578 佛說苦陰經
Fo-shwo-khu-yin-kiṅ.
'Sûtra spoken by Buddha on the Duḥkha-skandha (?).'

Translated under the Eastern Hân dynasty, A. D. 25–220; but the translator's name is lost. 6 leaves. This is an earlier translation of No. 542 (99), i. e. part 1 of the Sûtra on the Duḥkha-skandha, in the Madhyamâgama. K'-yuen-lu, fasc. 6, fol. 25 a.

579 佛說苦陰因事經
Fo-shwo-khu-yin-yin-sh'-kiṅ.
'Sûtra spoken by Buddha on the cause of the Duḥkha-skandha.'

Translated by Fâ-kü, of the Western Tsin dynasty, A. D. 265–316. 6 leaves.

580 佛說釋摩男本經
Fo-shwo-shih-mo-nân-pan-kiṅ.
'Sûtra on the cause spoken by Buddha to Sâkya Mahânâman.'

Translated by K' Khien, of the Wu dynasty, A. D. 222–280. 5 leaves.

The above two works are earlier translations of No. 542 (100), i. e. part 2 of the Sûtra on the Duḥkha-skandha, in the Madhyamâgama. K'-yuen-lu, fasc. 6, fol. 25 a.

581 佛說鞞摩肅經
Fo-shwo-pi-mo-suh-kiṅ.
'Sûtra spoken by Buddha to Vimanas (?).'

Translated by Guṇabhadra, of the earlier Suṅ dynasty, A. D. 420–479. 5 leaves. This is a later translation of No. 542 (209), i. e. the Sûtra spoken to Vimanas (?), in the Madhyamâgama. K'-yuen-lu, fasc. 7, fol. 2 b.

582 佛說婆羅門子命終愛念不離經
Fo-shwo-pho-lo-man-tsz'-miṅ-kuṅ-âi-nien-pu-li-kiṅ.
'Sûtra spoken by Buddha to a Brâhmaṇa who could not become free from tender thoughts at the death of his son.'

Translated by Ân Shi-kâo, of the Eastern Hân dynasty, A. D. 25–220. 5 leaves. This is an earlier translation of No. 542 (216), i. e. the Sûtra on the production of love, in the Madhyamâgama. K'-yuen-lu, fasc. 7, fol. 2 b.

583 佛說十支居士八城人經
Fo-shwo-shi-k'-kü-sh'-pâ-khân-žan-kiṅ.
'Sûtra spoken by Buddha to the Gṛhapati, being a man possessed of eight cities and ten families (?).'

Translated by Ân Shi-kâo, of the Eastern Hân dynasty, A. D. 25–220. 4 leaves. This is an earlier translation of No. 542 (217), i. e. the Sûtra spoken by Ânanda to the Grihapati possessed of eight cities (?), in the Madhyamâgama. *K'*-yuen-lu, fasc. 7, fol. 2 b.

584 佛說邪見經

Fo-shwo-siê-*k*ien-*k*iṅ.

'Sûtra spoken by Buddha on the unjust views.'

Translated under the Eastern Tsin dynasty, A. D. 317–420; but the translator's name is lost. 2 leaves. This is a later translation of No. 542 (220), i. e. the Sûtra on the view of the Tathâgata, in the Madhyamâgama. *K'*-yuen-lu, fasc. 7, fol. 3 a.

585 佛說箭喩經

Fo-shwo-tsien-yü-*k*iṅ.

'Sûtra spoken by Buddha on the arrow comparison.'

Translated under the Eastern Tsin dynasty, A. D. 317–420; but the translator's name is lost. 4 leaves. This is a similar translation of No. 542 (221), i. e. the Sûtra of the same title as that of No. 585, in the Madhyamâgama. *K'*-yuen-lu, fasc. 7, fol. 3 a.

586 佛說普法義經

Fo-shwo-phu-fâ-i-*k*iṅ.

'Sûtra spoken by Buddha on the universal meaning of the law.'

Translated by Ân Shi-kâo, A. D. 152, of the Eastern Hân dynasty, A. D. 25–220. 10 leaves.

587 佛說廣義法門經

Fo-shwo-kwâṅ-i-fâ-man-*k*iṅ.

'Sûtra spoken by Buddha on the gate of the law of wide meaning.'

Translated by Paramârtha, of the *Kh*an dynasty, A. D. 557–589. 10 leaves.

The above two works are similar translations of a chapter in the Madhyamâgama, No. 542; but the title of the chapter is not mentioned in *K'*-yuen-lu, fasc. 6, fol. 3 a; Piâo-mu, fasc. 6, fol. 28 b; *K'*-tsiṅ, fasc. 31, fol. 3 a.

588 佛說戒德香經

Fo-shwo-*k*iê-töh-hhiâṅ-*k*iṅ.

'Sûtra spoken by Buddha on the fragrance of the virtue of *S*îla.'

Translated by Thân-wu-lân (Dharmaraksha ?), of the Eastern Tsin dynasty, A. D. 317–420. 2 leaves. This is a similar translation of No. 543 (23), i. e. the chapter on the Lord of the earth, in the Ekottarâgama. *K'*-yuen-lu, fasc. 7, fol. 3 b.

589 佛說四人出現世間經

Fo-shwo-sz'-zan-*kh*u-hhien-shi-*k*ien-*k*iṅ.

'Sûtra spoken by Buddha on four men's appearance in the world.'

Translated by Guṇabhadra, of the earlier Suṅ dynasty, A. D. 420–479. 4 leaves. This is a later translation of No. 543 (26), i. e. the chapter on the four kinds of the cutting of thought, in the Ekottarâgama. *K'*-yuen-lu, fasc. 6, fol. 3 b.

590 佛說諸法本經

Fo-shwo-*k*u-fâ-pan-*k*iṅ.

'Sûtra spoken by Buddha on the origin of Sarva-dharma.'

Translated by *K' Kh*ien, of the Wu dynasty, A. D. 222–280. 1 leaf. This is an earlier translation of No. 542 (113), i. e. the Sûtra of the same title as that of No. 590, in the Madhyamâgama. *K'*-yuen-lu, fasc. 6, fol. 26 a.

591 佛說瞿曇彌記果經

Fo-shwo-*kh*ü-thân-mi-*k*i-kwo-*k*iṅ.

'Sûtra spoken by Buddha on the prophecy of Gautamî.'

Translated by Hwui-*k*ien, A. D. 457, of the earlier Suṅ dynasty, A. D. 420–479. 8 leaves. This is a later translation of No. 542 (116), i. e. the Sûtra on Gautamî, in the Madhyamâgama. *K'*-yuen-lu, fasc. 6, fol. 26 a. There is another translation similar to Nos. 542 (116) and 591, viz. chap. 9 of No. 556.

592 佛說梵志阿颰經

Fo-shwo-fân-*k'*-ö-fu-*k*iṅ.

'Sûtra spoken by Buddha on the Brahma*k*ârin Ambash*th*a (?).'

Translated by *K' Kh*ien, of the Wu dynasty, A. D. 222–280. 1 fasciculus. This is an earlier translation of No. 545 (20), i. e. the Sûtra on (the Mânava) Ambash*th*a (?), in the Dirghâgama. *K'*-yuen-lu, fasc. 6, fol. 21 a.

593 佛說寂志果經

Fo-shwo-tsi-*k'*-kwo-*k*iṅ.

'Sûtra spoken by Buddha on the fruit of the calm-minded (i. e. *S*râmaṇya-phala).'

Translated by Thân-wu-lân (Dharmaraksha ?), of the Eastern Tsin dynasty, A. D. 317–420. 1 fasciculus. This is a similar translation of No. 545 (27), i. e. the *S*râmaṇya-phala-sûtra, in the Dirghâgama. *K'*-yuen-lu, fasc. 6, fol. 21 a.

594 佛說賴吒和羅經

Fo-shwo-lâi-*kh*â-hö-lo-*k*iṅ.

'Sûtra spoken by Buddha on (the Grihapati) Râsh*t*rapâla (?).'

Translated by K' Khien, of the Wu dynasty, A. D. 222–280. 12 leaves. This is an earlier translation of No. 542 (132), i. e. the Sûtra of the same title as that of No. 594, in the Madhyamâgama. K'-yuen-lu, fasc. 6, fol. 27 a.

595   佛說善生子經

Fo-shwo-shân-shan-tsz'-kiṅ.

'Sûtra spoken by Buddha to the son of Sugâta.'

Translated by Ku Fâ-hu (Dharmaraksha), of the Western Tsin dynasty, A. D. 265–316. 9 leaves. This is a similar translation of No. 542 (135), i. e. the Sûtra spoken to Sugâta in the Madhyamâgama, and also Nos. 545 (16), 555, being the Sigâlo (or Srigâla ?)-vâda. Cf. K'-yuen-lu, fasc. 6, fol. 27 a.

596   佛說數經

Fo-shwo-shu-kiṅ.

'Sûtra spoken by Buddha to Sankhya (-maudgalyâyana).'

Translated by Fâ-kü, of the Western Tsin dynasty, A. D. 265–316. 6 leaves. This is an earlier translation of No. 542 (144), i. e. the Sûtra spoken to Saṅkhya-maudgalyâyana, in the Madhyamâgama. K'-yuen-lu, fasc. 6, fol. 27 a.

597   佛說梵志頞波羅延問種尊經

Fo-shwo-fân-k'-nŏ-po-lo-yen-wan-kuṅ-tsun-kiṅ.

'Sûtra spoken by Buddha on the superiority of the caste (of Brâhmanas) in answer to the Brahmakârin Nŏ-po-lo-yen (?).'

Translated by Thân-wu-lân (Dharmaraksha), of the Eastern Tsin dynasty, A. D. 317–420. 8 leaves. This is a similar translation of No. 542 (151), i. e. the Sûtra spoken to Asva (?) in the Madhyamâgama. K'-yuen-lu, fasc. 6, fol. 27 b.

598   佛說四諦經

Fo-shwo-sz'-ti-kiṅ.

'Sûtra spoken by Buddha on the four truths.'

Katus-satya-sûtra.

A. R., p. 476; A. M. G., p. 279. Translated by Ân Shi-kâo, of the Eastern Hân dynasty, A. D. 25–220. 10 leaves. This is an earlier translation of No. 542 (31), i. e. the Sûtra on the explanation of the holy truths, in the Madhyamâgama. K'-yuen-lu, fasc. 6, fol. 22 b.

599   佛說恒水經

Fo-shwo-haṅ-shui-kiṅ.

'Sûtra spoken by Buddha on the river Gaṅgâ (comparison).'

Translated by Fâ-kü, of the Western Tsin dynasty, A. D. 265–316. 4 leaves. This is an earlier translation of No. 542 (37), i. e. the Sûtra on (the country of) Kampâ (?), in the Madhyamâgama. K'-yuen-lu, fasc. 6, fol. 23 a.

600   佛說瞻婆比丘經

Fo-shwo-kan-pho-pi-khiu-kiṅ.

'Sûtra spoken by Buddha on the Bhikshu Kampa.'

Translated by Fâ-kü, of the Western Tsin dynasty, A. D. 265–316. 4 leaves. This is an earlier translation of No. 542 (122), i. e. the Sûtra on Kampa, in the Madhyamâgama. K'-yuen-lu, fasc. 6, fol. 26 a.

601   佛說本相倚致經

Fo-shwo-pan-siâṅ-i-k'-kiṅ.

'Sûtra spoken by Buddha on the fundamental relationship (or causation).'

Translated by Ân Shi-kâo, of the Eastern Hân dynasty, A. D. 25–220. 3 leaves.

602   佛說緣本致經

Fo-shwo-yuen-pan-k'-kiṅ.

'Sûtra spoken by Buddha on the fundamental causation.'

Translated under the Eastern Tsin dynasty, A. D. 317–420; but the translator's name is lost. 2 leaves. The above two works are similar translations of No. 542 (51), i. e. the Sûtra on the fundamental limit, in the Madhyamâgama. K'-yuen-lu, fasc. 6, fol. 23 a.

603   佛說頂生王故事經

Fo-shwo-tiṅ-shaṅ-wâṅ-ku-sh'-kiṅ.

'Sûtra spoken by Buddha on the former account of the King Mûrdhaga.'

Translated by Fâ-kü, of the Western Tsin dynasty, A. D. 265–316. 7 leaves.

604   佛說文陀竭王經

Fo-shwo-wan-tho-kiê-wâṅ-kiṅ.

'Sûtra spoken by Buddha on the King Mândhâtri.'

Translated by Dharmaraksha, of the Northern Liâṅ dynasty, A. D. 397–439. 4 leaves.

The above two works are similar translations of No. 542 (60), i. e. the Sûtra on the four continents, in the Madhyamâgama. K'-yuen-lu, fasc. 6, fol. 23 a. Cf. Burnouf, 'Introduction,' p. 65 seq., translated from the Divyâvadâna. For the Sanskrit text, see the Catalogue of the Hodgson Manuscripts, III. 25, 26; V. 51; VI. 46.

605 三歸五戒慈心厭離功德經

Sân-kwêi-wu-*k*iê-tshz'-sin-yen-li-kun-töh-*k*in.

'Sûtra on the merits of the Trisarana (three-refuges), Pa*ñk*asîla (five precepts), compassionate thought and disliking and becoming free (from the world).'

Translated under the Eastern Tsin dynasty, A. D. 317–420; but the translator's name is lost. 1 leaf.

606 佛說須達經

Fo-shwo-sü-tâ-*k*in.

'Sûtra spoken by Buddha to Sudatta.'

Translated by Gu*n*av*ri*ddhi, A. D. 495, of the Tshi dynasty, A. D. 479–502. 4 leaves.

The above two works are similar translations of No. 542 (155), i. e. the Sûtra spoken to Sudatta, in the Madhyamâgama. *K'*-yuen-lu, fasc. 6, fol. 27 b.

607 佛爲黃竹園老婆羅門說學經

Fo-wêi-kwân-*k*u-yuen-lâo-pho-lo-man-shwo-hhiâo-*k*in.

'Sûtra on learning addressed by Buddha to the old Brâhma*n*a of the yellow bamboo garden (Pitave*n*uvana ?).'

Translated under the earlier Sun dynasty, A. D. 420–479; but the translator's name is lost. 5 leaves. This is a later translation of No. 542 (157), i. e. the Sûtra spoken in the yellow reed garden, in the Madhyamâgama. *K'*-yuen-lu, fasc. 6, fol. 28 a.

608 佛說梵摩喩經

Fo-shwo-fân-mo-yü-*k*in.

'Sûtra spoken by Buddha on the Brahma comparison (?).'

Translated by *K' Kh*ien, of the Wu dynasty, A. D. 222–280. 11 leaves. This is an earlier translation of No. 542 (161), i. e. the Sûtra on (the conversion of the Brahma*k*ârin) Brahman (?), in the Madhyamâgama. *K'*-yuen-lu, fasc. 7, fol. 1 a.

609 佛說尊上經

Fo-shwo-tsun-shân-*k*in.

'Sûtra spoken by Buddha on the honourable one (?).'

Translated by *K*u Fâ-hu (Dharmaraksha), of the Western Tsin dynasty, A. D. 265–316. 4 leaves. This is an earlier translation of No. 542 (166), i. e. the Sûtra on the worthy in the Vihâra of *S*âkya(muni ?), in the Madhyamâgama. *K'*-yuen-lu, fasc. 7, fol. 1 a.

610 佛說鸚鵡經

Fo-shwo-yin-wu-*k*in.

'Sûtra spoken by Buddha to (the Brâhma*n*a) named *S*uka (parrot).'

Translated by Gu*n*abhadra, of the earlier Sun dynasty, A. D. 420–479. 10 leaves.

611 佛說兜調經

Fo-shwo-teu-thiâo-*k*in.

'Sûtra spoken by Buddha on or to Teu-thiâo (Devadatta ?).'

Translated under the Western Tsin dynasty, A. D. 265–316; but the translator's name is lost. 4 leaves.

The above two works are similar translations of No. 542 (170), i. e. the Sûtra spoken to *S*uka, in the Madhyamâgama. *K'*-yuen-lu, fasc. 7, fol. 1 a. These Sûtras relate, that there was a white dog in the house of a G*ri*hapati or Brâhma*n*a named *S*uka, in *S*râvastî. This dog barked at Buddha, when the latter approached the house for alms. Then the dog was told by Buddha, that he was a Brahma*k*ârin named Teu-thiâo (?) in his former birth, and constantly made a noise in asking food; but now having been born as a dog, he could simply bark, and that he should be silent. Afterwards *S*uka, the son of the former Brahma*k*ârin, and the master of the present dog, was very angry with Buddha, having learnt that his favourite dog was greatly offended by Buddha. Then Buddha taught him the doctrine of Karma.

The two characters 分衞 Fan-wêi are used in No. 610 and some other works (e.g. No. 16) in the sense of 'going about in the search of alms.' This term may literally be rendered as 'to divide an outpost or frontier town and garrison,' but not streets in general, as Mr. Beal translates in his Catalogue, p. 48, l. 5. Moreover, Fan-wêi is generally understood as a transliteration, the original of which may be Pai*nd*apâtika, one of the twelve Dhûtas. Cf. col. 108.

612 佛說意經

Fo-shwo-i-*k*in.

'Sûtra spoken by Buddha on thought.'

Translated by *K*u Fâ-hu (Dharmaraksha), of the Western Tsin dynasty, A. D. 265–316. 3 leaves. This is an earlier translation of No. 542 (172), i. e. the Sûtra on thought, in the Madhyamâgama. *K'*-yuen-lu, fasc. 7, fol. 1 b.

613 佛說應法經

Fo-shwo-yin-fâ-*k*in.

'Sûtra spoken by Buddha on the law of the fitness (of cause and effect).'

Translated by *K*u Fâ-hu (Dharmaraksha), of the Western Tsin dynasty, A. D. 265–316. 5 leaves. This is an earlier translation of No. 542 (174), i. e. the Sûtra on the law of receiving, in the Madhyamâgama. *K'-yuen-lu*, fasc. 7, fol. 1 b.

614 佛說波斯匿王太后崩塵土坌身經
Fo-shwo-po-sz'-ni-wâṅ-thâi-heu-paṅ-khân-tu-fan-shan-kiṅ.
'Sûtra spoken by Buddha to the King Prasenagit, who put dust on his body at the death of his mother (and came to see Buddha).'

Translated by Fâ-kü, of the Western Tsin dynasty, A. D. 265–316. 4 leaves. This is an earlier translation of a Sûtra in No. 543 (26), i. e. the chapter on the four kinds of the cutting of thought, in the Ekottarâgama. *K'-yuen-lu*, fasc. 7, fol. 4 a.

615 須摩提女經
Sü-mo-thi-nü-kiṅ.
'Sûtra on Sumati, the daughter (of Anâthapindada).'

Translated by K' Khien, of the Wu dynasty, A. D. 222–280. 20 leaves.

616 佛說三摩竭經
Fo-shwo-sân-mo-kiê-kiṅ.
'Sûtra spoken by Buddha on Sumati (?).'

Translated by Ku Lüh-yen, of the Wu dynasty, A. D. 222–280. 9 leaves.

The above two works are earlier translations of a Sûtra in No. 543 (30), i. e. the chapter on Suda, in the Ekottarâgama. *K'-tsiṅ*, fasc. 26, fol. 22 b.

617 佛說婆羅門避死經
Fo-shwo-pho-lo-man-pi-sz'-kiṅ.
'Sûtra spoken by Buddha on some Brâhmanas (who mean) to avoid death.'

Translated by Ân Shi-kâo, of the Eastern Hân dynasty, A. D. 25–220. 1 leaf. This is an earlier translation of a Sûtra in No. 543 (31), i. e. the chapter on the higher increasing, in the Ekottarâgama. *K'-yuen-lu*, fasc. 7, fol. 4 a.

618 施食獲五福報經
Sh'-shi-kwo-wu-fu-pâo-kiṅ.
'Sûtra on obtaining five happy rewards by giving food.'

Translated under the Eastern Tsin dynasty, A. D. 265–316; but the translator's name is lost. 2 leaves. This is a similar translation of a Sûtra in No. 543 (32), i. e. the chapter on the collection of good (qualities), in the Ekottarâgama. *K'-yuen-lu*, fasc. 7, fol. 4 a.

619 頻毗娑羅王詣佛供養經
Phin-phi-shâ-lo-wâṅ-i-fo-kuṅ-yâṅ-kiṅ.
'Sûtra on the King Bimbisâra's coming to worship Buddha.'

Translated by Fâ-kü, of the Western Tsin dynasty, A. D. 265–316. 5 leaves. This is an earlier translation of a Sûtra in No. 543 (34), i. e. the chapter on equanimity, in the Ekottarâgama. *K'-yuen-lu*, fasc. 7, fol. 4 b.

620 佛說長者子六過出家經
Fo-shwo-khâṅ-kö-tsz'-liu-kwo-khu-kiâ-kiṅ.
'Sûtra spoken by Buddha on the son of a Sreshthin (elder or rich merchant) who forsook home six times (liu-kwo; and who, for the seventh time, became a disciple of Buddha).'

Translated by Hwui-kien, A. D. 457, of the earlier Suṅ dynasty, A. D. 420–479. 3 leaves. This is a later translation of a Sûtra in No. 543 (35), i. e. the chapter on the collection of unjust things, in the Ekottarâgama. *K'-yuen-lu*, fasc. 7, fol. 4 b.

621 佛說鴦崛摩經
Fo-shwo-yâṅ-küê-mo-kiṅ.
'Sûtra spoken by Buddha on Aṅgulimâlya.'

Translated by Ku Fâ-hu (Dharmaraksha), of the Western Tsin dynasty, A. D. 265–316. 7 leaves.

622 佛說鴦崛髻經
Fo-shwo-yâṅ-küê-ki-kiṅ.
'Sûtra spoken by Buddha on Aṅgulimâlya.'

Translated by Ku Fâ-hu (Dharmaraksha), of the Western Tsin dynasty A. D. 265–316. 7 leaves.

The above two works are earlier translations of No. 543 (38), i. e. the chapter on the (six) powers, in the Ekottarâgama. *K'-yuen-lu*, fasc. 7, fol. 4 b seq.; where No. 622 is said to have been translated by Fâ-kü, of the Western Tsin dynasty. Nos. 621 and 622 do not agree with each other, so that they may most probably be different parts of a text.

623 佛說力士移山經
Fo-shwo-li-sh'-i-shân-kiṅ.
'Sûtra spoken by Buddha on the (500) Mallas or wrestlers who were trying to move a mountain.'

Translated by Ku Fâ-hu (Dharmaraksha), of the Western Tsin dynasty, A. D. 265–316. 6 leaves.

624 佛說四未曾有法經
Fo-shwo-sz'-wêi-tshaṅ-yiu-fâ-kiṅ.
'Sûtra spoken by Buddha on the four Adbhutadharmas.'

Translated by *K*u Fâ-hu (Dharmaraksha), of the Western Tsin dynasty, A.D. 265–316. 2 leaves.

The above two works are earlier translations of Sûtras in No. 543 (42), i.e. the chapter on the eight difficulties, in the Ekottarâgama. *K'*-yuen-lu, fasc. 7, fol. 5 a.

625 佛說舍利弗目犍連遊四衢經

Fo-shwo-shö-li-fu-mu-*k*ien-lien-yiu-sz'-*kh*ü-*k*iṅ.

'Sûtra spoken by Buddha on *S*âriputra and Maudgalyâyana's going through four roads.'

Translated by Khâṅ Maṅ-siâṅ, of the Eastern Hân dynasty, A.D. 25–220. 4 leaves. This is an earlier translation of a Sûtra in No. 543 (45), i.e. the chapter on the horse-king, in the Ekottarâgama. *K'*-yuen-lu, fasc. 7, fol. 5 a.

626 七佛父母姓字經

Tshi-fo-fu-mu-siṅ-tsz'-*k*iṅ.

'Sûtra on the names and surnames of the parents of the seven Buddhas.'

Translated under the Wêi dynasty, A.D. 220–265; but the translator's name is lost. 4 leaves. This is an earlier translation of a Sûtra in No. 543 (48), i.e. the chapter on the ten bad (actions), in the Ekottarâgama. *K'*-yuen-lu, fasc. 7, fol. 5 b.

627 佛說放牛經

Fo-shwo-fâṅ-niu-*k*iṅ.

'Sûtra spoken by Buddha on letting cows go.'

Translated by Kumâra*g*îva, of the Latter Tshin dynasty, A.D. 384–417. 5 leaves.

628 緣起經

Yuen-*kh*i-*k*iṅ.

'Nidâna-sûtra.'

Translated by Hhüen-*k*wâṅ (Hiouen-thsang), A.D. 661, of the Thâṅ dynasty, A.D. 618–907. 3 leaves.

The above two works are similar translations of a Sûtra in No. 543 (49), i.e. the chapter on pasturing cows, in the Ekottarâgama. *K'*-yuen-lu, fasc. 7, fol. 5 b.

629 佛說十一想思念如來經

Fo-shwo-shi-yi-siâṅ-sz'-nien-*z*u-lâi-*k*iṅ.

'Sûtra spoken by Buddha on eleven (methods of) thinking of the Tathâgata.'

Translated by Gu*n*abhadra, of the earlier Suṅ dynasty, A.D. 420–479. 2 leaves.

630 佛說四泥犂經

Fo-shwo-sz'-ni-li-*k*iṅ.

'Sûtra spoken by Buddhá on four Narakas.'

Translated by Thân-wu-lân (Dharmaraksha ?), of the Eastern Tsin dynasty, A.D. 317–420. 2 leaves.

The above two works are similar translations of a Sûtra in No. 543 (50), i.e. the chapter on the worship of the Triratna, in the Ekottarâgama. *K'*-yuen-lu, fasc. 7, fol. 6 a.

631 舍衛國王夢見十事經

Shö-wêi-kwo-wâṅ-maṅ-*k*ien-shi-sz'-*k*iṅ.

'Sûtra on ten different dreams of the King of the country *S*râvastî (Prasena*g*it).'

Translated under the Western Tsin dynasty, A.D. 265–316; but the translator's name is lost. 5 leaves.

632 佛說國王不黎先尼十夢經

Fo-shwo-kwo-wâṅ-pu-li-sien-ni-shi-maṅ-*k*iṅ.

'Sûtra spoken by Buddha on the ten dreams of Prasena*g*it, the King of the country (*S*râvastî).'

Translated by Thân-wu-lân (Dharmaraksha ?), of the Eastern Tsin dynasty, A.D. 317–420. 5 leaves.

The above two works are similar translations of a Sûtra in No. 543 (52), i.e. the chapter on the Parinirvâ*n*a of Mahâpra*g*âpatî. *K'*-yuen-lu, fasc. 7, fol. 6 b.

633 阿難同學經

Ö-nân-thuṅ-hhiâo-*k*iṅ.

'Sûtra on Ânanda's fellow-student (named Gupta).'

Translated by Ân Shi-kâo, of the Eastern Hân dynasty, A.D. 25–220. 4 leaves. This is an earlier translation of a part of the Ekottarâgama, No. 543. *K'*-yuen-lu, fasc. 7, fol. 7 a.

634 五蘊皆空經

Wu-yun-*k*iê-khuṅ-*k*iṅ.

'Sûtra on the emptiness of all the five Skandhas.'

Translated by I-tsiṅ, A.D. 710, of the Thâṅ dynasty, A.D. 618–907. 1 leaf. This is a later translation of a part of fasc. 2 of the Sa*m*yuktâgama, No. 544. *K'*-yuen-lu, fasc. 7, fol. 7 a.

635 阿難問事佛吉凶經

Ö-nân-wan-sh'-fo-*k*i-hhiüṅ-*k*iṅ.

'Sûtra asked by Ânanda on the difference of lucky and unlucky conditions of those who serve Buddha.'

Translated by Ân Shi-kâo, of the Eastern Hân dynasty, A.D. 25–220. 7 leaves.

636 慢法經
Mân-fâ-*kiṅ*.
'Sûtra on disregarding the law.'

Translated by Fâ-*kü*, of the Western Tsin dynasty, A.D. 265–316. 2 leaves.

637 阿難分別經
Ö-nân-fan-pieh-*kiṅ*.
'Sûtra on Ânanda's thinking.'

Translated by Shâṅ-*k*ien, of the Western Tshin dynasty, A.D. 385–431. 7 leaves.

The above three works are similar translations, and they are wanting in Tibetan. *K'*-yuen-lu, fasc. 7, fol. 10 b.

638 五母子經
Wu-mu-tsz'-*kiṅ*.
'Sûtra on the son of five mothers.'

Translated by *K' Kh*ien, of the Wu dynasty, A.D. 222–280. 2 leaves.

639 沙彌羅經
Shâ-mi-lo-*kiṅ*.
'Sûtra on a *Srâ*maṇera (viz. the son of five mothers).'

Translated under the three Tshin dynasties, A.D. 350–431; but the translator's name is lost. 2 leaves.

The above two works are similar translations, and they are wanting in Tibetan. *K'*-yuen-lu, fasc. 7, fol. 11 a.

640 玉耶經
Yü-ye-*kiṅ*.
'Sûtra on Yü-ye (lit. 'is (she) a gem?'—the name of the wife of a son of Anâthapiṇḍada).'

Translated by Thân-wu-lân (Dharmaraksha?), of the Eastern Tsin dynasty, A.D. 317–420. 5 leaves.

641 玉耶女經
Yü-ye-nü-*kiṅ*.
'Sûtra on the woman Yü-ye.'

Translated under the Western Tsin dynasty, A.D. 265–316; but the translator's name is lost. 4 leaves.

642 阿遬達經
Ö-su-tâ-*kiṅ*.
'Sûtra on Astha(lâ?—the name of a woman).'

Translated by Guṇabhadra, of the earlier Suṅ dynasty, A.D. 420–479. 2 leaves.

The above three works are similar translations, and they agree with Tibetan. *K'*-yuen-lu, fasc. 7, fol. 11 a.

643 摩鄧女經
Mo-taṅ-nü-*kiṅ*.
'Sûtra (spoken to) a Mâtaṅga (outcast) girl.'
Mâtaṅgî-sûtra.

Cf. Böhtlingk und Roth, Sanskrit Dictionary, s.v. Mâtaṅga°. Translated by Ân Shi-kâo, of the Eastern Hân dynasty, A.D. 25–220. 3 leaves. It has been translated into English by Mr. Beal, in his Buddhist Literature in China, pp. 166–170.

644 摩鄧女解形中六事經
Mo-taṅ-nü-*k*iê-hhiṅ-*k*uṅ-liu-sh'-*kiṅ*.
'Sûtra (spoken to) a Mâtaṅga girl on six different objects in explaining (the impurity of body, viz. eye, nose, mouth, ear, voice, and walking).'
Mâtaṅgî-sûtra.

Translated under the Western or Eastern Tsin dynasty, A.D. 265–316 or 317–420; but the translator's name is lost. 3 leaves.

The above two works are similar translations of chap. 1 of No. 645. *K'*-tsiṅ, fasc. 30, fol. 11 a.

645 摩登伽經
Mo-taṅ-*k*iê-*kiṅ*.
Mâtaṅgî-sûtra.

Translated by *K*u Lüh-yen, together with *K' Kh*ien, of the Wu dynasty, A.D. 222–280. 2 fasciculi; 21 and 18 leaves; 7 chapters.

646 舍頭諫經
Shö-theu-*k*ien-*kiṅ*.
'Sûtra on *S*ârdûlakarṇa ("tiger's ear," i.e. the former name of Ânanda).'
Mâtaṅgî-sûtra.

Translated by *K*u Fâ-hu (Dharmaraksha), of the Western Tsin dynasty, A.D. 265–316. 1 fasciculus; 33 leaves.

The above four works are similar translations complete and incomplete, and they are wanting in Tibetan. *K'*-yuen-lu, fasc. 7, fol. 9 b. They all give a history of the Mâtaṅgî or outcast girl named Prakriti, who was asked by Ânanda to give him water to drink, etc. Cf. Burnouf, 'Introduction' (ed. 1876), p. 183 seq., mentioned in Beal, Catalogue, p. 46. Nos. 643–646 are to be compared with the Divyâvadâna. For the Sanskrit text, see Catalogue of the Hodgson Manuscripts, III. 25, 26; V. 51; VI. 46.

647 治禪病祕要經
K'-shân-piṅ-pi-yâo-*kiṅ*.
'Sûtra on the secret importance of curing the (heart) disease of those who engage in contemplation.'

Translated by Tsü-*kh*ü *K*iṅ-shân, A. D. 455, of the earlier Suṅ dynasty, A. D. 420–479. 2 fasciculi. This is said to be a similar translation of a part of the Samyuktâgama, No. 544; but a corresponding part in No. 544 as well as Tibetan is not found. *K'*-yuen-lu, fasc. 7, fol. 9 a seq. Moreover it explains the doctrine of the Mahâyâna. *K'*-tsiṅ, fasc. 30, fol. 8 b seq.

648 佛說七處三觀經

Fo-shwo-tshi-*kh*u-sân-*k*wân-*k*iṅ.

'Sûtra spoken by Buddha on seven places (Âyatanas) and three subjects for contemplation.'

Translated by Ân Shi-kâo, A. D. 151, of the Eastern Hân dynasty, A. D. 25–220. 2 fasciculi. This is an earlier translation of a part of fasciculi 2 and 34 of the Samyuktâgama, No. 544. *K'*-yuen-lu, fasc. 7, fol. 7 a; *K'*-tsiṅ, fasc. 29, fol. 9 b.

649 阿那邠邸化七子經

Ö-nâ-pin-ti-hwâ-tshi-tsz'-*k*iṅ.

'Sûtra on the conversion of his seven children caused by Anâthapiṇḍada (by means of giving them money).'

Translated by Ân Shi-kâo, of the Eastern Hân dynasty, A. D. 25–220. 5 leaves. This is an earlier translation of a Sûtra in No. 543 (51), i. e. the chapter on the Anitya, in the Ekottarâgama. *K'*-yuen-lu, fasc. 7, fol. 6 a.

650 大愛道般涅槃經

Tâ-âi-tâo-pân-niê-phân-*k*iṅ.

'Mahâpragâpatî-parinirvâṇa-sûtra.'

Translated by Po Fâ-tsu, of the Western Tsin dynasty, A. D. 265–316. 8 leaves.

651 佛母般泥洹經

Fo-mu-pân-ni-yuen-*k*iṅ.

'Buddhamâtri (Mahâpragâpatî)-parinirvâṇa-sûtra.'

Translated by Hwui-*kh*ien, A. D. 457, of the earlier Suṅ dynasty, A. D. 420–479. 5 leaves.

The above two works are similar translations of a Sûtra in No. 543 (52), i. e. the chapter on the same subject, in the Ekottarâgama. *K'*-yuen-lu, fasc. 7, fol. 6 b.

There is an appendix to No. 651, entitled 'a record of changes after Buddha's Parinirvâṇa,' which describes a character of each of ten centuries. Cf. No. 123.

652 佛說聖法印經

Fo-shwo-shaṅ-fâ-yin-*k*iṅ.

'Sûtra spoken by Buddha on the holy seal of the law.'

Translated by *K*u Fâ-hu (Dharmaraksha), of the Western Tsin dynasty, A. D. 265–316. 2 leaves.

This is an earlier translation of a Sûtra in fasc. 3 of No. 544, i. e. the Samyuktâgama. *K'*-yuen-lu, fasc. 7, fol. 7 b.

653 五陰譬喩經

Wu-yin-phi-yü-*k*iṅ.

'Sûtra on the comparison of the five Skandhas (with foam, a bubble, flame, a plantain, and vision).'

Translated by Ân Shi-kâo, of the Eastern Hân dynasty, A. D. 25–220. 3 leaves.

654 佛說水沫所漂經

Fo-shwo-shui-mo-su-phiâo-*k*iṅ.

'Sûtra spoken by Buddha on the floating bubble or foam on water (i. e. the first of five comparisons).'

Translated by Thân-wu-lân (Dharmaraksha ?), of the Eastern Tsin dynasty, A. D. 317–420. 3 leaves.

The above two works are similar translations of a Sûtra in fasc. 10 of No. 544, i. e. the Samyuktâgama. *K'*-tsiṅ, fasc. 29, fol. 10 b.

655 佛說不自守意經

Fo-shwo-pu-tsz'-sheu-i-*k*iṅ.

'Sûtra spoken by Buddha on not guarding one's own thought.'

Translated by *K' Kh*ien, of the Wu dynasty, A. D. 222–280. 1 leaf. This is an earlier translation of a part of fasc. 11 of No. 544, i. e. the Samyuktâgama. *K'*-yuen-lu, fasc. 7, fol. 8 a.

656 佛說滿願子經

Fo-shwo-mân-yuen-tsz'-*k*iṅ.

'Sûtra spoken by Buddha on Pûrṇamaitrâyaṇîputra.'

Translated under the Eastern Tsin dynasty, A. D. 317–420; but the translator's name is lost. 3 leaves. This is a similar translation of a Sûtra in fasc. 13 of No. 544, i. e. the Samyuktâgama. *K'*-yuen-lu, fasc. 7, fol. 8 a. Cf. Burnouf, 'Introduction,' p. 209 seq., where a longer history of Pûrṇa is given.

657 轉法輪經

*K*wân-fâ-lun-*k*iṅ.

Dharma*k*akra-pravartana (-sûtra).

A. R., p. 485; A. M. G., p. 288. Translated by Ân Shi-kâo, of the Eastern Hân dynasty, A. D. 25–220. 2 leaves.

658 佛說三轉法輪經
Fo-shwo-sân-kwân-fâ-lun-kiṅ.
'Buddhabhâshita-tripravartana-dharmakakra-sûtra.'
Dharmakakra-pravartana (-sûtra).

Translated by I-tsiṅ, A.D. 710, of the Thâṅ dynasty, A.D. 618–907. 2 leaves.

The above two works are similar translations of a Sûtra in fasc. 15 of No. 544, i. e. the Samyuktâgama. K'-yuen-lu, fasc. 7, fol. 8 b; K'-tsiṅ, fasc. 29, fol. 11 a. Nos. 657 and 658 are to be compared with the Pâli text of the Dhammakakka-ppavatana-sutta. An English translation of the latter is given in the Sacred Books of the East, vol. xi.

659 佛說八正道經
Fo-shwo-pâ-kâṅ-tâo-kiṅ.
'Buddhabhâshita-ashtâṅga-samyaṅ-mârga-sûtra.'

Translated by Ân Shi-kâo, of the Eastern Hân dynasty, A.D. 25–220. 2 leaves. This is an earlier translation of a Sûtra in fasc. 28 of No. 544, i. e. the Samyuktâgama. K'-yuen-lu, fasc. 7, fol. 8 b.

660 難提釋經
Nân-thi-shih-kiṅ.
'Sûtra (addressed to) Nandi (or Nanda) of the Sâkya family.'
Nanda-pravragyâ-sûtra (?).

A.R., p. 478; A.M.G., p. 280. Translated by Fâ-kü, of the Western Tsin dynasty, A.D. 265–316. 5 leaves. This is an earlier translation of a Sûtra in fasc. 30 of No. 544, i. e. the Samyuktâgama. K'-yuen-lu, fasc. 7, fol. 8 b.

661 佛說馬有三相經
Fo-shwo-mâ-yiu-sân-siâṅ-kiṅ.
'Sûtra spoken by Buddha on three characteristic marks of a (good) horse.'

Translated by K' Yâo, A.D. 185, of the Eastern Hân dynasty, A.D. 25–220. 1 leaf.

662 佛說馬有八態譬人經
Fo-shwo-mâ-yiu-pâ-thâi-phi-zan-kiṅ.
'Sûtra spoken by Buddha on eight characters of a (bad) horse compared with those of a (bad) man (or Bhikshu).'

Translated by K' Yâo, A.D. 185, of the Eastern Hân dynasty, A.D. 25–220. 2 leaves.

The above two works are earlier translations of a Sûtra or Sûtras in fasc. 33 of No. 544, i. e. the Samyuktâgama. K'-yuen-lu, fasc. 7, fol. 9 a.

663 佛說相應相可經
Fo-shwo-siâṅ-yiṅ-siâṅ-kho-kiṅ.
'Sûtra spoken by Buddha on suitableness.'

Translated by Fâ-kü, of the Western Tsin dynasty, A.D. 265–316. 2 leaves. This is a later translation of a Sûtra in No. 547, i. e. the Samyuktâgama in 1 fasciculus. K'-yuen-lu, fasc. 7, fol. 9 a. In No. 663, Buddha explains that both good and bad people consort with their own classes. K'-tsiṅ, fasc. 29, fol. 12 b.

664 修行本起經
Siu-hhiṅ-pan-khi-kiṅ.
'Sûtra on the origin of practice (of the Bodhisattva).'

Translated by Ku Tâ-li (Mahâbala ?), together with Khâṅ Maṅ-siâṅ, A.D. 197, of the Eastern Hân dynasty, A.D. 25–220. 2 fasciculi; 7 chapters. This is a life of Sâkyamuni. Chap. 1 is on 'manifesting a strange (phenomenon).' Chap. 2 is on 'Bodhisattva's causing his spirit to descend,' i. e. his coming down from the Tushita heaven to be born in this world. Chap. 7 is on 'subduing the Mâra.'

665 太子瑞應本起經
Thâi-tsz'-zui-yiṅ-pan-khi-kiṅ.
'Sûtra on the origin of the lucky fulfilment of the Crown-Prince.'

Translated by K' Khien, of the Wu dynasty, A.D. 222–280. 2 fasciculi. No division of chapters. This is a later translation of No. 664. The narration reaches as far as the conversion of the three brothers of Kâsyapa.

666 過去現在因果經
Kwo-khü-hhien-tsâi-yin-kwo-kiṅ.
'Sûtra on the cause and effect of the past and present.'

Translated by Guṇabhadra, of the earlier Suṅ dynasty, A.D. 420–479. 4 fasciculi. No division of chapters. This is a later and fuller translation of Nos. 664, 665. Deest in Tibetan. K'-yuen-lu, fasc. 7, fol. 11 b. The narration reaches as far as the conversion of Mahâkâsyapa; and it ends with a Gâtaka of Buddha, in which he was a Rishi named Shân-hwui (Sumati ?), at the time of the Tathâgata Samantaprabha.

667 佛說奈女耆域因緣經
Fo-shwo-nâi-nü-khi-yü-yin-yuen-kiṅ.
'Sûtra spoken by Buddha on the Avadâna of the woman of the Nâi tree (a kind of plum, i. e. Âmrapâlî (?), and her son) Gîva.'

Translated by Ân Shi-kâo, of the Eastern Hân dynasty, A.D. 25–220. 1 fasciculus.

668 佛說奈女耆婆經
Fo-shwo-nâi-nü-*k*hi-pho-*k*iṅ.
'Sûtra spoken by Buddha on the woman of the Nâi tree (Âmrapâlî?, and her son) *G*îva.'

Translated by Ân Shi-kâo, of the Eastern Hân dynasty, A.D. 25–220. 1 fasciculus.

The above two works are similar translations, but No. 668 is less complete. *K*'-tsiṅ, fasc. 30, fol. 11 b. The subject is the story of the woman of the Nâi tree (a kind of plum, i.e. Âmrapâlî?), and her son *G*îva. She was called so, because she was miraculously born in a flower of this tree, in the garden of the King of Vaisâlî. She was afterwards a favourite of the King Bimbisâra, and gave birth to *G*îva, who became a famous physician. *K*'-yuen-lu (fasc. 7, fol. 12 a) mentions No. 667 only, and says that it agrees with Tibetan.

669 佛說生經
Fo-shwo-shaṅ-*k*iṅ.
'Sûtra spoken by Buddha on former Births (i.e. *G*âtaka).'
*G*âtaka-nidâna.

A. R., p. 485; A. M. G., p. 288. Translated by *K*u Fâ-hu (Dharmaraksha), A.D. 285, of the Western Tsin dynasty, A.D. 265–316. 5 fasciculi; 55 Sûtras collected. Deest in Tibetan. *K*'-yuen-lu, fasc. 7, fol. 14 b. See, however, the authorities mentioned under the title.

670 萍沙王五願經
Phiṅ-shâ-wâṅ-wu-yuen-*k*iṅ.
'Bimbisâra-râ*g*a-pañ*k*a-pranidhâna-sûtra.'

Translated by *K*' *Kh*ien, of the Wu dynasty, A.D. 222–280. 8 leaves. It agrees with Tibetan. *K*'-yuen-lu, fasc. 7, fol. 14 b.

671 瑠璃王經
Liu-li-wâṅ-*k*iṅ.
'Vaidûrya-râ*g*a-sûtra.'

Translated by *K*u Fâ-hu (Dharmaraksha), of the Western Tsin dynasty, A.D. 265–316. 8 leaves. It agrees with Tibetan. *K*'-yuen-lu, fasc. 7, fol. 14 b.

672 佛說海八德經
Fo-shwo-hâi-pâ-töh-*k*iṅ.
'Sûtra spoken by Buddha on the eight good qualities of the sea.'

Translated by Kumâra*g*îva, of the Latter Tshin dynasty, A.D. 384–417. 3 leaves.

673 佛說法海經
Fo-shwo-fâ-hâi-*k*iṅ.
'Sûtra spoken by Buddha on the sea of the law.'

Translated by Fâ-*k*ü, of the Western Tsin dynasty, A.D. 265–316. 4 leaves.

The above two works are similar translations, and they are wanting in Tibetan. *K*'-yuen-lu, fasc. 7, fol. 12 a.

674 佛說義足經
Fo-shwo-i-tsu-*k*iṅ.
'Sûtra spoken by Buddha on the fulness of meaning.'

Translated by *K*' *Kh*ien, of the Wu dynasty, A.D. 222–280. 2 fasciculi; 16 Sûtras collected. Deest in Tibetan. *K*'-yuen-lu, fasc. 7, fol. 15 a.

675 鬼問目連經
Kwêi-wan-mu-lien-*k*iṅ.
'Sûtra on the questions addressed by Pretas (departed spirits) to Maudgalyâyana.'

Translated by Ân Shi-kâo, of the Eastern Hân dynasty, A.D. 25–220. 4 leaves.

676 雜藏經
Tsâ-tsâṅ-*k*iṅ.
'Samyukta-pitaka-sûtra.'

Translated by Fâ-hhien (Fa-hian), of the Eastern Tsin dynasty, A.D. 317–420. 11 leaves.

677 餓鬼報應經
Ṅö-kwêi-pâo-yiṅ-*k*iṅ.
'Preta (lit. hungry-demon)-phala-sûtra.'

Translated under the Eastern Tsin dynasty, A.D. 317–420; the translator's name is lost. 7 leaves.

The above three works are similar translations, and they are wanting in Tibetan. *K*'-yuen-lu, fasc. 7, fol. 10 a.

678 佛說四十二章經
Fo-shwo-sz'-shi-'rh-*k*âṅ-*k*iṅ.
'Sûtra of Forty-two Sections spoken by Buddha.'

Translated by Kâsyapa Mâtaṅga, together with *K*u Fâ-lân (Dharmaraksha?), A.D. 67, of the Eastern Hân dynasty, A.D. 25–220. 1 fasciculus; 8 leaves. This is the first translation of a Buddhist Sûtra made in China. It is stated in an old record, that this Sûtra consists of extracts from a larger work. 'As it was just the time when Buddhism was first introduced into China (A.D. 67), and the people did not yet believe in it deeply, Mâtaṅga concealed his good understanding and did not translate many works; but he simply selected this Sûtra for teaching others.' Khâi-yuen-lu, fasc. 1, fol. 4 b seq. Cf. Nêi-tien-lu, fasc. 1, fol. 6 a; Thu-*k*i, fasc. 1, fol. 3 a. 'There was a later translation of No. 678, made by *K' Khien*, of the Wu dynasty, A.D. 222–280; but it was lost already in A.D. 730. It is said to have differed little from the earlier translation, i.e. No. 678.' Khâi-yuen-lu, fasc. 15 a, fol. 14 b. Cf. Thu-*ki*, fasc. 1, fol. 20 a; *K'*-yuen-lu, fasc. 7, fol. 15 a. In the last authority, however, the usual reference to the Tibetan version is left out. But see M. L. Feer's edition, entitled, Le Sûtra en Quarante-deux Articles, Textes Chinois, Tibétain et Mongol. An English translation by Rev. S. Beal is given in his Catena of Buddhist Scriptures from Chinese, pp. 190–203. A French translation by M. L. Feer. See also Professor Max Müller's Selected Essays, vol. ii, p. 320, note 4.

CLASS II.

單譯經 Tân-yi-*k*in, or Sûtras of single translation, excluded from the preceding Class.

679 正法念處經

*K*ân-fâ-nien-*kh*u-*k*in.

Saddharmasm*ri*tyupasthâna-sûtra.

K'-yuen-lu, fasc. 7, fol. 15 a; Conc. 694; A. R., pp. 470–472; A. M. G., pp. 274–275. Translated by Gautama Pra*gñ*âru*k*i, A.D. 539, of the Eastern Wêi dynasty of the Yuen family, A.D. 534–550. 70 fasciculi; 7 chapters. It agrees with Tibetan. *K'*-yuen-lu, s. v. The subjects of the 7 chapters are—

(1) The results of the ten kinds of good conduct (i.e. contrary to the Dush*k*arita).
(2) Birth and death.
(3) The different hells (earthly prison).
(4) The condition of Pretas (hungry demons).
(5) The birth as a beast.
(6) The condition of Devas.
(7) The Kâya-smrity-upasthâna.

Cf. Beal, Catalogue, p. 53.

680 佛本行集經

Fo-pan-hhiṅ-tsi-*k*iṅ.

'Buddha-pûrvakaryâ-saṅgraha-sûtra.'

Buddha*k*aritra.

K'-yuen-lu, fasc. 7, fol. 15 b; Conc. 167.

Abhinishkramana-sûtra.

A. R., p. 474; A. M. G., p. 277; Wassiljew, p. 114. Translated by *G*ñânagupta, A.D. 587, of the Sui dynasty, A.D. 589 (or 581)–618. 60 fasciculi; 60 chapters. It agrees with Tibetan. *K'*-yuen-lu, s. v. The following titles of the Life of Buddha, such as No. 680, are mentioned at the end of this work, as adopted by five different schools:—

(1) Tâ-sh' (great matter, i.e. Mahâvastu?) by the Mahâsaṅghikas.
(2) Tâ-*k*wâṅ-yen (great adornment, i.e. Mahâvyûha or Lalitavistara (?), cf. the title of No. 159) by the Sarvâstivâdas.
(3) Fo-wâṅ-yin-yuen (Buddha's former Nidâna or Avadâna) by the Kâsyapîyas.
(4) Shih-kiâ-mâu-ni-pan-hhiṅ (Sâkyamuni's former practice, i.e. Buddhakaritra) by the Dharmaguptas.
(5) Phi-ni-tsâṅ-ken-pan (Vinayapiṭaka-mûla) by the Mahîsâsakas.

An abstract English translation of No. 680 by Beal, entitled the Romantic History of Buddha, in one volume.

The following nine works were translated by Ân Shi-kâo, of the Eastern Hân dynasty, A.D. 25–220:—

681 佛說大安般守意經

Fo-shwo-tâ-ân-pân-sheu-i-*k*iṅ.

'Sûtra spoken by Buddha on keeping thought, in the (manner of) great Ân-pân or Ânâpâna.' Cf. No. 543 (17). 2 fasciculi.

682 佛說罵意經

Fo-shwo-mâ-i-*k*iṅ.

'Sûtra spoken by Buddha on the thought of abuse.' 1 fasciculus.

683 禪行法想經

Shân-hhiṅ-fâ-siâṅ-*k*iṅ.

'Sûtra on perception in the law of practice of meditation.' 1 leaf.

684 佛說處處經

Fo-shwo-*kh*u-*kh*u-*k*iṅ.

'Sûtra spoken by Buddha on several places or objects.' 1 fasciculus.

685 佛說分別善惡所起經

Fo-shwo-fan-pieh-shân-ṅoh-su-*kh*i-*k*iṅ.

'Sûtra spoken by Buddha on the division of the results of good and bad (conducts or deeds).'

Karmavibhâga-dharmagrantha (?).

A. R., p. 479; A. M. G., p. 282. 1 fasciculus. There is an enumeration of thirty-six faults, as the result of drinking intoxicating liquor. *K'*-tsiṅ, fasc. 30, fol. 14 a.

686 佛說出家緣經
Fo-shwo-*kh*u-*k*iâ-yuen-*k*iṅ.
'Sûtra spoken by Buddha on the Nidâna of leaving the house (in order to become an anchorite, i. e. Abhinishkramana).' 2 leaves.

There is an enumeration of thirty-five faults, as the result of drink. *K'*-tsiṅ, fasc. 31, fol. 21 a.

687 佛說阿含正行經
Fo-shwo-ŏ-hân-*k*âṅ-hhiṅ-*k*iṅ.
'Sûtra spoken by Buddha on the right practice (taught) in the Âgama (?).' 4 leaves.

688 佛說十八泥犁經
Fo-shwo-shi-pâ-ni-li-*k*iṅ.
'Sûtra spoken by Buddha on eighteen Narakas or hells.' 6 leaves.

689 佛說法受塵經
Fo-shwo-fâ-sheu-*kh*an-*k*iṅ.
'Sûtra spoken by Buddha on the condition (Dharma) which receives dust or impurity.' 1 leaf.

Buddha exhorts both sexes of mankind to desist from their impure attachment to each other. *K'*-tsiṅ, fasc. 31, fol. 14 a.

690 佛說進學經
Fo-shwo-tsin-hhio-*k*iṅ.
'Sûtra spoken by Buddha on advancement in learning.'

Translated by Tsü-*kh*ü *K*iṅ-shaṅ, A. D. 455, of the earlier Suṅ dynasty, A. D. 420–479. 1 leaf.

691 佛說得道梯隥錫杖經
Fo-shwo-töh-tâo-thi-taṅ-si-*k*âṅ-*k*iṅ.
'Sûtra spoken by Buddha on (the use of) the tin-staff (Khakkhara, or a Bhikshu's staff, the top being armed with metal rings) as a ladder or path for obtaining Bodhi.'

Translated under the Eastern Tsin dynasty, A. D. 317–420; but the translator's name is lost. 3 leaves. There is an appendix on the law or rules for holding this staff. This work is to be compared with a Tibetan version or work, mentioned in A. R., p. 479, and A. M. G., p. 281, as No. 32, with the following note: 'No Sanskrit title. On the use of a staff (with some tinkling ornaments on it) by the priests.'

692 佛說貧窮老公經
Fo-shwo-phin-*kh*iüṅ-lâo-kuṅ-*k*iṅ.
'Sûtra spoken by Buddha to a poor old man.'

Translated by Hwui-*k*ien, of the earlier Suṅ dynasty, A. D. 420–479. 3 leaves. The sixth character of the title is written 翁 waṅ, an old man, in *K'*-yuen-lu, fasc. 7, fol. 14 a.

693 須摩提長者經
Sü-mo-thi-*kh*âṅ-*k*ö-*k*iṅ.
'Sûtra (spoken to) the *S*reshṭhin Sumati.'

Translated by *K' Kh*ien, of the Wu dynasty, A. D. 222–280. 11 leaves.

The following two works were translated by Ân Shi-kâo, of the Eastern Hân dynasty, A. D. 25–220:—

694 長者(子)懊惱三處經
*Kh*âṅ-*k*ö(-tsz')-âo-nâo-sân-*kh*u-*k*iṅ.
'Sûtra on (the son of) a *S*reshṭhin (rich merchant) who caused three places (of Devas, men, and Nâgas) to be harassed (at one and the same time).' 3 leaves.

The third character of the title is left out in the present edition, but according to the contents it must be put in, as it exists in *K'*-yuen-lu, fasc. 7, fol. 17 b; *K'*-tsiṅ, fasc. 31, fol. 8 b.

695 犍陀國王經
*K*ien-tho-kwo-wâṅ-*k*iṅ.
'Gândhâra-desa-râ*g*a-sûtra.' 2 leaves.

696 阿難四事經
Ö-nân-sz'-sh'-*k*iṅ.
'Sûtra (spoken to ?) Ânanda on four matters.'

Translated by *K' Kh*ien, of the Wu dynasty, A. D. 222–280. 3 leaves. The four matters are—1. To support men and feed animals with a pitiful heart. 2. To help the poor with a compassionate heart. 3. To abstain from eating meat, and to keep the five precepts. 4. To honour the *S*râmanas. If one practises these, it is the same as worshipping Buddha. *K'*-tsiṅ, fasc. 31, fol. 20 b.

697 分別經
Fan-pieh-*k*iṅ.
'Sûtra on the division or distinction (of results).'

Translated by *K*u Fâ-hu (Dharmaraksha), of the Western Tsin dynasty, A. D. 265–316. 6 leaves. There are those who keep the moral precepts and obtain happiness; and those who keep the same precepts, but fall into misfortune. There are three classes of those who serve Buddha. Then the Sûtra states that many lawless Chinamen are among the subjects of the Mâra! *K'*-tsiṅ, fasc. 31, fol. 20 a.

The following three works were translated by *K' Kh*ien, of the Wu dynasty, A. D. 222–280:—

698 未生怨經
Wêi-shaṅ-yuen-kiṅ.
'Sûtra on (the King) Agâtasatru.' 4 leaves.

It states the murder of the King Bimbisâra. The account is similar to that which is given in the Vinaya-piṭaka. K'-tsiṅ, fasc. 30, fol. 18 b.

699 四願經
Sz̈'-yuen-kiṅ.
'Sûtra on four wishes (of mankind).' 5 leaves.

It seems that some passages are left out, as the composition is not consecutive. K'-tsiṅ, fasc. 31, fol. 15 a.

700 猘狗經
K'-keu-kiṅ.
'Sûtra on the fierce dog (comparison).' 2 leaves.

Those who receive instruction in moral precepts and envy or dislike their teachers are compared to a fierce dog that bites his master. K'-tsiṅ, fasc. 31, fol. 19 b.

The above twenty works are wanting in Tibetan. K'-yuen-lu, fasc. 7, fol. 14 a seq. For Nos. 685 and 691, see, however, the authorities mentioned under the titles respectively.

701 八關齋經
Pâ-kwân-kâi-kiṅ.
'Sûtra on the eight kinds of fasting.'

Translated by Tsü-khü Kiṅ-shaṅ, A.D. 455, of the earlier Suṅ dynasty, A.D. 420–479. 2 leaves. This is somewhat similar to Nos. 542 (202), 576, 577. K'-tsiṅ, fasc. 28, fol. 20 a. It agrees with Tibetan. K'-yuen-lu, fasc. 7, fol. 18 b.

702 孝子經
Hhiâo-tsz̈'-kiṅ.
'Sûtra on the filial child.'

Translated under the Western Tsin dynasty, A.D. 265–316; but the translator's name is lost. 2 leaves.

703 黑氏梵志經
Hêi-sh'-fân-k'-kiṅ.
'Sûtra on the Brahmakârin Black-family (Krishna or Kâla ?).'

Translated by K' Khien, of the Wu dynasty, A.D. 222–280. 4 leaves.

704 阿鳩留經
Ö-kiu-liu-kiṅ.
'Sûtra on (the merchant) Akuru.'

Translated under the Eastern Hân dynasty, A.D. 25–222; but the translator's name is lost. 4 leaves.

The above three works are wanting in Tibetan. K'-yuen-lu, fasc. 7, fol. 18 a seq.

705 佛爲阿支羅迦葉(說)自化(read 他)作苦經
Fo-wêi-ö-k'-lo-kiâ-yeh (-shwo)-tsz̈'-hwâ (read thâ)-tso-khû-kiṅ.
'Sûtra spoken by Buddha to Akira (?)-kâsyapa on pain caused by oneself or by another.'

Translator's name is lost. 3 leaves. But in K'-tsiṅ (fasc. 31, fol. 6 a) this work is said to have been translated by Ân Shi-kâo, of the Eastern Hân dynasty, A.D. 25–220. The Chinese title is given there correctly, while in the present edition the eighth character (shwo) is left out, and the ninth (thâ) is written wrongly (as hwâ). Unless these faults are corrected, the title is quite unintelligible. The subject of Buddha's sermon in this work is this, that pain is caused neither by oneself nor by another, nor by both, nor is it without a cause. Thus he caused Akira (?)-kâsyapa to perceive the truth and obtain the way. K'-tsiṅ, s. v.

706 佛說罪業報應教化地獄經
Fo-shwo-tsui-yeh-pâo-yiṅ-kiâo-hwâ-ti-yü-kiṅ.
'Sûtra spoken by Buddha on teaching of hells as the results of sinful actions (?).'

Translated by Ân Shi-kâo, of the Eastern Hân dynasty, A.D. 25–220. 6 leaves.

The following four works were translated by K' Khien, of the Wu dynasty, A.D. 222–280:—

707 佛說龍王兄弟經
Fo-shwo-luṅ-wâṅ-hhiüṅ-ti-kiṅ.
'Sûtra spoken by Buddha on the elder and younger brothers of the Nâga-kings (subdued by Maudgalyâyana).' 3 leaves.

708 佛說長者音悅經
Fo-shwo-khâṅ-kö-yin-yueh-kiṅ.
'Sûtra spoken by Buddha on the Sreshthin named Mañgughosha.' 5 leaves.

709 佛說七女經
Fo-shwo-tshi-nü-kiṅ.
'Sûtra spoken by Buddha on seven women.' 7 leaves.

710 佛說八師經
Fo-shwo-pâ-sh'-kiṅ.
'Sûtra spoken by Buddha on eight teachers.' 5 leaves.

Buddha answered the question of a Brahmakârin named Yagña (?), as to who is the teacher of Buddha. The following eight subjects are noticed carefully: killing, stealing, adultery, lying, drinking intoxicating liquor, old age, disease, and death. K'-tsiṅ, fasc. 31, fol. 7 a.

711 佛說越難經
Fo-shwo-yueh-nân-kiṅ.
'Sûtra spoken by Buddha on (the Sreshṭhin) Vana.'

Translated by Nieh Khân-yuen, of the Western Tsin dynasty, A.D. 265–316. 2 leaves.

712 佛說所欲致患經
Fo-shwo-su-yü-k'-hwân-kiṅ.
'Sûtra spoken by Buddha on desire being the cause of affliction.'

Translated by Ku Fâ-hu (Dharmaraksha), A.D. 304, of the Western Tsin dynasty, A.D. 265–316. 6 leaves.

The above seven works are wanting in Tibetan. K'-yuen-lu, fasc. 7, fol. 12 b seq.

713 阿闍世王問五逆經
Ö-shö-shi-wâṅ-wan-wu-ni-kiṅ.
'Sûtra on the five deadly sins, in answer to the King Agâtasatru.'

Translated by Fâ-kü, of the Western Tsin dynasty, A.D. 265–316. 6 leaves. It agrees with Tibetan. K'-yuen-lu, fasc. 7, fol. 13 b. The five deadly sins or the Pañkânantaryas are—

Sanskrit (Mahâvyutpatti, § 118).

(1) Mâtrighâta,
(2) Pitrighâta,
(3) Arhadghâta,
(4) Saṅghabheda,
(5) Tathâgatasyântike dushṭakittarudhirotpâdana. The Mahâvyutpatti places the third sin before the second. The following six crimes or deadly sins are enumerated in Childers' Pâli Dictionary, p. 7 b, s.v. Abhiṭṭhânam :—
(1) Mâtughâto, matricide;
(2) Pitughâto, parricide;
(3) Arhantaghâto, killing an Arhat;
(4) Lohituppâdo, shedding the blood of a Buddha;
(5) Saṅghabhedo, causing divisions among the priesthood;
(6) Aññasatthuuddeso, following other teachers.

714 本事經
Pan-sh'-kiṅ.
'Mûla-vastu-sûtra (?).'

Translated by Hhüen-kwâṅ (Hiouen-thsang), of the Thâṅ dynasty, A.D. 618–907. 7 fasciculi; 3 chapters. It agrees with Tibetan. K'-yuen-lu, fasc. 7, fol. 16 a.

The following five works were translated by Thân-wu-lân (Dharmaraksha ?), of the Eastern Tsin dynasty, A.D. 317–420 :—

715 佛說中心經
Fo-shwo-kuṅ-sin-kiṅ.
'Sûtra spoken by Buddha on the middle heart (Madhya-hridaya ?).' 6 leaves.

716 佛說見正經
Fo-shwo-kien-kaṅ-kiṅ.
'Sûtra addressed by Buddha to (the Bhikshu named) Seeing-right (?).' 9 leaves.

717 佛說大魚事經
Fo-shwo-tâ-yü-sh'-kiṅ.
'Sûtra spoken by Buddha on the matter (or comparison) of a great fish.' 2 leaves.

718 佛說阿難七夢經
Fo-shwo-ö-nân-tshi-maṅ-kiṅ.
'Sûtra addressed by Buddha to Ânanda on seven dreams.' 2 leaves.

The above four works agree with Tibetan. K'-yuen-lu, fasc. 7, fol. 19 b seq.

719 佛說呵鵰阿那含經
Fo-shwo-hö-tiâo-ö-nâ-hân-kiṅ.
'Sûtra spoken by Buddha on (the praise of) the Anâgâmin Hö-tiâo (?).' 2 leaves.

Deest in Tibetan. K'-yuen-lu, fasc. 7, fol. 20 a.

720 佛說燈指因緣經
Fo-shwo-taṅ-k'-yin-yuen-kiṅ.
'Sûtra spoken by Buddha on the Avadâna of (the Sreshṭhi-putra) Dîpâṅguli (? Lamp-finger).'

Translated by Kumâragîva, of the Latter Tshin dynasty, A.D. 384–417. 11 leaves.

721 佛說婦人遇辜經
Fo-shwo-fu-zan-yü-ku-kiṅ.
'Sûtra spoken by Buddha on a woman who met with ill fate (by the death of all her relations at one and the same time).'

Translated by Shaṅ-kien, of the Western Tshin dynasty, A.D. 385–431. 2 leaves.

722 佛說四天王經
Fo-shwo-sz'-thien-wâṅ-kiṅ.

'Sûtra spoken by Buddha on the four heavenly kings (Katurmahârâgas, who go round the world on six fasting days every month, and who, observing the good or bad actions of mankind, raise their joy or grief).'

Translated by K'-yen, together with Pâo-yun, of the earlier Suṅ dynasty, A.D. 420–479. 3 leaves.

723 佛說摩訶迦葉度貧母經
Fo-shwo-mo-hö-kiâ-yeh-tu-phin-mu-kiṅ.

'Sûtra spoken by Buddha on Mahâkâsyapa's saving a poor mother.'

Translated by Guṇabhadra, of the earlier Suṅ dynasty, A.D. 420–479. 5 leaves.

The above four works agree with Tibetan. K'-yuen-lu, fasc. 7, fol. 20 b seq.

724 佛說禪行三十七品經
Fo-shwo-shân-hhiṅ-sân-shi-tshi-phin-kiṅ.

'Sûtra spoken by Buddha on the thirty-seven articles of the practice of meditation.'

Translated by Ân Shi-kâo, of the Eastern Hân dynasty, A.D. 25–220. 3 leaves.

725 比丘避女惡名欲自殺經
Pi-khiu-pi-nü-ṅoh-miṅ-yü-tsz'-shâ-kiṅ.

'Sûtra on a Bhikshu who intended to commit suicide for the purpose of avoiding ill-fame concerning a woman.'

Translated by Fâ-kü, of the Western Tsin dynasty, A.D. 265–316. 2 leaves.

726 佛說身觀經
Fo-shwo-shan-kwâṅ-kiṅ.

'Sûtra spoken by Buddha on the meditation on (the impurity of) the human body.'

Translated by Ku Fâ-hu (Dharmaraksha), of the Western Tsin dynasty, A.D. 265–316. 3 leaves.

The above three works are wanting in Tibetan. K'-yuen-lu, fasc. 7, fol. 24 b seq.

The following two works were translated by I-tsiṅ, A.D. 701, of the Thâṅ dynasty, A.D. 618–907. They agree with Tibetan. K'-yuen-lu, fasc. 7, fol. 25 a:—

727 佛說無常經
Fo-shwo-wu-khâṅ-kiṅ.

'Sûtra spoken by Buddha on Impermanency (Anitya).' 3 leaves.

There is an appendix entitled Lin-kuṅ-fâṅ-küê, or Rules for treating a dying person. 4 leaves.

728 佛說八無暇有暇經
Fo-shwo-pâ-wu-hhiâ-yiu-hhiâ-kiṅ.

'Sûtra spoken by Buddha on eight (classes of beings) born in time or out of time (Ashtâkshaṇa-kshaṇa).' 5 leaves.

The Ashtâkshaṇas or eight classes of beings born out of time are those in the following states or conditions:—

(1) Naraka, living in hell;
(2) Preta, hungry demon, departed spirit;
(3) Tiryagyoni, lower animal;
(4) Dîrghâyusha-deva, god of long life;
(5) Pratyantaganapada, born in a bordering country;
(6) Indriyavaikalya, deficient in the organs of senses;
(7) Mithyâdarsana, having false views or belief;
(8) Tathâgatânutpâda, born at a time when there is no Buddha.

K'-tsiṅ, fasc. 31, fol. 14 b. Cf. Mahâvyutpatti, § 116.

729 五百弟子自說本起經
Wu-pâi-ti-tsz'-tsz'-shwo-pan-khi-kiṅ.

'Sûtra on five hundred disciples' telling their own Nidâna, or Gâtaka.'

Translated by Ku Fâ-hu (Dharmaraksha), A.D. 303, of the Western Tsin dynasty, A.D. 265–316. 1 fasciculus; 30 chapters: the first 29 chapters contain the stories of the 500 disciples of Buddha; and in the 30th chapter Buddha speaks on the origin of human passion; this last chapter seems to be incomplete. K'-tsiṅ, fasc. 30, fol. 9 b. Deest in Tibetan. K'-yuen-lu, fasc. 7, fol. 19 a.

730 佛說五苦章句經
Fo-shwo-wu-khu-kaṅ-kü-kiṅ.

'Sûtra spoken by Buddha (beginning with) the section on the pain of five (states of existence).'

Translated by Thân-wu-lân (Dharmaraksha ?), of the Eastern Tsin dynasty, A.D. 317–420. 15 leaves. This work is doubtful in Tibetan. K'-yuen-lu, fasc. 7, fol. 13 b.

731 佛說堅意經
Fo-shwo-kien-i-kiṅ.

'Sûtra spoken by Buddha on keeping thought firm.'

Translated by Ân Shi-kâo, of the Eastern Hân dynasty, A.D. 25–220. 2 leaves.

732 佛說淨飯王般涅槃經
Fo-shwo-tsiṅ-fân-wâṅ-pân-niê-phân-kiṅ.

'Sûtra spoken by Buddha on the Parinirvâṇa of the King Suddhodana.'

Translated by Tsü-khü Kiṅ-shaṅ, A.D. 455, of the earlier Suṅ dynasty, A.D. 420–479. 9 leaves.

The above two works are wanting in Tibetan. K'-yuen-lu, fasc. 7, fol. 14 a.

733 佛說興起行經

Fo-shwo-hhiṅ-*kh*i-hhiṅ-*k*iṅ.

'Sûtra spoken by Buddha on the former practice (of Buddha).'

Translated by Khâṅ Maṅ-siâṅ, of the Eastern Hân dynasty, A.D. 25–220. 2 fasciculi; 10 short Sûtras collected. Each Sûtra relates a Nidâna or former cause of a certain event that happened to Buddha, such as his headache, pain in his back, Devadatta's throwing a stone at him, a Brâhmaṇî's abuse, his eating the horse barley, and penance, etc. It agrees with Tibetan. *K'*-yuen-lu, fasc. 7, fol. 16 a.

The following two works were translated by I-tsiṅ, A.D. 700 and 710, of the Thâṅ dynasty, A.D. 618–907. They agree with Tibetan. *K'*-yuen-lu, fasc. 7, fol. 25 b:—

734 長爪梵志請問經

*Kh*âṅ-*k*âo-fân-*k'*-tshiṅ-wan-*k*iṅ.

'Dîrghanakha-brahma*k*âri-paripri*kkh*â-sûtra.'

Dîrghanakha-parivra*g*aka-paripri*kkh*â.

A. R., p. 480; A. M. G., p. 280. 3 leaves.

735 佛說譬喻經

Fo-shwo-phi-yü-*k*iṅ.

'Sûtra spoken by Buddha on (eight) comparisons.' 2 leaves.

736 佛說比丘聽施經

Fo-shwo-pi-*kh*iu-thiṅ-*k'*-*k*iṅ.

'Sûtra addressed by Buddha to the Bhikshu Thiṅ-*k'* (hearing-giving).'

Translated by Thân-wu-lân (Dharmaraksha), of the Eastern Tsin dynasty, A.D. 317–420. 3 leaves. Deest in Tibetan. *K'*-yuen-lu, fasc. 7, fol. 25 a.

The following two works were translated by I-tsiṅ, A.D. 711 and 710 respectively, of the Thâṅ dynasty, A.D. 618–907. They agree with Tibetan. *K'*-yuen-lu, fasc. 7, fol. 25 b:—

737 佛說略教誡經

Fo-shwo-liâo-*k*iâo-*k*iê-*k*iṅ.

'Sûtra spoken by Buddha, being an abridged instruction.' 2 leaves.

738 佛說療痔病經

Fo-shwo-liâo-*k'*-piṅ-*k*iṅ.

'Sûtra spoken by Buddha on curing the disease of piles.' 2 leaves.

739 佛說業報差別經

Fo-shwo-yeh-pâo-*kh*â-pieh-*k*iṅ.

'Sûtra spoken by Buddha on the difference of the results of Karman.'

Translated by Thân Fâ-*k'* (Gautama Dharmapra*gñ*a), A.D. 582, of the Sui dynasty, A.D. 589 (or 581)–618. 15 leaves. Deest in Tibetan. *K'*-yuen-lu, fasc. 7, fol. 16 a.

The following two works were translated by Guṇabhadra, of the earlier Suṅ dynasty, A.D. 420–479. They agree with Tibetan. *K'*-yuen-lu, fasc. 7, fol. 20 b seq.:—

740 佛說十二品生死經

Fo-shwo-shi-'rh-phin-shaṅ-sz'-*k*iṅ.

'Sûtra spoken by Buddha on twelve differences of birth and death (between the holy and common men or beings).' 1 leaf.

741 佛說輪轉五道罪福報應經

Fo-shwo-lun-*k*wâṅ-wu-tâo-tsui-fu-pâo-yiṅ-*k*iṅ.

'Sûtra spoken by Buddha on transmigration throughout the five states of existence, being the result of both virtuous and sinful actions.' 5 leaves.

The following three works were translated by Tsü-*kh*ü *K*iṅ-shaṅ, A.D. 455, of the earlier Suṅ dynasty, A.D. 420–479:—

742 佛說五無返復經

Fo-shwo-wu-wu-fân-fu-*k*iṅ.

'Sûtra spoken by Buddha on the five (elements) not returning again (i. e. death).' 3 leaves.

743 The same as No. 742. 3 leaves.

744 佛說佛大僧大經

Fo-shwo-fo-tâ-saṅ-tâ-*k*iṅ.

'Sûtra spoken by Buddha on (two brothers named) Buddha-great (Buddhamahat?) and Saṅgha-great (Saṅghamahat?).' 8 leaves.

They were the sons of a rich man in Râ*g*agriha. When the younger brother became an ascetic, the elder wished to marry the wife of the former, but she did not follow him. Then the elder sent an assassin to kill his younger brother, who, at the moment when his four limbs were separated, obtained the fruits of the four holy paths, and whose wife was born in heaven, having died from excessive lamentation. The wicked elder brother at last fell into hell. *K'*-tsiṅ, fasc. 31, fol. 9 a.

The following two works were translated by *K*u Fâ-hu (Dharmaraksha), of the Western Tsin dynasty, A.D. 265–316:—

745 佛說大迦葉本經

Fo-shwo-tâ-*k*iâ-yeh-pan-*k*iṅ.

'Sûtra addressed by Buddha to Mahâkâsyapa on the origin (or the law of controlling the mind).' 6 leaves.

746 佛說四自侵經
Fo-shwo-sz'-tsz'-tshin-kiṅ.
'Sûtra spoken by Buddha on four (articles of) self-injuring.'
5 leaves.

The four articles are—1. Negligence in learning; 2. Continuation of lust in old age; 3. Want of generosity; and 4. Not receiving the words of Buddha.

The following three works were translated by Fâ-kü, of the Western Tsin dynasty, A. D. 265–316:—

747 佛說羅云忍辱經
Fo-shwo-lo-yun-zan-zu-kiṅ.
'Sûtra addressed by Buddha to Râhula on forbearance.' 4 leaves.

748 佛爲年少比丘說正事經
Fo-wêi-nien-siâo-pi-khiu-shwo-kaṅ-sh'-kiṅ.
'Sûtra addressed by Buddha to young Bhikshus on the right matter.' 2 leaves.

749 佛說沙曷比丘功德經
Fo-shwo-shâ-hö-pi-khiu-kuṅ-töh-kiṅ.
'Sûtra spoken by Buddha on the good qualities of the Bhikshu Shâ-hö (?).' 3 leaves.

The above eight works are wanting in Tibetan. K'-yuen-lu, fasc. 7, fol. 19 a seq.

750 佛說時非時經
Fo-shwo-sh'-fê-sh'-kiṅ.
'Sûtra spoken by Buddha on time and not-time (i. e. proper and improper time ?).'

Translated by Zo-lo-yen, of the Western Tsin dynasty, A. D. 265–316. (K'-tsiṅ, fasc. 31, fol. 17 a.) 4 leaves.

751 佛說自愛經
Fo-shwo-tsz'-âi-kiṅ.
'Sûtra spoken by Buddha on self-love.'

Translated by Thân-wu-lân (Dharmaraksha ?), of the Eastern Tsin dynasty, A. D. 317–420. 5 leaves.

The above two works agree with Tibetan. K'-yuen-lu, fasc. 7, fol. 19 b.

752 佛說賢者五福德經
Fo-shwo-hhien-kö-wu-fu-töh-kiṅ.
'Sûtra spoken by Buddha on five kinds of happiness and virtue of the wise men.'

Translated by Po Fâ-tsu, of the Western Tsin dynasty, A. D. 265–316. 2 leaves. The seventh character of the title (töh, virtue) is left out in K'-yuen-lu, fasc. 7, fol. 22 b; K'-tsiṅ, fasc. 31, fol. 11 b.

753 天請問經
Thien-tshiṅ-wan-kiṅ.
'Deva-paripṛikkhâ-sûtra.'
Devatâ-sûtra (?).

A. R., p. 478; A. M. G., p. 281. Translated by Hhüen-kwâṅ (Hiouen-thsang), A. D. 648, of the Thâṅ dynasty, A. D. 618–907. 4 leaves. There are nine questions and answers in this Sûtra.

The following four works were translated under the Eastern Tsin dynasty, A. D. 317–420; but the translators' names are lost:—

754 佛說護淨經
Fo-shwo-hu-tsiṅ-kiṅ.
'Sûtra spoken by Buddha on the protection of purity.' 3 leaves.

755 佛說木槵經
Fo-shwo-mu-hwân-kiṅ.
'Sûtra spoken by Buddha on the tree Hwân (the seeds of which, 108 in number, are used for rosaries).' 2 leaves.

This Sûtra gives an account concerning the use of a rosary made of these seeds.

756 佛說無上處經
Fo-shwo-wu-shâṅ-khu-kiṅ.
'Sûtra spoken by Buddha on the highest place (or object worshipped (?), i. e. the Triratna).' 1 leaf.

The above five works are wanting in Tibetan (?). K'-yuen-lu, fasc. 7, fol. 22 b.

757 盧至長者因緣經
Lu-k'-khâṅ-kö-yin-yuen-kiṅ.
'Sûtra on the Nidâna or Avadâna of the Sreshṭhin Ruki (?).'
12 leaves.

It agrees with Tibetan. K'-yuen-lu, fasc. 7, fol. 23 a.

The following three works were translated under the Western Tsin dynasty, A. D. 265–316; but the translators' names are lost:—

758 佛說普達王經
Fo-shwo-phu-tâ-wâṅ-kiṅ.
'Sûtra spoken by Buddha on the King Samantaprâpta (?).'
4 leaves.

Deest in Tibetan. K'-yuen-lu, fasc. 7, fol. 23 b.

759 佛說鬼子母經
Fo-shwo-kwâi-tsz'-mu-kiṅ.
'Sûtra spoken by Buddha on the mother of (500) demon-children (i. e. Hâritî).' 4 leaves.

It agrees with Tibetan. K'-yuen-lu, fasc. 7, fol. 24 a.

760 佛說梵摩難國王經

Fo-shwo-fân-mo-nân-kwo-wâṅ-*k*iṅ.

'Sûtra spoken by Buddha on the King of the country Brâhmaṇa (?).' 2 leaves.

761 佛說孫多耶致經

Fo-shwo-sun-to-ye-*k*'-*k*iṅ.

'Sûtra addressed by Buddha to (the Brahma*k*ârin) Sun-to-ye-*k*' (?).'

Translated by *K*' *Kh*ien, of the Wu dynasty, A. D. 222–280. 3 leaves.

762 佛說父母恩難報經

Fo-shwo-fu-mu-an-nân-pâo-*k*iṅ.

'Sûtra spoken by Buddha on the kindness of parents difficult to be returned.'

Translated by Ân Shi-kâo, of the Eastern Hân dynasty, A. D. 25–220. 1 leaf.

763 佛說新歲經

Fo-shwo-sin-sui-*k*iṅ.

'Sûtra spoken by Buddha on the new year (i. e. the time when the varshâs or rainy season is over).'

Translated by Thân-wu-lân (Dharmaraksha ?), of the Eastern Tsin dynasty, A. D. 317–420. 6 leaves.

764 佛說羣牛譬經

Fo-shwo-*kh*iün-niu-phi-*k*iṅ.

'Sûtra spoken by Buddha on the cow-herd comparison.'

Translated by Fâ-*k*ü, of the Western Tsin dynasty, A. D. 265–316. 2 leaves.

765 佛說九橫經

Fo-shwo-*k*iu-huṅ-*k*iṅ.

'Sûtra spoken by Buddha on nine (causes of) unexpected or untimely (death).'

Translated by Ân Shi-kâo, of the Eastern Hân dynasty, A. D. 25–220. 2 leaves.

The following two works were translated by Tsü-*kh*ü *K*iṅ-shaṅ, A. D. 455, of the earlier Suṅ dynasty, A. D. 420–479:—

766 佛說五恐怖世經

Fo-shwo-wu-khuṅ-pu-shi-*k*iṅ.

'Sûtra spoken by Buddha on five states of fear (concerning the disorder of Bhikshus in future time).' 2 leaves.

767 佛說弟子死復生經

Fo-shwo-ti-tsz'-sz'-fu-shaṅ-*k*iṅ.

'Sûtra spoken by Buddha on a pupil who revived (seven days after) his death.' 7 leaves.

The above eight works are wanting in Tibetan. *K*'-yuen-lu, fasc. 7, fol. 21 b seq.

768 佛說懈怠耕者經

Fo-shwo-hhiê-tâi-kaṅ-*k*ö-*k*iṅ.

'Sûtra spoken by Buddha on a slow and idle farmer.'

Translated by Hwui-*k*ien, of the earlier Suṅ dynasty, A. D. 420–479. 2 leaves. It agrees with Tibetan. *K*'-yuen-lu, fasc. 7, fol. 22 a.

769 佛說辨意長者子所問經

Fo-shwo-pien-i-*kh*âṅ-*k*ö-tsz'-su-wan-*k*iṅ.

'Sûtra spoken by Buddha (answering) the question of the son of the *S*reshthin Pien-i (?).'

Translated by Fâ-*kh*âṅ, of the Northern Wêi dynasty, A. D. 386–534. 11 leaves.

770 無垢優婆夷問經

Wu-keu-yiu-pho-i-wan-*k*iṅ.

'Sûtra (answering) the question of the Upâsikâ Vimalâ.'

Translated by Gautama Pra*gñ*âru*k*i, A. D. 542, of the Eastern Wêi dynasty, A. D. 534–550. 3 leaves.

The following four works were translated by Tsü-*kh*ü *K*iṅ-shaṅ, A. D. 455, of the earlier Suṅ dynasty, A. D. 420–479:—

771 佛說耶祇經

Fo-shwo-ye-*k*'-*k*iṅ.

'Sûtra spoken by Buddha on (the Brâhmaṇa) Ye-*k*' (?).' 3 leaves.

772 佛說末羅王經

Fo-shwo-mo-lo-wâṅ-*k*iṅ.

'Sûtra spoken by Buddha on the King Mo-lo (?).' 2 leaves.

773 佛說摩達國王經

Fo-shwo-mo-tâ-kwo-wâṅ-*k*iṅ.

'Sûtra spoken by Buddha on the King of a country Mo-tâ (?).' 2 leaves.

774 佛說旃陀越國王經

Fo-shwo-*k*ân-tho-yueh-kwo-wâṅ-*k*iṅ.

'Sûtra spoken by Buddha on the King of a country Kandanavat (?).' 3 leaves.

The above six works are wanting in Tibetan. *K*'-yuen-lu, fasc. 7, fol. 21 a seq.

775 佛說五王經

Fo-shwo-wu-wâṅ-*k*iṅ.

'Sûtra spoken by Buddha on five Kings.'

Translated under the Eastern Tsin dynasty, A. D. 317–420; but the translator's name is lost. 5 leaves.

776 佛說出家功德經

Fo-shwo-*kh*u-*k*iâ-kuṅ-töh-*k*iṅ.

'Sûtra spoken by Buddha on the merit of leaving the house (in order to become an anchorite).'

Translated under the three Tshin dynasties, A. D. 350–431; but the translator's name is lost. 6 leaves.

The above two works agree with Tibetan. *K'*-yuen-lu, fasc. 7, fol. 23 a.

777 佛說旃檀樹經

Fo-shwo-*k*ân-thân-shu-*k*iṅ.

'Sûtra spoken by Buddha on the *K*andana tree.'

Translated under the Eastern Hân dynasty, A. D. 25–220; but the translator's name is lost. 3 leaves.

778 佛說頞多和多耆經

Fo-shwo-ṅö-to-hö-to-*kh*i-*k*iṅ.

'Sûtra spoken by Buddha entitled Ṅö-to-hö-to-*kh*i (a transliteration of a certain term?).'

Translated under the Western Tsin dynasty, A. D. 265–316; but the translator's name is lost. 2 leaves. Buddha, being asked by a Deva, told his disciples eight things concerning gifts, and ten causes of a foolish man's not knowing gifts. *K'*-tsiṅ, fasc. 31, fol. 9 b.

The above two works are wanting in Tibetan. *K'*-yuen-lu, fasc. 7, fol. 23 b.

779 禪秘要法經

Shân-pi-yâo-fâ-*k*iṅ.

'Sûtra on the law of secret importance of meditation.'

Translated by Kumâragîva, of the Latter Tshin dynasty, A. D. 384–417. 3 fasciculi.

780 陰持入經

Yin-*kh*'-*z*u-*k*iṅ.

'Skandha-dhâtv-âyatana-sûtra.'

Translated by Ân Shi-kâo, of the Eastern Hân dynasty, A. D. 25–220. 2 fasciculi. Deest in Tibetan. *K'*-yuen-lu, fasc. 7, fol. 16 b.

781 佛說因緣僧護經

Fo-shwo-yin-yuen-saṅ-hu-*k*iṅ.

'Buddhabhâshita-nidâna-saṅghapâla-sûtra.'

Translated under the Eastern Tsin dynasty, A. D. 317–420; but the translator's name is lost. 1 fasciculus. Deest in Tibetan. *K'*-yuen-lu, fasc. 7, fol. 22 b.

PART III.

宋元入藏諸大小乘經 Suṅ-yuen-ʐu-tsâṅ-ku-tâ-siâo-shaṅ-kiṅ, or the Sûtras of the Mahâyâna and Hînayâna, admitted into the Canon during the later (or Northern) and Southern Suṅ (A. D. 960–1127 and 1127–1280) and Yuen (1280–1368) dynasties.

Note—There are fifty-nine Sûtras of the Hînayâna out of three hundred works in this Part. They will be distinguished by an h within parentheses added after their Chinese titles. They are the works mentioned under the heading of the Sûtras of the Hînayâna, except five, viz. Nos. 808, 817, 823, 824, 923, which are under that of the Vinaya-piṭaka of the same school, in the K'-yuen-lu and K'-tsiṅ.

The following two works were translated by Thien-si-tsâi, A. D. 980–1001, of the later Suṅ dynasty, A. D. 960–1127:—

782 佛說大乘莊嚴寶王經
Fo-shwo-tâ-shaṅ-kwâṅ-yen-pâo-wâṅ-kiṅ.
'Buddhabhâshita-mahâyâna-vyûha-ratnarâga-sûtra.'
Karaṇḍavyûha-sûtra.

K'-yuen-lu, fasc. 5, fol. 18 a; A.R., p. 437; A.M.G., p. 243.

Ghanavyûha-sûtra.

Conc. 592. 4 fasciculi. It agrees with Tibetan. K'-yuen-lu, s.v. Cf. Nos. 168, 169.

783 分別善惡報應經
Fan-pieh-shan-ṅoh-pâo-yiṅ-kiṅ. (h)
'Sûtra on the division or explanation of the results of good and bad (actions).' 2 fasciculi.

This is a later translation of Nos. 610, 611. Deest in Tibetan. K'-yuen-lu, fasc. 7, fol. 27 b.

784 佛說守護大千國土經
Fo-shwo-sheu-hu-tâ-tshien-kwo-tu-kiṅ.
'Sûtra spoken by Buddha on the protection of the great-thousand world.'
Mahâsahasrapramardana (?)-sûtra.

K'-yuen-lu, fasc. 5, fol. 19 a; A. R., p. 516; A.M.G., p. 316.

Mahâsahasramaṇḍala-sûtra.

Conc. 64. Translated by Sh'-hu (Dânapâla?), A. D. 980–1000, of the later Suṅ dynasty, A. D. 960–1127. 3 fasciculi. It agrees with Tibetan. K'-yuen-lu, s.v.

The following four works were translated by Fâ-thien (Dharmadeva?), A. D. 973–981, of the later Suṅ dynasty, A. D. 960–1127:—

785 大方廣總持寶光明經
Tâ-fâṅ-kwâṅ-tsuṅ-kh'-pâo-kwâṅ-miṅ-kiṅ.
'Mahâvaipulya-dhâraṇî-ratnaprabhâsa-sûtra.' 5 fasciculi.

This is a later translation of the fifteenth chapter on the ten dwellings (not the Dasabhûmis, but the lower steps of a Bodhisattva) in fasc. 16 of No. 88. K'-yuen-lu, fasc. 5, fol. 15 a.

786 佛說大乘聖無量壽決定光明王如來陀羅尼經
Fo-shwo-tâ-shaṅ-shaṅ-wu-liâṅ-sheu-kiê-tiṅ-kwâṅ-miṅ-wâṅ-ʐu-lâi-tho-lo-ni-kiṅ.
'Buddhabhâshita-mahâyânâryâmitâyurniskitaprabhâsarâga-tathâgata-dhâraṇî-sûtra.' 7 leaves.

It agrees with Tibetan. K'-yuen-lu, fasc. 5, fol. 19 b.

787 佛說大乘聖吉祥持世陀羅尼經
Fo-shwo-tâ-shaṅ-shaṅ-ki-siâṅ-kh'-shi-tho-lo-ni-kiṅ.
'Buddhabhâshita-mahâyânâryasrî-vasudhara-dhâraṇî-sûtra.'
Vasudhara-dhâraṇî.

See No. 492. 9 leaves. This is a later translation of Nos. 492, 962. Deest in Tibetan. *K'*-yuen-lu, fasc. 6, fol. 1. But see Nos. 492, 962.

788 佛說大乘日子王所問經

Fo-shwo-tâ-shañ-*s*ih-tsz'-wâñ-su-wan-*k*iñ.

'Buddhabhâshita-mahâyâna-sûryaputra (or, Udayana)-râga-pariprikkhâ-sûtra.'

Udayâna (or Udayana)-vatsarâ*g*a-paripr*ikkh*â.

See No. 38. 14 leaves. This is a later translation of Nos. 23 (29), 38. Deest in Tibetan. *K'*-yuen-lu, fasc. 4, fol. 14 b. But see No. 23 (29).

789 佛說金耀童子經

Fo-shwo-*k*iñ-yâo-thuñ-tsz'-*k*iñ.

'Buddhabhâshita-suvarnarasmi-kumâra-sûtra.'

Translated by Thien-si-tsâi, A.D. 980–1001, of the later Suñ dynasty, A.D. 960–1127. 9 leaves. It agrees with Tibetan. *K'*-yuen-lu, fasc. 4, fol. 14 a.

790 佛頂放無垢光明入普門觀察一切如來心陀羅尼經

Fo-tin-fâñ-wu-keu-kwâñ-miñ-*s*u-phu-man-kwâñ-tsâ-yi-tshiê-*s*u-lâi-sin-tho-lo-ni-*k*iñ.

Samantamukha - pravesa - rasmivimaloshnîsha - prabhâ-sarvatathâgatahr*i*daya-samaviro*k*ana-dhâra*n*î(-sûtra).

K'-yuen-lu, fasc. 5, fol. 20 a. Conc. 172 reads wrongly arhatâya for hridaya. Translated by Sh'-hu (Dânapâla ?), A.D. 980–1000, of the later Suñ dynasty, A.D. 960–1127. 2 fasciculi. It agrees with Tibetan. *K'*-yuen-lu, s.v.

The following two works were translated by Thien-si-tsâi, A.D. 980–1001, of the later Suñ dynasty, A.D. 960–1127:—

791 佛說樓閣正法甘露鼓經

Fo-shwo-leu-kwo-*k*añ-fâ-kân-lu-ku-*k*iñ.

'Buddhabhâshita-vimânasaddharmâmrita-dundubhi-sûtra.' 5 leaves.

Deest in Tibetan. *K'*-yuen-lu, fasc. 5, fol. 22 b.

792 佛說大乘善見變化文殊師利問法經

Fo-shwo-tâ-shañ-shân-*k*ien-pien-hwâ-wan-shu-sh'-li-wan-fâ-*k*iñ.

'Buddhabhâshita-mahâyâna-sudarsanavikriyâ-mañgusrî-dharma-pariprikkhâ-sûtra.'

Bodhivaksho-mañ*g*usrî-nirdesa-sûtra.

K'-yuen-lu, fasc. 4, fol. 12 a.

Bodhivakâ (?)-nirdesa.

A.R., p. 451; A.M.G., p. 256; Conc. 566. 7 leaves. It agrees with Tibetan. *K'*-yuen-lu, s.v.

The following two works were translated by Fâ-thien (Dharmadeva ?), A.D. 973–981, of the later Suñ dynasty, A.D. 960–1127:—

793 聖虛空藏菩薩陀羅尼經

Shañ-hhü-khuñ-tsâñ-phu-sâ-tho-lo-ni-*k*iñ.

'Âryâkâsagarbha-bodhisattva-dhâranî-sûtra.'

Saptabuddhaka-sûtra.

See No. 367. 9 leaves. This is a later translation of Nos. 367, 368. Deest in Tibetan. *K'*-yuen-lu, fasc. 5, fol. 21 b. But see Nos. 367, 368.

794 佛說大護明大陀羅尼經

Fo-shwo-tâ-hu-miñ-tâ-tho-lo-ni-*k*iñ.

'Buddhabhâshita-mahâprabhâpâla-mahâdhâranî-sûtra.' 7 leaves.

Deest in Tibetan. *K'*-yuen-lu, fasc. 5, fol. 21 b.

795 佛說無能勝幡王如來莊嚴陀羅尼經

Fo-shwo-wu-nañ-shañ-fâñ-wâñ-*s*u-lâi-*k*wâñ-yen-tho-lo-ni-*k*iñ.

'Buddhabhâshita-durgayadhvagarâga (?)-tathâgata-vyûha-dhâranî-sûtra.'

Dhva*g*âgrakeyûra-dhâra*n*î.

K'-yuen-lu, fasc. 5, fol. 25 b; Conc. 841; A.R., p. 525; A.M.G., p. 324. Translated by Sh'-hu (Dânapâla ?), A.D. 980–1000, of the later Suñ dynasty, A.D. 960–1127. 4 leaves. It agrees with Tibetan. *K'*-yuen-lu, s.v.

796 最勝佛頂陀羅尼經

Tsui-shâñ-fo-tiñ-tho-lo-ni-*k*iñ.

'The most excellent (or Vigaya-) Buddhoshnîsha-dhâranî-sûtra.'

Sarvadurgati-parisodhanoshn*î*shavi*g*aya-dhâra*n*î.

See No. 348. 3 leaves. Translated by Fâ-thien (Dharmadeva ?), A.D. 973–981, of the later Suñ dynasty, A.D. 960–1127. This is a later translation of Nos. 348–352. *K'*-yuen-lu, fasc. 4, fol. 25 b.

797 聖佛母小字般若波羅蜜多經

Shañ-fo-mu-siâo-tsz'-pân-*z*o-po-lo-mi-to-*k*iñ.

'Ârya-buddhamâtrikâlpâkshara-pragñâpâramitâ-sûtra.'

Alpâkshara-pra*g*ñâpâramitâ.

A.R., p. 512; A.M.G., p. 312. Translated by Thien-si-tsâi, A.D. 980–1001, of the later Suṅ dynasty, A.D. 960–1127. 4 leaves. It agrees with Tibetan. *K'-yuen-lu*, fasc. 1, fol. 19 b.

The following two works were translated by Sh'-hu (Dânapâla?), A.D. 980–1000, of the later Suṅ dynasty, A.D. 960–1127:—

798 消除一切閃電障難隨求如意陀羅尼經

Siâo-*k*hu-yi-tshiê-shân-tien-*k*âṅ-nân-sui-*k*hiu-*z*u-i-tho-lo-ni-*k*iṅ.

'Sûtra of the Dhâraṇî destroying all the obstacles of a flash of lightning according to wish and thought (?).' 5 leaves.

It agrees with Tibetan. *K'-yuen-lu*, fasc. 5, fol. 25 a.

799 聖最上燈明如來陀羅尼經

Shaṅ-tsui-shâṅ-taṅ-miṅ-*z*u-lâi-tho-lo-ni-*k*iṅ.

'Âryânuttaradîpa-tathâgata-dhâraṇî-sûtra.' 8 leaves.

It agrees with Tibetan. *K'-yuen-lu*, fasc. 6, fol. 2 a.

The following two works were translated by Fâ-thien (Dharmadeva?), A.D. 973–981, of the later Suṅ dynasty, A.D. 960–1127:—

800 大寒林聖難拏陀羅尼經

Tâ-hân-lin-shaṅ-nân-nâ-tho-lo-ni-*k*iṅ.

'Mahâsîtavanârya-daṇḍa-dhâraṇî-sûtra.'

Mahâdaṇḍa-dhâraṇî.

K'-yuen-lu, fasc. 5, fol. 21 a; Conc. 618; A.R., p. 525; A.M.G., p. 324. 6 leaves. It agrees with Tibetan. *K'-yuen-lu*, s.v.

801 佛說諸行有爲經

Fo-shwo-*k*u-hhiṅ-yiu-wêi-*k*in. (h)

'Buddhabhâshita-sarvasaṃskârâ-saṃskṛita-sûtra.' 2 leaves.

Deest in Tibetan. *K'-yuen-lu*, fasc. 8, fol. 4 b.

The following two works were translated by Sh'-hu (Dânapâla?), A.D. 980–1000, of the later Suṅ dynasty, A.D. 960–1127:—

802 息除中夭陀羅尼經

Si-*kh*u-*k*uṅ-yâo-tho-lo-ni-*k*iṅ.

'Sûtra of the Dhâraṇî stopping premature death.'

*K*intâmaṇinâma-sarvaghâtamṛityu-vâraṇita (or -vâraṇa)-dhâraṇî.

K'-yuen-lu, fasc. 6, fol. 3 a; Conc. 518, where however this Sanskrit title is not fully restored from the Chinese transliteration given on the former authority. 3 leaves. This Sûtra exists in Tibetan. *K'yuen-lu*, s.v.

803 一切如來正法秘密篋印心陀羅尼經

Yi-tshiê-*z*u-lâi-*k*aṅ-fâ-pi-mi-*kh*iê-yin-sin-tho-lo-ni-*k*iṅ.

'Sarvatathâgata-saddharma-guhyakaraṇḍa-mudrâ-hṛidaya-dhâraṇî-sûtra.' 10 leaves.

804 妙法聖念處經

Miâo-fâ-shaṅ-nien-*kh*u-*k*iṅ. (h)

Saddharma-(ârya)-smṛityupasthâna-sûtra.

Cf. No. 679. Translated by Fâ-thien (Dharmadeva?), A.D. 973–981, of the later Suṅ dynasty, A.D. 960–1127. 8 fasciculi. This is somewhat similar to No. 679, though it is much shorter. Cf. *K'-tsiṅ*, fasc. 30, fol. 2 a. According to *K'-yuen-lu* (fasc. 4, fol. 11 a), this is a later translation of No. 23 (43). But this note ought to belong to No. 805. Cf. *K'-tsiṅ*, fasc. 3, fol. 18 b.

805 佛說大迦葉問大寶積正法經

Fo-shwo-tâ-*k*iâ-yeh-wan-tâ-pâo-tsi-*k*aṅ-fâ-*k*iṅ.

'Buddhabhâshita-mahâkâsyapa-paripṛi*kkh*â-mahâratnakûta-saddharma-sûtra.' Cf. Conc. 623.

Kâsyapa-parivarta.

Translated by Sh'-hu (Dânapâla?), A.D. 980–1000, of the later Suṅ dynasty, A.D. 960–1127. 5 fasciculi. This is a later translation of Nos. 23 (43), 57, 58. *K'-tsiṅ*, fasc. 3, fol. 18 b. Deest in Tibetan. *K'-yuen-lu*, fasc. 1, fol. 37 a. But see No. 23 (43).

806 嗟韈曩法天子受三歸依獲免惡道經

Tsie-wâ-nâṅ-fâ-thien-tsz'-sheu-sân-kwêi-i-kwo-mien-ṅoh-tâo-*k*iṅ. (h)

'Sûtra on a Devaputra named Tsie-wâ-nâṅ-fâ (?), who escaped from (falling into) an evil state (to be reborn as a boar), on account of receiving (the instruction in) the Trisaraṇa (from Indra).'

Translated by Fâ-thien (Dharmadeva?), A.D. 937–981, of the later Suṅ dynasty, A.D. 960–1127. 3 leaves. Deest in Tibetan. *K'-yuen-lu*, fasc. 8, fol. 2 a.

807 佛說較量壽命經
Fo-shwo-kiâo-liâṅ-sheu-miṅ-kiṅ. (h)
'Sûtra spoken by Buddha on counting (the length of) the life (of beings in the Saha world).'

Translated by Thien-si-tsâi, A.D. 980–1001, of the later Suṅ dynasty, A.D. 960–1127. 11 leaves. Deest in Tibetan. K'-yuen-lu, fasc. 8, fol. 4 a.

The following two works were translated by Sh'-hu (Dânapâla?), A.D. 980–1000, of the later Suṅ dynasty, A.D. 960–1127:—

808 佛說沙彌十戒儀則經
Fo-shwo-shâ-mi-shi-kiê-i-tsö-kiṅ. (h)
'Sûtra spoken by Buddha on the ceremonial rules for the ten precepts (Sikshâpadas) of the Srâmanera.' 6 leaves.

Deest in Tibetan. K'-yuen-lu, fasc. 8, fol. 20 b, where this work is mentioned under the heading of the Vinaya of the Hînayâna.

809 佛說聖持世陀羅尼經
Fo-shwo-shaṅ-kh'-shi-tho-lo-ni-kiṅ.
'Buddhabhâshitârya-vasudhara-dhâranî-sûtra.'
Vasudhara-dhâranî.

K'-yuen-lu, fasc. 5, fol. 22 a; Conc. 112. 8 leaves. Cf. Nos. 492, 787, 962.

The following two works were translated by Fâ-thien (Dharmadeva?), A.D. 973–981, of the later Suṅ dynasty, A.D. 960–1127:—

810 佛說布施經
Fo-shwo-pu-sh'-kiṅ. (h)
'Buddhabhâshita-dâna-sûtra.' 3 leaves.

It agrees with Tibetan. K'-yuen-lu, fasc. 4, fol. 14 a.

811 佛說聖曜母陀羅尼經
Fo-shwo-shaṅ-yâo-mu-tho-lo-ni-kiṅ.
'Buddhabhâshitârya-grahamâtrikâ-dhâranî-sûtra.'
Grahamâtrikâ-dhâranî.

K'-yuen-lu, fasc. 6, fol. 2 b; Conc. 100; A. R., p. 530; A. M. G., p. 328. 5 leaves. It agrees with Tibetan. K'-yuen-lu, s. v.

812 法集名數經
Fâ-tsi-miṅ-shu-kiṅ.
'Sûtra of the number of names, being the Dharmasaṅgraha.'

Translated by Sh'-hu (Dânapâla?), A.D. 980–1000, of the later Suṅ dynasty, A.D. 960–1127. 7 leaves. This work is mentioned under the heading of the Works of the Western or Indian Sages, in K'-yuen-lu, fasc. 10, fol. 4 b. It is to be compared with the Sanskrit text of the Dharmasaṅgraha, mentioned in Catalogue of the Hodgson Manuscripts, II, 21. There is a similar MS. in the University Library, Cambridge.

813 聖多羅菩薩一百八名陀羅尼經
Shaṅ-to-lo-phu-sâ-yi-pâi-pâ-miṅ-tho-lo-ni-kiṅ.
'Ârya-târâ-(bhadra)-bodhisattva-nâmâshtasataka-dhâranî-sûtra.'
Cf. No. 515.

Translated by Fâ-thien (Dharmadeva?), A.D. 973–981, of the later Suṅ dynasty, A.D. 960–1127. 8 leaves. It agrees with Tibetan. K'-yuen-lu, fasc. 5, fol. 19 b.

814 十二緣生祥瑞經
Shi-'rh-yuen-shaṅ-siâṅ-sui-kiṅ. (h)
'Sûtra on lucky omens produced from twelve causes.'

Translated by Sh'-hu (Dânapâla?), A.D. 980–1000, of the later Suṅ dynasty, A.D. 960–1127. 2 fasciculi. It is doubtful or wanting in Tibetan. K'-yuen-lu, fasc. 8, fol. 4 a.

The following two works were translated by Thien-si-tsâi, A.D. 980–1001, of the later Suṅ dynasty, A.D. 960–1127. They agree with Tibetan. K'-yuen-lu, fasc. 5, fol. 19 b seq.:—

815 讚揚聖德多羅菩薩一百八名經
Tsân-yâṅ-shaṅ-töh-to-lo-phu-sâ-yi-pâi-pâ-miṅ-kiṅ.
'Sûtra on praising a hundred and eight names of the holy Bodhisattva Târâbhadra.'
Târâbhadra-nâmâshtasataka.

K'-yuen-lu, fasc. 5, fol. 19 b; Conc. 759; A. R., p. 534; A. M. G., p. 332. 6 leaves.

816 聖觀自在菩薩一百八名經
Shaṅ-kwâṅ-tsz'-tsâi-phu-sâ-yi-pâi-pâ-miṅ-kiṅ.
'Ârya-avalokitesvara-bodhisattva-nâmâshtasataka-sûtra.'
Avalokitesvara-nâmâshtasataka.

A. R., p. 533; A. M. G., p. 331. 6 leaves.

The following three works were translated by Fâ-thien (Dharmadeva?), A.D. 973–981, of the later Suṅ dynasty, A.D. 960–1127:—

817 佛說目連所問經
Fo-shwo-mu-lien-su-wan-*k*iṅ. (h)
'Sûtra spoken by Buddha on the request of Maudgalyâyana.'
2 leaves.

Deest in Tibetan. *K'*-yuen-lu, fasc. 8, fol. 20 b, where this work is mentioned under the heading of the Vinaya of the Hînayâna.

818 外道問聖大乘法無我義經
Wâi-tâo-wan-shaṅ-tâ-shaṅ-fâ-wu-wo-i-*k*iṅ.
'Ârya-mahâyâna-sûtra on the meaning of the Anâtma in (Sarva)-dharma, asked by a Tîrthaka.'
*S*âlisambhava-sûtra.

Conc. 787. 4 leaves. This is a later translation of Nos. 280, 281. *K'*-yuen-lu, fasc. 4, fol. 12 b.

819 毗俱胝菩薩一百八名經
Phi-*k*ü-*k'*-phu-sâ-yi-pâi-pâ-miṅ-*k*iṅ.
'Vikauta(ka?)-bodhisattva-nâmâshṭaśataka-sûtra.' 5 leaves.
It agrees with Tibetan. *K'*-yuen-lu, fasc. 5, fol. 20 a.

820 勝軍化世百喻伽陀經
Shaṅ-*k*iün-hwâ-shi-pâi-yü-*k*iê-tho-*k*iṅ.
'Sûtra of the Gâthâs of a hundred comparisons (or Avadânaśataka, composed by?) Gayasena for converting the world (to the law of Buddha).'

Translated by Thien-si-tsâi, A.D. 980–1001, of the later Suṅ dynasty, A.D. 960–1127. 10 leaves.

The following five works were translated by Fâ-thien (Dharmadeva?), A.D. 973–981, of the later Suṅ dynasty, A.D. 960–1127:—

821 六道伽陀經
Liu-tâo-*k*iê-tho-*k*iṅ.
'Sûtra of the Gâthâs on six paths.' 8 leaves.

The above two works are mentioned under the heading of the Works of the Indian Sages, in *K'*-yuen-lu, fasc. 10, fol. 6 b.

822 妙臂菩薩所問經
Miâo-phi-phu-sâ-su-wan-*k*iṅ.
'Subâhu-bodhisattva-paripr*i*kkhâ-sûtra.'
Subâhu-paripr*i*kkhâ.

K'-yuen-lu, fasc. 5, fol. 18 b; Conc. 361. 4 fasciculi. This is a later translation of No. 531. It agrees with Tibetan. *K'*-yuen-lu, s. v.

823 佛說苾芻五法經
Fo-shwo-pi-*k*hu-wu-fâ-*k*iṅ. (h)
'Buddhabhâshita-bhikshu-pañkadharma-sûtra.' 3 leaves.

824 佛說苾芻迦尸迦十法經
Fo-shwo-pi-*k*hu-*k*iâ-sh'-*k*iâ-shi-fâ-*k*iṅ. (h)
'Buddhabhâshita-bhikshuka-siksha (?)-dasadharma-sûtra.' 3 leaves.

The above two works are mentioned under the heading of the Vinaya of the Hînayâna, in *K'*-yuen-lu, fasc. 8, fol. 20 a.

825 諸佛心印陀羅尼經
*K*u-fo-sin-yin-tho-lo-ni-*k*iṅ.
'Sarvabuddha-hr*i*daya-mudrâ-dhâra*n*î-sûtra.'
Buddhahr*i*daya-dhâra*n*î.

This is a later translation of No. 489. Deest in Tibetan. *K'*-yuen-lu, fasc. 6, fol. 3 a. But see No. 489. 2 leaves.

The following two works were translated by Sh'-hu (Dânapâla?), A.D. 980–1000, of the later Suṅ dynasty, A.D. 960–1127:—

826 大乘寶月童子問法經
Tâ-shaṅ-pâo-yueh-thuṅ-tsz'-wan-fâ-*k*iṅ.
'Mahâyâna-ratnakandra-kumâra-paripr*i*kkhâ-dharma-sûtra.'
5 leaves.

Deest in Tibetan. *K'*-yuen-lu, fasc. 4, fol. 13 a.

827 佛說蓮華眼陀羅尼經
Fo-shwo-lien-hwâ-yen-tho-lo-ni-*k*iṅ.
'Buddhabhâshita-pu*nd*arikakakshur-dhâra*n*î-sûtra.' 1 leaf.
Deest in Tibetan. *K'*-yuen-lu, fasc. 5, fol. 24 b.

828 佛說觀想佛母般若波羅蜜多菩薩經
Fo-shwo-kwâṅ-siâṅ-fo-mu-pân-zo-po-lo-mi-to-phu-sâ-*k*iṅ.
'Sûtra spoken by Buddha on meditating on and thinking of the Bodhisattva Buddhamâtrikâ-pragñâpâramitâ (?).'

Translated by Thien-si-tsâi, A.D. 980–1001, of the later Suṅ dynasty, A.D. 960–1127. 3 leaves. It agrees with Tibetan. *K'*-yuen-lu, fasc. 1, fol. 18 b.

The following four works were translated by Sh'-hu (Dânapâla?), A.D. 980–1001, of the later Suṅ dynasty, A.D. 960–1127:—

829 佛說如意摩尼陀羅尼經
Fo-shwo-*z*u-i-mo-ni-tho-lo-ni-*k*iṅ.
'Buddhabhâshita-p°.'
Padma*k*intâma*n*i-dhâra*n*î-sûtra.

Conc. 247 a. 4 leaves. This is a later translation of Nos. 321–324. K'-yuen-lu, fasc. 4, fol. 20 b.

830 佛說聖大總持王經
Fo-shwo-shaṅ-tâ-tsun-*kh*'-wâṅ-*k*iṅ.
'Buddhabhâshitârya-mahâdhâra*n*îrâ*g*a-sûtra.' 4 leaves.

831 佛說最上意陀羅尼經
Fo-shwo-tsui-shâṅ-i-tho-lo-ni-*k*iṅ.
'Buddhabhâshita-anuttaramati-dhâra*n*î-sûtra.' 6 leaves.

832 佛說持明藏八大總持王經
Fo-shwo-*kh*'-miṅ-tsâṅ-pâ-tâ-tsuṅ-*kh*'-wâṅ-*k*iṅ.
'Buddhabhâshita-prabhâdhara-pi*t*aka (or -garbha)-ash*t*amahâdhâra*n*îrâ*g*a-sûtra.' 7 leaves.

The above three works are wanting in Tibetan. K'-yuen-lu, fasc. 5, fol. 22 b seq.

833 聖無能勝金剛火陀羅尼經
Shaṅ-wu-naṅ-shaṅ-*k*in-kâṅ-hwo-tho-lo-ni-*k*iṅ.
'Ârya-durgaya-va*g*râgnî-dhâra*n*î-sûtra.'

Translated by Fâ-thien (Dharmadeva?), A.D. 973–981, of the later Suṅ dynasty, A.D. 960–1127. 5 leaves. It agrees with Tibetan. K'-yuen-lu, fasc. 5, fol. 25 b.

The following five works were translated by Sh'-hu (Dânapâla?), A.D. 980–1000, of the later Suṅ dynasty, A.D. 960–1127:—

834 佛說尊勝大明王經
Fo-shwo-tsun-shaṅ-tâ-miṅ-wâṅ-*k*iṅ.
'Buddhabhâshita-âryottama-mahâvidyârâ*g*a-sûtra.' 4 leaves.

Deest in Tibetan. K'-yuen-lu, fasc. 6, fol. 4 a.

835 佛說智光滅一切業障陀羅尼經
Fo-shwo-*k*'-kwâṅ-mieh-yi-tshiê-yeh-*k*âṅ-tho-lo-ni-*k*iṅ.
'Buddhabhâshita-*g*ñânolkâ-sarvagati-parisodhana-dhâra*n*î-sûtra.'
*G*ñânolkâ-dhâra*n*î-sarvagati-pari*s*odhanî.

This is a later translation of No. 496. Deest in Tibetan. K'yuen-lu, fasc. 5, fol. 23 a. But see No. 496.

836 佛說如意寶總持王經
Fo-shwo-*z*u-i-pâo-tsuṅ-*kh*'-wâṅ-*k*iṅ.
'Buddhabhâshita-*k*intâ(ma*n*i)-ratna-dhâra*n*î-râ*g*a-sûtra.' 4 leaves.

It agrees with Tibetan. K'-yuen-lu, fasc. 4, fol. 12 b.

837 佛說大自在天子因地經
Fo-shwo-tâ-tsz'-tsâi-thien-tsz'-yin-ti-*k*iṅ.
'Buddhabhâshita-mahesvara-devaputra-hetubhûmi-sûtra.' 9 leaves.

Deest in Tibetan. K'-yuen-lu, fasc. 4, fol. 11 b.

838 佛說寶生陀羅尼經
Fo-shwo-pâo-shaṅ-tho-lo-ni-*k*iṅ.
'Buddhabhâshita-ratna*g*âta-dhâra*n*î-sûtra.' 2 leaves.

839 佛說十號經
Fo-shwo-shi-hâo-*k*iṅ.
'Sûtra spoken by Buddha on the ten names or epithets (of Buddha).'

Translated by Thien-si-tsâi, A.D. 980–1001, of the later Suṅ dynasty, A.D. 960–1127. 3 leaves. It agrees with Tibetan. K'-yuen-lu, fasc. 4, fol. 12 a.

840 佛爲娑伽羅龍王所說大乘法經
Fo-wêi-so-*k*iê-lo-luṅ-wâṅ-su-shwo-tâ-shaṅ-fâ-*k*iṅ.
'Sûtra addressed by Buddha to the Nâgarâ*g*a Sagara on the law of the Mahâyâna.'
Sagara-nâgarâ*g*a-pari*pri*kk*h*â-sûtra.

K'-yuen-lu, fasc. 4, fol. 13 b; Conc. 178. Translated by Sh'-hu (Dânapâla?), A.D. 980–1000, of the later Suṅ dynasty, A.D. 960–1127. 10 leaves. It agrees with Tibetan. K'-yuen-lu, s.v. No. 840 is mentioned under the heading of the Vinaya of the Mahâyâna, in K'-tsiṅ, fasc. 32, fol. 5 a.

841 佛說普賢菩薩陀羅尼經
Fo-shwo-phu-hhien-phu-sâ-tho-lo-ni-*k*iṅ.
'Buddhabhâshita-samantabhadra-bodhisattva-dhâra*n*î-sûtra.'

Translated by Fâ-thien (Dharmadeva?), A.D. 973–981, of the later Suṅ dynasty, A.D. 960–1127. 3 leaves. Deest in Tibetan. K'-yuen-lu, fasc. 5, fol. 21 b.

The following two works were translated by Sh'-hu (Dânapâla?), A.D. 980–1000, of the later Suṅ dynasty, A.D. 960–1127:—

842 大金剛妙高山樓閣陀羅尼經

Tâ-*k*in-kâṅ-miâo-kâo-shân-leu-kwo-tho-lo-ni-*k*iṅ.

Mahâva*g*rameru-*s*ikhara-kû*t*âgâra-dhâra*n*î(-sûtra).

K'-yuen-lu, fasc. 6, fol. 1 b; Conc. 626; A. R., p. 539; A. M. G., p. 337. 10 leaves. It agrees with Tibetan. *K*'-yuen-lu, s. v.

843 廣大蓮華莊嚴曼拏羅滅一切罪陀羅尼經

Kwâṅ-tâ-lien-hwâ-*k*wâṅ-yen-man-nâ-lo-mieh-yi-tshiê-tsâi-tho-lo-ni-*k*iṅ.

'Mahâ-pundarikavyûha-mandala-sarvapâpa-vinâsa-dhâranî-sûtra.'

11 leaves.

844 佛說大摩里支菩薩經

Fo-shwo-tâ-mo-li-*k*'-phu-sâ-*k*iṅ.

'Buddhabhâshita-mahâmarî*k*i-bodhisattva-sûtra.'

Translated by Thien-si-tsâi, A. D. 980–1001, of the later Suṅ dynasty, A. D. 960–1127. 7 fasciculi. It agrees with Tibetan. *K*'-yuen-lu, fasc. 5, fol. 17 a.

The following two works were translated by Amoghava*g*ra, A. D. 746–771, of the Thâṅ dynasty, A. D. 618–907:—

845 佛說末利支提婆華鬘經

Fo-shwo-mo-li-*k*'-thi-pho-hwâ-mân-*k*iṅ.

'Buddhabhâshita-marî*k*i-devî-pushpamâlâ-sûtra.'

14 leaves. Deest in Tibetan. *K*'-yuen-lu, fasc. 4, fol. 10 a. But see No. 847.

846 佛說摩利支天經

Fo-shwo-mo-li-*k*'-thien-*k*iṅ.

'Buddhabhâshita-marî*k*i-devî-sûtra.'

5 leaves. It agrees with Tibetan. *K*'-yuen-lu, fasc. 5, fol. 17 a.

847 佛說摩利支天陀羅尼咒經

Fo-shwo-mo-li-*k*'-thien-tho-lo-ni-*k*heu-*k*iṅ.

'Buddhabhâshita-marî*k*i-devî-dhâranî-mantra-sûtra.'

Marî*k*iye (Marî*k*i?)-dhâranî.

A. R., p. 518; A. M. G., p. 318. Translated under the Liâṅ dynasty, A. D. 502–557; but the translator's name is lost. 2 leaves. This is an earlier translation of a part of the Marî*k*i-sûtra in fasc. 10 of No. 363. *K*'-yuen-lu, fasc. 4, fol. 23 a.

But according to *K*'-tsiṅ (fasc. 14, fol. 23 b), the above three works are earlier translations of a part of No. 844.

The following five works were translated by Fâ-thien (Dharmadeva?), A. D. 973–981, of the later Suṅ dynasty, A. D. 960–1127:—

848 佛說長者施報經

Fo-shwo-*k*hâṅ-*k*ö-*k*'-pâo-*k*iṅ. (h)

'Buddhabhâshita-sresh*th*i-dânaphala-sûtra.'

8 leaves. Deest in Tibetan. *K*'-yuen-lu, fasc. 7, fol. 27 a. But, according to *K*'-tsiṅ (fasc. 28, fol. 18 a), this is a later translation of the Sudatta-sûtra in the Madhyamâgama, i. e. No. 542 (155).

849 佛說毗沙門天王經

Fo-shwo-phi-shâ-man-thien-wâṅ-*k*iṅ.

'Buddhabhâshita-vaisramana-divyarâ*g*a-sûtra.'

9 leaves. It agrees with Tibetan. *K*'-yuen-lu, fasc. 5, fol. 20 a.

850 毗婆尸佛經

Phi-pho-sh'-fo-*k*iṅ. (h)

'Vipasyi-buddha-sûtra.'

2 fasciculi. It agrees with Tibetan. *K*'-yuen-lu, fasc. 8, fol. 1 b. According to *K*'-tsiṅ (fasc. 29, fol. 5 a), this is a later translation of the latter part of the Mahânidâna-sûtra in the Dîrghâgama, i. e. No. 545 (1).

851 佛說大三摩惹經

Fo-shwo-tâ-sân-mo-*z*o-*k*iṅ. (h)

'Buddhabhâshita-mahâsamaya-sûtra.'

6 leaves. Deest in Tibetan. *K*'-yuen-lu, fasc. 7, fol. 26 b. But, according to *K*'-tsiṅ (fasc. 29, fol. 7 b), this is a later translation of the Mahâsamaya-sûtra in the Dîrghâgama, i. e. No. 545 (15).

852 佛說月光菩薩經

Fo-shwo-yueh-*k*wâṅ-phu-sâ-*k*iṅ. (h)

'Buddhabhâshita-*k*andraprabha-bodhisattva-sûtra.'

*K*andraprabha-bodhisattvâvadâna-sûtra.

K'-yuen-lu, fasc. 4, fol. 14 b; Conc. 869; A. R., p. 482; A. M. G., p. 286. 6 leaves. It agrees with Tibetan. *K*'-yuen-lu, s. v.

The following six works were translated by Sh'-hu (Dânapâla?), A. D. 980–1000, of the later Suṅ dynasty, A. D. 960–1127:—

853 佛說普賢曼拏羅經
Fo-shwo-phu-hhien-mân-nâ-lo-*k*iṅ.
'Buddhabhâshita-samantabhadra-maṇḍala-sûtra.'

10 leaves. Deest in Tibetan. *K'*-yuen-lu, fasc. 5, fol. 18 b.

854 佛說聖莊嚴陀羅尼經
Fo-shwo-shaṅ-*k*wâṅ-yen-tho-lo-ni-*k*iṅ.
'Buddhabhâshita-ârya-vyûha-dhâraṇî-sûtra.'

2 fasciculi. Deest in Tibetan. *K'*-yuen-lu, fasc. 5, fol. 20 b.

855 佛說聖六字大明王陀羅尼經
Fo-shwo-shaṅ-liu-tsz'-tâ-miṅ-wâṅ-tho-lo-ni-*k*iṅ.
'Buddhabhâshita-ârya-shaḍakshara-mahâvidyâ-râ*g*a-dhâraṇî-sûtra.'

2 leaves.

856 千轉大明陀羅尼經
Tshien-*k*wâṅ-tâ-miṅ-tho-lo-ni-*k*iṅ.
'Sahasrapravartana-mahâvidyâ-dhâraṇî-sûtra.'

4 leaves.

857 佛說華積樓閣陀羅尼經
Fo-shwo-hwâ-tsi-leu-kwo-tho-lo-ni-*k*iṅ.
'Buddhabhâshita-pushpakûṭa-vimâna-dhâraṇî-sûtra.'
Pushpakûṭa-dhâraṇî.

K'-yuen-lu, fasc. 5, fol. 23 a; Conc. 203; A. R., p. 526; A. M. G., p. 325. 4 leaves. This is a later translation of Nos. 337-389. *K'*-yuen-lu, s. v.; *K'*-tsiṅ, fasc. 13, fol. 1 a.

858 佛說勝旛瓔珞陀羅尼經
Fo-shwo-shaṅ-fâṅ-yiṅ-lo-tho-lo-ni-*k*iṅ.
'Buddhabhâshita-*g*ayadhva*g*amâlâ-dhâraṇî-sûtra.'

3 leaves.

859 衆許摩訶帝經
*K*uṅ-hhü-mo-hö-ti-*k*iṅ. (h)
'Samadatta-mahârâ*g*a-sûtra.'

Translated by Fâ-hhien, A. D. 982-1001, of the later Suṅ dynasty, A. D. 960-1127. 13 fasciculi. Deest in Tibetan. *K'*-yuen-lu, fasc. 7, fol. 26 a. It contains a history of Sâkyamuni, from the origin of the world, and a list of his ancestors, beginning with the first 'lord of the field' or ruler, Sân-mo-tâ-to-wâṅ, i. e. Samadatta-râ*g*a (fasc. 1, fol. 6 a, col. 5 seq.), and ending with Buddha's visit to his father after his becoming the enlightened, and his telling the story of a former king of Vârâṇasî, Brahmâyus by name. In the Chinese title, the first two characters 衆許 *K*uṅ-hhü, 'multitude-assent,' are used for a translation of the name Samadatta. The celebrated Pâsz*e*pa explains this name in his work entitled *K*aṅ-su-*k'*-lun (No. 1320, fasc. 1, fol. 19 b). He says, 'The ruler was called Tâ-sân-mo-to-wâṅ, i. e. Mahâ-Samadatta-râ*g*a, because he was chosen to become so (or elected as the first lord) by the multitude.' He uses the three characters 衆所許 *K*uṅ-su-hhü, 'he who is chosen by the multitude,' both for the explanation and translation of the name Samadatta. The first and third characters of this term are exactly the same as the first two characters in the present title as above mentioned; while the second one, 所 su, is merely a sign of the passive voice. Then the next three characters 摩訶帝 Mo-hö-ti in the title evidently stand for Mahârâ*g*a, which again agree with the first and last characters of the name 大三末多王 Tâ-sân-mo-to-wâṅ, i. e. Mahâ-Samadatta-râ*g*a, given in No. 1320. It is by no means certain, whether this Chinese title, 'Samadatta-mahârâ*g*a-sûtra,' is a literal rendering of the Sanskrit title, or not. But this Chinese title cannot be meant to represent 'the Mahâvastu according to the version of the Mahâsaṅghikas,' as Mr. Beal says in his Catalogue, p. 54.

The following two works were translated by Fâ-thien (Dharmadeva?), A. D. 973-981, of the later Suṅ dynasty, A. D. 960-1127:—

860 佛說七佛經
Fo-shwo-tshiê-fo-*k*iṅ. (h)
'Buddhabhâshita-saptabuddha-sûtra.'
Saptabuddhaka.

A. R., p. 511; A. M. G., p. 311. 15 leaves. It agrees with Tibetan. *K'*-yuen-lu, fasc. 8, fol. 1 a. According to *K'*-tsiṅ (fasc. 29, fol. 4 b), this is a later translation of the first part of the Mahânidâna-sûtra in the Dîrghâgama, i. e. No. 545 (1).

861 佛說解憂經
Fo-shwo-*k*iê-yiu-*k*iṅ. (h)
'Sûtra spoken by Buddha on alleviating sorrow or grief.'

4 leaves. Deest in Tibetan. *K'*-yuen-lu, fasc. 8, fol. 5 a.

862 佛說徧照般若波羅蜜經
Fo-shwo-pien-*k*âo-pân-*z*o-po-lo-mi-*k*iṅ.
'Buddhabhâshita-samantaprakâsamâna-pra*gñ*âpâramitâ-sûtra.'

Translated by Sh'-hu (Dânapâla?), A.D. 980–1000, of the later Suṅ dynasty, A.D. 960–1127. 8 leaves. Deest in Tibetan. *K'*-yuen-lu, fasc. 1, fol. 19 a. But No. 862 is to be compared with the Tibetan version of the Pra*gñ*âpâramitâ-va*g*rapâ*n*i, mentioned in A. R., p. 397; A. M. G., p. 203. No. 862 is addressed by Buddha to the Bodhisattva Va*g*rapâ*n*i. *K'*-tsiṅ, fasc. 12, fol. 7 b.

The following two works were translated by Fâ-hhien, A.D. 982–1001, of the later Suṅ dynasty, A.D. 960–1127:—

863 佛說大乘無量壽莊嚴經
Fo-shwo-tâ-shaṅ-wu-liâṅ-sheu-*k*wâṅ-yen-*k*iṅ.
'Buddhabhâshita-mahâyânâmitâyur-vyûha-sûtra.'
Amitâyusha-vyûha, or Sukhâvatî-vyûha.

Cf. No. 23 (5). 3 fasciculi. This is the last translation of this Sûtra, similar to Nos. 23 (5), 25, 26, 27. *K'*-yuen-lu, fasc. 4, fol. 11 a; *K'*-tsiṅ, fasc. 3, fol. 12 b.

864 佛母寶德藏般若波羅蜜經
Fo-mu-pâo-töh-tsâṅ-pân-*z*o-po-lo-mi-*k*iṅ.
'Buddhamâtrika-ratnagunagarbha-pra*gñ*âpâramitâ-sûtra.'
Pra*gñ*âpâramitâ-sa*ñ*kayagâthâ.

A. R., p. 395; A. M. G., p. 201. 3 fasciculi.

The following four works were translated by Sh'-hu (Dânapâla?), A.D. 980–1000, of the later Suṅ dynasty, A.D. 960–1127:—

865 佛說帝釋般若波羅蜜多心經
Fo-shwo-ti-shih-pân-*z*o-po-lo-mi-to-sin-*k*iṅ.
'Buddhabhâshita-indra-sakra-pra*gñ*âpâramitâ-hridaya-sûtra.'
Kau*s*ika-pra*gñ*âpâramitâ.

A. R., p. 514; A. M. G., p. 314. 5 leaves. Deest in Tibetan. *K'*-yuen-lu, fasc. 1, fol. 19 a. See, however, the authorities mentioned under the title.

866 佛說諸佛經
Fo-shwo-*k*u-fo-*k*iṅ. (h)
'Sûtra spoken by Buddha on Buddhas.'

4 leaves. It agrees with Tibetan. *K'*-yuen-lu, fasc. 4, fol. 11 b. According to *K'*-tsiṅ (fasc. 29, fol. 17 b), this is a later translation of the first chapter of No. 680.

867 大乘舍黎娑擔摩經
Tâ-shaṅ-shö-li-so-tân-mo-*k*iṅ.
'Mahâyâna-sâlisambhava-sûtra.'
Sâlisambhava-sûtra.

Conc. 565 reads the sixth character 擔 tân as 檐 yen, which latter seems to be right, though the former is given in the Chinese authorities. 8 leaves. This is a later translation of Nos. 280, 281, 818. *K'*-yuen-lu, fasc. 4, fol. 12 b.

868 佛說大金剛香陀羅尼經
Fo-shwo-tâ-*k*iṅ-kâṅ-hhiâṅ-tho-lo-ni-*k*iṅ.
'Buddhabhâshita-mahâva*g*ragandha-dhâra*n*î-sûtra.'

4 leaves. Deest in Tibetan. *K'*-yuen-lu, fasc. 5, fol. 24 b.

869 最上大乘金剛大教寶王經
Tsui-shâṅ-tâ-shaṅ-*k*iṅ-kâṅ-tâ-*k*iâo-pâo-wâṅ-*k*iṅ.
'Anuttara-mahâyâna-va*g*ra-mahâtantra-ratnarâ*g*a-sûtra.'
Va*g*ragarbha-ratnarâ*g*a-tantra.

K'-yuen-lu, fasc. 5, fol. 16 b; Conc. 781. Translated by Fâ-thien (Dharmadeva?), A.D. 973–981, of the later Suṅ dynasty, A.D. 960–1127. 2 fasciculi. It agrees with Tibetan. *K'*-yuen-lu, s. v.

870 佛說薩鉢多酥哩踰捺野經
Fo-shwo-sâ-po-to-su-li-yü-nâh-ye-*k*iṅ. (h)
'Buddhabhâshita-saptasûryanaya-sûtra.'

Translated by Fâ-hhien, A.D. 982–1001, of the later Suṅ dynasty, A.D. 960–1127. 4 leaves. It agrees with Tibetan. *K'*-yuen-lu, fasc. 8, fol. 4 b. According to *K'*-tsiṅ (fasc. 28, fol. 10 b), this is a later translation of the Saptasûrya-sûtra in the Madhyamâgama, i. e. No. 542 (8).

The following two works were translated by Fâ-thien (Dharmadeva?), A.D. 973–981, of the later Suṅ dynasty, A.D. 960–1127:—

871 佛說一切如來烏瑟膩沙最勝總持經
Fo-shwo-yi-tshiê-*z*u-lâi-wu-seh-nî-shâ-tsui-shaṅ-tsuṅ-*kh'*-*k*iṅ.
'Buddhabhâshita-sarvatathâgatoshnîsha-vi*g*aya-dhâra*n*î-sûtra.'
Sarvadurgati-pari*s*odhanosh*n*îsha-vi*g*aya-dhâra*n*î.

9 leaves. This is a similar translation of Nos. 348–352, 796. *K'*-yuen-lu, fasc. 5, fol. 24 b.

872 菩提心觀釋
Phu-thi-sin-kwân-shih.
'Bodhihridaya-dhyâya-vyâkhyâ.'

3 leaves. This work is mentioned under the heading of the Works of the Indian Sages, in *K'*-yuen-lu, fasc. 10, fol. 4 b.

The following seven works were translated by Sh'-hu (Dânapâla?), A. D. 980–1000, of the later Suṅ dynasty, A. D. 960–1127:—

873 佛說護國尊者所問大乘經
Fo-shwo-hu-kwo-tsun-*k*ö-su-wan-tâ-shaṅ-*k*iṅ.
'Buddhabhâshita-ârya-râshtrapâla-pariprikkhâ-mahâyâna-sûtra.'
Râshtrapâla-paripri*kk*hâ.

4 fasciculi. It agrees with Tibetan. *K'*-yuen-lu, fasc. 4, fol. 11 a. According to *K'*-tsiṅ (fasc. 3, fol. 14 a), this is a later translation of No. 23 (18).

874 佛說四無所畏經
Fo-shwo-sz'-wu-su-wêi-*k*iṅ. (h)
'Sûtra spoken by Buddha on four kinds of fearlessness (Vaisâradya).'

2 leaves. Deest in Tibetan. *K'*-yuen-lu, fasc. 4, fol. 11 b.

875 增慧陀羅尼經
Tsaṅ-hwui-tho-lo-ni-*k*iṅ.
'*G*ñânavriddhikara-dhâraṇî-sûtra.'

1 leaf.

876 聖六字增壽大明陀羅尼經
Shaṅ-liu-tsz'-tsâṅ-sheu-tâ-miṅ-tho-lo-ni-*k*iṅ.
'Ârya-shadaksharâyurvriddhikara-mahâvidyâ-dhâraṇî-sûtra.'

2 leaves.

877 佛說大乘戒經
Fo-shwo-tâ-shaṅ-*k*iê-*k*iṅ.
'Buddhabhâshita-mahâyâna-sîla-sûtra.'

2 leaves. Deest in Tibetan. *K'*-yuen-lu, fasc. 8, fol. 7 b, where this work is mentioned under the heading of the Vinaya-piṭaka of the Mahâyâna.

878 佛說聖最勝陀羅尼經
Fo-shwo-shaṅ-tsui-shaṅ-tho-lo-ni-*k*iṅ.
'Buddhabhâshita-âryânuttaravi*g*aya-dhâraṇî-sûtra.'

5 leaves. Deest in Tibetan. *K'*-yuen-lu, fasc. 6, fol. 1 a. This is perhaps a similar translation of No. 831. *K'*-tsiṅ, fasc. 14, fol. 5 a.

879 佛說五十頌聖般若波羅蜜經
Fo-shwo-wu-shi-suṅ-shaṅ-pân-*z*o-po-lo-mi-*k*iṅ.
'Buddhabhâshita-pañkâsadgâthârya-pra*g*ñâpâramitâ-sûtra.'
Pra*g*ñâpâramitâ ardhasatikâ.

A. R., p. 396; A. M. G., p. 201. Cf. No. 18. 2 leaves. It agrees with Tibetan. *K'*-yuen-lu, fasc. 1, fol. 18 b.

The following forty-six works, Nos. 880–925, were translated by Fâ-hhien, A. D. 982–1001, of the later Suṅ dynasty, A. D. 960–1127.

880 大乘八大曼拏羅經
Tâ-shaṅ-pâ-tâ-mân-nâ-lo-*k*iṅ.
'Mahâyânâshtamahâmaṇḍala-sûtra.'
Ashtamandalaka-sûtra.

*K'*yuen-lu, fasc. 5, fol. 12 a; Conc. 579; A. R., p. 511; A. M. G., p. 312. 2 leaves. It agrees with Tibetan. *K'*-yuen-lu, s. v.

881 佛說較量一切佛剎功德經
Fo-shwo-*k*iâo-liâṅ-yi-tshiê-fo-*k*khâ-kuṅ-töh-*k*iṅ.
'Sûtra spoken by Buddha on comparing and measuring the good qualities of all Buddha-kshetras.'

2 leaves. It agrees with Tibetan. *K'*-yuen-lu, fasc. 4, fol. 12 a. According to *K'*tsiṅ (fasc. 1, fol. 10 a), this work is a similar translation of No. 95. But the principal speaker of No. 95 is the Tathâgata, and that of No. 881 is the Bodhisattva A*k*intyaprabhâsarâ*g*a.

882 囉嚩拏說救療小兒疾病經
Lo-foh-nâ-shwo-*k*iu-liâo-siâo-'rh-tsi-piṅ-*k*iṅ.
'Sûtra spoken by Ravaṇa on the curing of the disease of a child.'

11 leaves. Deest in Tibetan. *K'*-yuen-lu, fasc. 5, fol. 19 a.

883 迦葉僊人說醫女人經
*K*iâ-yeh-siân-*z*an-shwo-i-nü-*z*an-*k*iṅ. (h)
'Sûtra spoken by the *Ri*shi Kâsya(pa?) on the curing (of the disease of) a woman.'

4 leaves. Deest in Tibetan. *K'*-yuen-lu, fasc. 8, fol. 4 b.

884 佛說俱枳羅陀羅尼經
Fo-shwo-*k*ü-*k'*-lo-tho-lo-ni-*k*iṅ.
'Buddhabhâshita-kû-*k*'-lo (?)-dhâraṇî-sûtra.'

2 leaves.

885 佛說消除一切災障寶髻陀羅尼經
Fo-shwo-siâo-*kh*u-yi-tshiê-tsâi-*k*âṅ-pâo-*k*i-tho-lo-ni-*k*iṅ.
'Sûtra spoken by Buddha on the Ratna*k*ûdâ(maṇi?)-dhâraṇî of destroying all obstacles and misfortunes.'
5 leaves.

886 佛說妙色陀羅尼經
Fo-shwo-miâo-seh-tho-lo-ni-*k*iṅ.
'Buddhabhâshita-suvarṇa-dhâraṇî-sûtra.'
1 leaf.

887 佛說旃檀香身陀羅尼經
Fo-shwo-*k*âṅ-thân-hhiâṅ-shan-tho-lo-ni-*k*iṅ.
'Buddhabhâshita-*k*andanagandhakâya-dhâraṇî-sûtra.'
2 leaves.

888 佛說鉢蘭那賒嚩哩大陀羅尼經
Fo-shwo-poh-lân-nâ-shö-foh-li-tâ-tho-lo-ni-*k*iṅ.
'Buddhabhâshita-prasânsabala (?)-mahâdhâraṇî-sûtra.'
3 leaves.

889 佛說宿命智陀羅尼經
Fo-shwo-su-miṅ-*k*'-tho-lo-ni-*k*iṅ.
'Buddhabhâshita-pûrvanivâsânusmṛitigñâna-dhâraṇî-sûtra.'
1 leaf.

890 佛說慈氏菩薩誓願陀羅尼經
Fo-shwo-tshz'-sh'-phu-sâ-shi-yuen-tho-lo-ni-*k*iṅ.
'Buddhabhâshita-maitreya-bodhisattva-praṇidhâna-dhâraṇî-sûtra.'
Maitrî-prati*gñ*â-dhâraṇî.

K'-yuen-lu, fasc. 5, fol. 24 a; Conc. 760; A. R., p. 528; A. M. G., p. 327. 1 leaf.

891 佛說滅除五逆罪大陀羅尼經
Fo-shwo-mieh-*kh*u-wu-ni-tsâi-tâ-tho-lo-ni-*k*iṅ.
'Buddhabhâshita-pa*ñk*ânantaryakarmavinâsa-dhâraṇî-sûtra.'
1 leaf.

892 佛說無量功德陀羅尼經
Fo-shwo-wu-liâṅ-kuṅ-töh-tho-lo-ni-*k*iṅ.
'Buddhabhâshitâmitaguṇa-dhâraṇî-sûtra.'
1 leaf.

893 佛說十八臂陀羅尼經
Fo-shwo-shi-pâ-phi-tho-lo-ni-*k*iṅ.
'Buddhabhâshita-ashṭâdasabâhu-dhâraṇî-sûtra.'
2 leaves.

894 佛說洛叉陀羅尼經
Fo-shwo-lö-*kh*â-tho-lo-ni-*k*iṅ.
'Buddhabhâshita-laksha-dhâraṇî-sûtra.'
2 leaves.

895 佛說辟除諸惡陀羅尼經
Fo-shwo-phi-*kh*u-*k*u-ṅoh-tho-lo-ni-*k*iṅ.
'Buddhabhâshita-sarvapâpavinâsa-dhâraṇî-sûtra.'
2 leaves.

The above twelve works are wanting in Tibetan. *K*'-yuen-lu, fasc. 5, fol. 23 b seq. But, for No. 890, see the last two authorities mentioned under the title.

896 佛說大愛陀羅尼經
Fo-shwo-tâ-âi-tho-lo-ni-*k*iṅ.
'Buddhabhâshita-mahâpriyâ-dhâraṇî-sûtra.'

2 leaves. It agrees with Tibetan. *K*'-yuen-lu, fasc. 5, fol. 22 b.

897 佛說阿羅漢具德經
Fo-shwo-ö-lo-hân-kü-töh-*k*iṅ. (h)
'Sûtra spoken by Buddha on the perfect good qualities of the Arhat.'

10 leaves. This is a later translation of chapters 4th–7th of the Ekottarâgama, i. e. No. 543. *K*'-yuen-lu, fasc. 8, fol. 1 a, where, however, it is stated that this work is wanting in Tibetan.

898 佛說八大靈塔名號經
Fo-shwo-pâ-tâ-liṅ-thâ-miṅ-hâo-*k*iṅ. (h)
'Sûtra spoken by Buddha on the names of eight great and auspicious *K*aityas.'

2 leaves. This work is mentioned under the heading of the Works of the Indian Sages, in *K*'-yuen-lu, fasc. 10, fol. 5 b, where the first two characters of the title Fo-shwo or Buddha-bhâshita are of course left out. They are however retained in *K*'-tsiṅ, fasc. 31, fol. 22 b, where the work is under the heading of the Sûtras of the Hînayâna.

The following are the names of the eight places where the great and auspicious *K*aityas are said to have been erected:—

(1) Lumbini garden, in Kapilavastu, where Buddha was born. (Cf. Lalitavistara, p. 94; Cunningham, Ancient Geography of India, pp. 414–416.)

(2) Underneath the Bodhi-tree (at Buddha-gayâ), on the bank of (or near) the river Nairañgana, in Magadha, where Buddha awoke to the perfect knowledge. (Cunningham, pp. 455–459.)

(3) Vârânasî (Benares), in the country of the Kâsis, where Buddha (first) turned the wheel of the law, i. e. he began to preach. (Lalitavistara, pp. 527–528; Cunningham, pp. 435–438.)

(4) *G*eta-grove, in *S*râvastî, where Buddha showed his great supernatural power. (Cunningham, pp. 407–414.)

(5) *K*hü-nü, 'hump-backed maiden,' i. e. Kânyakubga (Kanog), where Buddha descended from the Trayastrimsa heaven. (Cunningham, pp. 376–382. But the more exact place is Sankisa or Kapitha. See Cunningham, pp. 369–376.)

(6) Râgagriha, where Buddha taught his disciples, whose division (also took place there (?). Cunningham, pp. 467–468).

(7) Kwâñ-yen, 'wide-array,' i. e. Vaisalî, where Buddha thought of the length of his life. (Cunningham, pp. 443–446. For Buddha's speaking to Ânanda concerning the length of his life, see Hhüen-*k*wâñ's (Hiouen-thsang's) Si-yü-*k*i, fasc. 7, fol. 13 a seq.)

(8) Sâla-grove—within which is the place between large couples of trees—in Kusinagara, where Buddha entered Nirvâna. (Cunningham, pp. 430–433.)

899 佛說尊那經
Fo-shwo-tsun-nâ-*k*iñ.

'Sûtra addressed by Buddha to (the venerable) Kunda.'

6 leaves. It agrees with Tibetan. *K*'-yuen-lu, fasc. 4, fol. 14 a.

900 佛說頻婆娑羅王經
Fo-shwo-phin-pho-sâ-lo-wâñ-*k*iñ. (h)

'Sûtra addressed by Buddha to King Bimbisâra.'

7 leaves. It agrees with Tibetan. *K*'-yuen-lu, fasc. 8, fol. 1 a. According to *K*'-tsiñ (fasc. 28, fol. 12 a), this is a later translation of the Sûtra on King Bimbisâra's coming to meet Buddha, in the Madhyamâgama, i. e. No. 542 (62).

901 佛說人仙經
Fo-shwo-zan-sien-*k*iñ. (h)

'Buddhabhâshita-ganesa-sûtra.'

9 leaves. Deest in Tibetan. *K*'-yuen-lu, fasc. 8, fol. 4 a. But according to *K*'-tsiñ (fasc. 29, fol. 6 a), this is a later translation of the *G*anesa-sûtra in the Dîrghâgama, i. e. No. 545 (4)

902 佛說舊城喻經
Fo-shwo-*k*iu-*kh*añ-yü-*k*iñ.

'Sûtra spoken by Buddha on the old city comparison.'

6 leaves. This work is mentioned under the heading of the Sûtras of the Hînayâna, in *K*'-yuen-lu, fasc. 8, fol. 3 b, where it is said to agree with Tibetan. But according to *K*'-tsiñ (fasc. 10, fol. 1 b), this is a later translation of Nos. 278, 279, which are Sûtras of the Mahâyâna.

903 佛說信解智力經
Fo-shwo-sin-*k*ie-*k*'-li-*k*iñ. (h)

'Buddhabhâshita-adhimukta-gñâna-bala-sûtra.'

7 leaves. It agrees with Tibetan. *K*'-yuen-lu, fasc. 7, fol. 27 a.

904 大正句王經
Tâ-*k*añ-*k*ü-wâñ-*k*iñ. (h)

'Mahâsatpâda (?)-râga-sûtra.'

2 fasciculi. Deest in Tibetan. *K*'-yuen-lu, fasc. 8, fol. 2 b. But according to *K*'-tsiñ (fasc. 28, fol. 12 b), this is a later translation of the Pi-sh' (râga)-sûtra in the Madhyamâgama, i. e. No. 542 (71).

905 佛說善樂長者經
Fo-shwo-shan-yâo-*kh*âñ-*k*ö-*k*iñ.

'Sûtra addressed by Buddha to the *S*reshthin Svâsaya (? "good-inclination").'

4 leaves. Deest in Tibetan. *K*'-yuen-lu, fasc. 5, fol. 22 b. But according to *K*'-tsiñ (fasc. 13, fol. 12 a), this is a later translation of No. 982.

906 佛說聖多羅菩薩經
Fo-shwo-shañ-to-lo-phu-sâ-*k*iñ.

'Buddhabhâshita-ârya-târâ-bodhisattva-sûtra.'

7 leaves. It agrees with Tibetan. *K*'-yuen-lu, fasc. 5, fol. 19 b.

907 佛說大吉祥陀羅尼經
Fo-shwo-tâ-*k*i-siâñ-tho-lo-ni-*k*iñ.

'Buddhabhâshita-mahâsrî-dhâranî-sûtra.'

2 leaves.

908 寶賢陀羅尼經
Pâo-hhien-tho-lo-ni-*k*iñ.

'Ratnabhadra-dhâranî-sûtra.'

2 leaves.

The above two works are wanting in Tibetan. *K*'-yuen-lu, fasc. 6, fol. 1 a.

909 佛說秘密八名陀羅尼經
Fo-shwo-pi-mi-pâ-miñ-tho-lo-ni-*k*iñ.

'Buddhabhâshita-guhyâshtanâma-dhâranî-sûtra.'

2 leaves. It agrees with Tibetan. *K'*-yuen-lu, fasc. 6, fol. 1 b. According to *K'*-tsiṅ (fasc. 13, fol. 18 b), this is a later translation of No. 491.

910 觀自在菩薩母陀羅尼經
Kwâṅ-tsz'-tsâi-phu-sâ-mu-tho-lo-ni-*k*iṅ.
'Avalokitesvara-bodhisattva-mâtrî-dhâraṇî-sûtra.'
Avalokitesvara-mâtâ (or mâtri?)-dhâraṇî.

A. R., p. 534; A. M. G., p. 331. 3 leaves. Deest in Tibetan. *K'*-yuen-lu, fasc. 6, fol. 2 b. See, however, the authorities mentioned under the title.

911 佛說戒香經
Fo-shwo-*k*iê-hhiâṅ-*k*iṅ. (h)
'Buddhabhâshita-sîlagandha-sûtra.'

2 leaves. Deest in Tibetan. *K'*-yuen-lu, fasc. 8, fol. 3 b. But according to *K'*-tsiṅ (fasc. 22, fol. 12 b), this is a later translation of No. 588.

912 佛說妙吉祥菩薩陀羅尼
Fo-shwo-miâo-*k*i-siâṅ-phu-sâ-tho-lo-ni.
'Buddhabhâshita-mañgusrî-bodhisattva-dhâraṇî.'

3 leaves.

913 佛說無量壽大智陀羅尼
Fo-shwo-wu-liâṅ-sheu-tâ-*k'*-tho-lo-ni.
'Buddhabhâshita-amitâyur-mahâgñâna-dhâraṇî.'

7 columns.

914 佛說宿命智陀羅尼
Fo-shwo-su-miṅ-*k'*-tho-lo-ni.
'Buddhabhâshita-pûrvanivâsagñâna-dhâraṇî.'

4 columns.

915 佛說慈氏菩薩陀羅尼
Fo-shwo-tshz'-sh'-phu-sâ-tho-lo-ni.
'Buddhabhâshita-maitreya-bodhisattva-dhâraṇî.'

4 columns.

916 佛說虛空藏菩薩陀羅尼
Fo-shwo-hhü-khuṅ-tsâṅ-phu-sâ-tho-lo-ni.
'Buddhabhâshita-âkâsagarbha-bodhisattva-dhâraṇî.'

6 columns.

The above five works are wanting in Tibetan. *K'*-yuen-lu, fasc. 5, fol. 26 a seq.

917 寶授菩薩菩提行經
Pâo-sheu-phu-sâ-phu-thi-hhiṅ-*k*iṅ.
'Ratnadatta (?)-bodhisattva-bodhi*k*aryâ-sûtra.'

13 leaves. Deest in Tibetan. *K'*-yuen-lu, fasc. 4, fol. 14 a.

918 佛說延壽妙門陀羅尼經
Fo-shwo-yen-sheu-miâo-man-tho-lo-ni-*k*iṅ.
'Sûtra spoken by Buddha on the Dhâraṇî of the wonderful gate of increasing the life.'

8 leaves. It agrees with Tibetan. *K'*-yuen-lu, fasc. 5, fol. 1 b. According to *K'*-tsiṅ (fasc. 13, fol. 9 b), this is a later translation of Nos. 369–371.

919 一切如來名號陀羅尼經
Yi-tshiê-zu-lâi-miṅ-hâo-tho-lo-ni-*k*iṅ.
'Sarvatathâgatanâma-dhâraṇî-sûtra.'

3 leaves.

920 佛說息除賊難陀羅尼經
Fo-shwo-si-*kh*u-tsö-nân-tho-lo-ni-*k*iṅ.
'Sûtra spoken by Buddha on the Dhâraṇî of stopping the danger of a thief.'

2 leaves.

The above two works agree with Tibetan. *K'*-yuen-lu, fasc. 6, fol. 2 a seq.

921 佛說法身經
Fo-shwo-fâ-shan-*k*iṅ.
'Buddhabhâshita-dharmasarîra-sûtra.'
Dharmasarîra-sûtra.

K'-yuen-lu, fasc. 4, fol. 11 b; Conc. 126. 5 leaves. It agrees with Tibetan. *K'*-yuen-lu, s. v.

922 信佛功德經
Sin-fó-kuṅ-töh-*k*iṅ. (h)
'Buddhasraddhaguṇa-sûtra.'

10 leaves. It agrees with Tibetan. *K'*-yuen-lu, fasc. 7, fol. 26 b. According to *K'*-tsiṅ (fasc. 29, fol. 7 b), this is a later translation of No. 545 (18).

923 佛說解夏經
Fo-shwo-*k*iê-hhiâ-*k*iṅ. (h)
'Sûtra spoken by Buddha on *K*iê-hhiâ (? lit. "explaining summer").'

4 leaves. This work is mentioned under the heading of the Vinayapiṭaka of the Hînayâna, in *K'*-yuen-lu, fasc. 8, fol. 20 b, where it is said to be wanting in Tibetan. But *K'*-tsiṅ (fasc. 31, fol. 11 b) mentions this work as a Sûtra of the Hînayâna.

Fo-shwo-ti-shih-su-wan-*kiṅ.*
'Buddhabhâshita-indra-sakra-pariprikkhâ-sûtra.'

15 leaves.   Deest in Tibetan.   K'-yuen-lu, fasc. 8,
fol. 2 a.   But according to K'-tsiṅ (fasc. 28, fol. 17 a),
this is a later translation of No. 545 (14).

925   佛説未曾有正法經
Fo-shwo-wêi-tshâṅ-yiu-kaṅ-fâ-kiṅ.
'Buddhabhâshita-adbhuta-saddharma-sûtra.'

6 fasciculi.   It agrees with Tibetan.   K'-yuen-lu,
fasc. 4, fol. 10 b.   According to K'-tsiṅ (fasc. 8, fol. 5 b),
this is a later translation of Nos. 174, 182.

The following two works were translated by Sh'-hu
(Dânapâla ?), A. D. 980–1000, of the later Suṅ dynasty,
A. D. 960–1127 :—

926   佛説大方廣善巧
       方便經
Fo-shwo-tâ-fâṅ-kwâṅ-shan-khiâo-
fâṅ-pien-kiṅ.
'Buddhabhâshita-mahâvaipulyopâyakausalya-sûtra.'
Gñânottara-bodhisattva-pariprikkhâ.

4 fasciculi.   This is a later translation of Nos. 23 (38),
52.   K'-tsiṅ, fasc. 3, fol. 17 b.   But it is stated in
K'-yuen-lu (fasc. 4, fol. 10 a), that this is a similar
translation of No. 23 (37).

927   佛母出生三法藏般若
       波羅蜜多經
Fo-mu-khu-shaṅ-sân-fâ-tsâṅ-pân-zo-
po-lo-mi-to-kiṅ.
'Buddhamâtrigñâ-tridharmapiṭaka-pragñâpâramitâ-sûtra.'
Daśasâhasrikâ pragñâpâramitâ.

25 fasciculi ; 32 chapters.   This is a later translation
of Nos. 1 (d), 5–8.   Cf. K'-yuen-lu, fasc. 1, fol. 18 a ;
K'-tsiṅ, fasc. 23, fol. 19 a.

The following two works were translated by Fâ-
hhien, A. D. 982–1001, of the later Suṅ dynasty, A. D.
960–1127 :—

928   佛説決定義經
Fo-shwo-kiê-tiṅ-i-kiṅ. (h)
'Sûtra spoken by Buddha on the determination of the meaning
(of the law).'

12 leaves.   Deest in Tibetan.   K'-yuen-lu, fasc. 7,
fol. 26 b.

929   佛説護國經
Fo-shwo-hu-kwo-kiṅ. (h)
'Buddhabhâshita-râshtrapâla-sûtra.'

10 leaves.   Deest in Tibetan.   K'-yuen-lu, fasc. 8,
fol. 4 a.   But according to K'-tsiṅ (fasc. 28, fol. 16 b),
this is a later translation of No. 542 (132).

930   佛説分別布施經
Fo-shwo-fan-pieh-pu-sh'-kiṅ. (h)
'Sûtra spoken by Buddha on the division or explanation of gifts
(Dâna).'

Translated by Sh'-hu (Dânapâla ?), A. D. 980–1000,
of the later Suṅ dynasty, A. D. 960–1127.   4 leaves.
Deest in Tibetan.   K'-yuen-lu, fasc. 4, fol. 13 a.   But
according to K'-tsiṅ (fasc. 28, fol. 19 b), this is a later
translation of No. 542 (180).

931   佛説分別緣生經
Fo-shwo-fan-pieh-yuen-shaṅ-kiṅ. (h)
'Sûtra spoken by Buddha on the division or explanation of
the (twelve) Nidânas.'

Translated by Fâ-thien (Dharmadeva ?), A. D. 973–
981, of the later Suṅ dynasty, A. D. 960–1127.   3 leaves.
Deest in Tibetan.   K'-yuen-lu, fasc. 7, fol. 26 b.

The following twenty-two works, Nos. 932–953,
were translated by Sh'-hu (Dânapâla ?), A. D. 980–1000,
of the later Suṅ dynasty, A. D. 960–1127 :—

932   佛説法印經
Fo-shwo-fâ-yin-kiṅ. (h)
'Buddhabhâshita-dharmamudrâ-sûtra.'

2 leaves.   Deest in Tibetan.   K'-yuen-lu, fasc. 4,
fol. 13 a.   But according to K'-yuen (fasc. 29, fol.
10 b), this is a later translation of a part of fasc. 3
of No. 544.

933   佛説大生義經
Fo-shwo-tâ-shaṅ-i-kiṅ. (h)
'Buddhabhâshita-mahâgâtârtha-sûtra.'

9 leaves.   Deest in Tibetan.   K'-yuen-lu, fasc. 7,
fol. 26 a.   But according to K'-tsiṅ (fasc. 28, fol. 14 a),
this is a later translation of No. 542 (97).

934   佛説發菩提心破諸魔經
Fo-shwo-fâ-phu-thi-sin-po-ku-mo-kiṅ.
'Sûtra spoken by Buddha on raising the thought towards the
Bodhi and destroying all the Mâras.'

2 fasciculi.   It agrees with Tibetan.   K'-yuen-lu,
fasc. 5, fol. 16 b.   According to K'-tsiṅ (fasc. 9, fol. 2 a),
this is a later translation of No. 450.

935 佛說聖佛母般若波羅蜜多經

Fo-shwo-shan-fo-mu-pân-zo-po-lo-mi-to-kin.

'Buddhabhâshita-ârya-buddhamâtri-pragñâpâramitâ-sûtra.'

Pragñâpâramitâ-hridaya-sûtra.

2 leaves. This is a later and longer translation of Nos. 19, 20. K'-yuen-lu, fasc. 1, fol. 18 b; K'-tsiṅ, fasc. 23, fol. 23 b. For the Sanskrit text, see Cat. Bodl. Japan., No. 63 (d).

936 佛說大乘不思議神通境界經

Fo-shwo-tâ-shaṅ-pu-sz'-i-shan-thuṅ-kiṅ-kiê-kiṅ.

'Buddhabhâshita-mahâyânâkintyarddhi-vishaya-sûtra.'

3 fasciculi. Deest in Tibetan. K'-yuen-lu, fasc. 5, fol. 17 a.

937 佛說給孤長者女得度因緣經

Fo-shwo-ki-ku-khâṅ-kö-nü-töh-tu-yin-yuen-kiṅ. (h)

'Sûtra spoken by Buddha on the Nidâna of the conversion of the daughter of the Sreshthin Anathâpiṇḍada.'

3 fasciculi. This is a later translation of chapter 30 of No. 543. K'-yuen-lu, fasc. 7, fol. 27 a.

938 佛說大集法門經

Fo-shwo-tâ-tsi-fâ-man-kiṅ. (h)

'Buddhabhâshita-mahâsaṅgîti-dharmaparyâya sûtra.'

2 fasciculi. Deest in Tibetan. K'-yuen-lu, fasc. 7, fol. 26 a. But according to K'-tsiṅ (fasc. 29, fol. 7 a), this is a later translation of No. 545 (9).

939 佛說光明童子因緣經

Fo-shwo-kwâṅ-miṅ-thuṅ-tsz'-yin-yuen-kiṅ. (h)

'Sûtra spoken by Buddha on the Nidâna of the boy Prabhâsa.'

4 fasciculi. Deest in Tibetan. K'-yuen-lu, fasc. 8, fol. 2 a.

940 佛說寶帶陀羅尼經

Fo-shwo-pâo-tâi-tho-lo-ni-kiṅ.

'Buddhabhâshita-ratnamekhalâ-dhâraṇî-sûtra.'

Mekhalâ-dhâraṇî.

K'-yuen-lu, fasc. 5, fol. 21 a; Conc. 412; A. R., p. 542; A. M. G., p. 339. 10 leaves. This is a similar translation of No. 854. K'-tsiṅ, fasc. 13, fol. 4 a. But K'-yuen-lu states that No. 940 is similar to No. 800, which seems to be wrong.

941 佛說金身陀羅尼經

Fo-shwo-kin-shan-tho-lo-ni-kiṅ.

'Buddhabhâshita-suvarṇakâya-dhâraṇî-sûtra.'

3 leaves. Deest in Tibetan. K'-yuen-lu, fasc. 5, fol. 21 b.

942 佛說入無分別法門經

Fo-shwo-zu-wu-fan-pieh-fâ-man-kiṅ.

'Buddhabhâshita-aprabhedâvatâra (?)-dharmaparyâya-sûtra.'

6 leaves. Deest in Tibetan. K'-yuen-lu, fasc. 4, fol. 14 a.

943 佛說淨意優婆塞所問經

Fo-shwo-tsiṅ-i-yiu-pho-sö-su-wan-kiṅ. (h)

'Buddhabhâshita-suddhamaty-upâsaka-paripṛikkhâ-sûtra.'

6 leaves. Deest in Tibetan. K'-yuen-lu, fasc. 8, fol. 2 a.

944 佛說金剛場莊嚴般若波羅蜜多教中一分

Fo-shwo-kin-kâṅ-khâṅ-kwâṅ-yen-pân-zo-po-lo-mi-to-kiao-kuṅ-yi-fan.

'A part of the teaching of the Vagramaṇḍalavyûha-pragñâpâramitâ spoken by Buddha.'

11 leaves. It agrees with Tibetan. K'-yuen-lu, fasc. 1, fol. 19 b.

945 佛說息諍因緣經

Fo-shwo-si-kâṅ-yin-yuen-kiṅ. (h)

'Sûtra spoken by Buddha on the Avadâna of stopping a quarrel.'

9 leaves. Deest in Tibetan. K'-yuen-lu, fasc. 8, fol. 1 b. But according to K'-tsiṅ (fasc. 28, fol. 19 b), this is a later translation of No. 542 (196).

946 佛說初分說經

Fo-shwo-khu-fan-shwo-kiṅ. (h)

'Buddhabhâshita-prathamavargavakana-sûtra.'

2 fasciculi. Deest in Tibetan. K'-yuen-lu, fasc. 8, fol. 1 b.

947 佛說無畏授所問大乘經

Fo-shwo-wu-wêi-sheu-su-wan-tâ-shaṅ-kiṅ.

'Buddhabhâshita-vîradatta-paripṛikkhâ-mahâyâna-sûtra.'

3 fasciculi; 17 leaves. It agrees with Tibetan. K'-yuen-lu, fasc. 4, fol. 15 a. According to K'-tsiṅ (fasc. 3, fol. 15 b), this is a later translation of Nos. 23 (28), 389.

948 佛說月喩經

Fo-shwo-yueh-yü-*k*iṅ. (h)

'Buddhabhâshita-*k*andropamâna-sûtra.'

3 leaves. It agrees with Tibetan. *K'*-yuen-lu, fasc. 8, fol. 3 a.

949 佛說醫喩經

Fo-shwo-i-yü-*k*iṅ. (h)

'Buddhabhâshita-bhishag-upamâna-sûtra.'

2 leaves. It agrees with Tibetan. *K'*-yuen-lu, fasc. 8, fol. 3 b.

950 佛說灌頂王喩經

Fo-shwo-kwân-tiṅ-wâṅ-yü-*k*iṅ. (h)

'Buddhabhâshita-mûrddhâbhishikta-râgopamâna-sûtra.'

1 leaf. Deest in Tibetan. *K'*-yuen-lu, fasc. 8, fol. 2 b.

951 佛說尼拘陀梵志經

Fo-shwo-ni-*k*ü-tho-fân-*k'*-*k*iṅ. (h)

'Buddhabhâshita-nyagrodha-brahma*k*âri-sûtra.'

2 fasciculi; 16 leaves. Deest in Tibetan. *K'*-yuen-lu, fasc. 8, fol. 2 b. But according to *K'*-tsiṅ (fasc. 29, fol. 6 b), this is a later translation of No. 545 (8).

952 佛說白衣金幢二婆羅門緣起經

Fo-shwo-po-i-*k*in-*k*wâṅ-'rh-pho-lo-man-yuen-*kh*i-*k*iṅ. (h)

'Buddhabhâshita-suklavastra-suvarṇadhvaga-dvibrâhmaṇa-nidâna-sûtra.'

3 fasciculi; 21 leaves. Deest in Tibetan. *K'*-yuen-lu, fasc. 8, fol. 5 a. But according to *K'*-tsiṅ (fasc. 29, fol. 6 b), this is a later translation of No. 545 (5).

953 佛說福力太子因緣經

Fo-shwo-fu-li-thâi-tsz'-yin-yuen-*k*iṅ. (h)

'Buddhabhâshita-puṇyabala-kumârâvadâna-sûtra.'

Puṇyabalâvadâna.

A. R., p. 482; A. M. G., p. 285. 3 fasciculi; 23 leaves. It agrees with Tibetan. *K'*-yuen-lu, fasc. 4, fol. 14 b.

954 佛說身毛喜豎經

Fo-shwo-shan-mâo-hhi-shu-*k*iṅ. (h)

'Buddhabhâshita-saṁharshitaromakûpa*g*âta-sûtra.'

Translated by Wei-tsiṅ, A.D. 1009–1050, of the later Suṅ dynasty, A.D. 960–1127. 3 fasciculi; 31 leaves. It agrees with Tibetan. *K'*-yuen-lu, fasc. 8, fol. 6 a.

955 大乘本生心地觀經

Tâ-shaṅ-pan-shaṅ-sin-ti-kwân-*k*iṅ.

'Mahâyâna-mûla*g*âta-h*ri*dayabhûmi-dhyâna-sûtra.'

Translated by Pra*gñ*a and others, A.D. 785–810, of the Thâṅ dynasty, A.D. 618–907. 8 fasciculi; 13 chapters. There is a preface added by the Emperor Hhien-tsuṅ, A.D. 806–820, of the same dynasty. Deest in Tibetan. *K'*-yuen-lu, fasc. 4, fol. 10 b.

The following four works were translated by Amoghava*g*ra, A.D. 746–771, of the Thâṅ dynasty, A.D. 618–907:—

956 佛說出生無邊門陀羅尼經

Fo-shwo-*kh*u-shaṅ-wu-pien-man-tho-lo-ni-*k*iṅ.

'Buddhabhâshita-*g*âtânantamukha-dhâraṇî-sûtra.'

13 leaves. This is a later translation of Nos. 353–360. *K'*-tsin, fasc. 13, fol. 20 b.

957 一切如來心祕密全身舍利寶篋印陀羅尼經

Yi-tshiê-*z*u-lâi-sin-pi-mi-*kh*üen-shan-shö-li-pâo-*kh*iê-yin-tho-lo-ni-*k*iṅ.

Sarvatathâgatâdhishṭhâna-h*ri*daya-guhya-dhâtu-karaṇḍamudrâ-dhâraṇî(-sûtra).

K'-yuen-lu, fasc. 5, fol. 10 b; Conc. 224. 7 leaves. It agrees with Tibetan. *K'*-yuen-lu, s. v.

958 佛說大吉祥天女十二名號經

Fo-shwo-tâ-*k*i-siâṅ-thien-nü-shi-'rh-miṅ-hâo-*k*iṅ.

'Buddhabhâshita-mahâsrî-devî-dvâdasanâma-sûtra.'

Mahâsrî-sûtra.

K'-yuen-lu, fasc. 5, fol. 14 a; Conc. 625.

Mahâsraya-sûtra.

A. R., p. 536; A. M. G., p. 333. 2 leaves.

959 佛說大吉祥天女十二契一百八名無垢大乘經

Fo-shwo-tâ-*k*i-siâṅ-thien-nü-shi-'rh-*kh*i-yi-pâi-pâ-miṅ-wu-keu-tâ-shaṅ-*k*iṅ.

'Buddhabhâshita-mahâsrî-devî-dvâdasa-bandhanâshṭasatanâma-vimala-mahâyâna-sûtra.'

8 leaves.

The above two works agree with Tibetan. *K'*-yuen-lu, fasc. 5, fol. 14 a.

960 佛說一切如來金剛壽命
陀羅尼經

Fo-shwo-yi-tshiê-ẑu-lâi-ḱin-kâṅ-sheu-miṅ-
tho-lo-ni-ḱiṅ.

'Buddhabhâshita-sarvatathâgata-vagrâyur-dhâraṇî-sûtra.'

Translated by Vagrabodhi, together with K'-tsaṅ
(Gñânakoṣa, i. e. another name of Amoghavagra), A. D.
723–730, of the Thâṅ dynasty, A. D. 618–907. 3 leaves.
Deest in Tibetan. K'-yuen-lu, fasc. 5, fol. 10 b. But
according to K'-tsiṅ (fasc. 12, fol. 21 a), this is a later
and shorter translation of No. 495.

The following three works were translated by
Amoghavagra, A. D. 746–771, of the Thâṅ dynasty,
A. D. 618–907 :—

961 佛說積廃棃童女經

Fo-shwo-ẑăṅ-yü-li-thuṅ-nü-ḱiṅ.

'Buddhabhâshita-gaṅgulî-bâlikâ-sûtra.'

Gaṅgulî-vidyâ.

K'-yuen-lu, fasc. 4, fol. 8 b; Conc. 230; A. R.,
p. 518; A. M. G., p. 318. 4 leaves. It agrees with
Tibetan. K'-yuen-lu, s. v.

962 佛說雨寶陀羅尼經

Fo-shwo-yü-pâo-tho-lo-ni-ḱiṅ.

'Buddhabhâshita-varsharatna-dhâraṇî-sûtra.'

Ratnamegha-dhâraṇî.

K'-yuen-lu, fasc. 5, fol. 10 b; Conc. 879. 5 leaves.
This is a similar translation of Nos. 492, 787. K'-yuen-
lu, s. v.; K'-tsiṅ, fasc. 13, fol. 13 b.

963 慈氏菩薩所說大乘緣生
稻萪喻經

Tshẑ'-sh'-phu-sâ-su-shwo-tâ-shaṅ-yuen-shaṅ-
tâo-kâṅ-yü-ḱiṅ.

Maitreya-bodhisasattva-bhâshita-mahâyâna-nidâna-sâlisambhava-
upamâna-sûtra.'

Sâlisambhava-sûtra.

K'-yuen-lu, fasc. 4, fol. 8 b; Conc. 761. 9 leaves.
This is a similar translation of Nos. 280, 281, 818, 867.
K'-yuen-lu, s. v.; K'-tsiṅ, fasc. 10, fol. 2 b.

964 佛說除蓋障菩薩所問經

Fo-shwo-ḱhu-kâi-ḱaṅ-phu-sâ-su-wan-ḱiṅ.

'Sûtra spoken by Buddha on the question of the Bodhisattva
Ḱ'hu-kâi-ḱaṅ ("he who destroys the obstacle of covering").'

Ratnamegha-sûtra.

Conc. 161, 723. Translated by Sh'-hu (Dânapâla ?),
Fâ-hu (Dharmaraksha ?), Wêi-tsiṅ, and others, about

A. D. 1000–1010, of the later Suṅ dynasty, A. D. 960–
1127. 20 fasciculi. This is a later and longer translation of Nos. 151, 152. Deest in Tibetan. K'-yuen-lu,
fasc. 4, fol. 15 b.

965 仁王護國般若波羅蜜多經

Zan-wâṅ-hu-kwo-pân-ẑo-po-lo-mi-to-ḱiṅ.

'Pragñâpâramitâ-sûtra on a benevolent king who protects
his country.'

Translated by Amoghavagra, A. D. 746–771, of the
Thâṅ dynasty, A. D. 618–907. 2 fasciculi; 8 chapters.
This is a later translation of No. 17. K'-yuen-lu, fasc. 1,
fol. 17 a. There is a preface added by the Emperor
Tâi-tsuṅ, A. D. 763–779, of the Thâṅ dynasty.

966 穢跡金剛說神通大滿陀
羅尼法術靈要門經

Wêi-tsi-ḱin-kâṅ-shwo-shan-thuṅ-tâ-mân-tho-
lo-ni-fâ-shu-liṅ-yâo-man-ḱiṅ.

'Sûtra spoken by Malapâda (? "dirty-footprint")-vagra on the
auspicious and important gate of the doctrine of supernatural and great perfect Dhâraṇî.'

Translated by Wu-naṅ-shaṅ, of the Thâṅ dynasty,
A. D. 618–907. 4 leaves.

967 穢跡金剛法禁百變法門經

Wêi-tsi-ḱin-kâṅ-fâ-ḱin-pâi-pien-fâ-man-ḱiṅ.

'Malapâda (?)-vagra-dharmanishedha-(law-prohibition)-
satavikriyâ-dharmaparyâya-sûtra.'

Translated by Ö-ḱih-tâ-sien, of the Thâṅ dynasty,
A. D. 618–907. 8 leaves.

The following two works were translated by Fâ-hu
(Dharmaraksha ?), A. D. 1004–1058, of the later Suṅ
dynasty, A. D. 618–907 :—

968 佛說大乘大方廣佛冠經

Fo-shwo-tâ-shaṅ-tâ-fâṅ-kwâṅ-fo-kwân-ḱiṅ.

'Buddhabhâshita-mahâyâna-mahâvaipulya-buddhamukuṭa-sûtra.'

2 fasciculi. Deest in Tibetan. K'-yuen-lu, fasc. 4,
fol. 15 a.

969 佛說八種長養功德經

Fo-shwo-pâ-kuṅ-ḱhâṅ-yâṅ-kuṅ-töh-ḱiṅ. (h)

'Sûtra spoken by Buddha on eight kinds of good qualities for
making grow and nourishing.'

2 leaves. It states briefly the rules for receiving
the moral precepts. K'-tsiṅ, fasc. 28, fol. 20 b.

The following two works were translated by Amoghavagra, A. D. 746–771, of the Thâṅ dynasty, A. D. 618–

970 大雲輪請雨經
Tâ-yun-lun-tsiṅ-yü-*k*iṅ.
'Sûtra on asking rain of the great cloud-wheel.'
Mahâmegha-sûtra.

Conc. 667. 2 fasciculi. This is a later translation of Nos. 186–188. *K*'-yuen-lu, fasc. 2, fol. 26 a.

971 大乘密嚴經
Tâ-shaṅ-mi-yen-*k*iṅ.
'Mahâyâna-ghanavyûha-sûtra.'
Ghanavyûha-sûtra.

K'-yuen-lu, fasc. 4, fol. 9 a; Conc. 577. 3 fasciculi; 8 chapters. This is a later translation of No. 444. *K*'-yuen-lu, s. v. There is a preface added by the Emperor Tâi-tsuṅ, A.D. 763–779, of the Thâṅ dynasty.

972 佛說大集會正法經
Fo-shwo-tâ-tsi-hwui-*k*aṅ-fâ-*k*iṅ.
'Buddhabhâshita-mahâsaṅgîti-saddharma-sûtra.'

Translated by Sh'-hu (Dânapâla?), A.D. 980–1000, of the later Suṅ dynasty, A.D. 960–1127. 5 fasciculi. It agrees with Tibetan, but the latter is shorter. *K*'-yuen-lu, fasc. 1, fol. 7 b. According to *K*'-tsiṅ (fasc. 5, fol. 10 b), this is a later translation of No. 449.

The following three works were translated by Amoghavagra, A.D. 746–771, of the Thâṅ dynasty, A.D. 618–907:—

973 葉衣觀自在菩薩經
Yeh-i-kwân-tsz'-tsâi-phu-sâ-*k*iṅ.
'Leaf-dressed Avalokitesvara-bodhisattva-sûtra.'
Par*n*asavari-dhâra*n*î.

K'-yuen-lu, fasc. 5, fol. 12 a; Conc. 857; A. R., p. 518; A. M. G., p. 318. 10 leaves. It agrees with Tibetan. *K*'-yuen-lu, s. v.

974 毗沙門天王經
Phi-shâ-man-thien-wâṅ-*k*iṅ.
'Vaisrama*n*a-divyarâga-sûtra.'

6 leaves. It agrees with Tibetan. *K*'-yuen-lu, fasc. 5, fol. 20 a. According to *K*'-tsiṅ (fasc. 6, fol. 17 b), this is a later translation of a part of chapter 12 of No. 126.

975 文殊問經字母品
Wan-shu-wan-*k*iṅ-tsz'-mu-phin.
'Mañgusrî-paripr*kkh*â-sûtra-akshara-mâtrikâdhyâya.'

3 leaves.

976 海意菩薩所問淨印法門經
Hâi-i-phu-sâ-su-wan-tsiṅ-yin-fâ-man-*k*iṅ.
'Sâgaramati-bodhisattva-paripr*kkh*â-suddhamudrâ-dharma-paryâya-sûtra.'
Sâgaramati-paripr*ikkh*â.

K'-yuen-lu, fasc. 4, fol. 15 b; Conc. 155, 181; A. R., p. 448; A. M. G., p. 253. Translated by Wei-tsiṅ, together with Fâ-hu (Dharmaraksha?), A.D. 1009–1058, of the later Suṅ dynasty, A.D. 960–1127. 9 fasciculi. This is a later translation of chapter 5 of No. 61 (fasc. 8–11). This work exists in Tibetan. *K*'-yuen-lu, s. v.

977 佛說如幻三摩地無量印法門經
Fo-shwo-*s*u-hwân-sân-mo-ti-wu-liâṅ-yin-fâ-man-*k*iṅ.
'Buddhabhâshita-mâyopama-samâdhy-amitamudrâ-dharma-paryâya-sûtra.'

Translated by Sh'-hu (Dânapâla?), A.D. 980–1000, of the later Suṅ dynasty, A.D. 960–1127. 3 fasciculi. It agrees with Tibetan. *K*'-yuen-lu, fasc. 4, fol. 11 a. According to *K*'-tsiṅ (fasc. 3, fol. 21 a), this is a later and longer translation of No. 395.

978 守護國界主陀羅尼經
Sheu-hu-kwo-*k*iê-*k*u-tho-lo-ni-*k*iṅ.
'Desântapâlapati-dhâra*n*î-sûtra.'

Translated by Pragña, A.D. 785–810, of the Thâṅ dynasty, A.D. 618–907. 10 fasciculi; 11 chapters. Deest in Tibetan. *K*'-yuen-lu, fasc. 6, fol. 5 b. According to *K*'-tsiṅ (fasc. 12, fol. 14 a seq.), this is a later translation of chapter 2 of No. 61.

The following seven works were translated by Amoghavagra, A.D. 746–771, of the Thâṅ dynasty, A.D. 618–907:—

979 佛說三十五佛名禮懺文
Fo-shwo-sân-shi-wu-fo-miṅ-li-*kh*ân-wan.
'Composition on the worship and confession concerning the names of thirty-five Buddhas spoken by Buddha.'

3 leaves. This is a later translation of a part of Nos. 23 (24), 36. It agrees with Tibetan. *K*'-yuen-lu, fasc. 4, fol. 8 b; *K*'-tsiṅ, fasc. 3, fol. 14 b.

980 觀自在菩薩說普賢陀羅尼經
Kwân-tsz'-tsâi-phu-sâ-shwo-phu-hhien-tho-lo-ni-*k*iṅ.
'Avalokitesvara-bodhisattva-bhâshita-samantabhadra-dhâra*n*î-sûtra.'

5 leaves. Deest in Tibetan. *K'*-yuen-lu, fasc. 5, fol. 12 b.

981 佛說八大菩薩曼荼羅經

Fo-shwo-pâ-tâ-phu-sâ-man-thu-lo-*k*in.

'Buddhabhâshita-ashtamahâbodhisattva-mandala-sûtra.'

Ash*t*aman*d*alaka-sûtra.

4 leaves. This is an earlier translation of No. 880. *K'*-yuen-lu, fasc. 5, fol. 12 a.

982 佛說能淨一切眼疾病陀羅尼經

Fo-shwo-nan-tsin-yi-tshiê-yen-tsi-pin-tho-lo-ni-*k*in.

'Sûtra spoken by Buddha on the Dhâra*n*î of purifying all the diseases of the eye.'

*K*akshuvisodhana-vidyâ-dhâra*n*î.

K'-yuen-lu, fasc. 5, fol. 11 b; Conc. 386. Cf. A. R., p. 525; A. M. G., p. 324. 2 leaves. It agrees with Tibetan. *K'*-yuen-lu, s. v. According to *K'*-tsin (fasc. 13, fol. 12 b), this is an earlier translation of No. 905. Cf. also No. 483.

983 佛說除一切疾病陀羅尼經

Fo-shwo-*kk*u-yi-tshiê-tsi-pin-tho-lo-ni-*k*in.

'Buddhabhâshita-sarva . . . . sûtra.'

Sarvarogaprasamani-dhâra*n*î.

K'-yuen-lu, fasc. 5, fol. 11 b; Conc. 722; A. R., p. 520; A. M. G., p. 320. 1 leaf. It agrees with Tibetan. *K'*-yuen-lu, s. v.

984 佛說救拔焰口餓鬼陀羅尼經

Fo-shwo-*k*iu-pâ-yen-kheu-ṅö-kwêi-tho-lo-ni-*k*in.

'Buddhabhâshita-*g*valavaktrapreta-paritrâ*n*a-dhâra*n*î-sûtra.'

*G*valaprasamani-dhâra*n*î (?).

A. R., p. 520; A. M. G., p. 320. 4 leaves. This is a later translation of No. 539. *K'*-yuen-lu, fasc. 5, fol. 8 b.

985 瑜伽集要救阿難陀羅尼焰口儀軌經

Yü-*k*iê-tsi-yâo-*k*iu-ö-nân-tho-lo-ni-yen-kheu-i-kwêi-*k*in.

'Yoga-mahârthasaṅgraha-ânanda-paritrâ*n*a-dhâra*n*î-*g*valavaktra (preta)-kalpa-sûtra.'

1 fasciculus. It contains many Mudrâs or certain positions or intertwinings of the fingers.

The following eight works were translated by Sh'-hu (Dânapâla ?), A. D. 980–1000, of the later Suṅ dynasty, A. D. 960–1127:—

986 佛說蟻喻經

Fo-shwo-i-yü-*k*in. (h)

'Buddhabhâshita-piptlikopamâna-sûtra.'

3 leaves. It agrees with Tibetan. *K'*-yuen-lu, fasc. 8, fol. 3 a.

987 聖觀自在菩薩不空王秘密心陀羅尼經

Shaṅ-kwân-tsz'-tsâi-phu-sâ-pu-khuṅ-wâṅ-pi-mi-sin-tho-lo-ni-*k*in.

'Ârya-avalokitesvara-bodhisattvâmoghara*g*a-guhya-hridaya-dhâra*n*î-sûtra.'

Amoghapâsa-dhâra*n*î.

12 leaves. This is a later translation of Nos. 312, 315, 316, and chapter 1 of No. 317. *K'*-yuen-lu, fasc. 5, fol. 16 b; *K'*-tsin, fasc. 14, fol. 8 b.

988 佛說勝軍王所問經

Fo-shwo-shaṅ-*k*iun-wâṅ-su-wan-*k*in.

'Buddhabhâshita-prasena*g*it-râ*g*a-paripri*kkh*â-sûtra.'

Râ*g*âvavâdaka-sûtra.

K'-yuen-lu, fasc. 7, fol. 27 b; Conc. 102; A. R., p. 459; A. M. G., p. 263. 8 leaves. It agrees with Tibetan. *K'*-yuen-lu, s. v. In this authority, No. 988 is mentioned under the heading of the Sûtras of the Hînayâna, though the Sanskrit title is fully transliterated, as Ârya-râ*g*âvavâdakanâma-mahâyâna-sûtra.

989 佛說輪王七寶經

Fo-shwo-lun-wâṅ-tshiê-pâo-*k*in. (h)

'Buddhabhâshita-*k*akra(varti)-râ*g*a-sapta-ratna-sûtra.'

5 leaves. Deest in Tibetan. *K'*-yuen-lu, fasc. 8, fol. 3 a. But according to *K'*-tsin (fasc. 28, fol. 3 a), this is a later translation of No. 542 (58).

990 佛說園生樹經

Fo-shwo-yuen-shaṅ-shu-*k*in. (h)

'Buddhabhâshita-ârâma*g*âtadruma-sûtra.'

2 leaves. Deest in Tibetan. *K'*-yuen-lu, fasc. 8, fol. 3 a. But according to *K'*-tsin (fasc. 28, fol. 10 a), this is a later translation of No. 542 (2).

991 佛說了義般若波羅蜜多經

Fo-shwo-liâo-i-pân-zo-po-lo-mi-to-*k*in.

'Buddhabhâshita-prasannârtha(? "clear-meaning")-pra*g*ñâpâramitâ-sûtra.'

3 leaves. This is an extract from a larger text of the Prag<i>ñ</i>âpâramitâ. <i>K</i>'-yuen-lu, fasc. 1, fol. 18 b.

992 佛說大方廣未曾有經善巧方便品

Fo-shwo-tâ-fâṅ-kwâṅ-wêi-tshâṅ-yiu-<i>k</i>iṅ-shan-<i>k</i>hiâo-fâṅ-pien-phin.

'Buddhabhâshita-mahâvaipulyâdbhuta-sûtra-upâyakaualyâdhyâya.'

5 leaves. Deest in Tibetan. <i>K</i>'-yuen-lu, fasc. 4, fol. 13 b.

993 佛說大堅固婆羅門緣起經

Fo-shwo-tâ-<i>k</i>ien-ku-pho-lo-man-yuen-<i>k</i>hi-<i>k</i>iṅ. (h)

'Buddhabhâshita-mahâsthira-brâhmaṇa-nidâna-sûtra.'

2 fasciculi; 22 leaves. Deest in Tibetan. <i>K</i>'-yuen-lu, fasc. 8, fol. 2 b. But according to <i>K</i>'-tsiṅ (fasc. 29, fol. 6 a), this is a later translation of No. 545 (3).

994 佛說巨力長者所問大乘經

Fo-shwo-<i>k</i>ü-li-<i>k</i>hâṅ-<i>k</i>ö-su-wan-tâ-shiṅ-<i>k</i>iṅ.

'Buddhabhâshita-mahâbala-sreshṭhi-paripṛi<i>k</i>kkâ-mahâyâna-sûtra.'

Translated by <i>K</i>'-<i>k</i>i-siâṅ (G<i>ñ</i>ânaśrî?), A.D. 1053, of the later Suṅ dynasty, A.D. 960-1127. 3 fasciculi; 27 leaves. Deest in Tibetan. <i>K</i>'-yuen-lu, fasc. 4, fol. 17 b.

The following three works were translated by Fâ-hhien, A.D. 982-1001, of the later Suṅ dynasty, A.D. 960-1127:—

995 佛說妙吉祥菩薩所問大乘法螺經

Fo-shwo-miâo-<i>k</i>i-siâṅ-phu-sâ-su-wan-tâ-shaṅ-fâ-lo-<i>k</i>iṅ.

'Buddhabhâshita-ma<i>ñ</i>gusrî-bodhisattva-paripṛi<i>k</i>kkâ-mahâyâna-dharmasaṅkha-sûtra.'

7 leaves. It agrees with Tibetan. <i>K</i>'-yuen-lu, fasc. 4, fol. 12 b. According to <i>K</i>'-tsiṅ (fasc. 10, fol. 5 a), this is a later translation of Nos. 264, 265.

996 佛說四品法門經

Fo-shwo-sz'-phin-fâ-man-<i>k</i>iṅ. (h)

'Buddhabhâshita-katurvarga-dharmaparyâya-sûtra.'

6 leaves. It agrees with Tibetan. <i>K</i>'-yuen-lu, fasc. 7, fol. 27 a.

997 佛說八大菩薩經

Fo-shwo-pâ-tâ-phu-sâ-<i>k</i>iṅ.

'Buddhabhâshita-ashṭamahâbodhisattva-sûtra.'

2 leaves. Deest in Tibetan. <i>K</i>'-yuen-lu, fasc. 4, fol. 13 a.

The following two works were translated by Sh'-hu (Dânapâla?), A.D. 980-1000, of the later Suṅ dynasty, A.D. 960-1127:—

998 佛說施一切無畏陀羅尼經

Fo-shwo-sh'-yi-tshiê-wu-wêi-tho-lo-ni-<i>k</i>iṅ.

'Buddhabhâshita-sarvâ . . . . sûtra.'
Sarvâbhaya-pradâna-dhâraṇî.

K'-yuen-lu, fasc. 6, fol. 2 a; Conc. 74; A.R., p. 524; A.M.G., p. 323. 3 leaves. It agrees with Tibetan. K'-yuen-lu, s. v.

999 聖八千頌般若波羅蜜多一百八名眞實圓義陀羅尼經

Shaṅ-pâ-tshien-suṅ-pân-<i>z</i>o-po-lo-mi-to-yi-pâi-pâ-miṅ-<i>k</i>an-shih-yuen-i-tho-lo-ni-<i>k</i>iṅ.

'Ârya-ashṭasahasra-gâthâ (or -śloka)-prag<i>ñ</i>âpâramitâ-nâmâshṭaśata-satyapûrnârtha-dhâraṇî-sûtra.'

3 leaves. It agrees with Tibetan. <i>K</i>'-yuen-lu, fasc. 1, fol. 19 a.

1000 佛說一髻尊陀羅尼經

Fo-shwo-yi-<i>k</i>i-tsun-tho-lo-ni-<i>k</i>iṅ.

'Buddhabhâshita-ekakûdârya-dhâraṇî-sûtra.'

Translated by Amoghavagra, A.D. 746-771, of the Thâṅ dynasty, A.D. 618-907. 16 leaves. Deest in Tibetan. <i>K</i>'-yuen-lu, fasc. 5, fol. 13 b.

1001 金剛摧碎陀羅尼

Kin-kâṅ-tshui-sui-tho-lo-ni.

'Vagra-bha<i>ñ</i>gana-dhâraṇî.'

Translated by Tshz'-hhien, of the later Suṅ dynasty, A.D. 960-1127. 3 leaves. Deest in Tibetan. <i>K</i>'-yueh-lu, fasc. 6, fol. 6 a, where the title is read Tâ-tshui-sui-tho-lo-ni-<i>k</i>iṅ, or 'Mahâ-bha<i>ñ</i>gana-dhâraṇî-sûtra.'

1002 不空羂索毗盧遮那佛大灌頂光眞言經

Pu-khuṅ-<i>k</i>ien-soh-phi-lu-<i>k</i>ö-nâ-fo-tâ-kwâṅ-tiṅ-kwâṅ-<i>k</i>an-yen-<i>k</i>iṅ.

'Amoghapâśa-vairokana-buddha-mahâbhishikta-prabhâsa-mantra-sûtra.'

Translated by Amoghavagra, A.D. 746-771, of the Thâṅ dynasty, A.D. 618-907. 2 leaves.

1003 地藏菩薩本願經

Ti-tsâṅ-phu-sâ-pan-yuen-*k*iṅ.

'Kshitigarbha-bodhisattva-pûrvapra*n*idhâna-sûtra.'

Translated by *S*ikshânanda, A. D. 695–700, of the Thâṅ dynasty, A. D. 618–907. 2 fasciculi; 13 chapters.

1004 大乘理趣六波羅蜜多經

Tâ-shaṅ-li-tshü-liu-po-lo-mi-to-*k*iṅ.

'Mahâyâna-buddhi (? "reason")-sha*t*pâramitâ-sûtra.'

Translated by Pra*gñ*a, A. D. 788, of the Thâṅ dynasty, A. D. 618–907. 10 fasciculi; 10 chapters. There is a preface added by the Emperor Tâi-tsuṅ, A. D. 763–779, of the same dynasty. This Emperor died in 779, so that he did not see the whole work, because the translation was not finished till 788.

1005 佛說大乘菩薩藏正法經

Fo-shwo-tâ-shaṅ-phu-sâ-tsâṅ-*k*aṅ-fâ-*k*iṅ.

'Buddhabhâshita-mahâyâna-bodhisattva-pi*t*aka-saddharma-sûtra.'

Bodhisattva-pi*t*aka.

Translated by Fâ-hu (Dharmaraksha?), A. D. 1004–1058, of the later Suṅ dynasty, A. D. 960–1127. 40 fasciculi; 11 chapters. This is a later translation of No. 23 (12). *K*'-yuen-lu, fasc. 4, fol. 16 a.

1006 佛爲優塡王說王法政論經

Fo-wêi-yiu-thien-wâṅ-shwo-wâṅ-fâ-*k*aṅ-lun-*k*iṅ.

'Sûtra addressed by Buddha to King Udayana on the law of kings and counsel for administration.'

Translated by Amoghava*g*ra, A. D. 746–771, of the Thâṅ dynasty, A. D. 618–907. 9 leaves. It agrees with Tibetan. *K*'-yuen-lu, fasc. 4, fol. 9 a.

1007 佛說五大施經

Fo-shwo-wu-tâ-sh'-*k*iṅ. (h)

'Buddhabhâshita-pañ*k*amahâpradâna-sûtra.'

Translated by Sh'-hu (Dânapâla?), A. D. 980–1000, of the later Suṅ dynasty, A. D. 960–1127. 9 leaves.

1008 佛說無畏陀羅尼經

Fo-shwo-wu-wêi-tho-lo-ni-*k*iṅ.

'Buddhabhâshita-abhaya-dhâra*n*î-sûtra.'

Translated by Fâ-hhien, A. D. 982–1001, of the later Suṅ dynasty, A. D. 960–1127. 3 leaves.

1009 佛說大威德金輪佛頂熾盛光如來消除一切災難陀羅尼經

Fo-shwo-tâ-wêi-töh-*k*in-lun-fo-tiṅ-*kh*'-shaṅ-kwâṅ-*z*u-lâi-siâo-*kh*u-yi-tshiê-tsâi-nân-tho-lo-ni-*k*iṅ.

'Buddhabhâshita-mahâbalagu*n*asuvar*n*a*k*akrabuddhoshnîshate*g*a-prabha-tathâgata-sarvâpadvinâsa-dhâra*n*î-sûtra.'

Translated under the Thâṅ dynasty, A. D. 618–907; but the translator's name is lost. 3 leaves.

1010 佛說熾盛光大威德消災吉祥陀羅尼經

Fo-shwo-*kh*'-shaṅ-kwâṅ-tâ-wêi-töh-siâo-tsâi-*k*i-siâṅ-tho-lo-ni-*k*iṅ.

'Buddhabhâshita-te*g*aprabhâmahâbalagu*n*âpadvinâsa-srî-dhâra*n*î-sûtra.'

Translated by Amoghava*g*ra, A. D. 746–771, of the Thâṅ dynasty, A. D. 618–907. 2 leaves. This is a similar and shorter translation of No. 1009. *K*'-tsiṅ, fasc. 13, fol. 15 a.

1011 佛說頂生王因緣經

Fo-shwo-tiṅ-shaṅ-wâṅ-yin-yuen-*k*iṅ.

'Buddhabhâshita-mûrdhagâta-râ*g*âvadâna-sûtra.'

Translated by Sh'-hu (Dânapâla?), A. D. 980–1000, of the later Suṅ dynasty, A. D. 960–1127. 6 fasciculi. This work exists in Tibetan. *K*'-yuen-lu, fasc. 4, fol. 15 a.

1012 佛說大乘隨轉宣說諸法經

Fo-shwo-tâ-shaṅ-sui-*k*wâṅ-süen-shwo-*k*u-fâ-*k*iṅ.

'Buddhabhâshita-mahâyâna-sarva .... sûtra.'

Sarvadharma-pravr*i*tti-nirdesa-sûtra.

Translated by Shâo-töh and others, of the later Suṅ dynasty, A. D. 960–1127. 3 fasciculi. Deest in Tibetan. *K*'-yuen-lu, fasc. 4, fol. 17 b. According to *K*'-tsiṅ (fasc. 7, fol. 6 a), this is a later translation of Nos. 163, 164.

1013 佛說大乘入諸佛境界智光明莊嚴經

Fo-shwo-tâ-shaṅ-*z*u-*kh*u-fo-*k*iṅ-*k*iê-*k*'-kwâṅ-miṅ-*k*wâṅ-yen-*k*iṅ.

'Buddhabhâshita-mahâyâna-sarva .... sûtra.'

Sarvabuddhavishayâvatâra-*gñ*ânâlokâlaṅkâra-sûtra.

K'-yuen-lu, fasc. 4, fol. 16 a; Conc. 158, 572; A. R., p. 428; A. M. G., p. 233. Translated by Fâ-hu (Dharmaraksha?), A. D. 1004–1058, and others, of the later Suṅ dynasty, A. D. 960–1127. 5 fasciculi. It agrees with Tibetan. K'-yuen-lu, s. v. According to K'-tsiṅ (fasc. 7, fol. 11 a seq.), this is a later translation of Nos. 56, 245.

1014 佛說大乘智印經
Fo-shwo-tâ-shaṅ-k'-yin-kiṅ.
'Buddhabhâshita-mahâyâna-gñâna-mudrâ-sûtra.'
Tathâgata-gñâna-mudrâ-sûtra.

K'-yuen-lu, fasc. 4, fol. 16 b; Conc. 589. Translated by K'-ki-siâṅ (Gñânasrî?), A. D. 1053, of the later Suṅ dynasty, A. D. 960–1127. 5 fasciculi. This is a later translation of Nos. 255, 256. K'-yuen-lu, s. v.

1015 佛說法乘義決定經
Fo-shwo-fâ-shaṅ-i-kiê-tiṅ-kiṅ. (h)
'Buddhabhâshita-dharma-(mahâ)yânârtha-viniskaya-sûtra.'
Arthaviniskaya-dharmaparyâya.

K'-yuen-lu, fasc. 4, fol. 18 a; Conc. 139; A. R., p. 476; A. M. G., p. 279. Translated by Kin-tsun-kh' (Suvarna-dhâranî?), about A. D. 1113, of the later Suṅ dynasty, A. D. 960–1127. 3 fasciculi. It agrees with Tibetan. K'-yuen-lu, s. v.

1016 佛說大白傘蓋總持陀羅尼經
Fo-shwo-tâ-po-sân-kâi-tsun-kh'-tho-lo-ni-kiṅ.
'Buddhabhâshita-mahâsitâtapatra-dhâranî-sûtra.'
Sitâtapatra-dhâranî.

Cf. K'-yuen-lu, fasc. 6, fol. 4 b, where an earlier translation made by Amoghavagra, A. D. 746–771, is mentioned; Conc. 427. Translated by Tsi-nâh-miṅ-töh-li-lien-töh-lo-mo-miṅ, together with Kan-k', of the Yuen dynasty, A. D. 1280–1368. 1 fasciculus.

1017 佛說一切如來眞實攝大乘現證三昧大教王經
Fo-shwo-yi-tshiê-zu-lâi-kan-shih-shö-tâ-shaṅ-hhien-kaṅ-sân-mêi-tâ-kiâo-wâṅ-kiṅ.
'Buddhabhâshita-sarvatathâgata-satya-saṅgraha-mahâyâna-pratyutpannâbhisambuddha-samâdhi-mahâtantrarâga-sûtra.'

Translated by Sh'-hu (Dânapâla?), A. D. 980–1000, of the later Suṅ dynasty, A. D. 960–1127. 30 fasciculi; 26 divisions. It is stated at the end that the Sanskrit text consists of 4000 slokas in verse, or an equivalent number of syllables in prose. It agrees with Tibetan. K'-yuen-lu, fasc. 6, fol. 3 b. The contents of No. 1017 are briefly mentioned by Wassiljew, in his Buddhismus, pp. 187, 188

1018 一切如來大秘密王未曾有最上微妙大曼拏羅經
Yi-tshiê-zu-lâi-tâ-pi-mi-wâṅ-wêi-tshâṅ-yiu-tsui-shâṅ-wêi-miâo-tâ-man-nâ-lo-kiṅ.
'Sarvatathâgata-mahâguhyarâgâdbhutâ-nuttaraprasasta-mahâmandala-sûtra.'

Translated by Thien-si-tsâi, A. D. 980–1001, of the later Suṅ dynasty, A. D. 930–1127. 5 fasciculi; 7 chapters.

1019 出生一切如來法眼徧照大力明王經
Khu-shaṅ-yi-tshiê-zu-lâi-fâ-yen-pien-kâo-tâ-li-miṅ-wâṅ-kiṅ.
'Gâta-sarvatathâgata-dharmakakshu-samantaprakâsamâna-mahâbala-vidyârâga-sûtra.'

Translated by Fâ-hu (Dharmaraksha?), A. D. 1004–1058, of the later Suṅ dynasty, A. D. 960–1127. 2 fasciculi; 21 leaves.

The following two works were translated by Amoghavagra, A. D. 746–771, of the Thâṅ dynasty, A. D. 618–907:—

1020 金剛頂一切如來眞實攝大乘現證大教王經
Kin-kâṅ-tiṅ-yi-tshiê-zu-lâi-kan-shih-shö-tâ-shaṅ-hhien-kaṅ-tâ-kiâo-wâṅ-kiṅ.
'Vagrasekhara-sarvatathâgata-satya-saṅgraha-mahâyâna-pratyutpannâbhisambuddha-mahâtantrarâga-sûtra.'

3 fasciculi. According to K'-tsiṅ (fasc. 11, fol. 4 b), this is an earlier translation of the first division of No. 1017.

1021 阿唎多羅陀羅尼阿嚕力經
Ö-li-to-lo-tho-lo-ni-ö-lu-li-kiṅ.
'Ârya-târâ (?)-dhâranî-ö-lu-li (?)-sûtra.'

1 fasciculus.

1022 佛說瑜伽大教王經
Fo-shwo-yü-kiê-tâ-kiâo-wâṅ-kiṅ.
'Buddhabhâshita-yoga-mahâtantrarâga-sûtra.'
Mâyâgâla-mahâtantra-mahâyâna-gambhîra-nâya-guhya-parâsi-sûtra.

K'-yuen-lu, fasc. 5, fol. 16 a; Conc. 878. Cf. A. R., p. 500; A. M. G., p. 301. Translated by Fâ-hhien,

A. D. 982–1001, of the later Suṅ dynasty, A. D. 960–1127. 5 fasciculi; 10 chapters. It agrees with Tibetan. K'-yuen-lu, s. v.

The following three works were translated by Amoghava*g*ra, A. D. 746–771, of the Thâṅ dynasty, A. D. 618–907:—

1023 一字奇特佛頂經
Yi-tsz'-*kh*i-thŏ-fo-tiṅ-*k*iṅ.
'Ekâkshara-prasasta-buddhoshnisha-sûtra.'
Ushnîsha*k*akravarti-tantra.

K'-yuen-lu, fasc. 5, fol. 13 b; Conc. 222. 3 fasciculi; 9 chapters. It agrees with Tibetan. K'-yuen-lu, s. v. There is an appendix, entitled, Yi-tsz'-tiṅ-lun-wâṅ-nien-suṅ-i-kwêi, or 'Ekâksharoshnîsha*k*akrarâ*g*âdhyâya-kalpa.' 10 leaves.

1024 菩提場所說一字頂輪王經
Phu-thi-*kh*âṅ-su-shwo-yi-tsz'-tiṅ-lun-wâṅ-*k*iṅ.
'Ekâksharoshnîsha*k*akrarâ*g*a-sûtra, spoken at the Bodhimanda.'

5 fasciculi; 13 chapters. It agrees with Tibetan. K'-yuen-lu, fasc. 5, fol. 10 a. According to K'-tsiṅ (fasc. 11, fol. 19 b), this is a later translation of No. 532.

1025 菩提場莊嚴陀羅尼經
Phu-thi-*kh*âṅ-*k*wâṅ-yen-tho-lo-ni-*k*iṅ.
Bodhimanda-vyûha-dhâranî-sûtra.'

1 fasciculus.

The following two works were translated by Sh'-hu (Dânapâla?), A. D. 980–1000, of the Suṅ dynasty, A. D. 960–1127:—

1026 佛說秘密相經
Fo-shwo-pi-mi-siâṅ-*k*iṅ.
'Sûtra spoken by Buddha on the secret form.'
Guhyagarbharâ*g*a.

K'-yuen-lu, fasc. 5, fol. 15 a; Conc. 157, 440. 3 fasciculi; 24 leaves.

1027 佛說一切如來金剛三業最上秘密大教王經
Fo-shwo-yi-tshiê-*z*u-lâi-*k*in-kâṅ-sân-yeh-tsui-shâṅ-pi-mi-tâ-*k*iâo-wâṅ-*k*iṅ.
Buddhabhâshita-sarvatathâgata-va*g*ra-trikarmânuttara-guhya-mahâtantrarâ*g*a-sûtra.'
*S*rî-guhya-sama*g*a-tantrarâ*g*a.

K'-yuen-lu, fasc. 5, fol. 14 b; Conc. 223; A. R., p. 496; A. M. G., p. 299. 7 fasciculi; 18 divisions. It agrees with Tibetan. K'-yuen-lu, s. v.

1028 大寶廣博樓閣善住秘密陀羅尼經
Tâ-pâo-kwâṅ-po-leu-kwo-shan-*k*u-pi-mi-tho-lo-ni-*k*iṅ.
'Mahâmani .... guhya-dhâranî-sûtra.'
Mahâma*n*i-vipula-vimâna-vi*s*va-supratish*th*ita-guhya-parama-rahasya-kalparâ*g*a-dhâra*n*î.

K'-yuen-lu, fasc. 5, fol. 11 a; Conc. 641; A. R., p. 509; A. M. G., p. 310. Translated by Amoghava*g*ra, A. D. 746–771, of the Thâṅ dynasty, A. D. 618–907. 3 fasciculi; 8 chapters. It agrees with Tibetan. K'-yuen-lu, s. v. According to K'-tsiṅ (fasc. 11, fol. 3 a), this is a later translation of Nos. 535, 536. 'There is a curious plate on the first page of this work, which illustrates the Thibetan Formula "Om mani padme houm."' Beal, Catalogue, p. 64.

The following two works were translated by Sh'-hu (Dânapâla?), A. D. 980–1000, of the later Suṅ dynasty, A. D. 960–1127:—

1029 佛說秘密三昧大教王經
Fo-shwo-pi-mi-sân-mêi-tâ-*k*iâo-wâṅ-*k*iṅ.
'Buddhabhâshita-guhya-samaya-mahâtantrarâ*g*a-sûtra.'
Guhyasamayagarbharâ*g*a.

K'-yuen-lu, fasc. 5, fol. 16 a; Conc. 156, 439. 4 fasciculi; 3 assemblies.

1030 佛說無二平等最上瑜伽大教王經
Fo-shwo-wu-'rh-piṅ-taṅ-tsui-shâṅ-yü-*k*iê-tâ-*k*iâo-wâṅ-*k*iṅ.
'Buddhabhâshita-asamasamânuttara-yoga-mahâtantrarâ*g*a-sûtra.'

6 fasciculi; 21 divisions.

The above two works agree with Tibetan. K'-yuen-lu, fasc. 5, fol. 16 a.

1031 佛說金剛手菩薩降伏一切部多大教王經
Fo-shwo-*k*in-kâṅ-sheu-phu-sâ-*k*iâṅ-fu-yi-tshiê-pu-to-tâ-*k*iâo-wâṅ-*k*iṅ.
'Buddhabhâshita-va*g*rapâni-bodhisattva-sarvabhûta*d*âmara-mahâtantrarâ*g*a-sûtra.'
*S*rî-sarvabhûta*d*âmara-tantra.

K'-yuen-lu, fasc. 5, fol. 17 b; Conc. 284.

Bhûta*d*âmara-mahâtantrarâ*g*a.

A. R., p. 536; A. M. G., p. 334; Conc. 284. Translated by Fâ-thien (Dharmadeva?), A. D. 973–981, of the later Suṅ dynasty, A. D. 960–1127. 3 fasciculi.

It agrees with Tibetan. *K'*-yuen-lu, s. v. For the Sanskrit text, see Catalogue of the Hodgson Manuscripts, I. 48; III. 39; V. 37.

1032 聖妙吉祥眞實名經
Shań-miâo-*k*i-siâń-*k*an-shih-miń-*k*iń.
'Ârya-mañgusrî-satyanâma-sûtra.'
Mañgusrî-nâma-nâh-*k*i-tiń (?), or Sûtra on reciting the true name of the Ârya Mañgusrî.

Thus the Sanskrit title, both in transliteration and translation, is given at the beginning. Translated by *K'*-hwui (Pragña ?), of the Yuen dynasty, A.D. 1280–1368. 1 fasciculus. There is another work translated by the same person and prefixed to this work, which is entitled Shań-kö-wan-shu-sh'-li-fâ-phu-thi-sin-wan, or 'Ârya-mañgusrî-bodhi-*k*ittotpâda-lekha.' A preface is added by the Emperor *Kh*âń-tsu, of the Miń dynasty, dated A.D. 1411.

1033 金剛頂瑜伽理趣般若經
*K*in-kâń-tiń-yü-*k*iê-li-tshü-pân-*z*o-*k*iń.
'Vagrasekhara-yoga-buddhi (?)-pragñâ(pâramitâ)-sûtra.'
Pragñâpâramitâ ardhasatikâ.

Translated by Vagrabodhi, A.D. 723–730, of the Thâń dynasty, A.D. 618–907, from the Sanskrit text, while he was in Central India. 13 leaves. Deest in Tibetan. *K'*-yuen-lu, fasc. 6, fol. 6 a.

1034 大樂金剛不空眞實三麼耶般若波羅蜜多理趣經
Tâ-lö-*k*in-kâń-pu-khuń-*k*an-shih-sân-mo-ye-pân-*z*o-po-lo-mi-to-li-tshü-*k*iń.
'Mahâsukhya-vagrâmoghasatyasamaya-pragñâpâramitâ-buddhi (?)-sûtra.'
Pragñâpâramitâ ardhasatikâ.

Translated by Amoghavagra, A.D. 746–771, of the Thâń dynasty, A.D. 618–907. 9 leaves. Deest in Tibetan. *K'*-yuen-lu, fasc. 6, fol. 9 a.

According to *K'*-tsiń (fasc. 11, fol. 12 a seq.), the above two works are later translations of No. 18. They are similar translations of a part of No. 1037.

1035 佛說佛母般若波羅密多大明觀想儀軌經
Fo-shwo-fo-mu-pân-*z*o-po-lo-mi-to-tâ-miń-kwân-siâń-i-kwêi-*k*iń.
'Buddhabhâshita-buddhamâtrikâ-pragñâpâramitâ-mahâvidyâ-dhyânasañgñâna-kalpa-sûtra.'

Translated by Sh'-hu (Dânapâla ?), A.D. 980–1000, of the later Suń dynasty, A.D. 960–1127. 5 leaves. It agrees with Tibetan. *K'*-yuen-lu, fasc. 1, fol. 19 b.

1036 金剛頂瑜伽念珠經
*K*in-kâń-tiń-yü-*k*iê-nien-shu-*k*iń.
'Sûtra on (the merit in the use of) a rosary, being (an extract from) the Vagrasekhara-yoga.'

Translated by Amoghavagra, A.D. 746–771, of the Thâń dynasty, A.D. 618–907. 2 leaves. It agrees with Tibetan. *K'*-yuen-lu, fasc. 5, fol. 13 b.

The following two works were translated by Fâ-hhien, A.D. 982–1001, of the later Suń dynasty, A.D. 960–1127:—

1037 佛說最上根本大樂金剛不空三昧大教王經
Fo-shwo-tsui-shâń-kân-pan-tâ-lö-*k*in-kâń-pu-khuń-sân-mêi-tâ-*k*iâo-wâń-*k*iń.
'Buddhabhâshita-anuttaramûla-mahâsukhya-vagrâmogha-samaya-mahâtantrarâga-sûtra.'

7 fasciculi; 25 divisions. Deest in Tibetan. *K'*-yuen-lu, fasc. 5, fol. 16 a. There is a preface added by the Emperor *K*an-tsuń, A.D. 998–1022, of the later Suń dynasty. The contents of No. 1037 are briefly mentioned by Wassiljew, in his Buddhismus, p. 188.

1038 佛說最上秘密那拏天經
Fo-shwo-tsui-shâń-pi-mi-nâ-nâ-thien-*k*iń.
'Buddhabhâshita-anuttaraguhya-nada-deva-sûtra.'
Sravanasya (?)-putra-nada-gupilâya (?)-kalpa-râga.

K'-yuen-lu, fasc. 5, fol. 18 b. Conc. 780 does not restore this Sanskrit title fully from the Chinese transliteration given by the former authority. 3 fasciculi; 9 divisions; 32 leaves. It agrees with Tibetan. *K'*-yuen-lu, s. v.

1039 金剛峰樓閣一切瑜伽瑜祇經
*K*in-kâń-fań-leu-kwo-yi-tshiê-yü-*k*iê-yü-*k'*-*k*iń.
'Vagrasekhara-vimâna-sarva-yoga-yogî-sûtra.'

Translated by Vagrabodhi, A.D. 723–730, of the Thâń dynasty, A.D. 618–907. 2 fasciculi; 12 chapters. Deest in Tibetan. *K'*-yuen-lu, fasc. 6, fol. 4 a.

1040 佛說妙吉祥最勝根本大教經
Fo-shwo-miâo-*k*i-siâń-tsui-shań-kân-pan-tâ-*k*iâo-*k*iń.
'Buddhabhâshita-mañgusry-anuttara-mûla-mahâtantra-sûtra.'
Mañgusrî-sadvritta-guhya-tantrarâgasya vimsatika-krodhavigayâñgana.

K'-yuen-lu, fasc. 5, fol. 17 b; Conc. 357. Translated by Fâ-hhien, A. D. 982–1001, of the later Suṅ dynasty, A. D. 960–1127. 3 fasciculi; 10 divisions. It agrees with Tibetan. *K'*-yuen-lu, s. v.

1041 妙吉祥平等秘密最上觀門大教王經

Miâo-*k*i-siâṅ-piṅ-taṅ-pi-mi-tsui-shâṅ-kwân-man-tâ-*k*iâo-wâṅ-*k*iṅ.

'Mañ*g*usrî-samaguhyânuttara-dhyânamukha-mahâtantrarâ*g*a-sûtra.'

Translated by Tshz'-hhien, of the later Suṅ dynasty, A. D. 960–1127. 5 fasciculi. Deest in Tibetan. *K'*-yuen-lu, fasc. 6, fol. 5 a. The contents of No. 1041 are briefly mentioned by Wassiljew, in his Buddhismus, p. 188.

1042 普徧光明燄鬘清淨熾盛如意寶印心無能勝大明王大隨求陀羅尼經

Phu-pien-kwân-miṅ-yen-mân-tshiṅ-tsiṅ-*kh*'-shaṅ-*z*u-i-pâo-yin-sin-wu-naṅ-shaṅ-tâ-miṅ-wâṅ-tâ-sui-*kh*iu-tho-lo-ni-*k*iṅ.

Buddhabhâshita-samanta*g*valamâlâ-visuddha-sphu*t*ik*ri*ta-*k*intâma*n*imudrâ-h*ri*dayâpara*g*ita-dhâra*n*î-pratisara-mahâvidyârâ*g*a.

Ku-kan-yen-yâo-tsi, fasc. 3, fol. 12 a.

Mahâpratisara-dhâra*n*î.

K'-yuen-lu, fasc. 5, fol. 13 a; Conc. 473.

Mahâpratisara-vidyârâ*g*ñî.

A. R., p. 517; A. M. G., p. 317. Translated by Amoghava*g*ra, A. D. 746–771, of the Thâṅ dynasty, A. D. 618–907. 2 fasciculi; 2 chapters. It agrees with Tibetan. *K'*-yuen-lu, s. v.

1043 佛說如來不思議秘密大乘經

Fo-shwo-*z*u-lâi-pu-sz'-i-pi-mi-tâ-shaṅ-*k*iṅ.

'Buddhabhâshita-tathâgatâ*k*intya-guhya-mahâyâna-sûtra.'

Tathâgatâ*k*intya-guhya-nirdesa.

Translated by Fâ-hu (Dharmaraksha?), A. D. 1004–1058, of the later Suṅ dynasty, A. D. 960–1127. 20 fasciculi; 25 chapters. This is a later and longer translation of No. 23 (3). *K'*-yuen-lu, fasc. 6, fol. 3 b.

1044 大乘瑜伽金剛性海曼殊室利千臂千鉢大教王經

Tâ-shaṅ-yü-*k*iê-*k*in-kâṅ-siṅ-hâi-mân-shu-shih-li-tshien-phi-tshien-poh-tâ-*k*iâo-wâṅ-*k*iṅ.

'Mahâyâna-yoga-va*g*ra-prak*ri*tisâgara-mañ*g*usrî-sahasrabâhu-sahasrapâtra-mahâtantrarâ*g*a-sûtra.'

Translated by Amoghava*g*ra, A. D. 740, of the Thâṅ dynasty, A. D. 618–907. 10 fasciculi. Deest in Tibetan. *K'*-yuen-lu, fasc. 6, fol. 3 a. The contents of No. 1044 are briefly mentioned by Wassiljew, in his Buddhismus, p. 183.

The following two works were translated by Fâ-thien (Dharmadeva?), A. D. 973–981, of the later Suṅ dynasty, A. D. 960–1127:—

1045 佛說聖寶藏神儀軌經

Fo-shwo-shaṅ-pâo-tsâṅ-shan-i-kwêi-*k*iṅ.

'Buddhabhâshita-ârya-ratnagarbharddhi-kalpa-sûtra.'

***G*ambhala-*g*alendra-yathâlabdha-kalpa.**

K'-yuen-lu, fasc. 6, fol. 13 a; Conc. 109; A. R., p. 541; A. M. G., p. 338. In the first authority 'labdha' is wanting, while in the last two it is read 'lasatâ' or 'bhavatâ.' 2 fasciculi.

1046 佛說寶藏神大明曼拏羅儀軌經

Fo-shwo-pâo-tsâṅ-shan-tâ-miṅ-mân-nâ-lo-i-kwêi-*k*iṅ.

'Buddhabhâshita-ratnagarbharddhi-mahâvidyâ-ma*nd*ala-kalpa-sûtra.'

2 fasciculi.

The above two works agree with Tibetan. *K'*-yuen-lu, fasc. 6, fol. 13 a seq.

1047 金剛恐怖集會方廣軌儀觀自在菩薩三世最勝心明王經

***K*in-kâṅ-khuṅ-pu-tsi-hwui-fâṅ-kwâṅ-kwêi-i-kwân-tsz'-tsâi-phu-sâ-sân-shi-tsui-shaṅ-sin-miṅ-wâṅ-*k*iṅ.**

'Va*g*rabhaya-sannipâta-vaipulya-kalpa-avalokitesvara-bodhi-sattva-tribhâvânuttarah*ri*daya-vidyârâ*g*a-sûtra.'

Translated by Amoghava*g*ra, A. D. 746–771, of the Thâṅ dynasty, A. D. 618–907. 1 fasciculus; 9 chapters. It agrees with Tibetan. *K'*-yuen-lu, fasc. 5, fol. 13 a.

1048 金剛恐怖集會方廣軌儀觀自在菩薩三世最勝心明王大威力烏樞瑟摩明王經

[The first twenty-two characters are exactly the same as those of No. 1047]-tâ-wêi-li-wu-shu-seh-mo-miṅ-wâṅ-*k*iṅ.

'Va*g*rabhaya . . . . vidyârâ*g*a-mahâbala-wu-shu-seh-mo (i. e. ushman ?)-vidyârâ*g*a-sûtra.'

Mahâbalava*g*rakrodha-sûtra (?).

Conc. 660. Cf. *K'*-yuen-lu, fasc. 5, fol. 9 b; A. R., p. 541; A. M. G., p. 338. Translated by Ö-*k*ih-tâ-sien, of the Thâṅ dynasty, A. D. 618–907. 3 fasciculi.

1049 佛說大乘觀想曼拏羅淨諸惡趣經

Fo-shwo-tâ-shaṅ-kwân-siâṅ-mân-nâ-lo-tsiṅ-*k*u-ṅoh-tshü-*k*iṅ.

'Buddhabhâshita-mahâyâna-dhyâna-sa*ṅg*ñâna-mandala-sarvadurbhâva-prasâdaka-sûtra.'

Translated by Fâ-hhien, A. D. 982–1001, of the later Suṅ dynasty, A. D. 960–1127. 2 fasciculi; 28 leaves.

1050 佛說大方廣曼殊室利經觀自在多羅菩薩儀軌經

Fo-shwo-tâ-fâṅ-kwâṅ-mân-shu-shih-li-*k*iṅ-kwân-tsz'-tsâi-to-lo-phu-sâ-i-kwêi-*k*iṅ.

'Buddhabhâshita-mahâvaipulya-ma*ñg*usrî-sûtra-avalokitesvaratam-bodhisattva-kalpa-sûtra.'

Translated by Amoghava*g*ra, A. D. 746–771, of the Thâṅ dynasty, A. D. 618–907. 15 leaves; 3 chapters.

1051 佛說一切佛攝相應大教王經觀自在菩薩念誦儀軌經

Fo-shwo-yi-tshiê-fo-shö-siâṅ-yiṅ-tâ-*k*iâo-wâṅ-*k*iṅ-kwân-tsz'-tsâi-phu-sâ-nien-suṅ-i-kwêi-*k*iṅ.

'Buddhabhâshita-sarvabuddha-sa*ṅ*graha-yukta-mahâtantrarâ*g*a-sûtra-avalokitesvara-bodhisattvâdhyâya-kalpa-sûtra.'

Translated by Fâ-hhien, A. D. 982–1001, of the later Suṅ dynasty, A. D. 960–1127. 11 leaves. Deest in Tibetan. *K'*-yuen-lu, fasc. 6, fol. 14 b.

1052 瑜伽金剛頂經釋字母品

Yü-*k*iê-*k*in-kâṅ-tiṅ-*k*iṅ-shih-tsz'-mu-phin.

'Yoga-va*g*rasekhara-sûtra-aksharamâtrikâ-vyâkhyâ-varga.'

Translated by Amoghava*g*ra, A. D. 746–771, of the Thâṅ dynasty, A. D. 618–907. 3 leaves. It gives a certain meaning to each letter of the Sanskrit alphabet. Deest in Tibetan. *K'*-yuen-lu, fasc. 6, fol. 7 b.

1053 佛說一切如來安像三昧儀軌經

Fo-shwo-yi-tshiê-*z*u-lâi-ân-siâṅ-sân-mêi-i-kwêi-*k*iṅ.

'Buddhabhâshita-sarvatathâgata-pratirûpapratish*th*â-samaya-kalpa-sûtra.'

Translated by Sh'-hu (Dânapâla ?), A. D. 980–1000, of the later Suṅ dynasty, A. D. 960–1127. 9 leaves. It agrees with Tibetan. *K'*-yuen-lu, fasc. 6, fol. 13 a.

The following two works were translated by Amoghava*g*ra, A. D. 746–771, of the Thâṅ dynasty, A. D. 618–907:—

1054 文殊師利菩薩根本大教王金翅鳥王經

Wan-shu-sh'-li-phu-sâ-kân-pan-tâ-*k*iâo-wâṅ-*k*in-*k*h'-niâo-wâṅ-*k*iṅ.

'Ma*ñg*usrî-bodhisattva-mûla-tantrarâ*g*a-garu*d*a-dvi*g*arâ*g*a-sûtra.'

Garu*d*agarbharâ*g*a.

K'-yuen-lu, fasc. 6, fol. 12 a, where the last character of the Chinese title is read phin, or varga or chapter.

Garu*d*agarbhatantra.

Conc. 807. Cf. Ma*ñg*usrî-mûla-tantra, mentioned in A. R., p. 512; A. M. G., p. 313. 14 leaves. It agrees with Tibetan. *K'*-yuen-lu, s. v. But No. 1054 is of course a part or chapter of the Ma*ñg*usrî-mûla-tantra.

1055 十一面觀自在菩薩心密言念誦儀軌經

Shi-yi-mien-kwân-tsz'-tsâi-phu-sâ-sin-mi-yen-nien-suṅ-i-kwêi-*k*iṅ.

'Ekâdasamukha-avalokitesvara-bodhisattva-h*r*idaya-mantra (?)-adhyâya-kalpa-sûtra.'

3 fasciculi; 28 leaves. It agrees with Tibetan. *K'*-yuen-lu, fasc. 6, fol. 8 b.

1056 大方廣菩薩藏文殊師利根本儀軌經

Tâ-fâṅ-kwâṅ-phu-sâ-tsâṅ-wan-shu-sh'-li-kân-pan-i-kwêi-*k*iṅ.

'Mahâvaipulya-bodhisattvapi*t*aka-ma*ñg*usrî-mûla-kalpa-sûtra.'

Bodhisattvapi*t*akâvatamsaka-ma*ñg*usrî-mûla-garbha-tantra.

K'-yuen-lu, fasc. 5, fol. 14 b; Conc. 602.

Mañ*g*usrî-mûla-tantra.

A. R., p. 512; A. M. G., p. 313. Translated by Thien-si-tsâi, A. D. 980–1001, of the later Suṅ dynasty, A. D. 960–1127. 20 fasciculi; 28 chapters. It agrees with Tibetan. *K*'-yuen-lu, s. v.

1057 佛說持明藏瑜伽大教尊那菩薩大明成就儀軌經

Fo-shwo-*kh*'-miṅ-tsâṅ-yü-*k*iê-tâ-*k*iâo-tsun-nâ-phu-sâ-tâ-miṅ-*kh*âṅ-tsiu-i-kwêi-*k*iṅ.

'Buddhabhâshita-te*g*odhara-piṭaka (?)-yoga-mahâtantra-*k*unda (?)-bodhisattva-mahâvidyâ-siddhi-kalpa-sûtra.'

Translated by Fâ-hhien, A. D. 982–1001, of the later Suṅ dynasty, A. D. 960–1127. 4 fasciculi; 6 divisions. This is an extract from the Te*g*odhara-piṭaka (?), made by Nâgâr*g*una. It agrees with Tibetan. *K*'-yuen-lu, fasc. 6, fol. 14 a.

1058 佛說金剛香菩薩大明成就儀軌經

Fo-shwo-*k*in-kâṅ-hhiâṅ-phu-sâ-tâ-miṅ-*kh*âṅ-tsiu-i-kwêi-*k*iṅ.

'Buddhabhâshita-va*g*ragandha-bodhisattva-mahâvidyâ-siddhi-kalpa-sûtra.'

Translated by Sh'-hu (Dânapâla ?), A. D. 980–1000, of the later Suṅ dynasty, A. D. 960–1127. 3 fasciculi.

1059 金剛薩埵說頻那夜迦天成就儀軌經

*K*in-kâṅ-sâ-to-shwo-phin-nâ-ye-*k*iâ-thien-*kh*âṅ-tsiu-i-kwêi-*k*iṅ.

'Va*g*rasattva-bhâshita-pinnayaka (?)-deva-siddhi-kalpa-sûtra.'

Translated by Fâ-hhien, A. D. 982–1001, of the later Suṅ dynasty, A. D. 960–1127. 4 fasciculi.

The above two works agree with Tibetan. *K*'-yuen-lu, fasc. 6, fol. 13 b.

1060 佛說大悲空智金剛大教王儀軌經

Fo-shwo-tâ-pêi-khuṅ-*k*'-*k*in-kâṅ-tâ-*k*iâo-wâṅ-i-kwêi-*k*iṅ.

'Buddhabhâshita-mahâkâruṇikâmogha-*g*ñâna-va*g*ra-mahâtantrarâ*g*a-kalpa-sûtra.'

He Va*g*ra-tantra.

K'-yuen-lu, fasc. 6, fol. 16 b; Conc. 646; A. R., p. 489; A. M. G., p. 293. Translated by Fâ-hu (Dharmaraksha ?), A. D. 1004–1058, of the later Suṅ dynasty, A. D. 960–1280. 5 fasciculi; 20 chapters. It agrees with Tibetan, but one chapter of the latter is wanting in No. 1060. *K*'-yuen-lu, s. v. For the Sanskrit text, see Catalogue of the Hodgson Manuscripts, III. 45, 46.

The following two works were translated by Fâ-hhien, A. D. 982–1001, of the later Suṅ dynasty, A. D. 960–1127:—

1061 佛說幻化網大瑜伽教十忿怒明王大明觀想儀軌經

Fo-shwo-hwân-hwa-wâṅ-tâ-yü-*k*iê-*k*iâo-shi-fan-nu-miṅ-wâṅ-tâ-miṅ-kwân-siâṅ-i-kwêi-*k*iṅ.

'Buddhabhâshita-mâyâ*g*âla-mahâyoga-tantra-dasakrodha-vidyârâ*g*a-mahâvidyâ-dhyânasañ*g*ñâna-kalpa-sûtra.'

1 fasciculus. Deest in Tibetan. *K*'-yuen-lu, fasc. 6, fol. 13 b.

1062 佛說妙吉祥瑜伽大教金剛陪羅嚩輪觀想成就儀軌經

Fo-shwo-miâo-*k*i-siâṅ-yü-*k*iê-tâ-*k*iâo-*k*in-kâṅ-phêi-lo-foh-lun-kwân-siâṅ-*kh*âṅ-tsiu-i-kwêi-*k*iṅ.

'Buddhabhâshita-mañ*g*usrî-yogatantra-va*g*ra-bhairava-*k*akra-dhyânasañ*g*ñâna-siddhi-kalpa-sûtra.'

Va*g*ra-bhairava-tantra-krodha-tattvarâ*g*a.

K'-yuen-lu, fasc. 6, fol. 14 a; Conc. 358. 1 fasciculus; 6 divisions. It agrees with Tibetan. *K*'-yuen-lu, s. v.

The following two works were translated by Amoghava*g*ra, A. D. 746–771, of the Thâṅ dynasty, A. D. 618–907:—

1063 底哩三昧耶不動尊威怒王使者念誦法

Ti-li-sân-mêi-ye-pu-tuṅ-tsun-wêi-nu-wâṅ-sh'-*k*ö-nien-suṅ-fâ.

'Trisamaya-akarârya-krodharâ*g*a-dûtâdhyâya-dharma (or -kalpa).'

1 fasciculus. It agrees with Tibetan. *K*'-yuen-lu, fasc. 6, fol. 8 b.

1064 聖迦柅忿怒金剛童子菩薩成就儀軌經

Shaṅ-*k*iâ-ni-fan-nu-*k*in-kâṅ-thuṅ-tsz'-phu-sâ-*kh*âṅ-tsiu-i-kwêi-*k*iṅ.

'Ârya-(dâ)kini (?)-krodha-va*g*rakumâra-bodhisattva-siddhi-kalpa-sûtra.'

Va*g*rakumâra-tantra.

K'-yuen-lu, fasc. 6, fol. 11 b; Conc. 101. 3 fasciculi. It agrees with Tibetan. *K*'-yuen-lu, s. v.

1065 七佛讚唄伽陀

Tshi-fo-tsân-pâi-kiê-tho.

'Gâthâ on the praise of the seven Buddhas (and Maitreya),' or 'Saptabuddha-stotra-gâthâ.'

Translated by Fâ-thien (Dharmadeva?), A.D. 973–981, of the later Suṅ dynasty, A.D. 960–1127. 3 leaves. It contains ten verses, nine of them being merely transliterated into Chinese.

1066 佛三身讚

Fo-sân-shan-tsân.

'Laudatory verse on the three bodies of Buddha,' or 'Buddha-trikâya-stotra.'

Translated by Fâ-hhien, A.D. 982–1001, of the later Suṅ dynasty, A.D. 960–1127. 2 leaves. The three bodies of Buddha are: 1. Dharma-kâya, 2. Sambhoga-kâya, 3. Nirmâna-kâya. See Eitel, Handbook of Chinese Buddhism, p. 148 b, s. v. Trikâya.

1067 佛一百八名讚經

Fo-yi-pâi-pâ-miṅ-tsân-kiṅ.

'Buddha-nâmâshṭaśataka-stotra-sûtra.'

Translated by Fâ-thien (Dharmadeva?), A.D. 973–981, of the later Suṅ dynasty, A.D. 960–1127. 3 leaves.

The above three works are mentioned under the heading of the Works of the Indian Sages, in K'-yuen-lu, fasc. 10, fol. 5 a seq.

1068 聖救度佛母二十一種禮讚經

Shaṅ-kiu-tu-fo-mu-'rh-shi-yi-kuṅ-li-tsân-kiṅ.

'Ârya-trâta-buddhamâtrikâ-viṁsati-pûga-stotra-sûtra.'

Translated by Ân Tsâṅ, of the Yuen dynasty, A.D. 1280–1368. 4 leaves. There are two Mantras, written in the Devanâgarî character, and transliterated into Chinese.

The following two works were translated by Sh'-hu (Dânapâla?), A.D. 980–1000, of the later Suṅ dynasty, A.D. 960–1127:—

1069 佛說一切如來頂輪王一百八名讚經

Fo-shwo-yi-tshiê-zu-lâi-tiṅ-lun-wâṅ-yi-pâi-pâ-miṅ-tsân-kiṅ.

'Buddhabhâshita-sarvatathâgatoshṇîshakakra-nâmâshṭaśataka-stotra-sûtra.'

2 leaves. Deest in Tibetan. K'-yuen-lu, fasc. 6, fol. 17 a. There are two appendices, both being Imperial compositions, though the Emperors' names are not given, namely: 1. Laudatory verses in honour of 'Trâta-buddhamâtrikâ (?),' and 2. Those of Buddha Śâkyamuni.

1070 讚法界頌

Tsân-fâ-kiê-suṅ.

'Dharmadhâtu-stotra.'

Composed by the Bodhisattva Nâgârguna. It consists of 87 verses.

The following two works were transliterated by Fâ-hhien, A.D. 982–1001, of the later Suṅ dynasty, A.D. 960–1127:—

1071 八大靈塔梵讚

Pâ-tâ-liṅ-thâ-fân-tsân.

'Laudatory verse in Sanskrit on the eight great auspicious Kaityas,' or 'Ashṭa-mahâ-śrî-kaitya-saṁskṛita-stotra.'

Composed by King Śîlâditya. 2 leaves.

1072 三身梵讚

Sân-shan-fân-tsân.

'Laudatory verse in Sanskrit on the three bodies (of Buddha),' or 'Trikâya-saṁskṛita-stotra.'

5 leaves.

1073 佛說文殊師利一百八名梵讚

Fo-shwo-wan-shu-sh'-li-yi-pâi-pâ-miṅ-fân-tsân.

'Buddhabhâshita-mañgusrî-nâmâshṭaśataka-saṁskṛita-stotra.'

Translated by Fâ-hhien, A.D. 982–1001, of the later Suṅ dynasty, A.D. 960–1127. 5 leaves. There are nineteen verses transliterated into Chinese, while a few others are translated. An Imperial composition is prefixed, namely: Laudatory verses in honour of Mañgusrî. The author is the Emperor Thâi-tsuṅ, i.e. Khâṅ-tsu, A.D. 1403–1424, of the Miṅ dynasty.

The above four works are mentioned under the heading of the Works of the Indian Sages, in K'-yuen-lu, fasc. 10, fol. 5 a seq., where the first two characters in the Chinese title of No. 1073 are of course left out.

The following two works were transliterated by Fâ-hhien, A.D. 982–1001, of the later Suṅ dynasty, A.D. 960–1127:—

1074 曼殊室利菩薩吉祥伽陀

Mân-shu-shih-li-phu-sâ-ki-siâṅ-kiê-tho.

'Mañgusrî-bodhisattva-srî-gâthâ.'

2 leaves.

1075 聖金剛手菩薩一百八名梵讚
Shan-kin-kân-sheu-phu-sâ-yi-pâi-pâ-min-fân-tsân.
'Ârya-vagrapâni-bodhisattva-nâmâshtasataka-samskrita-stotra.'

5 leaves. Deest in Tibetan. *K*'-yuen-lu, fasc. 6, fol. 17 a.

1076 聖觀自在菩薩功德讚
Shan-kwân-tsz'-tsâi-phu-sâ-kun-töh-tsân.
'Ârya-avalokitesvara-bodhisattva-guna-stotra.'

Collected by a Western or Indian sage; and translated by Sh'-hu (Dânapâla?), A.D. 980-1000, of the later Sun dynasty, A.D. 960-1127. 5 leaves; 184 lines. Two Imperial compositions are prefixed, both written by the Emperor Thâi-tsun, i.e. *Khân*-tsu, A.D. 1403-1424, of the Min dynasty. They are both laudatory verses in honour of the Bodhisattva Avalokitesvara.

1077 讚觀世音菩薩頌
Tsân-kwân-shi-yin-phu-sâ-sun.
'Avalokitesvara-bodhisattva-stotra.'

Translated by Hwui-*k*', A.D. 692, of the Thân dynasty, A.D. 618-907. 5 leaves.

1078 佛說聖觀自在菩薩梵讚
Fo-shwo-shan-kwân-tsz'-tsâi-phu-sâ-fân-tsân.
'Buddhabhâshita-ârya-avalokitesvara-bodhisattva-samskrita-stotra.'

Translated by Fâ-thien (Dharmadeva?), A.D. 973-981, of the later Sun dynasty, A.D. 960-1127. 3 leaves. There are eight verses transliterated into Chinese, while only another one is translated.

1079 聖多羅菩薩梵讚
Shan-to-lo-phu-sâ-fân-tsân.
'Ârya-târâ-bodhisattva-samskrita-stotra.'

Transliterated by Sh'-hu (Dânapâla?), A.D. 980-1000, of the later Sun dynasty, A.D. 960-1127. 8 leaves.

1080 事師法五十頌
Sh'-sh'-fâ-wu-shi-sun.
'Fifty verses on the law or rules for serving a teacher.'

Composed by the Bodhisattva Asvaghosha; and translated by *Z*ih-*kh*an, A.D. 1004-1058, of the later Sun dynasty, A.D. 960-1127. 4 leaves.

1081 犍椎梵讚
*K*ien-*kh*ui-fân-tsân.
'Ghanti(kâ?)-samskrita-stotra.'
Ghanti-sûtra (?).

A. R., p. 486; A. M. G., p. 289. Transliterated by Fâ-thien (Dharmadeva?), A.D. 973-981, of the later Sun dynasty, A.D. 960-1127. 10 leaves.

The above six works are mentioned under the heading of the Works of the Indian Sages, in *K*'-yuen-lu, fasc. 10, fol. 2 b seq., where the first two characters in the Chinese title of No. 1078 are of course left out.

SECOND DIVISION.

律藏 Lüh-tsân, or Vinaya-pitaka.

PART I.

大乘律 Tâ-shan-lüh, or the Vinaya of the Mahâyâna.

The following two works were translated by Gunavarman, A. D. 431, of the earlier Sun dynasty, A. D. 420–479:—

1082 佛說菩薩內戒經
Fo-shwo-phu-sâ-nêi-kiê-kin.
'Sûtra spoken by Buddha on the internal Sîla of the Bodhisattva.'
1 fasciculus.

1083 菩薩優婆塞五戒威儀經
Phu-sâ-yiu-pho-sö-wu-kiê-wêi-i-kin.
'Sûtra on the manners concerning the five Sîlas of the Bodhisattva-upâsaka.'
Spoken by the Bodhisattva Maitreya. 1 fasciculus.

The above two works are wanting in Tibetan. K'-yuen-lu, fasc. 8, fol. 8 b. For No. 1083, see, however, Nos. 1096, 1098, and 1170.

1084 佛說文殊師利淨律經
Fo-shwo-wan-shu-sh'-li-tsin-lüh-kin.
'Buddhabhâshita-mañgusri-suddhavinaya-sûtra.'
Paramârthasamvarti (-varta?)-satyanirdesanâma-mahâyâna-sûtra.

K'-yuen-lu, fasc. 8, fol. 9 a; Conc. 809. Translated by Ku Fâ-hu (Dharmaraksha), A. D. 289, of the Western Tsin dynasty, A. D. 265–316. 1 fasciculus; 4 chapters. It agrees with Tibetan. K'-yuen-lu, s. v.

1085 菩薩善戒經
Phu-sâ-shân-kiê-kin.
'Bodhisattva-bhadrasîla-sûtra.'
Bodhisattva-karyâ-nirdesa.

A. R., p. 452; A. M. G., p. 257; Conc. 476, 487. Translated by Gunavarman, A. D. 431, of the earlier Sun dynasty, A. D. 420–479. 10 fasciculi; 30 chapters. The first chapter is similar to No. 36. The rest is similar to the fifteenth part on the Bodhisattva-bhûmi in the first division of No. 1170. No. 1085 is the Sûtra on which the Bodhisattva Maitreya spoke No. 1170. K'-tsin, fasc. 32, fol. 3 a.

1086 菩薩地持經
Phu-sâ-ti-kh'-kin.
'Bodhisattva-bhûmidhara-sûtra.'
Bodhisattva-karyâ-nirdesa.

Conc. 488. Spoken by the Bodhisattva Maitreya. Translated by Dharmaraksha, A. D. 414–421, of the Northern Liân dynasty, A. D. 397–439. 8 fasciculi; 27 chapters. This work is similar to No. 1085. But, according to K'-tsin (fasc. 37, fol. 14 b), No. 1086 is an earlier translation of the fifteenth part on the Bodhisattva-bhûmi in the first division of No. 1170. The last character of the Chinese title is sometimes read 論 lun or sâstra. Khâi-yuen-lu, fasc. 12 b, fol. 12 a.

The above two works are wanting in Tibetan. K'-yuen-lu, fasc. 8, fol. 6 b. For No. 1086, see, however, No. 1170.

1087 梵網經
Fân-wân-kin.
Brahmagâla-sûtra.

Cf. A. R., p. 483; A. M. G., p. 286; Conc. 142. Translated by Kumâragîva, A. D. 406, of the Latter Tshin dynasty, A. D. 384–417. 2 fasciculi. It is stated in the preface by San-kâo, the disciple of the translator, that this work is the tenth chapter on the Bodhisattva-hridayabhûmi, in a Sanskrit text, consisting of 120 fasciculi, 61 chapters.

1088 優婆塞戒經
Yiu-pho-sö-kiê-kiṅ.
'Upâsaka-sîla-sûtra.'

Translated by Dharmaraksha, A.D. 428, of the Northern Liâṅ dynasty, A.D. 397–439. 7 fasciculi; 28 chapters.

The above two works are wanting in Tibetan. K'-yuen-lu, fasc. 8, fol. 7 b.

1089 寂調音所問經
Tsi-thiâo-yin-su-wan-kiṅ.
'Munivinayasvara (? devaputra)-paripṛkkhâ-sûtra.'
Paramârthasamvarti(-varta ?)-satyanirdesanâma-mahâyâna-sûtra.

Cf. No. 1084. Translated by Fâ-hâi, of the earlier Suṅ dynasty, A.D. 420–479. 1 fasciculus. This is a later translation of No. 1084. K'-yuen-lu, fasc. 8, fol. 9 b.

1090 大乘三聚懺悔經
Tâ-shaṅ-sân-tsü-khan-hwui-kiṅ.
'Mahâyâna-trirâsi-kshamâ (? confession)-sûtra.'
Karmâvarana-pratisarana (or -pratikkhedana).

K'-yuen-lu, fasc. 8, fol. 9 b; Conc. 585; A.R., p. 458; A.M.G., p. 262.

Triskandhaka.

Conc. 585. Translated by Gñânagupta and Dharmagupta, about A.D. 590, of the Sui dynasty, A.D. 589–618. 1 fasciculus. It agrees with Tibetan. K'-yuen-lu, s.v.

1091 佛說文殊悔過經
Fo-shwo-wan-shu-hwui-kwo-kiṅ.
'Buddhabhâshita-mañgusrî-kshamâ (? confession)-sûtra.'

Translated by Ku Fâ-hu (Dharmaraksha), A.D. 266–313, of the Western Tsin dynasty, A.D. 265–316. 1 fasciculus.

1092 菩薩瓔珞本業經
Phu-sâ-yiṅ-lo-pan-yeh-kiṅ.
'Sûtra on the original action of the garland of the Bodhisattva.'

Translated by Ku Fo-nien, of the Latter Tshin dynasty, A.D. 384–417. 2 fasciculi; 8 chapters. It agrees with Tibetan. K'-yuen-lu, fasc. 8, fol. 7 b.

1093 佛說受十善戒經
Fo-shwo-sheu-shi-shân-kiê-kiṅ.
'Sûtra spoken by Buddha on receiving the ten good Sîlas or the Sikshâpada.'

Translated under the Eastern Hân dynasty, A.D. 25–220; but the translator's name is lost. 1 fasciculus; 2 chapters. Deest in Tibetan. K'-yuen-lu, fasc. 8, fol. 7 b.

1094 佛說淨業障經
Fo-shwo-tsiṅ-yeh-kaṅ-kiṅ.
'Buddhabhâshita-karmâvarana-visuddhi-sûtra.'
Karmâvarana-visuddhi-mahâyâna-sûtra.

K'-yuen-lu, fasc. 8, fol. 7 a; A.R., p. 458; A.M.G., p. 262. Translated under the (three) Tshin dynasties, A.D. 350–431; but the translator's name is lost. 1 fasciculus. It agrees with Tibetan. K'-yuen-lu, s.v.

1095 佛藏經
Fo-tsâṅ-kiṅ.
'Buddhapiṭaka-sûtra.'
Buddhapiṭaka-nigrahanâma-mahâyâna-sûtra.

K'-yuen-lu, fasc. 8, fol. 8 a; Conc. 176. Cf. A.R., p. 458; A.M.G., p. 263. Translated by Kumâragîva, A.D. 405, of the Latter Tshin dynasty, A.D. 384–417. 4 fasciculi; 10 chapters. It agrees with Tibetan. K'-yuen-lu, s.v.

1096 菩薩戒本經
Phu-sâ-kiê-pan-kiṅ.
'Bodhisattva-pratimoksha-sûtra.'

Spoken by the Bodhisattva Maitreya. Translated by Dharmaraksha, A.D. 414–421, of the Northern Liâṅ dynasty, A.D. 397–439. 12 leaves. This is an earlier translation of Nos. 1083 and 1098. K'-yuen-lu, fasc. 8, fol. 8 a; K'-tsiṅ, fasc. 32, fol. 13 a.

The following two works were translated by Hhüen-kwâṅ (Hiouen-thsang), A.D. 649, of the Thâṅ dynasty, A.D. 618–907:—

1097 菩薩戒羯磨文
Phu-sâ-kiê-kiê-mo-wan.
'A composition or treatise on the Bodhisattva's Sîla-karma.'

Spoken by the Bodhisattva Maitreya. 7 leaves; 3 parts. This is an extract from No. 1170. K'-tsiṅ, fasc. 32, fol. 12 b.

1098 菩薩戒本
Phu-sâ-kiê-pan.
'Bodhisattva-pratimoksha.'

Spoken by the Bodhisattva Maitreya. 1 fasciculus. This translation was made in A.D. 649, and it is similar to Nos. 1083, 1096, and a portion of the fifth part on the Bodhisattva-bhûmi in the first division of No. 1170.

1099 佛說法律三昧經

Fo-shwo-fâ-lüh-sân-mêi-*k*iñ.

'Buddhabhâshita-vinayasamâdhi-sûtra.'

Translated by *K' Kh*ien, A. D. 223–253, of the Wu dynasty, A. D. 222–280. 9 leaves.

1100 佛說十善業道經

Fo-shwo-shi-shân-yeh-tâo-*k*iñ.

'Buddhabhâshita-dasabhadrakarmamârga-sûtra.'

Translated by *S*ikshânanda, A. D. 695–700, of the Thâñ dynasty, A. D. 618–907. 7 leaves.

1101 清淨毗尼方廣經

Tshiñ-tsiñ-phi-ni-fâñ-kwâñ-*k*iñ.

'*S*addhavinaya-vaipulya-sûtra.'

Paramârthasamvarti (-varta?)-satyanirdesanâma-mahâyâna-sûtra.

Cf. Nos. 1084, 1089, of which this is a similar translation. Translated by Kumâra*g*îva, A. D. 401–409, of the Latter Tshin dynasty, A. D. 384–417. 1 fasciculus.

1102 菩薩五法懺悔經

Phu-sâ-wu-fâ-*kh*an-hwui-*k*iñ.

'Bodhisattva-pañkadharma-kshamâ (? confession)-sûtra.'

Translated under the Liâñ dynasty, A. D. 502–557; but the translator's name is lost. 2 leaves.

1103 菩薩藏經

Phu-sâ-tsâñ-*k*iñ.

'Bodhisattva-pitaka-sûtra.'

Translated by Sañghapâla, A. D. 506–520, of the Liâñ dynasty, A. D. 502–557. 11 leaves.

The following two works were translated by Nieh Tâo-*k*an, A. D. 280–315, of the Western Tsin dynasty, A. D. 265–316:—

1104 三曼陀颰陀羅菩薩經

Sân-mân-tho-fu-tho-lo-phu-sâ-*k*iñ.

'Samantabhadra-bodhisattva-sûtra.'

8 leaves; 6 chapters.

1105 菩薩受齋經

Phu-sâ-sheu-*k*âi-*k*iñ.

'Sûtra on the Bodhisattva's receiving or observing the Upavasatha or Uposhadha fast.'

3 leaves. For the word Uposhadha, see Childers' Pâli Dictionary, p. 535 a, s. v. Uposatha.

1106 舍利弗悔過經

Shö-li-fu-hwui-kwo-*k*iñ.

'*S*âriputra-kshamâ (? confession)-sûtra.'

Triskandhaka.

K'-yuen-lu, fasc. 8, fol. 10 a; Conc. 48; A. R., p. 470; A. M. G., p. 274. Translated by Ân Shi-kâo, A. D. 148–170, of the Eastern Hân dynasty, A. D. 25–220. 6 leaves. This is an earlier and shorter translation of Nos. 1090 and 1103. *K'*-tsiñ, fasc. 32, fol. 11 b.

PART II.

小乘律 Siâo-shañ-lüh, or the Vinaya of the Hînayâna.

1107 佛阿毗曇經
Fo-ŏ-phi-thân-*k*iñ.
'Buddhâbhidharma-sûtra.'

Translated by Paramârtha, A. D. 557–569, of the *Kh*an dynasty, A. D. 557–589. 2 fasciculi; 2 chapters. Deest in Tibetan. *K*'-yuen-lu, fasc. 8, fol. 8 a.

1108 解脫戒本經
*K*iâ-tho-*k*iê-pan-*k*iñ.
'Pratimoksha-sûtra,' of the Kâsyapîya-nikâya.
Pratimoksha-vinaya (or -sûtra?).

Conc. 277. Translated by Gautama Pra*g*ñâru*k*i, A. D. 543, of the Eastern Wêi dynasty, A. D. 534–550. 1 fasciculus. Deest in Tibetan. *K*'-yuen-lu, fasc. 8, fol. 14 a.

1109 優波離問經
Yiu-po-li-wan-*k*iñ.
'Upâli-pariprikkhâ-sûtra.'

Translated by Gu*n*avarman, A. D. 431, of the earlier Suñ dynasty, A. D. 420–479. 1 fasciculus. It agrees with Tibetan. *K*'-yuen-lu, fasc. 8, fol. 15 b, where this translation is said to have been made by an unknown translator under the Eastern Hân dynasty, A. D. 25–220.

1110 根本說一切有部戒經
Kan-pan-shwo-yi-tshiê-yiu-pu-*k*iê-*k*iñ.
Mûlasarvâstivâda(-nikâya)-vinaya (or pratimoksha)-sûtra. Conc. 255.
Pratimoksha-sûtra (?).

A. R., p. 43; A. M. G., p. 146. Translated by I-tsiñ, A. D. 710, of the Thâñ dynasty, A. D. 618–907. 1 fasciculus. It agrees with Tibetan. *K*'-yuen-lu, fasc. 8, fol. 13 b.

1111 佛說迦葉禁戒經
Fo-shwo-*k*iâ-yeh-*k*in-*k*iê-*k*iñ.
'Sûtra spoken by Buddha on the forbidding precepts of the Kâsyapîya (-nikâya?).'

Translated by Tsü-*k*hü *K*iñ-shañ, A. D. 455, of the earlier Suñ dynasty, A. D. 420–479. 4 leaves.

1112 佛說犯戒罪輕重經
Fo-shwo-fân-*k*iê-tsâi-*kh*iñ-*k*uñ-*k*iñ.
'Sûtra spoken by Buddha on the lightness and heaviness of the sin of transgressing the *S*îla.'

Translated by Ân Shi-kâo, A. D. 148–170, of the earlier Hân dynasty, A. D. 25–220. 2 leaves. This is an earlier translation of No. 817. *K*'-tsiñ, fasc. 33, fol. 8 a.

1113 佛說戒消災經
Fo-shwo-*k*iê-siâo-tsâi-*k*iñ.
'Sûtra spoken by Buddha on the *S*îla destroying misfortune.'

Translated by *K*' *Kh*ien, A. D. 223–253, of the Wu dynasty, A. D. 222–280. 4 leaves.

1114 佛說優婆塞五戒相經
Fo-shwo-yiu-pho-sö-wu-*k*iê-siañ-*k*iñ.
'Buddhabhâshita-upâsaka-pañkasîla-rûpa-sûtra.'

Translated by Gu*n*avarman, A. D. 431, of the earlier Suñ dynasty, A. D. 420–479. 17 leaves.

The above four works are wanting in Tibetan. *K*'-yuen-lu, fasc. 8, fol. 16 b.

1115 十誦律
Shi-suñ-lüh.
'Dasâdhyâya-vinaya,' or 'Vinaya of ten recitations.'
Sarvâstivâda-vinaya.

K'-yuen-lu, fasc. 8, fol. 11 a; Conc. 82. Translated by Pu*n*yatara, together with Kumâra*g*îva, A. D. 404, of the Latter Tshin dynasty, A. D. 384–417. 65 fasciculi; 10 adhyâyas or divisions; 29 sections. This is similar to Tibetan, but the latter is shorter. *K*'-yuen-lu, s. v. For the Tibetan Vinaya, see the Analysis of the Dulva by Csoma in the Asiatic Researches, vol. xx, especially p. 45 seq. 'That the Tibet Vinaya belongs to the Mahâsarvâstivâdinas is stated by Wassiljew (Buddhismus, p. 96).' See Professor Oldenberg's Introduction to the Vinayapi*t*akam, vol. i, p. xlvii, note 1. But, according to I-tsiṅ (Nân-hâi-ki-kwêi-*k*whân, fasc. 1, fol. 8 a), No. 1115 is not the Vinaya of the Mûlasarvâstivâda-nikâya; for which latter, see No. 1118.

1116 尼羯磨
Ni-*k*ie-mo.
'Bhikshunî-karman,' of the Dharmagupta-nikâya.

Compiled by Kwâi-su, disciple of Hiouen-thsang, of the Thâṅ dynasty, A. D. 618–907. 5 fasciculi. This is an extract from No. 1117. It agrees with Tibetan. *K*'-yuen-lu, fasc. 8, fol. 16 a.

1117 四分律藏
Sz'-fan-lüh-tsâṅ.
'*Katurvarga-vinayapiṭaka*.'
Dharmagupta-vinaya.

K'-yuen-lu, fasc. 8, fol. 12 b; Conc. 545. Translated by Buddhayasas, together with *K*u Fo-nien, A. D. 405, of the Latter Tshin dynasty, A. D. 384–417. 60 fasciculi; 4 vargas or divisions; 20 skandhas or sections. This is similar to Tibetan, but the latter is shorter. *K*'-yuen-lu, s. v.

1118 根本說一切有部毗奈耶
Kan-pan-shwo-yi-tshie-yiu-pu-phi-nâi-ye.
Mûlasarvâstivâda-nikâya-vinaya.

Cf. Conc. 258. Translated by I-tsiṅ, A. D. 703, of the Thâṅ dynasty, A. D. 618–907. 50 fasciculi. Deest in Tibetan. *K*'-yuen-lu, fasc. 8, fol. 11 b.

1119 摩訶僧祇律
Mo-hö-saṅ-*kh*i-lüh.
Mahâsaṅgha (or -saṅghika)-vinaya.

K'-yuen-lu, fasc. 8, fol. 10 b; Conc. 368. Translated by Buddhabhadra, together with Fâ-hhien (Fa-hian), A. D. 416, of the Eastern Tsin dynasty, A. D. 317–420. 46 fasciculi; 18 sections. It agrees with Tibetan. *K*'-yuen-lu, s. v.

1120 曇無德部四分律删補隨機羯磨
Thân-wu-töh-pu-sz'-fan-lüh-shân-pu-sui-*k*i-*k*ie-mo.
'A revised Karman according to the disposition (of the disciples?) in the *Katurvarga-vinaya* of the Dharmagupta-nikâya.'

Compiled by Tâo-süen, about A. D. 660, of the Thâṅ dynasty, A. D. 618–907. 4 fasciculi. This is an extract from No. 1117. It agrees with Tibetan. *K*'-yuen-lu, fasc. 8, fol. 16 a.

1121 根本說一切有部毗奈耶雜事
Kan-pan-shwo-yi-tshie-yiu-pu-phi-nâi-ye-tsâ-sh'.
'Mûlasarvâstivâda-nikâya-vinaya-samyuktavastu.'

Translated by I-tsiṅ, A. D. 710, of the Thâṅ dynasty, A. D. 618–907. 40 fasciculi; 8 parts. Deest in Tibetan. *K*'-yuen-lu, fasc. 8, fol. 12 a.

1122 彌沙塞部五分律
Mi-shâ-sö-pu-wu-fan-lüh.
'Mahîsâsaka-nikâya-pañkavarga-vinaya.'
Mahîsâsaka-vinaya.

K'-yuen-lu, fasc. 8, fol. 12 b; Conc. 342. Translated by Buddhagîva, together with *K*u Tâo-shaṅ, A. D. 423–424, of the earlier Suṅ dynasty, A. D. 420–479. 30 fasciculi; 5 vargas or divisions. This is similar to Tibetan, but the latter is shorter. *K*'-yuen-lu, s. v. For the contents of No. 1122, see Mr. Beal's letter quoted by Professor Oldenberg in his Introduction to the Vinayapiṭakam, vol. i, pp. xliv–xlvi.

The following two works were translated by I-tsiṅ, A. D. 710, of the Thâṅ dynasty, A. D. 618–907:—

1123 根本說一切有部毗奈耶破僧事
Kan-pan-shwo-yi-tshie-yiu-pu-phi-nâi-ye-po-saṅ-sh'.
'Mûlasarvâstivâda-nikâya-vinaya-saṅghabhedakavastu.'
Saṅghabhedakavastu.

K'-yuen-lu, fasc. 8, fol. 19 a; Conc. 261, where 'bheda' is wrongly read 'piṭaka.' 20 fasciculi. It agrees with Tibetan. *K*'-yuen-lu, s. v.

1124 根本說一切有部苾芻尼毗奈耶
Kan-pan-shwo-yi-tshie-yiu-pu-pi-*kh*u-ni-phi-nâi-ye.
Mûlasarvâstivâda-nikâya-bhikshunî-vinaya.

Cf. Conc. 259. 20 fasciculi. Deest in Tibetan. *K*'-yuen-lu, fasc. 8, fol. 11 b.

1125 善見毗婆沙律
Shân-*k*ien-phi-pho-shâ-lüh.
'Sudarsana-vibhâshâ-vinaya.'
Vibhâshâ-vinaya.

Conc. 55, 55 a. Translated by Saṅghabhadra, A. D. 489, of the Tshi dynasty, A. D. 479–502. 18 fasciculi.

According to the *K'*-yuen-lu (fasc. 8, fol. 18 a), this is somewhat similar to No. 1109, though the latter is much shorter.

1126 大比丘三千威儀
Tâ-pi-*kh*iu-sân-tshien-wêi-i.
'Mahâbhikshu-trisahasra-karma (?).'

Translated by Ân Shi-kâo, A.D. 148–170, of the Eastern Hân dynasty, A.D. 25–220. 2 fasciculi. Deest in Tibetan. *K'*-yuen-lu, fasc. 8, fol. 18 b.

1127 根本薩婆多部律攝
Kan-pan-sâ-pho-to-pu-lüh-shö.
'Mûlasarvâstivâda-nikâya-vinaya-saṅgraha.'
Sarvâstivâda-vinaya-saṅgraha.

K'-yuen-lu, fasc. 8, fol. 17 b; Conc. 269. Compiled by the venerable *G*inamitra. Translated by I-tsiṅ, A.D. 700, of the Thâṅ dynasty, A.D. 618–907. 14 fasciculi. It agrees with Tibetan. *K'*-yuen-lu, s. v.

1128 四分僧羯磨
Sz'-fan-saṅ-*k*iê-mo.
'*Katurvarga*(-vinaya)-saṅgha-karman.'
Dharmagupta-bhikshu-karman.

Conc. 548. Compiled by Kwâi-su, disciple of Hiouen-thsang, of the Thâṅ dynasty, A.D. 618–907. 5 fasciculi; 17 chapters. This is an extract from No. 1117. It agrees with Tibetan. *K'*-yuen-lu, fasc. 8, fol. 16 a.

1129 四分比丘尼羯磨法
Sz'-fan-pi-*kh*iu-ni-*k*iê-mo-fâ.
'*Katurvarga*(-vinaya)-bhikshuṇî-karmavâkâ.'
Dharmagupta-bhikshuṇî-karman.

Conc. 549. Translated by Guṇavarman, A.D. 431, of the earlier Suṅ dynasty, A.D. 420–479. 1 fasciculi. This is an extract from No. 1117. Deest in Tibetan. *K'*-yuen-lu, fasc. 8, fol. 15 b.

1130 戒因緣經
*K*iê-yin-yuen-*k*iṅ.
Vinayanidâna-sûtra.

Conc. 276. Translated by *K*u Fo-nien, A.D. 378, of the latter Tshin dynasty, A.D. 384–417, under the Former Tshin dynasty, A.D. 350–394. 10 fasciculi. Deest in Tibetan. *K'*-yuen-lu, fasc. 8, fol. 18 a.

1131 根本說一切有部百一羯磨
Kan-pan-shwo-yi-tshiê-yiu-pu-pâi-yi-*k*iê-mo.
Mûlasarvâstivâdaikaśatakarman.

Conc. 257. Translated by I-tsiṅ, A.D. 703, of the Thâṅ dynasty, A.D. 618–907. 10 fasciculi. Deest in Tibetan. *K'*-yuen-lu, fasc. 8, fol. 15 a.

1132 薩婆多部毗尼摩得勒伽
Sâ-pho-to-pu-phi-ni-mo-töh-lö-*k*iâ.
Sarvâstivâda-nikâya-vinaya-mâtrikâ.

Cf. Conc. 442. Translated by Saṅghavarman, A.D. 445, of the earlier Suṅ dynasty, A.D. 420–479. 10 fasciculi. It agrees with Tibetan. *K'*-yuen-lu, fasc. 8, fol. 17 b.

The following two works were translated by I-tsiṅ, A.D. 703, of the Thâṅ dynasty, A.D. 618–907:—

1133 根本說一切有部尼陀那
Kan-pan-shwo-yi-tshiê-yiu-pu-ni-tho-nâ.
Mûlasarvâstivâda-nikâya-nidâna.

Cf. Conc. 260. 5 fasciculi.

1134 根本說一切有部目得迦
Kan-pan-shwo-yi-tshiê-yiu-pu-mu-töh-*k*iâ.
Mûlasarvâstivâda-nikâya-mâtrikâ.

Cf. Conc. 260. 5 fasciculi.

The above two works are similar to Tibetan, but the latter is shorter. Nos. 1118, 1121, 1124, 1133, and 1134 are somewhat different from No. 1115. *K'*-yuen-lu, fasc. 8, fol. 12 a.

The following two works were translated under the three Tshin dynasties, A.D. 350–431; but the translators' names are lost:—

1135 薩婆多毗尼毗婆沙
Sâ-pho-to-phi-ni-phi-pho-shâ.
Sarvâstivâda-vinaya-vibhâshâ.

Conc. 502. 8 fasciculi.

1136 續薩婆多毗尼毗婆沙
Suh-sâ-pho-to-phi-ni-phi-pho-shâ.
'A continuation of the Sarvâstivâda-vinaya-vibhâshâ.'

1 fasciculus.

The above two works are wanting in Tibetan. *K'*-yuen-lu, fasc. 8, fol. 18 b.

1137 根本說一切有部出家授近圓羯磨儀範
Kan-pan-shwo-yi-tshiê-yiu-pu-*kh*u-*k*iâ-sheu-*k*in-yuen-*k*iê-mo-i-fân.
'Mûlasarvâstivâda-nikâya-pravragyâ-upasampadâ-karmavâkâ (?).'

Compiled by Pâszepa (Bâshpa), A.D. 1271, of the Yuen dynasty, which dynasty was established in A.D. 1260, and was the sole ruler of China from A.D. 1280 till 1368. 1 fasciculus, with an appendix on brief rules for the learning and practice of a Bhikshu.

1138 毗尼母論
Phi-ni-mu-lun.
'Vinaya-mâtrikâ-sâstra.'

Translated under the (three) Tshin dynasties, A.D. 350–431; but the translator's name is lost. 8 fasciculi.

1139 律二十二明了論
Lüh-'rh-shi-'rh-miṅ-liâo-lun.
'Vinaya-dvâvimsati-prasannârtha (?)-sâstra.'

Composed by Buddhatrâta, of the Sammatîya-nikâya. Translated by Paramârtha, A.D. 568, of the *Kh*an dynasty, A.D. 557–589. 1 fasciculus. There are 22 verses, each comprising a clear meaning of the principle of the Vinayapitaka.

The above two works are wanting in Tibetan. *K'*-yuen-lu, fasc. 8, fol. 18 b.

The following two works were translated by I-tsiṅ, A.D. 710, of the Thâṅ dynasty, A.D. 618–907:—

1140 根本說一切有部毗奈耶尼陀那目得迦攝頌
Kan-pan-shwo-yi-tshiê-yiu-pu-phi-nâi-ye-ni-tho-nâ-mu-töh-*k*iâ-shö-suṅ.
Mûlasarvâstivâda-nikâya-vinaya-nidâna-mât*r*ikâ-gâthâ.

Cf. Conc. 263. 15 leaves.

1141 根本說一切有部毗奈耶雜事攝頌
Kan-pan-shwo-yi-tshiê-yiu-pu-phi-nâi-ye-tsâ-sh'-shö-suṅ.
'Mûlasarvâstivâda-nikâya-vinaya-samyuktavastu-gâthâ.'

10 leaves.

The above two works agree with Tibetan. *K'*-yuen-lu, fasc. 9, fol. 20 b.

1142 普賢菩薩行願讃
Phu-hhien-phu-sâ-hhiṅ-yuen-tsan.
'Samantabhadra-bodhisattva-*k*aryâ-pranidhâna-stotra.'
Bhadra*k*arî-pra*n*idhâna.

Translated by Amoghavagra, A.D. 746–771, of the Thâṅ dynasty, A.D. 618–907. 7 leaves. It consists of 62 verses and a Mantra. Deest in Tibetan. *K'*-yuen-lu, fasc. 6, fol. 16 b, where this work is properly mentioned under the heading of the Mahâyâna-sûtras. For the Sanskrit text, see Catalogue of the Hodgson Manuscripts, I. 33, and Catal. Bodl. Japan., No. 56. No. 1142 is a later translation of the 62 verses of No. 89.

1143 根本說一切有部毗奈耶頌
Kan-pan-shwo-yi-tshiê-yiu-pu-phi-nâi-ye-suṅ.
Mûlasarvâstivâda-nikâya-vinaya-gâthâ.

Cf. Conc. 262. Composed by the venerable Visâkhya. Translated by I-tsiṅ, A.D. 710, of the Thâṅ dynasty, A.D. 618–907. 4 fasciculi. It agrees with Tibetan. *K'*-yuen-lu, fasc. 8, fol. 17 a.

1144 十誦律毗尼序
Shi-suṅ-lüh-phi-ni-sü.
'Dasâdhyâya-vinaya-nidâna (?),' or 'the preface to the Dasâdhyâya-vinaya.'

Translated by Vimalâkshas, A.D. 405–418, of the Eastern Tsin dynasty, A.D. 317–420. 3 fasciculi. This is a continuation of No. 1115.

1145 沙彌十戒法并威儀
Shâ-mi-shi-*k*iâ-fâ-piṅ-wêi-i.
'Srâmanera-dasasîla (or sikshâpada)-dharma-karmavâkâ (?).'

Translated under the Eastern Tsin dynasty, A.D. 317–420; but the translator's name is lost. 1 fasciculus.

1146 羯磨
*K*iê-mo.
'Karman,' of the Dharmagupta-nikâya.

Compiled or translated by Thân-ti (Dharmasatya?), A.D. 254, of the Wêi dynasty, A.D. 220–265. 2 fasciculi; 9 sections. This is an earlier translation of an extract from No. 1117.

1147 佛說大愛道比丘尼經
Fo-shwo-tâ-âi-tâo-pi-*kh*iu-ni-*k*iṅ.
'Buddhabhâshita-mahâpragâpatî-bhikshunî-sûtra.'

Translated under the Northern Liâṅ dynasty, A.D. 397–439; but the translator's name is lost. 2 fasciculi.

1148 佛說目連問戒律中五百輕重事經
Fo-shwo-mu-lien-wan-*k*iê-lüh-*k*uṅ-wu-pâi-*kh*iṅ-*k*uṅ-sh'-*k*iṅ.
'Sûtra spoken by Buddha at the request of Maudgalyâyana on 500 light and heavy matters concerning the Vinaya.'

Translated under the Eastern Tsin dynasty, A. D. 317–420; but the translator's name is lost. 2 fasciculi; 17 chapters. According to the *K'*-tsiṅ (fasc. 33, fol. 10 b), this work is doubtful, as it differs from all other works on the Vinaya.

The above four works are wanting in Tibetan. *K'*-yuen-lu, fasc. 8, fol. 14 b seq..

1149 根本說一切有部苾芻尼戒經

Kan-pan-shwo-yi-tshiê-yiu-pu-pi-*kh*u-ni-*k*iê-*k*iṅ.

Mûlasarvâstivâda (-nikâya)-bhikshu*n*î-vinaya (or prâtimoksha)-sûtra. Conc. 256.

Bhikshu*n*î-pratimoksha-sûtra (?).

A. R., p. 43; A. M. G., p. 146. Translated by I-tsiṅ, A. D. 710, of the Thâṅ dynasty, A. D. 618–907. 2 fasciculi.

1150 比丘尼僧祇律波羅提木叉戒經

Pi-*kh*iu-ni-saṅ-*kh*i-lüh-po-lo-thi-mu-*kh*â-*k*iê-*k*iṅ.

'Bhikshu*n*î-saṅghikavinaya-prâtimoksha-sûtra.'

Mahâsaṅgha-bhikshu*n*î-vinaya.

Conc. 514. Translated by Fâ-hhien (Fâ-hian), together with Buddhabhadra, A. D. 414, of the Eastern Tsin dynasty, A. D. 317–420. 1 fasciculus.

The above two works agree with Tibetan. *K'*-yuen-lu, fasc. 8, fol. 13 a, b.

1151 沙彌尼戒經

Shâ-mi-ni-*k*iê-*k*iṅ.

'*S*ramaṇerikâ-sîla (or prâtimoksha)-sûtra.'

Translated under the Eastern Hân dynasty, A. D. 25–220; but the translator's name is lost. 5 leaves. Deest in Tibetan. *K'*-yuen-lu, fasc. 8, fol. 14 b.

1152 舍利弗問經

Shö-li-fu-wan-*k*iṅ.

*S*âriputra-paripri*kkh*â-sûtra.

Conc. 50. Translated under the Eastern Tsin dynasty, A. D. 317–420; but the translator's name is lost. 12 leaves. It agrees with Tibetan. *K'*-yuen-lu, fasc. 8, fol. 15 a.

1153 彌沙塞羯磨本

Mi-shâ-sö-*k*iê-mo-pan.

Mahî*s*âsaka-karman.

Conc. 343. Compiled by Âi-thuṅ, about A. D. 700, of the Thâṅ dynasty, A. D. 618–907. 2 fasciculi. This is an extract from No. 1122. Deest in Tibetan. *K'*-yuen-lu, fasc. 8, fol. 15 b.

1154 四分戒本

Sz'-fan-*k*iê-pan.

'*K*aturvarga(-vinaya)-prâtimoksha,' or Prâtimoksha of the Dharmagupta-nikâya.

Compiled by Kwâi-su, disciple of Hiouen-thsang, of the Thâṅ dynasty, A. D. 618–907. 1 fasciculus. This is an extract from No. 1117; and cf. No. 1155.

1155 The same title as No. 1154.

Translated by Buddhayasas, A. D. 403–413, of the Latter Tshin dynasty, A. D. 384–417. 1 fasciculus. An English translation of No. 1155 is given by Mr. Beal in his Catena of Buddhist Scriptures from the Chinese, pp. 206–239.

1156 四分比丘尼戒本

Sz'-fan-pi-*kh*iu-ni-*k*iê-pan.

'*K*aturvarga(-vinaya)-bhikshu*n*î-prâtimoksha,' or Bhikshu*n*î-prâtimoksha of the Dharmagupta-nikâya.

Compiled by Kwâi-su, disciple of Hiouen-thsang, of the Thâṅ dynasty, A. D. 618–907. 2 fasciculi. This is an extract from No. 1117.

1157 五分戒本

Wu-fan-*k*iê-pan.

'Pañ*k*avarga(-vinaya)-prâtimoksha,' or Prâtimoksha of the Mahî*s*âsaka-nikâya.

Translated by Buddha*g*îva, A. D. 423–424, of the earlier Suṅ dynasty, A. D. 420–479. 1 fasciculus.

1158 五分比丘尼戒本

Wu-fan-pi-*kh*iu-ni-*k*iê-pan.

'Pañ*k*avarga(-vinaya)-bhikshu*n*î-prâtimoksha,' or Bhikshu*n*î-prâtimoksha of the Mahî*s*âsaka-nikâya.

Compiled by Miṅ-hwui, A. D. 522, of the Liâṅ dynasty, A. D. 502–557.

The above two works are extracts from No. 1122.

1159 波羅提木叉僧祇戒本

Po-lo-thi-mu-*kh*â-saṅ-*kh*i-*k*iê-pan.

'Prâtimoksha-saṅghika-vinayamûla.'

Translated by Buddhabhadra, about A. D. 416, of the Eastern Tsin dynasty, A. D. 317–420. 1 fasciculus. This is an extract from No. 1119.

1160 十誦律比丘戒本

Shi-suṅ-lüh-pi-*kh*iu-*k*iê-pan.

'Dasâdhyâya-vinaya-bhikshu-pratimoksha,' or Pratimoksha of the Sarvâstivâda-nikâya.

Pratimoksha-sûtra (?).

A. R., p. 43; A. M. G., p. 146. Translated by Kumâra*g*îva, about A. D. 404, of the Latter Tshin dynasty, A. D. 384–417. 1 fasciculus.

1161 十誦律比丘尼戒本

Shi-suṅ-lüh-pi-*kh*iu-ni-*k*iê-pan.

'Dasâdhyâya-vinaya-bhikshunî-pratimoksha,' or Pratimoksha of the Sarvâstivâda-nikâya.

Bhikshunî-pratimoksha-sûtra (?).

A. R., p. 43; A. M. G., p. 146. Compiled by Fâ-yiṅ, of the earlier Suṅ dynasty, A. D. 420–479. 1 fasciculus.

1162 大沙門百一羯磨法

Tâ-shâ-man-pâi-yi-*k*iê-mo-fâ.

'Mahâsrâmanaikasatakarmavâkâ.'

Translated under the earlier Suṅ dynasty, A. D. 420–479; but the translator's name is lost. 1 fasciculus.

The above three works are extracts from No. 1115.

The above nine works agree with Tibetan. *K'*-yuen-lu, fasc. 8, fol. 13 a seq.

1163 曇無德律部雜羯磨

Thân-wu-töh-lüh-pu-tsâ-*k*iê-mo.

'Dharmagupta-vinaya-nikâya-samyukta-karman.'

Cf. No. 1146. Translated by Khâṅ Saṅ-khâi (Saṅghavarman), A. D. 252, of the Wêi dynasty, A. D. 220–265. 2 fasciculi.

1164 沙彌威儀

Shâ-mi-wêi-i.

'*Sramanera-karmavâkâ* (?).'

Cf. No. 1145. Translated by Gunavarman, A. D. 431, of the earlier Suṅ dynasty, A. D. 420–479. 11 leaves.

1165 沙彌尼離 (for 雜) 戒文

Shâ-mi-ni-li (for tsâ)-*k*iê-wan.

'*Sramanerikâ-sîla-bheda* (for samyukta)-vâkâ (?).'

Cf. No. 1151. Translated under the Eastern Tsin dynasty, A. D. 317–420; but the translator's name is lost. 5 leaves. For the correction of the fourth character of the title, see *K'*-yuen-lu, fasc. 8, fol. 14 b.

The above three works are wanting in Tibetan. *K'*-yuen-lu, s. v.

1166 十誦羯磨比丘要用

Shi-suṅ-*k*iê-mo-pi-*kh*iu-yâo-yuṅ.

'An important use for the Bhikshu concerning the Karman of the Dasâdhyâya(-vinaya).'

Compiled by Saṅ-*kh*ü, of the earlier Suṅ dynasty, A. D. 420–479. 1 fasciculus; 20 sections. This is an extract from No. 1115. It agrees with Tibetan. *K'*-yuen-lu, fasc. 8, fol. 15 a.

THIRD DIVISION.

論藏 Lun-tsâṅ, or Abhidharma-piṭaka.

PART I.

大乘論 Tâ-shaṅ-lun, or the Abhidharma of the Mahâyâna.

1167 金剛般若波羅蜜經論
*K*in-kâṅ-pân-*z*o-po-lo-mi-*k*iṅ-lun.
'Vagra(*kkh*edikâ)-pragñâpâramitâ-sûtra-sâstra.'
Va*g*ra*kkh*edikâ-sûtra-sâstra.

K'-yuen-lu, fasc. 8, fol. 23 a; Conc. 286. This is a commentary on Nos. 10–15, compiled by the Bodhisattva Asaṅga. Translated by Dharmagupta, A. D. 590–616, of the Sui dynasty, A. D. 589–618. 3 fasciculi.

1168 The same title as No. 1167.

Conc. 285. This is a commentary on No. 1167, compiled by the Bodhisattva Vasubandhu. Translated by Bodhiruki, A. D. 509, of the Northern Wêi dynasty, A. D. 386–534. 3 fasciculi. 'This work explains the Sûtra and Asaṅga's verses on it, and makes twenty-seven doubtful questions clear.' *K*'-tsiṅ, fasc. 34, fol. 9 b.

The above two works agree with Tibetan. *K*'-yuen-lu, fasc. 8, fol. 23 a, b.

1169 大智度論
Tâ-*k*'-tu-lun.
'Mahâpragñâpâramitâ(-sûtra)-sâstra.'

This is a commentary on Nos. 1 (b), 2–4, compiled by the Bodhisattva Nâgâr*g*una. Translated by Kumâra*g*îva, A. D. 402–405, of the Latter Tshin dynasty, A. D. 384–417. 100 fasciculi. It is stated in the preface by Saṅ-zui, disciple of the translator, that the Sanskrit text of this *S*âstra consists of 100,000 slokas in verse, or a corresponding number of syllables in prose; but the first chapter of the *S*âstra only is fully translated in the first 34 fasciculi, while an abstract is given of the remaining 89 chapters. Deest in Tibetan. *K*'-yuen-lu, fasc. 8, fol. 21 b. No. 1169 is generally, in short, called Tâ-lun ('great *S*âstra'), *K*'-lun, or *K*'-tu-lun.

1170 瑜伽師地論
Yü-*k*iê-sh'-ti-lun.
Yogâ*k*âryabhûmi-sâstra. Conc. 876.
Saptadasabhûmi-sâstra-yogâ*k*âryabhûmi.

K'-yuen-lu, fasc. 8, fol. 26 a. Addressed by the Bodhisattva Maitreya (to Asaṅga). Translated by Hhüen-*k*wâṅ (Hiouen-thsang), A. D. 646–647, of the Thâṅ dynasty, A. D. 618–907. 100 fasciculi; 5 divisions; 17 Bhûmis in the first division. The Sanskrit text consists of 40,000 slokas in verse, or a corresponding number of syllables in prose. It agrees with Tibetan. *K*'-yuen-lu, s. v. This is the principal work of the Yogâ*k*ârya school founded by Asaṅga.

1171 攝大乘論釋
Shö-tâ-shaṅ-lun-shih.
'Mahâyânasamparigraha-sâstra-vyâkhyâ.'

48 fasciculi. Deest in Tibetan. *K*'-yuen-lu, fasc. 9, fol. 3 a seq. No. 1171 is a collection of four different translations of two Vyâkhyâs or commentaries on Asaṅga's Mahâyânasamparigraha-sâstra (Nos. 1183, 1184, 1247). The following is a list of the four translations:—

(1) Translation by Hhüen-*k*wâṅ (Hiouen-thsang), A. D. 647–649, of the commentary by the Bodhisattva Wu-siṅ ('without-nature,' or 'Agotra?'). 10 fasciculi (fasc. 1–10).

(2) Translation by Paramârtha, A. D. 563, of the commentary by the Bodhisattva Vasubandhu. 18 fasciculi (fasc. 11–20, 41–48).

(3) Translation by Dharmagupta, A. D. 590–616, of the same commentary as before. 10 fasciculi (fasc. 21–30).

(4) Translation by Hhüen-*k*wâṅ (Hiouen-thsang), A.D. 648–649, of the same commentary as before. 10 fasciculi (fasc. 31–40).

Thus the latter three works are similar translations, but Paramârtha's version (2) has an additional part in 8 fasciculi (fasc. 41–48).

1172 無相思塵論
Wu-siâṅ-sz'-*kh*an-lun.
'Anâkâra-*k*intâ-ragas (?)-sâstra,' or '*Sâstra on the dust of shapeless thought.*'

Composed by the Bodhisattva *G*ina. Translated by Paramârtha, A.D. 557–569, of the *Kh*an dynasty, A.D. 557–589. 4 leaves.

1173 觀所緣緣論
Kwân-su-yuen-yuen-lun.
'Âlambanapratyayadhyâna-sâstra.'

Composed by the Bodhisattva *G*ina. Translated by Hhüen-*k*wâṅ (Hiouen-thsang), A.D. 657, of the Thâṅ dynasty, A.D. 618–907. 3 leaves.

The above two works are similar translations, and they agree with Tibetan. *K*'-yuen-lu, fasc. 9, fol. 9 b.

1174 觀所緣緣論釋
Kwân-su-yuen-yuen-lun-shih.
'Âlambanapratyayadhyâna-sâstra-vyâkhyâ,' i. e. a commentary on No. 1173.

Compiled by the Bodhisattva Dharmapâla. Translated by I-tsiṅ, A.D. 710, of the Thâṅ dynasty, A.D. 618–907. 11 leaves. It agrees with Tibetan. *K*'-yuen-lu, fasc. 9, fol. 9 b.

1175 大乘廣五蘊論
Tâ-shaṅ-kwâṅ-wu-yun-lun.
'Mahâyânavaipulya-pañ*k*askandha-sâstra.'
Pañ*k*askandhavaipulya-sâstra.

Conc. 574. This is a commentary on No. 1176, compiled by the Bodhisattva Sthitamati. Translated by Divâkara, A.D. 685, of the Thâṅ dynasty, A.D. 618–907. 17 leaves. Deest in Tibetan. *K*'-yuen-lu, fasc. 9, fol. 8 a.

1176 大乘五蘊論
Tâ-shaṅ-wu-yun-lun.
'Mahâyâna-pañ*k*askandha-sâstra.'
Pañ*k*askandhaka-sâstra.

K'-yuen-lu, fasc. 9, fol. 8 a; Conc. 578. Composed by the Bodhisattva Vasubandhu. Translated by Hhüen-*k*wâṅ (Hiouen-thsang), A.D. 647, of the Thâṅ dynasty, A.D. 618–907. 10 leaves. It agrees with Tibetan. *K*'-yuen-lu, fasc. 9, fol. 8 a.

1177 顯揚聖教論
Hhien-yâṅ-shaṅ-*k*iâo-lun.
'Prakaranâryavâkâ (?)-sâstra,' or '*Sâstra on expounding the holy teaching.*'

Composed by the Bodhisattva Asaṅga. Translated by Hhüen-*k*wâṅ (Hiouen-thsang), A.D. 645–646, of the Thâṅ dynasty, A.D. 618–907. 20 fasciculi; 11 chapters. This *Sâstra* contains the principles of No. 1170.

1178 大乘阿毗達磨雜集論
Tâ-shaṅ-ŏ-phi-tâ-mo-tsâ-tsi-lun.
'Mahâyânâbhidharma-samyuktasaṅgîti-sâstra.'

This is a commentary on No. 1199, compiled by the Bodhisattva Sthitamati. Translated by Hhüen-*k*wâṅ (Hiouen-thsang), A.D. 646, of the Thâṅ dynasty, A.D. 618–907. 16 fasciculi.

The above two works are wanting in Tibetan. *K*'-yuen-lu, fasc. 8, fol. 26 b seq.

1179 中論
*K*uṅ-lun.
'Madhyamaka-sâstra.'
Prâ*n*yamûla-sâstra-*t*îkâ.

K'-yuen-lu, fasc. 8, fol. 27 b; Conc. 711. Composed by the Bodhisattvas Nâgârgunas and Nila*k*akshus (? 'blue-eye,' or Piṅgalanetra), the latter explaining 500 verses of the former. Translated by Kumâra*g*îva, A.D. 409, of the Latter Tshin dynasty, A.D. 384–417. 4 fasciculi; 27 chapters. It agrees with Tibetan. *K*'-yuen-lu, s. v. This is the principal work of the Madhyamika school, founded by Nâgâr*g*una.

1180 十住毗婆沙論
Shi-*k*u-phi-pho-shâ-lun.
'Dasabhûmi-vibhâshâ-sâstra.'

This is a commentary on the first two of the ten Bhûmis in Nos. 87 (chap. 22), 88 (chap. 26), 105, 110, compiled by the Bodhisattva Nâgâr*g*una. Translated by Kumâra*g*îva, about A.D. 405, of the Latter Tshin dynasty, A.D. 384–417. 15 fasciculi; 35 chapters. In the ninth chapter, Nâgâr*g*una explains the doctrine of Amitâyus or Amitâbha as taught by Buddha in Nos. 23 (5), 25, 26, 27, 863. Nâgâr*g*una is therefore looked upon as the first patriarch after Buddha in teaching this doctrine. Deest in Tibetan. *K*'-yuen-lu, fasc. 9, fol. 1 a.

1181 菩提資糧論
Phu-thi-tsz'-liâṅ-lun.
'Sâstra on the provision for (obtaining) the Bodhi.'

Composed by the Bodhisattva Nâgârguna, and explained by the Bhikshu Îsvara. Translated by Dharmagupta, A. D. 590-616, of the Sui dynasty, A. D. 589-618. 6 fasciculi.

1182 大莊嚴經論
Tâ-kwâṅ-yen-kiṅ-lun.
'Mahâlaṅkâra-sûtra-sâstra.'
Sûtrâlaṅkâra-sâstra.

K'-yuen-lu, fasc. 9, fol. 2 a; Conc. 656. Composed by the Bodhisattva Asvaghosha. Translated by Kumâragîva, about A. D. 405, of the Latter Tshin dynasty, A. D. 384-417. 15 fasciculi. Some extracts from No. 1182 are given by Mr. Beal, in his Buddhist Literature in China, pp. 31, 101, 105.

1183 攝大乘論
Shö-tâ-shaṅ-lun.
Mahâyânasamparigraha-sâstra.

Eitel, Handbook, p. 68 b. Composed by the Bodhisattva Asaṅga. Translated by Paramârtha, A. D. 563, of the Khan dynasty, A. D. 557-589. 3 fasciculi.

1184 The same title as No. 1183.

Translated by Buddhasânta, A. D. 531, of the Northern Wei dynasty, A. D. 386-534. 2 fasciculi.

The above four works agree with Tibetan. Nos. 1183 and 1184 are similar translations. K'-yuen-lu, fasc. 9, fol. 1 b seq.

1185 般若燈論
Pân-zo-taṅ-lun.
'Pragñâdîpa-sâstra.'
Pragñâpradîpa-sâstra-kârikâ (or -vyâkhyâ?).

Conc. 402. Composed by the Bodhisattvas Nâgârguna and Nirdesaprabha (? 'distinct-brightness,' or Piṅgalanetra), the latter explaining 500 verses of the former. Translated by Prabhâkaramitra, A. D. 630-632, of the Thâṅ dynasty, A. D. 618-907. 15 fasciculi; 27 chapters. Deest in Tibetan. K'-yuen-lu, fasc. 8, fol. 27 b, where it is stated that Nâgârguna's text is the same as that of No. 1179, and this commentary is different from that of No. 1179. But No. 1185 may be a later and fuller translation of No. 1179.

1186 十二門論
Shi-'rh-man-lun.
Dvâdasanikâya (or -mukha)-sâstra.

Conc. 69. Composed by the Bodhisattva Nâgârguna. Translated by Kumâragîva, A. D. 408, of the Latter Tshin dynasty, A. D. 384-417. 1 fasciculus.

1187 十八空論
Shi-pâ-khuṅ-lun.
Ashtâdasâkâsa (or °dasa-sûnyatâ)-sâstra.

Conc. 79. Composed by the Bodhisattva Nâgârguna. Translated by Paramârtha, A. D. 557-569, of the Khan dynasty, A. D. 557-589. 1 fasciculus.

1188 百論
Pâi-lun.
Sata-sâstra.

Eitel, Handbook, p. 126 b. Composed by the Bodhisattvas Deva and Vasubandhu, the latter explaining the text of the former. Translated by Kumâragîva, A. D. 404, of the Latter Tshin dynasty, A. D. 384-417. 2 fasciculi; 10 chapters.

1189 廣百論本
Kwâṅ-pâi-lun-pan.
Sata-sâstra-vaipulya.

Eitel, Handbook, p. 126 b. Composed by the Bodhisattva Deva. Translated by Hhüen-kwâṅ (Hiouen-thsang), A. D. 650, of the Thâṅ dynasty, A. D. 618-907. 1 fasciculus; 8 chapters.

The above four works are wanting in Tibetan. K'-yuen-lu, fasc. 8, fol. 28 a, b.

1190 大乘莊嚴經論
Tâ-shaṅ-kwâṅ-yen-kiṅ-lun.
'Mahâyânâlaṅkâra-sûtra-sâstra.'
Sûtrâlaṅkâra-tîkâ.

K'-yuen-lu, fasc. 9, fol. 1 b; Conc. 591. Composed by the Bodhisattva Asaṅga. Translated by Prabhâkaramitra, A. D. 630-633, of the Thâṅ dynasty, A. D. 618-907. 13 fasciculi; 24 chapters. It agrees with Tibetan. K'-yuen-lu, s. v.

1191 文殊師利菩薩問菩提經論
Wan-shu-sh'-li-phu-sâ-wan-phu-thi-kiṅ-lun.
'Mañgusrî-bodhisattva-paripriKkhâ-bodhi-sûtra-sâstra.'
Gayâsîrsha-sûtra-tîkâ.

This is a commentary on Nos. 238-241, compiled by the Bodhisattva Vasubandhu. Translated by Bodhiruki, A. D. 535, of the Northern Wei dynasty, A. D. 386-534. 2 fasciculi.

1192 金剛般若波羅蜜經破取著不壞假名論

*K*in-kâṅ-pân-zo-po-lo-mi-*k*iṅ-po-tshü-*k*u-pu-hwâi-*k*iâ-miṅ-lun.

'Va*gr*a(*kkh*edikâ)-pra*gñ*âpâramitâ-sûtra-sâstra, on the refutation of grasping and attachment to the undestroyed and artificial name.'

Composed by the Bodhisattva Gu*n*ada (?). Translated by Divâkara, A.D. 683, of the Thâṅ dynasty, A.D. 618–907. 2 fasciculi. Deest in Tibetan. *K*'-yuen-lu, fasc. 8, fol. 23 b. For the Sûtra, see Nos. 10–15.

1193 勝思惟梵天所問經論

Shaṅ-sz'-wêi-fân-thien-su-wan-*k*iṅ-lun.

Vi*s*esha*k*inta-brâhma*n*a (or -brahma)-pari*prikkh*â-sûtra-*t*îkâ (or -*s*âstra).

K'-yuen-lu, fasc. 8, fol. 24 b; Conc. 111. This is a commentary on Nos. 189, 190, compiled by the Bodhisattva Vasubandhu. Translated by Bodhiru*k*i, A.D. 531, of the Northern Wêi dynasty, A.D. 386–534. 3 fasciculi.

1194 十地經論

Shi-ti-*k*iṅ-lun.

Dasabhûmika(-sûtra)-sâstra.

K'-yuen-lu, fasc. 8, fol. 21 b; Conc. 91. This is a commentary on Nos. 87 (chap. 22), 88 (chap. 26), 105, 110, compiled by the Bodhisattva Vasubandhu. Translated by Bodhiru*k*i, A.D. 508–511, of the Northern Wêi dynasty, A.D. 386–534. 12 fasciculi.

1195 佛地經論

Fo-ti-*k*iṅ-lun.

Buddhabhûmi-sûtra-*s*âstra.

K'-yuen-lu, fasc. 8, fol. 22 b; Conc. 170. This is a commentary on No. 502, compiled by the Bodhisattva Bandhuprabha (? or Prabhâmitra, see Conc. 170) and others. Translated by Hhüen-*k*wâṅ (Hiouen-thsang), A.D. 649, of the Thâṅ dynasty, A.D. 618–907. 7 fasciculi.

The above three works agree with Tibetan. *K*'-yuen-lu, s.v.

1196 三具足經優波提舍

Sân-*k*ü-tsu-*k*iṅ-yiu-po-thi-shö.

'Tripûr*n*a-sûtropadesa.'

Composed by the Bodhisattva Vasubandhu. Translated by the *R*ishi Vimokshapra*gñ*a (?) and others, A.D. 541, of the Eastern Wêi dynasty, A.D. 534–550. 1 fasciculus. Deest in Tibetan. *K*'-yuen-lu, fasc. 8, fol. 25 b.

1197 成唯識論

*Kh*aṅ-wêi-shi-lun.

Vidyâmâtrasiddhi(-*s*âstra).

Eitel, Handbook, p. 166 a. Compiled by the Bodhisattva Dharmapâla and (nine) others. Translated by Hhüen-*k*wâṅ (Hiouen-thsang), A.D. 659, of the Thâṅ dynasty, A.D. 618–907. 10 fasciculi. This is the famous commentary on No. 1215, but the Sanskrit text is said to have consisted of ten different commentaries on the same text, No. 1215, by as many different authors. This translation is an abstract of the ten commentaries mixed together, which was made by the translator. See the preface by *Kh*an Hhüen-miṅ, a contemporary of the translator. 'In the Tibetan Catalogue, No. 1197 is said to agree with the Tibetan version, but the latter is not found.' *K*'-yuen-lu, fasc. 9, fol. 7 a.

1198 廣百論釋論

Kwâṅ-pâi-lun-shih-lun.

'Vaipulya-*s*ata-*s*âstra-vyâkhyâ.'

Composed by the Bodhisattvas Deva and Dharmapâla, the latter explaining the text of the former, i.e. No. 1189. Translated by Hhüen-*k*wâṅ (Hiouen-thsang), A.D. 650, of the Thâṅ dynasty, A.D. 618–907. 10 fasciculi; 8 chapters. Deest in Tibetan. *K*'-yuen-lu, fasc. 9, fol. 1 a.

1199 大乘阿毗達磨集論

Tâ-shaṅ-ŏ-phi-tâ-mo-tsi-lun.

Mahâyânâbhidharma-saṅgîti-*s*âstra.

Eitel, Handbook, p. 68 b. Composed by the Bodhisattva Asaṅga. Translated by Hhüen-*k*wâṅ (Hiouen-thsang), A.D. 652, of the Thâṅ dynasty, A.D. 618–907. 7 fasciculi; 2 divisions; 8 chapters.

1200 王法正理論

Wâṅ-fâ-*k*aṅ-li-lun.

'Râ*g*adharma-nyâya-*s*âstra.'

Composed (or spoken ?) by the Bodhisattva Maitreya. Translated by Hhüen-*k*wâṅ (Hiouen-thsang), A.D. 649, of the Thâṅ dynasty, A.D. 618–907. 1 fasciculus. This translation is similar to No. 1170, second division, second Bhûmi. *K*'-tsiṅ, fasc. 37, fol. 15 a.

1201 瑜伽師地論釋
Yü-kiê-sh'-ti-lun-shih.
Yogâkâryabhûmi-sâstra-kârikâ (or -vyâkhyâ).

Conc. 877. This is a brief commentary on No. 1170, compiled by the Bodhisattva Ginaputra and others. Translated by Hhüen-kwân (Hiouen-thsang), A.D. 654, of the Thân dynasty, A.D. 618–907. 1 fasciculus.

1202 顯揚聖教論頌
Hhien-yân-shan-kiâo-lun-sun.
'Prakaranâryavâkâ (?)-sâstra-kârikâ.'

Composed by the Bodhisattva Asaṅga. Translated by Hhüen-kwân (Hiouen-thsang), A.D. 645, of the Thân dynasty, A.D. 618–907. 1 fasciculus. This is the collection of the verses of No. 1177.

1203 彌勒菩薩所問經論
Mi-lö-phu-sâ-su-wan-kin-lun.
'Maitreya-bodhisattva-pariprikkhâ-sûtra-sâstra.'

This is a commentary on Nos. 23 (41), 54, but the compiler's name is unknown. Translated by Bodhiruki, A.D. 508–535, of the Northern Wêi dynasty, A.D. 386–534. 7 fasciculi.

The above five works are wanting in Tibetan. K'-yuen-lu, fasc. 8, fol. 22 a seq.

1204 無量壽經優波提舍
Wu-liân-sheu-kin-yiu-po-thi-shö.
'Amitâyus-sûtropadesa.'
Aparimitâyus-sûtra-sâstra.

K'-yuen-lu, fasc. 8, fol. 25 a; Conc. 832. This is a short treatise on Nos. 23 (5), 25, 26, 27, 863, composed by the Bodhisattva Vasubandhu. Translated by Bodhiruki, A.D. 529, of the Northern Wêi dynasty, A.D. 386–534. 9 leaves. It agrees with Tibetan. K'-yuen-lu, s.v. On account of the authorship of No. 1204, Vasubandhu is looked upon as the second patriarch in teaching the doctrine of Amitâyus or Amitâbha, Nâgârjuna being the first.

1205 轉法輪經優波提舍
Kwân-fâ-lun-kin-yiu-po-thi-shö.
'Dharmakakrapravartana-sûtropadesa.'

Composed by the Bodhisattva Vasubandhu. Translated by the Rishi Vimokshapragña (?) and others, A.D. 541, of the Eastern Wêi dynasty, A.D. 534–550. 12 leaves.

1206 大般涅槃經論
Tâ-pân-niê-phân-kin-lun.
'Mahâparinirvâna-sûtra-sâstra.'
Nirvâna-sâstra.

Wassiljew, p. 149. This is a short commentary on Nos. 113, 114, 120, compiled by the Bodhisattva Vasubandhu. Translated by Dharmabodhi, of the Northern or Eastern Wêi dynasty, A.D. 386–550. 12 leaves.

1207 涅槃經本有今無偈論
Niê-phân-kin-pan-yiu-kin-wu-kiê-lun.
'Nirvâna-sûtra-pûrvabhûtotpannâbhûta(?)-gâthâ-sâstra,' or 'Sâstra on the Gâthâ on the state of being formerly existing and now extinct (etc.) in the Nirvâna-sûtra (No. 113, fasc. 17).'

Composed by the Bodhisattva Vasubandhu. Translated by Paramârtha, A.D. 550, of the Liân dynasty, A.D. 502–557. 7 leaves.

The above three works are wanting in Tibetan. K'-yuen-lu, fasc. 8, fol. 24 b seq.

1208 能斷金剛般若波羅蜜多經論頌
Nan-twân-kin-kân-pân-zo-po-lo-mi-to-kin-lun-sun.
'Vagrakkhedikâ-pragñâpâramitâ-sûtra-sâstra-gâthâ (or -kârikâ).'

Composed by the Bodhisattva Asaṅga. Translated by I-tsin, A.D. 711, of the Thân dynasty, A.D. 618–907. 6 leaves. This is the collection of 77 verses explained in No. 1231.

1209 遺教經論
I-kiâo-kin-lun.
'Sâstra on the Sûtra of (Buddha's) last teaching (No. 122).'

Composed by the Bodhisattva Vasubandhu. Translated by Paramârtha, A.D. 557–569, of the Khan dynasty, A.D. 557–589. 1 fasciculus. Deest in Tibetan. K'-yuen-lu, fasc. 8, fol. 25 a.

1210 成唯識寶生論
Khan-wêi-shi-pâo-shan-lun.
'Vidyâmâtrasiddhi-ratnagâti-sâstra.'

This is a commentary on Nos. 1238, 1239, 1240, compiled by the Bodhisattva Dharmapâla. Translated by I-tsin, A.D. 710, of the Thân dynasty, A.D. 618–907. 5 fasciculi. Deest in Tibetan. K'-yuen-lu, fasc. 9, fol. 7 a.

1211 十二因緣論
Shi-'rh-yin-yuen-lun.
'Dvâdasa-nidâna-sâstra.'
Pratîtyasamutpâda-sâstra.

K'-yuen-lu, fasc. 9, fol. 10 b; Conc. 68. Composed by the Bodhisattva *S*uddhamati. Translated by Bodhiru*k*i, A.D. 508–535, of the Northern Wêi dynasty, A.D. 386–534. 4 leaves. It agrees with Tibetan. *K'*-yuen-lu, s.v.

1212 壹輸盧迦論
Yi-shu-lu-*k*iâ-lun.
'Ekasloka-sâstra.'

Composed by the Bodhisattva Nâgâr*g*una. Translated by Gautama Pra*g*ñâru*k*i, A.D. 538–543, of the Eastern Wêi dynasty, A.D. 534–550. 4 leaves. Deest in Tibetan. *K'*-yuen-lu, fasc. 9, fol. 10 b.

1213 大乘百法明門論
Tâ-shañ-pâi-fâ-miñ-man-lun.
'Mahâyâna-satadharmavidyâdvâra-sâstra.'

Composed by the Bodhisattva Vasubandhu. Translated by Hhüen-*k*wâñ (Hiouen-thsang), A.D. 648, of the Thâñ dynasty, A.D. 618–907. 2 leaves. This is a list of the technical terms used in the first division of No. 1170. It agrees with Tibetan. *K'*-yuen-lu, fasc. 9, fol. 12 a.

1214 轉識論
*K*wân-shi-lun.
'Vidyâpravartana-sâstra.'

Author's name unknown. Translated by Paramârtha, A.D. 557–569, of the *Kh*an dynasty, A.D. 557–589. 8 leaves. Deest in Tibetan. *K'*-yuen-lu, fasc. 9, fol. 6 a.

1215 唯識三十論
Wêi-shi-sân-shi-lun.
Vidyâmâtrasiddhi-tridasa-sâstra (or -trimsak-*kh*âstra)-kârikâ.

Eitel, Handbook, p. 166 a. Composed by the Bodhisattva Vasubandhu. Translated by Hhüen-*k*wâñ (Hiouen-thsang), A.D. 648, of the Thâñ dynasty, A.D. 618–907. 6 leaves. It consists of 30 verses explained in No. 1197. It agrees with Tibetan. *K'*-yuen-lu, fasc. 9, fol. 6 b.

1216 因明入正理論
Yin-miñ-*z*i-*k*añ-li-lun.
Hetuvidyâ-nyâyapravesa-sâstra.
Nyâyapravesatâraka-sâstra.

K'-yuen-lu, fasc. 9, fol. 5 b; Conc. 225. Composed by the Bodhisattva *S*añkarasvâmin (cf. the commentary on No. 1216, fasc. 1, fol. 6 a, by Kwhêi-*k*i, a disciple of Hiouen-thsang). Translated by Hhüen-*k*wâñ (Hiouen-thsang), A.D. 647, of the Thâñ dynasty, A.D. 618–907. 6 leaves. It agrees with Tibetan. *K'*-yuen-lu, s.v.

1217 顯識論
Hhien-shi-lun.
'Vidyânirdesa-sâstra.'

Author's name unknown. Translated by Paramârtha, A.D. 557–569, of the *Kh*an dynasty, A.D. 557–569. 15 leaves. Deest in Tibetan. *K'*-yuen-lu, fasc. 9, fol. 6 a.

1218 發菩提心論
Fâ-phu-thi-sin-lun.
'Bodhi*k*ittotpâdana-sâstra.'

Composed by the Bodhisattva Vasubandhu. Translated by Kumâra*g*îva, about A.D. 405, of the Latter Tsin dynasty, A.D. 384–417. 2 fasciculi. It agrees with Tibetan. *K'*-yuen-lu, fasc. 9, fol. 9 a.

1219 三無性論
Sân-wu-siñ-lun.
'Try-alakshana (?)-sâstra.'

Author's name unknown. Translated by Paramârtha, A.D. 557–569, of the *Kh*an dynasty, A.D. 557–589. 2 fasciculi. Deest in Tibetan. *K'*-yuen-lu, fasc. 9, fol. 9 a. The third character of the title is sometimes written 相 siâñ.

1220 佛性論
Fo-siñ-lun.
'Buddha-gotra-sâstra,' or 'Sâstra on Buddha's nature.'

Composed by the Bodhisattva Vasubandhu. Translated by Paramârtha, A.D. 557–569, of the *Kh*an dynasty, A.D. 557–589. 4 fasciculi. Deest in Tibetan. *K'*-yuen-lu, fasc. 9, fol. 3 b.

1221 大乘成業論
Tâ-shañ-*kh*añ-yeh-lun.
'Mahâyâna-karmasiddha-sâstra.'
Karmasiddhaprakara*n*a-sâstra.

K'-yuen-lu, fasc. 9, fol. 5 a; Conc. 590. Composed by the Bodhisattva Vasubandhu. Translated by Hhüen-*k*wâñ (Hiouen-thsang), A.D. 651, of the Thâñ dynasty, A.D. 618–907. 1 fasciculus.

1222 業成就論
Yeh-*kh*añ-tsui-lun.
Karmasiddhaprakara*n*a-sâstra.

Conc. 390. Composed by the Bodhisattva Vasubandhu. Translated by the *Rishi* Vimokshapra*gñ*a, A. D. 541, of the Eastern Wêi dynasty, A. D. 534–550. 1 fasciculus. It consists of 4,872 Chinese characters.

The above two works are similar translations, and they agree with Tibetan. *K'*-yuen-lu, fasc. 9, fol. 5 a.

1223 因明正理門論
Yin-miṅ-*k*aṅ-li-man-lun.
'Hetuvidyâ-nyâyadvâra-sâstra.'
Nyâyadvâratarka-*s*âstra.

K'-yuen-lu, fasc. 9, fol. 5 b. Composed by the Bodhisattva Nâgârguna. Translated by I-tsiṅ, A. D. 711, of the Thâṅ dynasty, A. D. 618–907. 1 fasciculus.

1224 因明正理門論本
Yin-miṅ-*k*aṅ-li-man-lun-pan.
'Hetuvidyâ-nyâyadvâra-sâstramûla.'
Nyâyadvâratarka-*s*âstra.

Conc. 226. Composed by the Bodhisattva Nâgâr*g*una. Translated by Hhüen-*k*wâṅ (Hiouen-thsang), A. D. 648, of the Thâṅ dynasty, A. D. 618–907. 1 fasciculus.

The above two works are similar translations. They agree with Tibetan. *K'*-yuen-lu, fasc. 9, fol. 5 b.

1225 止觀門論頌
K'-kwân-man-lun-suṅ.
'*S*amatha-vipassanâ (or -vidarsana)-dvâra-sâstra-kârikâ.'

Composed by the Bodhisattva Vasubandhu. Translated by I-tsiṅ, A. D. 711, of the Thâṅ dynasty, A. D. 618–907. 6 leaves. It consists of 77 verses. For the words *S*amatha and Vipassanâ, see Childers' Pâli Dictionary, pp. 429 and 580.

1226 手杖論
Sheu-*k*aṅ-lun.
'Hastada*n*da-sâstra.'

Composed by the venerable *S*âkyayasas. Translated by I-tsiṅ, A. D. 711, of the Thâṅ dynasty, A. D. 618–907. 8 leaves. It refutes the heretical belief in the existence of a newly-born being. *K'*-tsiṅ, fasc. 38, fol. 15 a.

1227 緣生論
Yuen-shaṅ-lun.
'Nidâna or pratîtyasamutpâda-sâstra.'

Composed by the venerable Ullaṅghya (?). Translated by Dharmagupta, A. D. 607, of the Sui dynasty, A. D. 589–618. 15 leaves.

1228 取因假設論
Tshü-yin-*k*iâ-shö-lun.
'Pra*gñ*âpti-hetu-saṅgraha (?)-sâstra.'

Composed by the Bodhisattva *G*ina. Translated by I-tsiṅ, A. D. 703, of the Thâṅ dynasty, A. D. 618–907. 10 leaves.

1229 觀總相論頌
Kwân-tsuṅ-siâṅ-lun-suṅ.
'Sarvalakshanadhyâna-sâstra-kârikâ.'

Composed by the Bodhisattva *G*ina. Translated by I-tsiṅ, A. D. 711, of the Thâṅ dynasty, A. D. 618–907. 1 leaf.

1230 六門教授習定論
Liu-man-*k*iâo-sheu-si-tiṅ-lun.
'Shaddvâropadish*t*a-dhyânavyavahâra (?)-sâstra.'

Composed by the Bodhisattvas Asaṅga and Vasubandhu, the latter explaining the text of the former. Translated by I-tsiṅ, A. D. 703, of the Thâṅ dynasty, A. D. 618–907. 12 leaves.

The above six works are wanting in Tibetan. *K'*-yuen-lu, fasc. 9, fol. 10 a seq.

1231 能斷金剛般若波羅蜜經論釋
Naṅ-twân-*k*in-kâṅ-pâṅ-*z*o-po-lo-mi-*k*iṅ-lun-shih.
Va*g*ra*kk*hedikâ-pra*gñ*âpâramitâ-sûtra-*s*âstra-(-vyâkhyâ).

Conc. 385. Composed by the Bodhisattvas Asaṅga and Vasubandhu, the latter explaining the text of the former (No. 1208). Translated by I-tsiṅ, A. D. 711, of the Thâṅ dynasty, A. D. 618–907. 3 fasciculi. This is a later translation of No. 1168, without quoting the Sûtra. *K'*-yuen-lu, fasc. 8, fol. 23 b; *K'*-tsiṅ, fasc. 34, fol. 9 b.

There is an appendix, added by I-tsiṅ, which is entitled 'A laudatory explanation of the last verse (in the Sûtra) which briefly illustrates the Pra*gñ*â,' in 5 leaves. This appendix is mentioned in the original Catalogue (Tâ-miṅ-sân-tsâṅ-shaṅ-*k*iâo-mu-lu, fasc. 3, fol. 15 b, col. 2) as an independent work, so as to be reckoned No. 1232. But it is merely the translator's own composition added to No. 1231; so that it is not mentioned separately in this Catalogue. Cf. *K'*-tsiṅ, fasc. 34, fol. 9 b.

1232 妙法蓮華經優波提舍
Miâo-fâ-lien-hwâ-*k*in-yiu-po-thi-shö.
'Saddharmapuṇḍarîka-sûtropadesa.'
Saddharmapu*nd*arîka-sûtra-*s*âstra.

K'-yuen-lu, fasc. 8, fol. 24 a; Conc. 130. This is a commentary on Nos. 134, 138, 139, compiled by the Bodhisattva Vasubandhu. Translated by Bodhiru*k*i, together with Thân-lin and others, A. D. 508–535, of the Northern Wêi dynasty, A. D. 386–534. 2 fasciculi.

1233 妙法蓮華經論優波提舍
Miâo-fâ-lien-hwâ-*k*in-lun-yiu-po-thi-shö.
'Saddharmapuṇḍarîka-sûtra-sâstropadesa.'
Saddharmapu*nd*arîka-sûtra-*s*âstra.

Conc. 355. This is the same commentary as No. 1232. Translated by Ratnamati, together with San-lân, A. D. 508, of the Northern Wêi dynasty, A. D. 386–534. 2 fasciculi.

The above two works are similar translations. They agree with Tibetan. *K'*-yuen-lu, fasc. 8, fol. 24 a, b.

1234 大寶積經論
Tâ-pâo-tsi-*k*in-lun.
'Mahâratnakûṭa-sûtra-sâstra.'
Ratnakû*t*a-*s*âstra.

K'-yuen-lu, fasc. 8, fol. 22 a; Conc. 580. This is a commentary on the forty-third Sûtra of No. 23 (fasc. 112), but the author's name is unknown. Translated by Bodhiru*k*i, A. D. 508–535, of the Northern Wêi dynasty, A. D. 386–534. 4 fasciculi. It agrees with Tibetan. *K'*-yuen-lu, s. v.; *K'*-tsin, fasc. 34, fol. 4 b.

1235 決定藏論
*K*iê-tin-tsân-lun.
'Vinirṇita (?)-piṭaka-sâstra.'

Spoken by the Bodhisattva Maitreya. Translated by Paramârtha, A. D. 557–569, of the *Kh*an dynasty, A. D. 557–589. 3 fasciculi. This is an earlier translation of No. 1170, second division, first Bhûmi. *K'*-tsin, fasc. 37, fol. 14 b. But according to the *K'*-yuen-lu (fasc. 9, fol. 4 a), the author's name is lost, and this work is wanting in Tibetan.

1236 究竟一乘寶性論
*K*iu-*k*in-yi-shan-pâo-sin-lun.
'Uttaraikayânaratnagotra (?)-sâstra.'
Mahâyânottaratantra-*s*âstra.

K'-yuen-lu, fasc. 9, fol. 4 b; Conc. 281. Author's name unknown. Translated by Ratnamati, A. D. 508, of the Northern Wêi dynasty, A. D. 386–534. 5 fasciculi; 11 chapters. The first fasc. is the text, and the rest a commentary. *K'*-tsin, fasc. 38, fol. 10 a.

1237 大乘掌珍論
Tâ-shan-*k*ân-*k*an-lun.
'Mahâyânatâlaratna-sâstra.'

Composed by the Bodhisattva Bhavaviveka. Translated by Hhüen-*k*wân (Hiouen-thsang), A. D. 643, of the Thân dynasty, A. D. 618–907. 2 fasciculi. Deest in Tibetan. *K'*-yuen-lu, fasc. 9, fol. 8 a.

1238 大乘楞伽經唯識論
Tâ-shan-lan-*k*iê-*k*in-wêi-shi-lun.
'Mahâyânalaṅka(-avatâra)-sûtra-vidyâmâtra-sâstra.'
Vidyâmâtrasiddhi.

K'-yuen-lu, fasc. 9, fol. 6 a; Conc. 793. This is a treatise on Nos. 175, 176, 177, composed by the Bodhisattva Vasubandhu. Translated by Bodhiru*k*i, A. D. 508–535, of the Northern Wêi dynasty, A. D. 386–534. 1 fasciculus; 24 leaves. For the Sûtra, see Nos. 175, 176, 177.

1239 大乘唯識論
Tâ-shan-wêi-shi-lun.
'Mahâyâna-vidyâmâtra-sâstra.'
Vidyâmâtrasiddhi.

Composed by the Bodhisattva Vasubandhu. Translated by Paramârtha, A. D. 557–569, of the *Kh*an dynasty, A. D. 557–589. 14 leaves.

1240 唯識二十論
Wêi-shi-'rh-shi-lun.
'Vidyâmâtra-viṃsati (-gâthâ)-sâstra.'
Vidyâmâtrasiddhi.

Composed by the Bodhisattva Vasubandhu. Translated by Hhüen-*k*wân (Hiouen-thsang), A. D. 661, of the Thân dynasty, A. D. 618–907. 11 leaves.

The above three works are similar translations. They agree with Tibetan. *K'*-yuen-lu, fasc. 9, fol. 6 b.

1241 寶髻經四法優波提舍
Pâo-*k*i-*k*in-sz'-fâ-yiu-po-thi-shö.
'Ratnakûḍa-sûtra-katurdharmopadesa.'

This is a treatise on No. 23 (47), composed by the Bodhisattva Vasubandhu. Translated by the *R*ishi Vimokshapra*gñ*a, A. D. 539 or 541, of the Eastern Wêi dynasty, A. D. 534–550. 13 leaves. It consists of 4,997 Chinese characters. Deest in Tibetan. *K'*-yuen-lu, fasc. 8, fol. 22 b.

1242　　大丈夫論
Tâ-*kaṅ*-fu-lun.
Mahâpurusha-sâstra.

K'-yuen-lu, fasc. 9, fol. 7 b; Conc. 652. Composed by the Bodhisattva Devala (or Deva?). Translated by Tâo-thâi, of the Northern Liâṅ dynasty, A. D. 397–439. 2 fasciculi; 29 chapters. It agrees with Tibetan. *K'*-yuen-lu, s. v.

1243　　入大乘論
Zu-tâ-shaṅ-lun.
'Mahâyânâvatâraka-sâstra.'

Composed by the Bodhisattva Sthiramati. Translated by Tâo-thâi, of the Northern Liâṅ dynasty, A. D. 397–439. 2 fasciculi; 3 chapters. Deest in Tibetan. *K'*-yuen-lu, fasc. 9, fol. 7 b.

1244　　辨中邊論
Pien-*kuṅ*-pien-lun.
Madhyânta-vibhâga-sâstra.

Conc. 455. Composed by the Bodhisattva Vasubandhu. Translated by Hhüen-*kwâṅ* (Hiouen-thsang), A. D. 661, of the Thâṅ dynasty, A. D. 618–907. 3 fasciculi; 7 chapters. Deest in Tibetan. *K'*-yuen-lu, fasc. 9, fol. 4 b.

1245　　辨中邊論頌
Pien-*kuṅ*-pien-lun-suṅ.
Madhyântavibhâga(-sâstra)-grantha.

K'-yuen-lu, fasc. 9, fol. 4 a; Conc. 454. Composed (or spoken) by the Bodhisattva Maitreya. Translated by Hhüen-*kwâṅ* (Hiouen-thsang), A. D. 661, of the Thâṅ dynasty, A. D. 618–907. 9 leaves; 7 chapters. It consists of verses, being the text of Nos. 1244 and 1248. It agrees with Tibetan. *K'*-yuen-lu, s. v.

1246　　順中論
Shun-*kuṅ*-lun.
'Madhyântânugama-sâstra.'

Composed by the Bodhisattvas Nâgârguna and Asaṅga, the latter explaining the text of the former. Translated by Gautama Pra*gñâruki*, A. D. 543, of the Eastern Wêi dynasty, A. D. 534–550. It consists of 13,727 Chinese characters. Deest in Tibetan. *K'*-yuen-lu, fasc. 9, fol. 2 a. No. 1246. treats of the doctrine of the first Varga of the Mahâpra*gñâ*pâramitâ-sûtra (No. 1). *K'*-tsiṅ, fasc. 38, fol. 7 a.

1247　　攝大乘論本
Shö-tâ-shaṅ-lun-pan.
'Mahâyânasamparigraha-sâstramûla.'

Composed by the Bodhisattva Asaṅga. Translated by Hhüen-*kwâṅ* (Hiouen-thsang), A. D. 648–649, of the Thâṅ dynasty, A. D. 618–907. 3 fasciculi; 11 divisions. This is a later translation of Nos. 1183 and 1184. *K'*-yuen-lu, fasc. 9, fol. 2 b.

1248　　中邊分別論
Kuṅ-pien-fan-pieh-lun.
Madhyântavibhâga-sâstra.

Composed by the Bodhisattva Vasubandhu. Translated by Paramârtha, A. D. 557–569, of the *Kh*an dynasty, A. D. 557–589. 2 fasciculi; 7 chapters. This is an earlier translation of No. 1244. *K'*-yuen-lu, fasc. 9, fol. 4 b.

1249　　大乘起信論
Tâ-shaṅ-*kh*i-sin-lun.
'Mahâyâna-sraddhotpâda-sâstra.'

Composed by the Bodhisattva Asvaghosha. Translated by Sîkshânanda, A. D. 695–700, of the Thâṅ dynasty, A. D. 618–907. 1 fasciculus; 28 leaves.

1250 The same title as No. 1249.

Translated by Paramârtha, A. D. 553, of the Liâṅ dynasty, A. D. 502–557. 2 fasciculi.

The above two works are similar translations, and they are wanting in Tibetan. *K'*-yuen-lu, fasc. 9, fol. 8 b. Towards the end of this Sâstra, Asvaghosha quotes a Sûtra (probably the Amitâyus-sûtra or Sukhâvatî-vyûha) on Buddha Amitâyus or Amitâbha and his Buddhakshetra Sukhâvatî.

1251　　回諍論
Hwui-*kaṅ*-lun.
'Vivâdasamana (?)-sâstra.'

Composed by the Bodhisattva Nâgârguna. Translated by the *Ri*shi Vimokshapra*gñâ* and others, A. D. 541, of the Eastern Wêi dynasty, A. D. 534–550. 1 fasciculus; 37 leaves. It consists of 11,098 Chinese characters. Deest in Tibetan. *K'*-yuen-lu, fasc. 9, fol. 10 a.

1252　　如實論
Zu-shih-lun.
'Tarka-sâstra.'

K'-yuen-lu, fasc. 9, fol. 9 b; Conc. 245. Composed by the Bodhisattva Vasubandhu. Translated by Para-

T

mârtha, A. D. 560, of the *Kh*an dynasty, A. D. 557–589. 1 fasciculus; 3 chapters. It agrees with Tibetan. *K'*-yuen-lu, s. v.

1253 寶行王正論
Pâo-hhiṅ-wâṅ-*k*aṅ-lun.
'Ratnakâryârâgadharma (?)-sâstra.'

Author's name unknown. Translated by Paramârtha, A. D. 557–569, of the *Kh*an dynasty, A. D. 557–589. 1 fasciculus; 5 chapters. Deest in Tibetan. *K'*-yuen-lu, fasc. 9, fol. 8 b.

1254 百字論
Pâi-tsz'-lun.
'Satâkshara-sâstra.'

Composed by the Bodhisattva Deva. Translated by Bodhiru*k*i, A. D. 508–535, of the Northern Wêi dynasty, A. D. 386–534. 10 leaves.

1255 解拳論
*K*iê-*kh*üen-lun.
'Mushti-prakarana (?)-sâstra.'

Composed by the Bodhisattva *G*ina. Translated by Paramârtha, A. D. 557–569, of the *Kh*an dynasty, A. D. 557–589. 1 fasciculus; 3 chapters.

1256 掌中論
*K*âṅ-*k*uṅ-lun.
'Tâlântaraka (?)-sâstra.'

Composed by the Bodhisattva *G*ina. Translated by I-tsiṅ, A. D. 703, of the Thâṅ dynasty, A. D. 618–907. 3 leaves.

The above three works agree with Tibetan. *K'*-yuen-lu, fasc. 9, fol. 12 a, b.

1257 方便心論
Fâṅ-pien-sin-lun.
'Upâyakausalyahridaya-sâstra.'

Composed by the Bodhisattva Nâgârguna. Translated by *K*i-*k*iâ-ye, together with Thân-yâo, A. D. 472, of the Northern Wêi dynasty, A. D. 386–534. 1 fasciculus; 4 chapters. Deest in Tibetan. *K'*-yuen-lu, fasc. 9, fol. 9 a.

1258 大乘法界無差別論
Tâ-shaṅ-fâ-*k*iê-wu-*kh*â-pieh-lun.
'Mahâyâna-dharmadhâtv-aviseshatâ (?)-sâstra.'

Composed by the Bodhisattva Sthiramati. Translated by Devapra*gñ*a and others, A. D. 691, of the Thâṅ dynasty, A. D. 618–907. 8 leaves. Deest in Tibetan. *K'*-yuen-lu, fasc. 9, fol. 11 b.

1259 提婆菩薩破楞伽經中外道小乘四宗論
Thi-pho-phu-sâ-po-laṅ-*k*iê-*k*iṅ-*k*uṅ-wâi-tâo-siâo-shaṅ-sz'-tsuṅ-lun.
'Sâstra by the Bodhisattva Deva on the refutation of four heretical Hînayâna schools mentioned in the Laṅka (-avatâra)-sûtra.'

Translated by Bodhiru*k*i, A. D. 508–535, of the Northern Wêi dynasty, A. D. 386–534. 6 leaves. The following are the four schools: 1. The Sâṅkhyas, who believe in oneness. 2. The Vaiseshikas, in difference. 3. The Nirgrantha-putras, in both. 4. The *Gñ*âti-putras, in neither. See *K'*-tsiṅ, fasc. 38, fol. 14 b. For the Sûtra, see Nos. 175, 176, 177.

1260 提婆菩薩釋楞伽經中外道小乘涅槃論
Thi-pho-phu-sâ-shih-laṅ-*k*iê-*k*iṅ-*k*uṅ-wâi-tâo-siâo-shaṅ-niê-phân-lun.
'Sâstra by the Bodhisattva Deva on the explanation of the Nirvâna by (twenty) heretical Hînayâna (teachers) mentioned in the Laṅka (-avatâra)-sûtra.'

Translated by Bodhiru*k*i, A. D. 508–535, of the Northern Wêi dynasty, A. D. 386–534. 6 leaves. The following is a list of the twenty teachers:

(1) The teacher of the Sâstra of the Hînayâna heresy.
(2) That of the direction or point of the compass.
(3) „ the wind *Ri*shi.
(4) „ the Vedas.
(5) „ the *Gñ*âti-putras.
(6) „ the naked heretics.
(7) „ the Vaiseshikas.
(8) „ the painful practice.
(9) „ the women (regarded) as the members of a family (?).
(10) „ practising the painful practice.
(11) „ the pure eye.
(12) „ the Madras (?).
(13) „ the Nirgrantha-putras.
(14) „ the Sâṅkhyas.
(15) „ Mahesvara.
(16) „ the absence of cause.
(17) „ time.
(18) „ drinking water.
(19) „ the power of the mouth.
(20) „ the Anda*g*ātaka, or 'the original birth from an egg.'

The above two works agree with Tibetan. *K'*-yuen-lu, fasc. 9, fol. 12 b.

PART II.

小乘論 Siâo-shaṅ-lun, or the Abhidharma of the Hînayâna.

1261 四諦論
Sz'-ti-lun.
*K*atursatya-*s*âstra.

Conc. 554. Composed by the venerable Vasuvarman. Translated by Paramârtha, A. D. 557–569, of the *Kh*an dynasty, A. D. 557–589. 4 fasciculi; 6 chapters.

1262 辟支佛因緣論
Phi-*k*'-fo-yin-yuen-lun.
Pratyekabuddha-nidâna-*s*âstra.

Conc. 447. Author's name unknown. Translated under the (three) Tshin dynasties, A. D. 350–431; but the translator's name is lost. 1 fasciculus; 26 leaves. This work gives eight Nidânas or Avâdanas.

The above two works are wanting in Tibetan. *K*'-yuen-lu, fasc. 9, fol. 23 b seq.

1263 阿毗達磨大毗婆沙論
Ö-phi-tâ-mo-tâ-phi-pho-shâ-lun.
Abhidharma-mahâvibhâshâ-*s*âstra.

K'-yuen-lu, fasc. 9, fol. 19 a; Conc. 21. Compiled by five hundred Arhats (beginning with the venerable Vasumitra), 400 years after Buddha's entering Nirvâ*n*a. Translated by Hhüen-*k*wâṅ (Hiouen-thsang), A. D. 656–659, of the Thâṅ dynasty, A. D. 618–907. 200 fasciculi; 8 kha*n*das or divisions; 43 vargas or chapters. It consists of 438,449 Chinese characters. This work is a commentary on Kâtyâyanîputra's *Gñ*ânaprasthâna-*s*âstra (No. 1275), of the Sarvâstivâda-nikâya.

1264 阿毗曇毗婆沙論
Ö-phi-thân-phi-pho-shâ-lun.
Abhidharma-vibhâshâ-*s*âstra.

This work is attributed to Kâtyâyanîputra, who is however the author of the text (No. 1275). Cf. No. 1263. Translated by Buddhavarman, together with Tâo-thâi, A. D. 437–439, of the Northern Liâṅ dynasty, A. D. 397–439. 82 fasciculi; 3 kha*n*das or divisions; 16 chapters.

'The above two works are similar translations, and they agree with Tibetan.' *K*'-yuen-lu, fasc. 9, fol. 19 a. But No. 1264 is incomplete.

1265 阿毗達磨順正理論
Ö-phi-tâ-mo-shun-*k*aṅ-li-lun.
'Abhidharma-nyâyânusâra-*s*âstra.'
Nyâyânusâra-*s*âstra.

K'-yuen-lu, fasc. 9, fol. 20 a; Conc. 125. Composed by the venerable Saṅghabhadra, of the Sarvâstivâda-nikâya, a contemporary of Vasubandhu. Translated by Hhüen-*k*wâṅ (Hiouen-thsang), A. D. 653–654, of the Thâṅ dynasty, A. D. 618–907. 80 fasciculi; 8 chapters. In this work Saṅghabhadra refutes Vasubandhu's Abhidharma-kosa-*s*âstra (Nos. 1267, 1269), quoting his 600 verses. It agrees with Tibetan. *K*'-yuen-lu, s. v.

1266 阿毗達磨藏顯宗論
Ö-phi-tâ-mo-tsâṅ-hhien-tsuṅ-lun.
Abhidharma(-pi*t*aka)-prakara*n*a*s*âsana-*s*âstra.

K'-yuen-lu, fasc. 9, fol. 20 b; Conc. 192. Composed by the venerable Saṅghabhadra. Translated by Hhüen-*k*wâṅ (Hiouen-thsang), A. D. 651–652, of the Thâṅ dynasty, A. D. 618–907. 40 fasciculi; 9 chapters. This is an abstract of the preceding work, but an introductory chapter is added. It agrees with Tibetan. *K*'-yuen-lu, s. v.

1267 阿毗達磨俱舍論
Ö-phi-tâ-mo-*k*ü-shö-lun.
Abhidharma-kosa-*s*âstra.

K'-yuen-lu, fasc. 9, fol. 19 b; Conc. 19, 298. Composed by the venerable Vasubandhu. Translated by Hhüen-*k*wâṅ (Hiouen-thsang), A. D. 651–654, of the Thâṅ dynasty, A. D. 618–907. 30 fasciculi; 9 chapters. In this work Vasubandhu refutes the views of the Vaibhâshikas. It agrees with Tibetan. *K*'-yuen-lu, s. v.

There exists a commentary in Sanskrit on this *Sâstra*, called Abhidharma-kosa-vyâkhyâ with the title of Sphutârthâ. The compiler is Yasomitra, who mentions two earlier commentators, Gunamati and his disciple Vasumitra. This Vasumitra seems not to be the same person as the author of the Mahâvibhâshâ (Nos. 1263, 1264), Prakaranapâda (Nos. 1277, 1292), and Dhâtukâyapâda (No. 1282); because these works are quoted in Vasubandhu's text (Nos. 1267, 1269). Moreover, in the list of twenty-eight Indian patriarchs (beginning with Mahâkâsyapa and ending with Bodhidharma, who arrived in China in A. D. 520), Vasumitra, the author of many *Sâstras* above mentioned, is the seventh, while Vasubandhu is the twenty-first. See Edkins, Chinese Buddhism, p. 435 seq., and index to it; Eitel, Handbook, p. 164 a. For Yasomitra's commentary, see Catalogue of the Hodgson Manuscripts, III. 42; V. 40. There is a MS. of the same work in the University Library, Cambridge.

1268 舍利弗阿毗曇論
Shö-li-fu-ö-phi-thân-lun.
*S*âriputrâbhidharma-sâstra.

Conc. 47. Translated by Dharmagupta, together with Dharmayasas, A. D. 414–415, of the Latter Tshin dynasty, A. D. 384–417. 30 fasciculi; 4 divisions; 33 chapters. Deest in Tibetan. *K'*-yuen-lu, fasc. 9, fol. 23 a. Cf. however No. 1276.

1269 阿毗達磨俱舍釋論
Ö-phi-tâ-mo-*k*ü-shö-shih-lun.
Abhidharma-kosa (-'vyâkhyâ')-*s*âstra.

Cf. No. 1267. Composed by the venerable Vasubandhu. Translated by Paramârtha, A. D. 564–567, of the *Kh*an dynasty, A. D. 557–589. 22 fasciculi; 9 chapters. This is an earlier translation of No. 1267. *K'*-yuen-lu, fasc. 9, fol. 19 b. According to the Sandai-zô-mok-rok (fasc. 2, fol. 75 a), the seventh character of the Chinese title is sometimes left out. If so, both Sanskrit and Chinese titles exactly agree with each other, i. e. without 'vyâkhyâ.'

1270 阿毗達磨俱舍論本頌
Ö-phi-tâ-mo-*k*ü-shö-lun-pan-sun.
Abhidharma-kosa-kârikâ.

K'-yuen-lu, fasc. 9, fol. 19 b; Conc. 299. Composed by the venerable Vasubandhu. Translated by Hhüen-*k*wân (Hiouen-thsang), A. D. 651, of the Thân dynasty, A. D. 618–907. 2 fasciculi; 8 chapters. This is the collection of 600 principal and 7 additional verses, explained in Nos. 1267 and 1269. It agrees with Tibetan. *K'*-yuen-lu, s. v.

1271 三法度論
Sân-fâ-tu-lun.
'Tridharmaka-sâstra.'

Composed by the venerable Giribhadra (?) or Vasubhadra (cf. No. 1381) and Saṅghasena, the latter explaining the text of the former. Translated by Gautama Saṅghadeva, together with Hwui-yuen, A. D. 391, of the Eastern Tsin dynasty, A. D. 317–420. 3 fasciculi; 3 chapters. Deest in Tibetan. *K'*-yuen-lu, fasc. 9, fol. 22 a.

1272 三彌底部論
Sân-mi-ti-pu-lun.
'Sammitîya-nikâya-sâstra.'

Author's name unknown. Translated under the (three) Tshin dynasties, A. D. 350–431; but the translator's name is lost. 3 fasciculi. Deest in Tibetan. *K'*-yuen-lu, fasc. 9, fol. 23 b.

1273 阿毗曇八犍度論
Ö-phi-thân-pâ-*k*ien-tu-lun.
'Abhidharmâshṭakhaṇḍa-sâstra.'
Abhidharma-*gñ*ânaprasthâna-*s*âstra.

K'-yuen-lu, fasc. 9, fol. 17 a; Conc. 31. Composed by the venerable Kâtyâyanîputra, 300 years after Buddha's entering Nirvâṇa. Translated by Gautama Saṅghadeva, together with *K*u Fo-nien, A. D. 383, of the Former Tshin dynasty, A. D. 350–394. 30 fasciculi; 8 khaṇḍas or divisions; 44 vargas or chapters. It is said that the Sanskrit text has consisted of 15,072 *s*lokas in verse, or a corresponding number in prose. This is the principal work of the Abhidharma-piṭaka of the Sarvâstivâda-nikâya. It agrees with Tibetan. *K'*-yuen-lu, s. v.

1274 成實論
*Kh*an-shih-lun.
'Satyasiddhi-sâstra.'

Composed by Harivarman. Translated by Kumâragîva, A. D. 417–418 (or 407–408?), of the Latter Tshin dynasty, A. D. 384–417. 20 fasciculi; 202 chapters. This work differs from the views of the Sarvâstivâda-nikâya. It agrees with Tibetan. *K'*-yuen-lu, fasc. 9, fol. 22 b.

1275 阿毗達磨發智論
Ö-phi-tâ-mo-fâ-*k'*-lun.
Abhidharma-*gñ*ânaprasthâna-*s*âstra.

Conc. 15. Composed by the venerable Kâtyâyanîputra. Translated by Hhüen-kwân (Hiouen-thsang), A.D. 657–660, of the Thân dynasty, A.D. 618–907. 20 fasciculi; 8 khandas or divisions; 44 vargas or chapters. This is a later translation of No. 1273. K'-yuen-lu, fasc. 9, fol. 17 a.

1276 阿毗達磨集異門足論
Ö-phi-tâ-mo-tsi-i-man-tsö-lun.
Abhidharma-saṅgîtiparyâyapâda(-sâstra).

K'-yuen-lu, fasc. 9, fol. 17 b; Conc. 23. Composed by the venerable Sâriputra. 20 fasciculi; 12 chapters. According to Yasomitra's Abhidharmakosavyâkhyâ, the author of No. 1276 is Mahâkaushṭhila. This is the first of the Six Pâda works of the Sarvâstivâda-nikâya.

1277 阿毗達磨品類足論
Ö-phi-tâ-mo-phin-lêi-tsö-lun.
Abhidharma-prakaraṇapâda(-sâstra).

K'-yuen-lu, fasc. 9, fol. 18 b; Conc. 20. Composed by the venerable Vasumitra. Translated by Hhüen-kwân (Hiouen-thsang), A.D. 659, of the Thân dynasty, A.D. 618–907. 18 fasciculi; 8 chapters. This is the second of the Six Pâda works of the Sarvâstivâda-nikâya.

1278 阿毗達磨甘露味論
Ö-phi-tâ-mo-kân-lu-wêi-lun.
Abhidharmâmrita(-rasa)-sâstra.

K'-yuen-lu, fasc. 9, fol. 21 b. Composed by the venerable Ghosha. Translated under the Wêi dynasty, A.D. 220–265. 2 fasciculi; 16 chapters.

The above three works agree with Tibetan. K'-yuen-lu, s. v.

1279 鞞婆沙論
Pi-pho-shâ-lun.
Vibhâshâ-sâstra.

Conc. 445. Composed by the venerable Kâtyâyanîputra. Translated by Saṅghabhûti, A.D. 383, of the Former Tshin dynasty, A.D. 350–394. 18 fasciculi; 42 chapters. Deest in Tibetan. K'-yuen-lu, fasc. 9, fol. 23 a.

1280 隨相論
Sui-siân-lun.
'Lakshaṇânusâra-sâstra.'

Composed by the venerable Guṇamati. Translated by Paramârtha, A.D. 557–569, of the Khan dynasty, A.D. 557–589. 2 fasciculi. Deest in Tibetan. K'-yuen-lu, fasc. 9, fol. 21 b.

1281 阿毗達磨識身足論
Ö-phi-tâ-mo-shi-shan-tsö-lun.
Abhidharma-vigñânakâyapâda(-sâstra).

K'-yuen-lu, fasc. 9, fol. 18 a; Conc. 22. Composed by the Arhat Devasarman, 100 years after Buddha's entering Nirvâṇa. Translated by Hhüen-kwân (Hiouen-thsang), A.D. 649, of the Thân dynasty, A.D. 618–907. 16 fasciculi; 6 chapters. This is the third of the Six Pâda works of the Sarvâstivâda-nikâya.

1282 阿毗達磨界身足論
Ö-phi-tâ-mo-kiê-shan-tsö-lun.
(Abhidharma-)dhâtukâyapâda(-sâstra).

K'-yuen-lu, fasc. 9, fol. 18 a; Conc. 17. Composed by the venerable Vasumitra, 300 years after Buddha's entering Nirvâṇa. Translated by Hhüen-kwân (Hiouen-thsang), A.D. 663, of the Thân dynasty, A.D. 618–907. 2 fasciculi; 2 chapters. This is the fourth of the Six Pâda works of the Sarvâstivâda-nikâya. According to Yasomitra's Abhidharmakosavyâkhyâ, the author of No. 1282 is Pûrṇa.

The above two works agree with Tibetan. K'-yuen-lu, s. v.

1283 五事毗婆沙論
Wu-sh'-phi-pho-shâ-lun.
'Pañkavastu-vibhâshâ-sâstra.'

Compiled by the venerable Dharmatrâta. Translated by Hhüen-kwân (Hiouen-thsang), A.D. 663, of the Thân dynasty, A.D. 618–907. 2 fasciculi; 3 chapters. This is a commentary on Vasumitra's 'Pañkavastu-sâstra.' Deest in Tibetan. K'-yuen-lu, fasc. 9, fol. 23 a.

1284 十八部論
Shi-pâ-pu-lun.
'Ashṭâdasanikâya-sâstra.'

Composed by the Bodhisattva Vasumitra. Translated by Paramârtha, A.D. 557–569, of the Khan dynasty, A.D. 557–589. 9 leaves.

1285 部執異論
Pu-kih-i-lun.
'Sâstra on the difference of the views of (18 or 20 Hînayâna) schools.'

This translation is similar to No. 1284.

1286 異部宗輪論
I-pu-tsuṅ-lun-lun.
'Sâstra on the wheel of the principles (or Dharmakakra?) of different schools.'

Composed by the Bodhisattva Vasumitra. Translated by Hhüen-kwâṅ (Hiouen-thsang), A. D. 662, of the Thâṅ dynasty, A. D. 618–907. 10 leaves.

The above three works are different translations of the same or a similar text, and they are wanting in Tibetan. K'-yuen-lu, fasc. 9, fol. 24 a. For the names of the different schools mentioned in No. 1285, see the List published by Julien in the Journal Asiatique, Octobre–Novembre 1859, pp. 327–361.

1287 雜阿毗曇心論
Tsâ-ŏ-phi-thân-sin-lun.
Saṃyuktâbhidharma-hṛidaya-sâstra.

Conc. 757. Compiled by the venerable Dharmatrâta. Translated by Saṅghavarman and others, A. D. 434, of the earlier Suṅ dynasty, A. D. 420–479. 16 fasciculi; 11 chapters. This is a commentary on No. 1288. Deest in Tibetan. K'-yuen-lu, fasc. 9, fol. 21 a.

1288 阿毗曇心論
Ŏ-phi-thân-sin-lun.
Abhidharma-hṛidaya (-sâstra).

K'-yuen-lu, fasc. 9, fol. 20 b; Conc. 33. Composed by the venerable Dharmagina (?). Translated by Gautama Saṅghadeva, together with Hwui-yuen, A. D. 391, of the Eastern Tsin dynasty, A. D. 317–420. 4 fasciculi; 10 chapters. It agrees with Tibetan. K'-yuen-lu, s. v.

1289 尊婆須蜜菩薩所集論
Tsun-pho-su-mi-phu-sâ-su-tsi-lun.
'Ârya-vasumitra-bodhisattva-saṅgîti-sâstra.'

Translated by Saṅghabhûti and others, A. D. 384, of the Former Tshin dynasty, A. D. 350–394. 15 fasciculi; 14 khandas or chapters.

1290 分別功德論
Fan-pieh-kuṅ-töh-lun.
'Guṇanirdesa (?)-sâstra.'

Compiler's name unknown. Translated under the Eastern Hâṅ dynasty, A. D. 25–220; but the translator's name is lost. 3 fasciculi. This is a commentary on the first and fourth chapters of the Ekottarâgama, No. 543.

1291 入阿毗達磨論
Zu-ŏ-phi-tâ-mo-lun.
'Abhidharmâvatâra-sâstra.'

Composed by the Arhat Sugandhara (?). Translated by Hhüen-kwâṅ (Hiouen-thsang), A. D. 658, of the Thâṅ dynasty, A. D. 618–907. 2 fasciculi; 16 leaves each. This work contains a brief explanation of the names of the Pañka-skandha and Try-asaṃskṛitas; the former are Rûpa, Vedanâ, Saṅgñâ, Saṃskâra, and Vigñâna; and the latter, Âkâsa, Pratisaṅkhyâ-nirodha, and Apratisaṅkhyâ-nirodha.

The above three works are wanting in Tibetan. K'-yuen-lu, fasc. 9, fol. 22 a seq.

1292 衆事分阿毗曇論
Kuṅ-sh'-fan-ŏ-phi-thân-lun.
Abhidharma-prakaraṇapâda (-sâstra).

Conc. 713. Composed by the venerable Vasumitra. Translated by Guṇabhadra, together with Bodhiyasas, A. D. 435–443, of the earlier Suṅ dynasty, A. D. 420–479. 12 fasciculi; 8 chapters. This is an earlier translation of No. 1277. K'-yuen-lu, fasc. 9, fol. 18 b.

1293 解脫道論
Kiê-to-tâo-lun.
'Vimokshamârga-sâstra.'

Composed by the Arhat Upatishya or Sâriputra. Translated by Saṅghapâla, A. D. 505, of the Liâṅ dynasty, A. D. 502–557. 12 fasciculi; 12 chapters.

1294 法勝阿毗曇心論
Fâ-shaṅ-ŏ-phi-thân-sin-lun.
(Dharmagina?)-abhidharma-hṛidaya (-sâstra).

Conc. 127. Compiled by the venerable Upasânta. Translated by Narendrayasas, A. D. 563, of the Northern Tshi dynasty, A. D. 550–577. 6 fasciculi; 10 chapters. This is a commentary on No. 1288.

The above two works are wanting in Tibetan. K'-yuen-lu, fasc. 9, fol. 21 a seq.

1295 勝宗十句義論
Shaṅ-tsuṅ-shi-kü-i-lun.
'Vaiseshikanikâya-dasapadârtha-sâstra.'

Composed by the Vaiseshika Gñânakandra. Translated by Hhüen-kwâṅ (Hiouen-thsang), A. D. 648, of the Thâṅ dynasty, A. D. 618–907. 1 fasciculus; 13 leaves. This is an enlarged work of the 'Shaṭpadârthâ' of the 'Vaiseshika-sâstra.' 'This is not the law of Buddha' (K'-yuen-lu, fasc. 10, fol. 4 a), but 'a Sâstra of the heretics' or the Vaiseshikas (K'-tsiṅ, fasc. 41, fol. 12 b). No. 1295 therefore ought to be arranged under the heading of the Miscellaneous Indian Works, i.e. the Fourth Division, Part I, in this Catalogue.

1296 阿毗達磨法蘊足論
Ö-phi-tâ-mo-fâ-yun-tsŏ-lun.
Abhidharma(-dharma)-skandhapâda (-sâstra).

K'-yuen-lu, fasc. 9, fol. 17 b; Conc. 16. Composed by the venerable Mahâmaudgalyâyana. Translated by Hhüen-kwân (Hiouen-thsang), A.D. 659, of the Thâṅ dynasty, A.D. 618–907. 12 fasciculi; 21 chapters. It agrees with Tibetan. K'-yuen-lu, s.v. This is the fifth of the Six Pâda works of the Sarvâstivâda-nikâya. According to Yosomitra's Abhidharmakosavyâkhyâ, the author of No. 1296 is Sâriputra.

1297 立世阿毗曇論
Li-shi-ö-phi-thân-lun.
'Lokasthiti (?)-abhidharma-sâstra.'

Author's name unknown. Translated by Paramârtha, A.D. 558, of the Khan dynasty, A.D. 557–589. 10 fasciculi; 25 chapters. This Sâstra is doubtful (or wanting) in Tibetan. K'-yuen-lu, fasc. 9, fol. 22 b. The subject of the first chapter is the motion of the earth, and that of the nineteenth is that of the sun and moon. The latter chapter is the principal text for some Buddhists who make astronomical calculations for the almanacs.

PART III.

宋元續入藏諸論 Suṅ-yuen-suh-zu-tsâṅ-*k*u-lun, or Works of the Abhidharma of the Mahâyâna and Hînayâna, successively admitted into the Canon during the later (or Northern) and Southern Suṅ (A.D. 960–1127 and 1127–1280) and Yuen (A.D. 1280–1368) dynasties.

1298 大乘集菩薩學論
Tâ-shaṅ-tsi-phu-sâ-hhiâo-lun.
'Mahâyâna-saṅgitibodhisattvavidyâ-sâstra.'

Composed by the Bodhisattva Dharmayasas. Translated by Fâ-hu (Dharmaraksha ?) and *Z*ih-*k*han (Sûryayasas), A.D. 1004–1058, of the later Suṅ dynasty, A.D. 960–1127. 25 fasciculi; 18 chapters.

1299 大宗地玄文本論
Tâ-tsuṅ-ti-hhüen-wan-pan-lun.
'Mahâyânabhûmiguhyavâkâmûla (?)-sâstra.'

Composed by the Bodhisattva Asvaghosha. Translated by Paramârtha, A.D. 557–569, of the *Kh*an dynasty, A.D. 557–589. 8 fasciculi; 40 chapters.

The above two works are wanting in Tibetan. *K*'-yuen-lu, fasc. 9, fol. 15 b seq.

1300 金七十論
*K*in-tshi-shi-lun.
(Suvarna-) Saptati (-sâstra).
Sâṅkhyakârikâ-bhâshya.

Translated by Paramârtha, A.D. 557–569, of the *Kh*an dynasty, A.D. 557–589. 3 fasciculi. It is stated in a note at the beginning, that 'this work was composed by the heretical *Ri*shi Kapila, explaining twenty-five tattvas or truths, and it is not the law of Buddha.' Towards the end (fasc. 3, fol. 20 b), however, we read that 'there were 60,000 verses, composed by Pañkasikha (Kâpileya), whose teacher Âsuri was the disciple of the *Ri*shi Kapila, and that afterwards a Brâhmana, Îsvara Krishna, selected 70 verses out of the 60,000.' This work is to be compared with the Sanskrit text of the Sâṅkhya-kârikâ, or memorial verses on the Sâṅkhya philosophy, by Îsvara Krishna, translated by Colebrooke; and also the Bhâshya, or commentary of Gaurapâda, translated and illustrated by an original comment, by Wilson. Published at Oxford, 1837. 'This is not the law of Buddha' (*K*'-yuen-lu, fasc. 10, fol. 3 b), but 'a *S*âstra of the heretics' or the Sâṅkhyas (*K*'-tsiṅ, fasc. 41, fol. 13 a). It ought therefore to be arranged somewhere else, as already alluded to under No. 1295.

1301 廣釋菩提心論
Kwâṅ-shih-phu-thi-sin-lun.
'Bodhihridayavaipulyaprakarana-sâstra.'

Composed by the Bodhisattva Padmasila (?). Translated by Sh'-hu (Dânapâla ?), A.D. 980–1000, of the later Suṅ dynasty, A.D. 960–1127. 4 fasciculi. It agrees with Tibetan. *K*'-yuen-lu, fasc. 9, fol. 14 a.

1302 集諸法寶最上義論
Tsi-*k*u-fâ-pâo-tsui-shâṅ-i-lun.
'Sarvadharmaratnottara (-artha)-saṅgiti-sâstra.'

Composed by the Bodhisattva Sumuni (?). Translated by Sh'-hu (Dânapâla ?), A.D. 980–1000, of the later Suṅ dynasty, A.D. 960–1127. 2 fasciculi.

1303 金剛針論
*K*in-kâṅ-*k*an-lun.
Vagrasûki (-sâstra).

Composed by the Bodhisattva Dharmayasas. Translated by Fâ-thien (Dharmadeva ?), A.D. 973–981, of the later Suṅ dynasty, A.D. 960–1127. 9 leaves. This work contains a refutation of the four Vedas. For the Sanskrit text, see Catalogue of the Hodgson Manuscripts, III. 54, 55; V. 64; VI. 66; VII. 91.

The above two works are wanting in Tibetan. *K*'-yuen-lu, fasc. 9, fol. 14 b seq.

The following seven works were trânslated by Sh'-hu (Dânapâla ?), A. D. 980–1000, of the later Suṅ dynasty, A. D. 960–1127:—

1304 菩提心離相論
Phu-thi-sin-li-siâṅ-lun.
'Lakshaṇavimukta (?)-bodhihṛdaya-śâstra.'

Composed by the Bodhisattva Nâgârguna. 9 leaves. It agrees with Tibetan. K'-yuen-lu, fasc. 9, fol. 14 a.

1305 大乘破有論
Tâ-shaṅ-po-yiu-lun.
'Mahâyâna-bhavabheda-śâstra.'

Composed by the Bodhisattva Nâgârguna. 2 leaves.

1306 集大乘相論
Tsi-tâ-shaṅ-siâṅ-lun.
'Mahâyâna-lakshaṇasaṅgîti-śâstra.'

Composed by the Bodhisattva Buddhaśrîgñâna (?). 2 fasciculi; 18 leaves.

The above two works are wanting in Tibetan. K'-yuen-lu, fasc. 9, fol. 14 b.

1307 六十頌如理論
Li-shi-suṅ-zu-li-lun.
'Gâthâshashṭi-yathârtha-śâstra.'

Composed by the Bodhisattva Nâgârguna. 5 leaves.

1308 大乘二十頌論
Tâ-shaṅ-'rh-shi-suṅ-lun.
'Mahâyâna-gâthâviṃśati-śâstra.'

Composed by the Bodhisattva Nâgârguna. 2 leaves.

The above two works agree with Tibetan. K'-yuen-lu, fasc. 9, fol. 14 a.

1309 佛母般若波羅蜜多圓集要義論
Fo-mu-pân-zo-po-lo-mi-to-yuen-tsi-yâo-i-lun.
'Buddhamâtṛkâ-pragñâpâramitâ-mahârtha-saṅgîti-śâstra.'

Composed by the Bodhisattva Tâ-yü-luṅ or Nâgârguna (? Cf. Nos. 1223, 1224). 4 leaves.

1310 佛母般若波羅蜜多圓集要義釋論
Fo-mu-pân-zo-po-lo-mi-to-yuen-tsi-yâo-i-shih-lun.
A commentary on the preceding Śâstra.

Composed by the Bodhisattva Triratnârya (?). 4 fasciculi.

1311 大乘寶要義論
Tâ-shaṅ-pâo-yâo-i-lun.
'Mahâyâna-ratnamahârtha-śâstra.'

Author's name lost. Translated by Fâ-hu (Dharmaraksha ?) and others, A. D. 1004–1058, of the later Suṅ dynasty, A. D. 960–1127. 10 fasciculi.

1312 菩薩本生鬘論
Phu-sâ-pan-shaṅ-mân-lun.
(Bodhisattva-)Gâtakamâlâ (-śâstra).

Composed or collected by the Bodhisattva Âryaśûra, and commented by Tsi-pien-shaṅ-thien or the Muni Ginadeva (?). Translated by Shâo-tôh, Hwui-sün, and others, of the later Suṅ dynasty, A. D. 960–1127. 16 fasciculi. The first 4 fasciculi contain fourteen Gâtakas of Sâkyamuni, being Âryaśûra's text; while the latter 12 fasciculi form a commentary, being divided into 34 sections. But this translation is not good. See the K'-tsiṅ, fasc. 38, fol. 13 b. For the Sanskrit text, see Catalogue of the Hodgson Manuscripts, III. 23; V. 24; VI. 14. The following is a list of thirty-five Gâtakas (C. H. M., III. 23):—

(1) Vyâghrî-gâtaka.
(2) Śivi.
(3) Kulmâshapiṇḍî.
(4) Śreshṭhi.
(5) Sahya (? or Avishagya-) śreshṭhi.
(6) Śaśa.
(7) Agastya.
(8) Maitribala.
(9) Viśvântara.
(10) Yagña.
(11) Śakra.
(12) Brâhmaṇa.
(13) Unmâdayantî.
(14) Supâraga (? or Suparâga)
(15) Matsya.
(16) Vartakâpotaka.
(17) Kakkhapa.
(18) Kumbha.
(19) Putra.
(20) Visa.
(21) Śreshṭhi.
(22) Buddhabodhi
(23) Haṃsa.
(24) Mahâbodhi.
(25) Mahâkapi.
(26) Śarabha.
(27) Ruru.
(28) Mahâkapi.
(29) Kshânti.
(30) Brahma.
(31) Hasti.
(32) Sutasoma.
(33) Ayogṛiha.
(34) Mahisha.
(35) Śatapatra.

For the above list, see also Five Jâtakas, edited by Fausböll, p. 59; Buddhist Birth Stories, translated by Rhys Davids, vol. i, p. xcviii.

The above four works (Nos. 1309–1312) are wanting in Tibetan. K'-yuen-lu, fasc. 9, fol. 13 b seq.

1313 聖佛母般若波羅蜜多九頌精義論
Shaṅ-fo-mu-pân-zo-po-lo-mi-to-kiu-suṅ-tsiṅ-i-lun.
'Âryabuddhamâtṛkâ-pragñâpâramitâ-navagâthâ-mahârtha-śâstra.'

Composed by the Bodhisattva *S*rîgunaraktâmbara (?). Translated by Fâ-hu (Dharmaraksha ?), A.D. 1004–1058, of the later Suṅ dynasty, A.D. 960–1127. 2 fasciculi; 10 leaves.

1314 大乘緣生論
Tâ-shaṅ-yuen-shaṅ-lun.
'Mahâyâna-nidâna-sâstra.'

Composed by the venerable Ullaṅgha. Translated by Amoghavagra, A.D. 746–771, of the Thâṅ dynasty, A.D. 618–907. 15 leaves. It agrees with Tibetan. *K'*-yuen-lu, fasc. 9, fol. 13 a. But, according to the *K'*-tsiṅ (fasc. 40, fol. 15 b), No. 1314 is a later translation of No. 1227, and it is a *S*âstra of the Hînayâna.

1315 諸教決定名義論
*K*u-*k*iâo-*k*iâ-tiṅ-miṅ-i-lun.
'Sarvasikshâ-sthita-nâmârtha-sâstra.'

Composed or spoken by the Bodhisattva Maitreya. Translated by Sh'-hu (Dânapâla ?), A.D. 980–1000, of the later Suṅ dynasty, A.D. 960–1127. 5 leaves. In this work the root letters or syllables in all the teaching (of the Tantra), such as Om, Hûm, A, etc., are enumerated or explained.

1316 大乘中觀釋論
Tâ-shaṅ-*k*uṅ-kwân-shih-lun.
'Mahâyâna-madhyadhyâna-vyâkhyâ-sâstra.'

Composed by the Bodhisattva Sthitamati. Translated by Wêi-tsiṅ and others, A.D. 1009–1050, of the later Suṅ dynasty, A.D. 960–1127. 9 fasciculi. This is a commentary on the first 13 chapters of Nâgârguna's Pramânyamûla-sâstra, No. 1179.

The above two works are wanting in Tibetan. *K'*-yuen-lu, fasc. 9, fol. 15 a, b.

1317 施設論
Sh'-shö-lun.
'Pragñâpti-sâstra.'
Pragñâptipâda-sâstra.

K'-yuen-lu, fasc. 9, fol. 24 b; Conc. 66. Composed by the venerable Mahâmaudgalyâyana. Translated by Fâ-hu (Dharmaraksha ?) and others, A.D. 1004–1058, of the later Suṅ dynasty, A.D. 960–1127. This is the last of the Six Pâda works of the Sarvâstivâda-nikâya, and therefore a *S*âstra of the Hînayâna. It agrees with Tibetan. *K'*-yuen-lu, s.v.

1318 大乘法界無差別論
Tâ-shaṅ-fâ-*k*iê-wu-*kh*â-pieh-lun.
'Mahâyâna-dharmadhâtv-avisesbatâ-sâstra.'

Composed by the Bodhisattva Sthiramati. Translated by Devapragña, A.D. 691, of the Thâṅ dynasty, A.D. 618–907. 8 leaves. This is another translation of No. 1258. *K'*-tsiṅ, fasc. 38, fol. 4 a. According to the *K'*-yuen-lu (fasc. 9, fol. 11 b), the translator's name is lost.

1319 金剛頂瑜伽中發阿耨多羅三藐三菩提心論
*K*in-kâṅ-tiṅ-yü-*k*iâ-*k*uṅ-fâ-ö-neu-to-lo-sân-miâo-sân-phu-thi-sin-lun.
'Vagrasekharayoga-anuttarasamyaksambodhikittotpâda-sâstra.'

Author's name unknown. Translated by Amoghavagra, A.D. 746–771, of the Thâṅ dynasty, A.D. 618–907. 8 leaves. It agrees with Tibetan. *K'*-yuen-lu, fasc. 9, fol. 13 a. According to the *K'*-tsiṅ (fasc. 34, fol. 8 a), No. 1319 seems to be the translator's own work.

1320 彰所知論
*K*aṅ-su-*k'*-lun.
'*S*âstra on explaining known objects.'

Composed by Pâ-sz'-pâ or Bashpa (died A.D. 1280), the teacher of the Emperor Shi-tsu or Kublai Khan of the Yuen dynasty, reigned A.D. 1260–1294, and actually seated on the throne of China from 1280. Translated by Shâ-lo-pâ (died A.D. 1314), disciple of Bashpa, of the Yuen dynasty, A.D. 1280–1368. 2 fasciculi; 5 chapters, on the Bhâgana-loka or vessel-world, Sattva-loka or being-world, Mârga-dharma or way-law, Phala-dharma or fruit-law, and Asamskrita-dharma or unmade-law respectively. This is a useful and interesting manual of the Buddhistic terminology, consisting of extracts from several Sûtras and *S*âstras, such as Nos. 62, 549, 550, 679, 1267, 1269. It was compiled by Bashpa for the sake of *K*an-*k*in, the Crown-prince of the Emperor Shi-tsu, in A.D. 1272(?). See the last passage of the work, where however the Chinese cycle only is mentioned without the name and order of the period; but this cycle (壬寅) must be an error, as it corresponds to A.D. 1242 and 1302, and the author died in 1280 as above mentioned, and the *K*an-*k*in was not elected as the Crown-prince till 1272. Then the cycle of the year 1272 is 壬申, which may most probably be a right reading. In the *K'*-tsiṅ (fasc. 40, fol. 16 a), No. 1320 is mentioned as a *S*âstra of the Hînayâna.

FOURTH DIVISION.

雜藏 Tsâ-tsân (Samyukta-pitaka ?), or Miscellaneous Works.

PART I.

INDIAN MISCELLANEOUS WORKS.

西土聖賢撰集 Si-thu-shan-hhien-kwân-tsi, or Works of the sages and wise men of the western country, i. e. India.

1321 出曜經
*Kh*u-yâo-*k*in.
Avadâna (-sûtra).

Composed by the Bodhisattva Dharmatrâta. Translated by *K*u Fo-nien, A.D. 398–399, of the Latter Tshin dynasty, A.D. 384–417. 20 fasciculi; 33 chapters. It is stated in the preface by San-zui, dated A.D. 399, that 'Dharmatrâta, the maternal uncle of Vasumitra, collected 1000 verses in 33 chapters, and called this collection 法句 Fâ-*k*ü or law-verse (i. e. Dharmapada or Dhammapada). Then he recorded the original account of each verse as a commentary, which he called 出曜 *Kh*u-yâo or coming-out light (i. e. Avadâna). This term was previously rendered into 譬喻 Phi-yü or comparison, being the sixth (or seventh ?) of twelve classes of the Sûtras or scriptures. In A.D. 383, there was a *S*râmana of *K*i-pin (Cabul) Sanghabhûti by name, who came to *Kh*ân-ân, the capital of the Former Tshin dynasty, A.D. 350–394 (bringing with him the MS. of this work (?). Cf. *K*âo-san-*k*whân, fasc. 1, fol. 21 a). Afterwards in A.D. 398, under the Latter Tshin dynasty, A.D. 384–417, he was asked to translate this work, which translation was finished in the following spring. In translating it, Sanghabhûti took the Sanskrit text in his hand, while Fo-nien (a Chinese priest) interpreted it.' This is the third of four Chinese versions of the Dhammapada (Nos. 1321, 1353, 1365, 1439), with a commentary; and the last chapter is on 梵志 Fân-*k*' or Brahma*k*ârin, or Brâhmana (?), if it is compared with the Pâli text. Cf. Beal, Dhammapada, p. 23 seq.; Sacred Books of the East, vol. x, Dhammapada, p. lii. According to the *K*'-yuen-lu (fasc. 9, fol. 26 a), this work is wanting in Tibetan. But for a Tibetan translation of a Dhammapada, see S. B. E., l. c. The Pâli text of the Dhammapada was published by Professor Fausböll, in Copenhagen, 1855, with Latin translation. Translated into German by Professor Weber, 'Zeitschrift der deutschen morgenländischen Gesellschaft,' vol. xiv, 1860; reprinted in 'Indische Streifen,' vol. i. Translated into English by Professor Max Müller, as introduction to 'Buddhaghosha's Parables,' 1870; reprinted in the Sacred Books of the East, vol. x, 1881.

1322 賢愚因緣經
Hhien-yü-yin-yuen-*k*in.
Damamûka (-nidâna-sûtra, or Sûtra on the cause or tales of the wise and the fool).

A.R., p. 480; A.M.G., p. 283. Translated by Hwui-*k*iâo and others, A.D. 445, of the Northern Wei dynasty, A.D. 386–534. 13 fasciculi; 69 chapters. It agrees with Tibetan. *K*'-yuen-lu, fasc. 9, fol. 26 a. Csoma says (A. R., l. c.): 'At the end it is stated that this work (viz. the Tibetan version), it seems, has been translated from Chinese.' See 'Der Weise und der Thor,' aus dem Tibetischen übersetzt und mit dem Original texte herausgegeben von I. J. Schmidt, St. Petersburg, 1843. No. 1322 is mentioned as a Hînayâna-sûtra in *K*'-tsin, fasc. 31, fol. 23 b.

1323 佛本行經
Fo-pan-hhin-*k*in.
'Buddhapûrvakaryâ-sûtra.'

Translated by Pâo-yun, A.D. 427–449, of the earlier Sun dynasty, A.D. 420–479. 7 fasciculi; 31 chapters. This is a life of Buddha in verse, but the author's name is unknown. It agrees with Tibetan. *K*'-yuen-lu, fasc. 9, fol. 25 b, where another title is also mentioned, viz. Pan-hhin-tsân-*k*whân or Life (of Buddha) in laudatory verses on his former practice.

1324 撰集百緣經

*K*wân-tsi-pâi-yuen-*k*iṅ.

'Selected and collected *S*atâvadâna-sûtra.'

Pûrnamukha-avadânasataka.

A. R., p. 481; A. M. G., p. 284. Translated by *K*' *Kh*ien, A.D. 223–253, of the Wu dynasty, A.D. 222–280. 10 fasciculi; 10 chapters, each chapter containing 10 Avadânas or stories. For the Sanskrit text, see Catalogue of the Hodgson Manuscripts, II. 19; V. 50; VII. 4, where three titles are mentioned, viz. 1. Avadânasataka, 2. *S*atâvadâna, and 3. *S*atakâvadânakathâ. No. 1324 agrees with Tibetan. See *K*'-yuen-lu, fasc. 9, fol. 25 b. For the Tibetan version, see 'Études Bud-dhiques.—Le Livre des cent légendes, par M. Léon Feer,' Paris, 1881. No. 1324 is mentioned as a Hînayâna-sûtra in *K*'-tsiṅ, fasc. 31, fol. 26 a.

1325 修行道地經

Siu-hhiṅ-tâo-ti-*k*iṅ.

'Karyâmârgabhûmi-sûtra.'

Composed by the Indian *S*râmana Saṅgharaksha, 700 years after Buddha's entering Nirvâna. Translated by *K*u Fâ-hu (Dharmaraksha), A.D. 284, of the Western Tsin dynasty, A.D. 265–316. 8 fasciculi; 30 chapters. The last 3 chapters depend on the Saddharmapundarîka. *K*'-tsiṅ, fasc. 38, fol. 19 a. This and the following work are mentioned as Mahâyâna-sâstras in *K*'-tsiṅ, fasc. 38, fol. 18 a seq.

1326 道地經

Tâo-ti-*k*iṅ.

'Mârgabhûmi-sûtra.'

Composed by Saṅgharaksha. Translated by Ân Shi-kâo, A.D. 148–170, of the Eastern Hân dynasty, A.D. 25–220. 1 fasciculus; 7 sections. This is an earlier translation of a part of No. 1325. *K*'-yuen-lu, fasc. 9, fol. 26 a.

1327 佛說佛醫經

Fo-shwo-fo-i-*k*iṅ.

'Sûtra spoken by Buddha on the Buddha-physician.'

Translated by Lüh-yen, together with *K*' Yueh, A.D. 230, of the Wu dynasty, A.D. 222–280. 5 leaves. This work is mentioned as a Hînayâna-sûtra in *K*'-tsiṅ, fasc. 31, fol. 13 b.

1328 惟日雜難經

Wêi-zih-tsâ-nân-*k*iṅ.

'Sûtra on several difficulties (or difficult questions) of Wêi-zih (name of a man?).'

Translated by *K*' *Kh*ien, A.D. 223–253, of the Wu dynasty, A.D. 222–280. 16 leaves. This work gives an account concerning several differences of the practice and virtue of Bhagavat, Bodhisattvas, Pratyekabuddhas, and *S*râvakas. This translation is not very readable. This work is mentioned as a Mahâyâna-sâstra in *K*'-tsiṅ, fasc. 38, fol. 16 a.

1329 雜寶藏經

Tsâ-pâo-tsâṅ-*k*iṅ.

'Samyuktaratnapitaka-sûtra.'

Translated by Ki-*k*iâ-ye, together with Thân-yâo, A.D. 472, of the Northern Wêi dynasty, A.D. 386–534. 8 fasciculi; 121 Avadânas or tales. The last tale is translated by Mr. Beal, in his Catalogue, pp. 85, 86. This work is mentioned as a Hînayâna-sûtra in *K*'-tsiṅ, fasc. 31, fol. 26 a.

1330 迦葉赴佛般涅槃經

*K*iâ-yeh-fu-fo-pân-niê-phân-*k*iṅ.

'Sûtra on Kâsyapa's coming up to the place where Buddha had just entered Nirvâna.'

Translated by Thân-wu-lân (Dharmaraksha?), A.D. 381–395, of the Eastern Tsin dynasty, A.D. 317–420. 3 leaves. This work is mentioned as a Hînayâna-sûtra in *K*'-tsiṅ, fasc. 29, fol. 21 b.

The above six works are wanting in Tibetan. *K*'-yuen-lu, fasc. 9, fol. 26 a seq.

1331 瑜伽翳迦訖沙羅烏瑟尼沙斫訖羅眞言安怛陀那儀則一字頂輪王瑜伽經

Yü-*k*iê-i-*k*iâ-*k*i-shâ-lo-wu-seh-ni-shâ-*k*ö-*k*i-lo-*k*an-yen-ân-tâ-tho-nâ-i-tsö-yi-tsz'-tiṅ-lun-wâṅ-yu-*k*iê-*k*iṅ.

'Yogaikâksharoshnîshakakramantrântadânakalpaikâksharoshnîshakakrarâgayoga-sûtra.'

Translated by Amoghavagra, A.D. 746–771, of the Thâṅ dynasty, A.D. 618–907. 7 leaves. This work is mentioned as a Mahâyâna-sûtra of the Vaipulya class in *K*'-tsiṅ, fasc. 15, fol. 4 a.

1332 佛入涅槃密跡金剛力士哀戀經

Fo-ʒu-niê-phân-mi-tsi-*k*in-kâṅ-li-sh'-âi-lien-*k*iṅ.

'Sûtra on the grief and ardent love of the Malla or wrestler Guhyapadavagra, when Buddha entered Nirvâna.'

Translated under the (three) Tshin dynasties, A.D. 350–431; but the translator's name is lost. 7 leaves.

This work is mentioned as a Hînayâna-sûtra in *K'*-tsiṅ, fasc. 29, fol. 22 a.

The following three works were translated under the Western Tsin dynasty, A.D. 265–316; but the translators' names are lost:—

1333 佛使比丘迦旃延說法沒盡偈經

Fo-sh'-pi-*kh*iu-*k*iâ-*k*ân-yen-shwo-fâ-mê-tsin-*k*iê-*k*iṅ.

'Sûtra on Buddha's causing the Bhikshu Kâtyâyana to preach the Gâthâ on the destruction of the law.'

9 leaves.

1334 佛說佛治身經

Fo-shwo-fo-*k*'-shan-*k*iṅ.

'Sûtra spoken by Buddha on Buddha's keeping the body in regular order.'

2 leaves. This and the following work are mentioned as Hînayâna-sûtras in *K'*-tsiṅ, fasc. 31, fol. 13 a, b.

1335 治意經

K'-i-*k*iṅ.

'Sûtra on keeping the mind or thought in regular order.'

2 leaves.

The above four works are wanting in Tibetan. *K'*-yuen-lu, fasc. 9, fol. 28 a.

1336 文殊師利發願經

Wan-shu-sh'-li-fâ-yuen-*k*iṅ.

'Mañ*g*usrî-pra*n*idhânotpâda-sûtra.'

Samantabhadrapra*n*idhâna, Bhadra*k*ari.

Translated by Buddhabhadra, A.D. 420, of the Eastern Tsin dynasty, A.D. 317–420. 4 leaves; 43 verses. This is an earlier and incomplete translation of the 62 verses of Nos. 89 and 1142. This work is mentioned as a Mahâyâna-sûtra of the Avatamsaka class in *K'*-tsiṅ, fasc. 1, fol. 11 a.

1337 六菩薩名亦當誦持經

Liu-phu-sâ-miṅ-yi-tâṅ-suṅ-*kh*'-*k*iṅ.

'Sûtra on six Bodhisattvas' names also to be recited and kept in mind.'

Translated under the Eastern Hân dynasty, A.D. 25–220; but the translator's name is lost. 2 leaves. This work is mentioned as a Mahâyâna-sûtra of the Vaipulya class in *K'*-tsiṅ, fasc. 5, fol. 27 b.

1338 小道地經

Siâo-tâo-ti-*k*iṅ.

'Kshullamârgabhûmi-sûtra.'

Translated by *K'* Yâo, A.D. 185, of the Eastern Hân dynasty, A.D. 25–220. 4 leaves. This work is mentioned as a Mahâyâna-sâstra in *K'*-tsiṅ, fasc. 38, fol. 18 a.

1339 阿含口解十二因緣經

Ö-hân-kheu-*k*iê-shi-'rh-yin-yuen-*k*iṅ.

'Sûtra on the twelve causes (Nidânas) as an oral explanation according to the Âgama.'

Translated by Ân Hhüen, A.D. 181, of the Eastern Hân dynasty, A.D. 25–220. 9 leaves. This work is mentioned as a Hînayâna-sâstra in *K'*-tsiṅ, fasc. 40, fol. 17 a.

The above four works are wanting in Tibetan. *K'*-yuen-lu, fasc. 10, fol. 1 b seq.

1340 付法藏因緣經 (or 傳)

Fu-fâ-tsâṅ-yin-yuen-*k*iṅ (or *k*whân).

'Sûtra (or record) on the Nidâna or cause of transmitting the Dharmapiṭaka.'

Translated by *K'*i-*k*iâ-ye, together with Thân-yâo, A.D. 472, of the Northern Wêi dynasty, A.D. 386–534. 6 fasciculi. This is a very well-known history of the succession of twenty-three patriarchs from Mahâkâsyapa to the Bhikshu Simha. Deest in Tibetan. *K'*-yuen-lu, fasc. 9, fol. 27 a. The following is a list of the names of 23 patriarchs, according to No. 1340, with reference to the pages of Eitel's Handbook of Chinese Buddhism, and Edkins' Chinese Buddhism, where the names are given:—

No. 1340.		EITEL.	EDKINS.
(1) 摩訶迦葉 Mo-ho-*k*iâ-yeh, Mahâkâsyapa.		64 b	63
(2) 阿難 Ö-nân, Ânanda.		9 a	64
(3) 商那和修 Shân-nâ-hö-siu, *S*anavâsa (?).		121 a	66
(4) 優波毱多 Yiu-po-*k*ü-to, Upagupta.		156 a	67
(5) 提多迦 Ti-to-*k*iâ, Dhritaka.		33 b	70
(6) 彌遮迦 Mi-*k*ö-*k*iâ, Mi*kk*haka.		76 b	71
		(7) Vasumitra, 164 a	72
(7) 佛陀難提 Fo-tho-nân-thi, Buddhanandi.	(8)	28 b	71
(8) 佛陀密多 Fo-tho-mi-to, Buddhamitra.	(9)	"	

No. 1340.

		Ei-tel.	Ed-kins.
(9) 脅比丘 Hhiê-pi-*kh*iu, Pârsva Bhikshu.	(10)	91 b	74
(10) 富那奢 Fu-nâ-shö, Puṇyayasas.	(11)	98 b	"
(11) 馬鳴菩薩 Mâ-miṅ-phu-sâ, Asvaghosha Bodhisattva.	(12)	16 b	"
(12) 比羅比丘 Pi-lo-pi-*kh*iu, Kapimala (?) Bhikshu.	(13)	52 a	76
(13) 龍樹菩薩 Luṅ-shu-phu-sâ, Nâgârguna Bodhisattva.	(14)	79 b	77
(14) 迦那提婆 *K*iâ-nâ-thi-pho, Kâṇadeva.	(15)	50 b	"
(15) 尊者羅睺羅 Tsun-*k*ö-lo-heu-lo, Ârya Râhulata (?).	(16)	101 b	78
(16) 尊者僧伽難提 Tsun-*k*ö-saṅ-*k*iê-nân-thi, Ârya Saṅghanandi.	(17)	117 b / 121 b	79
(17) 僧伽耶舍 Saṅ-*k*iê-ye-shö, Saṅghayasas.	(18)		80
(18) 鳩摩羅馱 *K*iu-mo-lo-tho, Kumârata (?).	(19)	59 a	81
(19) 闍夜多 Shö-yê-to, *G*ayata.	(20)	42 a	82
(20) 婆修槃陀 Pho-siu-phân-tho, Vasubandhu.	(21)	164 a	In Index only.
(21) 摩奴羅 Mo-nu-lo, Manura.	(22)		82
(22) 鶴勒那夜奢 Hâo-lö-nâ-yê-shö, Haklenayasas.	(23)	87 b	83
(23) 師子比丘 Sh'-tsz'-pi-*kh*iu, Simha Bhikshu.	(24)		84
	(25)		Basiasita (?), 85
	(26)		Putnomita (?), 85
	(27) Pragñâtara,	95 a	85
	(28) Bodhidharma,	24 b	86

1341 達磨多羅禪經

Tâ-mo-to-lo-shân-*k*iṅ.

Dharmatara (or Dharmatrâta)-dhyâna-sûtra.

Conc. 636. Translated by Buddhabhadra, A. D. 398–421, of the Eastern Tsin dynasty, A. D. 317–420. 2 fasciculi; 17 divisions.

1342 禪法要解經

Shân-fâ-yâo-*k*iê-*k*iṅ.

'Sûtra on the important explanation of the law of meditation.'

Translated by Kumâragîva, about A. D. 405, of the Latter Tshin dynasty, A. D. 384–417. 2 fasciculi. This work is mentioned as a Mahâyâna-sâstra in *K*'-tsiṅ, fasc. 38, fol. 16 b.

1343 阿育王經

Ö-yü-wâṅ-*k*iṅ.

'Asoka-râga-sûtra.'

Translated by Saṅghapâla, A. D. 512, of the Liâṅ dynasty, A. D. 502–557. 10 fasciculi; 8 chapters. This may be a translation of the Asokâvadana. For the Sanskrit text, see Catalogue of the Hodgson Manuscripts, V. 23; VI. 12; VII. 3.

1344 阿育王譬喻經

Ö-yü-wâṅ-phi-yü-*k*iṅ.

'Asoka-râgâvadâna-sûtra.'

Translated under the Eastern Tsiṅ dynasty, A. D. 317–420; but the translator's name is lost. 8 leaves. According to *K*'-yuen-lu (fasc. 9, fol. 30 a), this is a shorter version of No. 1366, which latter is said to have been compiled by the Bhikshu Tâo-lüeh (or -phi). No. 1344 may be a translation of a part of the Asokâvadâna, mentioned under No. 1343.

The above four works are wanting in Tibetan. *K*'-yuen-lu, fasc. 9, fol. 29 a seq.

1345 三慧經

Sân-hwui-*k*iṅ.

'Trigñâna-sûtra.'

Translated under the Northern Liâṅ dynasty, A. D. 397–439; but the translator's name is lost. 14 leaves. The three kinds of knowledge (Trigñâna) are belief, hearing, and practice.

1346 阿毗曇五法行經

Ö-phi-thân-wu-fâ-hhiṅ-*k*iṅ.

'Abhidharma-pañkadharmakaryâ-sûtra.'

Translated by Ân Shi-kâo, A.D. 148–170, of the Eastern Hân dynasty, A.D. 25–220. 12 leaves. This work is mentioned as a Hînayâna-sâstra in *K'*-tsin, fasc. 40, fol. 13 a.

The above two works are wanting in Tibetan. *K'*-yuen-lu, fasc. 10, fol. 1 b.

1347 賓頭盧突羅闍爲優陀延王說法緣經

Pin-theu-lu-tu-lo-shö-wêi-yiu-tho-yen-wân-shwo-fâ-yuen-*k*in.

'Sûtra on the cause (Nidâna) of the preaching of the law by Pindola (?) Bharadvâga to the King Udâyana.'

Translated by Gunabhadra, A.D. 435–443, of the earlier Sun dynasty, A.D. 420–479. 9 leaves. This work is mentioned as a Hînayâna-sûtra in *K'*-tsin, fasc. 31, fol. 26 b.

1348 請賓頭盧經

Tshin-pin-theu-lu-*k*in.

'Sûtra on inviting Pindola (?).'

Translated by Hwui-*k*ien, A.D. 457, of the earlier Sun dynasty, A.D. 420–479. 2 leaves.

1349 大勇菩薩分別業報略經

Tâ-yun-phu-sâ-fan-pieh-yeh-pâo-lüeh-*k*in.

'Sûtra on the fruits of Karma briefly explained by the Bodhisattva Âryasûra.'

Translated by Sanghavarman, A.D. 434, of the earlier Sun dynasty, A.D. 420–479. 12 leaves.

1350 坐禪三昧法門經

Tso-shân-sân-mêi-fâ-man-*k*in.

'Dhyânanishthita (?)-samâdhi-dharmaparyâya-sûtra.'

Composed by Sangharaksha. Translated by Kumâragîva (first in A.D. 402, and afterwards revised in A.D. 407), of the Latter Tshin dynasty, A.D. 384–417. 2 fasciculi; 8 divisions. Deest in Tibetan. *K'*-yuen-lu, fasc. 9, fol. 27 b.

1351 佛所行讚經

Fo-su-hhin-tsân-*k*in.

Buddha*k*arita-kâvya (-sûtra).

Composed by the Bodhisattva Asvaghosha. Translated by Dharmaraksha, A.D. 414–421, of the Northern Liân dynasty, A.D. 397–439. 5 fasciculi; 28 chapters. This is a metrical work on the life of Buddha, from his birth till the division of his relics (*S*arîra). It has been translated into English by Mr. Beal, and will appear in a volume of the Sacred Books of the East. For the Sanskrit text, see Catalogue of the Hodgson Manuscripts, V. 34; VII. 10. There is a MS. of the same work in the University Library, Cambridge, which MS. is marked Add. 1387. The Sanskrit text consists of 17 chapters only, the titles and contents of which agree with those of the first 17 chapters of No. 1351 (except the titles of the 11th, 16th, and 17th chapters), though the latter omits some verses. The following Sanskrit titles of the 17 chapters are taken from two MSS., at Paris (C. H. M., V. 34) and Cambridge above alluded to:—

(1) Bhagavat-prasûti.
(2) Antahpura-vihâra.
(3) Samvegotpatti.
(4) Strî-vighâtana.
(5) Abhinishkramana.
(6) *Kh*andaka-nivartana.
(7) Tapovana-pravesa.
(8) Antahpura-vilâpa.
(9) Kumârânveshana.
(10) *S*renya (or *S*renika, i. e. Bimbisâra)-abhigamana.
(11) Kâma-vigarhana.
(12) Arâda-darsana.
(13) Mâra-vigaya.
(14) Abhisambodhana-samstava.
(15) Dharma*k*akrapravartanâdhyeshana.
(16) Dharma*k*akrapravartana.
(17) Lumbinîyâgâdika (or °yâtrikâ ?).

For the Chinese titles of the 28 chapters of No. 1351, see Mr. Beal's translation. According to *K'*-yuen-lu (fasc. 9, fol. 25 b), No. 1351 is wanting in Tibetan.

1352 僧伽羅刹所集佛行經

San-*k*iê-lo-*k*hâ-su-tsi-fo-hhin-*k*in.

'Sûtra on the practice of Buddha (or Buddha-*k*arita-sûtra), compiled by Sangharaksha.'

Translated by Sanghabhûti, A.D. 384, of the Former Tshin dynasty, A.D. 350–394. 5 fasciculi. Deest in Tibetan. *K'*-yuen-lu, fasc. 9, fol. 26 b.

1353 法句譬喩經

Fâ-*k*ü-phi-yü-*k*in.

'Dharmapadâvadâna-sûtra.'

Compiled by the venerable Dharmatrâta. Cf. Nos. 1321, 1365, 1439. Translated by Fâ-*k*ü, together with Fâ-li, A.D. 290–306, of the Western Tsin dynasty, A.D. 265–316. 4 fasciculi; 39 chapters; 68 Avadânas or parables, illustrating the teaching of the verses. This is the second of four Chinese versions of the Dhammapada, being different in order from No. 1321. The verses are less complete than those in No. 1365. Deest in Tibetan. See *K'*-yuen-lu, fasc. 10, fol. 1 a; *K'*-tsiṅ, fasc. 41, fol. 2 b. No. 1321 has been translated by Mr. Beal. 'The Dhammapada from the Buddhist Canon,' London, 1878. In his version, the verses in No. 1321 are fully translated, but of the parables an abstract only is given. See also the Sacred Books of the East, vol. x, Introduction to the Dhammapada, pp. l–lii.

1354 菩提行經

Phu-thi-hhiṅ-*k*iṅ.

'Bodhikaryâ-sûtra.'

Composed by the Bodhisattva Nâgârguna, in verse. Translated by Thien-si-tsâi, A. D. 980–1001, of the later Suṅ dynasty, A. D. 960–1127. 4 fasciculi; 8 chapters. This work is mentioned as a Mahâyâna-sâstra in *K'*-tsiṅ, fasc. 38, fol. 19 b.

The following two works were translated by Amoghavagra, A. D. 746–771, of the Thâṅ dynasty, A. D. 618–907:—

1355 金剛頂一切如來眞實攝大乘現證大教王經

*K*in-kâṅ-tiṅ-yi-tshiê-*z*u-lâi-*k*an-shih-shö-tâ-shaṅ-hhien-*k*aṅ-tâ-*k*iâo-wâṅ-*k*iṅ.

'Vagrasekhara-sarvatathâgata-satyasaṅgraha-mahâyâna-pratyutpannâbhisambuddha-mahâtantrarâga-sûtra.'

2 fasciculi. This is an earlier translation of the first division of No. 1017. *K'*-tsiṅ, fasc. 15, fol. 1 a, where this work is accordingly mentioned as a Mahâyâna-sûtra of the Vaipulya class.

1356 文殊菩薩及諸仙所說吉凶時日善惡宿曜經

Wan-shu-phu-sâ-*k*i-*k*u-sien-su-shwo-*k*i-hhiüṅ-sh'-*z*ih-shân-ṅoh-su-yâo-*k*iṅ.

'Sûtra on the goodness and badness concerning the Nakshatras or constellations, and lucky and unlucky days and times, spoken by the Bodhisattva Mañgusrî and many other Rishis.'

2 fasciculi. This translation was made in A. D. 759. It is a work on astrology.

1357 僧伽斯那所撰菩薩本緣經

Saṅ-*k*iê-sz'-nâ-su-*k*wân-phu-sâ-pan-yuen-*k*iṅ.

'Sûtra on the former causes (Pûrva-nidâna or -avadâna) of the Bodhisattva compiled by Saṅghasena.'

Translated by *K' Kh*ien, A. D. 223–253, of the Wu dynasty, A. D. 222–280. 4 fasciculi; 8 chapters.

1358 那先比丘經

Nâ-sien-pi-*kh*iu-*k*iṅ.

'Nâgasena-bhikshu-sûtra.'

Translated under the Eastern Tsin dynasty, A. D. 317–420; but the translator's name is lost. 3 fasciculi; 23, 21, and 14 leaves. The principal speakers are the Bhikshu Nâgasena and the Râga Mi-lân, i. e. Milinda (?); so that it seems to be a translation of a text similar to the Milinda-pañho, though the introductory part is not exactly the same as that of the Pâli text, published by Dr. Trenckner in his Pâli Miscellany, part 1, with English translation.

1359 舊雜譬喩經

*K*iu-tsâ-phi-yü-*k*iṅ.

'An old (version of the) Samyuktâvadâna-sûtra.'

Collected by the sages and the wise. Translated by Khâṅ Saṅ-hwui, A. D. 251, of the Wu dynasty, A. D. 222–280. 2 fasciculi. This work is mentioned as a Mahâyâna-sâstra in *K'*-tsiṅ, fasc. 38, fol. 19 a.

The following two works were translated under the Eastern Hân dynasty, A. D. 25–220; but the translators' names are lost:—

1360 禪要訶欲經

Shân-yâo-hö-yü-*k*iṅ.

'Sûtra on blaming human desire or lust, and on the importance of the meditation.'

4 leaves. This work is mentioned as a Mahâyâna-sâstra in *K'*-tsiṅ, fasc. 38, fol. 17 b.

1361 內身觀章句經

Nêi-shan-kwân-*k*âṅ-*k*ü-*k*iṅ.

'Sûtra consisting of sections and verses on meditation on the inner body.'

4 leaves.

1362 法觀經

Fâ-kwân-*k*iṅ.

'Sûtra of meditation on the law.'

Translated by *K*u Fâ-hu (Dharmaraksha), A. D. 266–313, of the Western Tsin dynasty, A. D. 265–316. 6 leaves. This translation is not readable. *K'*-tsiṅ, fasc. 41, fol. 6 b.

The above six works are wanting in Tibetan. *K'*-yuen-lu, fasc. 9, fol. 27 a seq.

1363 迦葉結經

*K*iâ-yeh-*k*iê-*k*iṅ.

'Sûtra on Kâsyapa's collection (of the Tripitaka).'

Translated by Ân Shi-kâo, A. D. 148–170, of the Eastern Hân dynasty, A. D. 25–220. 11 leaves. Mention is made in this work of Kâsyapa's reproach of nine faults committed by Ânanda. Deest in Tibetan. K'-yuen-lu, fasc. 10, fol. 1 a.

1364 百喻經

Pâi-yü-*k*in.

'Sûtra of a hundred comparisons.'

Composed by Saṅghasena. Translated by Guṇavṛiddhi, A. D. 492, of the Tshi dynasty, A. D. 479–502. 2 fasciculi; 98 comparisons, not Avadânas. For the Satâvadâna or Avadânasataka, see No. 1324. No. 1364 ends with the following words: 'Ârya Saṅghasena made this garland for the fool (?).'

1365 法句經

Fâ-*k*ü-*k*in.

'Dharmapada-sûtra,' or Dhammapada.

Composed or collected by Dharmatrâta. Translated by 維祇難 Wei-*k*hi-nân, i. e. Vighna, and others, A. D. 224, of the Wu dynasty, A. D. 222–280. 2 fasciculi; 39 chapters; 752 verses. This version is also called Fâ-tsi-*k*in, or Dharma-saṅgraha-sûtra. See K'-yuen-lu, fasc. 9, fol. 31. In the same work (fasc. 10, fol. 2 a), No. 1365 is said to be wanting in Tibetan. In the preface to No. 1365, this text is called 曇鉢偈 Thân-po-*k*ie, or Dharma-pada-gâthâ. For this preface as well as the version, see Mr. Beal's 'Dhammapada from the Buddhist Canon,' pp. 3–30. No. 1365 is the first of four Chinese versions of the Dhammapada. See also the Sacred Books of the East, vol. x, Introduction to Dhammapada, pp. l–lii. As to the character of the translator of No. 1365, the following account is given in the Kâo-san-*k*whân, or Memoirs of Eminent Priests (compiled in A. D. 519), fasc. 1, fol. 14 a, b: 'Vighna was an Indian Sramaṇa, who was at first a fire-worshipper, and afterwards converted to Buddhism. In A. D. 224, he together with *K*u Lüh-yen brought to China a Sanskrit text of the 曇鉢經 Thân-po-*k*in, or Dharma-pada-sûtra; then they were asked by the Chinese to translate it. At this time, both Vighna and Lüh-yen were not yet well acquainted with the language of the country (China), nevertheless they translated the text into Chinese in 2 fasciculi. Their translation is, therefore, somewhat difficult in its expression, owing to the simplicity of their words, though their intention was to retain the meaning of the text. Afterwards, in the reign of Hwui-ti (A. D. 290–306) of the Western Tsin dynasty (A. D. 265–316), Fâ-li, together with Fâ-*k*ü, made a better translation of the same work in 5 fasciculi (No. 1353), and the latter also translated a shorter Sûtra, consisting of about 100 verses. This shorter translation was lost, during the civil war towards the end of the Yun-*k*iâ period (A. D. 307–312).' No. 1365 is therefore an earlier translation of the verses of No. 1353; in the latter however the verses are less complete.

1366 衆經撰雜譬喻經

*K*uṅ-*k*iṅ-*k*wân-tsâ-phi-yü-*k*iṅ.

'Samyuktâvadâna-sûtra, selected from various Sûtras.'

Compiled by the Bhikshu Tâo-lüeh (or -phi). Translated by Kumâragîva, A. D. 405, of the Latter Tshin dynasty, A. D. 384–417. 2 fasciculi. This work is mentioned as a Mahâyâna-sâstra in K'-tsiṅ, fasc. 38, fol. 19 a.

1367 阿育王子法益壞目因緣經

Ö-yü-wâṅ-tsz'-fâ-yi-hwâi-mu-yin-yuen-*k*iṅ.

'Sûtra on the Nidâna or cause of the eye-destruction of Fâ-yi (Dharmavardhana ?) the prince of Asoka.'

Translated by Dharmanandi, A. D. 384, of the Former Tshin dynasty, A. D. 350–394. 1 fasciculus; 36 leaves. The Sanskrit text is said to have consisted of 343 slokas in verse, which are now translated into 10,880 Chinese characters. See preface to No. 1367.

1368 雜譬喻經

Tsâ-phi-yü-*k*iṅ.

'Samyuktâvadâna-sûtra.'

Cf. No. 1366. Translated under the Eastern Hân dynasty, A. D. 25–220; but the translator's name is lost. 2 fasciculi. This work is mentioned as a Mahâyâna-sâstra in K'-tsiṅ, fasc. 38, fol. 19 b.

The above three works are wanting in Tibetan. K'-yuen-lu, fasc. 9, fol. 30 a seq.

1369 無明羅剎經

Wu-miṅ-lo-*k*hâ-*k*iṅ.

'Avidyârâksha-sûtra.'

Translated under the (three) Tshin dynasties, A. D. 350–431; but the translator's name is lost. 1 fasciculus; 28 leaves. Deest in Tibetan. K'-yuen-lu, fasc. 10, fol. 2 a.

1370 文殊所說最勝名義經

Wan-shu-su-shwo-tsui-shaṅ-miṅ-i-*k*iṅ.

'Mañgusrî-bhâshitottamanâmârtha-sûtra.'

Mañgusrî-nâmasaṅgîti.

K'-yuen-lu, fasc. 5, fol. 15 b; Conc. 799.

Mañgusrî-gñâna-sattvasya paramârthânâm saṅgîti.

A. R., p. 488; A.M.G., p. 291; Conc. 799. Translated by *K*in-tsun-*kh'* (Suvarnadhâranî), about A. D. 1113, of the later Sun dynasty, A. D. 960–1127. 2 fasciculi; 18 leaves. It agrees with Tibetan. *K'*-yuen-lu, s. v. No. 1370 is mentioned as Mahâyâna-sûtra of the Vaipulya class in *K'*-tsin, fasc. 15, fol. 14 a.

1371 迦丁比丘說當來變經

*K*iâ-tiṅ-pi-*kh*iu-shwo-tâṅ-lâi-pien-*k*iṅ.

'Sûtra on the changes of the future, spoken by the Bhikshu Kiâ-tiṅ (?).'

Translated under the earlier Suṅ dynasty, A. D. 420–479; but the translator's name is lost. 10 leaves.

1372 雜譬喩經

Tsâ-phi-yü-*k*iṅ.

'Samyuktâvadâna-sûtra.'

Cf. Nos. 1366 and 1368. Translated by *K'* Leu-*k*iâ-*kh*ân (Lokarakshaa?), A. D. 147–186, of the Eastern Hân dynasty, A. D. 25–220. 11 leaves.

1373 思惟要略法

Sz'-wêi-yâo-*l*üeh-fâ.

'An abridged law on the importance of thinking or meditation.'

Translated by Kumâragîva, A. D. 405, of the latter Tshin dynasty, A. D. 384–417. 12 leaves.

The above two works are mentioned as Mahâyâna-sâstras in *K'*-tsin, fasc. 38, fol. 19 b and 17 a respectively.

1374 十二遊經

Shi-'rh-yiu-*k*iṅ.

'Dvâdasa (-varsha)-viharana-sûtra.'

Translated by Kâlodaka, A. D. 392, of the Eastern Tsin dynasty, A. D. 317–420. 6 leaves. It gives an account concerning the life of Buddha, from his birth till the twelfth year from his becoming Buddha. Piâo-mu, fasc. 3, fol. 23 a.

The above three works are wanting in Tibetan. *K'*-yuen-lu, fasc. 9, fol. 29 b.

1375 賢聖集伽陀一百頌

Hhien-shaṅ-tsi-*k*iê-tho-yi-pâi-suṅ.

'A hundred Gâthâs collected by the sages and the wise.'

Translated by Thien-si-tsâi, A. D. 980–1001, of the later Suṅ dynasty, A. D. 960–1280. 8 leaves. The Gâthâs explain the happy rewards of the action of giving gifts to Buddha and Saṅgha.

1376 廣發大願頌

Kwâṅ-fâ-tâ-yuen-suṅ.

'Mahâpranidhânotpâda-gâthâ.'

Composed by the Bodhisattva Nâgârguna. Translated by Sh'-hu (Dânapâla?), A. D. 980–1000, of the later Suṅ dynasty, A. D. 960–1127. 3 leaves. In *K'*-yuen-lu, fasc. 10, fol. 6 a, the second character of the Chinese title is placed after the third one, which reading is adopted in the literal translation of the title above.

The following two works were translated by Fâ-thien (Dharmadeva?), A. D. 973–981, of the later Suṅ dynasty, A. D. 960–1127:—

1377 無能勝大明陀羅尼經

Wu-naṅ-shaṅ-tâ-miṅ-tho-lo-ni-*k*iṅ.

'Ageyamahâvidyâ-dhâranî-sûtra.'

10 leaves. This and the following work are mentioned as Mahâyâna-sûtras of the Vaipulya class in *K'*-tsin, fasc. 15, fol. 12 b.

1378 無能勝大明心陀羅尼經

Wu-naṅ-shaṅ-tâ-miṅ-sin-tho-lo-ni-*k*iṅ.

'Ageyamahâvidyâhridaya-dhâranî-sûtra.'

2 leaves.

1379 十不善業道經

Shi-pu-shân-yeh-tâo-*k*iṅ.

'Dasadushtakarmamârga-sûtra.'

Composed by the Bodhisattva Asvaghosha. Translated by *Z*ih-*k*âṅ (Sûryayasas?), A. D. 1004–1058, of the later Suṅ dynasty, A. D. 960–1127. 2 leaves.

1380 大乘修行菩薩行門諸經要集

Tâ-shaṅ-siu-hhiṅ-phu-sâ-hhiṅ-man-*k*u-*k*iṅ-yâo-tsi.

'Mahâyâna-karana-bodhisattva-karyâdvâra-sarvasûtra-mahârtha-saṅgraha.'

Translated by *K'*-yen, A. D. 721, of the Thâṅ dynasty, A. D. 618–907. 3 fasciculi. It consists of sixty-six articles on the practice of a Bodhisattva, collecting passages from forty-two different Sûtras.

1381 四阿含暮抄解

Sz'-ö-hân-mu-*kh*âo-*k*iê.

'Explanation of an extract from the four Âgamas.'

Composed or compiled by the Arhat Vasubhadra. Translated by Kumârabuddhi, A. D. 382, of the Former Tshin dynasty, A. D. 350–394. 2 fasciculi; 9 chapters. This is an earlier translation of No. 1271. See *K'*-tsiṅ, fasc. 40, fol. 16 b, where this work is accordingly mentioned as a Hînayâna-sâstra.

1382 五門禪經要用法
Wu-man-shân-*k*iṅ-yâo-yuṅ-fâ.
'Pañkadvâra-dhyânasûtra-mahârthadharma.'

Composed by the 'Mahâdhyânaguru' Buddhamitra. Translated by Dharmamitra, A. D. 424–441, of the earlier Suṅ dynasty, A. D. 420–479. 1 fasciculus. This work is mentioned as a Mahâyâna-sâstra in *K'*-tsiṅ, fasc. 38, fol. 16 a.

The above four works are wanting in Tibetan. *K'*-yuen-lu, fasc. 9, fol. 27 a seq.

1383 金剛頂瑜伽千手千眼觀自在菩薩修行儀軌經
*K*in-kâṅ-tiṅ-yü-*k*iê-tshien-sheu-tshien-yen-kwân-tsz'-tsâi-phu-sâ-siu-hhiṅ-i-kwêi-*k*iṅ.
'Vagrasekharayoga-sahasrabâhu-sahasrâksha-avalokitesvara-bodhisattva-karyâ-kalpa-sûtra.'

Translated by Amoghavagra, A. D. 746–771, of the Thâṅ dynasty, A. D. 618–907. 1 fasciculus. This work is mentioned as a Mahâyâna-sûtra in *K'*-tsiṅ, fasc. 15, fol. 9 a.

1384 密跡力士大權神王經偈頌
Mi-tsi-li-sh'-tâ-*kh*üen-shan-wâṅ-*k*iṅ-*k*iê-suṅ.
'Guhyapadamalla-mahardhirâga-sûtra-gâthâ.'

Collected by *K*u-pâ, A. D. 1314–1320, of the Yuen dynasty, A. D. 1280–1368. 1 fasciculus; 175 verses.

1385 一切秘密最上名義大教王儀軌
Yi-tshiê-pi-mi-tsui-shâṅ-miṅ-i-tâ-*k*iâo wâṅ-i-kwêi.
'Sarvaguhyânuttaranâmârtha-mahâtantra-râga-kalpa.'

Translated by Sh'-hu (Dânapâla ?), A. D. 980–1000, of the later Suṅ dynasty, A. D. 960–1127. 2 fasciculi; 21 leaves.

1386 大樂金剛薩埵修行成就儀軌
Tâ-lö-*k*in-kâṅ-sâ-to-siu-hhiṅ-*kh*aṅ-tsiu-i-kwêi.
'Mahâsukha-vagrasattva-karyâsiddhi-kalpa.'

Translated by Amoghavagra, A. D. 746–771, of the Thâṅ dynasty, A. D. 618–907. 16 leaves.

1387 曼殊室利菩薩吉祥伽陀
Mân-shu-shih-li-phu-sâ-*k*i-siâṅ-*k*iê-tho.
'Mañgusri-bodhisattva-srigâthâ.'

Transliterated by Fâ-hhien, A. D. 982–1001, of the later Suṅ dynasty, A. D. 960–1127. 2 leaves. This is another transliteration of No. 1074. *K'*-tsiṅ, fasc. 15, fol. 15 b.

The following three works were translated by Amoghavagra, A. D. 746–771, of the Thâṅ dynasty, A. D. 618–907:—

1388 成就妙法蓮華經王瑜伽觀智儀軌
*Kh*aṅ-tsiu-miâo-fâ-lien-hwâ-*k*iṅ-wâṅ-yü-*k*iê-kwân-*k'*-i-kwêi.
'Saddharmapundarika-sûtrarâga-siddhi-yoga-dhyânagñâna-kalpa.'

1 fasciculus.

1389 金剛頂瑜伽降三世成就極深密門
*K*in-kâṅ-tiṅ-yü-*k*iê-*k*iâṅ-sân-shi-*kh*aṅ-tsiu-*k*i-shan-mi-man.
'Vagrasekhara-yoga-tribhavavigaya-siddhi-mahâguhyadvâra.'

5 leaves. This translation was made by Amoghavagra, together with Pien-*k'* (Sarvagña ?).

1390 金剛頂瑜伽他化自在天理趣會普賢修行念誦儀
*K*in-kâṅ-tiṅ-yü-*k*iê-thâ-hwâ-tsz'-tsâi-thien-li-tshü-hwui-phu-hhien-siu-hhiṅ-nien-suṅ-i.
'Vagrasekhara-yoga-parinirmitavasavartisatyatâ-parshat-samantabhadrakaryâdhyâya-kalpa.'

16 leaves.

1391 金剛壽命陀羅尼念誦法
*K*in-kâṅ-sheu-miṅ-tho-lo-ni-nien-suṅ-fâ.
'Vagrâyur-dhârany-adhyâya-kalpa.'

Translated by Vagrabodhi, together with Amoghavagra, A. D. 723–730, of the Thâṅ dynasty, A. D. 618–907. 3 leaves.

1392 大藥叉女歡喜母幷愛子成就法
Tâ-yo-*kh*â-nü-kwân-hhi-mu-piṅ-âi-tsz'-*kh*aṅ-tsiu-fâ.
'Mahâyakshamâtr-ânandâ (?)-puriyaputra-siddhi-kalpa.'

Translated by Amoghavagra, A.D. 746–771, of the Thân dynasty, A.D. 618–907. 12 leaves.

1393 佛說帝釋巖秘密成就儀軌

Fo-shwo-ti-shih-yen-pi-mi-khan-tsiu-i-kwêi.

'Buddhabhâshita-indrasakra-silâ-guhya-siddhi-kalpa.'

Translated by Sh'-hu (Dânapâla?), A.D. 980–1000. of the later Sun dynasty, A.D. 960–1127. 5 leaves. In this work, Buddha tells Vagrapâni how man can see the Bodhisattva Maitreya in the Indra cave (?). *K'*-tsin, fasc. 12, fol. 9 a.

The following fourteen works were translated by Amoghavagra, A.D. 746–771, of the Thân dynasty, A.D. 618–907 :—

1394 觀自在菩薩如意輪念誦儀軌

Kwân-tsz'-tsâi-phu-sâ-su-i-lun-nien-sun-i-kwêi.

'Avalokitesvara-bodhisattva-kintâkakra (or -mani-dhâranî?)-adhyâya-kalpa.'

10 leaves.

1395 大毗盧遮那成佛神變加持經略示七支念誦隨行法

Tâ-phi-lu-kö-nâ-khan-fo-shan-pien-kiâ-kh'-kin-lüêh-sh'-tshiê-k'-nien-sun-sui-hhin-fâ.

'An abridgment, showing the law (kalpa) of seven sorts of recitation and practice, of (the 7th fasciculus of) the Mahâvairokanâbhisambuddhy-riddhiyugandhara-sûtra (No. 530).'

5 leaves.

1396 速疾立驗摩醯首羅天說阿尾奢法

Su-tsi-li-yen-mo-hhi-sheu-lo-thien-shwo-ö-wêi-shö-fâ.

'Sîghraphalodaya-mahesvara-deva-bhâshitâvisha-kalpa.'

5 leaves.

1397 大聖曼殊室利童子五字瑜伽法

Tâ-shan-mân-shu-shih-li-thun-tsz'-wu-tsz'-yü-kiê-fâ.

'Mahârya-mañgusrî-kumâra(bhûta)-pañkâkshara-yoga-kalpa.'

5 leaves. Thirty-five mantras are given in Nepalese letters.

1398 大威怒烏芻澀麼儀軌

Tâ-wêi-nu-wu-khu-seh-mo-i-kwêi.

'Mahâbalakrodha-wu-khu-seh-mo (?)-kalpa.'

17 leaves.

1399 大孔雀明王畫像壇場儀軌

Tâ-khun-tshioh-min-wân-hwâ-siân-thân-khân-i-kwêi.

'Mahâmayûrî-vidyârâgñî-kitrapratibimba-mandala-kalpa.'

6 leaves.

1400 金剛頂瑜伽金剛薩埵儀軌

Kin-kân-tin-yü-kiê-kin-kân-sâ-to-i-kwêi.

'Vagrasekhara-yoga-vagrasattva-kalpa.'

13 leaves.

1401 一字金輪王佛頂要略念誦法

Yi-tsz'-kin-lun-wân-fo-tin-yâo-lüêh-nien-sun-fâ.

'Ekâkshara-suvarnakakrarâga-buddhoshnîsha-mahârtha-sankshepâdhyâya-kalpa.'

5 leaves.

1402 觀自在菩薩如意輪瑜伽念誦法

Kwân-tsz'-tsâi-phu-sâ-su-i-lun-yü-kiê-nien-sun-fâ.

'Avalokitesvara-bodhisattva-kintâkakra (or -mani)-yogâdhyâya-kalpa.'

14 leaves. This is a later translation of No. 538. *K'*-tsin, fasc. 15, fol. 9 a.

1403 大聖大歡喜雙身毗那耶迦法

Tâ-shan-tâ-kwân-hhi-shwân-shan-phi-nâ-ye-kiâ-fâ.

'Mahârya-mahâbhirati-dvâkâya-vinayaka-kalpa.'

4 leaves. This is a later translation of a part of the 11th fasciculus of No 363. *K'*-tsin, fasc. 14, fol. 28 a.

1404 大日經略攝念誦隨行法

Tâ-zih-kin-lüêh-shö-nien-sun-sui-hhin-fâ.

'Mahâvairokana-sûtra-sankshepasangrahâdhyâya-karyâ-kalpa.'

4 leaves. For the Sûtra, see No. 530.

1405 五字陀羅尼頌

Wu-tsz'-tho-lo-ni-suṅ.

'Paṅkâkshara-dhâraṇî-gâthâ.'

11 leaves.

The above twenty-one works are mentioned as Mahâyâna-sûtras of the Vaipulya class in K'-tsiṅ, fasc. 12–15.

1406 仁王般若陀羅尼釋

Zan-waṅ-pân-zo-tho-lo-ni-shih.

'Kârunikarâga-pragñâ (pâramitâ)-dhâraṇî-vyâkhyâ.'

8 leaves. For the Pragñâpâramitâ, see Nos. 17, 965.

1407 大樂金剛不空眞實三昧
耶經般若波羅蜜多理趣釋

Tâ-lö-kin-kâṅ-pu-khuṅ-kan-shih-sân-mêi-ye-kiṅ-pân-zo-po-lo-mi-to-li-tshü-shih.

'Mahâsukha-vagrâmoghasatyasamaya-sûtra-pragñâpâramitâ-buddhi-vyâkhyâ.'

2 fasciculi. For the Sûtra, see No. 1034.

The above two works are mentioned as Mahâyâna-sâstras in K'-yuen, fasc. 34, fol. 7 a, b.

1408 佛說最勝妙吉祥根本智
最上秘密一切名義三摩地分

Fo-shwo-tsui-shaṅ-miâo-ki-siâṅ-kan-pan-k'-tsui-shâṅ-pi-mi-yi-tshiê-miṅ-i-sân-mo-ti-fan.

'Buddhabhâshita-anuttara-mañgusrî-mûlagñânânuttaraguhya-sarvanâmârtha-samâdhi-varga.'

Translated by Sh'-hu (Dânapâla?), A.D. 980–1000, of the Thâṅ dynasty, A.D. 618–907. 2 fasciculi; 21 leaves. This is an earlier translation of No. 1370. K'-yuen-lu, fasc. 5, fol. 15 b.

The following seven works were translated by Amoghavagra, A.D. 746–771, of the Thâṅ dynasty, A.D. 618–907:—

1409 金剛王菩薩秘密念誦儀軌

Kin-kâṅ-waṅ-phu-sâ-pi-mi-nien-suṅ-i-kwêi.

'Vagrarâga-bodhisattva-guhyâdhyâya-kalpa.'

15 leaves.

1410 金剛頂勝初瑜伽普賢菩
薩念誦法經

Kin-kâṅ-tiṅ-shaṅ-khu-yü-kiê-phu-hhien-phu-sâ-nien-suṅ-fâ-kiṅ.

'Vagrasekharânuttarayoga-samantabhadra-bodhisattvâdhyâya-kalpa-sûtra.'

11 leaves.

1411 金剛頂瑜伽金剛薩埵五
秘密修行念誦儀軌

Kin-kâṅ-tiṅ-yü-kiê-kin-kâṅ-sâ-to-wu-pi-mi-siu-hhiṅ-nien-suṅ-i-kwêi.

'Vagrasekhara-yoga-vagrasattva-pañkaguhya-karyâdhyâya-kalpa.'

14 leaves. This is another translation of No. 1400. K'-tsiṅ, fasc. 15, fol. 1 b.

1412 無量壽如來修觀行供
養儀軌

Wu-liâṅ-sheu-zu-lâi-siu-kwân-hhiṅ-kuṅ-yâṅ-i-kwêi.

'Amitâyus-tathâgata-dhyâna-karyâ-pûgâ-kalpa.'

15 leaves.

1413 甘露軍茶利菩薩供養念
誦成就儀軌

Kân-lu-kiün-thu-li-phu-sâ-kuṅ-yâṅ-nien-suṅ-khaṅ-tsiu-i-kwêi.

'Amṛitakuṇḍali-bodhisattva-pûgâdhyâya-siddhi-kalpa.'

1 fasciculus.

1414 觀自在多羅瑜伽念誦法

Kwân-tsz'-tsâi-to-lo-yü-kiê-nien-suṅ-fâ.

'Avalokitesvaratârâ-yogâdhyâya-kalpa.'

14 leaves. This is a metrical work.

1415 聖觀自在菩薩心眞言瑜
伽觀行儀軌

Shaṅ-kwân-tsz'-tsâi-phu-sâ-sin-kan-yen-yü-kiê-kwân-hhiṅ-i-kwêi.

'Ârya-avalokitesvara-bodhisattva-hṛidaya-mantra-yoga-dhyâna-karyâ-kalpa.'

6 leaves. This is an extract from No. 530.

The above eight works are mentioned as Mahâyâna-sûtras in K'-tsiṅ, fasc. 12 and 15.

1416 菩薩訶色欲法

Phu-sâ-hö-seh-yü-fâ.

'Law of the Bodhisattva's blaming the lustful desire.'

Translated by Kumâragîva, about A.D. 405, of the Latter Tshin dynasty, A.D. 384–417. 1 leaf. This work is mentioned as a Mahâyâna-sâstra in K'-tsiṅ, fasc. 38, fol. 17 b.

1417 四品學法

Sz'-phin-hhio-fâ.

'Katurvarga-sikshâ-dharma.'

Translated by Gunabhadra, A.D. 435–443, of the earlier Sun dynasty, A.D. 420–479. 3 leaves. This work is mentioned as a Hînayâna-sâstra in K'-tsiṅ, fasc. 40, fol. 17 b.

The above two works are wanting in Tibetan. K'-yuen-lu, fasc. 9, fol. 27 b seq.

The following seven works were translated by Amoghavagra, A.D. 746–771, of the Thâṅ dynasty, A.D. 618–907:—

1418 大虛空藏菩薩念誦法

Tâ-hhiu-khuṅ-tsâṅ-phu-sâ-nien-suṅ-fâ.

'Mahâkâsagarbha-bodhisattva (-dhâranî ?)-adhyâya-kalpa.'

6 leaves. For the Dhâranî, see Nos. 67–70.

1419 仁王般若念誦法

Zan-wâṅ-pân-zo-nien-suṅ-fâ.

'Kârunikarâga-pragñâ (pâramitâ)-adhyâya-kalpa.'

7 leaves. For the Pragñâpâramitâ, see Nos. 17, 965.

1420 阿閦如來念誦供養法

Ö-shö-zu-lâi-nien-suṅ-kuṅ-yâṅ-fâ.

'Akshobhya-tathâgatâdhyâya-pûgâ-kalpa.'

17 leaves.

1421 佛頂尊勝陀羅尼念誦儀軌

Fo-tiṅ-tsun-shaṅ-tho-lo-ni-nien-suṅ-i-kwêi.

'Buddhoshnîshavigaya-dhârany-adhyâya-kalpa.'

11 leaves. For the Dhâranî, see Nos. 348–352, 796.

1422 聖閻曼德迦威怒王立成大神驗念誦法

Shaṅ-yen-mân-töh-kiâ-wêi-nu-wâṅ-li-khaṅ-tâ-shan-yen-nien-suṅ-fâ.

'Ârya-ganmântaraka (?)-balakrodharâga-sighrodayamahardddhi-phala-adhyâya-kalpa.'

9 leaves.

1423 大乘方廣曼殊室利菩薩華嚴本教讚閻曼德迦忿怒王眞言大威德儀軌品

Tâ-shaṅ-fâṅ-kwâṅ-mân-shu-shih-li-phu-sâ-hwâ-yen-pan-kiâo-tsân-yen-mân-töh-kiâ-fan-nu-wâṅ-kan-yen-tâ-wêi-töh-i-kwêi-phin.

'Mahâyâna-vaipulya-mañgusrî-bodhisattvâvatamsaka-mûlatantra-ganmântaraka (?)-krodharâga-mantra-mahâbalaguna-kalpavarga.

4 leaves.

1424 大方廣曼殊室利童眞菩薩華嚴本教讚閻曼德迦忿怒王眞言阿毗遮嚕迦儀軌品

Tâ-fâṅ-kwâṅ-mân-shu-shih-li-thuṅ-kan-phu-sâ-hwâ-yen-pan-kiâo-tsân-yen-man-töh-kiâ-fan-nu-wâṅ-kan-yen-ö-phi-kö-lu-kiâ-i-kwêi-phin.

'Mahâvaipulya-mañgusrî-kumârabhûta-bodhisattvâvatamsaka-mûlatantra-ganmântaraka (?)-krodharâga-prasamsâ-mantra-avikalaka (?)-kalpavarga.'

12 leaves.

1425 蘇悉地羯羅供養法

Su-shih-ti-kiê-lo-kuṅ-yâṅ-fâ.

'Sushiddhikâra (-sûtra)-pûgâ-kalpa.'

Translated by Subhakarasimha, A.D. 717–724, of the Thâṅ dynasty, A.D. 618–907. 3 fasciculi. Deest in Tibetan. K'-yuen-lu, fasc. 6, fol. 16 b.

The following two works were translated by Vagrabodhi, A.D. 723–730, of the Thâṅ dynasty, A.D. 618–907:—

1426 不動使者陀羅尼秘密法

Pu-thuṅ-sh'-kö-tho-lo-ni-pi-mi-fâ.

'Akala-dûta-dhâranî-guhya-kalpa.'

15 leaves.

1427 金剛頂瑜伽修習毗盧遮那三摩地法

Kin-kâṅ-tiṅ-yü-kiê-siu-si-phi-lu-kö-nâ-sân-mo-ti-fâ.

'Vagrasekhara-yoga-karyâ-vairokana-samâdhi-kalpa.'

17 leaves.

The following two works were translated by Amoghavagra, A.D. 746–771, of the Thâṅ dynasty, A.D. 618–907:—

1428 金剛頂瑜伽經文殊師利菩薩儀軌供養法

Kin-kâṅ-tiṅ-yü-kiê-kiṅ-wan-shu-sh'-li-phu-sâ-i-kwêi-kuṅ-yâṅ-fâ.

'Vagrasekhara-yoga-sûtra-mañgusrî-bodhisattva-kalpa-pûgâ-dharma.'

14 leaves.

1429 瑜伽蓮華部念誦法

Yü-*k*iê-lien-hwâ-pu-nien-sun-fâ.

'Yoga-pundarika-vargâdhyâya-kalpa.'

8 leaves.

1430 金剛頂經瑜伽觀自在王如來修行法

*K*in-kâṅ-tiṅ-*k*iṅ-yü-*k*iê-kwâṅ-tsz'-tsâi-wâṅ-*z*u-lâi-siu-hhiṅ-fâ.

'Va*g*rasekhara-sûtra-yogâvalokitesvararâ*g*a-tathâgata-*k*aryâ-kalpa.'

Translated by Va*g*rabodhi, A.D. 723–730, of the Thâṅ dynasty, A.D. 618–907. 1 fasciculus.

The following six works were translated by Amogha-va*g*ra, A.D. 746–771, of the Thâṅ dynasty, A.D. 618–907:—

1431 金剛頂經觀自在王如來修行法

*K*in-kâṅ-tiṅ-*k*iṅ-kwân-tsz'-tsâi-wâṅ-*z*u-lâi-siu-hhiṅ-fâ.

'Va*g*rasekhara-sûtra-avalokitesvararâ*g*a-tathâgata-*k*aryâ-kalpa.'

8 leaves. This is a later translation of No. 1430. *K*'-tsiṅ, fasc. 15, fol. 10 a.

1432 金剛手光明灌頂經最勝立印聖無動尊大威怒王念誦儀軌

*K*in-kâṅ-sheu-kwâṅ-miṅ-kwân-tiṅ-*k*iṅ-tsui-shaṅ-li-yin-shaṅ-wu-thuṅ-tsun-tâ-wêi-nu-wâṅ-nien-suṅ-i-kwêi.

'Va*g*rapâniprabhâbhisheka-sûtrânuttarapratish*th*itamudrâryâ*k*ala-mahâbalakrodharâ*g*âdhyâya-kalpa.'

1 fasciculus. This translation was made by Amogha-va*g*ra, together with Pien-*k*' (Sarva*g*ña ?).

The above fifteen works are mentioned as Mahâyâna-sûtras in *K*'-tsiṅ, fasc. 12–15.

1433 略述金剛頂瑜伽分別聖位修證法門

Lüêh-shu-*k*in-kâṅ-tiṅ-yü-*k*iê-fan-pieh-shaṅ-i-siu-*k*aṅ-fâ-man.

'Saṅkshepa-va*g*rasekhara-yogâryapadanirdesa-*k*aryâbhisambuddha-dharmaparyâya.'

14 leaves. This is mentioned as a Mahâyâna-sâstra in *K*'-tsiṅ, fasc. 34, fol. 6 b.

1434 一字佛頂輪王念誦儀軌

Yi-tsz'-fo-tiṅ-lun-wâṅ-nien-suṅ-i-kwêi.

'Ekâkshara-buddhoshnishaka*k*rarâ*g*âdhyâya-kalpa.'

12 leaves.

1435 仁王護國般若波羅蜜多經道場念誦儀軌

*Z*an-wâṅ-hu-kwo-pân-*z*o-po-lo-mi-to-*k*iṅ-tâo-*kh*âṅ-nien-suṅ-i-kwêi.

'Kârunikarâ*g*a-râsh*t*rapâla-pra*g*ñâpâramitâ-sûtra-bodhima*nd*â-dhyâya-kalpa.'

1 fasciculus; 5 divisions. For the Sûtra, see Nos. 17, 965.

1436 金剛頂蓮華部心念誦儀軌

*K*in-kâṅ-tiṅ-lien-hwâ-pu-sin-nien-suṅ-i-kwêi.

'Va*g*rasekhara-pu*nd*arikavargahr*i*dayâdhyâya-kalpa.'

1 fasciculus.

The following two works were translated by Tsz'-hhien, of the later Suṅ dynasty, A.D. 960–1127:—

1437 佛說如意輪蓮華心如來修行觀門儀

Fo-shwo-*z*u-i-lun-lien-hwâ-sin-*z*u-lâi-siu-hhiṅ-kwân-man-i.

'Buddhabhâshita-*k*intâ*k*akra (or -mani)-pu*nd*arika-hr*i*daya-tathâgata-*k*aryâ-dhyânadvâra-kalpa.'

14 leaves.

1438 妙吉祥平等瑜伽秘密觀身成佛儀軌

Miâo-*k*i-siâṅ-piṅ-tâṅ-yü-*k*iê-pi-mi-kwân-shan-*kh*aṅ-fo-i-kwêi.

'Mañ*g*usrî-samantayoga-guhya-dhyânakâyâbhisambuddha-kalpa.'

15 leaves.

The above five works are mentioned as Mahâyâna-sûtras of the Vaipulya class in *K*'-tsiṅ, fasc. 15.

1439 法集要頌經

Fâ-tsi-yâo-suṅ-*k*iṅ.

'Dharmasaṅgraha-mahârthagâthâ-sûtra,' or Dhammapada.

Collected by the venerable Dharmatrâta. Translated by Thien-si-tsâi, A.D. 980–1001, of the later Suṅ dynasty, A.D. 960–1127. 4 fasciculi; 33 chapters. This is the last of four Chinese versions of the Dhammapada. It is a collection of those verses in No. 1321, being all spoken by Buddha. See *K*'-tsiṅ, fasc. 41, fol. 3 a. For No. 1439, see the Sacred Books of the East, vol. x, p. lii.

1440 勸發諸王要偈

Kwân-fâ-*k*u-wân-yâo-*k*iê.

'Important Gâthâs or verses on persuading and encouraging kings (or King Sadvâhana).'

Ârya-nâgârguna-bodhisattva-suh*r*illekha.

Note at the end of No. 1441. Composed by the Bodhisattva Nâgârguna. Translated by Saṅghavarman, A. D. 534, of the earlier Suṅ dynasty, A. D. 420–479. 10 leaves.

1441 龍樹菩薩勸誡王頌

Luṅ-shu-phu-sâ-kwân-*k*iê-wâṅ-suṅ.

'Verses on persuading and cautioning King (Sadvâhana), (composed) by the Bodhisattva Nâgârguna.'

Ârya-nâgârguna-bodhisattva-suh*r*illekha.

Translated by I-tsiṅ, A. D. 700–712, of the Thâṅ dynasty, A. D. 618–907. 9 leaves. This is a later translation of No. 1440. *K'*-tsiṅ, fasc. 41, fol. 9 a.

The following three works were translated by Amoghavagra, A. D. 746–771, of the Thâṅ dynasty, A. D. 618–907:—

1442 普賢金剛薩埵瑜伽念誦儀

Phu-hhien-*k*in-kâṅ-sâ-to-yü-*k*iê-nien-suṅ-i.

'Samantabhadra-vagrasattva-yogâdhyâya-kalpa.'

14 leaves.

Fogg Mus. has a Fujiwara ms. scroll.

1443 金剛頂瑜伽護摩儀軌

*K*in-kâṅ-tiṅ-yü-*k*iê-hu-mo-i-kwêi.

'Vagrasekhara-yoga-homa-kalpa.'

14 leaves; 5 different kalpas or ceremonial rules.

1444 大悲心陀羅尼修行念誦略儀

Tâ-pêi-sin-tho-lo-ni-siu-hhiṅ-nien-suṅ-lüêh-i.

'Mahâkâruṇikahr*i*daya-dhâraṇî-*k*aryâdhyâya-saṅkshepakalpa.'

10 leaves. For the Dhâraṇî, see No. 320.

1445 妙吉祥平等觀門大教王經略出護摩儀

Miâo-*k*i-siâṅ-piṅ-tâṅ-kwân-man-tâ-*k*iâo-wâṅ-*k*iṅ-lüêh-*kh*u-hu-mo-i.

'Homa-kalpa, being an abridged translation of the Mañgusrî-samantadhyânadvâra-mahâtantrarâga-sûtra (No. 1041).'

Translated by Tshz'-hhien, of the later Suṅ dynasty, A. D. 960–1127. 10 leaves.

The following ten works were translated by Amoghavagra, A. D. 746–771, of the Thâṅ dynasty, A. D. 618–907:—

1446 金剛頂超勝三界經說文殊五字眞言勝相

*K*in-kâṅ-tiṅ-*k*âo-shaṅ-sân-*k*iê-*k*iṅ-shwo-wan-shu-wu-tsz'-*k*an-yen-shaṅ-siâṅ.

'An excellent mark of Mañgusrî's Mantra of five letters, spoken (by Buddha) in the Vagrasekhara-trilokâtikramaṇa-sûtra.'

3 leaves.

1447 金剛頂經瑜伽文殊師利菩薩法一品

*K*in-kâṅ-tiṅ-*k*iṅ-yü-*k*iê-wan-shu-sh'-li-phu-sâ-fâ-yi-phin.

'Vagrasekhara-sûtra-yoga-mañgusrî-bodhisattva-dharmaikavarga.'

3 leaves.

1448 金剛頂瑜伽經十八會指歸

*K*in-kâṅ-tiṅ-yü-*k*iê-*k*iṅ-shi-pâ-hwui-sh'-kwêi.

'An outline of eighteen assemblies in the Vagrasekhara-yoga-sûtra.'

10 leaves.

1449 訶利帝母眞言法

Hö-li-ti-mu-*k*an-yen-fâ.

'Hâritî-mâtri-mantra-kalpa.'

4 leaves.

The above eight works are mentioned as Mahâyâna-sûtras of the Vaipulya class in *K'*-tsiṅ, fasc. 14, 15.

1450 大方廣佛華嚴經入法界品四十二字觀

Tâ-fâṅ-kwâṅ-fo-hwâ-yen-*k*iṅ-*z*u-fâ-*k*iê-phin-sz'-shi-'rh-tsz'-kwân.

'Mahâvaipulya-buddhâvataṃsaka-sûtra (Nos. 87, 88)-dharmadhâtvavatârâdhyâya-dvâkatvârimsad-akshara-dhyâna.'

8 leaves. It agrees with Tibetan. *K'*-yuen-lu, fasc. 2, fol. 14 b.

1451 般若波羅蜜多理趣經大安樂不空三昧眞實金剛菩薩等一十七聖大曼荼羅義述

Pân-*z*o-po-lo-mi-to-li-tshü-*k*iṅ-tâ-ân-lö-pu-khuṅ-sân-mêi-*k*an-shih-*k*in-kâṅ-phu-sâ-tâṅ-yi-shi-tshiê-shaṅ-tâ-man-thu-lo-i-shu.

'Pragñâpâramitâ-buddhi-sûtra (No. 1033 ?)-mahâsukhâmogha-samayasatyavagra-bodhisattvâdi-saptadasârya-mahâmaṇḍala-vyâkhyâ.'

3 leaves.

The above two works are mentioned as Mahâyâna-sâstras in *K'*-tsin, fasc. 34.

1452 陀羅尼門諸部要目
Tho-lo-ni-man-*k*u-pu-yâo-mu.
'Important names or articles of many classes of the Dhâranî-dvâra.'

5 leaves.

1453 金剛頂瑜伽三十七尊禮
*K*in-kân-tin-yü-*k*iê-sân-shi-tshiê-tsun-li.
'Vagrasekhara-yoga-saptatrimsadârya-pûgâ.'

5 leaves.

1454 受菩提心戒儀
Sheu-phu-thi-sin-*k*iê-i.
'Bodhihridayasîlâdâna (?)-kalpa.'

Compiled by the Yogâkârya Samantabhadra. Translated by Amoghavagra, as mentioned in col. 319. 5 leaves.

The above three works are mentioned as Mahâyâna-sûtras of the Vaipulya class in *K'*-tsin, fasc. 14, 15.

1455 大聖文殊師利菩薩讚佛法身禮
Tâ-shan-wan-shu-sh'-li-phu-sâ-tsân-fo-fâ-shan-li.
'Mahârya-mañgusrî-bodhisattva-buddha-dharmakâya-prasamsâ-pûgâ.'

4 leaves. This translation was made in A.D. 765.

1456 一百五十讚佛頌
Yi-pâi-wu-shi-tsân-fo-sun.
'Sârdhasataka-buddhaprasamsâ-gâthâ (?),' or '150 verses on the praise of Buddha.'

Composed by the venerable Mâtrikêta. Translated by I-tsin, of the Thân dynasty, A.D. 618–907, while staying in the Nâlanda Vihâra, Central India. 11 leaves. I-tsin left China for India in A.D. 671, and returned to China in 695. According to Khâi-yuen-lu (fasc. 9, fol. 21 a), I-tsin revised his translation in A.D. 708. Deest in Tibetan. *K'*-yuen-lu, fasc. 10, fol. 2 a.

1457 百千頌大集經地藏菩薩請問法身讚
Pâi-tshien-sun-tâ-tsi-*k*in-ti-tsân-phu-sâ-tshin-wan-fâ-shan-tsân.
'Satasahasragâthâ-mahâsannipâta-sûtra (No. 61)-kshitigarbha-bodhisattva-pariprikkhâ-dharmakâya-stotra.'

Translated by Amoghavagra, A.D. 746–771, of the Thân dynasty, A.D. 618–907. 9 leaves. Deest in Tibetan. *K'*-yuen-lu, fasc. 6, fol. 17 a. In the *K'*-yuen-lu, fasc. 2, fol. 7 b, a similar title, ending with 'tsân-*k*in' or 'stotra-sûtra,' is mentioned, and it is said to agree with Tibetan.

1458 佛吉祥德讚
Fo-*k*i-siân-töh-tsân.
'Buddha-sriguna-stotra.'

Composed by Munimitra (?). Translated by Sh'-hu (Dânapâla ?), A.D. 980–1000, of the later Sun dynasty, A.D. 960–1127. 3 fasciculi.

The above four works are mentioned under the heading of the Mahâyâna-sâstras in *K'*-tsin, fasc. 38.

1459 阿育王傳
Ö-yü-wân-*k*whân.
'Life of King Asoka.'

Translated by Ân Fâ-*kh*in, A.D. 281–306, of the Western Tsin dynasty, A.D. 265–316. 5 fasciculi; 11 Avadânas. This is an earlier translation of No. 1343. *K'*-yuen-lu, fasc. 9, fol. 30 b.

The following three works were translated by Kumâragîva, about A.D. 405, of the Latter Tshin dynasty, A.D. 384–417:—

1460 馬鳴菩薩傳
Mâ-min-phu-sâ-*k*whân.
'Life of the Bodhisattva Asvaghosha.'

4 leaves. Cf. Wassiljew, Buddhismus, p. 211, and elsewhere.

1461 龍樹菩薩傳
Lun-shu-phu-sâ-*k*whân.
'Life of the Bodhisattva Nâgârguna.'

5 leaves. Cf. Wassiljew, Buddhismus, p. 212, and elsewhere.

1462 提婆菩薩傳
Thi-pho-phu-sâ-*k*whân.
'Life of the Bodhisattva Deva (or Âryadeva).'

5 leaves. Cf. Wassiljew, Buddhismus, p. 214, and elsewhere.

1463 婆藪槃豆傳
Pho-seu-phân-teu-*k*whân.
'Life of Vasubandhu.'

Translated by Paramârtha, A.D. 557–569, of the *Kh*an dynasty, A.D. 557–589. 12 leaves. Cf. Wassiljew, Buddhismus, p. 215, and elsewhere.

1464 龍樹菩薩爲禪陀迦王說法要偈

Luṅ-shu-phu-sâ-wêi-shân-tho-kiâ-wân-shwo-fâ-yâo-kiê.

'Gâthâs or verses on the importance of the law, spoken (or composed) by the Bodhisattva Nâgârguna to (or for) King Shân-tho-kiâ (Gńâtaka, of the Sadvâhana family?).'

Ârya-nâgârguna-bodhisattva-suhrillekha.

Cf. Nos. 1440, 1441. Translated by Gunavarman, A.D. 431, of the earlier Suṅ dynasty, A.D. 420–479. 12 leaves. This is an earlier translation of Nos. 1440, 1441. K'-yuen-lu, fasc. 10, fol. 2 b; K'-tsiṅ, fasc. 41, fol. 8 b. In the Nân-hâi-ki-kwâi-kwhân (fasc. 4, fol. 5 b), I-tsiṅ (A.D. 671–712) says that this Suhrillekha was sent by the Bodhisattva Nâgârguna to his old Dânapati, a great King of the South (India), who was called 娑多婆漢那 So-to-pho-hân-nâ, i.e. Sadvâhana, and whose proper name was 市演得迦 Sh'-yen-töh-kiâ, i.e. Gńâtaka (? cf. Shân-tho-kiâ, in the title of No. 1464). I-tsiṅ also says that the Buddhists in the five parts of India first commit these verses to memory when they begin to study their religion.

1465 撰集三藏及雜藏傳

Kwân-tsi-sân-tsâṅ-kiu-tsâ-tsâṅ-kwhân.

'Record of the collection of the Tripitaka and Samyukta-pitaka.' Cf. No. 1363.

Translated under the Eastern Tsin dynasty, A.D. 317–420; but the translator's name is lost. 15 leaves. Deest in Tibetan. K'-yuen-lu, fasc. 10, fol. 1 a.

1466 大阿羅漢難提蜜多羅所說法住記

Tâ-ö-lo-hân-nân-thi-mi-to-lo-su-shwo-fâ-ku-ki.

'Record on the duration of the law, spoken by the great Arhat Nandimitra.'

Translated by Hhüen-kwân (Hiouen-thsang), A.D. 654, of the Thâṅ dynasty, A.D. 618–907. 8 leaves. It begins: 'As handed down by tradition, in the time when eight hundred years had elapsed since the Bhagavat entered Parinirvâṇa, there lived an Arhat named Nandimitra, in the capital of King Prasenagit, of the country of Simhala or Simhaladvipa.' The names of sixteen great Arhats and their dwelling-places are mentioned in this work.

1467 瑜伽集要燄口施食儀

Yü-kiâ-tsi-yâo-yen-kheu-sh'-shi-i.

'Ceremonial rules for giving food to the Flaming-mouth (Preta), in the collection of important (articles) of Yoga.'

Translated by Amoghavagra, A.D. 746–771, of the Thâṅ dynasty, A.D. 618–907. 1 fasciculus; 42 leaves. The Buddhoshnishavigaya-dhâranî (Nos. 348–351, 796) is given in the Devanâgarî character with a Chinese transliteration in parallel columns. There are two appendices. The one is, 'Writing on ten sorts of departed spirits or Pretas;' and the other, Trisarana-stotra, or Laudatory verses on taking refuge with the Triratna, viz. Buddha, Dharma, and Saṅgha. No. 1467 is mentioned under the heading of the Mahâyâna-sûtras of the Vaipulya class in K'-tsiṅ, fasc. 15, fol. 17 a.

PART II.

CHINESE MISCELLANEOUS WORKS.

(a) 此土著述 Tshz'-thu-ku-shu, or Works of 'this country,' i. e. China.

1468 釋迦譜
Shih-kiâ-fu.
'A record or history of the Sâkya (family).'

Compiled by San-yiu, about A. D. 500, under the Tshi dynasty, A. D. 479–502, from various Sûtras and Vinaya works of the Mahâyâna and Hînayâna. 10 fasciculi; 34 chapters. It consists of 112,734 Chinese characters. It begins with a genealogy of the Sâkya family, and ends with a record of the state of the destruction of the law of Sâkyamuni. There are given separately the lives of Sâkyamuni and his parents, relations and disciples, and the records of the Vihâras and Kaityas.

The following three works were compiled by Tâo-süen, A. D. 650–667, of the Thân dynasty, A. D. 618–907:—

1469 釋迦氏譜
Shih-kiâ-sh'-fu.
'A record or history of the Sâkya family.'

2 fasciculi; 5 chapters. This work is similar to No. 1468. Dated A. D. 665.

1470 釋迦方誌
Shih-kiâ-fân-k'.
'A record of the country of Sakya(muni),' i. e. India.

3 fasciculi; 8 chapters. Dated A. D. 650.

1471 集古今佛道論衡實錄
Tsi-ku-kin-fo-tâo-lun-han-shih-lu.
'A collection of the authentic records of the controversies between Buddhists and Taoists in ancient and modern times (from A. D. 71 till about 620).'

4 fasciculi; 33 chapters. The first three fasciculi are dated A. D. 661, and the fourth, 664.

1472 續集古今佛道論衡
Suh-tsi-ku-kin-fo-tâo-lun-han.
'A continued collection of the controversies between Buddhists and Taoists in ancient and modern times.'

Compiled by K'-shan, A. D. 730, of the Thân dynasty, A. D. 618–907. 1 fasciculus; 23 leaves. This is a supplement to No. 1471. It gives an account concerning the first controversy between the two schools after Buddhism was introduced into China (A. D. 67), which controversy took place in A. D. 71. Cf. Fân-i-min-i-tsi, fasc. 3, fol. 2 b.

1473 經律異相
Kin-lüh-i-siân.
'(A collection of extracts) on different subjects from Sûtras and Vinaya works.'

Compiled by San-min, Pâo-khân, and others, A. D. 516, of the Liân dynasty, A. D. 502–557, under the Imperial order. 50 fasciculi; 21 classes subdivided into 40; 639 articles. The order of the subjects treated in this work is heaven, earth, Buddha, Bodhisattvas, Srâvakas, Kakravartirâga, kings, queens, princes, Sreshthins or rich merchants, Upâsakas, Upâsikâs, Tirthikas and Rishis, Brahmakârins, Brâhmanas, Grihapatis, merchants, common men and women, gods and demons, beasts, birds, insects, and hells.

1474 諸經要集
Ku-kin-yâo-tsi.
'A collection of (extracts on) important (doctrinal questions) from various Sûtras.'

Compiled by Tâo-shi, A. D. 656–660, of the Thân dynasty, A. D. 618–907. 30 fasciculi; 30 chapters; 1000 articles.

1475 陀羅尼雜集
Tho-lo-ni-tsâ-tsi.
'A mixed collection of Dhâranîs.'

This work is mentioned in a catalogue compiled under the Liân dynasty, A. D. 502–557; but the collector's name is unknown. 10 fasciculi; 185 Dhâranîs.

1476 出三藏記集

*Kh*u-sân-tsâṅ-*k*i-tsi.

'A collection of the records of translations of the Tripitaka.'

Compiled by Saṅ-yiu, about A. D. 520, of the Liâṅ dynasty, A. D. 502–557. 17 fasciculi. This is a catalogue of the Tripiṭaka translated into Chinese from A. D. 67 till about A. D. 520. There are several interesting records added to the catalogue.

1477 顯密圓通成佛心要集

Hhien-mi-yuen-thuṅ-*kh*aṅ-fo-sin-yâo-tsi.

'A collection of important (accounts concerning) the thought of becoming Buddha, perfect in both hidden and apparent (doctrines?).'

Compiled by Tâo-*kh*an, of the later Suṅ dynasty, A. D. 960–1127. 2 fasciculi.

1478 密咒圓因往生集

Mi-*kh*eu-yuen-yin-wâṅ-shaṅ-tsi.

'A collection of (33) Mantras (to be recited?) for the perfect cause of going to be born (in Buddha's country).'

Collected by *K*'-kwâṅ and Hwui-*k*an, and translated by Vagraketu (?), of the later (or Northern) or Southern Suṅ dynasty, A. D. 960–1127, or 1127–1280. There is a preface dated A. D. 1200, under the great Hhiâ, i. e. a contemporaneous dynasty with the Suṅ. 1 fasciculus; 26 leaves.

1479 弘明集

Huṅ-miṅ-tsi.

'A collection of (miscellaneous writings on) propagation and illustration (of the teaching of Buddha).'

Collected by Saṅ-yiu, about A. D. 520, of the Liâṅ dynasty, A. D. 502–557. 14 fasciculi.

1480 集沙門不應拜俗等事

Tsi-shâ-man-pu-yiṅ-pâi-su-tâṅ-sh'.

'A collection of (miscellaneous writings for asserting) that *S*râmanas ought not to bow before laymen.'

Compiled by Yen-tshuṅ, A. D. 662, of the Thâṅ dynasty, A. D. 618–907. 6 fasciculi; 6 chapters.

1481 廣弘明集

Kwâṅ-huṅ-miṅ-tsi.

'An enlarged collection of (miscellaneous writings on) propagation and illustration (of the teaching of Buddha).'

Collected by Tâo-süen, A. D. 650–667, of the Thâṅ dynasty, A. D. 618–907. 40 fasciculi. This work is similar to No. 1479.

1482 法苑珠林

Fâ-wân-shu-lin.

'Pearl-grove of the garden of the law.'

Compiled by Tâo-shi, A. D. 668, of the Thâṅ dynasty, A. D. 618–907. 100 fasciculi; 100 chapters, subdivided into many parts. This is a large Encyclopædia, containing extracts from the Tripiṭaka.

The following two works were compiled by Tâo-süen, A. D. 664, of the Thâṅ dynasty, A. D. 618–907:—

1483 大唐內典錄

Tâ-thâṅ-nêi-tien-lu.

'A catalogue of the Buddhist books, (compiled) under the great Thâṅ dynasty, A. D. 618–907.

16 fasciculi. It contains all the titles of the Tripiṭaka translated into Chinese, from A. D. 67 till about 664, whether in existence or lost, and those of the works of Chinese Buddhists, together with short biographical accounts of the translators and authors. No. 1483 is generally called Nêi-tien-lu.

1484 集神州塔寺三寶感通錄

Tsi-shan-*k*eu-thâ-sz'-sân-pâo-kân-thuṅ-lu.

'A collection of accounts concerning the influential power of the three precious things or Triratna (Buddha, Dharma, and Saṅgha) in the pagodas and monasteries in the "spiritual" country,' i. e. China.

4 fasciculi.

The following two works were compiled by *K*'-shaṅ, A. D. 730, of the Thâṅ dynasty, A. D. 618–907:—

1485 開元釋教錄

Khâi-yuen-shih-*k*iâo-lu.

'A catalogue of (the books on) the teaching of *S*âkyamuni, (compiled) in the Khâi-yuen period, A. D. 713–741.'

30 fasciculi. In A. D. 730 there were in existence 1142 works in 5048 fasciculi; translated into Chinese, from A. D. 67 till 730. No. 1485 is generally called Khâi-yuen-lu. This work is similar to but fuller than No. 1483.

1486 開元釋教錄略出

Khâi-yuen-shih-*k*iâo-lu-lüeh-*kh*u.

'An abridged reproduction' of the preceding catalogue.

5 fasciculi. This is the last part of No. 1485. In this catalogue the order of all the works then admitted into the Canon is marked with the characters of the 千字文 Tshien-tsz'-wan, or Thousand-character-classic.

1487 古今譯經圖紀
Ku-*k*in-i-*k*iṅ-thu-*k*i.
'A record of the picture (of the events) of ancient and modern translations of the Sûtras (etc.).'

Compiled by Tsiṅ-mâi, about A. D. 664, of the Thâṅ dynasty, A. D. 618–907. 4 fasciculi. It contains all the titles of translations from the venerable Kâsyapa Mâtaṅga, A. D. 67, to Hhüen-*k*wâṅ (Hiouen-thsang), A. D. 645–664, together with short biographical notes. This work is said to have written on the figures of those translators, drawn on the wall of the 'translation hall' in the Tâ-tshz'-an-sz' monastery, in which Hiouen-thsang lived. See Khâi-yuen-lu, fasc. 8 b, fol. 19 a.

1488 續古今譯經圖紀
Suh-ku-*k*in-i-*k*iṅ-thu-*k*i.
'A continuation' of the preceding catalogue.

Compiled by *K*'-shaṅ, A. D. 730, of the Thâṅ dynasty, A. D. 618–907. 1 fasciculus; 22 leaves.

1489 宗鏡錄
Tsuṅ-*k*iṅ-lu.
'Records as the mirror of the (Dhyâna) school.'

Compiled by Yen-sheu, of the later (or Northern) or Southern Suṅ dynasty, A. D. 960–1127, or 1127–1280. 100 fasciculi; 3 parts. This is a metaphysical work of the Shân or Dhyâna school, founded by Bodhidharma, the twenty-eighth Indian patriarch, who arrived in China in A. D. 520.

1490 高僧傳
Kâo-saṅ-*k*whân.
'Memoirs of eminent priests.'

Compiled by Hwui-*k*iâo, A. D. 519, of the Liâṅ dynasty, A. D. 502–557. 14 fasciculi; 10 classes. 257 men are mentioned separately, while 239 are added in course of narration. They were either Indian or Chinese, and not only priests but also laymen, who lived in China some time between A. D. 67 and 519.

The following two works were compiled by I-tsiṅ, while staying in the South Sea country of Shi-li-fo-shi (?), and sent to China in A. D. 692, under the Thâṅ dynasty, A. D. 618–907:—

1491 大唐西域求法高僧傳
Tâ-thâṅ-si-yü-*k*iu-fâ-kâo-saṅ-*k*whân.
'Memoirs of eminent priests under the great Thâṅ dynasty, A. D. 618–907, who visited the Western region or India and its neighbouring countries, to search for the law.'

2 fasciculi. There are mentioned fifty-six priests who went from China to India and its neighbouring countries during the seventh century A. D.; and four others, who were companions of I-tsiṅ on his second voyage to the South Sea country of Shi-li-fo-shi, and studied there. An extract from No. 1491 has been published by Mr. Beal in Journal of the Royal Asiatic Society, 1881, pp. 558–572.

1492 南海寄歸內法傳
Nân-hâi-ki-kwêi-nêi-fâ-*k*whân.
'Records of the "inner law" or religion, sent from the South Sea country through one who returns (to China).'

4 fasciculi; 40 chapters. This is a work on the Vinaya. I-tsiṅ depends on the Vinaya-pi*t*aka of the Mûlasarvâstivâda-nikâya, and describes the actual practice of the priests in India and the South Sea countries. It is the practice which he has witnessed himself. At the same time, he refutes the former Chinese misinterpretations. He does not give any account concerning the Buddhists of Ceylon, except one passage (fasc. 1, fol. 3 b, col. 5), where he says that 'those of the Si*m*hala island all belong to the Sthavira school, and those of the Mahâsaṅgha (or -saṅghika) school are expelled (or not found there ?).' The term South Sea is used in this work to denote the China Sea, though it may include the Indian Ocean also.

1493 續高僧傳
Suh-kâo-saṅ-*k*whân.
'A continuation of the memoirs of eminent priests,' or a continuation of No. 1490.

Compiled by Tâo-süen, about A. D. 645–667, of the Thâṅ dynasty, A. D. 618–907. 40 fasciculi; 10 classes. 331 persons are mentioned separately, while 160 are added in course of narration. They lived in China some time between A. D. 519 and 645.

1494 大慈恩寺三藏法師傳
Tâ-tshz'-an-sz'-sân-tsâṅ-fâ-sh'-*k*whân.
'Life of the teacher of the law of Tripi*t*aka, (who lived) in the Tâ-tshz'-an (great-compassionate-favour) monastery,' i. e. Hhüen-*k*wâṅ (Hiouen-thsang).

Compiled by Hwui-li, and annotated by Yen-tshuṅ, A. D. 665, of the Thâṅ dynasty, A. D. 618–907. 10 fasciculi. According to Khâi-yuen-lu (fasc. 9, fol. 7 a), Houi-li left his work unfinished at his death, and Yen-tshuṅ made it complete. This teacher (H. T.) spent seventeen years on his journey from China to India, A. D. 629–645, and died in 664. This work has been translated into French by Julien, with the title of Voyages des Pèlerins Bouddhistes, vol. i. For this

French translation, see Professor Max Müller's Buddhist Pilgrims, in his Selected Essays, vol. ii, pp. 234–279.

1495 宋高僧傳
Suṅ-kâo-sañ-kwhân.
'Memoirs of eminent priests, (compiled) under the later (or Northern) Suṅ dynasty, A. D. 960–1127,' or a continuation of No. 1493.

Compiled by Tsan-niṅ, A. D. 988, of the later Suṅ dynasty, A. D. 960–1127. 30 fasciculi; 10 classes. 533 priests are mentioned separately, while thirty are added in course of narration. They lived in China some time between A. D. 645–988.

1496 法顯傳
Fâ-hhien-kwhân.
'Record (on the journey) of Fâ-hhien (Fâ-hian).'

Compiled by Fâ-hhien, A. D. 414, of the Eastern Tsin dynasty, A. D. 317–420, after he returned from India to China. He left China in A. D. 399, and spent fifteen years on his journey, A. D. 399–413. 1 fasciculus; 36 leaves. This work is otherwise called Fo-kwo-ki, or Record of Buddha's Country. It has been translated into French by A. Rémusat, and into English by Rev. S. Beal.

1497 比丘尼傳
Pi-khiu-ni-kwhân.
'Memoirs of (celebrated) Bhikshunîs.'

Compiled by Pâo-khân, about A. D. 526, of the Liâṅ dynasty, A. D. 502–557. 4 fasciculi. 65 Chinese Bhikshunîs are mentioned, who lived some time between A. D. 326–526.

1498 十門辯惑論
Shi-man-pien-hwo-lun.
'A treatise on explanation of (another's) doubts, in ten divisions.'

Composed by Fu-li, A. D. 681, of the Thâṅ dynasty, A. D. 618–907. 2 fasciculi. This is an answer to a work entitled 釋典稽疑 Shih-tien-ki-i, or 'a consideration on doubts in the Buddhist books,' by Khüen Wu-'rh, an official attached to the Prince Imperial.

1499 甄正論
Kan-kañ-lun.
'A treatise or dialogue between Kan-kañ, or one who "distinguishes what is right" from false (and Tâi-su, or one who "is attached to the common or popular views").'

Composed by Hhüen-i, of the Thâṅ dynasty, A. D. 618–907. 3 fasciculi. This work confutes several false Sûtras and names, such as Liṅ-pâo-kiṅ, or 'Sûtra of a marvellous gem,' and Thien-tsun, or 'heavenly-honour,' which latter had been probably used for an epitnet of Buddha.

The following two works were composed by Fâ-lin, A. D. 624–640, of the Thâṅ dynasty, A. D. 618–907:—

1500 破邪論
Po-siê-lun.
'A treatise on the confutation of heresy.'

2 fasciculi. This work confutes the sceptical opinions of Fu Yi, a contemporary of the author. Fu Yi was 'an imperial historiographer under Thâṅ Kâo-tsu (the first sovereign of the Thâṅ dynasty, reigned A. D. 618–626), and one of the most determined adversaries of the doctrines of Buddhism.' See Mayers' Chinese Reader's Manual, p. 44, No. 145.

1501 辯正論
Pien-kañ-lun.
'A treatise on the explanation of the truth.'

9 fasciculi; 12 chapters. This work chiefly confutes the opinions of the Taoists. A preface and commentary are added by Khan Tsz'-liâṅ, of the Thâṅ dynasty, A. D. 618–907.

1502 護法論
Hu-fâ-lun.
'A treatise on the preservation or protection of the Law.'

Composed by Kâṅ Shâṅ-yiṅ, about A. D. 1170, who was the prime minister under the Southern Suṅ dynasty, A. D. 1127–1280. 1 fasciculus, consisting of 12,345 Chinese characters. This work confutes the sceptical opinions of Eu-yâṅ Siu, who died in A. D. 1072. For this latter celebrated statesman and scholar, see Mayers' Chinese Reader's Manual, p. 165, No. 529.

1503 大唐西域記
Tâ-tâṅ-si-yü-ki.
'Records of the Western regions (made) under the great Thâṅ dynasty, A. D. 618–907.'

Compiled by Hhüen-kwân (Hiouen-thsang), together with his assistant Pien-ki, A. D. 646, of the Thâṅ dynasty, A. D. 618–907. 12 fasciculi. In this work, both the characters and usages of the people, and the sacred places of Buddhism, of 138 states in India and its neighbourhood are mentioned; most of which the author visited himself on his journey in A. D. 629–645. The country of Magadha is most minutely described in fasciculi 8 and 9. This work has been translated into French by Julien, with the title of Voyages des Pèlerins Bouddhistes, vols. ii and iii. It is to be compared with No. 1494, and its French translation by the same scholar. See Professor Max Müller's 'Buddhist Pilgrims,' in his Selected Essays, vol. ii, pp. 234–279; also Cunningham's Ancient Geography of India.

1504 歷代三寶紀
Li-tâi-sân-pâo-ki.

'Record concerning the three precious things (Triratna, viz. Buddha, Dharma, and Saṅgha) under successive dynasties.'

Compiled by Fêi *Kh*ân-fân, A.D. 597, of the Sui dynasty, A.D. 587–618. 15 fasciculi. The first three fasc. contain a general history of Buddhism, from the birth of Buddha down to the time of tne compilation of this work. The next eleven fasc. form a catalogue of the Tripitaka translated into Chinese from A.D. 67 till 587. The fifteenth fasc. is an index or a minute list of the contents of this work, No. 1504.

1505 集諸經禮懺悔文
Tsi-*k*u-*k*iṅ-li-*kh*ân-hwui-wan.

'A collection of writings on worship and confession from several Sûtras.'

Collected by *K*'-shan, A.D. 730, of the Thân dynasty, A.D. 618–907. 4 fasciculi.

The following three works were compiled by I-tsiṅ, who died in A.D. 713, of the Thân dynasty, A.D. 618–907:—

1506 說罪要行法
Shwo-tsui-yâo-hhiṅ-fâ.

'Rules for the important practice of confessing crimes or faults.'

5 leaves.

1507 受用三水要行法
Sheu-yuṅ-sân-shui-yâo-hhiṅ-fâ.

'Rules for an important practice of the use of three kinds of water.'

4 leaves. The three kinds of water are (1) pure water for a fixed time, (2) that for an unfixed time—both for drink—and (3) water for washing hands, etc. Cf. the sixth chapter of No. 1492 by the same author, where however the chapter is entitled Shui-yiu-'rh-piṅ, or 'two (different) vessels to be used for water.'

1508 護命放生軌儀法
Hu-miṅ-fâṅ-shaṅ-kwêi-i-fâ.

'Rules for letting living things go for their lives' preservation sake.'

3 leaves.

1509 慈悲道場懺法
Tsz'-pêi-tâo-*kh*âṅ-*kh*ân-fâ.

'Rules for confession in the religious place of the merciful and compassionate one, or in the temple of Buddha.'

No author's name given. 10 fasciculi; 40 chapters. According to the statement of the preface, dated A.D. 1267, this work was first compiled by a prince named Siâo Tsz'-liâṅ, in the Yuṅ-piṅ period, A.D. 483–493, of the Tshi dynasty, A.D. 479–502, when it was in 20 fasciculi, 30 chapters. Afterwards it was revised by an eminent priest in the Thien-*k*ien period, A.D. 502–519, of the Liâṅ dynasty, A.D. 502–557. But in No. 1493 it is stated that there was a writing on confession by Wu-ti, the first sovereign of the latter dynasty. Then a priest named *K*an-kwân or Hwui-shih enlarged it and called it by the present title.

1510 法華三昧懺儀
Fâ-hwâ-sân-mêi-*kh*ân-i.

'Ceremonial rules for confession and Samâdhi or meditation on (the merit of) the Saddharmapuṇḍarîka-sûtra, No. 134.'

Compiled by *K*'-i, who died A.D. 597, under the Sui dynasty, A.D. 589–618. 1 fasciculus; 5 chapters. The author lived on the Thien-thâi hill (in modern Che-kiang), where he founded his new school; so that he is generally known by the title Thien-thâi-tâ-sh', or 'the great teacher of the Thien-thâi hill.' His posthumous title is *K*'-*k*ö-tâ-sh', or 'the great teacher who was wise.' See No. 1522. His school is still called Thien-thâi-tsuṅ (Ten-dai-shu, in Japan).

1511 法華三昧行事運想補助儀
Fâ-hwâ-sân-mêi-hhiṅ-sh'-yun-siâṅ-pu-*k*u-i.

'Additional ceremonial rules for one who conveys his concept (towards the object worshipped?) while in the practice of the Saddharmapuṇḍarîka-samâdhi (as taught in No. 1510).'

Compiled by Tsân-zân, of the Thien-thâi school, who died A.D. 782, of the Thân dynasty, A.D. 618–907. 4 leaves.

The following four works were compiled by Tsun-shih, of the Thien-thâi school, about A.D. 1000, of the later Suṅ dynasty, A.D. 960–1127:—

1512 金光明懺法補助儀
*K*in-kwâṅ-miṅ-*kh*ân-fâ-pu-*k*u-i.
'Additional rules for confession (and recital of) the Suvarnaprabhâsa-sûtra, No. 127.'
1 fasciculus; 6 chapters.

1513 往生淨土懺願儀
Wâṅ-shaṅ-tsiṅ-thu-*kh*ân-yuen-i.
'Ceremonial rules for confession and prayer for going to be born in the Pure Land or Sukhâvatî.'
16 leaves.

1514 往生淨土決疑行願二門
Wâṅ-shaṅ-tsiṅ-thu-*k*iê-i-hhiṅ-yuen-'rh-man.
'(A treatise on) two subjects for going to be born in the Pure Land or Sukhâvatî, namely, determination of doubts and practice of prayer.'
12 leaves.

1515 請觀世音菩薩消伏毒害陀羅尼三昧儀
Tshiṅ-kwân-shi-yin-phu-sâ-siâo-fu-tu-hâi-tho-lo-ni-sân-mâi-i.
'Ceremonial rules for the Samâdhi or meditation on (the merit of) the Dhâranî asking the Bodhisattva Avalokitesvara for making poisonous injuries perish, No. 326.'
19 leaves.

The following three works were compiled by *K*'-li, of the Thien-thâi school, of the later Suṅ dynasty, A. D. 960–1127:—

1516 金光明最勝懺儀
*K*in-kwâṅ-miṅ-tsui-shaṅ-*kh*ân-i.
'Ceremonial rules for confession (and recital of) the Suvarnaprabhâsottama-(râga)-sûtra, No. 126 (or No. 127, cf. No. 1512).'
8 leaves.

1517 千手眼大悲心咒行法
Tshien-sheu-yeṅ-tâ-pêi-sin-*kh*eu-hhiṅ-fâ.
'Rules for the practice or recital of the Dhâranî of the heart of the great compassionate one who is possessed of a thousand arms and eyes, i. e. Avalokitesvara, No. 320.'
20 leaves.

1518 禮法華經儀式
Li-fâ-hwâ-*k*iṅ-i-shih.
'Ceremonial rules for worshipping the Saddharmapundarîka-sûtra, No. 134.'
2 leaves.

1519 熾盛光道場念誦儀
Kh'-shaṅ-kwâṅ-tâo-*k*âṅ-nien-suṅ-i.
'Ceremonial rules for the recital of (a Dhâranî entitled) *Kh*'-shaṅ-kwâṅ, etc., No. 1010, in the religious place or temple.'

Compiled by Tsun-shih, of the Thien-thâi school, about A. D. 1000, of the later Suṅ dynasty, A. D. 960–1127. 17 leaves.

The following two are the works of *Z*ân-yo, of the Thien-thâi school, of the later Suṅ dynasty, A. D. 960–1127:—

1520 釋迦如來涅槃禮讚文
Shih-*k*iâ-*z*u-lâi-niê-phân-li-tsân-wan.
'Laudatory composition for the worship on (the anniversary of) the Tathâgata Sâkyamuni's entrance into Nirvâna.'
8 leaves.

1521 觀自在菩薩如意輪咒課法
Kwân-tsz'-tsâi-phu-sâ-*z*u-i-lun-*kh*eu-*kh*ö-fâ.
'Rules for the recital of the Avalokitesvara-bodhisattva-(padma)-*k*intâmani-dhâranî, No. 324.'
8 leaves.

1522 天台智者大師齋忌禮讚文
Thien-thâi-*k*'-*k*ö-tâ-sh'-*k*âi-*k*i-li-tsân-wan.
'Laudatory composition (for the worship) on the anniversary of the death of *K*'-*k*ö-tâ-sh', or "the great teacher who was wise" (*K*'-i), of the Thien-thâi (hill or school).' Cf. No. 1510.

Composed by Tsun-shih, of the Thien-thâi school, about A. D. 1000, of the later Suṅ dynasty, A. D. 960–1127. 8 leaves.

1523 慈悲水懺法
Tshz'-pêi-shui-*kh*ân-fâ.
'Rules for the confession of water of mercy and compassion.'

Compiled by *K*'-hhüen, who died in A. D. 881, of the Thâṅ dynasty, A. D. 618–907. 3 fasciculi. The author is said to have met with the Ârya Kanaka, and they both purified their enmity with the so-called water of Samâdhi or meditation. Then *K*'-hhüen composed a confessional writing, and explained the meaning of the Law. This singular account is given in the preface by the Emperor *Kh*aṅ-tsu, of the Miṅ dynasty, dated A. D. 1416.

1524 景德傳燈錄
*K*iṅ-töh-*k*whân-tâṅ-lu.
'Records of the transmission of the lamp (of the Law) up to the *K*iṅ-töh period, A. D. 1004–1007, under the later Suṅ dynasty.

Compiled by Tâo-yuen, of the Shân or Dhyâna school, of the later Suṅ dynasty, A.D. 960-1127. 30 fasciculi. This is a history of the Indian and Chinese patriarchs of the Dhyâna school, which school was established in China by Bodhidharma, who arrived in that country from India in A.D. 520. In the first 26 fasciculi, 1712 persons are mentioned; and in the remaining fasciculi, accounts of twenty-two eminent priests and their verses and compositions are collected. See *K*'-tsiṅ, fasc. 42, fol. 10 b seq. But in a preface to No. 1524, a less number of these patriarchs is given, viz. 1701, which number is said to include that of the seven Buddhas, mentioned at the beginning of this work. The statement of this preface seems to be incorrect. No. 1524 was presented to the Emperor *K*an-tsuṅ, by the author, in A.D. 1006. See Thuṅ-*k*i, fasc. 44, fol. 4 a.

1525 六祖大師法寶壇經

Liu-tsu-tâ-sh'-fâ-pâo-thân-*k*iṅ.

'Sûtra (spoken) on the high seat of the gem of the Law (or Dharmaratna) by Liu-tsu-tâ-sh',' or 'the great teacher who was the sixth patriarch (from Bodhidharma, viz. Hwui-naṅ).'

Compiled by his disciple Tsuṅ-pâo, of the Shân or Dhyâna school, of the Thâṅ dynasty, A.D. 618-907. 1 fasciculus. This is a sacred book among the Southern Dhyâna school, i.e. the followers of this patriarch. Hwui-naṅ was born in A.D. 638, and succeeded his teacher Huṅ-*z*ân, the fifth patriarch, in patriarchate in 661, and died in 713. See the addendum by his disciple Fâ-hâi. Cf. Mayers' Chinese Reader's Manual, p. 137, No. 428. The succession of this patriarch makes a great epoch in the history of the Dhyâna school, as this school was then subdivided into two, namely, Southern and Northern, under Hwui-naṅ and his rival priest Shan-siu, who both established themselves in their respective parts in China. Cf. Edkins' Chinese Buddhism, p. 160 seq.

1526 宗門統要續集

Tsuṅ-man-thuṅ-yâo-suh-tsi.

'A continuation of the collection of important (accounts concerning) the lineage of the doctrinal school.'

Collected originally by Tsuṅ-yuṅ, about A.D. 1133, of the Southern Suṅ dynasty, A.D. 1127-1280; and continued or added by Tshiṅ-meu, about A.D. 1320, of the Yuen dynasty, A.D. 1280-1368. 21 fasciculi. This is a history of the patriarchs and other eminent priests of the Shân or Dhyâna school.

1527 明覺禪師語錄

Miṅ-*k*iâo-shân-sh'-yü-lu.

'Records of the sayings of the Dhyâna teacher Miṅ-*k*iâo ("clear understanding").'

Compiled by his disciples Wêi-*k*âi, Yun-*kh*aṅ, Yuen-yiṅ, Wan-*k*aṅ, *K*an, and others, of the Shân or Dhyâna school, of the later Suṅ dynasty, A.D. 960-1127 6 fasciculi. Miṅ-*k*iâo in the title is the posthumous name of Phu-*k*âo, given by the Emperor *K*an-tsuṅ, in A.D. 1012. See Thuṅ-*k*i, fasc. 44, fol. 11 a.

The following three are the works of *Kh*i-suṅ, of the Shân or Dhyâna school, of the later Suṅ dynasty, A.D. 960-1127:—

1528 傳法正宗論

*K*whân-fâ-*k*aṅ-tsuṅ-lun.

'A treatise on the right school of transmitting the Law.'

2 fasciculi. The author asserts that Bodhidharma was a patriarch of the orthodox school; and confutes a remark on this subject, by Shan-*k*i, a *S*râmana of the Thâṅ dynasty, A.D. 618-907, as well as an Indian work, Fu-fâ-tsâṅ-yin-yuen-*k*iṅ, or History of the Indian Patriarchs, No. 1340, in which work Bodhidharma is not mentioned.

1529 傳法正宗記

*K*whân-fâ-*k*aṅ-tsuṅ-*k*i.

'Records of the right school of transmitting the Law.'

10 fasciculi. This is a history of the patriarchs and eminent priests of the Shân or Dhyâna school.

1530 輔教編

Fu-*k*iâo-pien.

'A collection (of miscellaneous compositions) on the preservation of the teaching (of Buddha).'

3 fasciculi. The author *Kh*i-suṅ was very famous by his literary talents, and it is stated in Thuṅ-*k*i (fasc. 45, fol. 18 a) that some celebrated literati of his time, such as Eu-yâṅ Siu and others, admired him very much when they saw the above three works. The Emperor *Z*an-tsuṅ (A.D. 1023-1063) was the first admirer of *Kh*i-suṅ, when the former read the following sentence in a composition of the latter: 爲法不爲身 wêi-fâ-pu-wêi-shan, or '(I do my best) for the sake of the Law, but not for my own sake.' The Emperor at once ordered to admit the works of *Kh*i-suṅ into the Canon, and gave the author the honourable title Miṅ-*k*iâo-tâ-sh', or 'the great teacher who illustrates the teaching (of Buddha).' This event took place in A.D. 1062.

1531 圓悟佛果禪師語錄

Yuen-yü-fo-*kh*ö-shân-sh'-yü-lu.

'Records of the sayings of the Dhyâna teacher Yuen-yü-fo-*kh*ö ("he who fully understood the fruit of Buddha").'

Compiled by his disciples Shâo-luṅ and others, about A.D. 1133, of the Southern Suṅ dynasty, A.D. 1127–1280. 17 fasciculi.

1532 大慧普覺禪師語錄

Tâ-hwui-phu-*k*iâo-shân-sh'-yü-lu.

'Records of the sayings of the Dhyâna teacher Tâ-hwui-phu-*k*iâo ("great-wisdom-full-understanding").'

Compiled by his disciple Yun-wan, in the *K*ien-tâo period, A.D. 1165–1173, of the Southern Suṅ dynasty, A.D. 1127–1280. 12 fasciculi. Besides this there are three other works relating to the same teacher, which works are however not mentioned separately in the original catalogue of the present collection of the Chinese Tripitaka (Tâ-miṅ-sâṅ-tsâṅ-shaṅ-kiâo-mu-lu, fasc. 4, fol. 16 a). But in the same catalogue, No. 1532 is said to be in 30 fasciculi, so as to include as it were the three other works. They are—

(a) 大慧覺禪師普說

Tâ-hwui-*k*iâo-shân-sh'-phu-shwo.

'General speech of the Dhyâna teacher Tâ-hwui (-phu)-*k*iâo.'

Recorded by his disciples Hwui-zan and Yun-wan, in A.D. 1190. 5 fasciculi.

(b) 大慧法語

Tâ-hwui-fâ-yü.

'Religious conversation of Tâ-hwui.'

Recorded by his disciple Tâo-sien. 3 fasciculi.

(c) 大慧書問

Tâ-hwui-shu-wan.

'Inquiring letters of Tâ-hwui.'

Collected by his disciple Hwui-zan. 1 fasciculus.

The latter two works were afterwards re-collected by Hwâṅ Wan-*kh*âṅ.

1533 天目中峰和尚廣錄

Thien-mu-*k*uṅ-fâṅ-hö-shaṅ-kwâṅ-lu.

'Large records of (the sayings of) the Upâdhyâya or teacher *K*uṅ-fâṅ ("middle peak"), of the Thien-mu hill (in modern Chekiang).'

Compiled by his disciple Tshz'-tsi, of the Shân or Dhyâna school, in the *K*'-*k*' period, A.D. 1321–1323, of the Yuen dynasty, A.D. 1280–1368. 30 fasciculi.

1534 妙法蓮華經玄義

Miâo-fâ-lien-hwâ-*k*iṅ-hhüen-i.

'A hidden meaning of (or introduction to) the Saddharmapundarîka-sûtra, No. 134.'

Spoken by *K*'-kö-tâ-sh' (*K*'-i), of the Thien-thâi hill or school, of the Sui dynasty, A.D. 589–618; and recorded by his disciple Kwân-tiṅ, who died in A.D. 632, under the Thâṅ dynasty, A.D. 618–907. 20 fasciculi.

1535 法華玄義釋籤

Fâ-hwâ-hhüen-i-shih-tshien.

A commentary on the preceding work.

Compiled by Tsân-zân, of the Thien-thâi school, who died in A.D. 782, of the Thâṅ dynasty, A.D. 618–907. 20 fasciculi.

1536 妙法蓮華經文句

Miâo-fâ-lien-hwâ-*k*iṅ-wan-*k*ü.

'(An explanation of) the words and sentences of the Saddharmapundarîka-sûtra, No. 134.'

Spoken by *K*'-kö-tâ-sh' (*K*'-i), of the Thien-thâi hill or school, of the Sui dynasty, A.D. 589–618; and recorded by his disciple Kwân-tiṅ. 20 fasciculi. The recorder says in his introduction that he heard this explanation or lecture at *K*in-liâṅ (Nanking) in his twenty-seventh year of age, and afterwards revised his record at Tân-*kh*iu ('red hill') in his sixty-ninth year.

1537 法華文句記

Fâ-hwâ-wan-*k*ü-*k*i.

A commentary on the preceding work.

Compiled by Tsân-zân, of the Thien-thâi school, of the Thâṅ dynasty, A.D. 618–907. 30 fasciculi.

1538 摩訶止觀

Mo-hö-*k*i-kwân.

'Mahâ-samatha-vipasyanâ (?),' or 'Great cessation and seeing clearly, or meditation and knowledge.'

Spoken by *K*'-kö-tâ-sh' (*K*'-i), of the Thien-thâi hill or school, in A.D. 594, under the Sui dynasty, A.D. 589–618; and recorded by his disciple Kwân-tiṅ. 20 fasciculi; 10 divisions. This work is said to contain the doctrine of *K*'-i's own understanding; so that it is essential in the teaching of the Thien-thâi school. The two Chinese characters *k*i-kwân in the title are generally understood to be a translation of two technical words, namely, *S*amatha and Vipasyanâ, or Samatha and Vipassana. See Childers' Pâli Dictionary, pp. 429 b, 580 a. Cf. Miṅ-i-tsi, fasc. 10, fol. 19 b seq.

But in No. 1538, the meditation and knowledge are repeatedly explained as those of the Mahâyâna. For this reason Mahâ (mo-hŏ) in the title may stand for the Mahâyâna (cf. No. 1542), or at least in the sense of not only 'great' but also 'excellent' or superior to those of the Hînayâna. For it is a very popular interpretation among the Chinese Buddhist literature, that the Sanskrit word Mahâ equals in meaning three Chinese words, namely, 大 tâ, great, 多 to, many or much, and 勝 shan, excellent. This interpretation is given in Kumâragîva's translation of the Mahâpragñâpâramitâ-sûtra-sâstra, i. e. the Tâ-*k*'-tu-lun, No. 1169. It is quoted under the term Mahâyâna, in Miṅ-i-tsi, fasc. 12, fol. 12 b. But it may equally be said that Mahâ in the title is used for the purpose of distinguishing this large work from No. 1540, which see.

Nos. 1534, 1536, and 1538 are so important works of the Thien-thâi school, that they are generally called Thien-thâi-sân-tâ-pu, or the 'three great works of the Thien-thâi.'

1539 止觀輔行傳弘訣

*K*i-kwân-fu-hhiṅ-*k*whân-huṅ-*k*iê.

A commentary on the preceding work.

Compiled by Tsân-zân, of the Thien-thâi school, of the Thâṅ dynasty, A. D. 618–907. 40 fasciculi.

1540 修習止觀坐禪法要

Siu-si-*k*i-kwân-tso-shân-fâ-yâo.

'An importance of the law of sitting in Dhyâna or the practice of meditation and knowledge.'

Composed by *K*'-i, of the Thien-thâi hill or school, of the Sui dynasty, A. D. 589–618. 2 fasciculi; 10 chapters. This work is otherwise called Thuṅ-maṅ-*k*i-kwân, or a book on meditation and knowledge for the use of an untaught youth; and also Siâo-*k*i-kwân, or a little or short book on meditation and knowledge. The first four chapters or sections have been translated by Mr. Beal, in his Catena, pp. 251–273.

1541 止觀義例

*K*i-kwân-i-lêi.

A short commentary on the Mo-hŏ-*k*i-kwân, No. 1538.

Compiled by Tsân-zân, of the Thien-thâi school, of the Thâṅ dynasty, A. D. 618–907. 2 fasciculi.

The following two works were composed by Hwui-sz', who died in A. D. 577, of the *Kh*an dynasty, A. D. 557–589:—

1542 大乘止觀法門

Tâ-shan-*k*i-kwân-fâ-man.

'Mahâyâna-samatha-vipasyanâ-dharmaparyâya,' or 'the doctrine of meditation and knowledge of the Mahâyâna.'

4 fasciculi.

1543 諸法無諍三昧法門

*K*u-fâ-wu-*k*aṅ-sân-mêi-fâ-man.

'Sarvadharmâranasamâdhi-dharmaparyâya,' or 'the doctrine of meditation on the absence of dispute concerning all the states of existence.'

2 fasciculi. The author Hwui-sz' was the disciple of Hwui-wan, and the teacher of *K*'-i, the founder of the Thien-thâi school. Hwui-wan first taught the doctrine of this school, depending on the Saddharmapu*nd*arîka-sûtra, No. 134.

The following two works were compiled by Kwân-tiṅ, of the Thien-thâi school, of the Thâṅ dynasty, A. D. 618–907:—

1544 大般涅槃經玄義

Tâ-pân-niê-phân-*k*iṅ-hhüen-i.

'A hidden meaning of (or introduction to) the Mahâparinirvâna-sûtra, Nos. 113, 114.'

2 fasciculi.

1545 大般涅槃經疏

Tâ-pân-niê-phân-*k*iṅ-shu.

'A commentary on the Mahâparinirvâna-sûtra, Nos. 113, 114.'

Revised by Tsân-zân, of the Thien-thâi school, of the Thâṅ dynasty, A. D. 618–907. 33 fasciculi.

1546 涅槃經玄義發源機要

Niê-phân-*k*iṅ-hhüen-i-fâ-yuen-*k*i-yâo.

A commentary on the Niê-phân-*k*iṅ-hhüen-i, No. 1544.

Compiled by *K*'-yuen, A. D. 1014, of the later Suṅ dynasty, A. D. 960–1127. 4 fasciculi. The last four characters in the title, being a special name for this commentary, may be translated into 'a secret importance for discovering the origin or truth(?).'

1547 法華經安樂行義

Fâ-hwâ-*k*iṅ-ân-lŏ-hhiṅ-i.

'(An explanation of) the meaning of the fourteenth (or thirteenth) chapter on the Sukhavihâra or "happy-walking" of the Saddharmapu*nd*arîka-sûtra, No. 134.' For the order of the chapter, see column 46 above.

Compiled by Hwui-sz', of the *Kh*an dynasty, A. D. 557–589. 1 fasciculus.

1548 金光明經玄義
*K*in-kwân-min-*k*in-hhüen-i.
'A hidden meaning of (or introduction to) the Suvarnaprabhâsa-sûtra, No. 127.'

Spoken by *K'-kö*-tâ-sh' (*K'*-i), of the Thien-thâi hill or school of the Sui dynasty, A.D. 589–618; and recorded by his disciple Kwân-tin. 2 fasciculi.

1549 金光明經玄義拾遺記
*K*in-kwân-min-*k*in-hhüen-i-shi-i-*k*i.
A commentary on the preceding work.

Compiled by *K'*-li, of the Thien-thâi school, of the later Sun dynasty, A.D. 960–1127. 6 fasciculi. The last three characters in the title, being a special name for this work, may be translated into 'record of picking up what has been left unrecorded.'

1550 金剛般若經疏
*K*in-kân-pân-zo-*k*in-shu.
'A commentary on the Vagrakkhedikâ-pragñâpâramitâ-sûtra, No. 10.'

Spoken by *K'-kö*-tâ-sh' (*K'*-i), of the Thien-thâi hill or school, of the Sui dynasty, A.D. 589–618; and recorded by his disciple Kwân-tin. 1 fasciculus.

1551 天台四教儀
Thien-thâi-sz'-*k*iâo-i.
'(A treatise on) four divisions of (Buddha's) teaching according to the Thien-thâi school.'

Composed by Ti-kwân, a learned Corean priest of the Thien-thâi school, under the later Sun dynasty, A.D. 960–1127. 1 fasciculus. This work depends on No. 1568. The four divisions are technically called 藏通別圓 tsân, thun, pieh, yuen. Edkins translates these into 'collection, progress, distinction, and completion.' See his Chinese Buddhism, p. 182.

1552 金光明經文句
*K*in-kwân-min-*k*in-wan-*k*ü.
'(An explanation of) the words and sentences of the Suvarnaprabhâsa-sûtra, No. 127.'

Spoken by *K'-kö*-tâ-sh' (*K'*-i), of the Thien-thâi hill or school, of the Sui dynasty, A.D. 589–618. 6 fasciculi.

1553 金光明經文句記
*K*in-kwân-min-*k*in-wan-*k*ü-*k*i.
A commentary on the preceding work.

Compiled by *K'*-li, of the Thien-thâi school, of the later Sun dynasty, A.D. 960–1127. 12 fasciculi.

The following two works were spoken by *K'-kö*-tâ-sh' (*K'*-i), of the Thien-thâi hill or school, of the Sui dynasty, A.D. 589–618; and recorded by his disciple Kwân-tin:—

1554 菩薩戒義疏
Phu-sâ-*k*iê-i-shu.
'A commentary on the Bodhisattva-pratimoksha(-sûtra, No. 1096).'
2 fasciculi.

1555 觀音玄義
Kwân-yin-hhüen-i.
'A hidden meaning of (or introduction to) the Avalokitesvara (-sûtra, No. 137, or the 25th chapter of No. 134).'

2 fasciculi. This work is a minute commentary on the title of the chapter, namely, Kwân-shi-yin-phu-sâ-phu-man-phin, i. e. Avalokitesvara-bodhisattva-samanta-mukha-parivarta. See No. 137.

1556 觀音玄義記
Kwân-yin-hhüen-i-*k*i.
A commentary on the preceding work.

Compiled by *K'*-li, of the Thien-thâi school, of the later Sun dynasty, A.D. 960–1127. 4 fasciculi.

1557 觀音義疏
Kwân-yin-i-shu.
'A commentary on the Avalokitesvara(-sûtra).' Cf. No. 1555.

Spoken by *K'-kö*-tâ-sh' (*K'*-i), of the Thien-thâi hill or school, of the Sui dynasty, A.D. 589–618. 2 fasciculi.

1558 觀音義疏記
Kwân-yin-i-shu-*k*i.
A commentary on the preceding work.

Compiled by *K'*-li, of the Thien-thâi school, of the later Sun dynasty, A.D. 960–1127. 4 fasciculi.

1559 觀無量壽佛經疏
Kwân-wu-liân-sheu-fo-*k*in-shu.
'A commentary on the Amitâyur-buddha-dhyâna (?)-sûtra, No. 198.'

Spoken by *K'-kö*-tâ-sh' (*K'*-i), of the Thien-thâi hill or school, of the Sui dynasty, A.D. 589–618. 1 fasciculus.

1560 觀無量壽佛經疏妙宗鈔
Kwân-wu-liân-sheu-fo-*k*in-shu-miâo-tsun-*kh*âo.
A commentary on the preceding work.

Compiled by *K'*-li, of the Thien-thâi school, in A. D. 1021, under the later Suṅ dynasty, A. D. 960–1127. 6 fasciculi. The last three characters in the title, being a special name of this work, may be translated into 'record of the wonderful principle.'

1561 天台智者大師禪門口訣
Thien-thâi-*k'*-*k*ö-tâ-sh'-shân-man-*kh*u-*k*üê.
'An oral transmission of the doctrine of Dhyâna or meditation, by *K'*-*k*ö-tâ-sh' (*K'*-i), of the Thien-thâi (hill or school).'

Recorder's name not mentioned. 1 fasciculus.

1562 請觀音經疏
Tshiṅ-kwân-yin-*k*iṅ-shu.
'A commentary on the Avalokitesvara-yâkana (?)-sûtra, No. 326.'

Spoken by *K'*-*k*ö-tâ-sh' (*K'*-i), of the Thien-thâi hill or school, of the Sui dynasty, A. D. 589–618. 1 fasciculus.

1563 請觀音經疏闡義鈔
Tshiṅ-kwân-yin-*k*iṅ-shu-shân-i-*kh*âo.
A commentary on the preceding work.

Compiled by *K'*-yuen, of the Thien-thâi school, of the later Suṅ dynasty, A. D. 960–1127. 4 fasciculi. The last three characters in the title being a special name of this work may be translated into 'record of opening the meaning.'

The following three works were spoken by *K'*-*k*ö-tâ-sh' (*K'*-i), of the Thien-thâi hill or school, of the Sui dynasty, A. D. 589–618; and No. 1566 was recorded by his disciple Kwân-tiṅ, but the recorders of Nos. 1564 and 1565 are not mentioned:—

1564 釋摩訶般若波羅蜜經覺意三昧
Shih-mo-hö-pân-*z*o-po-lo-mi-*k*iṅ-*k*iâo-i-sân-mâi.
'An explanation of the Samâdhi or meditation called understanding-thought (explained in) the Mahâpragñâpâramitâ-sûtra, No. 3.'

1 fasciculus.

1565 四念處
Sz'-nien-*kh*u.
'(A discourse or work) on the *K*atur-smrity-upasthâna, or four subjects of thoughts.'

4 fasciculi. The subject of this work is the first division of the thirty-seven constituents of true knowledge, or the Bodhipakshika-dharma. See Childers' Pâli Dictionary, pp. 92 b, 466 b.

1566 仁王護國般若經疏
*Z*an-wâṅ-hu-kwo-pân-*z*o-*k*iṅ-shu.
'A commentary on the Kârunikarâga-desapâla (?)-pragñâpâramitâ-sûtra, No. 17.'

5 fasciculi.

1567 佛說仁王護國般若波羅蜜經疏神寶記
Fo-shwo-*z*an-wâṅ-hu-kwo-pân-*z*o-po-lo-mi-*k*iṅ-shu-shan-pâo-*k*i.
A commentary on the preceding work.

Compiled by Shân-yueh, of the Thien-thâi school, A. D. 1230, under the Southern Suṅ dynasty, A. D. 1127–1280. 4 fasciculi. The last three characters in the title, being a special name of this work, may be translated into 'record of spiritual gems.'

1568 天台八教大意
Thien-thâi-pâ-*k*iâo-tâ-i.
'An outline of eight divisions of (Buddha's) teaching according to the Thien-thâi school.'

Drawn by Kwân-tiṅ, of the Thien-thâi school, of the Thâṅ dynasty, A. D. 618–907. 1 fasciculus. The eight divisions are technically called 頓, 漸, 秘密, 不定, 藏, 通, 別, 圓, tun, tsien, pi-mi, pu-tiṅ, tsâṅ, thuṅ, pieh, yuen. Edkins translates these into 'the compliant, gradual, secret, indeterminate, collection, progress, distinction, and completion.' See his Chinese Buddhism, p. 182. The first four are styles of teaching considered as medical compounds, while the last four are those of the law taught as the taste or power of medicine. The last four are fully explained in Nos. 1551 and 1569.

1569 四教義
Sz'-*k*iâo-i.
'(A work on) the meaning of four divisions of (Buddha's) teaching.' Cf. Nos. 1551, 1568.

Composed by *K'*-*k*ö (*K'*-i), of the Thien-thâi hill or school, of the Sui dynasty, A. D. 589–618. 6 fasciculi.

1570 國清百錄
Kwo-tshiṅ-pâi-lu.
'A collection of a hundred (compositions of the teacher) of the Kwo-tshiṅ (monastery, viz. *K'*-i, of the Thien-thâi hill or school).'

Collected by his disciple Kwân-tiṅ, of the Thâṅ dynasty, A. D. 618–907. 4 fasciculi.

1571 釋禪波羅蜜次第法門
Shih-shân-po-lo-mi-tshz'-ti-fâ-man.
'An explanation of the gradual doctrine of the Dhyâna-pâramitâ.'

Spoken by *K'-kö-tâ-sh'* (*K'*-i), of the Thien-thâi hill or school, of the Sui dynasty, A.D. 589–618, and recorded by his disciple Fâ-*k*an, and revised by Kwân-tiṅ. 10 fasciculi.

1572 法界次第初門
Fâ-*k*iê-tshz'-ti-*k*u-man.
'The first gate or step to the order or degree of the state of existence (Dharmadhâtu).'

Composed by *K'-kö* (*K'*-i), of the Thien-thâi hill or school, of the Sui dynasty, A.D. 589–618. 3 fasciculi. This is a useful work on the Buddhist technical terms.

The following two works were spoken by *K'-kö-tâ-sh'* (*K'*-i), of the Thien-thâi hill or school, of the Sui dynasty, A.D. 589–618, and No. 1573 was recorded by his disciple Kwân-tiṅ, but the recorder of No. 1574 is not mentioned:—

1573 方等三昧行法
Fân-tan-sân-mêi-hhiṅ-fâ.
'Rules for the practice of the Vaipulya-samâdhi or extended meditation.'

1 fasciculus.

1574 淨土十疑論
Tsiṅ-thu-shi-i-lun.
'A treatise on ten doubts about the Pure Land (Sukhâvatî).'

1 fasciculus. This treatise explains ten doubts about being born in Sukhâvatî of Amitâyus or Amitâbha, and removes them, according to *K'*i's own view on this doctrine. The ten doubts are—(1) Those who wish to be born in the Pure Land seem to be in want of great mercy and compassion. (2) Their wish to be born seems to be contrary to the reason or law of wu-shaṅ or 'without birth' (Anutpanna?). (3) They seem to wish partially to be born in one land. (4) They seem to believe partially in one Buddha. (5) Even those who are not free from worldly thirst are allowed to be born there. (6) They are said to attain to the state of freedom from return (Avinivartanîya). (7) They do not wish to be born in the inner palace (of the Tushita heaven, where the future Buddha Maitreya lives now). (8) They are allowed to be born there only by meditating or thinking intensely on Amitâyus or Amitâbha ten times. (9) Women and the deformed are not allowed to be born there. (10) Whether any other action or practice is needed for going to be born there. As to the eighth doubt, the term 十念 shi-nien is generally explained by others as 'repetitions of Buddha's name ten times;' but *K'*-i takes it in the sense of 'intense thought on Buddha ten times.' Cf. No. 1559, where his whole view is fully explained.

1575 觀心論疏
Kwân-sin-lun-shu.
'A commentary on the treatise about meditation on the heart (composed by *K'*-i).'

Compiled by Kwân-tiṅ, of the Thien-thâi school, of the Thâṅ dynasty, A.D. 618–907. 5 fasciculi.

1576 南嶽思大禪師立誓願文
Nân-yo-sz'-tâ-shân-sh'-li-shi-yuen-wan.
'Prayer by Hwui-sz', the great Dhyâna teacher of the Nân-yo, or the southern high mountain.'

1 fasciculus. For the author Hwui-sz', see Nos. 1542, 1543, 1547.

1577 天台智者大師別傳
Thien-thâi-*k'-kö-tâ-sh'*-pieh-*k*whân.
'A separate or special life of *K'-kö-tâ-sh'* (*K'*-i), of the Thien-thâi (hill or school).'

Compiled by his disciple Kwân-tiṅ, of the Thâṅ dynasty, A.D. 618–907. 1 fasciculus.

The following two works were composed by Tsân-zân, of the Thien-thâi school, of the Thâṅ dynasty, A.D. 618–907:—

1578 止觀大意
*K*i-kwân-tâ-i.
'An outline of (Mo-hö-)*k*i-kwân, No. 1538.'

21 leaves.

1579 始終心要
Sh'-*k*uṅ-sin-yâo.
'(A treatise on) the beginning and end of the importance concerning the heart.'

2 leaves.

1580 修懺要旨
Siu-*k*hân-yâo-*k'*.
'(A treatise on) the importance of the practice of confession.'

Composed by *K'*-li, of the Thien-thâi school, of the later Suṅ dynasty, A.D. 960–1127. 17 leaves.

1581 十不二門
Shi-pu-'rh-man.
'(A treatise on) ten inseparable ("not two") subjects.'

Composed by Tsân-zân, of the Thien-thâi school, of the Thâṅ dynasty, A. D. 618–907. 14 leaves. This work is a part of, or an extract from No. 1535. See *K'*-tsiṅ, fasc. 42, fol. 9 a.

1582 指要鈔
Sh'-yâo-*kh*âo.
'Record of pointing out importance.'
A commentary on the preceding work.

Compiled by *K'*-li, of the Thien-thâi school, of the later Suṅ dynasty, A. D. 960–1127. 2 fasciculi.

1583 金剛錍
*K*in-kâṅ-pi.
'A diamond probe.' A metaphysical work.

Composed by Tsân-zân, of the Thien-thâi school, of the Thâṅ dynasty, A. D. 618–907. 1 fasciculus; 37 leaves.

1584 法智遺編觀心二百問
Fâ-*k'*-i-pien-kwân-sin-'rh-pâi-wan.
'Two hundred questions on (the treatise about) meditation on the heart (cf. No. 1575), being a work left by Fâ-*k'* (unfinished?) at his death.'

Compiled by *K*i-*k*uṅ, of the Thien-thâi school, of the later Suṅ dynasty, A. D. 960–1127. 1 fasciculus; 27 leaves.

1585 永嘉集
Yuṅ-*k*iâ-tsi.
'A compilation (of general accounts of the Law, made by a priest) of Yuṅ-*k*iâ (name of a place).'

Compiled by Hhüen-*k*iâo, of the Thien-thâi school, of the Thâṅ dynasty, A. D. 618–907. 2 fasciculi. This work does not belong to the Shân or Dhyâna school, though its full title has the two characters Shân-tsuṅ or 'Dhyâna school.'

The following two works were composed by Hwâi-tsö, of the Thien-thâi school, of the Yuen dynasty, A. D. 1280–1368:—

1586 天台傳佛心印記
Thien-thâi-*k*whân-fo-sin-yin-*k*i.
'A record of the transmission of the seal of Buddha's heart (Buddha-hridaya-mudrâ), of the Thien-thâi school.'

10 leaves.

1587 淨土境觀要門
Tsiṅ-thu-*k*iṅ-kwân-yâo-man.
'An important gate or doctrine of meditation on the state of the Pure Land (Sukhâvatî).'

18 leaves.

1588 首楞嚴經義海
Sheu-lâṅ-yen-*k*iṅ-i-hâi.
'The sea of the meaning of (or a commentary on) the Sûraṅgama-sûtra, No. 446.'

Compiled or collected by Hhien-kwei, about A. D. 1165, under the Southern Suṅ dynasty, A. D. 1127–1280. 30 fasciculi. It contains three older commentaries, which are arranged one after the other under each sentence or passage of the Sûtra. The respective titles and compilers of these three commentaries are—(1) I-shu, or 'a statement of the meaning,' by Tsz'-sûen, about A. D. 1030. (2) Piâo-sh'-yâo-i, or 'a mark for pointing out the important meaning,' by Hhiâo-yueh, about A. D. 1073. (3) Tsi-*k*ieh, or 'a collection of explanations,' by *Z*an-yo, about A. D. 1059.

The following two works were compiled by *Kh*an-kwân, the fourth patriarch of the Hwâ-yen or Avatamsaka school, who died in A. D. 806, under the Thâṅ dynasty, A. D. 618–907:—

1589 大方廣佛華嚴經疏
Tâ-fâṅ-kwâṅ-fo-hwâ-yen-*k*iṅ-shu.
'A commentary on the Buddhâvatamsaka-vaipulya-sûtra, No. 88.'

60 fasciculi.

1590 大方廣佛華嚴經隨疏演義鈔
Tâ-fâṅ-kwâṅ-fo-hwâ-yen-*k*iṅ-sui-shu-yen-i-*kh*âo.
A commentary on the preceding work.

90 fasciculi.

The following three works were composed by Fâ-tsâṅ, the third patriarch of the Hwâ-yen school, now called 賢首宗 Hhien-sheu-tsuṅ, after the posthumous name of this patriarch, who died in A. D. 712, under the Thâṅ dynasty, A. D. 618–907:—

1591 華嚴一乘教義分齊章
Hwâ-yen-yi-shaṅ-*k*iâo-i-fan-tshi-*k*âṅ.
'A treatise on the distinction of the meaning of the doctrine of one vehicle (Ekayâna), of the Buddhâvatamsaka-sûtra, Nos. 87, 88.'

4 fasciculi; 10 chapters.

1592 華嚴經明法品內立三寶章
Hwâ-yen-*k*iṅ-miṅ-fâ-phin-nêi-li-sân-pâo-*k*âṅ.
'A treatise on the Triratna established or explained in the Min-fâ ("clear law") chapter of the Buddhâvataṃsaka-sûtra, Nos. 87 (fasc. 10), 88 (fasc. 18).'

2 fasciculi.

1593 修華嚴奧旨妄盡還源觀
Siu-hwâ-yen-âo-*k*'-wân-tsin-hwân-yuen-kwân.
'(A treatise on) the deepest meaning of the Buddhâvataṃsaka-sûtra, Nos. 87, 88, viz. when falseness comes to an end, it is the return to its origin.'

16 leaves; 6 chapters.

1594 原人論
Yuen-*z*an-lun.
'A treatise on the origin of man.'

Composed by Tsuṅ-mi, the fifth patriarch of the Hwâ-yen school, who died in A. D. 841, under the Thâṅ dynasty, A. D. 618–907. 11 leaves; 4 chapters. The first chapter confutes Confucianism; the second does the same with the Hînayâna school, and even some of the followers of the Mahâyâna who still believe in only a part of the Law; the third explains the true doctrine of Buddha; and the fourth unites all those before confuted, and treats them as if they were all the right teachings, being produced from one and the same source. This is a very well-known work.

1595 華嚴經指歸
Hwâ-yen-*k*iṅ-*k*'-kwêi.
'An outline of the contents of the Buddhâvataṃsaka-sûtra, Nos. 87, 88.'

Drawn by Fâ-tsâṅ, the third patriarch of the Hwâ-yen school, of the Thâṅ dynasty, A. D. 618–907. 1 fasciculus; 27 leaves; 10 chapters.

1596 註華嚴法界觀門
*K*u-hwâ-yen-fâ-*k*iê-kwân-man.
'A commentary on (the treatise about) the meditation on the state of existence, according to the Buddhâvataṃsaka-sûtra, Nos. 87, 88.'

Compiled by Tsuṅ-mi, the fifth patriarch of the Hwâ-yen school, of the Thâṅ dynasty, A. D. 618–907. 1 fasciculus. The text was composed by Tu Fâ-shun, the first patriarch or the founder of this school in China, who died in A. D. 640.

1597 佛遺教經論疏節要
Fo-i-*k*iâo-*k*iṅ-lun-shu-shwo-yâo.
'An extract from a commentary on the *S*âstra, No. 1209, of the Sûtra of Buddha's last teaching, No. 122.'

Made by Tsiṅ-yuen, a Corean priest of the Hwâ-yen school, of the later Suṅ dynasty, A. D. 960–1127. 1 fasciculus; 63 leaves. The original commentator is not mentioned. The *S*âstra is wrongly ascribed to Asvaghosha, instead of Vasubandhu. See *K*'-tsiṅ, fasc. 36, fol. 18 b.

1598 華嚴法界玄鏡
Hwâ-yen-fâ-*k*iê-hhüen-*k*iṅ.
'A hidden mirror of the state of existence (Dharmadhâtu) according to the Buddhâvataṃsaka-sûtra, Nos. 87, 88.'
A commentary on No. 1596.

Compiled by *Kh*an-kwân, the fourth patriarch of the Hwâ-yen school, of the Thâṅ dynasty, A. D. 618–907. 2 fasciculi.

1599 般若波羅蜜多心經略疏
Pân-*z*o-po-lo-mi-to-sin-*k*iṅ-liâo-shu.
'An abridged or brief commentary on the *Pragñâpâramitâ-hridaya*-sûtra, No. 20.'

Compiled by Fâ-tsâṅ, the third patriarch of the Hwâ-yen school, in A. D. 702, under the Thâṅ dynasty, A. D. 618–907. 1 fasciculus; 13 leaves.

1600 般若心經略疏連珠記
Pân-*z*o-sin-*k*iṅ-liâo-shu-lien-shu-*k*i.
A commentary on the preceding work.

Compiled by Sh'-hwui, of the Hwâ-yen school, who died in A. D. 946, under the Latter Tsin dynasty, A. D. 936–946. 2 fasciculi. The last three characters in the title, being a special name for this work, mean 'a record of pearls united together by a string.'

1601 盂蘭盆經疏
Yü-lân-phan-*k*iṅ-shu.
'A commentary on the Ullambana-sûtra, No. 303.'

Compiled by Tsuṅ-mi, the fifth patriarch of the Hwâ-yen school, of the Thâṅ dynasty, A. D. 618–907. 2 fasciculi.

1602 華嚴金師子章雲間類解
Hwâ-yen-*k*in-sh'-tsz'-*k*âṅ-yun-*k*ien-lêi-*k*iê.
'A brief commentary on the treatise about the Buddhâvataṃsaka-sûtra compared with a golden lion.'

Compiled by Tsiṅ-yuen, a Corean priest of the Hwâ-yen school, of the later Suṅ dynasty, A. D. 960–1127. 19 leaves. The text is the work of Fâ-tsâṅ, the third patriarch of the Hwâ-yen school, who wrote this treatise at the request of the Empress Wu Tsö-thien, A. D. 684–705, of the Thâṅ dynasty. The golden lion referred to in the title is said to have been an ornament placed in the Imperial garden. The last four characters in the title, being a special name for this commentary, may mean 'explanation (as imperfect) as (a dragon appears) in the midst of a cloud(?).'

1603 佛說阿彌陀經疏
Fo-shwo-ö-mi-tho-*k*iñ-shu.
'A commentary on the Buddhabhâshita-amitâyus-sûtra, i.e. the short Sukhâvatîvyûha, No. 200.'

Compiled by Yuen-hhiâo, a Corean priest, of the Thâñ dynasty, A. D. 618–907. 9 leaves.

1604 紹興重雕大藏音
Shâo-hhiñ-*k*uñ-tiâo-tâ-tsâñ-yin.
'Sounds of (the words of) the great repository, or a dictionary of the Buddhist Canon, republished in the Shâo-hhiñ period, A. D. 1131–1162 (under the Southern Suñ dynasty, A. D. 1127–1368).'

Compiled (originally?) by *Kh*u-kwân, in about A. D. 1094, under the later or Northern Suñ dynasty, A. D. 960–1127. 3 fasciculi.

1605 一切經音義
Yi-tshiê-*k*iñ-yin-i.
'A dictionary ("sound and meaning") of the whole Canon.'

Compiled by Hhüen-yiñ, in about A. D. 649, under the Thâñ dynasty, A. D. 618–907. 26 fasciculi.

1606 華嚴經音義
Hwâ-yen-*k*iñ-yin-i.
'A dictionary ("sound and meaning") of the Buddhâvatamsaka-sûtra, No. 88.'

Compiled by Hwui-wân, in about A. D. 700, under the Thâñ dynasty, A. D. 618–907. 4 fasciculi.

1607 辯僞錄
Pien-wêi-lu.
'Records of explanation or confutation of the falseness (of Taoism).'

Compiled by Siâñ-mâi, of the Shan or Dhyâna school, of the Yuen dynasty, in A. D. 1291, under the Yuen dynasty, A. D. 1280–1368. 5 fasciculi.

1608 隋衆經目錄
Sui-*k*uñ-*k*iñ-mu-lu.
'A catalogue of Buddhist sacred books (collected) under the Sui dynasty, A. D. 589–618.'

Compiled by priests and literati, in A. D. 603, who had been appointed by the Emperor as translators of the Tripi*t*aka. 5 fasciculi. The total number of the books mentioned in this catalogue is 2109 works, in 5058 fasciculi; of which 402 works, in 747 fasciculi, had then been lost.

1609 The same title as No. 1608.

Compiled by Fâ-*k*iñ and others, in A. D. 594. 7 fasciculi. The total number of the books mentioned in this catalogue is 2257 works, in 5310 fasciculi; of which the number missing may be about the same as that in the preceding work.

1610 武周刋定衆經目錄
Wu-*k*eu-khân-tiñ-*k*uñ-*k*iñ-mu-lu.
'A revised catalogue of Buddhist sacred books (collected) under the *K*eu dynasty, of the Wu family, A. D. 690–705 (or the rightful but then nominal Thâñ dynasty, A. D. 618–907).'

Compiled by Miñ-*kh*üen and others, in A. D. 695. 15 fasciculi. The total number of the books mentioned in this catalogue is 3616 works, in 8641 fasciculi; of which that of the translations of the Tripi*t*aka of the Mahâyâna and Hînayâna is 1470 works, in 2406 fasciculi.

The *K*eu dynasty of the Wu family fills the latter part of the reign of the Empress Wu Tsö-thien, who set aside the rightful sovereign *Z*ui-tsuñ, the fifth Emperor of the Thâñ dynasty, and usurped the throne for twenty years. In A. D. 690, she adopted the dynastic title of *K*eu in lieu of Thâñ. See Mayers' Chinese Reader's Manual, p. 256, No. 862, and p. 381, col. 1.

1611 大藏聖教法寶標目
Tâ-tsâñ-shañ-*k*iâo-fâ-pâo-piâo-mu.
'A catalogue of the Dharmaratna, being the holy teaching of the great repository, or Buddhist sacred books.'

Compiled originally by Wâñ Ku, of the later (or Northern) or Southern Suñ dynasty, A. D. 960–1280; and continued by Kwân-*k*u-pâ, in A. D. 1306, under the Yuen dynasty, A. D. 1280–1368. 10 fasciculi. This catalogue entirely depends on No. 1612, and adds a short account of the contents of each book.

1612 至元法寶勘同總錄
K'-yuen-fâ-pâo-*k*ien-thuñ-tsuñ-lu.
'A comparative catalogue of the Dharmaratna or Buddhist sacred books (collected) in the *K*'-yuen period, A. D. 1264–1294 (under the Yuen dynasty, which ruled over the whole of China, from A. D. 1280 till 1368).'

Compiled by *K*iñ-*k*i-siâñ and others, in A. D. 1285–1287. 10 fasciculi. The total number of the translations of the Tripiṭaka mentioned in this catalogue is 1440 works, in 5586 fasciculi. Besides this number, there are some miscellaneous Indian and Chinese works. All the translations of the Tripiṭaka and other Indian works are compared with the Tibetan translations. The Sanskrit titles, being taken from the latter translations, are transliterated into Chinese and added to the Chinese ones. This catalogue is generally called *K'*-yuen-lu.

The following three works were compiled by Tsuṅ-lŏ and *Ẕu-kh*i, in A.D. 1378, under the Miṅ dynasty, A.D. 1368–1644:—

1613 楞伽阿跋多羅寶經註解

Laṅ-*k*iā-ŏ-poh-to-lo-pâo-*k*iṅ-*k*u-*k*iâ.

'A commentary on the Laṅkâvatâra-ratna-sûtra, No. 175.'

8 fasciculi.

1614 般若波羅蜜多心經註解

Pân-*ẕ*o-po-lo-mi-to-sin-*k*iṅ-*k*u-*k*iâ.

'A commentary on the Pragñâpâramitâ-hridaya-sûtra, No. 20.'

4 leaves.

1615 金剛般若波羅蜜經註解

*K*in-kâṅ-pân-*ẕ*o-po-lo-mi-*k*iṅ-*k*u-*k*iâ.

'A commentary on the Vagrakkhedikâ-pragñâpâramitâ-sûtra, No. 10.'

28 leaves.

The above three commentaries were compiled under an Imperial order of the first Emperor of the Miṅ dynasty, reigned A.D. 1368–1398. In A.D. 1377 he, by a decree, caused all the Buddhist priests in China to study these three Sûtras; and at the same time he called together the priests of the Shân or Dhyâna school to compile these works. This is one of the reasons why these Sûtras have become so popular in China.

The names of the collectors or compilers of the following four works are unknown:—

1616 大明太宗文皇帝御製序讚文

Tâ-miṅ-thâi-tsuṅ-wan-hwâṅ-ti-yü-shi-sü-tsâṅ-wan.

'The Imperial prefaces and laudatory verses of the Emperor Thâi-tsuṅ Wan (*Kh*aṅ-tsu), of the great Miṅ dynasty, reigned A.D. 1403–1424.'

1 fasciculus; 12 leaves; 10 compositions, both in prose and verse, dated some time between A.D. 1410–1415.

1617 諸佛世尊如來菩薩尊者神僧名經

*K*u-fo-shi-tsun-*ẕ*u-lâi-phu-sâ-tsun-*k*ö-shan-saṅ-miṅ-*k*iṅ.

'Sûtra of the names of Buddhas Bhagavat Tathâgatas, Bodhisattvas, Âryas, and Riddhi-saṅgha or spiritual priests.'

40 fasciculi. The preface dates from A.D. 1415.

1618 諸佛世尊如來菩薩尊者名稱歌曲

*K*u-fo-shi-tsun-*ẕ*u-lâi-phu-sâ-tsun-*k*ö-miṅ-*kh*âṅ-ko-*kh*ü.

'Verses on the names of the Buddhas Bhagavat Tathâgatas, Bodhisattvas, and Âryas.'

51 fasciculi. The preface dates from A.D. 1415.

1619 感應歌曲

Kân-yiṅ-ko-*kh*ü.

'Verses on the influential power or favour (of Buddha).'

1 fasciculus. The Imperial preface dates from A.D. 1420.

1620 神僧傳

Shan-saṅ-*k*whân.

'Memoirs of spiritual priests.'

Compiled by the Emperor *Kh*aṅ-tsu, the third sovereign of the Miṅ dynasty, reigned A.D. 1403–1424. 9 fasciculi. The preface by the compiler dates from A.D. 1417. 209 priests, both foreign and native, are mentioned, from Kâsyapa Mâtaṅga of the Eastern Hân dynasty, A.D. 25–220, to Phu-ân of the Southern Suṅ dynasty, A.D. 1127–1280, who are in the narration preceded by some priests of the Yuen dynasty, A.D. 1280–1368. The Emperor selects these priests, whose actions seem very wonderful and almost supernatural, as they are described in older memoirs.

1621 大明三藏法數

Tâ-miṅ-sân-tsâṅ-fâ-shu.

'(A concordance of) numerical (terms and phrases) of the Law of the Tripiṭaka (collected) under the great Miṅ dynasty, A.D. 1368–1644.'

Collected and annotated by Yi-*ẕ*u, a priest of the Shâṅ-thien-*k*u ('upper India') hill (in China), and others. 40 fasciculi. In this useful concordance many technical terms and phrases are arranged according to the order of their own number, and they extend from 1 (i.e. terms and phrases beginning with one) up to 84,000.

(b) 大明續入藏諸集 Tà-miṅ-suh-ẑu-tsàṅ-ḳu-tsi, or Several Chinese Works successively admitted into the Canon during the great Miṅ dynasty, A.D. 1368–1644 (in or before A.D. 1584).

1622 華嚴懸談會玄記
Hwâ-yen-hhüen-thân-hwui-hhüen-ki.

'A record of the explanation of the hidden meaning of (or a commentary on) the introductory part of (the commentary on) the Buddhâvataṃsaka-sûtra, No. 1589.'

Compiled by Phu-ẑui, of the Yuen dynasty, A.D. 1280–1368. 40 fasciculi.

1623 妙法蓮華經要解
Miâo-fâ-lien-hwâ-kiṅ-yâo-kiĕ.

'An important explanation of (or a commentary on) the Saddharmapuṇḍarîka-sûtra, No. 134.'

Compiled by Kiĕ-hwân, of the later or Northern, or Southern Suṅ dynasty, A.D. 960–1280. 7 fasciculi.

1624 大佛頂萬行首楞嚴經會解
Tà-fo-tiṅ-wân-hhiṅ-sheu-laṅ-yen-kiṅ-hwui-kiĕ.

'A compilation of explanations of (or nine earlier commentaries on) the Mahâbuddhoshṇîsha-sarvakâryâ-sûraṅgama-sûtra, No. 446.'

Compiled by Wêi-tsö, in A.D. 1342, under the Yuen dynasty, A.D. 1280–1368. 20 fasciculi.

1625 大乘起信論疏
Tà-shaṅ-khi-sin-lun-shu.

'A commentary on the Mahâyâna-sraddhotpâda-sâstra, No. 1249.'

Compiled by Fâ-tsâṅ, the third patriarch of the Hwâ-yen school, of the Thâṅ dynasty, A.D. 618–907. 5 fasciculi.

1626 大乘起信論筆削記
Tà-shaṅ-khi-sin-lun-pi-sio-ki.

'A revised record' or commentary on the preceding work.

Compiled by Tsï-süen, of the later Suṅ dynasty, A.D. 960–1127. 15 fasciculi.

The following two works were compiled by Wan-tshâi, who died in A.D. 1302, under the Yuen dynasty, A.D. 1280–1368:—

1627 肇論新疏
Kâo-lun-sin-shu.

'A new commentary on the treatise by Saṅ-kâo (a famous disciple of Kumâragîva).'

3 fasciculi.

1628 肇論新疏游刃
Kâo-lun-sin-shu-yiu-ẑan.

A commentary on the preceding work.

10 fasciculi. The last two characters in the title, being a special name for this work, may mean 'playing with a strong and well-tempered weapon.'

1629 圓覺經略疏之鈔
Yuen-kiâo-kiṅ-liâo-shu-k'-khâo.

'An extract from an abridged or brief commentary on the Pûrṇa-buddha-sûtra, No. 427.'

Made by Tsuṅ-mi, the fifth patriarch of the Hwâ-yen school, of the Thâṅ dynasty, A.D. 618–907. 30 fasciculi; 10 divisions. The original commentary is said to have been compiled by the same author, but it is not found in this collection.

1630 金剛經論疏纂要
Kin-kâṅ-kiṅ-lun-shu-tswân-yâo.

'An extract from a commentary on the Vagrakkhedikâ-sûtra-sâstra, Nos. 1167, 1168, 1231.'

Made by Tsuṅ-mi (see No. 1629); and revised by Tsï-süen, of the later Suṅ dynasty, A.D. 960–1127. 2 fasciculi.

1631 釋金剛經刊定記
Shih-kin-kâṅ-kiṅ-khân-tiṅ-ki.

'A revised record' or commentary on the preceding work.

Compiled by Tsï-süen (see No. 1630), in A.D. 1024. 7 fasciculi.

1632 維摩詰所說經註
Wêi-mo-khiĕ-su-shwo-kiṅ-ku.

'A commentary on the Vimalakîrti-nirdesa-sûtra, No. 146.'

Compiled by Saṅ-ḳâo, of the Latter Tshin dynasty, A.D. 384–417. 10 fasciculi. This work is generally quoted by the short name of Ku-wêi-mo; and it is a very well-known comment.

1633 華嚴原人論解
Hwâ-yen-yuen-ẑan-lun-kiĕ.

'A commentary on the treatise on the origin of man according to the Hwâ-yen school, No. 1594.'

Compiled by Yuen-*k*iâo, in A. D. 1322, under the Yuen dynasty, A. D. 1280–1368. 3 fasciculi.

1634 折疑論
*K*ŏ-i-lun.
'A treatise on the eradication of doubt.'

Composed by Tsz'-*kh*âṅ, a Chinese Bhikshu, and annotated by Sh'-tsz' (Si*m*ha), a Bhikshu of the Western region, both under the Miṅ dynasty, A. D. 1368–1644. 5 fasciculi; 20 chapters. The third chapter answers the question, why Buddha is so called without mentioning his family and personal name. All other chapters relate and explain several sceptical views. It is a very interesting work.

1635 天台四教儀集註
Thien-thâi-sz'-*k*iâo-i-tsi-*k*u.
'A commentary on (the treatise on) the four divisions of (Buddha's) teaching according to the Thien-thâi school, No. 1551.'

Compiled by Man-zun, of the Nân-thien-*k*u ('south India') monastery (in China), in A. D. 1334, under the Yuen dynasty, A. D. 1280–1368. 10 fasciculi.

1636 教乘法數
*K*iâo-shan-fâ-shu.
'(A concordance of) numerical (terms and phrases) of the Law in the vehicle of the teaching, or the Tripi*t*aka.'

Collected by Yuen-tsiṅ, in about A. D. 1431, under the Miṅ dynasty, A. D. 1368–1644. 12 fasciculi. This is a later collection similar to No. 1621.

1637 佛祖歷代通載
Fo-tsu-li-tâi-thuṅ-tsâi.
'A complete statement concerning Buddha and Patriarchs in all ages.'
A history of Buddhism.

Compiled by Nien-*kh*âṅ, of the Yuen dynasty, A. D. 1280–1368. 36 fasciculi. The narration of this work begins with the so-called first ruler of China, Phân-ku, down to A. D. 1333 or 1344, when the compilation was completed. It relates several events concerning not only Buddhism, but also Confucianism and Taoism.

1638 禪林寶訓
Shân-lin-pâo-hhün.
'Precious instruction of the Shân or Dhyâna school.'

Collected by Miâo-hhi and *K*u-ân, of the later (or Northern) or Southern Suṅ dynasty, A. D. 960–1280; and re-collected or added by Tsiṅ-shan, of the Miṅ dynasty, A. D. 1368–1644. 4 fasciculi; about 300 compositions.

1639 大方廣佛華嚴經疏鈔
Tâ-fâṅ-kwâṅ-fo-hwâ-yen-*k*iṅ-shu-*kh*âo.
'An extract from two commentaries on the Buddhâvata*m*saka-vaipulya-sûtra, Nos. 1589, 1590.'

Made by *Kh*an-kwân, the fourth patriarch of the Hwâ-yen school, of the Thâṅ dynasty, A. D. 618–907. 30 fasciculi.

1640 翻譯名義集
Fân-i-miṅ-i-tsi.
'A collection of the meanings of the (Sanskrit) names translated (into Chinese).'

Collected by Fâ-yun, in A. D. 1151, under the Southern Suṅ dynasty, A. D. 1127–1368. 20 fasciculi; 64 chapters. This is a very useful dictionary of the technical names both in the Sanskrit and Chinese Buddhist literature, though much correction is required.

1641 禪宗正脈
Shân-tsuṅ-*k*âṅ-mo.
'A right line of succession of the Shân or Dhyâna school.' A collection of extracts from an older compilation (perhaps No. 1526) of the sayings of the eminent priests of this school.

Collected by *Z*u-pâ, in about A. D. 1488–1505, under the Miṅ dynasty, A. D. 1368–1644. 20 fasciculi.

1642 百丈清規
Pâi-*k*âṅ-tshiṅ-kwêi.
'Pure rules (established) by Pâi-*k*âṅ (of the Thâṅ dynasty, A. D. 618–907).'

Re-collected by Tŏh-hwui, and revised by Tâ-su, both under the Yuen dynasty, A. D. 1280–1368. 8 fasciculi; 9 chapters. 'Most of these rules however refer to worldly matters; so that they are not only far from the Vinaya, but also from the original rules of Pâi-*k*âṅ.' *K*'-tsiṅ, fasc. 43, fol. 12 b.

1643 三教平心論
Sân-*k*iâo-piṅ-sin-lun.
'An impartial ("even-mind") treatise on the three teachings or doctrines,' viz. Confucianism, Taoism, and Buddhism.

Composed by Liu Mi, of the Yuen dynasty, A. D. 1280–1368. 2 fasciculi. In the first place it asserts that all the three doctrines should not be despised, because they equally have the influence of causing man to practise goodness and avoid evil. In the second place it explains a difference of the final result of these teachings. In the third place it confutes widely the opinions of Hân Yü (A. D. 768–824), Eu-yâṅ Siu (1017–1072), *Kh*eṅ Hâo (1032–1085), *Kh*eṅ I (1033–1107), and *K*u Hhi (1130–1200). These five Chinese literati and philosophers are very well-known as sceptical authors who wrote against Buddhism. See Mayers' Chinese Reader's Manual, p. 50, No. 158; p. 165, No. 529; p. 34, No. 107; p. 34, No. 108; p. 25, No. 79 respectively.

1644 緇門警訓

Tsz'-man-*k*iṅ-hhün.

'Cautious instructions to priests.'

A collection of about 200 compositions.

Collected by *Z*u-pâ, in about A.D. 1488–1505 (cf. No. 1641), under the Miṅ dynasty, A.D. 1368–1644. 10 fasciculi.

1645 鐔津文集

Sün-tsiṅ-wan-tsi.

'A collection of the compositions of (a priest of) Sün-tsiṅ (name of a place in China).'

Composed (and collected) by *K*ie-suṅ, who died in A.D. 1072, under the later Suṅ dynasty, A.D. 960–1127. 19 fasciculi. The first three fasciculi are the same as No. 1530.

1646 八識規矩

Pâ-shi-kwêi-*k*ü.

'(A commentary on) the rules for (treating) the eight kinds of consciousness (Vigñânas).'

Compiled by Phu-thâi, also called Hân-shân-tâ-sh', of the Miṅ dynasty, A.D. 1368–1644. 1 fasciculus; 33 leaves. For the name of the compiler, see *K*'-tsiṅ, fasc. 42, fol. 22 a, where the two characters Pu-*k*u, or 'additional commentary,' are added to the title of this work. The text consists of twelve verses, and it is said to have been composed by the famous Hhüen-*k*wâṅ (Hiouen-thsang), of the Thâṅ dynasty, A.D. 618–907. See a recent Chinese edition of 相宗八要直解 Siâṅ-tsuṅ-pâ-yâo-*k*ih-*k*ie (fasc. 2, part 7), published in Nanking, 1870. The following is a list of the eight Vigñânas:—

Sanskrit.	Pâli.	Chinese.	Translation.
(1) *K*akshur-vigñâna	*K*akkhu-viññâna	眼識 Yen-shi	Eye-consciousness
(2) *S*rotas	Sota	耳 'rh	Ear
(3) Ghrâna	Ghâna	鼻 Pi	Nose
(4) *G*ihvâ	*G*ivhâ	舌 Shö	Tongue
(5) Kâya	Kâya	身 Shan	Body
(6) Manas	Mano	意 I	Mind
(7) Klish*t*a-manas		訖利瑟吒耶末那識 *K*i-li-seh-*k*hâ-ye-mo-no-shi; 染汙意識 *Z*an-wu-i-shi	Spoiled mind
(8) Âlaya		阿賴耶識 Ŏ-lâi-ye-shi; 藏識 Tsân-shi	Receptical (like)

The last two Vigñânas are not explained in the books of the Hînayâna.

There seems to have been another work after No. 1646 originally in this collection, viz. a commentary on 百法明門論 Pâi-fâ-miṅ-man-lun, or '*S*ata-dharma-vidyâdvâra-sâstra,' No. 1213, compiled by Kwêi-*k*i, a celebrated disciple of Hhüen-*k*wâṅ (Hiouen-thsang). See the original catalogue of the collection, last part, fol. 26 b, col. 6, where however two works (No. 1646 and the other) are mentioned as if one and the same book. Cf. *K*'-tsiṅ, fasc. 39, fol. 20 a. But this work seems to be wanting in the present Japanese edition, or in the copy of it in the India Office Library.

1647 禪源諸詮集都序

Shân-yue 1-*k*u-*k*hüen-tsi-tu-sü.

'A general introduction to a collection of explanations on the origin of Dhyâna or meditation.'

Composed by Tsuṅ-mi, the fifth patriarch of the Hwâ-yen school, of the Thâṅ dynasty, A.D. 618–907. 4 fasciculi.

1648 修心訣

Siu-sin-*k*üê.

'(A treatise on) the secret of cultivating the heart.'

Composed by Phu-*k*âo, a Corean priest of the Shân or Dhyâna school, under the Yuen dynasty, A.D. 1280–1368. 1 fasciculus.

1649 眞心直說
*K*an-sin-*k*ih-shwo.
'An honest speech with the true heart.'

Composed by *K*'no, of the Shân or Dhyâna school, of the Yuen dynasty, A.D. 1280–1368. 1 fasciculus; 15 sections.

1650 晉僧肇法師寶藏論
Tsin-sañ-*k*âo-fâ-sh'-pâo-tsâñ-lun.
'A treatise on the precious repository (or Ratna-pitaka-sâstra, written) by Sañ-*k*âo, a teacher of the Law or a Buddhist priest of the (Eastern) Tsin dynasty, A.D. 317–420.'

1 fasciculus; 3 chapters. The author lived in *Kh*âñ-ân, the capital of the Latter Tshin dynasty, A.D. 384–417.

1651 廬山蓮宗寶鑑
Lu-shân-lien-tsuñ-pâo-*k*ien.
'A precious mirror of the Lotus school, being (a work of a priest of) Lu-shân.'

Compiled by Phu-tu, about A.D. 1314, of the Yuen dynasty, A.D. 1280–1368. 10 fasciculi.

1652 永明智覺禪師唯心訣
Yuñ-miñ-*k*'-*k*iâo-shân-sh'-wêi-sin-*k*üê.
'(A treatise on) the secret of "only mind or heart," (written) by *K*'-*k*iâo, a teacher of the Dhyâna school, of the Yuñ-miñ monastery.'

1 fasciculus. *K*'-*k*iâo is the posthumous or honourable title of Yen-sheu, who died in A.D. 975, under the later Suñ dynasty, A.D. 960–1127.

1653 禪宗決疑集
Shân-tsuñ-*k*iê-i-tsi.
'A compilation of (explanations for) determining doubts according to the Shân or Dhyâna school.'

Compiled by *K*'-*kh*ŏ, of the Shân or Dhyâna school, of the Yuen dynasty, A.D. 1280–1368. 1 fasciculus. It gives some rules for thinking or meditating on a subject.

1654 黄檗傳心法要
Hwâñ-poh-*k*whân-sin-fâ-yâo.
'The doctrine of the transmission of the heart (of Buddha, being the sayings of a teacher) of the Hwâñ-poh hill.'

Compiled or recorded by Fê Hhiu, about A.D. 842–848, of the Thâñ dynasty, A.D. 618–907. 1 fasciculus. The recorder was a minister of state under four successive reigns, A.D. 826–856. He constantly heard the preaching of the teacher Hhi-yun, and took note of it each time; the result is the present work. He added a preface in A.D. 857. The teacher Hhi-yun was a disciple of a disciple of the sixth patriarch of the Shân or Dhyâna school, Hwui-nañ, and lived on the Hwâñ-poh hill, in the Kâo-ân district of Huñ-*k*eu. His school has consequently been called Hwâñ-poh-tsuñ (Wô-bak-shu, in Japanese sound). This school was established in Japan in A.D. 1654 by a Chinese priest Yin-yuen (In-gen), and it is one of ten existing Buddhist sects in that country at the present day. The Japanese editor of this collection of the Chinese Tripi*t*aka, Dôkô, better known by another name Tetsugen ('iron eye'), belonged to this school.

1655 萬善同歸集
Wân-shân-thuñ-kwêi-tsi.
'A compilation or work on the principle that several different kinds of goodness have but the same final object, i.e. truth.'

Compiled or composed by Yen-sheu, of the Shân or Dhyâna school, of the later Suñ dynasty, A.D. 960–1127. 3 fasciculi.

1656 華嚴法界觀通玄記頌註
Hwâ-yen-fâ-*k*iê-kwân-thun-hhüen-*k*i-suñ-*k*u.
'A commentary on the verses in the Thuñ-hhüen-*k*i ("record of passing through the hidden meaning") of the work on the meditation on the Dharmadhâtu, according to the Avatamsaka-sûtra,' cf. Nos. 1596, 1598.

The verses were composed by Pan-suñ, about A.D. 1088, of the later Suñ dynasty, A.D. 960–1127; and annotated by Tsuñ-tsân, of the Yuen dynasty, A.D. 1280–1368. 2 fasciculi.

1657 大明仁孝皇后夢感佛說第一希有大功德經
Tâ-miñ-zan-hhiâo-hwâñ-heu-mañ-kan-fo-shwo-ti-yi-hhi-yiu-tâ-kuñ-tŏh-*k*iñ.
'Buddhabhâshita-paramârtha-sudurlabha-mahâguna-sûtra, obtained in a dream by the Empress Zan-hhiâo, of the great Miñ dynasty, A.D. 1368–1644.'

2 fasciculi. The Empress was the consort of *Kh*añ-tsu, the third Emperor of the Miñ dynasty, who reigned A.D. 1403–1424. She wrote a preface in A.D. 1403, in which she says 'that on the new-year's day of the thirty-first year of the Huñ-wu period, A.D. 1398, she burnt incense and sat down quietly in her chamber and was reading some old sacred books, and when her mind was serene, there appeared suddenly a light of the purple-golden colour,' etc. In that strange way she obtained this Sûtra. This is, however, called rightly in *K*'-tsiñ (fasc. 41, fol. 13 a) 'a doubtful or false Sûtra.'

(c) 北藏缺南藏函號附 Pe-tsâṅ-*kh*üê-nân-tsâṅ-hân-hâo-fu, or Works wanting in the Northern Collection and now added from the Southern Collection with their 'case-marks.'

1658 續傳燈錄

Suh-*k*whân-tañ-lu.

'A continuation of the records of the transmission of the lamp (of the Law), No. 1524.'

Compiler's name is not mentioned; but it is stated in a work entitled Wêi-mu-i-man, that this was compiled by *K*ü-tiñ, a *S*râmaṇa of the Liñ-ku monastery, under the Yuen dynasty, A.D. 1280–1368 (?). See *K'*-tsiñ, fasc. 42, fol. 11 a. 36 fasciculi. 3118 eminent priests of the Shân or Dhyâna school are enumerated.

1659 古尊宿語錄

Ku-tsun-su-yü-lu.

'Records of the sayings of the Sthaviras or (forty-three) eminent priests (of the Shân or Dhyâna school) of the former ages.'

Collected by Tsö-tsâñ-*k*u, of the Southern Suñ dynasty, A.D. 1127–1280 (?). 48 fasciculi.

1660 禪宗頌古聯珠通集

Shân-tsuñ-suñ-ku-lien-shu-thuñ-tsi.

'A complete collection of verses as a gathering of pearls on praise of the former (patriarchs) of the Shân or Dhyâna school.'

Collected by Fâ-yiñ, about A.D. 1174–1189, under the Southern Suñ dynasty, A.D. 1127–1280; and continued by Phu-hwui, A.D. 1295–1318, of the Yuen dynasty, A.D. 1280–1368. 40 fasciculi. The first collection consists of 325 articles, and 2100 verses by 122 teachers of the school; and the continuation, of 493 articles, and 3050 verses by 426 teachers.

1661 佛祖統紀

Fo-tsu-thuñ-*k*i.

'Records of the linage of Buddha and Patriarchs.'

A history of Chinese Buddhism.

Compiled by *K'*-phân, of the Thien-thâi school, about A.D. 1269–1271, of the Southern Suñ dynasty, A.D. 1127–1280. 54 fasciculi.

1662 大明三藏聖教目錄

Tâ-miñ-sân-tsâñ-shan-*k*iâo-mu-lu.

'A record of the titles or catalogue of the sacred teaching of the three repositories or Tripiṭaka, (collected) under the great Miñ dynasty, A.D. 1368–1644.'

Compiler's name is not mentioned. 4 fasciculi. This was originally the Catalogue of the Southern Collection of the Chinese Tripiṭaka, published in A.D. 1368–1398, under the reign of the first Emperor of the Miñ dynasty; in 3 fasciculi. See *K'*-tsiñ, fasc. 45, fol. 15 a. But it is now in 4 fasciculi, and employed for this reproduction of the Northern Collection (Nos. 1–1621), first issued in A.D. 1403–1424, under the reign of the third Emperor of the same dynasty, together with some additional works (Nos. 1622–1662), published by Mi-tsâñ, in China, at the beginning of the seventeenth century of the Christian era. Differences in the order of works in both Collections are marked above each title.

Our Catalogue is based on this work, No. 1662, and the divisions and subdivisions of the 1662 works mentioned in it are adopted with a slight modification. See the table of contents above. It is the same work which Mr. Beal calls the Index, giving its contents minutely, in his own Catalogue, pp. 2–4, under Case 1. Besides the fly-leaf and a list of contents, there are six compositions added at the beginning, namely:—

(1) A memorial by the Japanese editor Dôkô to the Japanese Emperor Reigen, A.D. 1663–1686, on the presentation of a copy of his new edition of this Collection. It dates from the sixth year of the Yempô (lit. Yen-hô) period, A.D. 1678. 4 leaves.

(2) Another memorial by the same author with his second name Tetsugen, to the Japanese Shiôgun or Commander-in-chief, Tokugawa Tsunayoshi, A.D. 1681–1709, on the same subject. It dates from the first year of the Tenna (lit. Ten-wa) period, A.D. 1681. 3 leaves.

(3) The first Imperial preface with laudatory verses on the Canon, by Thâi-tsuñ (*Kh*an-tsu), the third Emperor of the Miñ dynasty, who reigned A.D. 1403–1424. It dates from the eighth year of the Yuñ-lö period, A.D. 1410. 2 leaves.

(4) The second Imperial preface to the Tripiṭaka, by Kuñ-tsuñ, the fourth Emperor of the Thâñ dynasty, who reigned A.D. 684–710. No date. 4 leaves. This preface was written to recommend the translations made by I-tsiñ, and a sketch of his life is therefore given in it.

(5) The third Imperial preface to the Tripiṭaka, by Thâi-tsuñ, the second Emperor of the later or

Northern Sun dynasty, who reigned A. D. 976–997. No date. 2 leaves.

(6) A letter by the Japanese editor Dôkô or Tetsugen, expressing his wish to receive donations for his intended reproduction of this Chinese Tripitaka. It dates from the ninth year of the Kwambun (lit. Kwan-bun) period, A. D. 1669. 2 leaves.

Towards the end of No. 1662 there are two more Imperial compositions added between the titles of Nos. 1621 and 1622, namely:—

(1) An addendum to the Canon, by the third Emperor of the Miṅ dynasty above mentioned. It dates from the ninth year of the Yuṅ-lö period, A. D. 1411. Half a leaf.

(2) A preface to a list of the works admitted into the Canon under the Miṅ dynasty, probably in A. D. 1584, by Shan-tsuṅ, the fifteenth Emperor of the dynasty. 1 leaf, with an extra column of the date of the twelfth year of the Wân-li period, A. D. 1584.

APPENDIX I.

LIST OF THE INDIAN AUTHORS, WITH THE TITLES OF THE WORKS ASCRIBED TO THEM.

Note—The date under the titles is that of the translation.

BODHISATTVAS.

1 Maitreya, whose name is transliterated 彌勒 Mi-lö, and translated 慈氏 Tshz'-sh', lit. he whose surname means benevolent. See Eitel, p. 70 a; Edkins, Chinese Buddhism, p. 240, and elsewhere. There are 10 works ascribed to him, namely:—

No. 1083	'Bodhisattvopâsaka-pa*ñk*asîlakarma-sûtra (V. M.).'	A. D.	431.
" 1086	Bodhisattva*k*aryânirdesa.	"	414-421.
" 1096	'Bodhisattvapratimoksha.'	"	" "
" 1097	'Bodhisattvasîlakarmalekha.'	"	649.
" 1098	'Bodhisattvapratimoksha.'	"	"
" 1170	Saptadasabhûmi-sâstra-yogâ*k*ârya (A.M.).	"	646-647.
" 1200	'Râgadharmanyâya-sâstra.'	"	649.
" 1235	'Vinirnîtapi*t*aka-sâstra.'	"	557-569.
" 1245	Madhyântavibhâga-grantha.	"	661.
" 1315	'Sarvasikshâsthitanâmârtha-sâstra.'	"	980-1000.

2 Asvaghosha, whose name is translated 馬鳴 Mâ-miñ, lit. a horse neighing. The twelfth patriarch. See No. 1460, i. e. a life of this Bodhisattva, translated by Kumâra*g*îva, A. D. 401–409; Wassiljew, p. 231; Eitel, p. 16 b; Edkins, pp. 74, 278; Beal, B.L.C., p. 95. There are 7 works ascribed to him, namely:—

No. 1080	'Fifty verses on the rules for serving a teacher (S. M.).'	A. D.	1004-1058.
" 1182	'Sûtrâlaṅkâra-sâstra (A. M.).'	"	405.
" 1249	'Mahâyânasraddhotpâda-sâstra.'	"	695-700.
" 1250	" "	"	553.
" 1299	'Mahâyânabhûmiguhyavâ*k*âmûla (?)-sâstra.'	"	557-569.
" 1351	Buddha*k*aritakâvya (I. M.).	"	414-421.
" 1379	'Dasadush*t*akarmamârga-sûtra.'	"	1004-1058.

3 Nâgâr*g*una, whose name is translated 龍樹 Luṅ-shu, lit. dragon-tree, 龍勝 Luṅ-shaṅ, lit. dragon-conqueror, or 龍猛 Luṅ-maṅ, lit. dragon the brave. The fourteenth patriarch. See No. 1461, i.e. a life of this Bodhisattva, translated by Kumâra*g*îva, A. D. 401–409; Wassiljew, p. 232; Eitel, p. 79 b; Edkins, p. 77; J. A. S. B., 1882, p. 115 et seq. There are 24 works ascribed to him, namely:—

No. 1070	'Dharmadhâtustotra (S. M.).'	A. D.	980-1000.
" 1169	'Mahâpra*g*ñâpâramitâ(sûtra)-sâstra (A. M.).'	"	402-405.
" 1179	Prâṇyamûla-sâstra (text).	"	409.
" 1180	'Dasabhûmivibhâshâ-sâstra.'	"	401-409.
" 1181	'Sâstra on the provisions for obtaining the Bodhi (text).'	"	590-616.
" 1185	Pra*g*ñâpradîpa-sâstra-kârikâ (text).	"	630-632.
" 1186	Dvâdasanikâya-sâstra.	"	408.
" 1187	Ash*t*âdasâkâsa-sâstra.	"	557-569.
" 1219	'Ekasloka-sâstra.'	"	538-543.
" 1223	Nyâyadvâratarka-sâstra.	"	711.
" 1224	" "		648.
" 1246	'Madhyântânugama-sâstra (text).'	"	543.
" 1251	'Vivâdasamana-sâstra.'	"	541.
" 1257	'Upâyakausalyahridaya-sâstra.'	"	472.
" 1304	'Lakshanavimukta-bodhih*ri*daya-sâstra.'	"	980-1000.
" 1305	'Mahâyâna-bhavabheda-sâstra.'	"	" "
" 1307	'Gâthâshash*t*i-yathârtha-sâstra.'	"	" "
" 1308	'Mahâyâna-gâthâvimsati-sâstra.	"	" "
" 1309	'Buddhamât*ri*kâ-pra*g*ñâpâramitâ-mahârthasaṅgîti-sâstra.'	"	" "
" 1354	'Bodhi*k*aryâ-sûtra (I. M.).'	"	980-1001.
" 1376	'Mahâpranidhânotpâda-gâthâ.'	"	980-1000.
" 1440	Ârya-nâgâr*g*una-bodhisattva-suh*ri*l-lekha.	"	434.
" 1441	" "	"	700-712.
" 1464	" "	"	431.

4 Deva, whose name is transliterated 提婆 Thi-pho, and sometimes translated 聖天 Shaṅ-thien, i. e. Âryadeva or Ârya Deva. A native of South India (not Ceylon, as in Eitel), and the disciple of Nâgâr*g*una. The fifteenth patriarch. See No. 1462, i. e. a life of this Bodhisattva, translated by Kumâra*g*îva, A. D. 401–409; Wassiljew, p. 234; Eitel, p. 30 b; Edkins, p. 77. 'Ârya Deva, also called Nîlanetra, on account of his having two spots, as large as the eyes, on his cheeks. His real name was *K*andrakîrti,' J. A. S. B., 1882, p. 96. The name Nîlanetra is translated 青目 Tshiṅ-mu, lit. blue-eye, or 分別明 Fan-pieh-miṅ, lit. distinct brightness. There are 9 works ascribed to him, namely:—

No. 1179	Prâṇyamûla-sâstra-*t*îkâ (A. M.).	A. D.	409.
" 1185	Pra*g*ñâpradîpa-sâstra-kârikâ (commentary).	"	630-632.
" 1188	*S*ata-sâstra (text).	"	404

No. 1189	*S*ata-sâstra-vaipulya.	A. D.	650.
" 1198	" "	"	"
" 1242	Mahâpurusha-sâstra.	"	397–439.
" 1254	'Satâkshara-sâstra.'	"	508–535.
" 1259	'*S*âstra on the refutation of the principles of four heretical Hînayâna schools mentioned in the Laṅkâvatâra-sûtra.'	"	" "
" 1260	'*S*âstra on the explanation of the Nirvâ*n*a of twenty heretical Hînayâna (teachers) mentioned in the Laṅkâvatâra-sûtra.'	"	" "

5 Asaṅga, whose name is translated 無著 Wu-*k*âo. See Eitel, p. 14 b; Edkins, p. 169. There are 12 works ascribed to him, namely:—

No. 1167	Va*g*ra*kkh*edikâ-sûtra-sâstra (A. M.).	A. D.	590–616.
" 1177	'Prakara*n*âryavâkâ (?)-sâstra.'	"	645–646.
" 1183	'Mahâyânasamparigraha-sâstra.'	"	563.
" 1184	" "	"	531.
" 1190	Sûtrâlaṅkâra-*t*îkâ.	"	630–633.
" 1199	Mahâyânâbhidharmasaṅgîti-sâstra.	"	652.
" 1202	'Prakara*n*âryavâkâ (?)-sâstra-kârikâ.'	"	645.
" 1208	'Va*g*ra*kkh*edikâ-pra*g*ñâpâramitâ-sûtra-sâstra-kârikâ.'	"	711.
" 1230	'Sha*dd*vâropadishtadhyânavyavahâra (?)-sâstra (text).'	"	703.
" 1231	Va*g*ra*kkh*edikâ-pra*g*ñâpâramitâ-sûtra-sâstra (text).	"	711.
" 1246	'Madhyântânugama-sâstra (commentary).'	"	543.
" 1247	Mahâyânasamparigraha-sâstra.	"	648–649.

6 Vasubandhu, whose name is transliterated 婆藪槃豆 Pho-su-phân-teu, and translated 天親 Thien-sin, lit. kindred with heaven, or 世親 Shi-sin, lit. kindred with the world. The younger brother of Asaṅga, and the twenty-first patriarch. See No. 1463, i. e. a life of this Bodhisattva, translated by Paramârtha, A. D. 557–569; Wassiljew, p. 235; Eitel, p. 164; Edkins, p. 278. It is stated in the Khâi-yuen-lu (fasc. 4 a, fol. 8 b), that there was an older translation of the life of Vasubandhu, made by Kumâra*g*îva, A. D. 401–409; but it was lost already in A. D. 730. There are 36 works ascribed to him, namely:—

No. 1168	Va*g*ra*kkh*edikâ-sûtra-sâstra (A. M.).	A. D.	509.
" 1171 (2)	'Mahâyânasamparigraha-sâstra-vyâkhyâ.'	"	563.
" " (3)	" "	"	590–616.
" " (4)	" "	"	648–649.
" 1176	Pañkaskandhaka-sâstra.	"	647.
" 1188	*S*ata-sâstra (commentary)[1].	"	404.
" 1191	Gayâsîrsha-sûtra-*t*îkâ.	"	535.
" 1193	Visesha*k*inta-brâhma*n*a-pariprikkhâ-sûtra-*t*îkâ.	"	531.
" 1194	Dasabhûmika-sâstra.	"	508–511.
" 1196	'Tripûr*n*a-sûtropadesa.'	"	541.
" 1204	Aparimitâyus-sûtra-sâstra.	"	529.

No. 1205	'Dharma*k*akrapravartana-sûtropadesa.'	A. D.	541.
" 1206	(Mahâpari)nirvâ*n*a-(sûtra)-sâstra.	"	386–550.
" 1207	'Nirvâ*n*a-sûtra-pûrvabhûtotpannâbhûta-gâthâ-sâstra.'	"	550.
" 1209	'*S*âstra on the Sûtra of Buddha's last teaching.'	"	557–569.
" 1213	'Mahâyânasatadharmavidyâdvâra-sâstra.'	"	648.
" 1215	'Vidyâmâtrasiddhi-tridasa-sâstra.'	"	"
" 1218	'Bodhi*k*ittotpâdana-sâstra[1].'	"	405.
" 1220	'Buddhagotra-sâstra.'	"	557–569.
" 1221	'Karmasiddhaprakara*n*a-sâstra.'	"	651.
" 1222	" "	"	541.
" 1225	'*S*amatha-vipasyanâ-dvâra-sâstra-kârikâ.'	"	711.
" 1230	'Sha*dd*vâropadishtadhyânavyavahâra (?)-sâstra (commentary).'	"	703.
" 1231	Va*g*ra*kkh*edikâ-pra*g*ñâpâramitâ-sûtra-sâstra (commentary).	"	711.
" 1232	'Saddharmapu*n*darîka-sûtra-sâstra.'	"	508–535.
" 1233	" "	"	508.
" 1238	Vidyâmâtrasiddhi.	"	508–535.
" 1239	"	"	557–569.
" 1240	"	"	661.
" 1241	'Ratnakû*t*a-sûtra-*k*aturdharmopadesa.'	"	539 or 541.
" 1244	Madhyântavibhâga-sâstra.	"	661.
" 1248	" "	"	557–569.
" 1252	Tarka-sâstra.	"	550.
" 1267	Abhidharmakosa-sâstra (A. H.).	"	651–654.
" 1269	" "	"	564–567.
" 1270	Abhidharmakosa-kârikâ.	"	651.

7 Sthiramati, whose name is translated 堅意 *K*ien-i, lit. solid thought, or 堅慧 *K*ien-hwui, lit. solid wisdom. A learned priest of Nâlanda (?). See Eitel, p. 133 a.

No. 1243	'Mahâyânâvatâraka-sâstra (A. M.).'	A. D.	397–439.
" 1258	'Mahâyâna-dharmadhâtvavisesha tâ-sâstra.'	"	691.
" 1318	" "	"	"

8 Âryasûra, whose name is translated 聖勇 Shan-yuṅ, lit. holy bravery, or 大勇 Tâ-yuṅ, lit. great bravery.

No. 1312	*G*âtakamâlâ (A. M.).	A. D.	960–1127.
" 1349	'Mahâvîra (or Âryasûra)-bodhisattva-karmaphala-saṅkshiptanirdesa-sûtra (I. M.).'	"	434.

9 *S*uddhamati (?), whose name is translated 淨意 Tsiṅ-i, lit. pure thought.

No. 1211	Pratîtyasamutpâda-sâstra (A. M.).	A. D.	508–535.

10 *G*ina, whose name is transliterated 陳那 *Kh*an-nâ. See Eitel, p. 37 b.

No. 1172	'Anâkâra*k*intâra*g*as (?)-sâstra (A. M.).'	A. D.	557–569.
" 1173	'Âlambanapratyayadhyâna-sâstra.'	"	657.
" 1228	'Pra*g*ñaptihetusaṅgraha (?)-sâstra.'	"	703.
" 1229	'Sarvalakshanadhyâna-sâstra-kârikâ.'	"	711.

[1] In No. 1188 the commentator's name is Vasu. It may therefore be another person.

[1] No. 1218 is ascribed either to Maitreya or Vasubandhu. See the Khâi-yuen-lu, fasc. 12 b, fol. 24 b.

No. 1255 '*Sâstra on the explanation of the fist.*' A. D. 557–569.
„ 1256 '*Tâlântaraka-sâstra.*' „ 703.

11 Sthitamati, whose name is translated 安慧 Ân-hwui, lit. quiet wisdom. The teacher of *G*aya-sena (?). See Eitel, p. 133 a.

No. 1175 Pañkaskandhavaipulya-sâstra (A. M.). A. D. 685.
„ 1178 'Mahâyânâbhidharmasamyuktasaṅgîti-sâstra.' „ 646.
„ 1316 'Prâyamûla-sâstra-*t*îkâ.' „ 1009–1050.

12 Agotra (?), whose name is translated 無性 Wu-siṅ, lit. without nature.

No. 1171 (4) 'Mahâyânasamparigraha-sâstra-vyâkhyâ (A. M.).' A. D. 647–649.

13 *S*aṅkarasvâmin, whose name is partly transliterated and partly translated 商羯羅主 Shâṅ-*k*ie-lo-*k*u, the last character means 'a lord.'

No. 1216 Nyâyapraveśatâraka-sâstra (A. M.). A. D. 647.

14 Bhavaviveka, whose name is translated 清辯 Tshiṅ-pien, lit. clear discussion. See Eitel, p. 23 b.

No. 1237 'Mahâyâna-tâlaratna-sâstra (A. M.).' A. D. 648.

15 Bandhuprabha (?), whose name is translated 親光 Sin-kwâṅ, lit. kindred light.

No. 1195 Buddhabhûmi-sûtra-sâstra (A. M.). A. D. 649.

16 Dharmapâla, whose name is translated 護法 Hu-fâ, lit. guardian of the law. See Eitel, p. 32 b.

No. 1174 'Âlambanapratyayadhyâna-sâstra-vyâkhyâ (A. M.).' A. D. 710.
„ 1197 Vidyâmâtrasiddhi (-sâstra). „ 659.
„ 1198 '*S*ata-sâstra-vaipulya-vyâkhyâ.' „ 650.
„ 1210 Vidyâmâtrasiddhi (-sâstra). „ 710.

17 *G*inaputra, whose name is translated 最勝子 Tsui-shaṅ-tsz', lit. son of the superior conqueror. See Eitel, p. 37 b.

No. 1201 Yogâkâryabhûmi-sâstra-kârikâ (or vyâkhyâ, A. M.). A. D. 654.

18 Gu*n*ada (?), whose name is translated 功德施 Kuṅ-töh-sh', lit. giver of the good qualities.

No. 1192 'Vagrakkhedikâ-sûtra-sâstra on the destruction of belief in an unbroken artificial name (? A. M.).' A. D. 683.

19 Dharmayasas (?), whose name is translated 法稱 Fâ-*kh*an, lit. law-fame.

No. 1298 'Mahâyâna-bodhisattvavidyâsaṅgîti-sâstra (A. M.).' A. D. 1004–1058.
„ 1303 Vagrasûki (-sâstra). „ 973–981.

20 Padmasîla (?), whose name is translated 蓮華戒 Lien-hwâ-*k*iâ, lit. lotus flower (like) morality.

No. 1301 'Bodhihr*i*daya-vaipulyavyâkhyâ-sâstra (A. M.).' A. D. 980–1000.

21 Sumuni (?), whose name is translated 善寂 Shan-tsi, lit. good calmness.

No. 1302 'Sarvadharmaratnottarârthasaṅgîti-sâstra (A. M.).' A. D. 980–1000.

22 Buddhasrig*ñ*âna (?), whose name is translated 覺吉祥 *K*iâo-*k*i-siâṅ, lit. lucky omen of understanding.

No. 1306 'Mahâyâna-lakshanasaṅgîti-sâstra (A. M.).' A. D. 980–1000.

23 Triratnârya (?), whose name is translated 三寶尊 Sân-pâo-tsun, lit. three gems worthy.

No. 1310 'Buddhamâtr*i*kâ-prag*ñ*âpâramitâ-mahârthasaṅgîti-sâstra-vyâkhyâ (A. M.).' A. D. 980–1000.

24 *S*rigu*n*araktâmbara (?), whose name is translated 勝德赤衣 Shaṅ-töh-*kh*ih-i, lit. excellent virtue and red dress.

No. 1313 'Ârya-buddhamâtr*i*kâ-prag*ñ*âpâramitâ-navagâthâ-mahârtha-sâstra (A. M.).' A. D. 1004–1058.

ARHATS AND ÂRYAS.

25 *S*âriputra, whose name is transliterated 舍利弗 Shö-li-fu, or partly transliterated and partly translated 舍利子 Shö-li-tsz', lit. son of *S*âri. See Eitel, p. 123 b.

No. 1268 *S*âriputrâbhidharma-sâstra (A. H.). A. D. 414–415.
„ 1276 Abhidharmasaṅgîtiparyâyapâda. „ 660–663.

26 Upatishya, whose name is transliterated 優波底沙 Yiu-po-ti-shâ. This may either be another name of *S*âriputra, or a different man. Cf. Eitel, p. 157 a.

No. 1293 'Vimokshamârga-sâstra (A. H.).' A. D. 505.

27 Mahâmaudgalyâyana, whose name is partly translated and partly transliterated 大目乾 (or 犍) 連 Tâ-mu-*k*ien (or *k*ien)-lien, i. e. the great Maudgalyâyana. See Eitel, p. 65 a.

No. 1296 Abhidharmaskandhapâda (A. H.). A. D. 659.
„ 1317 Prag*ñ*aptipâda-sâstra. „ 1004–1058.

28 Kâtyâyanîputra, whose name is partly transliterated and partly translated 迦旃延子 *K*iâ-*k*ân-yen-tsz', or 迦多衍尼子 *K*iâ-to-yen-ni-tsz', i. e. son of Kâtyâyanî. Cf. Eitel, pp. 54 b, 64 b.

No. 1264 Abhidharma(mahâ)vibhâshâ-sâstra (A. H. text, i. e. No. 1273). A. D. 437–439.
„ 1273 Abhidharmagñânaprasthâna-sâstra. „ 383.
„ 1275 „ „ „ 657–660.
„ 1279 Vibhâshâ-sâstra. „ 383.

29 Devasarman, whose name is transliterated 提婆設摩 Thi-pho-shö-mo. He is said to have lived 100 years after Buddha's entering Nirvâna. See also Eitel, p. 31 a.

No. 1281 Abhidharmavigñânakâyapâda (A. H.). A. D. 649.

30 Ghosha, whose name is transliterated 瞿沙 *Khü*-shâ. See Eitel, p. 42 a.

No. 1278 Abhidharmâmrita-sâstra (A. H.). A. D. 220–265.

31 Dharmatrâta, whose name is transliterated 達磨多羅 Tâ-mo-to-lo, and translated 法救 Fâ-*kiu*, lit. protected by the law. The maternal uncle of Vasumitra (see No. 33 below). See Eitel, p. 33 b.

No. 1283 'Pañkavastu-vibhâshâ-sâstra (A. H.). A. D. 663.
„ 1287 'Samyuktâbhidharmahridaya-sâstra.' „ 434.
„ 1321 Avadâna-sûtra (I. M.), or Dharmapada with Avadâna. „ 398–399.
„ 1341 Dharmatrâta-dhyâna-sûtra. „ 398–421.
„ 1353 Dharmapadâvadâna, or Dharmapada with Avadâna. „ 290–306.
„ 1365 Dharmapada, or Dhammapada. „ 224.
„ 1439 „ „ „ 980–1001.

32 Pañka mahârhakkhatâni (?), 五百大羅漢 Wu-pâi-tâ-lo-hân, i. e. 500 great Arhats, who formed the synod convoked by King Kanishka. See Eitel, p. 2 b, s. v. Abhidharmavibhâshâ-sâstra.

No. 1263 Abhidharmamahâvibhâshâ-sâstra (A. H.). A. D. 656–659.
„ 1264 „ „ „ 437–439.

33 Vasumitra, whose name is transliterated 婆須蜜 Pho-shu-mi, and translated 天友 Thien-yiu, lit. friend of heaven or Deva, or 世友 Shi-yiu, lit. friend of the world. He was one, if not the chief, of the 500 Arhats above mentioned. See No. 1494, i. e. the life of Hiouen-thsang, fasc. 2, fol. 19 a. See also Wassiljew, p. 53, and some other places; Eitel, p. 164 a.

No. 1277 Abhidharmaprakaranapâda (A. H.). A. D. 659.
„ 1282 (Abhidharma-)dhâtukâyapâda. „ 663.
„ 1284 'Ashtâdasanikâya-sâstra.' „ 557–569.
„ 1285 'Sâstra on the difference of the principles of (twenty Hînayâna) schools.' „ 557–569.
„ 1286 'Sâstra of the Dharmakakra (?) or the principles of different schools.' „ 662.
„ 1289 'Ârya-vasumitra-bodhisattva-saṅgîti-sâstra.' „ 384.
„ 1292 Abhidharmaprakaranapâda. „ 435–443.

34 Tâo-lüeh 道略, lit. abridgment of the way, whose name appears in this translation only.

No. 1344 Asokâvadâna (-sûtra, I. M.). A. D. 317–420.
„ 1366 'Samyuktâvadâna-sûtra, selected from various Sûtras.' „ 405.
„ 1368 'Samyuktâvadâna-sûtra.' „ 25–220.
„ 1372 „ „ „ 147–186.

35 Saṅgharaksha, whose name is transliterated 僧伽羅刹 Saṅ-*kiê*-lo-*khâ*. He is said to have lived 700 years after Buddha's entering Nirvâna.

No. 1325 'Karyâmârgabhûmi-sûtra (I. M.).' A. D. 284.
„ 1326 'Mârgabhûmi-sûtra.' „ 148–170.
„ 1350 'Dhyânanishthitasamâdhi-dharma-paryâya-sûtra.' „ 402–407.
„ 1352 'Saṅgharaksha-samkaya-buddhakarita-sûtra.' „ 384.

36 Vasubhadra, whose name is transliterated 婆素跋陀 Pho-su-poh-tho, and translated 山賢 Shân-hhien, lit. the wise of a mountain. But this translation may be that of another name.

No. 1271 'Tridharmaka-sâstra (A. H.).' A. D. 391.
„ 1381 'Explanation of an extract from the four Âgamas (I. M.).' „ 382.

37 Saṅghasena, whose name is transliterated 僧伽斯那 Saṅ-*kiê*-sz'-nâ, or 僧伽先 Saṅ-*kiê*-sien.

No. 1271 'Tridharmaka-sâstra (A. H.).' A. D. 391.
„ 1357 'Saṅghasena-samkaya-bodhisattva-pûrvanidâna-sûtra (I. M.).' „ 223–253.
„ 1364 'Satâvadâna-sûtra.' „ 492.

38 Nâgasena, whose name is transliterated 那先 Nâ-sien.

No. 1358 'Nâgasena-bhikshu-sûtra (I. M.),' or Milinda-prasna. A. D. 317–420.

39 Upasânta, whose name is transliterated 優波扇多 Yiu-po-shân-to, and translated 法勝 Fâ-shaṅ, lit. excellence of the law. But this translation may be that of another name.

No. 1288 Abhidharmahridaya(-sâstra, A. H.). A. D. 391.
„ 1294 „ „ „ 563.

40 Harivarman, whose name is transliterated 訶梨跋摩 Hö-li-poh-mo.

No. 1274 'Satyasiddhi (?)-sâstra (A. H.).' A. D. 407–408.

41 *Kiâ*-tiṅ 迦丁 (?) a transliteration.

No. 1371 'Sûtra on the changes of the future, spoken by the Bhikshu *Kiâ*-tiṅ (I. M.).' A. D. 420–479.

42 Buddhamitra, whose name is transliterated 佛陀密多 Fo-tho-mi-to. Cf. Eitel, p. 28 b.

No. 1382 'Pañkadvâradhyâna-sûtra-mahârtha-dharma (? I. M.).' A. D. 424–441.

43 Buddhatrâta, whose name is transliterated 佛陀多羅多 Fo-tho-to-lo-to. A teacher of the Sammatîya school.

No. 1139 'Vinayadvâvimsati-prasannârtha (?)-sâstra (V. H.).' A. D. 568.

44 Vasuvarman, whose name is transliterated 婆藪跋摩 Pho-su-poh-mo.

No. 1261 *Katussatya-sâstra* (A. H.). A. D. 557–569.

45 Gunamati, whose name is translated 德慧 Töh-hwui, lit. virtue and wisdom. See Eitel, p. 43 b.

No. 1280 'Lakshanânusâra-sâstra (A. H.).' A. D. 557–569.

46 Îsvara, whose name is translated 自在 Tsh'-tsâi, lit. self-existence.

No. 1181 '*Sâstra* on the provision for obtaining the Bodhi (A. M. commentary).' A. D. 590–616.

47 Ullangha, whose name is transliterated 鬱迦 Yü-*k*iâ, or 鬱楞伽 Yü-lan-*k*iê.

No. 1227 'Nidâna-sâstra (A. M.).' A. D. 607.
„ 1314 'Mahâyâna-nidâna-sâstra.' „ 746–771.

48 Sanghabhadra, whose name is translated 衆賢 *K*un-hhien, lit. the wise of the assembly. See Eitel, p. 117 b.

No. 1265 Nyâyânusâra-sâstra (A. H.). A. D. 653–654.
„ 1266 Abhidharmaprakaranasâsana-sâstra. „ 651–652.

49 Nandimitra, whose name is transliterated 難提蜜多羅 Nân-thi-mi-to-lo.

No. 1466 'Prophecy on the duration of the law, spoken by the great Arhat Nandimitra (I. M.).' A. D. 654.

50 Sugandhara (?), whose name is transliterated 塞建地羅 Sâi-*k*ien-thi-lo.

No. 1291 'Abhidharmâvatâra-sâstra (A. H.).' A. D. 658.

51 *G*inamitra, whose name is translated 勝友 Shan-yiu, lit. friend of the conqueror. This may be the same as the priest mentioned by Eitel, p. 37 b, viz. 'a priest famous for his eloquence, who lived about 630 A. D. in Nâlanda.'

No. 1127 Sarvâstivâdavinaya-sangraha (V. H.). A. D. 700.

52 Vaisâkhya, whose name is transliterated 毗舍佉 Phi-shö-*kh*ü.

No. 1143 Mûlasarvâstivâdanikâyavinaya-gâthâ (V. H.). A. D. 710.

53 Mât*rik*eta, whose name is transliterated 摩咥哩制吒 Mo-*k*'-li-*k*'-*kh*â.

No. 1456 'Buddhastotrârdhasataka (I. M.).' A. D. 708.

54 *S*âkyayasas, whose name is partly transliterated and partly translated 釋迦稱 Shih-*k*iâ-*kh*an.

No. 1226 'Hastadanda-sâstra (A. M.).' A. D. 711.

55 Samantabhadra, whose name is translated 普賢 Phu-hhien, lit. the wide-spreading wise. A Yogâkârya or a teacher of the Yoga school.

No. 1454 'Bodhihridayasilâdana(?)-kalpa (I. M.).' A. D. 746–771.

56 Munimitra (?), whose name is translated 寂友 Tsi-yiu, lit. friend of a solitary man.

No. 1458 'Buddhasrigunas-stotra (I. M.).' A. D. 980–1000.

A RÂGA OR KING.

57 *S*îlâditya, whose name is translated 戒日 *K*iê-zih, lit. the sun of morality. See Eitel, p. 127 b.

No. 1071 'Laudatory verses in Sanskrit (transliteration) on the eight great auspicious *K*aityas (S. M.).' A. D. 982–1001.

TÎRTHAKAS OR HERETICS.

58 Kapila, whose name is transliterated 迦毗羅 *K*iâ-phi-lo. A *R*ishi, the author of the Sânkhya philosophy. See Eitel, p. 51 b.

No. 1300 (Suvarna-)Saptati(-sâstra, A. H.), i. e. Sânkhyakârikâ with a commentary. A. D. 557–569.

59 *G*ñânakandra (?), whose name is translated 慧月 Hwui-yueh, lit. the moon of wisdom. A teacher of the Vaiseshika philosophy.

No. 1295 'Vaiseshikanikâya-dasapadârtha-sâstra (A. H.).' A. D. 648.

APPENDIX II.

LIST OF THE TRANSLATORS OF THE CHINESE BUDDHIST TRIPIṬAKA,

BOTH FOREIGN AND NATIVE, UNDER SUCCESSIVE AND CONTEMPORANEOUS DYNASTIES, WITH SHORT BIOGRAPHICAL NOTES AND THE TITLES OF THEIR TRANSLATIONS WHICH ARE STILL IN EXISTENCE.

Note.—The figures preceded by 'No.' and followed by 'above' or 'below' refer to the figures in this Appendix II, and those without this distinction refer to the figures in the Catalogue.

後漢 Heu-hân, or the Latter Hân dynasty, of the 劉 Liu family, also styled 東漢 Tuṅ-hân, or the Eastern Hân, from its capital at 洛陽 Lo-yâṅ. A.D. 25–220.

1 迦葉摩騰 *K*iâ-yeh Mo-thaṅ, i.e. Kâsyapa (or Kâsya) Mâtaṅga, also written 竺攝 (or 葉) 摩騰 *K*u Shö (or Yeh)-mo-thaṅ, or without 竺 *K*u, i.e. the last character of 天竺 Thien-*k*u, India, which character is prefixed to the names of other Indian priests, living in China, as their surname, e.g. *K*u Fâ-lân, No. 2 below. (See the 百家姓考略 Pâi-*k*iâ-siṅ-khâo-lüeh, fol. 37 a. Selected Essays, vol. ii, p. 320.) He was a *S*râmaṇa of Central India and a Brâhmaṇa by cast. He came to China in A.D. 67, having been invited by the Chinese envoy 蔡愔 Tsâi Yin (who was sent to India, in A.D. 65, by 明帝 Miṅ-ti, the second sovereign of the dynasty, reigned A.D. 58–75). In the same year he translated one Sûtra, in 白馬寺 Po-mâ-sh', or the White Horse Monastery, at Lo-yâṅ, where shortly after he died. This Sûtra is said to consist of some extracts from a Sûtra or Sûtras made in a foreign country, probably India. See the Saṅ-*k*whân, fasc. 1, fol. 1 b; Sui-shu, fasc. 35, fol. 21 a; Nêi-tien-lu, fasc. 1, fol. 6 a; Thu-*k*i, fasc. 1, fol. 2 b; Khâi-yuen-lu, fasc. 1, fol. 4 b; Miṅ-i-tsi, fasc. 3, fol. 4 a; Selected Essays, vol. ii, p. 319; Beal, B.L.C., p. 5.

No. 678 The Sûtra of forty-two sections (S.H.).

2 竺法蘭 *K*u Fâ-lân,—the last two characters, being a proper name, mean literally 'law-orchid;' but the last character 'lân' might possibly be a transliteration, while the first character 'Fâ' is one which is always used for the translation of the Sanskrit word 'Dharma' (cf. the name Thân-wu-lân, i.e. Dharma + lân, No. 37 below). In this case Fâ-lân may be restored into Dharmaraksha. But *K*u Fâ-lân seems to be called Gobharaṇa or Bhâraṇa by Tibetans. (See Le Sûtra en Quarante-deux Articles, Textes Chinois, Tibétain et Mongol, p. 38, col. 2, l. 3, where the last syllable is written 'na;' Selected Essays, vol. ii, p. 320; J.A.S.B., 1882, p. 89.) He was a *S*râmaṇa of Central India, well versed in Vinaya. When invited to go to China, the king would not let him depart. He, however, left secretly, and arrived in China after Kâsyapa Mâtaṅga (No. 1 above), in A.D. 67. They both together translated the Sûtra of forty-two sections (No. 678). After Mâtaṅga died, Fâ-lân translated five works, in A.D. 68–70; and died in Lo-yâṅ, when he was more than sixty years old. See the Saṅ-*k*whân, fasc. 1, fol. 2 a; Sui-shu, fasc. 35, fol. 21 a; Nêi-tien-lu, fasc. 1, fol. 6 b; Thu-*k*i, fasc. 1, fol. 3 a; Khâi-yuen-lu, fasc. 1, fol. 6 a; Miṅ-i-tsi, fasc. 3, fol. 4 b; Selected Essays, vol. ii, p. 320; Beal, B.L.C., p. 5. The Nêi-tien-lu and Thu-*k*i mention the following five works:—

(1) 佛本行經 Fo-pan-hhiṅ-*k*iṅ, or the Buddha*k*arita-sûtra (?) (taken by Julien for a translation of the Lalita-vistara), 5 fasc. A.D. 68.

(2) 十地斷結經 Shi-ti-twân-*k*ie-*k*iṅ, or the Dasabhûmi-klesa*kkh*edikâ (?)-sûtra, 4 fasc. A.D. 70.

(3) 法海藏經 Fâ-hâi-tsâṅ-*k*iṅ, or the Dharmasamudrakosha-sûtra (?), 3 fasc.

(4) 佛本生經 Fo-pan-shaṅ-*k*iṅ, or the *G*âtaka, 2 fasc.

(5) 二百六十戒合異 'rh-pâi-li-shi-*k*ie-hö-i, lit. 'a gathering of differences of 260 (articles of) *S*îla or moral precepts,' 2 fasc.

But the Saṅ-*k*whân and Khâi-yuen-lu ascribe to him the first four works only in a different order, and a compiler of the latter work adds that these translations have long been lost. (See the Selected Essays, vol. ii, pp. 320–321.) The fifth translation had also been lost in A.D. 730. See the Khâi-yuen-lu, fasc. 15 b, fol. 15 b.

3 支婁迦讖 *K*' Leu-*k*iâ-*k*hân,—the last three characters seem to be used for a transliteration of a Sanskrit name, such as Lokaraksha (?), and 支 *K*' is

the second character of 月支 Yueh-*k'*, which character is prefixed to the names of other translators of the Yueh-*k'*, living in China, as their surname, e.g. *K' Kh*ien, No. 18 below. But cf. *K*ilukâksha, in J.A.S.B., 1882, p. 90. He was a *S*râmana of the country of Yueh-*k'*, who came to China in A.D. 147, or 164, and worked at translations till A.D. 186 in Lo-yân. See San-*k*whân, fasc. 1, fol. 7 a; Sui-shu, fasc. 35, fol. 21 b; Nêi-tien-lu, fasc. 1, fol. 15 a; Thu-*k*i, fasc. 1, fol. 3 b; Khâi-yuen-lu, fasc. 1, fol. 7 a; Selected Essays, vol. ii, p. 322; Beal, B.L.C., p. 6. The Nêi-tien-lu and Thu-*k*i ascribe to him 21 distinct translations in 63 fasciculi; but the Khâi-yuen-lu mentions 23 works in 67 fasciculi, and states that 11 works in 26 fasciculi only were in existence in A.D. 730. There are, however, 12 translations ascribed to him in this Collection, namely:—

No. 5 Dasasâhasrikâ pra*g*ñâpâramitâ (S.M.).
„ 25 Amitâyusha (or -âbha)-vyûha, or Sukhâvatî-vyûha (long).
„ 28 Akshobhyasya tathâgatasya vyûha.
„ 57 Kâsyapa-parivarta.
„ 73 Pratyutpanna-buddhasammukhâvasthita-samâdhi.
„ 76 Bhadrapâla-sûtra.
„ 102 'Tathâgata-viseshana (?)-sûtra.'
„ 112 'Sûtra on the office of the Bodhisattva asked by Mañgusrî.'
„ 161 Mahâdruma-kinnararâ*g*a-paripri*kkh*â.
„ 174 A*g*âtasatru-kaukritya-vinodana.
„ 386 Lokânuvartana, or Lokânusamânâvatâra.
„ 1372 'Samyuktâvadâna-sûtra (I.M.).'

4 安世高 Ân Shi-kâo,—the last two characters are said to be a literary appellation (字) by which he is most usually designated, and 安 Ân is the first character of 安息 Ân-si (Eastern Persia or Parthia or Arsak), which character is prefixed to the names of other translators of the same country, living in China, as their surname, e.g. Ân Hhüen, No. 6 below. The cognomen of Ân Shi-kâo is 淸 Tsin or 靜 Tsin, so that he is mentioned in the Sui-shu (fasc. 35, fol. 21 b) as 安靜 Ân Tsin. He was a prince royal of the country of Ân-si. When his father died he gave up the kingdom to his uncle and became a *S*râmana. He came to China in A.D. 148 and worked at translations till A.D. 170. See San-*k*wân, fasc. 1, fol. 3 a; Sui-shu, fasc. 35, fol. 21 b; Nêi-tien-lu, fasc. 1, fol. 7 b; Thu-*k*i, fasc. 1, fol. 4 b; Khâi-yuen-lu, fasc. 1, fol. 10 a; Selected Essays, vol. ii, p. 321; Beal, B.L.C., p. 7. The Nêi-tien-lu and Thu-*k*i ascribe to him 176 distinct translations in 197 fasciculi; but the Khâi-yuen-lu mentions 95 works in 115 fasciculi only, and states that 54 works in 59 fasciculi only were in existence in A.D. 730. There are, however, 55 translations ascribed to him in this Collection, namely:—

No. 54 Maitreya-paripri*kkh*â-dharmâshta (S.M.).
„ 220 'Kumâra-mûka-sûtra.'
„ 227 '*S*reshthi-putra-*g*eta (?)-sûtra.'
„ 251 Ratnakûta-sûtra.
„ 282 'Sûtra on the Samâdhi called Vow.'
„ 387 'Sûtra on (*G*îvas inviting) many priests to wash themselves in a bath-house.'
„ 438 'Sûtra on fifty countings of clear measure (?).'
„ 451 'Buddhamudrâ-samâdhi-sûtra.'
„ 512 'Sûtra on the eight understandings of great men.'
„ 548 'Sûtra on the law of ten rewards in the Dîrghâgama (S.H.).'
„ 553 'Sûtra on the Avidyâ, Trishnâ, and *G*âti of man.'
„ 555 Sri*g*âla-vâda.
„ 559 'Sûtra on the cause of all sins.'
„ 565 'Sûtra on the law true and not true.'
„ 567 'Sûtra on the explanation of Âsrava (?).'
„ 582 'Sûtra addressed by Buddha to a Brâhmana who could not become free from loving thoughts at the death of his son.'
„ 583 'Sûtra spoken by Buddha to the *G*rihapati, being a man possessed of eight cities and ten families (?).'
„ 586 'Samantadharmârtha-sûtra.'
„ 598 '*K*atussatya-sûtra.'
„ 601 'Sûtra on the fundamental relationship.'
„ 617 'Sûtra on a Brâhmana who wished to avoid death.'
„ 633 'Sûtra on Ânanda's fellow-student.'
„ 635 'Sûtra on a question asked by Ânanda about the difference of the lucky and unlucky condition of those who serve Buddha.'
„ 643 'Mâtangî-sûtra.'
„ 648 'Saptâyatana-tridhyâna-sûtra.'
„ 649 'Sûtra on the conversion of Anâthapindada's seven sons.'
„ 653 'Pa*ñk*askandhâvadâna-sûtra.'
„ 657 Dharma*k*akra-pravartana-sûtra.
„ 659 'Ashtâṅgasamyañmârga-sûtra.'
„ 667 'Âmrapâlî-*g*îva-nidâna-sûtra.'
„ 668 „ „ „
„ 675 'Sûtra of the question addressed by Pretas to Maudgalyâyana.'
„ 681 'Mahânâpâna-dhyâna-sûtra.'
„ 682 'Sûtra on the mind of reproaching.'
„ 683 'Dhyâna*k*aryâ-dharmasa*ñg*ñâna-sûtra.'
„ 684 'Sûtra on several places or objects.'
„ 685 'Sûtra on thinking of the origin of goodness and evil.'
„ 686 'Abhinishkramana-nidâna-sûtra.'
„ 687 'Âgamasamyak*k*aryâ-sûtra.'
„ 688 'Ashtâdasanaraka-sûtra.'
„ 689 'Dharmasa*ñg*ñânara*g*as-sûtra.'
„ 694 'Sûtra on a *S*reshthiputra's causing three places to be harassed.'
„ 695 'Gândhâradesa-râ*g*a-sûtra.'
„ 705 'Sûtra addressed by Buddha to A*k*ira(?)-kâsyapa on pain either caused by oneself or by another.'
„ 706 'Sûtra on teaching of hells as the recompense of sinful actions.'
„ 724 'Dhyâna*k*aryâ-saptatrimsadvarga-sûtra.'
„ 731 'Sthiramati-sûtra.'
„ 762 'Sûtra on the kindness of parents which is difficult to be returned.'

No. 765 'Sûtra on the nine causes of untimely death.'
„ 780 'Skandha-dhâtvâyatana-sûtra.'
„ 1112 'Sûtra on the lightness and heaviness of the sin of transgressing the *S*îla or precepts (V. H.).'
„ 1126 'Mahâbhikshu-trisahasrakarman.'
„ 1326 'Mârgabhûmi-sûtra (I. M.).'
„ 1346 'Abhidharmapa*k*kadharmakaryâ-sûtra.'
„ 1363 'Sûtra on Kâsyapa's collection of the Tripi*t*aka.'

5 竺佛朔 *K*u Fo-soh, an Indian *S*râmana, who translated two Sûtras (one and two fasciculi respectively) at Lo-yâṅ in A. D. 172 and 183; but these translations had long been lost in A. D. 730. See Saṅ-*k*whân, fasc. 1, fol. 7 b; Sui-shu, fasc. 35, fol. 21 b; Nêi-tien-lu, fasc. 1, fol. 18 a; Thu-*k*i, fasc. 1, fol. 10 b; Khâi-yuen-lu, fasc. 1, fol. 24 a; Selected Essays, vol. ii, p. 322; Beal, B. L. C., p. 9.

6 安玄 Ân Hhüen, an Upâsaka of Ân-si, who was also called 安侯 Ân-heu, or the Marquis or prince Ân, and 騎都尉 *Kh*i-tu-wêi, or the head officer of cavalry. This official title was given to him by the Emperor of China. He together with Yen Fo-thiâo, No. 9 below, translated two works at Lo-yâṅ in A. D. 181. See Saṅ-*k*whân, fasc. 1, fol. 7 b; Nêi-tien-lu, fasc. 1, fol. 17 b; Thu-*k*i, fasc. 1, fol. 11 a; Khâi-yuen-lu, fasc. 1, fol. 24 b; Beal, B. L. C., p. 9.

No. 33 Ugraparipri*kkh*â (S. M.).
„ 1339 'Dvâdasanidâna-sûtra as an oral explanation according to the Âgama (? I. M.).'

7 支曜 *K*' Yâo, a *S*râmana of the western region, probably from the Yueh-*k*', who worked at translations at Lo-yâṅ in A. D. 185. See Saṅ-*k*whân, fasc. 1, fol. 8 a; Nêi-tien-lu, fasc. 1, fol. 18 b; Thu-*k*i, fasc. 1, fol. 11 b; Khâi-yuen-lu, fasc. 1, fol. 25 a; Beal, B. L. C., p. 9. The Nêi-tien-lu and Thu-*k*i ascribe to him 11 distinct translations in 12 or 13 fasciculi; but the Khâi-yuen-lu mentions 10 works in 11 fasciculi, and states that 5 works in 6 fasciculi were lost already in A. D. 730.

No. 381 'Purnaprabhâsa-samâdhimati-sûtra (S. M.).'
„ 563 'Sûtra on the eight intense thoughts of Anuruddha (S. H.).'
„ 661 'Sûtra on the three marks of a good horse.'
„ 662 'Sûtra on the eight points of resemblance between man and horse.'
„ 1338 'Small Mârgabhûmi-sûtra (I. M.).'

8 康巨 Khâṅ *K*ü, a *S*râmana of the western region, probably of Tibetan descent, as 康 Khâṅ is the first character of 康居 Khâṅ-*k*ü, i. e. Kambu or Ulterior Tibet (see Wells Williams' Chinese Dictionary, p. 744),—or Kambo*g*a (see Childers' Pâli Dictionary, p. 177 b),—which character (康) is prefixed to the names of other translators of the same descent living in China as their surname, e. g. Khâṅ Maṅ-siâṅ, No. 10 below. He translated one Sûtra at Lo-yâṅ in A. D. 187; but this translation had been lost in A. D. 730. See Saṅ-*k*whân, fasc. 1, fol. 8 a; Nêi-tien-lu, fasc. 1, fol. 19 a; Thu-*k*i, fasc. 1, fol. 11 b; Khâi-yuen-lu, fasc. 1, fol. 26 a; Beal, B. L. C., p. 9.

9 嚴佛調 Yen Fo-thiâo, a *S*râmana (or an Upâsaka, according to the Nêi-tien-lu and Thu-*k*i) of 臨淮 Lin-hwâi, in China, who was an assistant of Ân Hhüen, No. 6 above, and well versed in Sanskrit. Afterwards he alone translated some works at Lo-yâṅ in A. D. 188. See Saṅ-*k*whân, fasc. 1, fol. 8 a; Nêi-tien-lu, fasc. 1, fol. 19 a; Thu-*k*i, fasc. 1, fol. 12 a; Khâi-yuen-lu, fasc. 1, fol. 26 b; Beal, B. L. C., p. 9. The Nêi-tien-lu and Thu-*k*i ascribe to him 7 distinct translations in 9 or 10 fasciculi; but the Khâi-yuen-lu mentions 5 works in 8 fasciculi, and states that 4 works in 7 fasciculi were lost already in A. D. 730.

No. 435 'Sûtra on the Bodhisattva's inner practice (?) of the six pâramitâ (S. M.).'

10 康孟詳 Khâṅ Maṅ-siâṅ, a *S*râmana of Tibetan descent, who came to China from Central India or the western region. In A. D. 194–199 he translated 6 works in 9 fasciculi, of which 4 works in 6 fasciculi had been lost in A. D. 730. Among these missing translations there were the Brahma*g*âla-sûtra, *K*atussatya-sûtra, and 'Kumâra-nidâna-sriphala-sûtra,' i. e. a life of Buddha. See Saṅ-*k*whân, fasc. 1, fol. 8 b; Nêi-tien-lu, fasc. 1, fol. 19 b; Thu-*k*i, fasc. 1, fol. 12 b; Khâi-yuen-lu, fasc. 1, fol. 27 b; Beal, B. L. C., p. 10.

No. 625 'Sûtra on Sâriputra and Maudgalyâyana's going through the four roads (for begging, S. H.).'
„ 733 'Nidânakaryâ-sûtra.'

11 竺大力 *K*u Tâ-li,—the last two characters mean literally 'great power,' so that they may possibly be a translation of the name Mahâbala. He was a *S*râmana of the western region, who together with Khâṅ Maṅ-siâṅ, No. 10 above, translated one Sûtra at Lo-yâṅ in A. D. 197. See Saṅ-*k*whân, fasc. 1, fol. 8 a; Nêi-tien-lu, fasc. 1, fol. 20 a; Thu-*k*i, fasc. 1, fol. 12 b; Khâi-yuen-lu, fasc. 1, fol. 28 a; Beal, B. L. C., p. 10.

No. 664 '*Karyâ*-nidâna-sûtra,' i. e. a life of Buddha (S. H.).

12 曇果 Thân-kwo (Dharmaphala ?), also written 釋曇果 Shih Thân-kwo,—釋 Shih is the first character of 釋迦 Shih-*k*iâ, i. e. *S*âkya, which character is prefixed to the names of some other Indian priests living in China and of Chinese priests as their surname. (See the Selected Essays, vol. ii, p. 320, note 3.) He was a *S*râmana of the western region, who brought with him one Sanskrit text from Kapila-

vastu, and together with Khân Mañ-siâñ, No. 10 above, translated it at Lo-yâñ in A. D. 207. See Sañ-*k*whân, fasc. 1, fol. 8 a; Nêi-tien-lu, fasc. 1, fol. 20 a; Thu-*k*i, fasc. 1, fol. 13 a; Khâi-yuen-lu, fasc. 1, fol. 28 b; Beal, B. L. C., p. 10.

No. 556 'Madhyama-ityukta-sûtra,' i. e. a life of Buddha (S. H.).

WORKS OF UNKNOWN TRANSLATORS.

The Thu-*k*i (fasc. 1, fol. 13 a seq.) mentions 123 works in 148 fasciculi; and the Khâi-yuen-lu (fasc. 1, fol. 28 b seq.) gives 141 works in 158 fasciculi, and adds that 16 works in 26 fasciculi were in existence in A. D. 730. There are the following 16 works in the Collection, which are, however, not exactly the same as those in the Khâi-yuen-lu:—

No. 202 'A later translation of the Sûtra consisting of verses on Amitâyus (S. M.).'
" 260 Adbhuta-dharmaparyâya.
" 289 Tathâgata-pratibimba-pratishtânusamsâ.
" 431 'Sûtra of the great and good means by which Buddha recompenses the favour (of his parents).'
" 478 'Sûtra on the spiritual Mantra for keeping the house safe.'
" 573 'Sûtra on Maudgalyâyana's temptation by the Mâra (S. H.).'
" 578 'Sûtra on Duhkha-skandha (?).'
" 704 'Akuru (?)-sûtra.'
" 777 '*K*andanadruma-sûtra.'
" 1093 'Sûtra on receiving the Dasabhadrasila,' i. e. *S*ikshâpada (V. M.).
" 1151 '*S*râmanerikâ-sila-sûtra (V. H.).'
" 1290 'Gunanirdesa-sâstra (A. H.).'
" 1337 'Sûtra on six Bodhisattvas' names, to be recited and remembered (I. M.).'
" 1360 'Sûtra on blaming lust, as an important action of meditation.'
" 1361 'Sûtra of sections about the meditation on the inner body.'
" 1368 'Samyuktâvadâna-sûtra.'

SUMMARY OF THE PRECEDING LIST OF TRANSLATIONS MADE UNDER THE LATTER OR EASTERN HÂN DYNASTY, A. D. 25–220.

Translators.	Nêi-tien-lu.	Thu-*k*i.	Khâi-yuen-lu.	In existence.
No. 1	1	1	1	1
" 2	5	5	4	0
" 3	21	21	23	12
" 4	176	176	95	55
" 5	2	2	2	0
" 6	2	2	2	2
" 7	11	11	10	5
" 8	1	1	1	0
" 9	7	7	5	1
" 10	6	6	6	2
" 11	1	1	1	1
" 12	1	1	1	1
	125	123	141	16
	359	357	292*	96

* In 395 fasciculi. In A. D. 730 there were 97 works in 131 fasciculi in existence, and 195 works in 264 fasciculi had been lost. See the Khâi-yuen-lu, fasc. 1, fol. 3 b.

魏 The Wêi dynasty, of the 曹 Tsho family, the northern of the Three Kingdoms, with its capital at Lo-yâñ. A. D. 220–265.

13 曇柯(or 摩)迦羅 Thân-kö (or mo)-*k*iâ-lo, i. e. Dharmakâla, whose name is translated 法時 Fâ-sh', lit. 'law-time.' He was a *S*ramana of Central India, who came to China in A. D. 222, and observed that the priests in China were then entirely ignorant of the rules of Vinaya. In A. D. 250, therefore, he translated the Prâtimoksha of the Mahâsaṅghikas, in one fasciculus. This was the first book of the Vinaya-pitaka, translated into Chinese; but it was lost in A. D. 730. See Sañ-*k*whân, fasc. 1, fol. 8 b; Nêi-tien-lu, fasc. 2, fol. 2 b; Thu-*k*i, fasc. 1, fol. 17 a; Khâi-yuen-lu, fasc. 1, fol. 41 b; Miñ-i-tsi, fasc. 3, fol. 4 b; Beal, B. L. C., p. 10. Cf. the Sui-shu, fasc. 35, fol. 21 b; Selected Essays, vol. ii, p. 322, fourth paragraph.

14 康僧鎧 Khâñ Sañ-khâi,—the last two characters are most probably employed for Saṅghavarman, because 僧 Sañ is the first character of 僧伽 Sañ-*k*iê, the very well-known transliteration of the word Saṅgha, and 鎧 khâi means 'armour,' i. e. varman (cf. the name Sañ-*k*iê-poh-mo, No. 80 below). He was an Indian *S*ramana of Tibetan descent, as the character 康 Khâñ being prefixed to his name implies. In A. D. 252 he translated some works in the White Horse Monastery at Lo-yâñ. See Sañ-*k*whân, fasc. 1, fol. 9 a (where it ascribes to him 4 Sûtras); Nêi-tien-lu, fasc. 2, fol. 3 a; Thu-*k*i, fasc. 1, fol. 17 b (both ascribe to him 2 Sûtras in 4 fasciculi); Khâi-yuen-lu, fasc. 1, fol. 42 a (where 3 works in 4 fasciculi are mentioned); Miñ-i-tsi, fasc. 3, fol. 5 a (where only 1 Sûtra is mentioned, viz. the Sukhâvatîvyûha); Selected Essays, vol. ii, pp. 322, 341, and 343; Beal, B. L. C., p. 11.

No. 23 (19) Ugrapariprikkhâ (S. M.).
" 27 Aparimitâyus-sûtra, or Amitâbha-vyûha, or Sukhâvatîvyûha (long).
" 1163 'Samyuktakarma of the Dharmagupta-nikâya (V. H.).'

15 曇諦 Thân-ti, or 曇無諦 Thân-wu-ti, i. e. Dharma-satya (?), whose name is translated 法實 Fâ-shih, lit. 'law-truth.' He was a *S*ramana of the country of Ân-si, who compiled or translated one work at Lo-yâñ in A. D. 254. See Sañ-*k*whân, fasc. 1, fol. 9 a; Nêi-tien-lu, fasc. 2, fol. 3 b; Thu-*k*i,

fasc. 1, fol. 17 b; Khâi-yuen-lu, fasc. 1, fol. 43 a; Beal, B. L. C., p. 11.

No. 1146 'Karman' (of the Dharmagupta-nikâya. V. H.).

16 白延 Po Yen, a *S*ramana of the western region, who translated some Sûtras in the White Horse Monastery at Lo-yâṅ in A. D. 257. See Saṅ-*k*whân, fasc. 1, fol. 9 a; Nêi-tien-lu, fasc. 2, fol. 4 a; Thu-*k*i, fasc. 1, fol. 18 a (these three authorities ascribe to him 6 Sûtras in 8 fasciculi); Khâi-yuen-lu, fasc. 1, fol. 43 a (where 5 Sûtras in 7 fasciculi are mentioned, and said to have long been lost in A. D. 730); Beal, B. L. C., p. 11. According to the Thu-*k*i, there were two versions of the larger Sukhâvatî-vyûha made by him; but one of them is not given in the Khâi-yuen-lu. There exists 1 Sûtra in the Collection, namely:—

No. 43 Surataparipri*kkh*â (S. M.).

17 安法賢 Ân Fa-hhien,—the last two characters mean literally 'law-wise,' i. e. Dharmabhadra (?). He was a *S*ramana of the western region, who translated 2 Sûtras in 5 fasciculi, but the date is not given. These translations had been lost in A. D. 730. See Nêi-tien-lu, fasc. 2, fol. 4 a; Thu-*k*i, fasc. 1, fol. 18 a; Khâi-yuen-lu, fasc. 1, fol. 43 b; Beal, B. L. C., p. 11. One of his translations was the Mahâparinirvâna-sûtra.

Works of Unknown Translators.

No. 626 'Sûtra of the patronymics and names of the parents of the seven Buddhas (S. H.).'

" 1278 Abhidharmâmrita-sâstra (A. H.).

Summary of the preceding List of Translations made under the Wêi dynasty, A. D. 220–265.

Translators.	Nêi-tien-lu.	Thu-*k*i.	Khâi-yuen-lu.	In existence.
No. 13	1	1	1	0
" 14	2	2	3	3
" 15	1	1	1	1
" 16	6	6	5	1
" 17	2	2	2	0
	0	0	0	2
	12	12	12*	7

* In 18 fasciculi. In A. D. 730 there were only 4 works in 5 fasciculi in existence, and 8 works in 13 fasciculi had been lost. See the Khâi-yuen-lu, fasc. 1, fol. 41 a. But the present Collection has 3 more works, one of them is however mentioned under the Wu dynasty in the older catalogues.

吳 The Wu dynasty, of the 孫 Sun family, the southern of the Three Kingdoms, with its capital at 建業 Kien-yeh, the modern 南京 Nanking. A. D. 222–280.

18 支謙 K' Khien, who had the literary appellation 恭明 Kuṅ-miṅ, and also another cognomen 越 Yueh. He was an Upâsaka of the country of Yueh-*k*', who came to China towards the end of the Eastern Hân dynasty, which came to an end in A. D. 220. Afterwards he took refuge in the Kingdom of Wu, where he was appointed as a professor by 孫權 Sun *Kh*üen, the first sovereign of the Wu dynasty, and assisted or taught his heir-apparent. He translated numerous works in A. D. 223–253. See Saṅ-*k*whân, fasc. 1, fol. 9 b (where it ascribes to him 49 Sûtras); Nêi-tien-lu, fasc. 2, fol. 6 b; Thu-*k*i, fasc. 1, fol. 18 b (both mention 129 works in 152 fasciculi); Khâi-yuen-lu, fasc. 2 a, fol. 2 b (where 88 works in 118 fasciculi are mentioned, and 51 works in 69 fasciculi are said to have been in existence in A. D. 730); Miṅ-i-tai, fasc. 3, fol. 5 a; Beal, B. L. C., p. 11. According to the Thu-*k*i (fasc. 1, fol. 20 a) and Khâi-yuen-lu (fasc. 2 a, fol. 7 a), there was a second translation of the Sûtra of 42 sections, made by him; but it had been lost in A. D. 730. There is a note under the title of this Sûtra in the Khâi-yuen-lu, namely:—'It is stated in a "Separate Record"—probably an old catalogue—that this translation differs a little from that made by (Kâsyapa) Mâtaṅga, being the second version (of the same text), as the meaning of the words is correct, and the composition is readable.' Now the following 49 works are in existence in this Collection, which number curiously corresponds to that which is given in the Saṅ-*k*whân as above alluded to:—

No. 8 Dasasâhasrikâ pra*g*ñâpâramitâ (S. M.).
" 26 Amitâyusha (or -âbha)-vyûha, or Sukhâvatî-vyûha (long).
" 100 'Sûtra on the original action of the Bodhisattva.'
" 147 Vimalakîrtti-nirdesa.
" 218 'Navavarnamri*g*a-sûtra.'
" 224 'Vriddhastrî-sûtra.'
" 233 Vatsa-sûtra.
" 256 Tathâgata*g*ñânamudrâsamâdhi.
" 278 Pratîtyasamutpâda-sûtra (?).
" 281 *S*âlisambhava-sûtra.
" 297 'Nâgadattâ-dârakâ-sûtra.'
" 299 Ashtabuddhaka.
" 337 Pushpakûta.
" 355 Anantamukha-sâdhaka-dhâranî (?).
" 364 'Padadhararddhimantra-sûtra.'
" 377 'Bodhisattva-bodhivriksha-sûtra.'
" 378 Kshâmâkâra-bodhisattva-sûtra.
" 379 'Sûtra on the history of Poh or Pushya (?).'
" 466 'Trivargasahya-sûtra.'
" 513 '*K*andraprabha-bodhisattva-sûtra.'
" 554 Brahma*g*âla-sûtra (S. H.).
" 557 'Sapta*g*ñâna-sûtra.'
" 574 'Sûtra on Maudgalyâyana's temptation by the wicked Mâra.'
" 577 'Sûtra on the Upavasatha.'

No. 580 'Sûtra on the cause addressed by Buddha to Sâkya Mahânâman.'
„ 590 'Sarvadharmamûla-sûtra.'
„ 592 'Sûtra on the Brahmakârin Ŏ-fu.'
„ 594 'Sûtra on the Grihapati Râshtravara (?).'
„ 608 'Sûtra on the Brahma comparison.'
„ 615 'Sumati-bâlikâ-sûtra.'
„ 638 'Sûtra on the son of five mothers.'
„ 645 Mâtaṅgî-sûtra.
„ 655 'Sûtra on one who is in want of guarding his thoughts.'
„ 665 'Kumârakusalaphalanidâna-sûtra,' i. e. a life of Buddha.
„ 670 'Bimbisâra-râga-pañkapranidhâna-sûtra.'
„ 674 'Sûtra on the sufficiency of truth.'
„ 693 'Sumati-sreshthi-sûtra.'
„ 696 'Sûtra (addressed to ?) Ânanda on four matters.'
„ 698 'Agâtasatru-sûtra.'
„ 699 'Katushpranidhâna-sûtra.'
„ 700 'Sûtra on a fierce dog.'
„ 703 'Kâla-brahmakâri-sûtra.'
„ 707 'Nâgarâga-bhrâtri-sûtra.'
„ 708 'Sreshthi-mañgughosha-sûtra.'
„ 709 'Saptastri-sûtra.'
„ 710 'Ashtaguru-sûtra.'
„ 761 'Sûtra addressed to a Brahmakârin called Sun-to-ye-k' (?).'
„ 1099 'Dharmavinaya-samâdhi-sûtra (V. M.).'
„ 1113 'Sûtra on Sîla or moral precepts which dispel misfortune (V. H.).'

19 維祇難 Wêi-khi-nân, i. e. Vighna, whose name is translated 障礙 Kân-ñâi, lit. 'partition-hindrance.' He was an Indian Sramana, who was originally a fire-worshipper, and afterwards converted to Buddhism. He, together with Ku Lüh-yen, No. 20 below, brought to China a Sanskrit text of the 曇鉢經 Thân-po-kiṅ, i. e. the Dharmapada-sûtra, or the Dhammapada-sutta, in A. D. 224, and translated it. See No. 1365, and Saṅ-kwhân, fasc. 1, fol. 14 a. Vighna also translated another Sûtra in 4 fasciculi, but it was lost in A. D. 730. See Nêi-tien-lu, fasc. 2, fol. 6 a; Thu-ki, fasc. 1, fol. 22 b; Khâi-yuen-lu, fasc. 2 a, fol. 1 b; Miṅ-i-tsi, fasc. 3, fol. 5 b; Beal, B. L. C., p. 12.

No. 1365 Dharmapada or Dhammapada (I. M.).

20 竺律炎 Ku Lüh-yen, an Indian Sramana, who, together with Vighna, No. 19 above, came to the Kingdom of Wu in A. D. 224. In A. D. 230 he alone translated some works. See Nêi-tien-lu, fasc. 2, fol. 6 b; Thu-ki, fasc. 1, fol. 22 b (both ascribe to him 3 works in 3 or 4 fasciculi); Khâi-yuen-lu, fasc. 2 a, fol. 2 a (where 4 works in 6 fasciculi are mentioned, and one of them is said to have been lost long before A. D. 730); Beal, B. L. C., p. 12.

No. 616 'Sumati (?)-sûtra (S. H.).'
„ 645 'Mâtaṅgî-sûtra.'
„ 1327 'Buddhavaidya-sûtra (I. M.).'

21 康僧會 Khân Saṅ-hwui, an Indian Sramana, who was the eldest son of the prime minister of the country of 康居 Khâṅ-kü, i. e. Kambu, or Ulterior Tibet or Kamboga, whose family was continuously resident in India. He came to the capital of the Kingdom of Wu in A. D. 241. In A. D. 247 he had the 建初寺 Kien-ku-sh', or the Kien-ku monastery built, by order of Sun Khüen, the first sovereign of the Wu dynasty, who gave the name 佛陀里 Fo-tho-li, or the Buddha village, to the place where this monastery was. In A. D. 251 he began his work of translation, and died in A. D. 280. See Saṅ-kwhân, fasc. 1, fol. 9 b; Sui-shu, fasc. 35, fol. 21 b; Nêi-tien-lu, fasc. 2, fol. 13 a; Thu-ki, fasc. 1, fol. 23 a (both ascribe to him 14 works in 29 fasciculi); Khâi-yuen-lu, fasc. 2 a, fol. 10 a (where only 7 works in 20 fasciculi are mentioned, and 5 works in 10 fasciculi are said to have been lost long before A. D. 730); Miṅ-i-tsi, fasc. 3, fol. 5 b; Selected Essays, vol. ii, p. 322; Beal, B. L. C., p. 12.

No. 143 'Shatpâramitâ-saṅgraha-sûtra (S. M.).'
„ 1359 'An old Samyuktâvadâna-sûtra (I. M.).'

22 支彊梁接 (or 樓) K' Khiâṅ-liâṅ-tsiê (or leu),—the last three characters are evidently used for a transliteration of a Sanskrit name, such as Kâlasivi (?), whose name is however translated 正無畏 Kaṅ-wu-wêi, lit. 'correct-without-fear.' He was a Sramana of the western region, who translated one work entitled 'Saddharmasamâdhi-sûtra,' in 6 fasciculi, in A. D. 255 or 256; but it was lost in A. D. 730. See Nêi-tien-lu, fasc. 2, fol. 4 a (where this translator is mentioned under the Wêi dynasty); Thu-ki, fasc. 1, fol. 24 a; Khâi-yuen-lu, fasc. 2 a, fol. 16 a; Beal, B. L. C., p. 12.

Works of Unknown Translators.

The Thu-ki (fasc. 1, fol. 24 b seq.) mentions 110 works[1] in 291 fasciculi, which are said to have been translated under the Wu dynasty, A. D. 222–280. See Beal, B. L. C., p. 12. The Khâi-yuen-lu (fasc. 2 a, fol. 1 b, and fol. 16 b seq.) gives 87 works in 261 fasciculi, which are said to have been produced under the Wêi and Wu dynasties, A. D. 220–280, but 4 works in 6 fasciculi only were in existence in A. D. 730. There is, however, only one translation of the kind in the Collection, namely:—

No. 547 Samyuktâgama (S. H.).

[1] Among these works, there was the oldest translation of the Lalita-vistara, in 8 fasciculi. This translation is said to have been made under the Latter Hân dynasty, one of the Three Kingdoms. A. D. 221–263. Cf. col. 51, under No. 159.

SUMMARY OF THE PRECEDING LIST OF TRANSLATIONS MADE UNDER THE WU DYNASTY, A.D. 222–280.

Translators.	Nêi-tien-lu.	Thu-ki.	Khâi-yuen-lu.	In existence.
No. 18	129	129	88	49
" 19	2	2	2	1
" 20	3	3	4	3
" 21	14	14	7	2
" 22	1	1	1	0
	110	110	87	1
	259	259	189*	56

* In 417 fasciculi. In A.D. 730 there were 61 works in 92 fasciculi in existence, and 128 works in 325 fasciculi had long been lost. See the Khâi-yuen-lu, fasc. 2 a, fol. 1 a.

西晋 Si-tsin, or the Western Tsin dynasty, of the 司馬 Sz'-mâ family, with its capital at Lo-yân. A.D. 265–316.

23 竺曇摩羅察 (or 剎) *K*u Thân-mo-lo-*k*â (or *k*hâ), i.e. Dharmaraksha, whose name is translated 法護 Fâ-hu, lit. 'law-protection.' He was a *S*ramana, whose family was continuously resident in the 燉煌 Thun-kwân district (the western extreme of the Great Wall in Kan-shuh in Nan-si-*k*eu, China. See Wells Williams' Chin. Dict. p. 930, col. 1). He was a descendant of a man of the country of Yueh-*k*', so that his original surname was 支 *K*', the second character of 月支 Yueh-*k*'. But he adopted 竺 *K*u, the second character of 天竺 Thien-*k*u, or India, having become a disciple of the foreign *S*ramana 竺高座 *K*u Kâo-tso. Hence he is always called 竺法護 *K*u Fâ-hu, in the Collection. He went to the western regions with his teacher, and was well acquainted with thirty-six different languages or dialects. In A.D. 266 he came to Lo-yân, where he worked at translations till A.D. 313 or 317; and afterwards died in his seventy-eighth year. He was the man who first translated several Sûtras of the Vaipulya class (方等 Fân-tân, lit. 'square-even or equal'). See San-*k*whân, fasc. 1, fol. 14 b (where it ascribes to him 165 works); Sui-shu, fasc. 35, fol. 21 b; Nêi-tien-lu, fasc. 2, fol. 22 a; Thu-*k*i, fasc. 2, fol. 1 a (both mention 210 works in 394 fasciculi); Khâi-yuen-lu, fasc. 2 a, fol. 22 a–fasc. 2 b, fol. 6 a (where 175 works in 354 fasciculi are mentioned, and 91 works in 208 fasciculi are said to have been in existence in A.D. 730); Min-i-tsi, fasc. 3 fol. 5 b; Selected Essays, vol. ii, p. 323; Beal, B.L.C., p. 13. The following 90 works are now in existence in the Collection:—

No. 4 Pa*ñk*avimsati-sâhasrikâ pra*gñ*âpâramitâ (S. M.).
" 23 (3) Tathâgatâ*k*intya-guhya-nirdesa.
" 23 (4) (Vini)sodhana-nirdesa, or Svapna-nirdesa.
" 23 (47) Ratnakûda-paripri*kkh*â.
" 30 Samantamukha-parivarta.
" 31 Ma*ñg*usri-buddhakshetragunavyûha.
" 32 Garbha-sûtra (?).
" 34 Ugra-paripri*kkh*â.
" 35 Bhadra-mâyâkâra-paripri*kkh*â, or -vyâkarana.
" 39 Sumati-dârikâ-paripri*kkh*â.
" 41 Vimaladattâ-paripri*kkh*â.
" 42 Asokadattâ-vyâkarana.
" 47 Sushthitamati-paripri*kkh*â, or Mâyopama-samâdhi.
" 49 Subâhu-paripri*kkh*â.
" 52 *Gñ*ânottara-bodhisattva-paripri*kkh*â.
" 55 Maitreya-paripri*kkh*â.
" 74 Aksharamati-nirdesa-sûtra.
" 79 Tathâgata-mahâkârunika-nirdesa.
" 80 'Ratnastri-paripri*kkh*â (?).'
" 81 'Mûka-kumâra-sûtra.'
" 92 'Sûtra on the appearance of the Tathâgata.'
" 104 'Sûtra of the chapter on going across the world.'
" 108 'Bodhisattvadasasthânakaryâdhyâya.'
" 110 Dasabhûmika-sûtra.
" 111 'Sama*k*akshus-paripri*kkh*â.'
" 116 *K*aturdâraka-samâdhi-sûtra.
" 125 'Sûtra on the rules for two annual festivals to be held after Buddha's entering Parinirvâna.'
128 Sarvapunyasamu*kk*aya-samâdhi-sûtra.
138 Saddharmapundarika-sûtra.
145 Vimalakîrtti-nirdesa.
" 150 Avaivartya (?) or Aparivartya-sûtra.
" 153 'Sûtra of Buddha's ascension to the Trayastrimsa heaven to preach the law for his mother's sake.'
" 160 Lalitavistara.
" 165 'Vasudhara-bodhisattva-paripri*kkh*â-sûtra.'
" 168 Ratnâkârandakavyûha-sûtra.
" 182 A*g*âtasatru-kaukritya-vinodana.
" 184 Ma*ñg*usri-vikridita-sûtra.
" 194 Hastikakshyâ.
" 197 Viseshakinta-brahma-paripri*kkh*â.
" 208 'Sûtra about the meditation on the Bodhisattva Maitreya's coming down to be born (in this world).'
" 214 Strîvivarta-vyâkarana-sûtra.
" 219 'Kumâra-mûka-sûtra.'
" 230 *K*andraprabha-kumâra-sûtra.
" 234 Vatsa-sûtra.
" 235 Strîvivartavyâkarana-sûtra.
" 242 'Determined-dhâranî.'
" 252 'Sarvavaipulyavidyâsiddha-sûtra.'
" 257 'Anantaratnasamâdhi-sûtra.'
" 283 'Sûtra on the Samâdhi called vow realised by the Tathâgata alone.'
" 298 'Nâgadattâ-bodhisattva-nidâna-sûtra.'
" 300 Ashtabuddhaka.
" 303 'Ullambanapâtra-sûtra.'
" 342 *S*rîmati-brâhmanî-paripri*kkh*â.
" 385 Ratna*g*âli-paripri*kkh*â.
" 388 'Sûtra on the characteristic marks on Buddha's person as the results of fifty causes of the practice of Bodhisattva.'
" 392 '*K*aturdurlabha-sûtra.'
" 393 'Su*k*inti (?)-devaputra-sûtra.'

No. 401 Buddhasaṅgîti-sûtra.
„ 403 Bhadrakalpika-sûtra.
„ 437 Anavatapta-nâgarâga-pariprikkhâ-sûtra.
„ 456 Sâgara-nâgarâga-pariprikkhâ.
„ 467 'Katurvarga (sishya)-sûtra.'
„ 468 'Anâgatavikriyâ-sûtra.'
„ 469 'Atîta-buddha-paindapâtika-sûtra.'
„ 514 'Kittaprabhâ (?)-sûtra.'
„ 515 'Dasadigandhakâra-vidhvamsana-sûtra.'
„ 516 'Mrigamâtri-sûtra.'
„ 517 'Sûtra on the opposition of the Mâra.'
„ 562 'Sûtra on the world and time of the past (S. H.).'
„ 564 'Sûtra on freedom from sleep (S. H.).'
„ 566 'Sûtra on the idea of happiness.'
„ 570 'Sûtra on receiving the year (?).'
„ 571 'Sûtra on a Brahmakârin who believes in the pureness of water.'
„ 609 'Sûtra on Pûgyottara (? a Deva).'
„ 612 'Sûtra on Manas.'
„ 613 'Sûtra on the proper law (?).'
„ 621 'Aṅgulimâlya-sûtra.'
„ 622 „ „
„ 623 'Sûtra on some wrestlers' intention on moving a mountain.'
„ 624 'Katuradbhutadharma-sûtra.'
„ 646 'Sârdûlakarna-sûtra or Mâtaṅgî-sûtra.
„ 652 'Âryadharmamudrâ-sûtra.'
„ 669 Gâtaka-nidâna (a collection of 55 short Sûtras).
„ 671 'Vaidûlyarâga-sûtra.'
„ 697 'Nirdesa (?)-sûtra.'
„ 712 'Sûtra on desire being the cause of affliction.'
„ 726 'Sûtra on the meditation on the body.'
„ 729 'Sûtra on 500 disciples (Srâvakas) telling their own Nidâna or history.'
„ 745 'Mahâkâsyapa-nidâna-sûtra.'
„ 746 'Sûtra on four kinds of self-injury.'
„ 1325 'Karyâmargabhûmi-sûtra (I. M.).'
„ 1362 'Dharma-dhyâna-sûtra.'

24 彊梁婁至 Khiâṅ-liâṅ-leu-k', i. e. Kâlaruki, whose name is translated 眞喜 Kan-hhi, lit. 'true-joy.' He was a Sramana of the western region, who in A. D. 281 translated one Sûtra in Kâṅkeu (Canton), China. His translation was lost already in A. D. 730. See Nêi-tien-lu, fasc. 2, fol. 31 a (where an earlier date of A. D. 266 is given instead of 281, and both the transliteration and translation of the name differ from those above mentioned); Thu-ki, fasc. 2, fol. 7 a; Khâi-yuen-lu, fasc. 2 b, fol. 7 b; Beal, B. L. C., p. 13.

25 安法欽 Ân Fâ-khin, a Sramana of the country of Ân-si, who translated 5 works in 12 or 16 fasciculi, at Lo-yâṅ, in A. D. 281–306. Three translations were lost in A. D. 730. See Nêi-tien-lu, fasc. 2, fol. 31 b; Thu-ki, fasc. 2, fol. 7 b; Khâi-yuen-lu, fasc. 2 b, fol. 7 b; Beal, B. L. C., p. 13.

No. 148 'Sûtra on unlimited changes of the supernatural footsteps (S. M.).'
„ 1459 Asokâvadâna (I. M.).

26 無羅叉 Wu-lo-khâ, or 無叉羅 Wu-khâ-lo, i. e. Mokshala (see Eitel, p. 77 a). He was a Sramana of 于闐 Yü-then, i. e. Kusutana (Khoten, Eitel, p. 60 b), who together with Ku Shu-lân, No. 27 below, translated one Sûtra in A. D. 291. See Nêi-tien-lu, fasc. 2, fol. 31 b; Thu-ki, fasc. 2, fol. 7 b; Khâi-yuen-lu, fasc. 2 b, fol. 8 a; Beal, B. L. C., p. 13, where a note is added which seems not quite correct.

No. 2 Pañkavimsati-sâhasrikâ pragñâpâramitâ (S. M.).

27 竺叔蘭 Ku Shu-lân, an Upâsaka of Indian descent, who was born in China, and translated 2 works in 5 fasciculi, under the reign of Hwui-ti, A. D. 290–306. His translations were lost in A. D. 730. See Nêi-tien-lu, fasc. 2, fol. 33 a; Thu-ki, fasc. 2, fol. 8 a (both say wrongly that Shu-lân was a Sramana of the western region); Khâi-yuen-lu, fasc. 2 b, fol. 9 b; Beal, B. L. C., p. 13.

28 白法祖 Po Fâ-tsu,—the last two characters are said to be a literary appellation (字) by which he is generally designated; his cognomen is 遠 Yuen, and his original surname was 萬 Wân. He was a Chinese Sramana of 河内 Ho-nêi. He translated several works under the reign of Hwui-ti, A. D. 290–306. See San-kwhân, fasc. 1, fol. 16 b; Nêi-tien-lu, fasc. 2, fol. 35 b; Thu-ki, fasc. 2, fol. 8 b (both ascribe to him 23 works in 25 fasciculi); Khâi-yuen-lu, fasc. 2 b, fol. 11 b (where 16 works in 18 fasciculi are mentioned, and 11 works in 12 fasciculi are said to have long been lost in A. D. 730).

No. 228 'Sûtra on the Bodhisattva Shi or Geta (? S. M.).'
„ 389 'Sûtra on the practice of Bodhisattva.'
„ 552 Mahâparinirvâna-sûtra (S. H.).
„ 650 'Mahâpragâpatî-parinirvâna-sûtra.'
„ 752 'Sûtra on five kinds of happiness and virtue of wise men.'

29 釋法立 Shih Fâ-li, a Sramana, whose native place is unknown. He, together with Fâ-kü, No. 30 below, translated 4 works in 12 fasciculi, at Lo-yâṅ, under the reign of Hwui-ti, A. D. 290–306. One of their translations was lost already in A. D. 730. See Nêi-tien-lu, fasc. 2, fol. 36 b; Thu-ki, fasc. 2, fol. 12 a; Khâi-yuen-lu, fasc. 2 b, fol. 13 b; Beal, B. L. C., p. 14.

No. 383 'Sarvagunapunyakshetra-sûtra (S. M.).'
„ 551 'Lokadhâtu (?)-sûtra (S. H.).'
„ 1353 Dharmapada, or Dhammapada (I. M.).

30 釋法炬 Shih Fâ-kü, a Sramana, whose native place is unknown. After the death of Fâ-li, No. 29 above, Fâ-kü alone translated several works

under the same reign as before. See Nêi-tien-lu, fasc. 2, fol. 37 b; Thu-*k*i, fasc. 2, fol. 12 a (both ascribe to him 132 works in 142 fasciculi); Khâi-yuen-lu, fasc. 2 b, fol. 14 a (where 40 works in 50 fasciculi are mentioned and 16 works in 26 fasciculi are said to have long been lost in A.D. 730); Beal, B. L. C., p. 14. The following 23 works are now in existence in the Collection:—

No. 38 Udayâna-vatsarâ*g*a-paripr*kkh*â (S. M.).
„ 270 'Sûtra on three changes of Buddha's former births.'
„ 272 'A*g*âtasatru-râ*g*a-vyâkarana-sûtra.'
„ 291 'Sûtra on sprinkling water on the images of Buddha.'
„ 569 'Sûtra on desire (S. H.).'
„ 572 'Sûtra on overcoming lust.'
„ 579 'Sûtra on the cause of Du*h*khaskandha.'
„ 596 'Sûtra on Shu ("number," a Brâhma*n*a).'
„ 599 'Gangânadi-sûtra.'
„ 600 '*K*ampa-bhikshu-sûtra.'
„ 603 'Murdhaga-râ*g*a-nidâna-sûtra.'
„ 614 'Sûtra on King Prasena*g*it, who put dust on his body at the death of his mother, the queen.'
„ 619 'Sûtra on King Bimbisâra's coming to worship Buddha.'
„ 636 'Sûtra on disregarding the law.'
„ 660 Nandi-pravra*g*yâ-sûtra (?).
„ 663 'Sûtra relating to what ought to be practised by the Bhikshus, and what ought not, in their relationship as associates.'
„ 673 'Dharmasagara-sûtra.'
„ 713 'A*g*âtasatru-paripr*kkh*â-pa*ñk*ânantarya-karma-sûtra.'
„ 725 'Sûtra on a Bhikshu who intended to commit suicide for the purpose of avoiding ill-fame concerning a woman.'
„ 747 'Râhula-kshânti-sûtra.'
„ 748 'Sûtra on the right matters spoken by Buddha for the sake of young Bhikshus.'
„ 749 'Shâ-hö (nâma)-bhikshu-guna-sûtra.'
„ 764 'Sûtra on the cow-herd comparison.'

31 聶承遠 Nieh *Kh*an-yuen, a Chinese Upâsaka, who assisted *K*u Fâ-hu, No. 23 above, while the latter was working at translations. In the meantime, he alone translated certain works under the reign of Hwui-ti, A.D. 290–306. See Nêi-tien-lu, fasc. 2, fol. 33 a (where 3 works in 4 fasciculi are ascribed to him); Khâi-yuen-lu, fasc. 2 b, fol. 19 b (where 2 works in 3 fasciculi are mentioned).

No. 397 'Sûrya-gihmîkarana-prabhâ-samâdhi-sûtra (S. M.).'
„ 711 'Vana (? nâma-sreshthi)-sûtra (S. H.).'

32 聶道眞 Nieh Tâo-*k*an, a Chinese Upâsaka, who was the son of the last, and also an assistant of *K*u Fâ-hu, No. 23 above, from A.D. 280 to 312. After the death of Fâ-hu (which happened in A.D. 313, or a little later), Tâo-*k*an alone translated several works. See Nêi-tien-lu, fasc. 2, fol. 35 b; Thu-*k*i, fasc. 2, fol. 9 b (both ascribe to him 54 works in 66 fasciculi); Khâi-yuen-lu, fasc. 2 b, fol. 20 a (where 24 works in 36 fasciculi are mentioned, and 6 works in 6 fasciculi are said to have been in existence in A.D. 730); Beal, B. L. C., p. 14. There are the following 4 works only now in existence in the Collection:—

No. 23 (33) Vimaladattâ-paripr*kkh*â (S. M.).
„ 107 'Sûtra on the original actions of the Bodhisattvas who are seeking the state of Buddha.'
„ 508 'Ma*ñg*usrî-parinirvâna-sûtra.'
„ 509 Abhinishkramana-sûtra (?).

33 支法度 *K*' Fâ-tu, a *S*ramana, whose native place is not known. In A.D. 301 he translated 4 works in 5 fasciculi, of which 2 works in 3 fasciculi were lost already in A.D. 730. See Nêi-tien-lu, fasc. 2, fol. 41 b; Thu-*k*i, fasc. 2, fol. 9 b; Khâi-yuen-lu, fasc. 2 b, fol. 23 a; Beal, B. L. C., p. 14.

No. 229 'Sûtra on the boy Shi or *G*eta (? S. M.).'
„ 595 Srigâla-vâda (S. H.).

34 若羅嚴 *Z*o-lo-yen, a foreign *S*ramana, who translated one Sûtra; but when he came to China is not known. See the Khâi-yuen-lu, fasc. 26, fol. 23 b.

No. 750 'Sûtra on time and not-time (? S. H.).'

Works of Unknown Translators.

The Thu-*k*i (fasc. 2, fol. 16 b) mentions 8 works in 15 fasciculi, and the Khâi-yuen-lu (fasc. 2 b, fol. 24 a seq.) enumerates 58 works in 59 fasciculi, of which 19 works in 19 fasciculi only were in existence in A.D. 730. There are now the following 20 works:—

No. 50 Subâhu-paripr*kkh*â (S. M.).
„ 124 'Sûtra on the funeral ceremony of Buddha.'
„ 136 Saddharmapu*nd*arîka (incomplete).
„ 216 'Sûtra on the Bodhisattva who was the son who took a look at his blind father.'
„ 454 'Dharmanityasthâna-sûtra.'
„ 455 'Dîrghâyû-râ*g*a-sûtra.'
„ 558 'Sûtra on the salt-water comparison (S. H.).'
„ 562 'Sûtra on the world and time of the past.'
„ 571 'Sûtra on a Brahma*k*ârin who believes in the pureness of water.'
„ 611 'Sûtra on a man named Teu-thiâo.'
„ 631 'Sûtra on the King of *S*râvasti's dreaming ten different things.'
„ 641 'Sûtra on a woman called Yü-ye.'
„ 702 'Sûtra on the filial child.'
„ 758 'Samantaprâpta (nâma)-râ*g*a-sûtra.'
„ 759 'Hâritî (lit. the mother of demon-children)-sûtra.'
„ 760 'Sûtra on a king of a country, Brâhmana by name (?).'
„ 778 'Nö-to-hö-to-*k*hi (?)-sûtra.'
„ 1333 'Sûtra on Buddha's causing Kâtyâyana to speak the Gâthâs on the destruction of the law (I. M.).'
„ 1334 'Sûtra on Buddha's keeping the body in regular order.'
„ 1335 'Sûtra on keeping the mind or thoughts in regular order.'

SUMMARY OF THE PRECEDING LIST OF TRANSLATIONS MADE UNDER THE WESTERN TSIN DYNASTY, A.D. 265–316.

Translators.	Nêi-tien-lu.	Thu-*k*i.	Khâi-yuen-lu.	In existence.
No. 23	210	210	175	90
„ 24	1	1	1	0
„ 25	5	5	5	2
„ 26	1	1	1	1
„ 27	2	2	2	0
„ 28	23	23	16	5
„ 29	4	4	4	3
„ 30	132	132	40	23
„ 31	3	0	2	2
„ 32	54	54	24	4
„ 33	4	4	4	2
„ 34	0	0	1	1
	8	8	58	20
	447	444	333*	153

* In 590 fasciculi. In A.D. 730 there existed 156 works in 321 fasciculi, and 177 works in 269 fasciculi had been lost. See the Khâi-yuen-lu, fasc. 2 a, fol. 21 b.

前涼 Tshien-liâṅ, or the Former Liâṅ dynasty, of the 張 *K*hâṅ family, with its capital at 姑臧 Ku-tsâṅ. A.D. 302–376.

35 支施崙 *K*' Sh'-lun, an Upâsaka of the country of Yueh-*k*', who translated 4 works in 6 fasciculi in A.D. 373, of which 3 works in 5 fasciculi were lost already in A.D. 730. See Khâi-yuen-lu, fasc. 4 b, fol. 7 a.

No. 44. Surata-paripri*kkh*â (S. M.).

東晉 Tuṅ-tsiṅ, or the Eastern Tsin dynasty, of the 司馬 Sz'-mâ family, with its capital at 建康 *K*ien-khâṅ, or 建業 *K*ien-yeh, the modern 南京 Nanking. A.D. 317–420.

36 帛尸梨蜜多羅 Poh Sh'-li-mi-to-lo, i.e. *S*rîmitra, whose name is translated 吉友 *K*i-yiu, lit. 'lucky friend.' He was a *S*ramana of the western region, who was the heir-apparent of a king of the country, but gave up his realm to his younger brother, and became a *S*ramana. He came to China in the Yuṅ-*k*iâ period, A.D. 307–312, under the Western Tsin dynasty, and translated 3 works at *K*ien-khâṅ (Nanking) under the reign of Yuen-ti, A.D. 317–322, and died at the age of about eighty, in the Hhien-khâṅ period, A.D. 335–342. See Saṅ-*k*whân, fasc. 1, fol. 18 b; Nêi-tien-lu, fasc. 3, fol. 4 a; Thu-*k*i, fasc. 2, fol. 17 a; Miṅ-i-tsi, fasc. 3, fol. 6 a; Beal, B. L. C., p. 15.

No. 167 'Mahâbhishekarddhidhâranî-sûtra (S. M.).'
„ 309 Mahâmayûrî-vidyârâ*g*ñî.
„ 310 „ „

37 支道根 (or 林) *K*' Tâo-kan (or lin), a (Chinese?) *S*ramana, who translated 2 works in 7 fasciculi, in A.D. 335, but both were lost already in A.D. 730. One of them was the Saddharmapu*nd*arîka, in 5 fasciculi. See Nêi-tien-lu, fasc. 3, fol. 4 b; Thu-*k*i, fasc. 2, fol. 17 b; Khâi-yuen-lu, fasc. 3, fol. 3 b; Beal, B. L. C., p. 15.

38 竺曇無蘭 *K*u Thân-wu-lân, i.e. Dharmaraksha (? cf. *K*u Fâ-lân, No. 2 above), whose name is translated 法正 Fâ-*k*an, lit. 'law-correct.' He was a *S*ramana of the western region, who translated several works in A.D. 381–395. See Nêi-tien-lu, fasc. 3, fol. 5 b (where 110 works in 112 fasciculi are ascribed to him); Thu-*k*i, fasc. 2, fol. 17 b (111 works in 112 fasciculi); Khâi-yuen-lu, fasc. 3, fol. 4 a (where 61 works in 63 fasciculi are mentioned, of which 24 works in 24 fasciculi were in existence in A.D. 730); Beal, B. L. C., p. 16. There are 29 works in the present Collection, namely:—

No. 273 'Sûtra of prophecy received from Buddha by one who offered a flower to Buddha, and did not follow King (Agâtasatru, S. M.).'
„ 365 'Dhâranî-pâtra (?)-sûtra.'
„ 479 'Mâyâkâra-bhadra-*r*iddhi-mantra-sûtra.'
„ 481 'Sûtra on relieving epidemic by a spell.'
„ 482 'Sûtra on relieving toothache by a spell.'
„ 483 'Sûtra on relieving eye-disease by a spell.'
„ 484 'Sûtra on relieving a sick child by a spell.'
„ 486 'Manirata (?)-sûtra.'
„ 487 'Danda-lo-mo-yiu-shu (?)-sûtra.'
„ 561 'Sûtra on the iron-castle Naraka (S. H.).'
„ 568 'Anupâta (?)-sûtra.'
„ 575 'Naraka-sûtra.'
„ 588 '*S*îlagandhagandha-sûtra.'
„ 593 '*S*râmanyaphala-sûtra.'
„ 597 'Sûtra on the Brahma*k*ârin Ṅö-po-lo-yen's question on the superiority of the caste (of Brâhmanas).'
„ 630 '*K*aturnaraka-sûtra.'
„ 632 'Sûtra on ten dreams of King Prasena*g*it.'
„ 640 'Sûtra on a woman named Yü-ye.'
„ 654 'Sûtra on the floating bubbles on water.'
„ 715 'Sûtra on the middle heart.'
„ 716 'Sûtra addressed to a Bhikshu named *K*ien-*k*aṅ (lit. "one who sees the right," i.e. Saddarsana?).'

No. 717 'Sûtra on the matter (or comparison) of a great fish.'
„ 718 'Sûtra addressed to Ânanda on seven dreams.'
„ 719 'Sûtra on an Anâgâmin named Hŏ-tiâo (?).'
„ 730 'Sûtra beginning with the section on the pain of five (states of existence).'
„ 736 'Sûtra on a Bhikshu named Thiñ-ki' (lit. "hearing-giving").'
„ 751 'Sûtra on self-loving.'
„ 763 'Sûtra on the new year.'
„ 1330 'Sûtra on Kâsyapa's going to the place where Buddha had just entered Parinirvâna (I. M.).'

39 瞿曇僧伽提婆 *Khü*-thân Sañ-*kiê*-ti-pho, i. e. Gautama Saṅghadeva, the second and proper name being translated 衆天 *Kuñ*-thien, lit. 'company-heaven or god.' He was a *S*ramana of the country of 罽賓 *Ki*-pin, i. e. Kubhâ (the Kophen of the Greeks, the modern Cabul,—Eitel, p. 58 a), who in A. D. 383 arrived at *Khâñ*-ân, then the capital of the Former Tsin dynasty of the Fu family, where he translated two works (see No. 56 below). In A. D. 391–398 he translated five other works, in two different places, belonging to the Eastern Tsin dynasty, namely, (1) the Lü mountain, and (2) *K*ien-khâñ, the capital. One of these five translations was lost in A. D. 730. See Sañ-*k*whân, fasc. 1, fol. 22 b; Sui-shu, fasc. 35, fol. 21 b; Nêi-tien-lu, fasc. 3, fol. 9 b; Thu-*ki*, fasc. 2, fol. 21 a; Miñ-i-tsi, fasc. 3, fol. 6 a; Selected Essays, vol. ii, p. 327; Beal, B. L. C., p. 16. There are 3 works in existence in the Collection, namely:—

No. 542 Madhyamâgama (S. H.).
„ 1271 'Tridharmaka (?)-sâstra (A. H.).'
„ 1288 Abhidharmahridaya-sâstra.

40 迦留陀伽 *Kiâ*-liu-tho-*kiê*, i. e. Kâlodaka, whose name is translated 時水 Sh'-shui, lit. 'time (kâla)-water (udaka).' He was a *S*ramana of the western region, who translated one work in A. D. 392. See Nêi-tien-lu, fasc. 2, fol. 9 b; Thu-*ki*, fasc. 2, fol. 22 a; Khâi-yuen-lu, fasc. 3, fol. 10 b; Beal, B. L. C., p. 16.

No. 1374 'Sûtra of twelve (years') going for pleasure (I. M.).'

41 康道和 Khâñ Tâo-hŏ, a *S*ramana (of Tibetan descent?), who translated one Sûtra, in 3 fasciculi, in A. D. 396, but it was lost already in A. D. 730. See Nêi-tien-lu, fasc. 2, fol. 9 a; Thu-*ki*, fasc. 2, fol. 22 b; Khâi-yuen-lu, fasc. 3, fol. 10 b; Beal, B. L. C., p. 16.

42 佛陀跋陀羅 Fo-tho-poh-tho-lo, i. e. Buddhabhadra, whose name is translated 覺賢 *Kiâo*-hhien, lit. 'intelligence-wise.' He was an Indian *S*ramana, and a descendant of Amritodana, an uncle of *S*âkyamuni. In A. D. 398–421 he translated 13 or 15 works (of which 8 works in 116 fasciculi only were in existence in A. D. 730), at two different places, namely, the Lü mountain, and *K*ien-khâñ, the capital. He met Kumâra*g*îva in China, and whenever the latter found any doubts, the former was always asked for an explanation. He made some translations with Fâ-hhien (Fa-hian). He died in A. D. 429 at the age of seventy-one. See Sañ-*k*whân, fasc. 2, fol. 16 b; Sui-shu, fasc. 35, fol. 22 b; Nêi-tien-lu, fasc. 3, fol. 11 a; Thu-*ki*, fasc. 2, fol. 22 b; Khâi-yuen-lu, fasc. 3, fol. 11 b; Miñ-i-tsi, fasc. 3, fol. 6 a; Selected Essays, vol. ii, p. 325; Beal, B. L. C., p. 16. There are 7 works in existence in the Collection, namely:—

No. 87 Buddhâvatamsaka-mahâvaipulya-sûtra (S. M.).
„ 356 Anantamukha-sâdhaka-dhârani (?).
„ 430 'Buddhadhyâna-samâdhisâgara-sûtra.'
„ 1119 Mahâsaṅgha (or °saṅghika)-vinaya (V. H.).
„ 1159 Prâtimoksha of the Mahâsaṅghikas.
„ 1336 'Mañgusrî-pranidhâna-sûtra,' or Samantabhadra-pranidhâna (I. M.).
„ 1341 'Dharmatrâta-dhyâna-sûtra.'

43 曇摩卑 Thân-mo-pi, i. e. Dharmapriya (?)—the last character is omitted in the Nêi-tien-lu and Khâi-yuen-lu—whose name is translated 法善 Fâ-shân, lit. 'law-goodness.' He was an (Indian?) *S*ramana, who was well versed in the Vinaya, and translated one work, called 'mixed questions on the matter of Vinaya,' in 2 fasciculi, in A. D. 400; but it was lost already in A. D. 730. See Nêi-tien-lu, fasc. 3, fol. 11 a; Thu-*ki*, fasc. 2, fol. 23 b; Khâi-yuen-lu, fasc. 3, fol. 16 a; Beal, B. L. C., p. 17.

44 卑摩羅叉 Pi-mo-lo-*khâ*, i. e. Vimalâksha, whose name is translated 無垢眼 Wu-keu-yen, lit. 'without-dirt-eye.' He was a *S*ramana of Kubhâ (Cabul), who was a great teacher of Vinaya in 龜玆 Kwei-tsz', i. e. Khara*k*ar or Ku*k*e (see Eitel, p. 56 a), where Kumâra*g*îva was one of his disciples. Afterwards, in A. D. 406, he arrived in China, and was respected by his former disciple Kumâra*g*îva, who was then flourishing there. After the latter's death, which happened between 409 and 415, Vimalâksha went southward in the I-hhi period, A. D. 405–418, and translated 2 works in 5 fasciculi; one of them was lost in A. D. 730. He died at the age of seventy-seven. See Sañ-*k*whân, fasc. 2, fol. 13 a; Nêi-tien-lu, fasc. 3, fol. 9 b; Thu-*ki*, fasc. 2, fol. 24 a; Khâi-yuen-lu, fasc. 3, fol. 16 b; Miñ-i-tsi, fasc. 3, fol. 6 a; Beal, B. L. C., p. 15.

No. 1144 'Sarvâstivâdavinayanidâna (V. H.).'

45 釋法顯 Shih Fâ-hhien (Fa-hian, or Fa-hien), a Chinese *S*ramana, whose original surname was 龔 Kuṅ, and who was a native of 武陽 Wu-yâṅ, at the 平陽 Piṅ-yâṅ district. He started from *Kh*âṅ-ân towards India in A. D. 399, and came back to China in A. D. 414. Then he, together with Buddhabhadra, No. 42 above, translated certain works, and he alone made some translations, and wrote his famous travels. He died at the age of eighty-six. See Saṅ-*k*whân, fasc. 3, fol. 1 b; Sui-shu, fasc. 35, fol. 22 b; Nêi-tien-lu, fasc. 3, fol. 12 a; Thu-*k*i, fasc. 2, fol. 24 b; Khâi-yuen-lu, fasc. 3, fol. 18 a; Miṅ-i-tsi, fasc. 3, fol. 6 b; Selected Essays, vol. ii, p. 325; Beal, B. L. C., p. 17. There are 4 works ascribed to him in the Collection, namely:—

No. 118 Mahâparinirvâṇa-sûtra (S. H.).
" 120 " " (S. M.).
" 676 'Samyuktapitaka-sûtra (S. H.).'
" 1150 Mahâsaṅgha-bhikshuṇî-vinaya (H. V.).

46 祇多蜜 *K*i-to-mi, or 祇蜜多 *K*i-mi-to, i. e. Gîtamitra, whose name is translated 謌友 Ko-yiu, lit. 'song-friend.' He was a *S*ramana of the western region, who translated 23 or 25 works under the Eastern Tsin dynasty, A. D. 317–420; but when he died is not known, and only 2 works were in existence in A. D. 730. See Nêi-tien-lu, fasc. 3, fol. 13 a; Thu-*k*i, fasc. 2, fol. 25 a; Khâi-yuen-lu, fasc. 3, fol. 22 a; Beal, B. L. C., p. 17.

No. 109 'Bodhisattva-dasasthâna-sûtra (S. M.).'
" 258 'Ratnatathâgata-samâdhi-sûtra.'

47 竺難提 *K*u Nân-ti, i. e. Nandi, whose name is translated 喜 Hhi, lit. 'joy.' He was a Grihapati (householder) of the western region, who in A. D. 419 and the following years translated 3 works, one of them was lost already in A. D. 730. See Nêi-tien-lu, fasc. 3, fol. 14 a; Thu-*k*i, fasc. 2, fol. 25 b; Khâi-yuen-lu, fasc. 3, fol. 24 a; Beal, B. L. C., p. 18.

No. 23 (38) *G*ñânottara-bodhisattva-paripri*kkh*â (S. M.).
" 326 'Dhâraṇî-mantra for asking the Bodhisattva Avalokitesvara to counteract the injury of a poison.'

48 竺法力 *K*u Fâ-li (Dharmabala?), a *S*ramana of the western region, who in A. D. 419 translated the 'Amitâyur-arhat-samyaksambuddha-sûtra,' i. e. the larger Sukhâvatî-vyûha, being the eighth of twelve different translations of the same or a similar text, in 1 fasciculus; but it was lost already in A. D. 730. See Nêi-tien-lu, fasc. 3, fol. 14 b; Thu-*k*i, fasc. 2, fol. 26 a; Khâi-yuen-lu, fasc. 3, fol. 24 b; Beal, B. L. C., p. 18. See also column 11, note, where for Tâ-li read Fâ-li.

49 釋嵩公 Shih Suṅ-kuṅ, or 高公 Kâo-kuṅ, a (Chinese?) *S*ramana, who towards the end of the Eastern Tsin dynasty (ended A. D. 420) translated 3 works in 3 fasciculi; but all of them were lost already in A. D. 730. See Nêi-tien-lu, fasc. 3, fol. 14 b; Thu-*k*i, fasc. 2, fol. 26 a; Khâi-yuen-lu, fasc. 3, fol. 24 b; Beal, B. L. C., p. 18.

50 釋退公 Shih Thui-kuṅ, a Chinese *S*ramana, who in about A. D. 420 translated one work in 1 fasciculus; but it was lost already in A. D. 730. See the four authorities above mentioned.

51 釋法勇 Shih Fâ-yuṅ, a (Chinese?) *S*ramana, who in about A. D. 420 translated one work in 1 fasciculus; but it was lost already in A. D. 730. See the four authorities above mentioned.

Works of Unknown Translators.

The Thu-*k*i (fasc. 2, fol. 26 b seq.) enumerates 52 works in 56 fasciculi, while the Khâi-yuen-lu (fasc. 3, fol. 25 b seq.) mentions 40 works in 48 fasciculi, of which 2 works in 3 fasciculi were lost already in A. D. 730. There are the following 35 works now in existence in the Collection; in some of them however the distinctive character 東 Tuṅ or Eastern before 晉 Tsin dynasty is omitted:—

No. 36 Vinayaviniskaya-upâli-paripri*kkh*â (S. M.).
" 58 Kâsyapa-parivarta.
" 119 Mahâparinirvâṇa-sûtra (S. H.).
" 206 Maitreya-vyâkaraṇa (S. M.).
" 280 *S*âlisambhava-sûtra.
" 290 Tathâgata-pratibimba-pratish*th*ânusamsâ.
" 304 'Sûtra on offering the vessel of eatables to Buddha and the Saṅgha, for recompensing the favour of the parents.'
" 338 Pushpakûta.
" 339 "
" 340 Shadakshara-vidyâmantra.
" 417 '(Ko)sala (?)-desa-sûtra.'
" 432 'Bodhisattva-pûrvakaryâ-sûtra.'
" 447 'Saptabuddhabhâshitarddhimantra.'
" 480 'Sûtra on the Vidyâ, or spell for avoiding and removing the injury caused by a thief.'
" 585 'Sûtra on the arrow comparison (S. H.).'
" 602 'Nidâna-sûtra (?).'
" 605 'Sûtra on the good qualities of Trisaraṇa, Pañkasîla, benevolent mind, and separation from (the world).'
" 618 'Sûtra on obtaining five happy rewards by giving food (to others).'
" 644 'Sûtra on six different things (or objects) in explaining (the impurity of) the body to a Mâtaṅgî,' or Mâtaṅgî-sûtra.
" 656 'Pûrṇamaitrâyaṇîputra-sûtra.'

No. 677 'Sûtra on the retribution of Pretas.'
" 691 'Sûtra on a Khakkhara (a Bhikshu's staff), as a ladder and path for obtaining Bodhi.'
" 754 'Sûtra on guarding pureness.'
" 755 'Sûtra on soap-berry seeds (for rosaries).'
" 756 'Sûtra on the highest place (or Anuttaravishaya).'
" 757 'Ruki(nâma)-sreshthi-nidâna-sûtra.'
" 775 'Pañka-râga-sûtra.'
" 781 'Nidâna-saṅghapâla-sûtra.'
" 1145 'Rules and ceremony concerning *S*râmaneradasasila or *S*ikshâpada (V. H.).'
" 1148 'Sûtra of Maudgalyâyana's questions on 500 light and heavy matters concerning Vinaya.'
" 1152 *S*âriputra-paripṛikkhâ-sûtra.
" 1165 '*S*râmanerikâ-samyuktasilavâkâ.'
" 1344 Asokâvadâna (I. M.).
" 1358 'Nâgasena-bhikshu-sûtra,' or Milindaprasna.
" 1465 'Record of the collection of the Tripitaka and miscellaneous works.'

Summary of the preceding List of Translations made under the Eastern Tsin dynasty, A. D. 317–420.

Translators.	Nêi-tien-lu.	Thu-*k*i.	Khâi-yuen-lu.	In existence.
No. 36	3	3	3	3
" 37	2	2	2	0
" 38	110	111	61	29
" 39	5	5	5	3
" 40	1	1	1	1
" 41	1	1	1	0
" 42	15	15	13	9
" 43	1	1	1	0
" 44	2	2	2	1
" 45	6	5	7	4
" 46	25	25	23	2
" 47	3	3	3	2
" 48	1	1	1	0
" 49	3	3	3	0
" 50	1	1	1	0
" 51	1	1	1	0
	53	52	40	38
	233	232	168 *	92

* In 468 fasciculi. In A. D. 730 there were 85 works in 336 fasciculi in existence, while 83 works in 132 fasciculi were lost already. See Khâi-yuen-lu, fasc. 3, fol. 1 a.

前秦 Tshien-tshien, or the Former Tshien dynasty, of the 苻 Fu family, with its capital at 長安 *Kh*âṅ-ân. A. D. 350–394.

52 曇摩持 (or 侍) Thân-mo-*kh*' (or sh'), i. e. Dharma + *kh*' (or sh'), whose name is translated 法慧 Fâ-hwui, lit. 'law-wisdom,' or 法海 Fâ-hâi, lit. 'law-sea.' He was a *S*ramana of the western region, who in A. D. 367 translated 2 or 3 works; all of them were lost already in A. D. 730. See Nâi-tien-lu, fasc. 3 b, fol. 2 b: Thu-*k*i, fasc. 3, fol. 1 a; Khâi-yuen-lu, fasc. 3, fol. 30 a; Beal, B. L. C., p. 18.

53 鳩摩羅佛提 *K*iu-mo-lo-fo-thi, i. e. Kumârabuddhi, whose name is translated 童覺 Thuṅ-*k*iâo, lit. 'boy-intelligence.' He was a *S*ramana of the western region, who translated one work at *Kh*âṅ-ân, in A. D. 369–371 or 382. See the four authorities above mentioned.

No. 1381 'An explanation or commentary on an extract from the four Âgamas (I. M.).'

54 僧伽跋澄 (or 橙) Saṅ-*k*iê-poh-*k*han (or *k*haṅ), i. e. Saṅghabhûti, whose name is translated 衆現 *K*uṅ-hhien, lit. 'company-appearing.' He was a *S*ramana of Kubhâ (Cabul), who translated 3 works in 27 or 37 fasciculi, in A. D. 381–385. See Saṅ-*k*whân, fasc. 1, fol. 20 b; Nâi-tien-lu, fasc. 3 b, fol. 4 a; Thu-*k*i, fasc. 3, fol. 1 b; Khâi-yuen-lu, fasc. 3, fol. 31 a; Beal, B. L. C., p. 18.

No. 1279 Vibhâshâ-sâstra (A. H.).
" 1289 'Âryâ-Vasumitra-bodhisattva-saṅgîti-sâstra.'
" 1352 'Saṅgharaksha-saṅkaya-buddhakarita-sûtra (I. M.).'

55 曇摩蜱 Thân-mo-pi, i. e. Dharmapriya, whose name is translated 法愛 Fâ-âi, lit. 'law-love' (cf. Eitel, p. 32 b, where a fuller transliteration of the same Sanskrit name with the same translation of a later Indian priest is given). He was an Indian *S*ramana, who translated one Sûtra in 5 fasciculi, in A. D. 382. See Nâi-tien-lu, fasc. 3 b, fol. 3 a; Thu-*k*i, fasc. 3, fol. 2 a; Khâi-yuen-lu, fasc. 3, fol. 32 a; Beal, B. L. C., p. 18. No. 55 may be the same person as No. 43 above.

No. 7 Dasasâhasrikâ pragñâpâramitâ (S. M.).

56 瞿曇僧伽提婆 *Kh*ü-thân Saṅ-*k*iê-thi-pho, i. e. Gautama Saṅghadeva, a *S*ramana of Kubhâ (Cabul), who was the same person as No. 39 above. He first arrived at *Kh*âṅ-ân, in A. D. 383; where he translated 2 or 3 works (one of them only was in existence in A. D. 730). In A. D. 391 he went southward and translated some more works, as already alluded to under No. 39 above. See Saṅ-*k*whân, fasc. 1, fol. 22 b; Nâi-tien-lu, fasc. 3 b, fol. 4 b; Thu-*k*i, fasc. 2, fol. 21 a; Khâi-yuen-lu, fasc. 3, fol. 32 b; Miṅ-ỳ-tsi, fasc. 3, fol. 6 a.

No. 1273 Abhidharmagñânaprasthâna-sâstra (A. H.).

57 曇摩難提 Thân-mo-nân-thi, i. e. Dharmanandin, whose name is translated 法喜 Fâ-hhi, lit. 'law-joy.' He was a *S*ramana of the country of

兜佉勒 Teu-*kh*ü-lö, i. e. Tukhâra (Eitel, p. 152 b). In A. D. 384 he arrived at *Kh*âṅ-ân, where he translated 5 works in 114 or 116 fasciculi (of which 4 works in 113 fasciculi were lost already in A. D. 730). Having finished his work of translation in A. D. 391, he went back westward; but where he died is not known. See Saṅ-*k*whân, fasc. 1, fol. 10 b; Sui-shu, fasc. 35, fol. 22 b; Nêi-tien-lu, fasc. 3 b, fol. 3 b; Thu-*k*i, fasc. 3, fol. 2 a; Khâi-yuen-lu, fasc. 3, fol. 33 a; Eitel, p. 32 a; Selected Essays, vol. ii, p. 327; Beal, B. L. C., p. 18. There are 2 works in existence in the Collection, though the first of the two is said to have long been lost in A. D. 730, in the Khâi-yuen-lu (fasc. 3, fol. 33 b), namely:—

No. 543 Ekottarâgama (S. H.).
" 1367 'Asoka-*râg*a-putra-*k*akshurbheda-nidâna-sûtra (I. M.).'

SUMMARY OF THE PRECEDING LIST OF TRANSLATIONS MADE UNDER THE FORMER TSHIN DYNASTY, A. D. 350–394.

Translators.	Nêi-tien-lu.	Thu-*k*i.	Khâi-yuen-lu.	In existence.
No. 52	2	2	3	0
" 53	1	1	1	1
" 54	3	3	3	3
" 55	1	1	1	1
" 56	3	3	2	3
" 57	5	5	5	2
	15	15	15*	10

* In 197 fasciculi. In A. D. 730 there were 7 works in 65 fasciculi in existence, while 8 works in 132 fasciculi were already lost. See the Khâi-yuen-lu, fasc. 3, fol. 29 b.

後秦 Heu-tshin, or the Latter Tshin dynasty, of the 姚 Yâo family, with its capital at *Kh*âṅ-ân. A. D. 384–417.

58 竺佛念 *K*u Fo-nien, a Chinese *S*ramana of 涼州 Liâṅ-*k*eu, who was a constant assistant of the foreign translators under the Former Tshin dynasty, A. D. 350–394. He also translated by himself 12 or 13 works from A. D. 374 till some time under the Latter Tshin dynasty, A. D. 384–417. Of his translations 7 works in 61 fasciculi only were in existence in A. D. 730, as they are at present. See Saṅ-*k*whân, fasc. 1, fol. 24 a; Nêi-tien-lu, fasc. 3 b, fol. 9 b; Thu-*k*i, fasc. 3, fol. 3 a; Khâi-yuen-lu, fasc. 4 a, fol. 1 b; Beal, B. L. C., p. 19.

No. 376 'Sûtra on the cutting of the tie of passions in the ten dwellings or steps (S. M.).'
" 433 Garbha-sûtra (?).
" 445 'Bodhisattvamâlâ-sûtra.'
" 463 Antarâ-bhava-sûtra.
" 1092 'Sûtra on the original action of Bodhisattvamâlâ (V. M.).'
No. 1130 Vinayanidâna-sûtra (V. H.)
" 1321 'Avadâna-sûtra,' or Dharmapada with Avadâna (I. M.).

59 鳩摩羅什 *K*iu-mo-lo-shi, or 鳩摩羅耆婆 *K*iu-mo-lo-*kh*i-pho, i. e. Kumâra*g*îva, whose name is translated 童壽 Thuṅ-sheu, lit. 'boy-age or longevity.' He was an Indian *S*ramana, whose forefathers were successively ministers of the country. His father *K*iu-mo-lo-yen (Kumârâyana ?) forsook this rank and went to Khara*k*ar, where he was married to *G*îvâ, a younger sister of the king of that country. The name of Kumâra*g*îva is said to consist of the names of his parents.

He was born in Khara*k*ar, and became a monk in his seventh year. Two years after, his mother, who had already become a nun, brought her son to Kubhâ (Cabul), where the young monk became the disciple of a famous priest, named Vandhudatta, a cousin of the king of Kubhâ. In his twelfth year, the mother of Kumâra*g*îva brought her son back to Khara*k*ar. On the way back, they met an Arhat, who told the mother, that 'she should carefully guard this *S*râmanera (Kumâra*g*îva) against disorder; because if he did not commit any sin till his thirty-fifth year, then he would greatly propagate the law of Buddha, and save innumerable people, just as Upagupta (the fourth patriarch) did; but on the contrary, if he could not keep moral precepts (*S*îla), he would not be more than a clever and skilful priest.'

Afterwards Kumâra*g*îva studied the Sarvâstivâda-vinaya, under the instruction of Vimalâksha, No. 44 above. Then, following Sûryasoma, he first heard the doctrine of Mahâyâna, and exclaimed: 'My former study of the Hînayâna was just like this, that one thought an ore resembling pure copper excellent, without knowing (the excellence of) gold!' From this time, he entirely devoted himself to the propagation of the Mahâyâna. Finally, by his discourse, his former teacher Vandhudatta was converted to it.

In A. D. 383, Khara*k*ar was destroyed by Lü Kwâṅ, the commander-in-chief under the Former Tshin dynasty, who killed the king of the country, and captured Kumâra*g*îva. On the way to China, Kumâra*g*îva was compelled by Lü Kwâṅ to sleep together with a daughter of the unfortunate king, when Kumâra*g*îva was still young, say, before his thirty-fifth year. He stayed with Lü Kwâṅ in Liâṅ-*k*eu, China, till A. D. 401. On the twentieth day of the twelfth month of the same year, he arrived at *Kh*âṅ-âṇ, being greatly welcomed by Yâo Hhiṅ, the second ruler of the Latter Tshin dynasty. From A. D. 402 to 412, he translated numerous works, and also wrote a treatise and some verses in Chinese. He is said to have had Chinese priests as his disciples more than three thousand in number, among whom there were about ten great disciples, who wrote several works. Kumâra*g*îva died in the Hun-sh' period, A.D. 399–415, but the exact date is uncertain, though the San-*k*whân (fasc. 2, fol. 11 b) gives a very minute date as the twentieth day of the eighth month of the eleventh year of the Hun-sh' period, A.D. 409. There are, however, some of his translations of a much later date. See Khâi-yuen-lu, fasc. 4 a, fol. 15 b. For a general account concerning Kumâra*g*îva, see San-*k*whân, fasc. 2, fol. 1 a; Sui-shu, fasc. 35, fol. 22 a; Nêi-tien-lu, fasc. 3 b, fol. 11 b; Thu-*k*i, fasc. 3, fol. 4 a (both ascribe to him 98 works in 421 or 425 fasciculi); Khâi-yuen-lu, fasc. 4 a, fol. 3 a (where 74 works in 384 fasciculi are mentioned, and 52 works in 302 fasciculi are said to have been in existence in A.D. 730); Min-i-tsi, fasc. 3, fol. 6 b; Eitel, p. 59 a; Selected Essays, vol. ii, p. 324; Beal, B. L. C., p. 19. There are fifty works in existence in the Collection, namely:—

No. 3 Pañkavimsati-sâhasrikâ pra*g*ñâpâramitâ (S. M.).
" 6 Dasasâhasrikâ pra*g*ñâpâramitâ.
" 10 Va*g*ra*kkh*edikâ pra*g*ñâpâramitâ.
" 17 'Pra*g*ñâpâramitâ-sûtra on a benevolent king who protects his country.'
" 19 Pra*g*ñâpâramitâ-h*r*idaya-sûtra.
" 23 (17) Pûrna-parip*rikkh*â.
" 23 (26) Subâhu-parip*rikkh*â.
" 40 Sumati-dârikâ-parip*rikkh*â.
" 82 'Îsvararâ*g*a-bodhisattva-sûtra.'
" 99 'Bodhih*r*idaya-vyûha-sûtra.'
" 105 Dasabhûmika-sûtra.
" 122 'Sûtra of Buddha's last instruction.'
" 129 Sarvapunyasamu*kk*aya-samâdhi-sûtra.
" 134 Saddharmapundarîka-sûtra.
" 137 Avalokitesvara-bodhisattva-samantamukha-parivarta (the twenty-fifth chapter of the preceding).
" 146 Vimalakîrtti-nirdesa.
" 162 Mahâdruma-kinnararâ*g*a-parip*rikkh*â.
" 164 Sarvadharma-pariv*r*itti-nirdesa-sûtra.
" 166 'Vasudhara-sûtra.'
" 190 Viseshakintâ-brahma-parip*rikkh*â.
" 200 Sukhâvaty-am*r*itavyûha-sûtra, or Sukhâvatîvyûha (short).
" 205 Maitreya-vyâkarana.
" 209 'Sûtra on Maitreya's becoming Buddha.'
" 238 Gayâsîrsha.
" 311 Mahâmayûrî-vidyârâ*g*ñî.
" 396 A*k*intyaprabhâsa-nirdesa-sûtra.
" 399 Sûrangama-samâdhi.
" 425 Kusalamûla-samparigraha (or -paridhara)-sûtra.
" 511 'Sahasrabuddhanidâna-sûtra.'
" 627 'Sûtra on a pastor (S. H.).'
" 672 'Sûtra on the eight good qualities of the sea.'
" 720 'Dîpankarâvadâna-sûtra (?).'
" 779 'Sûtra on the hidden and important law of meditation.'
" 1160 Sarvâstivâda-prâtimoksha (V. H.).
No. 1169 'Mahâpra*g*ñâpâramitâ (sûtra)-sâstra (A. M.).'
" 1179 Prânyamûla-sâstra-*t*îkâ.
" 1180 'Dasabhûmi-vibhâshâ-sâstra.'
" 1182 Sûtrâlankâra-sâstra.
" 1186 Dvâdasanikâya-sâstra.
" 1188 *S*ata-sâstra.
" 1218 'Sâstra on raising the thought towards the Bodhi.'
" 1274 'Satyasiddhi-sâstra (A. H.).'
" 1342 '*S*ûtra on the important explanation of the law of meditation (I. M.).'
" 1350 'Sûtra on the doctrine of sitting in meditation.'
" 1366 'Samyuktâvadâna-sûtra.'
" 1373 'Abridged law for importance of thinking or meditation.'
" 1416 'Law of Bodhisattva's blaming lust.'
" 1460 Life of the Bodhisattva Asvaghosha.
" 1461 Life of the Bodhisattva Nâgâr*g*una.
" 1462 Life of the Bodhisattva Deva.

60 弗若多羅 Fu-*z*o-to-lo, i.e. Pu*n*yatara, whose name is translated 功德華 Kun-töh-hwâ, lit. 'action-virtue-flower.' He was a *S*ramana of Kubhâ (Cabul), who arrived in China in the Hun-sh' period, A.D. 399–415, and in A.D. 404 he, together with Kumâra*g*îva, No. 59 above, translated one work in 58 fasciculi. See San-*k*whân, fasc. 2, fol. 11 b; Nêi-tien-lu, fasc. 3 b, fol. 11 b; Thu-*k*i, fasc. 3, fol. 9 a; Khâi-yuen-lu, fasc. 4 a, fol. 17 b; Beal, B. L. C., p. 19.

No. 1115 Sarvâstivâdavinaya (V. H.).

61 佛陀耶舍 Fo-tho-ye-shö, i.e. Buddhayasas, whose name is translated 覺明 *K*iâo-min, lit. 'intelligence-brightness.' He was a *S*ramana of Kubhâ (Cabul), who translated 4 works in A.D. 403–413. See San-*k*whân, fasc. 2, fol. 14 a; Sui-shu, fasc. 35, fol. 22 b; Nêi-tien-lu, fasc. 3 b, fol. 17 a; Thu-*k*i, fasc. 3, fol. 8 b; Khâi-yuen-lu, fasc. 4 a, fol. 19 a; Selected Essays, vol. ii, p. 327; Beal, B. L. C., p. 19.

No. 68 Âkâsagarbha-bodhisattva-sûtra (S. M.).
" 545 Dîrghâgama (S. H.).
" 1117 Dharmagupta-vinaya (V. H.).
" 1155 Dharmagupta-prâtimoksha.

62 曇摩耶舍 Thân-mo-ye-shö, i.e. Dharmayasas, whose name is translated 法稱 Fâ-*kh*an, lit. 'law-fame.' He was a *S*ramana of Kubhâ (Cabul), who translated 2 or 3 works in A.D. 407–415. See San-*k*whân, fasc. 1, fol. 24 b; Sui-shu, fasc. 35, fol. 23 b; Nêi-tien-lu, fasc. 3 b, fol. 11 a; Thu-*k*i, fasc. 3, fol. 3 b; Khâi-yuen-lu, fasc. 4 b, fol. 1 a; Min-i-tsi, fasc. 3, fol. 6 b; Selected Essays, vol. ii, p. 327; Beal, B. L. C., p. 19. There are two works in existence in the Collection, namely:—

No. 215 Strîvivarta-vyâkarana-sûtra (S. M.).
" 1268 *S*âriputrâbhidharma-sâstra (A. H.).

SUMMARY OF THE PRECEDING LIST OF TRANSLATIONS MADE UNDER THE LATTER TSHIN DYNASTY, A. D. 384-417.

Translators.	Nêi-tien-lu.	Thu-ki.	Khâi-yuen-lu.	In existence.
No. 58	13	13	12	9
" 59	98	98	74	50
" 60	1	1	1	1
" 61	4	4	4	5
" 62	2	2	3	2
	118	118	94*	67

* In 624 fasciculi. In A.D. 730 there were 66 works in 528 fasciculi in existence, while 28 works in 96 fasciculi were already lost. See the Khâi-yuen-lu, fasc. 4 a, fol. 1 a.

西秦 Si-tshin, or the Western Tshin dynasty, of the 乞伏 *Kh*i-fu family, with its capital at 苑川 Wân-*k*whân. A. D. 385-431.

63 釋聖堅 Shih Shań-*k*ien, or 法堅 Fâ-*k*ien, or 堅公 *K*ien-kuṅ, a (Chinese?) *S*ramana, who in A. D. 388-407 translated 14 or 15 works, of which 10 works in 12 fasciculi have been in existence since A. D. 730. See Nêi-tien-lu, fasc. 3 b, fol. 20 a; Thu-*k*i, fasc. 3, fol. 9 b; Khâi-yuen-lu, fasc. 4 b, fol. 3 a; Beal, B. L. C., p. 19.

No. 106 'Râmaka-sûtra (S. M.).'
" 217 'Sâmaputra (?)-sûtra.'
" 254 'Kumâra-sudâna-sûtra.'
" 292 'Buddhâbhishikta-sûtra.'
" 374 'Anantadhâranî-dharmaparyâya-sûtra.'
" 398 *S*rîkan*th*a-sûtra.
" 415 'Sûtra on an explanation of the actions of priests and laymen.'
" 510 'Bhadrasrî-sûtra.'
" 637 'Sûtra on Ânanda's thinking (or question on serving Buddha. S. H.)'
" 721 'Sûtra on a woman's meeting with a misfortune.'

WORKS OF UNKNOWN TRANSLATORS.

The Khâi-yuen-lu (fasc. 4 b, fol. 4 b seq.) mentions 41 works in 86 fasciculi (of which 22 works in 67 fasciculi were in existence in A. D. 730), which are said to have been translated under the Three Tshin (Former, Latter, and Western) dynasties, A. D. 350-431. But there are now the following 18 works only in existence in the Collection; some of them are said to have been translated under the Tshin dynasty, without any distinction of Former, Latter, or Western:—

No. 85 Sarvatathâgatavishayâvatâra (S. M.).
" 180 Mahâkarunâpu*nd*arîka-sûtra.
" 413 'Vagrasamâdhi-sûtra.'
" 414 'Simhakandra-buddha-*g*âtaka-sûtra.'
No. 418 'Dasasrî-sûtra.'
" 443 Tathâgata-garbha-sûtra.
" 472 'Divyarâgakumâra-Phi-lo (?)-sûtra.'
" 546 Saktavargâgama-sûtra (? S. H.).
" 639 '*S*râmanera-sûtra.'
" 776 'Abhinishkramana-guna-sûtra.'
" 1135 Sarvâstivâda-vinaya-vibhâshâ (V. H.).
" 1136 A continuation of the preceding work.
" 1138 'Vinayamâtrikâ-sâstra.'
" 1262 Pratyekabuddha-nidâna-sâstra (A. H.).
" 1272 'Sammitîya-nikâya-sâstra.'
" 1284 'Ash*t*âdasa-nikâya-sâstra.'
" 1332 'Sûtra on the grief and ardent love of the Malla or wrestler Guhyapadavagra on account of Buddha's entering Nirvâna (I. M.).'
" 1369 'Avidyâ-raksha-sûtra.'

SUMMARY OF THE PRECEDING LIST OF TRANSLATIONS MADE UNDER THE WESTERN TSHIN DYNASTY, A. D. 385-431, OR THE THREE TSHIN DYNASTIES, A. D. 350-431.

Translators.	Nêi-tien-lu.	Thu-ki.	Khâi-yuen-lu.	In existence.
63	15	14	15	10
	8	0	41	18
	23	14	56*	28

* In 110 fasciculi. In A. D. 730 there were 32 works in 79 fasciculi in existence, while 24 works in 31 fasciculi were already lost. See Khâi-yuen-lu, fasc. 4 b, fol. 2 b.

北凉 Pe-liâṅ, or the Northern Liâṅ dynasty, of the 沮渠 Tsü-*kh*ü family, with its capital first at 張掖 *Kh*âṅ-ye, and afterwards at 姑臧 Ku-tsâṅ. A. D. 397-439.

64 釋道龔 Shih Tâo-kuṅ, a (Chinese?) *S*ramana, who in A. D. 402-412 translated 2 works in 12 fasciculi, one of them was lost already in A. D. 730. See Nêi-tien-lu, fasc. 3 b, fol. 23 a; Thu-*k*i, fasc. 3, fol. 11 a; Khâi-yuen-lu, fasc. 4 b, fol. 9 a; Beal, B. L. C., p. 20.

No. 23 (44) Ratnarâsi or -parâsi (S. M.).

65 釋法衆 Shih Fâ-*k*uṅ, a Chinese priest of the 高昌 Kâo-*kh*âṅ district, who translated one work in 4 fasciculi, in A. D. 402-412. See the four authorities above mentioned.

No. 421 Pratyutpanna-buddha-sammukhâvasthita-samâdhi-sûtra (S. M.).

66 僧伽陀 Saṅ-kiâ-tho, i.e. Saṅghâta (?), whose name is translated 饒善 Zâo-shân, lit. 'plenty-goodness.' He was a *S*ramana of the western region, who translated one work in 2 fasciculi, in the same period as before, but it was lost already in A.D. 730. See the four authorities above mentioned.

67 曇無讖 Thân-wu-khân, or 曇摩讖 Thân-mo-khân, or 曇謨讖 Thân-mu-khân, or 曇摩羅讖 Thân-mo-lo-khân, i.e. Dharmaraksha, whose name is translated 法豐 Fâ-fan, lit. 'law-prosperity.' He was a *S*ramana of Central India, who arrived in China in A.D. 414, and translated several works till A.D. 421, at the request of Tsü-khü Man-sun, the second ruler of the Northern Liâṅ dynasty, A.D. 403–433. In his forty-ninth year (A.D. 433), Dharmaraksha was invited by Thâi-wu-ti, the third sovereign of the Northern Wêi dynasty, who reigned A.D. 424–452. But when he went off just 40 li from the capital of the Northern Liâṅ, Man-sun sent an assassin and killed him, on the suspicion that this Indian priest might have made a plan against the Northern Liâṅ for the sake of the Northern Wêi. This happened in the third month of the third year of the I-hö period, A.D. 433, of Man-sun's reign, and in the following month, Man-sun himself died, and was succeeded by his heir, who lost his kingdom in A.D. 439. See Saṅ-kwhân, fasc. 2, fol. 21 a; Sui-shu, fasc. 35, fol. 22 a; Nêi-tien-lu, fasc. 3 b, fol. 23 b (where 24 works in 151 fasciculi are ascribed to him); Thu-ki, fasc. 3, fol. 11 b (23 works in 148 fasciculi); Khâi-yuen-lu, fasc. 4 b, fol. 10 a (19 works in 131 fasciculi); Miṅ-i-tsi, fasc. 3, fol. 8 b; Selected Essays, vol. ii, pp. 325, 326; Beal, B.L.C., p. 20. There are the following 12 works in the Collection, as they existed in A.D. 730:—

No. 24 Trisambaranirdesa (S.M.).
„ 61 Mahâvaipulyamahâsannipâta-sûtra.
„ 113 Mahâparinirvâna-sûtra.
„ 127 Suvarnaprabhâsa-sûtra.
„ 142 Karunâpundarîka-sûtra.
„ 236 Strîvivarta-vyâkarana-sûtra.
„ 244 Mahâmegha-sûtra.
„ 604 'Mûrddhaka (or Mândhâtri)-râga-sûtra (S.H.).'
„ 1086 Bodhisattva-karyâ-nirdesa (V.M.).'
„ 1088 'Upâsakasîla-sûtra.'
„ 1096 Bodhisattva-pratimoksha-sûtra.
„ 1351 Buddhakaritakâvya, by Asvaghosha (I.M.).

68 沮渠京聲 Tsü-khü Kiṅ-shan,—安陽侯 Ân-yâṅ-heu, or the prince of Ân-yâṅ, who was a cousin of Tsü-khü Man-sun, the second ruler of the Northern Liâṅ dynasty. In his youth, he went to Kustana (Khoten), where he met the Indian priest Buddhasena, and could recite some Sanskrit text. Having come back to the dominion of the Northern Liâṅ, he translated one work in 2 or 3 fasciculi, entitled 'An important explanation of the law of meditation,' in A.D. 433–439, but it was lost already in A.D. 730. After the destruction of the Northern Liâṅ, A.D. 439, he went southward and took refuge in the realm of the Suṅ dynasty, where he translated some more works, for which see No. 83 below. See Saṅ-kwhân, fasc. 2, fol. 25 a; Nêi-tien-lu, fasc. 3 b, fol. 25 a; Thu-ki, fasc. 3, fol. 13 a; Khâi-yuen-lu, fasc. 4 b, fol. 15 b; Beal, B.L.C., p. 20, where the name of this translator and an account of his earlier life seem to be left out between the sixth and seventh lines from the bottom of the page.

69 浮陀跋摩 Feu-tho-poh-mo, or 佛陀跋摩 Fo-tho-poh-mo, i.e. Buddhavarman, whose name is translated 覺鎧 Kiâo-khâi, lit. 'intelligence-armour.' He was a *S*ramana of the western region, who translated one work in 100 fasciculi, in A.D. 437–439; but 40 fasciculi were lost at the destruction of the Northern Liâṅ, A.D. 439. There is an earlier date for this translation in the preface, namely, A.D. 425–427. See, however, the Saṅ-kwhân, fasc. 3, fol. 7 a; Nêi-tien-lu, fasc. 3 b, fol. 25 b; Thu-ki, fasc. 3, fol. 14 b; Khâi-yuen-lu, fasc. 4 b, fol. 16 a; Miṅ-i-tsi, fasc. 3, fol. 9 a; Beal, B.L.C., p. 21.

No. 1264 Abhidharma-mahâvibhâshâ-sâstra (A.H.).

70 釋智猛 Shih K'-man, a Chinese *S*ramana of 新豐 Sin-fan, of 京兆 Kiṅ-kâo, who started from Khâṅ-ân towards India in A.D. 404 with fourteen friends; nine of them returned from the Himâlaya mountain, and one died on the way. K'-man with four remaining friends went as far as Pâtaliputra, where he obtained the Nirvâna-sûtra, Mahâsaṅghika-vinaya, and some other texts, from the very same house of a Brâhmana, from which Fa-hhien (Fahian) had obtained the Nirvâna-sûtra in 6 fasciculi (in his Chinese translation?). On the way back to China in A.D. 424, K'-man again lost three more friends, and arrived at Liâṅ-ken with the only surviving companion Thân-tsân. In A.D. 433–439 he translated the Nirvâna-sûtra in 20 fasciculi, and died in about A.D. 453. His translation was lost already in A.D. 730. See Sui-shu, fasc. 35, fol. 22 a; Thu-ki, fasc. 3, fol. 14 b; Khâi-yuen-lu, fasc. 4 b, fol. 16 b; Miṅ-i-tsi, fasc. 3, fol. 9 a; Selected Essays, vol. ii, p. 325; Beal, B.L.C., p. 21.

71 釋道泰 Shih Tâo-thâi, a (Chinese) *S*ramana, who went to the west of the Himâlaya mountain, and obtained the text of the Vibhâshâ, and some Sûtras and *S*âstras. Having returned eastward to China, he met Buddhavarman, No. 69 above, and together with him translated the Vibhâshâ. Afterwards he alone made the translation of two other works. See Nêi-tien-lu, fasc. 3 b, fol. 26 b; Thu-*k*i, fasc. 3, fol. 14 b; Khâi-yuen-lu, fasc. 4 b, fol. 18 b.

No. 1242 Mahâpurusha-sâstra (A. M.).
" 1243 'Mahâyânâvatâraka-sâstra.'

72 釋法盛 Shih Fâ-shan, a Chinese *S*ramana of the 高昌 Kâo-*kh*an district, who went to a foreign country. Having returned to China, he translated one work under the Northern Liân dynasty, A. D. 397–439. See San-*k*whân, fasc. 2, fol. 26 a; Khâi-yuen-lu, fasc. 4 b, fol. 19 a.

No. 436 'Sûtra on the Nidâna of the *K*aitya erected in the place where the Bodhisattva threw his body to feed a hungry tiger (S. M.).'

Works of Unknown Translators.

The Khâi-yuen-lu (fasc. 4 b, fol. 20 a seq.) mentions 53 works in 75 fasciculi. There are 7 works in the Collection, namely:—

No. 65 Dasa*k*akra-kshitigarbha (S. M.).
" 157 Avaivartya (?), or Aparivartya-sûtra.
" 416 'Sûtra on the wife of the *S*resh*th*in Fâ-*k*, or Dharma*k*ârin.'
" 429 'Va*g*rasamâdhi-sûtra.'
" 506 'Upâsikâ-brahma*k*aryâ-dharmaparyâya-sûtra.'
" 1147 'Mahâpra*g*âpati-bhikshunî-sûtra (V. H.).'
" 1345 'Tri*g*ñâna-sûtra (I. M.).'

Summary of the preceding List of Translations made under the Northern Liân dynasty, A.D. 397–439.

Translators.	Nêi-tien-lu.	Thu-*k*i.	Khâi-yuen-lu.	In existence.
No. 64	2	2	2	1
" 65	1	1	1	1
" 66	1	1	1	0
" 67	24	23	19	12
" 68	1	1	1	0
" 69	1	1	1	1
" 70	1	1	1	0
" 71	1	2	2	2
" 72	0	0	1	1
	5	5	53	7
	37	37	82*	25

* In 311 fasciculi. In A. D. 730 there were 25 works in 209 fasciculi in existence, while 57 works in 102 fasciculi were already lost. See the Khâi-yuen-lu, fasc. 4 b, fol. 8 a.

宋劉 The earlier Sun dynasty, of the Liu family, with its capital at 建業 *K*ien-yeh, the modern Nanking. A. D. 420–479.

73 佛陀什 Fo-tho-shi, i. e. Buddha*g*îva, whose name is translated 覺壽 *K*iâo-sheu, lit. 'intelligence-age or longevity.' He was a *S*ramana of Kubhâ (Cabul), who arrived in China in A. D. 423, and translated 3 works in 32 or 36 fasciculi; one of them was lost already in A. D. 730. See San-*k*whân, fasc. 3, fol. 6 b; Nêi-tien-lu, fasc. 4 a, fol. 4 a; Thu-*k*i, fasc. 3, fol. 15 b; Khâi-yuen-lu, fasc. 5 a, fol. 2 b; Beal, B. L. C., p. 21.

No. 1122 Mahîsâsaka-vinaya (V. H.).
" 1157 Prâtimoksha of the Mahîsâsakas.

74 畺良耶舍 *Kh*iân-liân-ye-shö, i. e. Kâlayasas, whose name is translated 時稱 Sh'-*kh*an, lit. 'time-fame.' He was a *S*ramana of the western region, who arrived in *K*ien-yeh, the capital, in A. D. 424, and translated 2 works in 2 or 3 fasciculi, and died in his sixtieth year, in A. D. 442. See San-*k*whân, fasc. 3, fol. 22 b; Nêi-tien-lu, fasc. 4 a, fol. 12 b; Thu-*k*i, fasc. 3, fol. 16 b; Khâi-yuen-lu, fasc. 5 a, fol. 3 a; Min-i-tsi, fasc. 3, fol. 9 b; Beal, B. L. C., p. 21.

No. 198 'Amitâyur-dhyâna-sûtra (S. M.).'
" 305 Bhaishagyarâ*g*a-bhaishagyasamudgati (or -gata)-sûtra.

75 曇摩蜜多 Thân-mo-mi-to, i. e. Dharmamitra, whose name is translated 法秀 Fâ-siu, lit. 'law-flourishing.' He was a *S*ramana of Kubhâ (Cabul), who arrived in China in A. D. 424, and worked there at translations till A.D. 441, and died in his eighty-seventh year, in A. D. 442. See San-*k*whân, fasc. 3, fol. 19 a; Nêi-tien-lu, fasc. 4 a, fol. 11 b; Thu-*k*i, fasc. 3, fol. 15 b (both ascribe to him 10 works); Khâi-yuen-lu, fasc. 5 a, fol. 3 b (where 12 works in 17 fasciculi are mentioned, of which 5 works in 10 fasciculi were lost already in A. D. 730); Min-i-tsi, fasc. 3, fol. 9 a; Beal, B. L. C., p. 21. There are 6 works in the Collection, namely:—

No. 69 Âkâsagarbha-bodhisattva-dhâranî-sûtra (S. M.).
" 70 'Âkâsagarbha-bodhisattva-dhyâna-sûtra (?).'
" 193 Hastikakshyâ.
" 213 'Sarvadharma-nirbhaya-râ*g*a-sûtra.'
" 237 Strîvivarta-vyâkarana-sûtra.
" 394 'Samantabhadra-bodhisattva-dhyâna-*k*aryâdharma-sûtra.'

76 釋智嚴 Shih *K'*-yen, a Chinese *S*ramana of the Western 涼州 Liâṅ-*k*eu, who went to Kubhâ (Cabul), and obtained some Sanskrit texts. He was a companion of Fâ-hhien (Fa-hian) on his journey to India. In A. D. 427 he, together with Pâo-yun, No. 77 below, translated 10 or 14 works (of which 4 works in 12 fasciculi only were in existence in A. D. 730). Then he again went to Kubhâ, where he died in his seventy-eighth year. See Saṅ-*k*whân, fasc. 3, fol. 7 b; Nêi-tien-lu, fasc. 4 a, fol. 5 a; Thu-*k*i, fasc. 3, fol. 16 b; Khâi-yuen-lu, fasc. 5 a, fol. 6 b; Miṅ-i-tsi, fasc. 3, fol. 9 b; Beal, B. L. C., p. 22.

No. 77 Akshramatinirdesa-sûtra (S. M.).
„ 135 'Saddharmapundarika-samâdhi-sûtra.'
„ 158 Avaivartya (?) or Aparivartya-sûtra.
„ 722 '*K*aturdivyarâga-sûtra (S. H.).'

77 釋寶雲 Shih Pâo-yun, a Chinese *S*ramana of 涼州 Liâṅ-*k*eu, who went to the western region with Fâ-hhien and *K'*-yen, Nos. 45 and 76 above, and together with the latter, he translated several Sûtras. After *K'*-yen's death, Pâo-yun alone produced his own translation of 4 works in the Yuen-*k*iâ period, A. D. 424–453, of which 3 works in 10 fasciculi were lost already in A. D. 730. He died in A. D. 449. See Saṅ-*k*whân, fasc. 3, fol. 9 b; Nêi-tien-lu, fasc. 4 a, fol. 5 b; Thu-*k*i, fasc. 3, fol. 18 b; Khâi-yuen-lu, fasc. 5 a, fol. 9 b; Miṅ-i-tsi, fasc. 3, fol. 11 a; Beal, B. L. C., p. 22.

No. 1323 'Buddha-pûrvakaryâ-sûtra (I. M.).'

78 伊葉波羅 I-yeh-po-lo, i. e. Îsvara, whose name is translated 自在 Tsz'-tsâi, lit. 'self-existence.' He was a *S*ramana of the western region, who translated the Samyukta-abhidharma-hridaya-sâstra, in 10 fasciculi, in A. D. 426, and in A. D. 431 his translation was continued by Gunavarman, so that it was complete in 13 fasciculi. But the whole translation was lost already in A. D. 730. See Nêi-tien-lu, fasc. 4 a, fol. 6 b; Thu-*k*i, fasc. 3, fol. 16 b; Khâi-yuen-lu, fasc. 5 a, fol. 11 a; Miṅ-i-tsi, fasc. 3, fol. 9 b; Beal, B. L. C., p. 21.

79 求那跋摩 *K*iu-nâ-poh-mo, i. e. Gunavarman, whose name is translated 功德鎧 Kuṅ-töh-khâi, lit. 'action-virtue (i. e. good-quality)-armour.' He was a *S*ramana of Kubhâ (Cabul), who was a younger son of the king of the country, and arrived in *K*ien-yeh (Nanking) in A. D. 431, and translated 10 works in 16 fasciculi. In the same year he died, in his sixty-fifth year. Of his ten translations, 2 works in 2 fasciculi were lost already in A. D. 730. See Saṅ-*k*whân, fasc. 3, fol. 10 b; Nêi-tien-lu, fasc. 4 a, fol. 7 a; Thu-*k*i, fasc. 3, fol. 17 b; Khâi-yuen-lu, fasc. 5 a, fol. 11 a; Miṅ-i-tsi, fasc. 3, fol. 9 b; Beal, B. L. C., p. 22. There are 5 works only in the Collection, namely:—

No. 1109 'Upâli-pariprikkhâ-sûtra (V. H.).'
„ 1114 'Upâsakapañkasîlarûpa-sûtra.'
„ 1129 Dharmagupta-bhikshunî-karman.
„ 1164 '*S*râmanera-karmavâkâ (?).'
„ 1464 Nâgârguna-bodhisattva-suhrillekha (I. M.).

80 僧伽跋摩 Saṅ-*k*iê-poh-mo, i. e. Saṅghavarman, whose name is translated 衆鎧 Kuṅ-khâi, lit. 'company-armour.' He was an Indian *S*ramana, who arrived in *K*ien-yeh (Nanking) in A. D. 433, and in the following year he translated 5 works. In A. D. 442 he went back westward, but where he died is not known. See Saṅ-*k*whân, fasc. 3, fol. 18 a; Nêi-tien-lu, fasc. 4 a, fol. 7 b; Thu-*k*i, fasc. 3, fol. 19 a; Khâi-yuen-lu, fasc. 5 a, fol. 17 a; Beal, B. L. C., p. 23. There are 4 works in the Collection, namely:—

No. 1132 Sarvâstivâda-nikâya-vinaya-mâtrikâ (V. H.).
„ 1287 Samyuktâbhidharma-hridaya-sâstra (A. H.).
„ 1349 'Mahâsûra-bodhisattva-nirdesa-karmaphala-saṅkshipta-sûtra (I. M.).'
„ 1440 Nâgârguna-bodhisattva-suhrillekha.

81 求那跋陀羅 *K*iu-nâ-poh-tho-lo, i. e. Gunabhadra, whose name is translated 功德賢 Kuṅ-töh-hhien, lit. 'action-virtue (i. e. good-quality)-wise.' He was a *S*ramana of Central India, who was a Brâhmana by caste, and nicknamed the Mahâyâna, on account of being well acquainted with the doctrine of Mahâyâna. In A. D. 435 he arrived in China and worked at translations till A. D. 443, and in A. D. 468 he died in his seventy-fifth year. See Saṅ-*k*whân, fasc. 3, fol. 23 b; Nêi-tien-lu, fasc. 4 a, fol. 8 a; Thu-*k*i, fasc. 3, fol. 20 a (both ascribe to him 78 works in 161 or 261 fasciculi); Khâi-yuen-lu, fasc. 5 a, fol. 18 b (where 52 works in 134 fasciculi are mentioned, of which 26 works in 100 fasciculi were in existence in A. D. 730); Miṅ-i-tsi, fasc. 3, fol. 11 a; Beal, B. L. C., p. 23. There are 28 works in the Collection, namely:—

No. 59 *S*rîmâlâ-devî-simhanâda (S. M.).
„ 154 Sandhinirmokana-sûtra.
„ 155 „ „
„ 169 Ratnakârandakavyûha-sûtra.
„ 175 Laṅkâvatâra-sûtra.
„ 178 'Bodhisattvakaritopâyavishayarddhivikriyâ-sûtra.'
„ 201 'A spiritual Dhâranî for uprooting all the obstacles of Karma, and for causing one to be born in the Pure Land (Sukhâvatî).'
„ 226 'Vriddhamâtri-shatpushpâ (?)-sûtra.
„ 231 *K*andraprabha-kumâra-sûtra.
„ 434 Aṅgulimâlîya-sûtra.

No. 440 Mahâbheri-hâraka-parivarta.
„ 452 'Dvâdasadhûta-sûtra.'
„ 453 '*G*yotishka (?)-sûtra.'
„ 527 'Mahâmati-sûtra.'
„ 544 Samyuktâgâma-sûtra (S. H.).
„ 581 'Vimanas (?)-sûtra.'
„ 589 'Sûtra on four men's appearance in the world.'
„ 610 '*S*uka-sûtra.'
„ 629 'Sûtra on eleven methods of thinking of the Tathâgata.'
„ 642 'Asutâ (?)-sûtra.'
„ 666 'Atîtapratyutpanna-hetuphala-sûtra.'
„ 723 'Sûtra on Mahâ*k*âsyapa's saving a poor mother.'
„ 740 'Dvâdasavarga-*g*âtimarana-sûtra.'
„ 741 'Sûtra on transmigration throughout the five paths or states of existence as rewards and recompense of virtue and evil.'
„ 1292 Abhidharma-prakarana-pâda (A. H.).
„ 1347 'Dharmanidâna-sûtra spoken by Pi*nd*ola (?)-bharadvâ*g*a for the sake of King Udayana (I. M.).'
„ 1417 'Four kinds of the law of learning.'

82 釋法勇 Shih Fâ-yuṅ, whose Sanskrit name is 曇無竭 Thân-wu-*k*ie, i. e. Dharmavikrama (?) or Dharma*s*ûra, which seems to be a translation of the name 法勇 Fâ-yuṅ, lit. 'law-bravery,' and whose original surname was 李 Li. He was a Chinese *S*ramana of the country or state of 黃龍 Hwâṅ-luṅ, in 幽州 Yiu-*k*eu. In A. D. 420 he, together with twenty-five friends, went to India, following the example of Fâ-hhien and Pâo-yun, and came back to China in about A. D. 453, and translated one work. See Saṅ-*k*whân, fasc. 3, fol. 5 a; Nêi-tien-lu, fasc. 4 a, fol. 13 a (where 2 works in 6 fasciculi are ascribed to him); Thu-*k*i, fasc. 3, fol. 23 a; Khâi-yuen-lu, fasc. 5 b, fol. 1 a; Miṅ-i-tsi, fasc. 3, fol. 11 b; Beal, B. L. C., p. 23.

No. 395 'Avalokitesvara-mahâsthâmaprâpta-vyâkarana-sûtra (S. M.).'

83 沮渠京聲 Tsü-*kh*ü *K*iṅ-shaṅ, a Chinese G*ri*hapati (householder or layman), who was the same person as No. 68 above. In A. D. 455 he translated 28 or 35 works (of which 15 works in 15 fasciculi were in existence in A. D. 730), and died in about A. D. 464. See Saṅ-*k*whân, fasc. 2, fol. 25 a; Nêi-tien-lu, fasc. 4 a, fol. 13 a; Thu-*k*i, fasc. 3, fol. 13 a; Khâi-yuen-lu, fasc. 5 b, fol. 2 b; Beal, B. L. C., p. 20, line 33 seq. There are 16 works in the Collection, namely:—

No. 204 'Sûtra on the meditation on the Bodhisattva Maitreya's going up to be born in the Tushita heaven (S. M.).'
„ 248 Râ*g*âvavâdaka.
„ 647 'Sûtra on the secret importance for curing the disease concerning meditation (? S. H.).'
„ 690 'Sûtra on advancement in learning.'
No. 701 'Ash*t*opavasatha-sûtra.'
„ 732 '*S*uddhodana-râ*g*a-parinirvâna-sûtra.'
„ 742 'Sûtra on the five (elements) not returning again (i. e. death ?).'
„ 743 „ „ „
„ 744 'Buddhamahat-saṅghamahat-sûtra.'
„ 766 'Sûtra on five states of fear.'
„ 767 'Sûtra on a pupil who revived.'
„ 771 'Ye-*k*' (-nâma-brâhmana)-sûtra.'
„ 772 'Mo-lo (-nâma-râ*g*a)-sûtra.'
„ 773 'Mo-tâ (-desa ?)-râ*g*a-sûtra.'
„ 774 '*K*andanavat (-desa ?)-râ*g*a-sûtra.'
„ 1111 'Sûtra on the forbidding precepts of the Kâsyapîya (-nikâya ?) (V. H.).'

84 釋惠簡 Shih Hwui-kien, a *S*ramana, whose native place is not known. In A. D. 457 he translated 10 or 15 works, of which 7 works in 7 fasciculi only were in existence in A. D. 730. See Nêi-tien-lu, fasc. 4 a, fol. 15 a; Thu-*k*i, fasc. 3, fol. 23 b; Khâi-yuen-lu, fasc. 5 b, fol. 5 a; Beal, B. L. C., p. 24. There are 6 works in the Collection, namely:—

No. 560 'Yama-râ*g*a-pañ*k*adivyadûta-sûtra (S. H.).'
„ 591 'Gautamî-vyâkarana-sûtra.'
„ 620 'Sresh*th*iputra-liu-kwo-abhinishkramana-sûtra.'
„ 651 'Buddhamât*ri*-parinirvâna-sûtra.'
„ 768 'Sûtra on a slow and idle farmer.'
„ 1348 'Sûtra on inviting Pi*nd*ola (?)-bharadvâ*g*a (I. M.).'

85 功德直 Kuṅ-töh-*k*ih, lit. 'good-quality-uprightness,' which three characters seem to be a translation of a Sanskrit name such as Guna*s*ila (?). He was a *S*ramana of the western region, who arrived in China in A. D. 462, and translated 2 works in 7 fasciculi. See Nêi-tien-lu, fasc. 4 a, fol. 14 b; Thu-*k*i, fasc. 3, fol. 24 b; Khâi-yuen-lu, fasc. 5 b, fol. 6 b; Miṅ-i-tsi, fasc. 3, fol. 12 a; Beal, B. L. C., p. 24.

No. 71 Bodhisattva-buddhânusm*ri*ti-samâdhi (S. M.).
„ 354 Anantamukha-sâdhaka-dhâranî (?).

86 竺法眷 *K*u Fâ-*k*ien, an Indian *S*ramana, who in A. D. 465–471 translated 6 works in 29 fasciculi; but all of them were lost already in A. D. 730. See Nêi-tien-lu, fasc. 4 a, fol. 16 b; Thu-*k*i, fasc. 3, fol. 24 b; Khâi-yuen-lu, fasc. 5 a, fol. 7 b; Beal, B. L. C., p. 24.

87 釋翔公 Shih Siâṅ-kuṅ, or 朔公 Soh-kuṅ, a (Chinese ?) *S*ramana, who translated one work in 2 fasciculi; but the exact date is not known, so it is with the following five translators. See Nêi-tien-lu, fasc. 4 a, fol. 16 b; Thu-*k*i, fasc. 3, fol. 25 a; Khâi-yuen-lu, fasc. 5 b, fol. 8 a; Beal, B. L. C., p. 24.

No. 16 Pañ*k*asatikâ pra*g*ñâpâramitâ (? S. M.).

88 釋道嚴 Shih Tâo-yen, a (Chinese?) *S*ramana, who translated 2 works in 3 fasciculi; but all of them were lost already in A. D. 730. For this and the following three translators, see the four authorities mentioned under No. 87 above.

89 釋勇公 Shih Yun-kun, a (Chinese?) *S*ramana, who translated 3 works in 3 fasciculi, or 4 works in 4 fasciculi; but all of them were lost already in A. D. 730.

90 釋法海 Shih Fâ-hâi, a (Chinese?) *S*ramana, who translated 2 works in 2 fasciculi, one of them was in existence in A. D. 730; but it is not found in the present Collection.

91 釋先公 Shih Sien-kun, a (Chinese?) *S*ramana, who translated one work in 1 fasciculus.

No. 192 '*K*andradîpa-samâdhi-sûtra (S. M.).'

92 僧伽跋彌 San-*k*iê-poh-mi, i. e. Sanghavarman (?), a *S*ramana of 師子國 Sh'-tsz'-kwo, or 'the country of the lion,' i. e. Simhala (Ceylon), who translated an extract from the Mahîsâsaka-vinaya in 1 fasciculus; but it was lost already in A. D. 730. See Nêi-tien-lu, fasc. 4 a, fol. 17 a; Khâi-yuen-lu, fasc. 5 b, fol. 9 b.

Works of Unknown Translators.

The Khâi-yuen-lu (fasc. 5 b, fol. 10 a seq.) mentions 307 works in 340 fasciculi, of which 9 works in 9 fasciculi only were in existence in A. D. 730, as they are now in the Collection, namely:—

No. 225 'V*r*iddhamât*ri*-sûtra (S. M.).'
" 255 'Tathâgata*g*ñânamudrâ-samâdhi-sûtra.'
" 470 'Dharmavinâsa-sûtra.'
" 471 'Sûtra on the very deep and great act of making the stocks of merits ripen.'
" 576 'Upâsikâ-to-shö-*k*iâ (?)-sûtra (S. H.).'
" 584 'Durd*r*ish*t*i-sûtra[1].'
" 607 'Sûtra on learning addressed by Buddha to the old Brâhmana of the yellow-bamboo-garden.'
" 1162 'Mahâsrâmanaikasatakarmavâkâ (V. H.).'
" 1371 'Sûtra on changes of the future, spoken by the Bhikshu *K*iâ-tiñ (? I. M.).'

[1] No. 584 is said to have been translated under the Eastern Tsin dynasty, A. D. 317–420, in a catalogue. But it is wrong. See the Khâi-yuen-lu, fasc. 5 b, fol. 10 a; *K*'-tsiñ, fasc. 28, fol. 21 a.

Summary of the preceding List of Translations made under the Sung dynasty, A. D. 420–479.

Translators.	Nêi-tien-lu.	Thu-*k*i.	Khâi-yuen-lu.	In existence.
No. 73	3	3	3	2
" 74	2	2	2	2
" 75	10	10	12	7
" 76	14	14	10	4
" 77	4	4	4	4
" 78	1	1	1	0
" 79	7	8	10	5
" 80	5	5	5	4
" 81	78	78	52	27
" 82	2	1	1	1
" 83	35	35	28	16
" 84	25	25	10	6
" 85	2	2	2	2
" 86	6	6	6	0
" 87	1	1	1	1
" 88	2	2	2	0
" 89	4	4	3	0
" 90	2	2	2	0
" 91	1	1	1	1
" 92	1	0	1	0
	0	0	307	9
	205	204	463 *	91

* In 713 fasciculi. In A. D. 730 there were 91 works in 239 fasciculi in existence, while 372 works in 474 fasciculi were lost already. Cf. the Khâi-yuen-lu, fasc. 5 a, fol. 1 a.

齊 The Tshi dynasty, of the 蕭 Siâo family, with its capital at *K*ien-yeh (Nanking), A. D. 479–502.

93 曇摩伽陀耶舍 Thân-mo-*k*iê-tho-ye-shö, i. e. Dharma*g*âtayasas, whose name is translated 法生稱 Fâ-shan-*kh*an, lit. 'law-birth-fame.' He was a *S*ramana of Central India, who in A. D. 481 translated one work in 1 fasciculi. See Nêi-tien-lu, fasc. 4 a, fol. 19 b; Thu-*k*i, fasc. 4, fol. 1 a; Khâi-yuen-lu, fasc. 6, fol. 1 b; Beal, B. L. C., p. 24.

No. 133 'Amitârtha-sûtra (S. M.).'

94 摩訶乘 Mo-hö-shan, i. e. Mahâyâna, a *S*ramana of the western region, who in A. D. 483–493 translated 2 works in 2 fasciculi, namely: (1) 'Sûtra of 500 *G*âtakas,' and (2) 'Vinaya of the Sthavira school.' But both translations were lost already in A. D. 730. See the four authorities mentioned under No. 93 above.

95 僧伽跋陀羅 San-*k*iê-poh-tho-lo, i. e. Sanghabhadra, whose name is translated 衆賢 *K*un-hhien, lit. 'company-wise.' He was a *S*ramana of the western region, who in A. D. 489 translated one work in 18 fasciculi. See the four authorities mentioned under No. 93 above.

No. 1125 (Sudarsana)-vibhâshâvinaya (V. H.).

96 達摩摩提 Tâ-mo-mo-thi, i.e. Dharmamati, whose name is translated 法意 Fâ-i, lit. 'law-thought.' He was a *S*ramana of the western region, who in A.D. 490 translated 2 works in 2 fasciculi, one of them was in existence in A.D. 730; but it was not found in the present Collection. See the four authorities mentioned under No. 93 above, and also Min-i-tsi, fasc. 3, fol. 12 a.

97 求那毗地 *Kh*iu-nâ-phi-ti, i.e. Gunavriddhi (?), whose name is translated 德進 Töh-sin, lit. 'virtue-advancing.' He was a *S*ramana of Central India, who in A.D. 492 and 495 translated 3 works in 6 or 12 fasciculi, but one of them was lost already in A.D. 730. See San-*k*whân, fasc. 3, fol. 28 a; Nêi-tien-lu, fasc. 4 a, fol. 27 a; Thu-*k*i, fasc. 4, fol. 1 b; Khâi-yuen-lu, fasc. 6, fol. 4 b; Min-i-tsi, fasc. 3, fol. 12 a; Beal, B.L.C., p. 25.

No. 606 Sudatta-sûtra (S. H.).
" 1364 Sûtra of a hundred comparisons (I. M.).

98 釋法度 Shih Fâ-tu, a (Chinese?) *S*ramana, who translated one Sûtra and one Vinaya work, in 1 fasciculus each, in A.D. 483–493; but they seem to have been lost some time before A.D. 730, as even the name of this translator is not mentioned in the Khâi-yuen-lu. See, however, the Nêi-tien-lu, fasc. 4 a, fol. 23 a; Thu-*k*i, fasc. 4, fol. 2 a; Beal, B. L. C., p. 25.

99 釋曇景 Shih Thân-*k*in, a *S*ramana, whose native place is not known, and who translated 2 works in 4 fasciculi, but the exact date is unknown. See Nêi-tien-lu, fasc. 4, fol. 25 a; Thu-*k*i, fasc. 4, fol. 2 b; Khâi-yuen-lu, fasc. 6, fol. 6 a; Beal, B. L. C., p. 25.

No. 382 Mahâmâyâ-sûtra (S. M.).
" 400 Adbhutadharmaparyâya (?).

100 釋法化 Shih Fâ-hwâ, or 法尼 Fâ-ni, a (Chinese?) *S*ramana, who in A.D. 499–500 translated one work in 1 fasciculus; but it was lost already in A.D. 730. See the four authorities mentioned under No. 99 above.

SUMMARY OF THE PRECEDING LIST OF TRANSLATIONS MADE UNDER THE TSHI DYNASTY, A.D. 479–502.

Translators.	Nêi-tien-lu.	Thu-*k*i.	Khâi-yuen-lu.	In existence.
No. 93	1	1	1	1
" 94	2	2	2	0
" 95	1	1	1	1*
" 96	2	2	2	0
" 97	3	3	3	2
" 98	2	2	0	0
" 99	2	2	2	2
" 100	1	1	1	0
	14	14	12*	6

* In 33 fasciculi. In A.D. 730 there were 7 works in 28 fasciculi in existence, while 5 works in 5 fasciculi were already lost. See the Khâi-yuen-lu, fasc. 6, fol. 1 a.

梁 The Lian dynasty, of the 蕭 Siâo family, with its capital at *K*ien-yeh (Nanking), A.D. 502–557.

101 曼陀羅 Mân-tho-lo, i.e. Mandra, whose name is translated 弱聲 *Z*o-shân, lit. 'weak-sound,' or 弘弱 Hun-*z*o, lit. 'spreading-weakness,' also written 曼陀羅仙 Mân-tho-lo-sien, i.e. Mandra *R*ishi (?). He is a *S*ramana of 扶南國 Fu-nân-kwo, or the country of Bunan (Siam?), who arrived in *K*ien-yeh (Nanking) in A.D. 503, and translated 3 works in 11 fasciculi. Although he worked at translations, yet he was not well acquainted with the Chinese language, so that his translation is not quite perfect. See Suh-san-*k*whân, fasc. 1, fol. 15 a; Nêi-tien-lu, fasc. 4 b, fol. 7 b; Thu-*k*i, fasc. 4, fol. 6 a; Khâi-yuen-lu, fasc. 6, fol. 8 a; Min-i-tsi, fasc. 3, fol. 12 b; Beal, B. L. C., p. 26. There are 4 works in the Collection, namely:—

No. 21 Saptasatikâ pragñâpâramitâ (S. M.).
" 23 (8) Dharmadhâtu-prakrity-asambheda-nirdesa.
" 23 (46) Saptasatikâ pragñâpâramitâ.
" 152 Ratnamegha-sûtra.

102 僧伽婆羅 San-*k*ie-pho-lo, i.e. Sanghapâla or Sanghavarman, whose name is translated 衆養 *K*un-yân, lit. 'company-nourishing,' or 僧鎧 San-khâi, lit. 'company-armour.' He was a *S*ramana of Fu-nân or Bunan (Siam?), who translated 10 or 11 works in A.D. 506–520; and his ten translations in 32 fasciculi were in existence in A.D. 730. He became a disciple of the Indian *S*ramana Gunabhadra, after he arrived in China, and died in his sixty-fifth year, in A.D. 520. See Suh-san-*k*whân, fasc. 1, fol. 4 b; Nêi-tien-lu, fasc. 4 b, fol. 8 a; Thu-*k*i, fasc. 4, fol. 6 a; Khâi-yuen-lu, fasc. 6, fol. 9 a; Beal, B. L. C., p. 26. There are 9 works in the Collection, namely:—

No. 22 Saptasatikâ pragñâpâramitâ (S. M.).
" 29 Dasadharmaka.
" 56 Sarvabuddhavishayâvatâra.
" 301 Ashtabuddhaka.
" 308 Mahâmayûrî-vidyârâgñî.
" 353 Anantamukha-sâdhaka-dhâranî (?).
" 442 'Mañgusrî-paripri*kkh*â-sûtra.'
" 1103 'Bodhisattva-pitaka-sûtra (V. M.).'
" 1293 'Vimokshamarga-sâstra (A. H.).'

103 月婆首那 (read 耶 ye) Yueh-pho-sheu-nâ, i.e. Upasûnya, whose name is translated 高空 Kâo-khun, lit. 'high-emptiness.' He was a son of the King of 優禪尼 Yiu-shân-ni, i.e. Udyâna, of Central India, who first translated 3 works

in A. D. 538–540 or 541, in the capital of the Eastern Wêi dynasty, for which, see No. 117 below. In A. D. 545 he came southward to the capital of the Liâṅ dynasty (Nanking), where he translated one work. Afterwards he produced one more translation under the *Kh*an dynasty, for which, see No. 106 below. See Suh-sań-*k*whân, fasc. 1, fol. 21 b; Nêi-tien-lu, fasc. 4 b, fol. 9 b; Thu-*k*i, fasc. 6, fol. 9 b; Khâi-yuen-lu, fasc. 6, fol. 11 b; Beal, B. L. C., p. 27.

No. 144 Vimalakîrttinirdesa (S. M.).

104 波羅末陀 Po-lo-mo-tho, i. e. Paramârtha, whose name is translated 眞諦 *K*an-ti, lit. 'true-truth,' by which latter Chinese name he is always designated in the Collection, just as *K*u Fâ-hu, instead of Dharmaraksha, of the Western Tsin dynasty. He had another name 拘那羅陀 *K*ü-nâ-lo-tho, i. e. Guṇarata (or Kü-lo-nâ-tho (?), i. e. Kulanâtha), which name is translated 親依 Tshin-i, lit. 'intimate-relying.' He was a *S*ramana of 優禪尼 Yiu-shân-ni, i. e. Uggayinî, of Western India, who arrived in *K*ien-yeh (Nanking) in A. D. 548, and till A. D. 557 he translated about 10 works (of which 6 works in 15 fasciculi were in existence in A. D. 730). Afterwards, in A. D. 557–569, he translated numerous works under the *Kh*an dynasty, for which, see No. 105 below. See Suh-sań-*k*whân, fasc. 1, fol. 17 b; Nêi-tien-lu, fasc. 4 b, fol. 9 b; Thu-*k*i, fasc. 4, fol. 7 a; Khâi-yuen-lu, fasc. 6, fol. 12 a; Miṅ-i-tsi, fasc. 3, fol. 13 a; Beal, B. L. C., p. 26.

No. 259 'Sûtra on the highest reliance (S. M.).'
" 1207 'Nirvâṇasûtra-sâstra on the gâthâ on the state of being originally in existence and now extinct (A. M.).'
" 1250 'Mahâyâna-sraddhotpâda-sâstra.'

Works of Unknown Translators.

The Khâi-yuen-lu (fasc. 6, fol. 15 a seq.) mentions 14 works in 25 fasciculi. There are 13 works in the Collection, namely:—

No. 341 Shaḍakshara-vidyâmantra (S. M.).
" 368 Saptabuddhaka-sûtra.
" 405 'Atîta-vyûhakalpa-sahasrabuddhanâma-sûtra.'
" 406 'Pratyutpanna-bhadrakalpa-sahasra°.'
" 407 'Anâgata-nakshatratârâkalpa-sahasra°.'
" 419 'Sreshṭhi-duhitṛ-ṅân-thi-kö(?)-simhanâda-sûtra.'
" 474 'Ö-*kh*â-pho-*k*ü-asurasena-dhâraṇî.'
" 475 Samantabhadra-dhâraṇî.
" 476 'Mahâsaptaratna-dhâraṇî.'
" 477 'Shaḍaksharamahâ-dhâraṇî.'
" 485 'Amitadundubhisvara-râga-dhâraṇî.'
" 536 Mahâmaṇi-vipulavimâna-visva-supratishṭhita-guhya-parama-rahasya-kalparâga-dhâraṇî.
" 847 'Marîki-devî-dhâraṇî.'

Summary of the preceding List of Translations made under the Liang dynasty, A. D. 502–557.

Translators.	Nêi-tien-lu.	Thu-*k*i.	Khâi-yuen-lu.	In existence.
No. 101	3	3	3	3
" 102	11	11	10	9
" 103	1	1	1	1
" 104	16	10	11	3
	0	0	14	14
	31	25	39*	30

* In 93 fasciculi. In A. D. 730 there were 34 works in 84 fasciculi in existence, while 5 works in 9 fasciculi were already lost. Cf. the Khâi-yuen-lu, fasc. 6, fol. 6 b seq.

陳 The *Kh*an dynasty, of the 陳 *Kh*an family, with its capital at *K*ien-yeh (Nanking), A. D. 557–589.

105 波羅末陀 Po-lo-mo-tho, i. e. Paramârtha, who was the same person as No. 104 above. In A. D. 557–569 he translated 38 or 40 works, of which 25 works in 83 fasciculi were in existence in A. D. 730. He died in his seventy-first year, in A. D. 569. See Suh-sań-*k*whân, fasc. 1, fol. 17 b; Nêi-tien-lu, fasc. 5 a, fol. 9 b; Thu-*k*i, fasc. 4, fol. 7 a; Khâi-yuen-lu, fasc. 7, fol. 4 a; Miṅ-i-tsi, fasc. 3, fol. 13 a; Beal, B. L. C., p. 26. There are 29 works in the Collection (one of which (No. 1252) is mentioned in the Khâi-yuen-lu, under the Liâṅ dynasty), namely:—

No. 12 Vagrakkhedikâ pragñâpâramitâ (S. M.).
" 156 Sandhinirmokana-sûtra.
" 587 'Mahârthadharmaparyâya-sûtra (S. H.).'
" 1107 'Buddhâbhidharma-sûtra (V. H.).'
" 1139 'Vinaya-dvâvimsatividyâ-sâstra.'
" 1171 (2) 'Mahâyânasamparigraha-sâstra-vyâkhyâ (A. M.).'
" 1172 'Anâkârakintâragas (?)-sâstra.'
" 1183 Mahâyâna-samparigraha-sâstra.
" 1187 Ashṭâdasasûnyatâ-sâstra.
" 1209 'Sâstra on the Sûtra of Buddha's last teaching.'
" 1214 'Vidyâpravartana-sâstra.'
" 1217 'Vidyâdarsana (?)-sâstra.'
" 1219 'Tryakâra (or -alakshaṇa)-sâstra.'
" 1220 'Buddhagotra-sâstra.'
" 1235 'Vinirṇîtapiṭaka-sâstra.'
" 1239 Vidyâmâtrasiddhi-sâstra.
" 1248 Madhyânta-vibhâga-sâstra.
" 1252 Tarka-sâstra.
" 1253 'Ratnakaryârâgadharma (?)-sâstra.'
" 1255 'Sâstra of an explanation of the fist.'
" 1261 *K*aturasatya-sâstra (A. H.).
" 1269 Abhidharmakosa-sâstra.
" 1280 'Lakshaṇânusâra-sâstra.'
" 1284 'Ashṭâdasanikâya-sâstra.'
" 1285 'Sâstra on the difference of the principles of (Hînayâna) schools.'
" 1297 'Lokasthity (?)-abhidharma-sâstra.'
" 1299 'Mahâyânabhûmiguhyavâkâmûla-sâstra,' by Asvaghosha (A. M.).

No. 1300 'Suvarna-Saptati-'sâstra,' i. e. the Sâṅkhya-kârikâ with a vyâkhyâ (I. M.).
„ 1463 Life of Vasubandhu.

106 月婆首那 Yueh-pho-sheu-nâ, i. e. Upasûnya, who was the same person as No. 103 above. In A.D. 565 he translated one Sûtra in 7 fasciculi; the Sanskrit text of which was obtained by him from a Sramana of Kustana (Khoten), whom he met in China in A.D. 558. See Suh-sañ-kwhân, fasc. 1, fol. 21 b; Nêi-tien-lu, fasc. 5 a, fol. 12 a; Thu-ki, fasc. 4, fol. 11 a; Khâi-yuen-lu, fasc. 7, fol. 9 a; Beal, B. L. C., p. 27.

No. 9 Suvikrântavikrami-paripriKKhâ (S. M.).

107 須菩提 Su-phu-thi, i. e. Subhûti, whose name is translated 善現 Shân-hhien, lit. 'good-appearance,' or 善吉 Shân-ki, lit. 'good-lucky,' or 善業 Shân-yeh, lit. 'good-action.' He was a Sramana of Fu-nân or Bunan (Siam?), who translated the 'Mahâyânaratnamegha-sûtra,' in 8 fasciculi, but it was lost already in A.D. 730. See Suh-sañ-kwhân, fasc. 1, fol. 22 a; Nêi-tien-lu, fasc. 5 a, fol. 12 a; Thu-ki, fasc. 4, fol. 11 b; Khâi-yuen-lu, fasc. 7, fol. 10 a.

Summary of the preceding List of Translations made under the Khan dynasty, A.D. 557–589.

Translators.	Nêi-tien-lu.	Thu-ki.	Khâi-yuen-lu.	In existence.
No. 105	38	40	38	29
„ 106	1	1	1	1
„ 107	1	1	1	0
	40	42	40*	30

* In 133 fasciculi. In A.D. 730 there were 26 works in 89 fasciculi in existence, while 14 works in 44 fasciculi were already lost. See the Khâi-yuen-lu, fasc. 7, fol. 3 b.

北魏 Pe-wêi, or the Northern Wêi dynasty, of the 元 Yuen family, with its capital at 恆安 Hañ-ân, or 中山 Kuñ-shân, till A.D. 493, and then 洛陽 Lo-yâñ, A.D. 386–534.

108 釋惠覺 Shih Hwui-kiâo, or 曇覺 Thân-kiâo, a Chinese Sramana of 凉州 Liâñ-keu, who translated one work in 13 fasciculi, in A.D. 445. See Nêi-tien-lu, fasc. 4 b, fol. 25 b; Thu-ki, fasc. 3, fol. 10 a; Khâi-yuen-lu, fasc. 6, fol. 17 a.

No. 1322 Damamûka (-nidâna-sûtra I. M.).

109 釋曇曜 Shih Thân-yâo, a Sramana, whose native place is not known. In A.D. 462 he translated 2 or 3 works; but only one of them was in existence after A.D. 730. See Suh-sañ-kwhân, fasc. 1, fol. 11 a; Nêi-tien-lu, fasc. 4 b, fol. 18 a; Thu-ki, fasc. 3, fol. 10 a; Khâi-yuen-lu, fasc. 6, fol. 17 b.

No. 473. 'Mahâaryartharddhimantra-sûtra (S. M.).'

110 吉迦夜 Ki-kiâ-yê, i. e. Kiṅkara (?), whose name is translated 何事 Hö-sh', lit. 'what-matter.' He was a Sramana of the western region, who in A.D. 472 translated 5 works in 19 or 25 fasciculi, for the sake of Thân-yâo, No. 109 above. See Nêi-tien-lu, fasc. 4 b, fol. 19 a; Thu-ki, fasc. 3, fol. 10 b; Khâi-yuen-lu, fasc. 6, fol. 18 b.

No. 103 'Mahâvaipulya-bodhisattva-dasabhûmi-sûtra (S. M.).'
„ 402 Kusumasañkaya-sûtra.
„ 1257 'Upâyahridaya-sâstra (A. M.).'
„ 1329 'Samyuktaratnapitaka-sûtra (I. M.).'
„ 1340 A history of the Indian patriarchs.

111 曇摩流支 Thân-mo-liu-k', i. e. Dharmaruki, whose name is translated 法希 Fâ-hhi, lit. 'law-wishing,' or 法樂 Fâ-lö, lit. 'law-joy.' He was a Sramana of Southern India, who translated 3 works in 8 fasciculi, in A.D. 501, 504, and 507; but one of them was lost already in A.D. 730. See Suh-sañ-kwhân, fasc. 1, fol. 17 b; Nêi-tien-lu, fasc. 4 b, fol. 19 a; Thu-ki, fasc. 4, fol. 2 b; Khâi-yuen-lu, fasc. 6, fol. 19 b; Miñ-i-tsi, fasc. 3, fol. 12 b; Beal, B. L. C., p. 25.

No. 90 Sraddhâbaladhânâvatâramudrâ-sûtra (S. M.).
„ 245 Sarvabuddha-vishayâvatâra.

112 釋法場 Shih Fâ-khâñ, a Sramana, whose native place is not known. He translated one work in 1 fasciculus in A.D. 500–515. See the first four and the last authorities mentioned under No. 111 above.

No. 769 'Pien-i(-nâma)-sreshthiputra-paripriKKhâ (S. H.).'

113 勒那摩提 Lö-nâ-mo-thi, i. e. Ratnamati, or 婆提 Pho-ti, i. e. Mati, whose name is translated 寶意 Pâo-i, lit. 'jewel-thought.' He was a Sramana of Central India, who in A.D. 508 translated 3 or more works; but only 2 of them remained after A.D. 730. See the six authorities mentioned under No. 111 above.

No. 1233 Saddharmapundarika-sûtra-sâstra (A. M.).
„ 1236 Mahâyânottaratantra-sâstra.

114 菩提留(or 流)支 Phu-thi-liu (or liu)-*k*, i. e. Bodhiru*k*i, whose name is translated 道希 Tâo-hhi, lit. 'way-wishing,' or 覺希 *K*iâo-hhi, lit. 'intelligence-wishing.' He was a *S*ramana of Northern India, who arrived at Lo-yâṅ in A. D. 508, and till A. D. 535 he translated 30 or more works, of which 29 works were in existence in A. D. 730. See the six authorities mentioned under No. 111 above. There are 30 works in the Collection, namely:—

No. 11 Va*g*ra*kkh*edikâ pra*g*ñâpâramitâ (S. M.).
" 23 (41) Maitreya-pariprikkhâ-dharmâshta(ka ?).
" 176 Laṅkâvatâra-sûtra.
" 179 'Mahâsatya (?)-nirgranthaputra-vyâkarana-sûtra.'
" 189 Viseshakintâ-brahma-pariprikkhâ.
" 221 Anakshara-granthaka-rokanagarbha-sûtra.
" 239 Gayâsîrsha.
" 243 'Buddhatiraskriyâ (?)-sûtra.'
" 246 Sandhinirmokana-sûtra.
" 285 Bhavasaṅkrâmita (?).
" 286 'Mañgusrî-parikarana-sûtra.'
" 391 'Dharmaparyâya-sûtra.'
" 404 'Buddhanâma-sûtra.'
" 426 Dharmasaṅgîti-sûtra.
" 461 Kshamâvatî-vyâkarana-sûtra.
" 488 'Sarvabâlapâla-dhâranî.'
" 524 'Sûtra on neither increasing nor decreasing.'
" 1168 Va*g*ra*kkh*edikâ-sûtra-sâstra (A. M.).
" 1191 Gayâsîrsha-sûtra-tîkâ.
" 1193 Viseshakintâ-brâhmana-pariprikkhâ-sûtra-tîkâ.
" 1194 Dasabhûmika-sâstra.
" 1203 'Maitreyapariprikkhâ-sûtra-sâstra.'
" 1204 Aparimitâyus-sûtra-sâstra.
" 1211 Pratîtyasamutpâda-sâstra.
" 1232 Saddharmapundarîka-sûtra-sâstra.
" 1234 'Ratnakûta(-sûtra)-sâstra.'
" 1238 Vidyâmâtrâsiddhi(-sâstra).
" 1254 'Satâkshara-sâstra.'
" 1259 'Sâstra by the Bodhisattva Deva on the refutation of four heretical Hînayâna schools, mentioned in the Laṅkâvatâra-sûtra.'
" 1260 'Sâstra by the Bodhisattva Deva on the Nirvâna of the heretical Hînayâna schools, mentioned in the Laṅkâvatâra-sûtra.'

115 佛陀扇多 Fo-tho-shân-to, i. e. Buddhasânta, whose name is translated 覺定 *K*iâo-tiṅ, lit. 'intelligence-fixedness.' He was a *S*ramana of Central India, who translated 10 works in 10 or 11 fasciculi, in A. D. 524–538 or 539; but one of them was lost already in A. D. 730. Some of these translations were made under the Eastern Wêi dynasty, A. D. 534–550. See Suh-saṅ-*k*whân, fasc. 1, fol. 15 b; Nêi-tien-lu, fasc. 4 b, fol. 20 a; Thu-*k*i, fasc. 3, fol. 5 a; Khâi-yuen-lu, fasc. 6, fol. 27 b; Beal, B. L. C., p. 26.

No. 23 (9) Dasadharmaka (S. M.).
" 23 (31) Asokadattâ-vyâkarana.
" 262 Simhanâdika-sûtra.
" 271 'Rûpyavarnastrî-sûtra.'
" 274 'Supûgâ-sûtra.'
" 284 Bhavasaṅkrâmita (?).
" 357 Anantamukha-sâdhaka-dhâranî (?).
" 373 Va*g*ramantra (or -mandala or -manda)-dhâranî.
" 1184 Mahâyânasamparigraha-sâstra (A. M.).

SUMMARY OF THE PRECEDING LIST OF TRANSLATIONS MADE UNDER THE NORTHERN WÊI DYNASTY, A. D. 386–534.

Translators.	Nêi-tien-lu.	Thu-*k*i.	Khâi-yuen-lu.	In existence.
No. 108	1	1	1	1
" 109	2	2	3	1
" 110	5	5	5	5
" 111	3	3	3	2
" 112	1	1	1	1
" 113	6	5	3	2
" 114	49	39	30	30
" 115	10	10	10	9
	77	66	56*	51

* In 169 fasciculi. In A. D. 730 there were 50 works in 157 fasciculi in existence, while 6 works in 12 fasciculi were already lost. Cf. the Khâi-yuen-lu, fasc. 6, fol. 16 a seq.

東魏 Tuṅ-wêi, or the Eastern Wêi dynasty, of the 元 Yuen family, with its capital at 鄴 Yeh, A. D. 534–550.

116 瞿曇般若流支 *Kh*ü-thân Pân-zo-liu-*k*, i. e. Gautama Pra*g*ñâru*k*i, whose second or proper name is translated 智希 *K*'-hhi, lit. 'wisdom-wishing.' He was a Brâhmana of Vârânasî of Central India, who in A. D. 538–541 or 543 translated 14 or 18 works; of which 15 works in 89 fasciculi were in existence in A. D. 730. See Suh-saṅ-*k*whân, fasc. 1, fol. 16 a; Nêi-tien-lu, fasc. 4 b, fol. 23 b; Thu-*k*i, fasc. 4, fol. 9 a; Khâi-yuen-lu, fasc. 6, fol. 28 b; Beal, B. L. C., p. 26. There are 13 works in the Collection, namely:—

No. 45 Vimaladattâ-pariprikkhâ (S. M.).
" 60 Vyâsa-pariprikkhâ.
" 83 'Isvararâgapariprikkhâ.'
" 132 Niyatâniyatagati-mudrâvatâra.
" 210 Paramârthadharmavigaya-sûtra.
" 212 'Sarvadharmokkarâga-sûtra.'
" 390 Kanakavarna-pûrvayoga.
" 410 Ashtabuddhaka-sûtra.
" 679 Saddharmasmrityupasthâna-sûtra (S. H.).
" 770 'Vimala(nâma)-upâsikâ pariprikkhâ.'
" 1108 Pratimoksha-vinaya (V. H.).
" 1212 'Ekasloka-sâstra (A. M.).'
" 1246 'Madhyântânugama-sâstra.'

117 月婆首那 Yueh-pho-sheu-nâ, i. e. Upasûnya, who was the same person as Nos. 103 and 106 above. In A. D. 538–540 or 541 he translated 3 works in 7 fasciculi; but one of them was lost

already in A.D. 730. See Suh-sañ-*k*whân, fasc. 1, fol. 21 b; Nêi-tien-lu, fasc. 4 b, fol. 24 b; Thu-*k*i, fasc. 4, fol. 11 a; Khâi-yuen-lu, fasc. 6, fol. 30 b; Beal, B. L. C., p. 27.

No. 23 (23) Mahâkâsyapa-saṅgîti (S. M.).
„ 449 Saṅghâti-sûtra-dharmaparyâya.

118 毗目智仙 Phi-mu-*k*'-sien, i. e. Vimokshaprag*ñ*a *R*ishi, or Vimokshasena (?), a *S*rama*n*a of 烏長 Ö-*kh*âñ, i. e. Udyâna (?) of Northern India, who was a descendant of the *S*âkya family of Kapilavastu. In A.D. 541 he, together with Prag*ñ*âru*k*i, No. 116 above, translated 5 works in 5 fasciculi. See Nêi-tien-lu, fasc. 4 b, fol. 25 b; Khâi-yuen-lu, fasc. 6, fol. 31 a. But there are 6 works ascribed to him in the present Collection (of which the first work is mentioned under Prag*ñ*âru*k*i, in the Khâi-yuen-lu), namely:—

No. 48 Sushthitamatiparipri*kkh*â (S. M.).
„ 1196 'Tripûrnasûtropadesa (A. M.).'
„ 1205 'Dharma*k*akrapravartana-sûtropadesa.'
„ 1222 Karmasiddha-prakarana-sâstra.
„ 1241 'Ratna*k*û*d*a-sûtra-*k*aturdharmopadesa.'
„ 1251 'Vivâdasamana-sâstra (?).'

119 達磨菩提 Tâ-mo-phu-thi, i. e. Dharmabodhi, whose name is translated 法覺 Fâ-*k*iâo, lit. 'law-intelligence.' He was an Indian (?) *S*rama*n*a, who translated one work, but the exact date is not known. See Nêi-tien-lu, fasc. 4 b, fol. 25 b; Khâi-yuen-lu, fasc. 6, fol. 32 b.

No. 1206 'Mahâparinirvâna-sûtra-sâstra (A. M.).'

SUMMARY OF THE PRECEDING LIST OF TRANSLATIONS MADE UNDER THE EASTERN WÊI DYNASTY, A. D. 534–550.

Translators.	Nêi-tien-lu.	Thu-*k*i.	Khâi-yuen-lu.	In existence.
No. 116	14	14	18	13
„ 117	3	3	3	2
„ 118	5	0	5	6
„ 119	1	0	1	1
	23	17	27*	22

* In 105 fasciculi. In A.D. 730 there were 23 works in 101 fasciculi in existence, while 4 works in 4 fasciculi were already lost. See the Khâi-yuen-lu, fasc. 6, fol. 16 a seq.

北齊 Pe-tshi, or the Northern Tshi dynasty, of the 高 Kâo family, with its capital at Yeh, A.D. 550–577.

120 那連提黎耶舍 Nâ-lien-thi-li-ye-shö (or without the fourth character 'li'), i. e. Narendrayasas, whose name is translated 尊稱 Tsun-*kh*an, lit. 'honourable-fame.' He was a *S*rama*n*a of Udyâna of Northern India, who, together with Fâ-*k*', No. 126 below, translated 7 works in 51 or 52 fasciculi in A.D. 557–568. See Suh-sañ-*k*whân, fasc. 2, fol. 1 b; Nêi-tien-lu, fasc. 4 b, fol. 25 b; Thu-*k*i, fasc. 4, fol. 10 a; Khâi-yuen-lu, fasc. 6, fol. 33 a; Beal, B. L. C., p. 26.

No. 23 (16) Pitâ-putra-samâgama (S. M.).
„ 63 *K*andragarbha-vaipulya.
„ 66 Sumerugarbha.
„ 117 Mahâkaru*n*âpu*nd*arîka-sûtra.
„ 191 '*K*andradîpa-samâdhi-sûtra.'
„ 428 Pradîpadânîya-sûtra.
„ 1294 Abhidharma-h*ri*daya-sâstra (A. H.).

121 萬天懿 Wân Thien-i, whose original surname was 拓跋 To-poh, or Toba, which was changed into 萬俟 Wân-i, as one of ten subdivisions of the Toba family, i. e. that of the rulers of the Northern Wêi dynasty, and it was afterwards shortened into 萬 Wân. He was a Chinese G*ri*hapati or Upâsaka (layman), who translated one work in A.D. 562–564. See the first four authorities mentioned under No. 120 above.

No. 375 'Ârya-*g*ina (?)-bodhisattvaparipri*kkh*â (S. M.).'

SUMMARY OF THE PRECEDING LIST OF TRANSLATIONS MADE UNDER THE NORTHERN TSHI DYNASTY, A. D. 550–577.

Translators.	Nêi-tien-lu.	Thu-*k*i.	Khâi-yuen-lu.	In existence.
No. 120	7	7	7	7
„ 121	1	1	1	1
	8	8	8*	8

* In 52 fasciculi. Thus there have been 8 works in 52 fasciculi in existence since A.D. 730. See the Khâi-yuen-lu, fasc. 6, fol. 32 b.

北周 Pe-*k*eu, or the Northern *K*eu dynasty, of the 宇文 Yü-wan family, with its capital at 長安 *Kh*âñ-ân, A.D. 557–581.

122 攘那跋陀羅 *Z*âñ-nâ-poh-tho-lo, i. e. G*ñ*ânabhadra, whose name is translated 智賢 *K*'-hhien, lit. 'wisdom-wise.' He was a *S*rama*n*a of the country of 波頭摩 Po-theu-mo, i. e. Padma (?). In A.D. 558 he, together with G*ñ*ânayasas, No. 123 below, translated one sâstra on the Pa*ñk*avidyâ, or the five sciences, in 1 fasciculus; but it was lost already in

A. D. 730. See Suh-saṅ-*k*whân, fasc. 1, fol. 17 a; Nêi-tien-lu, fasc. 5 a, fol. 3 a; Thu-*k*i, fasc. 4, fol. 12 a; Khâi-yuen-lu, fasc. 7, fol. 1 b; Beal, B. L. C., p. 27.

123 闍那耶舍 Shö-nâ-ye-shö, i. e. *G*ñânayasas, whose name is translated 藏稱 Tsân-*kh*an, lit. 'concealed-fame,' or 勝名 Shan-miṅ, lit. 'excellent-name.' He was a *S*ramana of Magadha of Central India. In A. D. 564–572 he, together with his two disciples, Yasogupta and *G*ñânagupta, Nos. 124 and 125 below, translated 6 works in 15 or 17 fasciculi; but 2 of the works in 3 fasciculi only have been in existence since A. D. 730. For this and the following two translators, see the five authorities mentioned under No. 122 above.

No. 187 Mahâmegha-sûtra (S. M.).
„ 195 Mahâyânâbhisamaya-sûtra.

124 耶舍崛多 Ye-shö-*k*üê-to, i. e. Yasogupta, whose name is translated 稱藏 *Kh*an-tsâṅ, lit. 'fame-concealed.' He was a *S*ramana of the country or state of 優婆 Yiu-pho (?). In A. D. 561–578 he, together with his fellow-scholar *G*ñânagupta, No. 125 below, translated 3 or 4 works; but 2 of the works in 6 fasciculi only were in existence in A. D. 730. There is, however, only 1 work in the Collection, namely:—

No. 327 Avalokitesvaraikâdasamukha-dhâra*n*î (S. M.).

125 闍那崛多 Shö-nâ-*k*üê-to, i. e. *G*ñânagupta, whose name is translated 志德 *K*'-töh, lit. 'purpose (or secret)-virtue.' He was a *S*ramana of Gandhâra of Northern India. In A. D. 561–578 he translated 4 works in 5 fasciculi; but only 2 of the works in 2 fasciculi have been in existence since A. D. 730. See also Miṅ-i-tsi, fasc. 3, fol. 13 a.

No. 137 Gâthâs of the Avalokitesvara-samanta-mukha-parivarta (i. e. the 24th or 25th chapter) of the Saddharma-pu*n*darîka (S. M.).
„ 347 'Nânâ-samyuktamantra-sûtra.'

Summary of the preceding List of Translations made under the Northern *K*eu dynasty, A. D. 557–581.

Translators.	Nêi-tien-lu.	Thu-*k*i.	Khâi-yuen-lu.	In existence.
No. 122	1	1	1	0
„ 123	6	6	6	2
„ 124	3	4	3	1
„ 125	4	4	4	1
	14	15	14*	4

* In 29 fasciculi. In A. D. 730 there were 6 works in 11 fasciculi in existence, while 8 works in 18 fasciculi were already lost. See the Khâi-yuen-lu, fasc. 7, fol. 1 a.

隋 The Sui dynasty, of the 楊 Yâṅ family, with its capital at *Kh*âṅ-ân or 大興 Tâ-hhiṅ, A. D. 589 (or 581)–618.

126 瞿曇達摩闍那 *Kh*ü-thân Tâ-mo-shö-nâ, or 達摩般若 Tâ-mo-pân-zo, or 達摩波若 Tâ-mo-po-zo, i. e. Gautama Dharma*g*ñâna, or -pra*g*ña, whose name is translated 法智 Fâ-*k*', lit. 'law-wisdom.' He was an Upâsaka of Vârâ*n*asî of Central India, and was the eldest son of the Brâhmana Pra*g*ñâru*k*i, No. 116 above. After the destruction of the Northern Tshi dynasty (which took place in A. D. 577) he was appointed by the Northern *K*eu dynasty as the governor of the 洋川 Yâṅ-sen district; so that he is more commonly called 曇法智 Thân Fâ-*k*', as his surname and cognomen, after the Chinese style. In A. D. 582, Wan-ti, the first Emperor of the Sui dynasty (who in A. D. 581 succeeded the Northern *K*eu dynasty, but did not become the sole ruler of China till A. D. 589, when the *Kh*an dynasty was destroyed by him), called back Dharmapra*g*ña or Thân Fâ-*k*' to the capital, where he translated one work. See Suh-saṅ-*k*whân, fasc. 2, fol. 10 a; Nêi-tien-lu, fasc. 5 a, fol. 16 a; Thu-*k*i, fasc. 4, fol. 14 b; Khâi-yuen-lu, fasc. 7, fol. 11 a; Beal, B. L. C., p. 27.

No. 739 'Sûtra on difference of the results of actions (S. H.).'

127 毗尼多流支 Phi-ni-to-liu-*k*', i. e. Vinitaru*k*i, whose name is translated 滅喜 Mieh-hhi, lit. 'destruction-joy.' He was a *S*ramana of Udyâna of Northern India, who in A. D. 582 translated 2 works. See the last four authorities mentioned under No. 126 above.

No. 240 Gayâsîrsha-sûtra (S. M.).
„ 253 'Mahâyânavaipulya-dhâra*n*î-sûtra.'

128 那連提黎耶舍 Nâ-lien-thi-li-ye-shö, i. e. Narendrayasas, who was the same person as No. 120 above. In A. D. 582–585 he translated 8 works in 23 or 28 fasciculi. He died in A. D. 589. See the Suh-saṅ-*k*whân, fasc. 2, fol. 1 b; Nêi-tien-lu, fasc. 5 a, fol. 17 a; Thu-*k*i, fasc. 4, fol. 10 a; Khâi-yuen-lu, fasc. 7, fol. 12 a; Beal, B. L. C., p. 26.

No. 62 Sûryagarbha-sûtra (S. M.).
„ 185 Ma*ñg*usrî-vikrîdita-sûtra.
„ 188 Mahâmegha-sûtra.
„ 232 *S*rîgupta-sûtra.

No. 409 'Balavyûha-samâdhi-sûtra.'
„ 411 'Sata-buddhanâma-sûtra.'
„ 465 'Padmamukha (?)-sûtra.'
„ 525 'Sthiradhi (?)-sûtra.'

129 闍那崛多 Shê-nâ-khüe-to, i. e. Gñânagupta, who was the same person as No. 125 above. In A. D. 585–592 he translated 39 works in 192 fasciculi, of which 2 works in 14 fasciculi were lost already in A. D. 730. He died in his seventy-eighth year, in A. D. 600. See Suh-sań-kwhân, fasc. 2, fol. 5 a; Nêi-tien-lu, fasc. 5 a, fol. 20 a; Thu-ki, fasc. 4, fol. 13 a; Khâi-yuen-lu, fasc. 7, fol. 14 b; Beal, B. L. C., p. 27. There are 36 works ascribed to him in the Collection, namely:—

No. 23 (18) Râshtrapâla-paripriKkhâ (S. M.).
„ 23 (39) Bhadrapâla-sreshthi-paripriKkhâ.
„ 37 Âdyâsaya-saṅkoda.
„ 51 Ratnakûta-sûtra.
„ 67 Âkâsagarbha-sûtra.
„ 75 Mahâvaipulya-mahâsannipâta-bhadrapâla-sûtra.
„ 78 'Mahâsannipâtâvadânarâga-sûtra.'
„ 91 Tathâgatagunagñânâkintyavishayâvatâra-nirdesa.
„ 121 Katurdâraka-samâdhi-sûtra.
„ 130 Two chapters of the Suvarnaprabhâsa-sûtra.
„ 139 Saddharmapundarika (with additional chapters or sections).
„ 163 Sarvadharma-pravritti-nirdesa-sûtra.
„ 181 Vimalakirtti-nirdesa.
„ 186 Mahâmegha-sûtra.
„ 211 Paramârthadharmavigaya-sûtra.
„ 268 'Sûtra on good qualities of rare comparison.'
„ 275 'Supûgyâ-sûtra.'
„ 287 'Mañgusri-parikarana-sûtra.'
„ 302 Ashtabuddhaka.
„ 312 Amoghapâsa-dhâranî.
„ 335 Dvâdasabuddhaka-sûtra.
„ 359 Anantamukha-sâdhaka-dhâranî (?).
„ 366 'Lokapâla-dhâranî.'
„ 367 Saptabuddhaka-sûtra.
„ 372 Vagramantra (or -mandala, or -manda)-dhâranî.
„ 408 'Pañkasahasra-pañkasata-buddhanâma-mantra-sûtra.'
„ 412 'Akintyaguna-sarvabuddha-parigraha-sûtra.'
„ 422 'Mahâdharmolkâ-dhâranî-sûtra.'
„ 423 'Mahâbaladharmika-dhâranî-sûtra.'
„ 424 'Sarvadharmakaryâ-dhyâna (?)-sûtra.'
„ 439 'Akiñkana (?)-bodhisattva-sûtra.'
„ 441 Kandrottarâ-dârikâ-vyâkarana-sûtra.
„ 450 'Utpâdita-bodhikitta-sûtra.'
„ 507 'Sarvadharmânuttararâga-sûtra.'
„ 519 'Banikpati (?)-devaputra-sûtra.'
„ 680 Buddhakaritra (S. H.).

130 菩提登 Phu-thî-tań, i. e. Bodhitań (?), a foreign Sramana, who translated one work, but the exact date is not known. See Nêi-tien-lu, fasc. 5 b, fol. 7 a; Khâi-yuen-lu, fasc. 7, fol. 24 b.

No. 464 'Sûtra on the consideration by divination about the results of good and bad actions (S. M.).'

131 達摩笈多 Tâ-mo-kiu-to, i. e. Dharmagupta, whose name is translated 法密 Fâ-mi, lit. 'law-secret,' or 法藏 Fâ-tsâń, lit. 'law-repository.' He was a Sramana of the 羅邏 Lo-lo country or state of Southern India. He translated several works in A. D. 590–616, and died in A. D. 619. See Suh-sań-kwhân, fasc. 8, fol. 10 b (where 7 works in 32 fasciculi are ascribed to him); Nêi-tien-lu, fasc. 5 a, fol. 10 (7 works in 23 fasciculi); Thu-ki, fasc. 4, fol. 15 a (18 works in 81 fasciculi); Khâi-yuen-lu, fasc. 7, fol. 26 b (9 works in 46 fasciculi, all of them were in existence in A. D. 730); Miń-i-tsi, fasc. 3, fol. 13 a; Beal, B. L. C., p. 27. There are 10 works in the Collection, namely:—

No. 15 VagrakkhedikâA pragñâpâramitâ (S. M.).
„ 23 (36) Sushthitamati-paripriKkhâ.
„ 72 Mahâvaipulya-mahâsannipâta-bodhisattva-buddhânusmriti-samâdhi.
„ 141 'Nidâna-sûtra.'
„ 170 Bheshagyaguru-pûrvapranidhâna.
„ 549 'Sûtra on the original cause of raising the world (? S. H.).'
„ 1167 Vagrakkhedikâ-sûtra-sâstra (A. M.).
„ 1171 (3) 'Mahâyânasamparigraha-sâstra-vyâkhyâ.'
„ 1181 'Sâstra on the provision for obtaining Bodhi.'
„ 1227 'Nidâna-sâstra.'

Summary of the preceding List of Translations made under the Sui dynasty, A. D. 589–618.

Translators.	Nêi-tien-lu.	Thu-ki.	Khâi-yuen-lu.	In existence.
No. 126	1	1	1	1
„ 127	2	2	2	2
„ 128	8	8	8	8
„ 129	37	31	39	36
„ 130	1	0	1	1
„ 131	7	18	9	10
	56	60	60*	58

* In 265 fasciculi. In A. D. 730 there were 60 works in 251 fasciculi in existence, while 2 works in 14 fasciculi were already lost. Cf. the Khâi-yuen-lu, fasc. 7, fol. 10 b seq.

唐 The Thâń dynasty, of the 李 Li family, with its capital at Khâń-ân, A. D. 618–907.

132 波羅頗迦羅蜜多羅 Po-lo-pho-kiâ-lo-mi-to-lo, or without the fourth and fifth characters 'kiâ-lo,' i. e. Prabhâkaramitra, or Prabhâmitra, whose name is translated 作明知識 Tso-miń-k'-shi, lit. 'making-bright-knowing-knowledge,' or shortly 明友 Miń-yiu, lit. 'bright-friend;' or 波頗 Po-pho, i. e. the first and third

characters of the fuller transliteration above mentioned, so that it is merely a short form of the same Sanskrit name transliterated, but it is translated differently, 光智 Kwân-k', lit. 'light-wisdom.' He was a *S*ramana of Central India, and a Kshatriya by caste. In A. D. 627 he arrived in China, and translated 3 works in 35 or 38 fasciculi, and died in his sixty-ninth year, in A. D. 633. See Suh-san-*k*whân, fasc. 3, fol. 1 a; Nêi-tien-lu, fasc. 5 b, fol. 15 a; Thu-*k*i, fasc. 4, fol. 16 b; Khâi-yuen-lu, fasc. 8 a, fol. 3 a; Miṅ-i-tsi, fasc. 3, fol. 13 b; Beal, B. L. C., p. 28.

No. 84 'Ratnatârâ-dhâranî-sûtra (S. M.).'
„ 1185 Pragñâpradîpa-sâstra-*t*îkâ (A. M.).
„ 1190 Sûtrâlaṅkâra-*t*îkâ.

133 釋玄奘 Shih Hhüen-*k*wâṅ (Hiouen-thsang), whose original surname and cognomen were 陳禕 *Kh*an I. He was a Chinese *S*ramana of 洛陽 Lo-yâṅ of 河南 Ho-nân, who received his ordination at 成都 *Kh*aṅ-tu, in A. D. 622. In A. D. 629 he started from China on his well-known journey towards India. On the twenty-fourth day of the first month of the nineteenth year of the 貞觀 *K*an-kwân period, A. D. 645, he returned to the capital of China. From the same year till his death, he diligently translated 75 different works in 1335 fasciculi. On the fourth day of the second month of the first year of the 麟德 Lin-töh period, A. D. 664, he died in his sixty-fifth year. See Suh-san-*k*whân, fasc. 4, fol. 1 a—fasc. 5, fol. 20 b (where 73 works in 1330 fasciculi are ascribed to him); Nêi-tien-lu, fasc. 5 b, fol. 19 a (65 works in 1308 fasciculi); Thu-*k*i, fasc. 4, fol. 17 a; Khâi-yuen-lu, fasc. 8 a, fol. 12 a—fasc. 8 b, fol. 17 a (both ascribe to him 75 works in 1235, or 1245, or 1335 fasciculi); Miṅ-i-tsi, fasc. 3, fol. 13 b; Beal, B. L. C., p. 28. See also the Tâ-thâṅ-si-yu-*k*i, No. 1503, and Tâ-tshz'-an-sz'-sân-tsâṅ-fâ-sh'-*k*whân, No. 1494, i. e. a life of Hiouen-thsang, by Hwui-li and Yen-tsuṅ. There are 75 works still in existence in the Collection, namely:—

No. 1 Mahâpragñâpâramitâ-sûtra (S. M.).
„ 13 Vagra*kkh*edikâ pragñâpâramitâ.
„ 20 Pragñâpâramitâ-hridaya-sûtra.
„ 23 (12) Bodhisattva-pitaka.
„ 64 Dasa*k*akra-kshitigarbha.
„ 95 'Anantabuddhakshetraguna-nirdesa-sûtra.
„ 123 Mahâparinirvâna.
„ 140 'Nidâna-sûtra.'
„ 149 Vimalakîrtti-nirdesa.
„ 171 Bheshagyaguru-vaidûryaprabhâsa-pûrvapranidhâna.
„ 199 Sukhâvatîvyûha (short).
„ 247 Sandhinirmo*k*ana-sûtra.
„ 249 Râgâvavâdaka.

No. 261 Adbhuta-dharmaparyâya.
„ 269 'Sûtra on the greatest incomparableness.'
„ 276 'Mahâyânagunastuti-sûtra.'
„ 279 Pratîtyasamutpâda-sûtra (?).
„ 316 Amoghapâsa-hridaya.
„ 328 Avalokitesvaraikâdasamukha-dhâranî.
„ 330 'Pa*ñk*amantra-sûtra.'
„ 361 'Subâhumudrâdhvagadhâranî-sûtra.'
„ 489 Buddha-hridaya-dhâranî.
„ 490 'Duhkhonmûlana-dhâranî.'
„ 491 'Ashtanâmasamantaguhya-dhâranî.'
„ 492 Vasudhara-dhâranî.
„ 493 Shanmukhî-dhâranî.
„ 502 Buddhabhûmi.
„ 522 Prasântavinis*k*aya-pratihârya-samâdhi-sûtra.
„ 528 'Sûtra on the merits produced from keeping the names of seven Buddhas.'
„ 628 'Nidâna-sûtra (S. H.).'
„ 714 'Itivritta-sûtra.'
„ 753 'Deva-paripri*kkh*â.'
„ 1097 'Bodhisattva-karman (V. M.).'
„ 1098 'Bodhisattva-pratimoksha.'
„ 1170 Saptadasabhûmi-sâstra-yogâ*k*ârya-bhûmi (A. M.).
„ 1171 (1) 'Mahâyânasamparigraha-sâstra-vyâkhyâ,' by Wu-siṅ.
„ 1171 (4) 'Mahâyânasamparigraha-sâstra-vyâkhyâ,' by Vasubandhu.
„ 1173 'Âlambanapratyaya-dhyâna-sâstra.'
„ 1176 Pa*ñk*askandhaka-sâstra.
„ 1177 'Âryavâ*k*âprakarana (?)-sâstra.'
„ 1178 'Mahâyânâbhidharmasamyukta-saṅgîti-sâstra.'
„ 1189 *S*atasâstra-vaipulya.
„ 1195 Buddhabhûmi-sûtra-sâstra.
„ 1197 Vidyâmâtrasiddhi(-sâstra).
„ 1198 '*S*ata-sâstra-vaipulya-vyâkhyâ.'
„ 1199 Mahâyânâbhidharmasaṅgîti-sâstra.
„ 1200 'Râgadharmanyâya-sâstra.'
„ 1201 Yogâ*k*âryabhûmi-sâstra-kârikâ (or vyâkhyâ).
„ 1202 'Âryavâ*k*âprakarana (?)-sâstra-kârikâ.'
„ 1213 'Mahâyânasatadharmavidyâmukha-sâstra.'
„ 1215 Vidyâmâtrasiddhi-tridasa-sâstra-kârikâ (thirty verses).
„ 1216 Nyâyapravesatâraka-sâstra.
„ 1221 Karmasiddhaprakarana-sâstra.
„ 1224 Nyâyadvâratâraka-sâstra.
„ 1237 'Mahâyânatâlaratna-sâstra.'
„ 1240 Vidyâmâtrasiddhi-sâstra (with twenty verses).
„ 1244 Madhyântavibhâga-sâstra.
„ 1245 Madhyântavibhâga-grantha.
„ 1247 'Mahâyânasamparigraha-sâstramûla.'
„ 1263 Abhidharma-mahâvibhâshâ-sâstra (A. H.).
„ 1265 Nyâyânusâra-sâstra.
„ 1266 Abhidharma-prakarana-sâsana-sâstra.
„ 1267 Abhidharma-kosa-sâstra.
„ 1270 Abhidharma-kosa-kârikâ.
„ 1275 Abhidharma-*g*ñânaprasthâna-sâstra.
„ 1276 Abhidharma-saṅgîtiparyâya-pâda.
„ 1277 Abhidharma-prakarana-pâda.
„ 1281 Abhidharma-vigñânakâya-pâda.
„ 1282 Abhidharma-dhâtukâya-pâda.
„ 1283 'Pa*ñk*avastu-vibhâshâ-sâstra.'
„ 1286 '*S*âstra on the Dharma*k*akra of different schools.'
„ 1291 'Abhidharmâvatâra-sâstra.'
„ 1295 'Vaiseshikanikâya-dasapadârtha-sâstra.'

No. 1296 Abhidharma-skandha-pâda.
„ 1466 'Record on the duration of the law, spoken by the great Arhat Nandimitra (I. M.).'

134 釋智通 Shih K'-thuṅ, whose original surname was 趙 Kâo. He was a Chinese Sramana, who translated 4 works in 5 fasciculi; one in 2 fasciculi in the Kan-kwân period, A. D. 627–649, and the rest in A. D. 653. See Suh-thu-ki, fol. 1 a; Khâi-yuen-lu, fasc. 8 b, fol. 19 a; Suṅ-saṅ-kwhân, fasc. 3, fol. 1 a.

No. 318 Nîlakantha (S. M.).
„ 325 'Avalokitesvara-bodhisattva-(saman)tabhadrânuhridaya (?)-dhâranî.'
„ 329 'Sahasrapravartana-dhâranî.'
„ 494 'Samantabhadra-dhâranî.'

135 伽梵達摩 Kiê-fân-tâ-mo, i. e. Bhagavaddharma (?), whose name is translated 尊法 Tsun-fâ, lit. 'honourable law.' He was a Sramana of Western India, who translated one work; but the exact date is not known. See Suh-thu-ki, fol. 1 b; Khâi-yuen-lu, fasc. 8 b, fol. 20 a; Miṅ-i-tsi, fasc. 3, fol. 14 a.

No. 320 'Sahasrabâhu-sahasrâksha-avalokitesvara-bodhisattva-mahâpûrnâpratihata-mahâkârunikahridaya-dhâranî (S. M.).'

136 阿地瞿多 Ô-ti-khü-to, i. e. Atigupta (?), whose name is translated 無極高 Wu-ki-kâo, lit. 'without-limit-height.' He was a Sramana of Central India, who arrived in China in A. D. 652, and in the following two years he translated one work. See the three authorities mentioned under No. 135 above, and also Suṅ-saṅ-kwhân, fasc. 2, fol. 15 b.

No. 363 'Dhâranî-saṅgraha-sûtra (S. M.).'

137 那提 Nâ-thi, i. e. Nadi, or 布如烏伐耶 Pu-zo-u-poh-ye, i. e. Punyopâya (?), which latter name is translated 福生 Fu-shan, lit. 'happiness-producing.' He was a Sramana of Central India, who arrived in China in A. D. 655, bringing with him a collection of more than 1500 different texts or copies of the Tripitaka of both the Mahâyâna and Hînayâna schools. He made this collection in travelling throughout India and Ceylon. In A. D. 656 he was sent by the Chinese Emperor to the country of 崑崙 Kwhun-lun, i. e. Pulo Condore Island in the China Sea (see Wells Williams' Dict. p. 494, col. 1), to find some strange medicine. Having returned to China in A. D. 663, he translated 3 works in 3 fasciculi, one of them was lost already in A. D. 730. See Suh-saṅ-kwhân, fasc. 5, fol. 20 b; Suh-thu-ki, fol. 2 a; Khâi-yuen-lu, fasc. 9, fol. 1 a; Miṅ-i-tsi, fasc. 3, fol. 14 b.

No. 462 'Simhavyûharâga-bodhisattva-pariprikkhâ (S. M.).'
„ 521 'Vimalagñâna-bodhisattva-pariprikkhâ.'

138 若那跋陀羅 Zo-nâ-poh-tho-lo, i. e. Gñânabhadra, whose name is translated 智賢 K'-hhien, lit. 'wisdom-wise.' He was a Sramana of the country of 波陵 Po-liâṅ, or 訶陵 Hö-liâṅ of the South Sea. In the 麟德 Lin-töh period, A. D. 664–665, the Chinese Sramana 會寧 Hwui-niṅ passed that country on his journey to India, and together with Gñânabhadra translated one work. See Suh-thu-ki, fol. 3 b; Khâi-yuen-lu, fasc. 9, fol. 2 b; Suṅ-saṅ-kwhân, fasc. 2, fol. 11 b.

No. 115 'A latter part of the Mahâparinirvâna-sûtra (S. M.).'

139 地婆訶羅 Ti-pho-hö-lo, i. e. Divâkara, whose name is translated 日照 Zih-kâo, lit. 'sun-shining.' He was a Sramana of Central India, who translated 18 works in 34 fasciculi, in A. D. 676–688. See Suh-thu-ki, fol. 3 b; Khâi-yuen-lu, fasc. 9, fol. 3 a; Suṅ-saṅ-kwhân, fasc. 2, fol. 18 a; Miṅ-i-tsi, fasc. 3, fol. 14 b. But there are now 19 works ascribed to him in the Collection, namely:—

No. 53 Bhadrapâla-sreshthi-pariprikkhâ (S. M.).
„ 101 'A continuation of the Dharmadhâtvavatârâdhyâya of the Buddhâvatamsakavaipulya-sûtra.'
„ 159 Lalita-vistara.
„ 196 Mahâyânâbhisamaya-sûtra.
„ 222 Anakshara-granthaka-rokanagarbha-sûtra.
„ 223 „ „ „
„ 263 Simhanâdika-sûtra.
„ 264 Mañgusrî-pariprikkhâ.
„ 265 „ „
„ 266 Katushka-nirhâra-sûtra.
„ 267 „ „
„ 332 'Trimantra-sûtra.'
„ 344 Kundî-devî-dhâranî.
„ 351 Sarvadurgatiparisodhana-ushnîsha-vigaya-dhâranî.
„ 352 „ „ „
„ 444 Ghanavyûha-sûtra.
„ 523 'Kaityakaranaguna-sûtra.'
„ 1175 Pañkaskandhavaipulya-sâstra (A. M.).
„ 1192 'Vagrakkhedikâ-sûtra-sâstra, etc.'

140 杜行顗 Tu Hhiṅ-i, a Chinese Upâsaka (layman), who was an official at the Foreign Office, and translated one work in A. D. 679. See Suh-thu-ki, fol. 5 a; Khâi-yuen-lu, fasc. 9, fol. 5 a.

No. 349 Sarvadurgatiparisodhana-ushnîsha-vigaya-dhâranî (S. M.).

141 佛陀多羅 Fo-tho-to-lo, i. e. Buddhatrâta, whose name is translated 覺救 Kiâo-kiu,

lit. 'intelligence-saving.' He was a *S*ramana of Kubhâ (Cabul), who translated one work; but the exact date is not known. See Suh-thu-*k*i, fol. 5 b; Khâi-yuen-lu, fasc. 9 fol. 8 a; Sun-san-*k*whân, fasc. 2, fol. 13 a; Miṅ-i-tsi, fasc. 3, fol. 14 b.

No. 42[illegible] 'Mahâvaipulya-pûrnabuddha-sûtra-prasannârtha-sûtra (S. M.).'

142 佛陀波利 Fo-tho-po-li, i.e. Buddhapâla, whose name is translated 覺護 *K*iâo-hu, lit. 'intelligence-protection.' He was a *S*ramana of Kubhâ (Cabul), who arrived in China in A.D. 676, and translated one work. See the four authorities mentioned under No. 141 above.

No. 348 Sarvadurgatiparisodhana-ushnisha-vigaya-dhâranî (S.M.).

143 提雲般若 Thi-yun-pân-*z*o, or 提曇陀若那 Thi-thân-tho-*z*o-nâ, i.e. Devapragña, whose name is translated 天智 Thien-*k*', lit. 'heaven or god-wisdom.' He was a *S*ramana of Kustana (Khoten), who translated 6 works in 7 fasciculi in A.D. 689–691. See the first three authorities mentioned under No. 141 above. There are now 8 works ascribed to him, namely:—

No. 94 'A part on the practice of compassion, in the Buddhâvatamsakavaipulya-sûtra (S. M.).'
" 96 'A part on the Akintya-vishaya,' in the same Sûtra as before.
" 288 Tathâgata-pratibimba-pratishthânusamsâ.
" 495 Sarvabuddhâṅgavatî-dhâranî.
" 496 Gñânolkâ-dhâranî-sarvadurgati-parisodhanî.
" 1258 'Mahâyânadharmadhâtvanantara-sâstra (A. M.).'
" 13[illegible]8 " "

144 釋慧智 Shih Hwui-*k*', a *S*ramana, whose father was an Indian, a Brâhmana by caste, and who was born in China while his father was staying there as an envoy. In A.D. 692 Hwui-*k*' translated one work. See the first three authorities mentioned under No. 141 above.

No. 1077 'Avalokitesvara-bodhisattva-stotra (S.M.).'

145 實叉難陀 Shih-*k*ha-nân-tho, or 施乞叉難陀 *K*'-*k*i-*k*hâ-nân-tho, i.e. *S*ikshânanda, whose name is translated 學喜 Hhio-hhi, lit. 'learning-joy.' He was a *S*ramana of Kustana (Khoten). In A.D. 695–700 he translated 19 works in 107 fasciculi, of which 5 works in 5 fasciculi were lost already in A.D. 730. He died in his fifty-ninth year, in A.D. 710. See Suh-thu-*k*i, fol. 8 a; Khâi-yuen-lu, fasc. 9, fol. 11 a; Sun-san-*k*whân, fasc. 2, fol. 17 a; Miṅ-i-tsi, fasc. 3, fol. 15 a. There are now 16 works ascribed to him in the Collection, namely:—

No. 23 (15) Mañgusrî-buddhakshetragunavyûha (S. M.).
" 88 Buddhâvatamsaka-mahâvaipulya-sûtra.
" 93 Tathâgatagunagñânâkintyavishayâvatâra-nirdesa.
" 97 'Mahâvaipulya-tathâgatâkintyavishaya-sûtra.'
" 98 'Mahâvaipulya-samantabhadra-nirdesa.'
" 177 Laṅkâvatâra-sûtra.
" 321 Padmakintâmani-dhâranî-sûtra.
" 362 'Subâhumudrâdhvaga-dhâranî.'
" 458 Kaitya-pradakshina-gâthâ.
" 503 'Satasahasramudrâ-dhâranî.'
" 520 Katushka-nirhâra-sûtra.
" 539 'Gvâlâmukha-preta-paritrâna-dhâranî.'
" 540 'Amrita-sûtra-dhâranî.'
" 1003 'Kshitigarbha-bodhisattva-pûrvapranidhâna-sûtra.'
" 1100 'Dasabhadrakarmamârga-sûtra (V. M.).'
" 1249 'Mahâyânasraddhotpâda-sâstra (A. M.).'

146 李無諂 Li Wu-thâo, a Brâhmana of the country or state of 嵐波 Lân-po, of Northern India, who translated one work in A.D. 700. See Suh-thu-*k*i, fol. 9 b; Khâi-yuen-lu, fasc. 9, fol. 13 b.

No. 314 'Amoghapâsa-dhâranî (S. M.).'

147 彌陀山 Mi-tho-shân, i.e. Mitrasânta (?), whose name is translated 寂友 Tsbi-yiu, lit. 'calm-friend.' He was a *S*ramana of the country of 覩貨邏 Tu-kwa-lo, i.e. Tukhâra, who translated one work in about A.D. 705. See the first two authorities mentioned under No. 146 above, and also Sun-san-*k*whân, fasc. 2, fol. 20 a.

No. 380 'Vimalasuddhaprabhâsa-mahâdhâranî (S. M.).'

148 阿儞眞那 Ô-ni-*k*an-nâ, i.e. Ratna*k*inta, whose name is translated 寶思惟 Pâo-sz'-wêi, lit. 'jewel-thinking-considering.' He was a *S*ramana of 迦濕彌羅 *K*iâ-shi-mi-lo, i.e. Kasmîra (Cashmere), of Northern India, who translated 7 works in 9 fasciculi in A.D. 693–706. He died in A.D. 721, when he was more than 100 years old. See the three authorities referred to under No. 147 above.

No. 293 'Pratibimbâbhishiktaguna-sûtra (S. M.).'
" 295 'Sûtra on counting the good qualities of a rosary.'
" 313 'Amoghapâsa-hridaya-mantrarâga-sûtra.'
" 322 Padmakintâmani-dhâranî-sûtra.
" 333 'Ekâkshara-dhâranî.'
" 497 'Sûtra on the Dhâranî-riddhimantra of great freedom to be obtained as soon as one wishes for it.'
" 541 'Ekâksharahridaya-mantra.'

149 釋義淨 Shih I-tsing, whose original surname was 張 *Kh*âṅ, and who had the literary appellation of 文明 Wan-miṅ. He was a Chinese *S*ramana of 范陽 Fân-yâṅ, of 齊州 Tshi-*k*eu. In A.D. 671 he started from China on his voyage

towards India, and travelled through more than thirty countries, and returned to China in A.D. 695. He brought with him nearly 400 different Sanskrit texts, equal to 500,000 slokas, and some relics. In A.D. 700–712 he translated 56 works in 230 fasciculi; some of them were made at an earlier date. In A.D. 713 he died in his seventy-ninth year. See Suh-thu-*k*i, fol. 11 a; Khâi-yuen-lu, fasc. 9, fol. 16 b; Suṅ-saṅ-*k*whân, fasc. 1, fol. 6 a; Miṅ-i-tsi, fasc. 3, fol. 15 b; Beal, B. L. C., p. 28.

No. 14 Vagrakkhedikâ pragñâpâramitâ (S. M.).
„ 23 (14) Garbha-sûtra (?).
„ 126 Suvarnaprabhâsottamarâga-sûtra.
„ 131 Niyatâniyatagati-mudrâvatâra.
„ 172 Saptatathâgata-pûrvapranidhâna-viseshavistara.
„ 207 Maitreya-vyâkarana.
„ 250 Râgâvavâdaka.
„ 294 'Pratibimbâbhishiktaguna-sûtra.'
„ 296 'Sûtra on counting the good qualities of a rosary.'
„ 306 Mahâmayûrî-vidyârâgñî.
„ 323 Padmak ntâmani-dhârani-sûtra.
„ 334 'Ekâkshara-mantrarâga-sûtra.'
„ 336 Dvâdasabuddhaka-dhâranî.
„ 350 Sarvadurgatiparisodhana-ushnisha-vigaya-dhâranî.
„ 457 Sâgara-nâgarâga-paripṛikkhâ.
„ 459 'Suvarna(varna)râga-nidâna-sûtra.'
„ 498 Sarvadharmagunavyûharâga.
„ 499 'Sûtra on the Mantra-râga of uprooting and removing sin and obstacles.'
„ 500 Bhadrakâ-râtrî.
„ 504 Sarvatathâgatâdhishthânasattvâvalokana-buddhakshetrasandarsana-vyûharâga-sûtra.
„ 505 'Gandharâga-bodhisattva-dhâranî.'
„ 526 Bhavasaṅkrâmita (or -krânti)-sûtra.
„ 634 'Sarvapañkaskandhasûnyatâ-sûtra (S. H.).'
„ 658 'Dharmakakrapravartana-sûtra.'
„ 727 'Anitya-sûtra.'
„ 728 'Ashtâkshana-kshana-sûtra.'
„ 734 Dîrghanakha-parivrâgaka-paripṛikkhâ.
„ 735 'Avadâna-sûtra.'
„ 737 'Sûtra on an abridged instruction.'
„ 738 'Sûtra on curing diseases of the anus.'
„ 1110 Mûlasarvâstivâda-vinaya-sûtra (V. H.).
„ 1118 Mûlasarvâstivâda-vinaya.
„ 1121 Mûlasarvâstivâda-samyukta-vastu.
„ 1123 Mûlasarvâstivâda-saṅghabhedaka-vastu.
„ 1124 Mûlasarvâstivâda-bhikshunî-vinaya.
„ 1127 Mûlasarvâstivâda-vinaya-saṅgraha.
„ 1131 Mûlasarvâstivâda-ekasatakarman.
„ 1133 Mûlasarvâstivâda-nidâna.
„ 1134 Mûlasarvâstivâda-mâtrikâ.
„ 1140 Mûlasarvâstivâda-vinayanidânamâtrikâ-gâthâ.
„ 1141 Mûlasarvâstivâda-vinayasamyuktavastu-gâthâ.
„ 1143 Mûlasarvâstivâda-vinaya-gâthâ.
„ 1149 Mûlasarvâstivâda-bhikshunî-vinaya-sûtra.
„ 1174 'Âlambanapratyayadhyâna-sâstra-vyâkhyâ (A. M.).'
„ 1208 'Vagrakkhedikâ-sûtra-sâstra-gâthâ.'
„ 1210 'Vidyâmâtrasiddhiratnagâti-sâstra.'
„ 1223 Nyâyadvâratâraka-sâstra.
„ 1225 'Samatha-vipasyanâ-dvâra-sâstra-gâthâ.'
No. 1226 'Hastadanda-sâstra.'
„ 1228 'Pragñapti-hetusaṅgraha (?)-sâstra.'
„ 1229 'Sarvalakshanadhyâna-sâstra-gâthâ.'
„ 1230 'Shaddvâropadishtadhyânavyavahâra-sâstra.'
„ 1231 Vagrakkhedikâ-pragñâpâramitâ-sûtra-sâstra.
„ 1256 'Tâlântaraka-sâstra.'
„ 1441 Nâgârguna-bodhisattva-suhṛillekha (I. M.).
„ 1456 'Satapañkâsad-buddhastotra.'

150 菩提流志 Phu-thi-liu-*k*', i. e. Bodhiruki, whose name is translated 覺愛 *K*iâo-âi, lit. 'intelligence-loving.' His original name was 達摩流支 Tâ-mo-liu-*k*', i. e. Dharmaruki, which name is translated 法希 Fâ-hhi, lit. 'law-wishing,' and which was changed into Bodhiruki by the order of the Empress Wu Tsö-thien, A.D. 684–705. He was a *S*ramana of Southern India, and a Brâhmana by caste, and of the Kâsyapa family. In A.D. 693–713 he translated 53 works in 111 fasciculi, of which 12 works in 12 fasciculi were already missing in A.D. 730. He died in his 156th year, in A.D. 727. See the Suh-thu-*k*i, fol. 15 b; Khâi-yuen-lu, fasc. 9, fol. 25 a; Suṅ-saṅ-*k*whân, fasc. 3, fol. 3 a; Miṅ-i-tsi, fasc. 3, fol. 15 b. There are now 41 works ascribed to him in the Collection, namely:—

No. 18 Pragñâpâramitâ ardhasatikâ (S. M.).
„ 23 (1) Trisambara-nirdesa-parivartta-sûtra.
„ „ (2) Anantamukha-vinisodhana-nirdesa.
„ „ (5) Amitâyusha (or -âbha) vyûha, or Sukhâvatîvyûha (long).
„ „ (6) Akshobhyasya tathâgatasya vyûha.
„ „ (7) Varmavyûha-nirdesa.
„ „ (10) Samantamukha-parivarta.
„ „ (11) Rasminirhâra-saṅgîrathî (or -saṅgîti ?).
„ „ (13) Garbha-sûtra (?).
„ „ (20) 'Aksharakosha-sûtra (?).'
„ „ (21) Bhadra-mâyâkâra-paripṛikkhâ.
„ „ (22) Mahâpratihâryopadesa.
„ „ (24) Vinayaviniskaya-upâli-paripṛikkhâ.
„ „ (25) Âdyâsaya-saṅkodana.
„ „ (27) Surata-paripṛikkhâ.
„ „ (28) Vîradatta-paripṛikkhâ.
„ „ (29) Udayana-vatsarâga-paripṛikkhâ.
„ „ (30) Sumati-dârikâ-paripṛikkhâ.
„ „ (31) Gaṅgottaropâsikâ-paripṛikkhâ.
„ „ (34) Gunaratnasaṅkusumita-paripṛikkhâ.
„ „ (35) Akintyabuddhavishaya-nirdesa.
„ „ (37) Simha or Subâhu-paripṛikkhâ.
„ „ (40) '*S*uddhasraddhâ-dârikâ-paripṛikkhâ.'
„ „ (42) Maitreya-paripṛikkhâ.
„ „ (45) Akshayamati-paripṛikkhâ.
„ „ (48) *S*rîmâlâ-devî-paripṛikkhâ.
„ „ (49) Vyâsa-paripṛikkhâ.
„ 86 'Mahâyâna-vagrakûdâmani-bodhisattvakaryâ-varga-sûtra (?).'
„ 151 Ratnamegha-sûtra.
„ 241 Gayâsîrsha.
„ 315 Amoghapâsa-hṛidaya-sûtra.

No. 317 Amoghapâsa-kalparâga.
„ 319 Nîlakantha.
„ 324 Padmakintâmani-dhârani-sûtra.
„ 331 Shadakshara-vidyâmantra.
„ 343 Srîmati-brâhmanî-paripri*kkh*â.
„ 371 'Âyushpâla-dharmaparyâyarddhimantra-sûtra.'
„ 448 'Mañgusrî-ratnagarbha-dhâranî.'
„ 529 'Vagraprabhâsa-dhâranî.'
„ 532 'Ekâkshara-buddhoshnîsharâga-sûtra.'
„ 535 Mahâmani-vipulavimâna-visva-supratishthita-guhya-parama-rahasya-kalparâga-dhâranî.

151 般剌蜜帝 Pân-lâ-mi-ti, i. e. Pramiti, whose name is translated into 極量 *K*i-liâṅ, lit. 'extreme-measure.' He was a *S*rama*n*a of Central India. He, together with 彌伽釋迦 Mi-*k*iê-shih-*k*iâ, or 彌迦鑠佉 Mi-*k*iâ-sho-*kh*ü, i. e. Meghasikha (see the Miṅ-i-tsi, fasc. 3, fol. 16 b), a *S*rama*n*a of Udyâna of India, and a Chinese *S*rama*n*a named 釋懷廸 Shih Hwâi-ti (see the Khâi-yuen-lu, fasc. 9 fol. 34 a; Suṅ-sań-*k*whân, fasc. 3, fol. 4 b), translated one work in A. D. 705. See Suh-thu-*k*i, fol. 19 a; Suṅ-sań-*k*whân, fasc. 2, fol. 16 a; Miṅ-i-tsi, fasc. 3, fol. 16 a.

No. 446 'Mahâbuddhoshnîsha - tathâgata-guhyahetu - sâkshâtkritaprasannârtha - sarvabodhisattvakaryâ - surangama-sûtra (S. M.).'

152 釋智嚴 Shih *K*'-yen, whose original surname and cognomen were 鬱遲樂 Yü-*kh*' Lö. He was a son of the King of Kustana (Khoten), and was sent to China as a hostage (質子 *K*i-tsz'), where he became a *S*rama*n*a in A. D. 707. In A. D. 721 he translated 4 works in 6 fasciculi. See Suh-thu-*k*i, fol. 19 b; Khâi-yuen-lu, fasc. 9, fol. 32 a; Suṅ-sań-*k*whân, fasc. 3, fol. 1 b.

No. 277 'Sûtra on the good law which determines the obstacle of Karman (S. M.).'
„ 360 Anantamukha-sâdhaka-dhâranî (?).
„ 460 'Sûtra on the lion-king Sudarsana's cutting his flesh to feed others.'
„ 1380 'A collection of important accounts taken from several Sûtras on the practice of a Bodhisattva who practises the Mahâyâna (I. M.).'

153 跋日羅菩提 Poh-zih-lo-phu-thi, i. e. Vagrabodhi, whose name is translated 金剛智 Kin-kâṅ-*k*', lit. 'diamond-wisdom,' by which latter name he is generally designated. He was a *S*rama*n*a of the country or state of 摩賴耶 Mo-lâi-ye, i. e. Malaya, of Southern India, and was a Brâhma*n*a by caste. In A. D. 719 he arrived in China, and reached the capital in the following year. In A. D. 723 and 730 he translated 2 works each year; so that there were 4 works in 7 fasciculi in A. D. 730, when the Khâi-yuen-lu was compiled. He died in his seventy-first year, in A. D. 732. See Suh-thu-*k*i, fol. 21 b; Khâi-yuen-lu, fasc. 9, fol. 33 a; Suṅ-sań-*k*whân, fasc. 1, fol. 9 b. There are 11 works ascribed to him in the Collection, namely:—

No. 345 Kundî-devî-dhâranî (S. M.).
„ 534 'Sûtra for reciting, being an abridged translation of the Vagra-sekhara-yoga(-tantra).'
„ 537 'Pañkâkshara-hridaya-dhâranî.'
„ 538 'Avalokitesvara - kintâmani - bodhisattva - yogadharma - mahârtha.'
„ 964 'Sarvatathâgata-vagrâyur-dhâranî.'
„ 1033 Pragñâpâramitâ ardhasatikâ.
„ 1039 'Vagrasekharavimânasarvayogayogi-sûtra.'
„ 1391 'Vagrâyur-dhârany-adhyâya-kalpa (I. M.).'
„ 1426 'Akala-dûta-dhâranî-guhyakalpa.'
„ 1427 'Vagrasekhara-yogakaryâ-vairokana-samâdhikalpa.'
„ 1430 'Vagrasekhara - sûtra - yogâvalokitesvararâga - tathâgata-karyâ-kalpa.'

154 戍婆揭羅僧訶 Shu-pho-*k*iê-lo-sań-hö, i. e. Subhakarasimha, whose name is translated literally 淨師子 Tsiṅ-sh'-tsz', lit. 'pure-lion,' and obliquely 善無畏 Shân-wu-wêi, lit. 'good-without-fear,' by which third name he is generally designated. His Sanskrit name is commonly mentioned as 輸波迦羅 Shu-po-*k*iâ-lo, i. e. Subhakara, which name is rendered 無畏 Wu-wêi, lit. 'without-fear,' or 善無畏 Shân-wu-wêi, as before explained. He was a *S*rama*n*a of Central India, and a descendant of Amritodana, an uncle of Sâkyamuni, and lived in the Nâlanda monastery. In A. D. 716 he arrived in *Kh*âṅ-ân, the capital of China, bringing with him many Sanskrit texts. He translated one work in the following year, and in A. D. 724 he made three more translations; so that there were 4 works in 14 fasciculi in A. D. 730, when the Khâi-yuen-lu was compiled. He died in his ninty-ninth year, in A. D. 735. See Suh-thu-*k*i, fol. 20 b; Khâi-yuen-lu, fasc. 9, fol. 35 a; Suṅ-sań-*k*whân, fasc. 2, fol. 1 a. There are 5 works ascribed to him in the Collection, namely:—

No. 501 'Law or rules for seeking to hear and remember the Dhâranî, ... belonging to the Bodhisattva Âkâsagarbha (S. M.).'
„ 530 Mahâvairokanâbhisambodhi.
„ 531 'Subâhu-kumâra-sûtra.'
„ 533 Susiddhikâra-mahâtantra.
„ 1425 'The law of worshipping the Susiddhikâra(-sûtra)(I. M.).'

155 阿目佉跋折羅 Ô-mu-*k*ü-poh-*k*ö-lo, i. e. Amoghavagra, whose name is translated 不空金剛 Pu-khuṅ-*k*in-kâṅ, i.e. lit. 'not-hollow-diamond,' which is again shortened to 不空

Pu-khuṅ ('not-hollow,' i. e. Amogha), by which latter Chinese name he is generally designated. He was a *S*ramaṇa of Northern India (not a Siṅghalese, as taken by Eitel and Mayers), and a Brâhmaṇa by caste. In A. D. 719 he first arrived in China following his teacher Va*g*rabodhi, No. 153 above. When the latter was dying in A. D. 732, the former was instructed to go to India and Ceylon for the purpose of collecting some texts. In A. D. 741, therefore, Amoghava*g*ra left China for his journey, and returned to the capital of China in A. D. 746. Then the Emperor Hhüen-tsuṅ, A. D. 713–756, gave him the title 智藏 *K*'-tsâṅ, lit. 'wisdom-repository,' which name is translated into Pra*gñ*âkosha. (See the 悉曇字記 Si-thân-tsz'-*k*i.) Afterwards he was allowed to go back to his own country in A. D. 749; but when he arrived at the South-sea district, he was ordered to stay in China by the Imperial command. In A. D. 756 he was called back to the capital, and resided in the 大興善寺 Tâ-hhiṅ-shân-sh', lit. the 'great-hhiṅ-shân-monastery.' In A. D. 765 he received, besides an official title, an honourable title of 大廣智三藏 Tâ-kwâṅ-*k*'-sân-tsâṅ, or the Tripi*t*aka-bhadanta Tâ-kwâṅ-*k*'. On the birthday of the Emperor, Tâi-tsuṅ (A. D. 763–779), in A. D. 771, he presented to the court his own translations with a memorial, in which latter the following passages occur:—'From my boyhood I served my late teacher (Va*g*rabodhi) for fourteen years (A. D. 719–732), and received his instruction in the doctrine of Yoga. Then I went to the five parts of India, and collected several Sûtras and *S*âstras, more than 500 different texts, which had hitherto not yet been brought to China. In A. D. 746 I came back to the capital. From the same year till the present time (A. D. 771) I translated 77 works in more than 120 fasciculi.' In A. D. 774 he died in his seventieth year, when the Emperor gave him, besides the official title of a minister of state, the postumous title 大辯正廣智三藏 Tâ-pien-*k*aṅ-kwâṅ-*k*'-sân-tsâṅ, or the Tripi*t*aka-bhadanta Tâ-pien-*k*aṅ-kwâṅ-*k*' ('great-eloquence-correct-wide-wisdom'). (See Suṅ-saṅ-*k*whân, fasc. 1, fol. 12 b seq.; Thuṅ-*k*i, fasc. 40, fol. 13 a, 15 a; fasc. 41, fol. 5 a.) Thus he 'was held in high veneration at the court of successive sovereigns of the Thâṅ dynasty. Under his influence the Tantra doctrines, dealing with talismanic forms and professions of supernatural power, first gained currency in China.'—Mayers, p. 172, No. 554. Cf. Eitel, p. 8 a. There are 108 works ascribed to Amoghava*g*ra in the Collection, namely:—

No. 307 Mahâmayûri-vidyârâ*g*ñî (S. M.).
" 346 *K*undî-devî-dhâra*n*î.
No. 845 'Mari*k*î-devî-pushpamâlâ-sûtra.'
" 846 Mari*k*î-dhâra*n*î.
" 956 '*G*ñânantamukha-dhâra*n*î.'
" 957 Sarvatathâgatâdhish*th*ânahr*i*dayaguhyadhâtukara*n*da-mudrâ-dhâra*n*î.
" 958 Mahâsrî-sûtra.
" 959 'Mahâsrîdevî-dvâdasabandhanâshtasatanâma-vimala-mahâyâna-sûtra.'
" 961 *G*aṅgulî-vidyâ.
" 962 Ratnamegha-dhâra*n*î.
" 963 *S*âlisambhava-sûtra.
" 965 'Râsh*t*rapâla-pra*gñ*âpâramitâ.'
" 970 Mahâmegha-sûtra.
" 971 Ghanavyûha-sûtra.
" 973 Par*n*asavarî-dhâra*n*î.
" 974 'Vaisrama*n*a-divyarâ*g*a-sûtra.'
" 975 'Mañ*g*usrî-paripr*i*kkhâ-sûtra-aksharamâtr*i*kâdhyâya.'
" 979 'Pañ*k*atrimsadbuddhanâma-pû*g*â-svikâra-lekha.'
" 980 'Avalokitesvara-bodhisattva-nirdesa-samantabhadra-dhâra*n*î.'
" 981 Ash*t*ama*nd*alaka-sûtra.
" 982 *K*akshurvisodhanavidyâ-dhâra*n*î.
" 983 Sarvarogaprasamana-dhâra*n*î.
" 984 *G*valaprasamana-dhâra*n*î.
" 985 'Yogasaṅgrahamahârtha-ânandaparitrâ*n*a-dhâra*n*î-*g*vala-vaktra (preta)-kalpa-sûtra.'
" 1000 'Eka*k*û*d*ârya-dhâra*n*î.'
" 1002 'Amoghapâsa-vairo*k*anabuddha-mahâbhishiktaprabhâsa-mantra-sûtra.'
" 1006 'Nîtisâstra-sûtra, spoken by Buddha for the sake of King Udayana.'
" 1010 'Te*g*asprabhâ-mahâbalagu*n*âpadvinâsasrî-dhâra*n*î.'
" 1020 'Va*g*rasekhara-sarvatathâgatasatyasaṅgraha-mahâyâna-pratyutpannâbhisambuddha-mahâtantra-sûtra.'
" 1021 'Ö-li-to-lo (?)-dhâra*n*î.'
" 1023 Ushnîsha*k*akravarti-tantra.
" 1024 'Bodhima*nd*a-nirdesaikâksharoshnîsha*k*akravarti-râ*g*a-sûtra.'
" 1025 'Bodhima*nd*a-vyûha-dhâra*n*î.'
" 1028 Mahâma*n*i-vipulavimâna-visvasupratish*th*ita-guhya-parama-rahasya-kalparâ*g*a-dhâra*n*î.
" 1034 Pra*gñ*âpâramitâ ardhasatikâ.
" 1036 'Va*g*rasekhara-yoga-sûtra (ä ry)-sûtra.'
" 1042 Mahâpratisara-dhâra*n*î.
" 1044 'Mahâyâna-yoga-va*g*raprakr*i*tisâgara-mañ*g*usrî-sahasrabâhu-sahasrapâtra-mahâtantrarâ*g*a-sûtra.'
" 1047 'Va*g*rabhayasannipâta-vaipulyakalpa-avalokitesvara-bodhisattva-tribhâvânuttarahr*i*dayavidyârâ*g*a-sûtra.'
" 1050 'Mahâvaipulya-mañ*g*usrî-sûtra-avalokitesvaratara-bodhisattva-kalpa-sûtra.'
" 1052 'Yogava*g*rasekhara-sûtrâksharamâtr*i*ka-vyâkhyâ-varga.'
" 1054 Garu*d*agarbharâ*g*a-tantra.
" 1055 'Ekâdasamukha-avalokitesvara-bodhisattva-hr*i*daya-mantra (?)-adhyâya-kalpa-sûtra.'
" 1063 'Trisamayâ*k*arârya-krodharâ*g*adûtâdhyâyadharma.'
" 1064 Va*g*rakumâra-tantra.
" 1142 Samantabhadra-pra*n*idhâna-stotra.
" 1314 'Mahâyâna-nidâna-sâstra (A. M.).'
" 1319 'Va*g*rasekharayogânuttarasamyaksambodhi*k*ittotpâda-sâstra.'
" 1331 'Yogaikâksharoshnîsha*k*akramantrântadânakalpaikâksharoshnîsha*k*akrarâ*g*ayoga-sûtra (I. M.).'

No. 1355 'Va*g*rasekhara-sarvatathâgata-satyasa*n*graha-mahâyâna-pratyutpannâbhisambuddha-mahâtantrarâ*g*a-sûtra.'

„ 1356 'Ma*ñg*usrî-bodhisattva-sarvarshi-nirdesa-punyâpunya-kâla-divasa-nakshatra-târâ-sûtra,' i.e. a work on astrology.

„ 1383 'Va*g*rasekharayoga-sahasrabâhu-sahasrâksha-avalokitesvara-bodhisattva-*k*aryâ-kalpa-sûtra.'

„ 1386 'Mahâsukhava*g*rasattva-*k*aryâ-siddhi-kalpa.'

„ 1388 'Saddharmapu*nd*arîka-sûtrarâ*g*a-siddhi-yoga-dhyâna-*gñ*âna-kalpa.'

„ 1389 'Va*g*rasekharayoga-tribhavavi*g*ayasiddhi-mahâguhya-dvâra.'

„ 1390 'Va*g*rasekharayoga-parinirmitavasavarti-satyatâ-parshat-samantabhadra-*k*aryâdhyâya-kalpa.'

„ 1392 'Mahâyakshamât*ri*-puriyaputra-siddhi-kalpa.'

„ 1394 'Avalokitesvara-*k*intâmani (-dhâranî ?)-adhyâya-kalpa.'

„ 1395 'An abridgment showing the law of seven sorts of reciting and practice of the Mahâvairo*k*ana-sûtra.'

„ 1396 'Sîghraphalodaya-mahesvaradeva-bhâshita-avisha-kalpa.'

„ 1397 'Mahârya-ma*ñg*usrî-kumâra-pa*ñk*âkshara-yoga-kalpa.'

„ 1398 'Mahâbalakrodha-ushma (?)-kalpa.'

„ 1399 'Mahâmayûrî-vidyârâ*gñ*î-*k*itrapratibimba-ma*nd*ala-kalpa.'

„ 1400 'Va*g*rasekharayoga-va*g*rasattva-kalpa.'

„ 1401 'Ekâkshara-suvarna*k*akrarâ*g*a-buddhoshnîsha-mahârtha-saṅkshepâdhyâya-kalpa.'

„ 1402 'Avalokitesvara-*k*intâmaniyogâdhyâya-kalpa.'

„ 1403 'Mahârya-mahâbhirati-dvikâya-vinayaka-kalpa.'

„ 1404 'A law of reciting and practice of an abridgment of the Mahâvairo*k*ana-sûtra.'

„ 1405 'Pa*ñk*âkshara-dhâranî-gâthâ.'

„ 1406 'Kârunikarâ*g*a-pra*gñ*âpâramitâ-dhâranî-vyâkhyâ.'

„ 1407 'Mahâsukhava*g*râmoghasatyasamayasûtra-pra*gñ*âpâramitâ-buddhi-vyâkhyâ.'

„ 1409 'Va*g*rarâ*g*a-bodhisattva-guhyâdhyâya-kalpa.'

„ 1410 'Va*g*rasekharânuttaraprathamayoga-samantabhadra-bodhisattvâdhyâya-kalpa-sûtra.'

„ 1411 'Va*g*rasekharayoga-va*g*rasattva-pa*ñk*aguhya*k*aryâdhyâya-kalpa.'

„ 1412 'Amitâyus-tathâgata-dhyâna-*k*aryâ-pû*g*â-kalpa.'

„ 1413 'Am*ri*takundali-bodhisattva-pû*g*âdhyâyasiddhi-kalpa.'

„ 1414 'Avalokitesvaratârâ-yogâdhyâya-kalpa.'

„ 1415 'Âryâvalokitesvara-bodhisattva-h*ri*daya-mantra-yoga-dhyâna-*k*aryâ-kalpa.'

„ 1418 'Mahâkâsagarbha-bodhisattva (-dhâranî ?)-adhyâya-kalpa.'

„ 1419 'Kârunikarâ*g*a-pra*gñ*âpâramitâdhyâya-kalpa.'

„ 1420 'Akshobhya-tathâgatâdhyâya-pû*g*â-kalpa.'

„ 1421 'Sarvadurgatibuddhoshnîshavi*g*ayadhârany-adhyâya-kalpa.'

„ 1422 'Ârya-yen-mân-tôh-*k*iâ-krodharâ*g*a-mahârddhi-phalodaya-siddhyadhyâya-kalpa.'

„ 1423 'Mahâyânavaipulya-ma*ñg*usrî-bodhisattva-buddhâvatamsaka-mûlatantra-yen-mân-tôh-*k*iâ-krodha-râ*g*a-mantra-mahâbalaguna-kalpâdhyâya.'

„ 1424 A work of a similar title as the preceding.

„ 1428 'Va*g*rasekharayoga-sûtra-ma*ñg*usrî-bodhisattva-kalpa-pû*g*â-dharma.'

„ 1429 'Yogapu*nd*arîka-vargâdhyâya-kalpa.'

„ 1431 'Va*g*rasekhara-sûtrâvalokitesvararâ*g*a-tathâgata*k*aryâ-kalpa.'

No. 1432 'Va*g*rapâ*n*i-prabhâsamûrdhâbhishikta-sûtrânuttaramudrâryâ*k*ala-mahâkrodharâ*g*âdhyâya-kalpa.'

„ 1433 'A brief explanation of the doctrine of practice and understanding of those in the Ârya ranks, explained in the Va*g*rasekhara-yoga.'

„ 1434 'Ekâkshara-buddhoshnîsha*k*akrarâ*g*âdhyâya-kalpa.'

„ 1435 'Kârunikarâ*g*arâshtrapâla-pra*gñ*âpâramitâ-sûtra-bodhima*nd*âdhyâya-kalpa.'

„ 1436 'Va*g*rasekhara-pu*nd*arîkavarga-h*ri*dayâdhyâya-kalpa.'

„ 1442 'Samantabhadrava*g*rasattvayogâdhyâya-kalpa.'

„ 1443 'Va*g*rasekharayoga-homa-kalpa.'

„ 1444 'Mahâkârunikah*ri*daya-dhâranî-*k*aryâdhyâya-saṅkshepa-kalpa.'

„ 1446 'An excellent form of the Ma*ñg*usrî-pa*ñk*âkshara-mantra, explained in the Va*g*rasekhara-sûtra, which excels the three worlds.'

„ 1447 'Va*g*rasekhara-sûtra-yoga-ma*ñg*usrî-bodhisattva-dharmaikavarga.'

„ 1448 A work on the eighteen assemblies of the Va*g*rasekhara-yoga-sûtra.

„ 1449 'Hâritî-mât*ri*-mantra-kalpa.'

„ 1450 'Mahâvaipulya-buddhâvatamsaka-sûtra-dharmadhâtvavatârâdhyâya-dvâ*k*atvârimsad-aksharadhyâna.'

„ 1451 'Pra*gñ*âpâramitâ-buddhi-sûtra-mahâsukhâmogha-samayasatyava*g*rabodhisattvâdi-saptadasârya-mahâma*n*-*d*ala-vyâkhyâ.'

„ 1452 'Important names of several parts of Dhâranîs.'

„ 1453 'Va*g*rasekharayoga-saptatrimsadârya-pû*g*â (or *stotra*).'

„ 1454 'Ceremonial rules for receiving the Sîla or moral precepts of the Bodhih*ri*daya.'

„ 1455 'Mahârya-ma*ñg*usrî-bodhisattva-buddhadharmakâya-prasamsâ-pû*g*â.'

„ 1457 '*S*atasahasrika-mahâsannipâta-sûtra-kshitigarbha-bodhisattva-dharmakâya-parip*ri*k*kh*â-stotra.'

„ 1467 'Yogamahârthasaṅgraha-*g*valavaktra (preta)-annada-kalpa.'

156 般若 Pân-*z*o, i.e. Pra*gñ*a, a *S*ramana of Kubhâ (Cabul), who translated 4 works in about A.D. 785–810. See Suṅ-saṅ-*k*whân, fasc. 3, fol. 9 b; Thuṅ-*k*i, fasc. 41, fol. 9 a.

No. 89 Buddhâvatamsaka-vaipulya-sûtra,—'Samantabhadra-pranidhânâdhyâya (S. M.).'

„ 955 'Mahâyâna-mûla*g*âtah*ri*dayabhûmi-dhyâna-sûtra.'

„ 978 'Desântapâlapati-dhâranî-sûtra.'

„ 1004 'Mahâyânabuddhi-shatpâramitâ-sûtra.'

157 無能勝 Wu-naṅ-shaṅ, these characters seem to be a translation of a Sanskrit name, meaning literally 'without-well-conquering.' He wás a *S*ramana of Northern India, whose exact date is not known. In their translations there is no mention of the name of the Chinese dynasty under which he and the next translator lived; but in the *K*'-tsiṅ (fasc. 14, fol. 22 a), both are said to have lived under the Thâṅ dynasty, A.D. 618–907.

No. 966 'Malapâdavagra-nirdesarddhimahâpûrna-dhârani-dharmasrimahârthamukha-sûtra (S. M.).'

158 阿質達霰 Ō-*k*ih-tâ-sien, these characters seem to be a transliteration of a Sanskrit name. He was a *S*ramana of Northern India, whose exact date is unknown. See *K*'-tsiṅ, fasc. 14, fol. 22 a.

No. 967 'Malapâdavagra-dharmasatavikrîyâ-dharma-paryâya-sûtra (S. M.).'

" 1048 'Wu-shu-seh-mo'-krodha, or Mahâbalavagrakrodha-sûtra.

Work of Unknown Translator.

No. 1009 'Mahâsrigusa-suvarnakakrabuddhoshnishategaâprabha-tathâgata-sarvâpadvinâsa-dhârani-sûtra (S. M.).'

Summary of the preceding List of Translations made under the Thâṅ dynasty, A. D. 618–907.

Translators.	Nêi-tien-lu.	Thu-*k*i.	Khâi-yuen-lu.	In existence.
No. 132	3	3	3	3
" 133	65	75	75	75
	68	78		
		Suh-thu-*k*i, & Khâi-yuen-lu.		
" 134			4	4
" 135			1	1
" 136			1	1
" 137			3	2
" 138			1	1
" 139			18	19
" 140			1	1
" 141			1	1
" 142			1	1
" 143			12	12
" 144			1	1
" 145			19	16
" 146			1	1
" 147			1	1
" 148			7	7
" 149			56	56
" 150			53	40
" 151			1	1
" 152			4	4
" 153			4	11
" 154			4	5
			272 *	
" 155				108
" 156				4
" 157				1
" 158				2
				1
				380

* In 1744 fasciculi. In A. D. 730 there were 252 works in 1717 fasciculi in existence, while 20 works in 27 fasciculi were already lost. Cf. the Khâi-yuen-lu, fasc. 8 a, fol. 1 a seq.

(北) 宋 (Pe) Suṅ, or the later (or Northern) Suṅ dynasty, of the 趙 *K*âo family, with its capital at 汴梁 Pien-liâṅ, the modern 開封 Khâi-fuṅ, the capital of 河南 Ho-nân, A. D. 960–1127.

159 法天 Fâ-thien (Dharmadeva ?), afterwards 法賢 Fâ-hhien, a *S*ramana of the Nâlanda monastery of Magadha in Central India, who translated numerous works in A. D. 973–1001. In A. D. 982 he received from the Emperor Thâi-tsuṅ (A. D. 976–997) the title 傳教大師 *K*whân-*k*iâo-tâ-sh'. In the same year he changed his name (Fâ-thien) into Fâ-hhien, so that the dates of his translations will be clearly divided into two periods, according to these two names, either of which is given in his translations. He died in A. D. 1001, and his postumous title is 玄覺禪師 Hhüen-*k*iâo-shân-sh'. See Thuṅ-*k*i, fasc. 43, fol. 10 a, 16 a, 21 b; fasc. 44, fol. 2 a. There are 118 works ascribed to him in the Collection, of which the following 46 works were made in the first period under the name of 法天 Fâ-thien, A. D. 973–981:—

No. 785 'Mahâvaipulya-dhârani-ratnaprabhâsa-sûtra (S. M.).'
" 786 'Mahâyânâryâmitâyurniskitaprabhâsarâga-tathâgata-dhârani-sûtra.'
" 787 Vasudharâ-dhârani.
" 788 Udayana-vatsarâga-pariprikkhâ.
" 793 Saptabuddhaka-dhârani-sûtra.
" 794 'Mahâprabhâpâlamahâdhârani-sûtra.'
" 796 Sarvadurgatiparisodhanoshnishavigaya-dhârani.
" 800 Mahâdanda-dhârani.
" 801 'Sarvasamskârasamskrita-sûtra.'
" 804 Saddharmârya-smrity-upasthâna-sûtra.
" 806 'Sûtra on a Devaputra, named Tsie-wâ-nâṅ-fâ (?), who escaped from an evil state on account of receiving the Trisarana.'
" 810 'Dâna-sûtra.'
" 811 Grahamâtrikâ-dhârani.
" 813 'Âryatârâ-bodhisattva-nâmâshtasataka-sûtra.'
" 817 'Maudgalyâyana-pariprikkhâ-sûtra (V. H.).'
" 818 *S*âlisambhava-sûtra (S. M.).
" 819 'Vikoti (?)-bodhisattva-nâmâshtasataka-sûtra.'
" 821 'Shadbhavagâthâ-sûtra.'
" 822 Subâhu-pariprikkhâ-sûtra.
" 823 'Bhikshu-pañkadharma-sûtra (V. H.).'
" 824 'Bhikshuka-sikshâpâda (?)-dasadharma-sûtra.'
" 825 'Buddhahridaya-dhârani (S. M.).'
" 833 'Ârya-durgaya-vagrâgni-dhârani-sûtra.'
" 841 'Samantabhadra-bodhisattva-dhârani-sûtra.'
" 848 '*S*reshthi-dânaphala-sûtra (S. H.).'
" 849 'Vaisramana-divyarâga-sûtra (S. M.).
" 850 'Vipasyi-buddha-sûtra.'
" 851 'Mahâsamaya-sûtra (S. H.).'

No. 852 *K*andraprabha-bodhisattvâvadâna (S. M.).
„ 860 Saptabuddhaka (S. H.).
„ 861 '*S*okavinâsa-sûtra.'
„ 869 Va*g*ragarbharatnarâ*g*a-tantra (S. M.).
„ 871 Sarvadurgatiparisodhanoshnîshavi*g*aya-dhâranî.
„ 872 'Bodhihr*i*dayadhyâna-vyâkhyâ (I. M.).'
„ 931 'Nidâna-sûtra (S. H.).'
„ 1031 *S*rîsarvabhûta*d*âmara-tantra (S. M.).
„ 1045 *G*ambhala*g*alendrayathâlabdhakalpa-sûtra.
„ 1046 'Ratnagarbharddhimahâvidyâman*d*ala-kalpa-sûtra.'
„ 1065 'Saptabuddhastutigâthâ.'
„ 1067 'Buddhanâmâsh*t*asatakastotra-sûtra.'
„ 1073 'Ma*ñg*usrî-nâmâsh*t*asataka-stotra.'
„ 1078 'Âryâvalokitesvara-bodhisattva-stotra.'
„ 1081 'Gha*n*ti-stotra.'
„ 1303 Va*g*rasû*k*i (A. M.).
„ 1377 '*A*geya-mahâvidyâ-dhâranî-sûtra (I. M.).'
„ 1378 '*A*geya-mahâvidyâ-hr*i*daya-dhâranî-sûtra.'

The following 72 works were translated in the second period under the name of 法賢 Fâ-hhien, A. D. 982–1001:—

No. 859 'Samadatta-mahârâ*g*a-sûtra (S. H.).'
„ 863 'Mahâyânâmitâyurvyûha-sûtra,' or Sukhâvatîvyûha (long. S. M.).
„ 864 Pra*g*ñâpâramitâ-sa*ñk*ayagâthâ.'
„ 870 'Saptasûryanaya-sûtra (S. H.).'
„ 880 Ash*t*aman*d*alaka-sûtra (S. M.).
„ 881 'Sarvabuddhakshetragunopamânasaṅkhyâna-sûtra.'
„ 882 'Râvana-bhâshita-bâlavyâdhibhisha*g*yâ-sûtra.'
„ 883 'Kâsyaparshi-bhâshita-stribhisha*g*yâ-sûtra (S. H.).'
„ 884 '*K*û-*k*'-lo (?)-dhâranî (S. M.).'
„ 885 'Sarvâpâdvinâsaratnoshnîsha-dhâranî.'
„ 886 'Suvarna-dhâranî.'
„ 887 '*K*andanagandhakâya-dhâranî.'
„ 888 'Prasâsabala (?)-mahâdhâranî.'
„ 889 'Pûrvanivâsânusmr*i*ti*g*ñâna-dhâranî.'
„ 890 Maitrî (or -eya)-prati*g*ñâ-dhâranî.
„ 891 'Pa*ñk*ânantaryakarmavinâsa-dhâranî.'
„ 892 'Amitaguna-dhâranî.'
„ 893 'Ash*t*âdasabâhu-dhâranî.'
„ 894 'Laksha-dhâranî.'
„ 895 'Sarvapâpavinâsa-dhâranî.'
„ 896 'Mahâpriyâ-dhâranî.'
„ 897 'Arhat-pûrnaguna-sûtra (S. H.).'
„ 898 'Ash*t*amahâsrî*k*aityanâma-sûtra (S. M.).'
„ 899 '*K*unda (?)-sûtra.'
„ 900 'Bimbisârarâ*g*a-sûtra (S. H.).'
„ 901 'Nararshi-sûtra.'
„ 902 'Purâ*n*anagaropamâna-sûtra.'
„ 903 'Adhimukti*g*ñânabala-sûtra.'
„ 904 'Mahâsatpada (?)-râ*g*a-sûtra.'
„ 905 'Svâsaya (?)-sresh*th*i-sûtra (S. M.).'
„ 906 'Âryatârâ-bodhisattva-sûtra.'
„ 907 'Mahâsrî-dhâranî.'
„ 908 'Ratnabhadra-dhâranî.'
„ 909 'Guhyâsh*t*anâma-dhâranî.'
„ 910 Avalokitesvara-mâtr*i*kâ-dhâranî.
„ 911 'Sîlagandha-sûtra (S. H.).'
„ 912 'Ma*ñg*usrî-bodhisattva-dhâranî (S. M.).'
No. 913 'Amitâyur-mahâ*g*ñâna-dhâranî.'
„ 914 'Pûrvanivâsa*g*ñâna-dhâranî.'
„ 915 'Maitreya-bodhisattva-dhâranî.'
„ 916 'Âkâsagarbha-bodhisattva-dhâranî.'
„ 917 'Ratnadatta (?)-bodhisattva-bodhi*k*aryâ-sûtra.'
„ 918 'Âyurvardhana-sadmukha-dhâranî.'
„ 919 'Sarvatathâgatanâma-dhâranî.'
„ 920 '*K*aurâpakâra-vinâsa-dhâranî.'
„ 921 Dharmasarîra-sûtra.
„ 922 'Buddhasraddhâguna-sûtra (S. H.).'
„ 923 'Grishma-nidarsana-sûtra (V. H.).'
„ 924 'Indra-sakra-paripr*i*kkhâ-sûtra (S. H.).'
„ 925 'Adbhuta-saddharma-sûtra (S. M.).'
„ 928 'Vinirnîtârtha-sûtra (S. H.).'
„ 929 'Râsh*t*rapâla-sûtra.'
„ 995 'Ma*ñg*usrî-bodhisattva-paripr*i*kkhâ-mahâyâna-dharma-saṅkha-sûtra (S. M.).'
„ 996 '*K*aturvarga-dharmaparyâya-sûtra (S. H.).'
„ 997 'Ash*t*amahâbodhisattva-sûtra (S. M.).'
„ 1008 'Abhaya-dhâranî.'
„ 1022 Mâyâ*g*âla-mahâtantra-mahâyâna-gambhîra-nâya-guhya-parâsi-sûtra.
„ 1037 'Anuttaramûla-mahâsaṅkhya-va*g*râmoghasamaya-mahâtantra-sûtra.'
„ 1038 *S*ravanasya (?)-putra-nada-gupilâya (?)-kalparâ*g*a-sûtra.
„ 1040 Ma*ñg*usrî-sadvr*i*ttaguhyatantrarâ*g*asya vimsatika-krodhavi*g*ayâ*g*ana-sûtra.
„ 1049 'Mahâyâna-dhyânasa*ñg*ñânaman*d*ala-sarvadurbhâva-prasâdaka-sûtra.'
„ 1051 'Sarvabuddhasaṅgrahayukta-mahâtantra-sûtra-avalokitesvara-bodhisattvâdhyâya-kalpa-sûtra.'
„ 1057 'Ta*g*odhara-pi*t*aka-yogamahâtantra-*k*unda (?)-bodhisattva-mahâvidyâsiddhikalpa-sûtra.'
„ 1059 'Va*g*rasattva-bhâshita-vinâyaka-deva-siddhi-kalpa-sûtra.'
„ 1061 'Mâyâ*g*âla-mahâyogatantra-dasakrodha-mahâvidyârâ*g*a-dhyânasa*ñg*ñâna-kalpa-sûtra.'
„ 1062 Va*g*rabhairava-tantra-krodhatattvarâ*g*a.
„ 1066 'Buddhatrikâya-stotra.'
„ 1071 'Ash*t*asrî*k*aitya-stotra.'
„ 1072 'Trikâya-stotra.'
„ 1074 'Ma*ñg*usrî-bodhisattva-srî-gâthâ.'
„ 1075 'Va*g*rapâni-bodhisattva-nâmâsh*t*asataka-stotra.'
„ 1387 'Ma*ñg*usrî-bodhisattva-srîgâthâ (I. M.).'

160 天息災 Thien-si-tsâi (? lit. 'heaven or god (= deva)-stopping-misfortune'), a *S*ramana of 惹爛馱囉 *Z*ö-lân-to-lo, i. e. *G*alandhara of Northern India, or of 迦濕彌羅 *K*iâ-si-mi-lo, i. e. Kâsmîra (Cashmere) of Northern India, who arrived in China in A. D. 980, and worked at translations for twenty years. In A. D. 982 he received the title 明教大師 Miṅ-*k*iâo-tâ-sh', and died in A. D. 1000. His postumous title is 慧辯法師 Hwui-pien-fâ-sh'. See Thuṅ-*k*i, fasc. 43, fol. 15 a, 16 a; fasc. 44, fol. 1 b. There are 18 works ascribed to him in the Collection, namely:—

No. 782 Ghanavyûha-sûtra (S. M.).
„ 783 'Sukarma-duhkarma-phalaviseshana-sûtra (S. H.).'
„ 789 'Suvarnarasmi-kumâra-sûtra (S. M.).'
„ 791 'Vimânasaddharmâmritadundubhi-sûtra.'
„ 792 Bodhivaksho-mañgusri-nirdesa-sûtra.
„ 797 Alpâkshara-pragñâpâramitâ.
„ 807 'Upamitâyus-sûtra.'
„ 815 Târâbhadra-nâmâshtasataka.
„ 816 Avalokitesvara-nâmâshtasataka.
„ 820 'Gayasena-lokâdhyâpanâvadânasataka-gâthâ-sûtra.'
„ 828 'Dhyânasaṅgñâna - buddhamâtrika - pragñâpâramitâ-sûtra.'
„ 839 'Dasanâma-sûtra.'
„ 844 'Mahâmarîki-bodhisattva-sûtra.'
„ 1018 'Sarvatathâgata-mahâguhyarâga-adbhutânuttaramahâmandala-sûtra.'
„ 1056 Bodhisattvapitakâvatamsaka - prasneta - mañgusri - mûlagarbha-tantra.
„ 1354 'Bodhikaryâ-sûtra (I. M.).'
„ 1375 'Âryasaṅgîti-gâthâsataka.'
„ 1439 Dharmapada.

161 施護 Sh'-hu (Dânapâla?), a *Sramana* of Udyâna of Northern India, who arrived in China in A. D. 980, and worked there at translations for some years. In A. D. 982 he received from the Chinese Emperor the title 顯教大師 Hhien-kiâo-tâ-sh'. See Thuṅ-*ki*, fasc. 43, fol. 15 a, 16 a. There are 111 works ascribed to him in the Collection, namely:—

No. 784 Mahâsahasra-pramardana (or -vartana?)-sûtra (S. M.).
„ 790 Samantamukhapravesarasmivimaloshnîshaprabhâ - sarvatathâgatahridaya-samavirokana-dhâranî.
„ 795 Dhvagâgrakeyûra-dhâranî.
„ 798 'Sarvavagrakilavipatpravritayathoshta-dhâranî-sûtra.'
„ 799 'Âryânuttaradîpa-tathâgata-dhâranî-sûtra.'
„ 802 Kintâmaninâma-sarvaghâtamrityu-vâranita (or -vârana)-dhâranî.
„ 803 'Sarvatathâgatasaddharmaguhya-karandamudrâhridaya-dhâranî-sûtra.'
„ 805 Kâsyapa-parivarta.
„ 808 'Srâmanera-sikshâpadaniyama-sûtra (V. H.).'
„ 809 Vasudhara-dhâranî (S. M.).
„ 812 'Dharmasaṅgraha-nâmasaṅkhyâ-sûtra.'
„ 814 'Dvâdasanidânagâtasri-sûtra (S. H.).'
„ 826 'Mahâyâna-ratnakandra-kumâra-paripṛikkhâ-sûtra (S. M.).'
„ 827 'Pundarîkakakshur-dhâranî-sûtra.'
„ 829 Padmakintâmani-dhâranî-sûtra.
„ 830 'Âryamahâdhâranîrâga-sûtra.'
„ 831 'Anuttaramati-dhâranî-sûtra.'
„ 832 'Prabhâsadharagarbhâshtamahâdhâranîrâga-sûtra.'
„ 834 'Âryottama-mahâvidyârâga-sûtra.'
„ 835 Gñânolkâ-dhâranî-sarvadurgati-parisodhanî.
„ 836 'Kintâmani-dhâranî-sûtra.'
837 'Mahesvara-devaputra-hetubhûmi-sûtra.'
„ 838 'Ratnagâta-dhâranî-sûtra.'
„ 840 Sâgara-nâgarâga-paripṛikkhâ-sûtra.
„ 842 Mahâvagramerusekharakûtâgâra-dhâranî.
„ 843 'Mahâ-pundarîkavyûhasarvapâpavinâsa-mandala-dhâranî-sûtra.'

No. 853 'Samantabhadra-mandala-sûtra.'
„ 854 'Âryavyûha-dhâranî-sûtra.'
„ 855 'Âryashadaksharamahâvidyârâga-dhâranî-sûtra.'
„ 856 'Sahasrapravartana-mahâvidyâ-dhâranî-sûtra.'
„ 857 Pushpakûta-dhâranî.
„ 858 'Gayadhvagamâlâ-dhâranî-sûtra.'
„ 862 'Samantaprakâsamâna-pragñâpâramitâ-sûtra.'
„ 865 Kausika-pragñâpâramitâ.
„ 866 'Sarvabuddha-sûtra.'
„ 867 Sâlisambhava-sûtra.
„ 868 'Mahâvagragandha-dhâranî-sûtra.'
„ 873 Râshtrapâla-paripṛikkhâ.
„ 874 'Katurvaisâradya-sûtra.'
„ 875 'Gñânavardhamâna-dhâranî-sûtra.'
„ 876 'Âryashadaksharâyurvardhamâna-mahâvidyâ-dhâranî-sûtra.'
„ 877 'Mahâyânasîla-sûtra (V. M.).'
„ 878 Sarvadurgatiparisodhanoshnîshavigaya-dhâranî (S. M.).
„ 879 Pragñâpâramitâ-ardhasatikâ.
„ 926 Gñânottara-bodhisattva-paripṛikkhâ.
„ 927 Dasasâhasrikâ pragñâpâramitâ.
„ 930 'Dânakintana-sûtra.'
„ 932 'Dharmamudrâ-sûtra.'
„ 933 'Mahâgâtârtha-sûtra (S. H.).'
„ 934 'Bodhihridayagâta-sarvamâravinâsa-sûtra (S. M.).'
„ 935 'Pragñâpâramitâ-hridaya-sûtra.'
„ 936 'Mahâyânâkintyarddhivishaya-sûtra.'
„ 937 'Anâthapindada-sreshthi-duhitri-paritrânaprâpta-nidâna-sûtra (S. H.).'
„ 938 'Mahâsaṅgrahadharmaparyâya-sûtra.'
„ 939 'Prabhâsa-kumâra-nidâna-sûtra.'
„ 940 Mekhalâ-dhâranî (S. M.).
„ 941 'Suvarnakâya-dhâranî-sûtra.'
„ 942 'Akintadharmaparyâyâvatâra-sûtra.'
„ 943 'Suddhamaty-upâsaka-paripṛikkhâ-sûtra (S. H.).'
„ 944 'A part of the teaching of Vagramandalavyûha-pragñâpâramitâ (S. M.).'
„ 945 'Vivâdavinâsa-nidâna-sûtra (S. H.).'
„ 946 'Prathamavargavakana-sûtra.'
„ 947 'Vaisâradyadatta-paripṛikkhâ-sûtra (S. M.).'
„ 948 'Kandropamâna-sûtra (S. H.).'
„ 949 'Bhishag-upamâna-sûtra.'
„ 950 'Mûrdhâbhishiktopamâna-sûtra.'
„ 951 'Nyagrodha-brahmakâri-sûtra.'
„ 952 'Suklavastra - suvarnadhvaga - dvibrâhmana - nidâna-sûtra.'
„ 953 Punyabalâvadâna (S. M.).
„ 964 Ratnamegha-sûtra.
„ 972 'Mahâsannipâta-saddharma-sûtra.'
„ 977 'Mâyopamasamâdhyamitamudrâdharmaparyâya-sûtra.'
„ 986 'Pipîlikopamâna-sûtra (S. H.).'
„ 987 Amoghapâsa-dhâranî (S. M.).
„ 988 Râgâvavâdaka-sûtra (S. H.).
„ 989 'Kakravarti-râga-saptaratna-sûtra.'
„ 990 'Ârâmagâtadruma-sûtra.'
„ 991 'Prasannârtha-pragñâpâramitâ-sûtra (S. M.).'
„ 992 'Mahâvaipulyâdbhuta-sûtra-upâyakausalyâdhyâya.'
„ 993 'Mahâsthira-brâhmana-nidâna-sûtra (S. H.).'
„ 998 Sarvâbhayapradâna-dhâranî (S. M.).
„ 999 'Ashtasâhasrikâpragñâpâramitâ-nâmâshtasatasatyapûrnârtha-dhâranî.'
„ 1007 'Pañkamahâdâna-sûtra (S. H.).'
„ 1011 'Mûrdhagâta-râgâvadâna-sûtra (S. M.).'

No. 1017 'Sarvatathâgata-satyasangraha-mahâyâna-pratyutpannâbhisambuddha-samâdhi-mahâtantra-sûtra.
„ 1026 Guhyagarbharâga.
„ 1027 *S*rîguhyasamaga (or -ya?) tantrarâga.
„ 1029 Guhyasamayagarbharâga.
„ 1030 'Asamasamânuttarayogamahâtantrarâga.'
„ 1035 'Buddhamât*ri*ka-pra*g*ñâpâramitâ-mahâvidyâ-dhyânamañ*g*ñâna-kalpa.'
„ 1053 'Sarvatathâgata-pratibimbapratish*th*â-sanaya-kalpa.'
„ 1058 'Vagragandha-bodhisattva-mahâvidyasiddhi-kalpa.'
„ 1069 'Sarvatathâgatoshnîsha*k*akrarâga - nâmâsh*t*asataka-stotra.'
„ 1070 'Dharmadhâtu-stotra.'
„ 1076 'Âryâvalokitesvara-bodhisattva-guna-stotra.'
„ 1079 'Âryatârâ-bodhisattva-stotra.'
„ 1301 'Bodhih*ri*dayasâstra-vaipulyavyâkhyâ (A. M.).'
„ 1302 'Sarvadharmaratnottarârthasangîti-sâstra.'
„ 1304 'Bodhih*ri*daya-rûpavimukta-sâstra.'
„ 1305 'Mahâyâna-bhavabheda-sâstra.'
„ 1306 'Mahâyâna-rûpasangîti-sâstra.'
„ 1307 'Shash*t*igâthâ-yathârtha-sâstra.'
„ 1308 'Mahâyâna-vimsatigâthâ-sâstra.'
„ 1309 'Buddhamât*ri*ka - pra*g*ñâpâramitâ - mahârtha - sangîti-sâstra.'
„ 1310 A commentary on the preceding *S*âstra.
„ 1315 'Sarvasikshana-sthitanâmârtha-sâstra.'
„ 1376 'Mahâpranidhâna-gâthâ (I. M.).'
„ 1385 'Sarvaguhyânuttara-nâmârtha-mahâtantra-kalpa.'
„ 1393 'Indra-sakra-silâ-guhya-siddhi-kalpa.'
„ 1408 'Anuttara-mañ*g*usri-mûla*g*ñânânuttaraguhyasarvanâmârthasamâdhivarga.'
„ 1458 'Buddhasriguna-stotra.'

162 法護 Fâ-hu (Dharmaraksha?), a *S*ramana of Magadha of Central India, who arrived in China in A. D. 1004, and worked at translations till A. D. 1058, when he died in his ninety-sixth year. In A. D. 1054 he received from the Emperor *Z*ân-tsun (A. D. 1023–1063) the special title 普明慈覺傳梵大師 Phu-min-tsz'-*k*iâo-*k*whân-fân-tâ-sh'. See Thun-*k*i, fasc. 44, fol. 4 a; fasc. 45, fol. 16 b, 17 a. There are 12 works ascribed to him in the Collection, namely:—

No. 964 Ratnamegha-sûtra (S. M.).
„ 968 'Mahâyâna-mahâvaipulya-buddhamukta-sûtra.'
„ 969 'Ash*t*avargavardhamânaguna-sûtra.'
„ 1005 Bodhisattvapi*t*aka.
„ 1013 Sarvabuddhavishayâvatâra*g*ñânâlokâlankâra-sûtra.
„ 1019 '*G*ñatasarvatathâgata-dharma*k*akshuh-samantasobhanamahâbalavidyârâ*g*a-sûtra.'
„ 1043 Tathâgatâ*k*intyaguhyanirdesa.
„ 1060 He Va*gra*-tantra.
„ 1298 'Mahâyâna-bodhisattva-vidyâsangîti-sâstra (A. M.).'
„ 1311 'Mahâyâna-ratnamahârtha-sâstra.'
„ 1313 'Âryabuddhamât*ri*ka-pra*g*ñâpâramitâ-navagâthâ-mahârtha-sâstra.'
„ 1317 Pra*g*ñaptipâda-sâstra (A. H.).

163 惟淨 Wêi-tsin, a Chinese *S*ramana, who, on the column next to the title of some of his translations in the present Collection, is wrongly said to have been a man of Central India. (Cf. Thun-*k*i, fasc. 45, fol. 6 a.) In A. D. 1009 he was ordered by Imperial command to become a member of translators, and received the title 光梵大師 Kwân-fân-tâ-sh'. (See Thun-*k*i, fasc. 44, fol. 8 a.) He seems chiefly to have worked together with the Indians before mentioned. There are 4 works in the Collection, which are either wholy or partly ascribed to him, namely:—

No. 954 'Sambarshitaromakûpagâta-sûtra (S. H.).'
„ 964 Ratnamegha-sûtra (S. M.).
„ 976 Sâgaramati-pariprikkhâ-sûtra.
„ 1316 Prânyamûla-sâstra-*t*îkâ (A. M.).

164 智吉祥 *K*'-*k*i-siân (*G*ñânasrî?), an Indian *S*ramana, who arrived in China in A. D. 1053. See Thun-*k*i, fasc. 45, fol. 16 a. There are 2 works ascribed to him in the Collection, namely:—

No. 994 'Mahâbala-sresh*th*i-pariprikkhâ-sûtra (S. M.).'
„ 1014 Tathâgata*g*ñânamudrâ-sûtra.

165 金總持 *K*in-tsun-*k*h' (Suvarnadhâranî?), a (foreign?) *S*ramana, who translated some works in about A. D. 1113. Cf. Thun-*k*i, fasc. 46, fol. 10 b.

No. 1015 Arthavinishaya-dharmaparyâya (S. M.).
„ 1370 Mañ*g*usri-nâmasangîti (I. M.).

166 慈賢 Tshz'-hhien (Maitreyabhadra?), a *S*ramana of Magadha of Central India, who is said to have been a 國師 Kwo-sh', lit. 'a national teacher,' i. e. the teacher of the Emperor, of 契丹 *K*ie-tân,—the original name of the Liâo dynasty, A. D. 907–1125, into which latter dynastic name it was changed in A. D. 1066. But the exact date of this translator is not known. There are 5 works ascribed to him, namely:—

No. 1001 'Va*g*rabhañ*g*ana-dhâranî (S. M.).'
„ 1041 'Mañ*g*usri - samaguhyânuttaradhyânadvâra - mahâtantrarâ*g*a-sûtra.'
„ 1437 '*K*intâmani*k*akrapun*d*arîkah*ri*daya-tathâgata*k*aryâdhyâna-dvâra-kalpa (I. M.).'
„ 1438 'Mañ*g*usri-samantayogaguhyakâya-dhyânâbhisambuddha-kalpa.'
„ 1445 'Ceremonial rules for the Homa sacrifice, being an abridged translation of, or extracts from, the Mañ*g*usri-samanta-dhyânadvâra-mahâtantra-sûtra.'

167 日稱 *Z*ih-*kh*an (Sûryayasas?), an Indian *S*ramana, who had the title 宣梵大師 Süen-fân-tâ-sh', and was a contemporary of Fâ-hu, No. 162 above. There are 2 works ascribed to him, namely:—

No. 1080 'Guru-sevâ-dharma-pañkâsadgâthâ (S. M.),' compiled by Asvaghosha.
" 1379 'Dasadushtakarmamârgasûtra,' compiled by the same as before (I. M.).

168 紹德 Shâo-töh, a Sramana, whose native place and date are unknown. He, together with another Sramana named 慧詢 Hwui-sün, and others, translated one work, originally in 16 fasciculi, now gathered into nine.

No. 1312 Bodhisattva-gâtakamâlâ-sâstra (A. M.).

Summary of the preceding List of Translations made under the later (or Northern) Sun dynasty, A. D. 960–1127.

Translators.	In existence.
No. 159	118
" 160	18
" 161	111
" 162	12
" 163	4
" 164	2
" 165	2
" 166	5
" 167	2
" 168	1
	275

元 The Yuen dynasty, of the 奇渥温 Khi-uh-wân family, with its capital at 燕京 Yen-kiṅ, now the 順天府 Shun-thien-fu, in Kihli, A. D. 1280 (or 1260)–1368.

169 拔合思巴 Pâ-hö-sz'-pâ, or 巴思巴 Pâ-sz'-pâ, or 發思八 Fâ-sz'-pâ, or 拔思發 Pâ-sz'-fâ, or Baahpa. He was a Sramana of the country of 土波 Tu-po (Tibet), and was the 帝師 Ti-sh', lit. 'emperor's teacher.' He translated one work in A. D. 1271, when the Yuen dynasty was not yet the sole ruler of China. On the twenty-second day of the eleventh month of the seventeenth year of the K'-yuen period, A. D. 1280, he died in his forty-second year. See Tsuṅ-tsâi, fasc. 32, fol. 24 b–26 a. The following note is given by Mayers (p. 166, No. 532), who puts every date just one year earlier than that mentioned in the Tsuṅ-tsâi:—'Baahpa, a Tibetan lâma of the hereditary sect or priesthood of Ssakia, who became a confidential adviser of Kublai Khan during the latter's career of conquest in China. In A. D. 1260 he was named 國師 (Kwo-sh') Preceptor or Hierarch of the State, and recognised as head of the Buddhist Church. In A. D. 1269 he constructed an alphabetic system for the Mongol language, which there first became committed to writing. In reward for his services he received the exalted title of 大寶法王 (Tâ-pâo-fâ-wâṅ) or Prince of the Great and Precious Law [of Buddha].'

No. 1137 'Mûlasarvâstivâda-nikâya-pravragyopasampadâ-karmavâkâ (V. H.).'

170 沙羅巴 Shâ-lo-pâ, a Sramana, who was a disciple of the preceding, and had the title 弘教佛智三藏法師 Huṅ-kiâo-fo-k'-sân-tsâṅ-fâ-sh', or the Tripitaka-bhadanta Huṅ-kiâo-fo-k'. He died in his fifty-sixth year, in A. D. 1314. See Tsuṅ-tsâi, fasc. 36, fol. 3 a–5 b; Miṅ-saṅ-kwhân, fasc. 1, fol. 1 a. He translated his teacher's work, namely:—

No. 1320 'Sâstra explaining known objects (A. H.).'

171 嚩嘌奈銘得哩連得囉磨寧 Tsi-nâh-miṅ-töh-li-lien-töh-lo-mo-niṅ, an Indian Sramana, who, together with a (Chinese?) Sramana named 真智 Kan-k', translated one work; but the exact date is unknown.

No. 1016 Sitâtapatra-dhâranî (S. M.).

172 釋智慧 Shih K'-hwui (Pragñâ?), a Sramana of 土蕃 Tu-fân (Tibet), whose exact date is unknown.

No. 1032 Mañgusri-nâma-nâh-li-tiâ (? S. M.).

173 安藏 Ân Tsâṅ, a Chinese official, who had two appointments; but the date is not known.

No. 1068 'Âryaparitrâna-buddhamâtrikaikavimsativargapûgâ-stotra-sûtra (S. M.).'

Summary of the preceding List of Translations made under the Yuen dynasty, A. D. 1280 (or 1260)–1268.

Translators.	In existence.
No. 169	1
" 170	1
" 171	1
" 172	1
" 173	1
	5

APPENDIX III.

LIST OF THE CHINESE AUTHORS.

UNDER THE EASTERN TSIN DYNASTY, A.D. 317–420.

1 法顯 Fâ-hhien (Fa-hian). For his translations, see Appendix II, No. 45. In A.D. 414 he wrote his well-known travels, No. 1496.

UNDER THE LATTER TSHIN DYNASTY, A.D. 384–417.

2 僧肇 Sań-*k*âo, a famous disciple of Kumâra*g*îva; for the latter, see Appendix II, No. 59. There are 3 works ascribed to him, viz. Nos. 1627 (text), 1632, 1650.

UNDER THE EARLIER SUŃ DYNASTY, A.D. 420–479.

3 惠嚴 Hwui-yen, 惠觀 Hwui-kwân, 謝靈運 Sie Liń-yun, the first two were priests, and the last a literary man. In A.D. 424–453 they revised a version of the Mahâparinirvâ*n*a-sûtra, No. 113, and their revision is No. 114.

4 僧璩 Sań-*kh*u, a priest, who in A.D. 463 compiled 1 work, viz. No. 1166. See Khâi-yuen-lu, fasc. 5 b, fol. 7 a.

5 法穎 Fâ-yiń, a priest, who in about A.D. 465–471 compiled 1 work, viz. No. 1161. See Khâi-yuen-lu, fasc. 5 b, fol. 7 a.

UNDER THE LIÂŃ DYNASTY, A.D. 502–557.

6 僧祐 Sań-yiu, a priest, who compiled 3 works; the first in about A.D. 500, under the Tshi dynasty, A.D. 479–502, and the last two in about A.D. 520, viz. Nos. 1468, 1476, 1479. See Khâi-yuen-lu, fasc. 6, fol. 7 a.

7 寶唱 Pâo-*kh*âń, a priest, who compiled 2 works in A.D. 516 and 526, viz. Nos. 1473, 1497. See Khâi-yuen-lu, fasc. 6, fol. 10 b.

8 慧皎 Hwui-*k*iâo, a priest, who in A.D. 519 compiled 1 work, viz. No. 1490. See Khâi-yuen-lu, fasc. 6, fol. 14 a.

9 明徽 Miń-hwui, a priest, who in A.D. 522 compiled 1 work, viz. No. 1158. See Khâi-yuen-lu, fasc. 6, fol. 11 a.

UNDER THE *KH*AN DYNASTY, A.D. 557–589.

10 慧思 Hwui-sz', the teacher of *K*'-i, the founder of the Thien-thâi school; for the latter, see No. 12 below. Hwui-sz' died in A.D. 577. See Suh-sań-*k*whân, fasc. 21, fol. 7 a. There are 4 works ascribed to him, viz. Nos. 1542, 1543, 1547, 1576. He is the third patriarch, according to the Thien-thâi school. See Thuń-*k*i, fasc. 6, fol. 5 b. Cf. Edkins, Chinese Buddhism, p. 156.

UNDER THE SUI DYNASTY, A.D. 589–618.

11 法經 Fâ-*k*iń, a priest, who was engaged in translations, and who also in A.D. 594 compiled 1 work, viz. No. 1609. See Khâi-yuen-lu, fasc. 7, fol. 23 a.

12 智顗 *K*'-i, the founder or fourth patriarch of the Thien-thâi school, whose postumous title is 智者大師 *K*'-*k*ö-tâ-sh'. In A.D. 597 he died in his sixty-seventh year. See No. 1577, i.e. a life of *K*'-i, compiled by his disciple Kwân-tiń; for the latter, see No. 15 below. See also Suh-sań-*k*whân, fasc. 21, fol. 12 b; Edkins, Chinese Buddhism, p. 140, etc. There are 22 works ascribed to him, viz. Nos. 1510, 1534, 1536, 1538, 1540, 1548, 1550, 1552, 1554, 1555, 1557, 1559, 1561, 1562, 1564, 1565, 1566, 1569, 1571, 1572, 1573, 1574.

13 寶貴 Pâo-kwêi, a priest, who in A.D. 597 made a compilation of three incomplete translations of the Suvar*n*aprabhâsa-sûtra, and added new chapters, so as to make it complete, viz. No. 130. See Khâi-yuen-lu, fasc. 7, fol. 24 a.

14 費長房 Fê *Kh*âń-fâń, a scholar, who was engaged in the translation of the Tripi*t*aka. In A.D. 597 he compiled 1 work, viz. No. 1504. See Khâi-yuen-lu, fasc. 7, fol. 25 b.

UNDER THE THÂṄ DYNASTY, A.D. 618–907.

15 灌頂 Kwân-tiṅ, the fifth patriarch and the principal disciple of *K'*-i, the founder of the Thien-thâi school; for the latter, see No. 12 above. In A.D. 632 Kwân-tiṅ died in his seventy-second year. See Suh-saṅ-*k*whân, fasc. 23, fol. 18 b. He was the recorder of many works of his teacher, viz. Nos. 1334, 1336, 1338, 1548, 1550, 1552, 1554, 1555, 1557, 1559, 1562, 1566, 1571, 1573. He also compiled or composed 6 works, viz. Nos. 1544, 1545, 1568, 1570, 1575, 1577.

16 杜法順 Tu Fâ-shun, the founder or first patriarch of the Hwâ-yen or Avatamsaka school. In A.D. 640 he died in his eighty-fourth year. He wrote a work, which was afterwards annoted by Tsuṅ-mi, the fifth patriarch; for the latter, see No. 38 below. For the text, see its commentary, viz. No. 1596.

17 法琳 Fâ-lin, a priest, who in A.D. 624–640 composed 2 works, viz. Nos. 1500, 1501. In A.D. 640 he died in his sixty-ninth year. See Suh-saṅ-*k*whân, fasc. 32, fol. 1 a; Khâi-yuen-lu, fasc. 8 a, fol. 6 b.

18 玄奘 Hhüen-*k*wâṅ (Hiouen-thsang). For his translations, see Appendix II, No. 133. There are 2 works ascribed to him, viz. Nos. 1503, 1646.

19 辨機 Pien-*k*i, a priest, who in A.D. 646 assisted Hhüen-*k*wâṅ (Hiouen-thsang), No. 18 above, when the latter compiled his famous work on the Western regions, viz. No. 1503.

20 玄應 Hhüen-yiṅ, a priest, who in about A.D. 649 compiled 1 work, viz. No. 1605. See Khâi-yuen-lu, fasc. 8 b, fol. 18 a.

21 道宣 Tâo-süen, the founder of the Lüh or Vinaya school. In A.D. 667 he died in his seventy-second year. There are eight works ascribed to him, viz. Nos. 1120, 1469, 1470, 1471, 1481, 1483, 1484, 1493. See Khâi-yuen-lu, fasc. 8 b, fol. 17 a; Suṅ-saṅ-*k*whân, fasc. 14, fol. 1 a.

22 道世 Tâo-shi, whose literary appellation is 玄惲 Hhüen-yun, by which he was called under the Thâṅ dynasty, because the second character of his cognomen Tâo-shi is the same as the first character of the name (Shi-min) of Thâi-tsuṅ, the second Emperor of that dynasty. In A.D. 656–660 and 668 he compiled 2 works, viz. Nos. 1474, 1482. See Khâi-yuen-lu, fasc. 8 b, fol. 21 a; Suṅ-saṅ-*k*whân, fasc. 4, fol. 5 a.

23 彥悰 Yen-tshuṅ, a priest, who in A.D. 662 compiled 1 work, and who in about A.D. 665 made Hwui-li's (No. 24 below) work complete, viz. Nos. 1480, 1494. See Khâi-yuen-lu, fasc. 8 b, fol. 21 b; Suṅ-saṅ-*k*whân, fasc. 4, fol. 13 a.

24 慧立 Hwui-li, a priest, who compiled a life of Hhüen-*k*wâṅ (Hiouen-thsang), but left it unfinished at his death, viz. No. 1494. See Khâi-yuen-lu, fasc. 9, fol. 6 b; Suṅ-saṅ-*k*whân, fasc. 17, fol. 3 a.

25 靖邁 Tsiṅ-mâi, a priest, who in about A.D. 664 compiled a work, viz. No. 1487. He is said to have written this work separately above each of the figures of translators from Kâsyapa Mâtaṅga down to Hhüen-*k*wâṅ (Hiouen-thsang). These figures were then drawn on the wall of the hall of translation within the Tâ-tsz'-ǹn monastery, in which the last great translator lived. See Khâi-yuen-lu, fasc. 8 b, fol. 19 a; Suṅ-saṅ-*k*whân, fasc. 4, fol. 9 b.

26 復禮 Fu-li, a priest, who in A.D. 681 composed 1 work, viz. No. 1498. See Khâi-yuen-lu, fasc. 9, fol. 6 a; Suṅ-saṅ-*k*whân, fasc. 17, fol. 2 a.

27 懷素 Hwâi-su, a disciple of Hhüen-*k*wâṅ (Hiouen-thsang). In A.D. 629 he was ordained, and in A.D. 682 he died in his seventy-fourth year. He compiled 4 works, viz. Nos. 1116, 1128, 1154, 1156. See Khâi-yuen-lu, fasc. 9, fol. 7 a; Suṅ-saṅ-*k*whân, fasc. 14, fol. 9 a.

28 玄嶷 Hhüen-i, a priest, who in about A.D. 684–905 composed 1 work, viz. No. 1499. See Khâi-yuen-lu, fasc. 9, fol. 14 b; Suṅ-saṅ-*k*whân, fasc. 17, fol. 4 a.

29 明佺 Miṅ-*kh*üen, a priest, who in A.D. 695 compiled 1 work, viz. No. 1610. See Khâi-yuen-lu, fasc. 9, fol. 10 b.

30 法藏 Fâ-tsâṅ, the third patriarch of the Hwâ-yen or Avatamsaka school. In A.D. 699 or 712 he died, and his postumous title is 賢首大師 Hhien-sheu-tâ-sh'. See Suṅ-saṅ-*k*whân, fasc. 5, fol. 1 a; Thuṅ-*k*i, fasc. 40, fol. 7 a. There are 7 works ascribed to him, viz. Nos. 1591, 1592, 1593, 1595, 1599, 1602 (text), 1625.

31 愛同 Âi-thuṅ, a priest, who in about A. D. 700 compiled 1 work, viz. No. 1153. See Khâi-yuen-lu, fasc. 9, fol. 31 b; Suṅ-saṅ-*k*whân, fasc. 14, fol. 21 b.

32 慧苑 Hwui-wân, a priest, who in about A. D. 700 compiled 1 work, viz. No. 1606. See Khâi-yuen-lu, fasc. 9, fol. 31 b; Suṅ-saṅ-*k*whân, fasc. 6, fol. 3 a.

33 義淨 I-tsiṅ. For his translations, see Appendix II, No. 149. He compiled 5 works, viz. Nos. 1491, 1492, 1506, 1507, 1508. See Khâi-yuen-lu, fasc. 9, fol. 24 b.

34 慧能 Hwui-naṅ, the sixth patriarch of the Shân or Dhyâna school. In A. D. 713 he died in his seventy-sixth year. See Suṅ-saṅ-*k*whân, fasc. 8, fol. 3 a; Mayers, p. 137, No. 428. There is 1 work ascribed to him, viz. No. 1525.

35 智昇 *K'*-shaṅ, a priest, who in A. D. 730 compiled 5 works, viz. Nos. 1472, 1485, 1486, 1488, 1505. See Khâi-yuen-lu, fasc. 9, fol. 36 a; Suṅ-saṅ-*k*whân, fasc. 5, fol. 7 b.

36 湛然 Tsân-sân, the ninth patriarch of the Thien-thâi school. In A. D. 782 he died in his seventy-second year. See Suṅ-saṅ-*k*whân, fasc. 6, fol. 4 b. There are 10 works ascribed to him, viz. Nos. 1511, 1535, 1537, 1539, 1541, 1545, 1578, 1579, 1581, 1583.

37 澄觀 *Kh*an-kwân, the fourth patriarch of the Hwâ-yen or Avataṁsaka school. He died in the Yuen-hô period, A. D. 806–820, when he was more than seventy years old. See Suṅ-saṅ-*k*whân, fasc. 5, fol. 18 a. There are 4 works ascribed to him, viz. Nos. 1589, 1590, 1598, 1639. His honourable or posthumous title is 清涼大師 Tshiṅ-liâṅ-tâ-sh'.

38 宗密 Tsuṅ-mi, the fifth patriarch of the Hwâ-yen or Avataṁsaka school. In A. D. 840 or 841 he died in his sixty-second year. See Suṅ-saṅ-*k*whân, fasc. 6, fol. 13 a; Thuṅ-*k*i, fasc. 42, fol. 6 b. There are 6 works ascribed to him, viz. Nos. 1594, 1596, 1601, 1629, 1630, 1647. He is respectfully called 圭峰大師 Kwêi-fâṅ-tâ-sh', or the great teacher who lived on a hill or mountain called Kwêi-fâṅ.

39 裴休 Fê Hhiu, a minister of state, who in about A. D. 842–848 compiled 1 work, viz. No. 1654. In A. D. 870 he died. See Thuṅ-*k*i, fasc. 42, fol. 17 b.

40 知玄 *K'*-hhüen, a priest, who compiled 1 work, viz. No. 1523. In A. D. 881 he died in his seventy-third year. See Suṅ-saṅ-*k*whân, fasc. 6, fol. 18 b.

41 玄覺 Hhüen-*k*iâo, a priest, who compiled 1 work, viz. No. 1585. He seems to have belonged to the Thien-thâi school.

42 元曉 Yuen-hhiâo, a Corean priest, who compiled 1 work, viz. No. 1603. See Suṅ-saṅ-*k*whân, fasc. 4, fol. 17 a.

UNDER THE LATTER TSIN DYNASTY, A. D. 936–947.

43 師會 Sh'-hwui, a priest, who compiled 1 work, viz. No. 1600. In A. D. 946 he died in his sixty-seventh year. See Suṅ-saṅ-*k*whân, fasc. 28, fol. 5 b.

UNDER THE LATER (OR NORTHERN) SUṄ DYNASTY, A. D. 960–1127.

44 諦觀 Ti-kwân, a learned Corean priest of the Thien-thâi school, who arrived in China in A. D. 960, bringing with him the principal books of the sect. These books, during the period of the Five Dynasties, A. D. 907–960, had been almost destroyed in China by constant civil war. At last, therefore, the King of Wu-yueh, the north-eastern part of China, sent an envoy to Corea and Japan for the missing books. Ti-kwân was accordingly sent to China by the Corean King, and saw an eminent Chinese priest; and his school was then re-established in China. See the Thuṅ-*k*i, fasc. 43, fol. 4 a. There is 1 work ascribed to this Corean priest, viz. No. 1551.

45 延壽 Yen-sheu, a priest of the Shân or Dhyâna school, who died in A. D. 975. See Suṅ-saṅ-*k*whân, fasc. 28, fol. 13 b. There are 3 works ascribed to him, viz. Nos. 1489, 1652, 1655.

46 贊寧 Tsân-niṅ, a priest, who in A. D. 988 compiled 1 work, viz. No. 1495. In A. D. 1001 he died in his eighty-second year. See Thuṅ-*k*i, fasc. 44, fol. 2 a.

47 遵式 Tsun-shih, a priest of the Thien-thâi school, who in A. D. 998–1022 compiled 6 works, viz. Nos. 1512, 1513, 1514, 1515, 1519, 1522.

48 智圓 *K'*-yuen, a priest of the Thien-thâi school, who in A. D. 998–1022 compiled 2 works, viz. Nos. 1546, 1563.

49 道原 Tâo-yuen, a priest of the Shân or Dhyâna school, who in A.D. 1006 compiled 1 work, viz. No. 1524.

50 明覺 Miṅ-kiâo, a priest of the Shân or Dhyâna school, to whom this postumous name was given by the Emperor Kan-tsuṅ, in A.D. 1012. See Thuṅ-ki, fasc. 44, fol. 11 a. His sayings were collected by his disciple 惟蓋 Wêi-kâi, and others, in 1 work, viz. No. 1527.

51 知禮 K'-li, a priest of the Thien-thâi school, who in about A.D. 1020 compiled 10 works, viz. Nos. 1516, 1517, 1518, 1549, 1553, 1556, 1558, 1560, 1580, 1582.

52 繼忠 Ki-kuṅ, a priest of the Thien-thâi, school, who in A.D. 998–1022 compiled 1 work, viz. No. 1584.

53 子璿 Tsz'-süen, a priest of the Hwâ-yen school, who in about A.D. 1020 compiled 3 works, viz. Nos. 1626, 1630, 1631.

54 契嵩 Kie-suṅ, a priest of the Shân or Dhyâna school, who died in A.D. 1071. See Thuṅ-ki, fasc. 45, fol. 22 a. There are 4 works ascribed to him, viz. Nos. 1528, 1529, 1530, 1645.

55 本嵩 Pan-suṅ, a priest of the Hwâ-yen or Avatamsaka school, who wrote some verses which were commented by 琮湛 Tsuṅ-tsân, of the Yuen dynasty, A.D. 1280–1368, viz. No. 1656.

56 處觀 Khu-kwân, a priest, who in A.D. 1094 compiled 1 work, viz. No. 1604.

57 仁岳 Zan-yo, a priest of the Thien-thâi school, who composed or compiled 2 works, viz. Nos. 1520, 1521.

58 淨源 Tsiṅ-yuen, a Corean priest of the Hwâ-yen or Avatamsaka school, who compiled 2 works, viz. Nos. 1597, 1602 (commentary).

UNDER THE SOUTHERN SUṄ DYNASTY, A.D. 1127–1280.

59 紹隆 Shâo-luṅ, a priest of the Shân or Dhyâna school, who in about A.D. 1133, together with others, collected the sayings of his teacher in 1 work, viz. No. 1531.

60 法雲 Fâ-yun, a priest, who in A.D. 1151 compiled 1 work, viz. No. 1640.

61 王日休 Wâṅ Zih-hhiu, a minister of state, who in A.D. 1160–1162 compiled 1 work, viz. No. 203.

62 蘊聞 Yun-wan, a priest of the Shân or Dhyâna school, who in A.D. 1165–1173 collected the sayings of his teacher in 1 work, viz. No. 1532.

63 咸輝 Hhien-hwui, a priest, who in A.D. 1165 compiled 1 work, viz. No. 1588.

64 張商英 Kâṅ Shâṅ-yiṅ, a minister of state, who in about A.D. 1170 composed a treatise, viz. No. 1502.

65 法應 Fâ-yiṅ, a priest, who in A.D. 1174–1189 compiled 1 work, viz. No. 1660.

66 智廣 K'-kwâṅ and 慧印 Hwui-kan, two priests, who both together in about A.D. 1200 compiled 1 work, viz. No. 1478.

67 善月 Shân-yueh, a priest of the Thien-thâi school, who in A.D. 1230 compiled 1 work, viz. No. 1567.

68 志磐 K'-phân, a priest of the Thien-thâi school, who in A.D. 1269–1271 compiled 1 work, viz. No. 1661.

69 道殿 Tâo-khan, a priest, who compiled 1 work, viz. No. 1477.

70 王古 Wâṅ Ku, a householder, who compiled 1 work, i.e. the greater part of No. 1611, which was afterwards continued by another; for the latter, see No. 78 below.

71 戒環 Kie-hwân, a priest of the Thien-thâi school, who compiled 1 work, viz. No. 1623.

72 妙喜 Miâo-hhi, and 竹庵 Ku-ân, two priests, who both together compiled 1 work, viz. No. 1638.

73 嘖藏主 Tsö-tsâṅ-ku, a priest, who compiled 1 work, viz. No. 1659.

UNDER THE YUEN DYNASTY, A.D. 1280 (OR 1260)–1368.

74 發合思巴 Fâ-hö-sz'-pâ, i.e. Pâ-sz'-pâ, or Bashpa. For his translation, see Appendix II, No. 169.

He composed 1 work, most probably in Tibetan, which was translated into Chinese by his disciple Shâ-lo-pâ, viz. No. 1320.

75 慶吉祥 *Kin-ki-sian*, a priest, who in A. D. 1285–1287 compiled 1 work, viz. No. 1612.

76 祥邁 Siân-mâi, a priest of the Shân or Dhyâna school, who in A. D. 1291 compiled 1 work, viz. No. 1607.

77 普會 Phu-hwui, a priest, who in A. D. 1295–1318 continued a collection of No. 1660.

78 管主八 Kwân *Ku*-pâ, a priest, who in about A. D. 1300 compiled 2 works, the one wholly and the other partly, viz. Nos. 1384, 1611.

79 文才 Wan-tshâi, a priest, who compiled 2 works, viz. Nos. 1627 (commentary), 1628. He died in A. D. 1302. See Min-sañ-*k*whân, fasc. 2, fol. 4 b.

80 普度 Phu-tu, a priest, who in A. D. 1314 compiled 1 work, viz. No. 1651.

81 清茂 Tshiñ-meu, a priest, who in A. D. 1320 continued an old compilation, viz. No. 1526.

82 慈寂 Tshz'-tsi, a priest, who in A. D. 1321–1323 compiled or collected the sayings of his teacher in 1 work, viz. No. 1533.

83 圓覺 Yuen-*k*iâo, a priest of the Hwâ-yen or Avatamsaka school, who in A. D. 1322 compiled 1 work, viz. No. 1633.

84 念常 Nien-*kh*âñ, a priest, who in A. D. 1333 compiled 1 work, viz. No. 1637.

85 蒙潤 Mañ-sun, a priest of the Thien-thâi school, who in A. D. 1334 compiled 1 work, viz. No. 1635.

86 惟則 Wâi-tsö, a priest of the Thien-thâi school, who in A. D. 1342 compiled 1 work, viz. No. 1624.

87 懷則 Hwâi-tsö, a priest of the Thien-thâi school, who compiled 2 works, viz. Nos. 1586, 1587.

88 普瑞 Phu-zui, a priest of the Hwâ-yen or Avatamsaka school, who compiled 1 work, viz. No. 1622.

89 德煇 Töh-hwui and 大訢 Tâ-su, two priests of the Shân or Dhyâna school, the former made a new collection of an old work, and the latter revised it, viz. No. 1642.

90 劉謐 Liu Mi, a scholar, who composed 1 work, viz. No. 1643.

91 普照 Phu-*k*âo, a Corean priest of the Shân or Dhyâna school, who composed a treatise, viz. No. 1648.

92 知訥 *K*'-no, a priest, who composed a treatise, viz. No. 1649.

93 智徹 *K*'-*kh*ö, a priest of the Shân or Dhyâna school, who compiled 1 work, viz. No. 1653.

94 居頂 *K*ü-tiñ, a priest of the Shân or Dhyâna school, who compiled 1 work, viz. No. 1658.

UNDER THE MIṄ DYNASTY, A. D. 1368–1644.

95 宗泐 Tsuñ-lö and 如玘 *Z*u-*kh*i, two priests of the Shân or Dhyâna school, who both together in A. D. 1378 compiled 3 works, viz. Nos. 1613, 1614, 1615. For *Z*u-*kh*i's life, see Miñ-sañ-*k*whân, fasc. 3, fol. 7 a.

96 成祖 *Kh*añ-tsu, the third Emperor of the Miñ dynasty, reigned A. D. 1403–1424. There are 2 works ascribed to him, viz. Nos. 1616, 1620. No. 1616 is however a collection of his own writings, which might have been collected by some one else.

97 圓瀞 Yuen-tsiñ, a priest, who in A. D. 1431 compiled 1 work, viz. No. 1636.

98 如巴 *Z*u-pâ, a priest, who in A. D. 1488–1505 compiled 2 works, viz. Nos. 1641, 1644.

99 一如 Yi-zu, a priest, who compiled 1 work, viz. No. 1621.

100 子成 Tsz'-*kh*añ, a priest, who compiled 1 work, which was commented on by another priest called 師子 Sh'-tsz', viz. No. 1634.

101 淨善 Tsiñ-shan, a priest, who made an addition to an old compilation, viz. No. 1638.

102 普泰 Phu-thâi, a priest, who in about A. D. 1622 added a commentary to an old work or works, viz. No. 1646.

INDEX

OF THE

AUTHORISED SANSKRIT TITLES.

The figures in this Index refer to the number attached to each work in this Catalogue.

× Vajraśekhara ... 1020, 1036, 1052 1319, 1355, 1383, 1389, 1390, 1400, 1410, 1411, 1428, 1431, 1436, 1443, 1447, 1453

INDEX

OF THE

PROPER NAMES OF THE AUTHORS AND TRANSLATORS

The numerals refer to the three Appendices, the figures to the numbers in each.

Pāramiti see next col. s.v. Pramiti (erroneous for Pāramiti)

THE END.

ND - #0123 - 111124 - C0 - 229/152/15 - PB - 9781528000574 - Gloss Lamination